THE
WORK
AND THE
GLORY

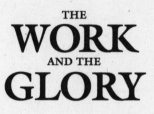

No
Unhallowed Hand

"It Is Time for Us to Leave"

VOLUME 7

THE
WORK
AND THE
GLORY

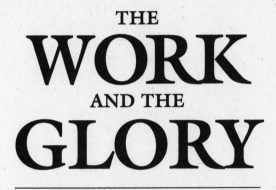

No
Unhallowed Hand

A HISTORICAL NOVEL

Gerald N. Lund

BOOKCRAFT
Salt Lake City, Utah

THE WORK AND THE GLORY

Volume 1: Pillar of Light
Volume 2: Like a Fire Is Burning
Volume 3: Truth Will Prevail
Volume 4: Thy Gold to Refine
Volume 5: A Season of Joy
Volume 6: Praise to the Man
Volume 7: No Unhallowed Hand
Volume 8: So Great a Cause
Volume 9: All Is Well

Visit us at www.deseretbook.com

Library of Congress Catalog Card Number: 96-86634

ISBN 1-57008-277-4
ISBN 1-57345-876-7 (softcover)

Printed in the United States of America   72082-6760

For behold, this is my work and my glory—to bring to pass the immortality and eternal life of man.

—Moses 1:39

Preface

On a hot, sultry afternoon late in June, 1844, four men sat in the upper bedroom of the small rock jail in Carthage, Illinois. Charged falsely with treason, they waited in a town that was filled with hate for a trial that offered them little hope of justice. Shortly after five p.m., a mob, many with their faces painted black, stormed the jail. The guards posted there, as much the enemy to the prisoners as the infuriated mob was, fired a shot or two in the air, then conveniently fled.

It took no more than minutes. The men rushed up the stairs, forced the door, and unleashed a withering hail of bullets into the room. Joseph and Hyrum Smith were killed; John Taylor lay severely wounded beneath the bed. Only Willard Richards miraculously escaped. With roars of delight, the killers left the jail and went home to congratulate one another and celebrate their triumph. Joseph was dead. His most likely successor was dead with him. They had done what many others had tried to do—in New York, in Ohio, in Missouri, and in Illinois. They had at last silenced the voice that was drawing people to The Church of Jesus Christ of Latter-day Saints in what outsiders saw as alarming numbers. They had struck down the man most responsible for the rise of this hated and abominable religion. Joe Smith was dead at last. And with him his work would die as well.

How little did they know!

When Joseph Smith went into that grove of trees a short distance west of his home in the spring of 1820, he learned in an instant that what he was about to do—and to become—would be implacably opposed by hell in all its fury. From that moment on, the opposition began. He was mocked, ridiculed, criticized, and condemned. As he moved forward, following the will of the Lord, opposition rose around him in endless, bitter processions. When the mockery and the ridicule were not sufficient to deter him, more serious means became the norm. He was slandered, vilified, shot at, beaten, thrown into court again and again, dragged from his home, cursed, spit upon, tarred and feathered.

Joseph had no illusions about how men felt about him. He once wrote: "As for the perils which I am called to pass through, they seem but a small thing to me, as the envy and wrath of man have been my common lot all the days of my life; and for what cause it seems mysterious, unless I was ordained from before the foundation of the world, for some good end, or bad, as you may choose to call it. Judge ye for yourselves. God knoweth all these things, whether it be good or bad. But, nevertheless, deep water is what I am wont to swim in; it all has become second nature to me. And I feel, like Paul, to glory in tribulation: for to this day has the God of my fathers delivered me out of them all, and will deliver me from henceforth; for behold, and lo, I shall triumph over all my enemies, for the Lord God hath spoken it." (*History of the Church* 5:143.)

From the beginning, however, the Lord also made it clear that there would be no ultimate triumph for those who sought to destroy the work. "The works, and the designs, and the purposes of God cannot be frustrated," he said in July of 1828, "neither can they come to naught. . . . Remember, remember that it is not the work of God that is frustrated, but the work of men." (D&C 3:1, 3.) And again he said, "I will not suffer that they shall destroy my work; yea, I will show unto them that my wisdom is greater than the cunning of the devil" (D&C 10:43).

It didn't take long for those who had shoved the muzzles of their rifles into the upper room of the Carthage jail to realize that while they had killed Joseph Smith, they had not slowed in any way the work he had begun. Stunned, horrified, shocked into numbness by the brutal loss of their beloved leader, for a time it looked as though the Saints were vulnerable to collapse. Who would lead the Church now? Who could possibly take over from one as gifted and inspired as Joseph Smith? Would the Church collapse into various splinters as this man or that stepped forward to ever so humbly claim that he was the one chosen to take over the reins? To the outside observer, for a time it looked as though the enemies had done their work well. But to those with eyes of faith, there was never any doubt. While Joseph was a prophet and leader of unusual and unique abilities—one of the greatest of all the prophets to ever live— the Church was not his, nor did the work depend on him alone. Joseph Smith was but an instrument in God's hands. He himself testified to that again and again during his lifetime. It was not the Church of Joseph Smith of Latter-day Saints. It was the Church of Jesus Christ, and Jesus Christ was still at the head.

Six weeks to the day following the Martyrdom, the Lord gave a miraculous and marvelous indication of how his church should be led and who should lead it. Brigham Young—barely known outside the circles of the Church, but long faithful in his service—would now step forward and take the Church onward. The work was only beginning, and it was time to move on to new tasks, new horizons, new visions, new places of settlement.

It didn't take long for the enemies of the Church to realize that they had not destroyed the work after all. Nauvoo did not disintegrate with Joseph's death. Instead, converts to the Church from all across America and Europe continued to flock to it. Over five hundred missionaries were sent into the world in 1844 alone! By the time of the exodus in early 1846, there was an estimated eleven to twelve thousand people in Nauvoo alone. There were more than a dozen other surrounding communities with another four or five thousand Latter-day Saints. That could hardly be defined as a collapse.

Soon the enemies were raging again. The Nauvoo Charter was revoked. Editorial writers fumed and foamed and once again began to use words like *expulsion* and *extermination*. Committees met, politicians lobbied, "law-abiding citizens" began to talk about law not being enough. Brigham Young and the Twelve became the target of frivolous lawsuits and criminal indictments.

And when none of that stopped the work, once again they turned to other means—the torch, the night rider, powder and ball, murder.

In this seventh volume of *The Work and the Glory*, the days and months and years following the deaths of Joseph and Hyrum Smith are depicted. The Steeds are part of the tumultuous events which unfold as the Church moves forward on its destined course. Two things become clearly evident during this time period. First, that this work is not the work of man, not even a man of Joseph Smith's greatness. Therefore, while his death is a great tragedy, it is not a termination. The second lesson is that just as before, when the enemies of the Church thought they had "solved the Mormon problem" once and for all, the Church comes through the smoke and haze of battle more majestic, more solid, and stronger than ever before. In Liberty Jail, Joseph was told: "As well might man stretch forth his puny arm to stop the Missouri river in its decreed course, or to turn it up stream, as to hinder the Almighty" (D&C 121:33). So it was here. As well might the mobs and the politicians and the lawless try to stop the mighty Mississippi as to halt the work of God. *No Unhallowed Hand* describes this time of great tragedy and ultimate triumph. The Saints' experience from 1844 to 1846 is a powerful testimony, after all else is said and done, of the declaration of God himself that it is *his* work and *his* glory, and no mere mortal shall ever stop it.

In each of the preceding volumes, acknowledgments of all of those who have made important contributions to this work have been given. They are not repeated here in print, but the feelings of gratitude and appreciation have only deepened all the more.

GERALD N. LUND

Bountiful, Utah
September 1996

Characters of Note in This Book

The Steed Family

Benjamin, father and grandfather; fifty-nine as the book begins.

Mary Ann Morgan, wife of Benjamin, and mother and grandmother; almost fifty-eight as the story opens.

Joshua, the oldest son (thirty-seven), and his wife, **Caroline
Mendenhall** (almost thirty-eight).

William ("Will"), from Caroline's first marriage; twenty.

Savannah; seven.

Charles Benjamin; four.

Livvy Caroline; two weeks old as the book opens.

Jessica Roundy Garrett (forty), Joshua's first wife, widow of
John Griffith, and her husband, **Solomon Garrett**
(thirty-nine).

Rachel, from marriage to Joshua; twelve.

Luke and Mark, sons from John Griffith's first marriage;
almost twelve and ten, respectively.

John Benjamin, from marriage to John; six.

Miriam Jessica, from marriage to Solomon; almost one.

Nathan, the second son (thirty-five), and his wife, **Lydia
McBride** (not quite thirty-five).

Joshua Benjamin ("Young Joshua"); thirteen.

Emily; not quite twelve.

Elizabeth Mary; six.

Josiah Nathan; three.

Nathan Joseph; one.

Melissa, the older daughter (thirty-three), and her husband,
Carlton ("Carl") Rogers (almost thirty-five).

Carlton Hezekiah; twelve.

David Benjamin; not quite ten.

Caleb John; almost eight.

Sarah; almost six.

Rebecca, the younger daughter (twenty-six), and her husband, **Derek Ingalls** (almost twenty-seven).

Christopher Joseph; five.

Benjamin Derek; two.

Matthew, the youngest son (not quite twenty-four), and his wife, **Jennifer Jo McIntire** (twenty-two).

Betsy Jo; two.

Peter Ingalls, Derek's younger brother; twenty.

Kathryn Marie McIntire, Jennifer Jo's sister; four years younger than Jennifer.

Note: Deceased children are not included in the above listing.

The Smiths

* Lucy Mack, the mother.
* Hyrum, Joseph's elder brother (almost six years older than Joseph), martyred at age forty-four.
* Mary Fielding, Hyrum's wife.
* Joseph, the Prophet, martyred at age thirty-eight and a half.
* Emma Hale, Joseph's wife; a year and a half older than Joseph.
* Joseph and Emma's children: Julia Murdock, Joseph III, Frederick Granger Williams, and Alexander Hale.
* Samuel, Joseph's younger brother; age thirty-six.
* William, Joseph's youngest living brother; age thirty-three.

Note: There are sisters to Joseph, but they do not play major roles in the novel.

*Designates actual people from Church history.

Others

* John C. Bennett, converted to the Church in 1840; elected mayor of Nauvoo in 1841; turned against the Church in 1842.

  Jean Claude Dubuque ("Frenchie"), Joshua's lumber foreman in Wisconsin.

* Thomas Ford, governor of the state of Illinois.

* Heber C. Kimball, friend of Brigham Young's and a member of the Quorum of the Twelve Apostles.

* Jane Manning, a free black who has joined the Church and lives in Nauvoo.

* Orson Pratt, member of the Quorum of the Twelve Apostles.

* Parley P. Pratt, member of the Quorum of the Twelve Apostles.

* Willard Richards, member of the Quorum of the Twelve Apostles.

* Sidney Rigdon, member of the First Presidency; age fifty-one.

* Orrin Porter Rockwell, close friend and bodyguard of the martyred prophet Joseph Smith.

  Alice Samuelson, daughter of Walter; age seventeen and a half as the story begins.

  Walter Samuelson and his wife, Judith, from St. Louis; Joshua's business partner.

* George A. Smith, member of the Quorum of the Twelve Apostles.

* Mercy Fielding Thompson Smith, sister to Mary, widowed plural wife of Hyrum Smith.

* John Taylor, member of the Quorum of the Twelve Apostles.

* Wilford Woodruff, member of the Quorum of the Twelve Apostles.

* Brigham Young, President of the Quorum of the Twelve Apostles; age forty-three as the novel opens.

*Designates actual people from Church history.

Though too numerous to list here, there are many other actual people from the pages of history who are mentioned by name in the novel. Thomas Sharp, Frank Worrell, Isaac Morley, Edmund Durfee, and many others mentioned in the book were real people who lived and participated in the events described in this work.

The Benjamin and Mary Ann Steed Family

Since the family continues to grow, it is felt that showing the various family groups separately will be less confusing. Therefore, each of Benjamin and Mary Ann's children has his or her own chart. (These charts do not include deceased children who play no part in the novel.)

BENJAMIN AND MARY ANN

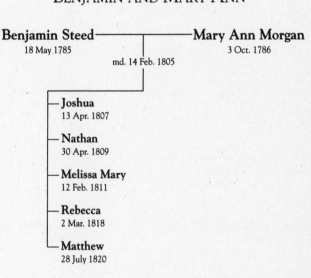

Benjamin Steed
18 May 1785

Mary Ann Morgan
3 Oct. 1786

md. 14 Feb. 1805

— **Joshua**
13 Apr. 1807

— **Nathan**
30 Apr. 1809

— **Melissa Mary**
12 Feb. 1811

— **Rebecca**
2 Mar. 1818

— **Matthew**
28 July 1820

JOSHUA AND CAROLINE

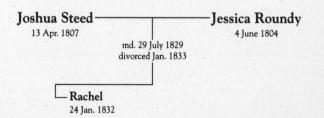

Joshua Steed
13 Apr. 1807

Jessica Roundy
4 June 1804

md. 29 July 1829
divorced Jan. 1833

— **Rachel**
24 Jan. 1832

Continued on following page

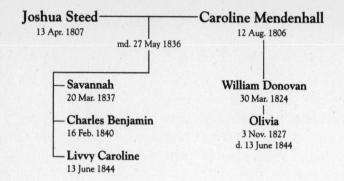

Joshua Steed ———— Caroline Mendenhall
13 Apr. 1807   12 Aug. 1806

md. 27 May 1836

— Savannah   William Donovan
  20 Mar. 1837   30 Mar. 1824

— Charles Benjamin   Olivia
  16 Feb. 1840   3 Nov. 1827
                                 d. 13 June 1844

— Livvy Caroline
  13 June 1844

JESSICA

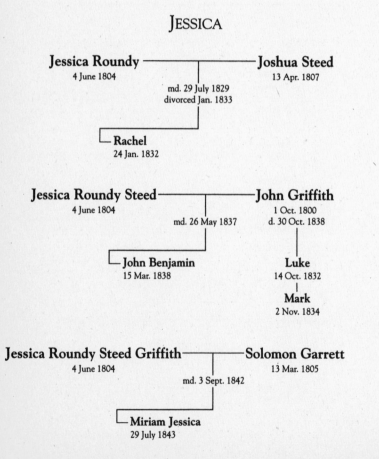

Jessica Roundy ———— Joshua Steed
4 June 1804   13 Apr. 1807

md. 29 July 1829
divorced Jan. 1833

— Rachel
  24 Jan. 1832

Jessica Roundy Steed ———— John Griffith
4 June 1804   1 Oct. 1800
                             d. 30 Oct. 1838

md. 26 May 1837

— John Benjamin   Luke
  15 Mar. 1838   14 Oct. 1832

                             Mark
                          2 Nov. 1834

Jessica Roundy Steed Griffith ———— Solomon Garrett
4 June 1804   13 Mar. 1805

md. 3 Sept. 1842

— Miriam Jessica
  29 July 1843

NATHAN AND LYDIA

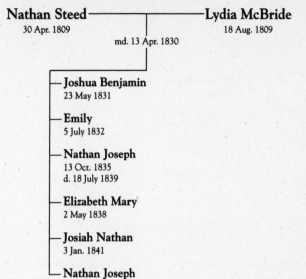

Nathan Steed —————————— Lydia McBride
30 Apr. 1809   18 Aug. 1809

md. 13 Apr. 1830

— **Joshua Benjamin**
23 May 1831

— **Emily**
5 July 1832

— **Nathan Joseph**
13 Oct. 1835
d. 18 July 1839

— **Elizabeth Mary**
2 May 1838

— **Josiah Nathan**
3 Jan. 1841

— **Nathan Joseph**
18 June 1843

MELISSA AND CARL

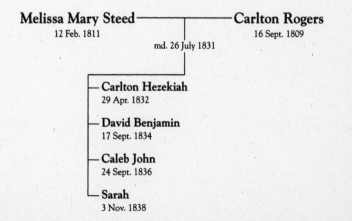

Melissa Mary Steed —————————— Carlton Rogers
12 Feb. 1811   16 Sept. 1809

md. 26 July 1831

— **Carlton Hezekiah**
29 Apr. 1832

— **David Benjamin**
17 Sept. 1834

— **Caleb John**
24 Sept. 1836

— **Sarah**
3 Nov. 1838

REBECCA AND DEREK

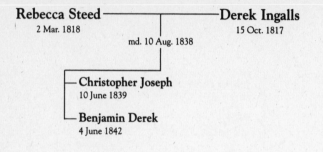

Rebecca Steed ——————————— **Derek Ingalls**
2 Mar. 1818   15 Oct. 1817
          md. 10 Aug. 1838

— **Christopher Joseph**
10 June 1839

— **Benjamin Derek**
4 June 1842

MATTHEW AND JENNY

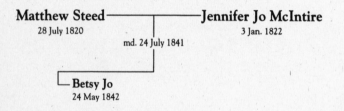

Matthew Steed ——————————— **Jennifer Jo McIntire**
28 July 1820   3 Jan. 1822
        md. 24 July 1841

— **Betsy Jo**
24 May 1842

Key to Abbreviations Used in Chapter Notes

Throughout the chapter notes, abbreviated references are given. The following key gives the full bibliographic data for those references.

American Moses   Leonard J. Arrington, *Brigham Young: American Moses* (New York: Alfred A. Knopf, 1985.)

CHFT   *Church History in the Fulness of Times* (Salt Lake City: The Church of Jesus Christ of Latter-day Saints, 1989.)

Edmund Durfee   William G. Hartley, *The Murder of Edmund Durfee* (Provo, Utah: Albert and Tamma Durfee Miner Family Organization, 1995.)

HC   Joseph Smith, *History of The Church of Jesus Christ of Latter-day Saints*, ed. B. H. Roberts, 7 vols. (Salt Lake City: The Church of Jesus Christ of Latter-day Saints, 1932–51.)

"Journal of Thomas Bullock"   Gregory R. Knight, ed., "Journal of Thomas Bullock," *BYU Studies* 31 (Winter 1991): 15–75.

Mack Hist.   Lucy Mack Smith, *History of Joseph Smith by His Mother*, ed. Preston Nibley (Salt Lake City: Bookcraft, 1954.)

Women of Nauvoo   Richard Neitzel Holzapfel and Jeni Broberg
Holzapfel, *Women of Nauvoo* (Salt Lake
City: Bookcraft, 1992.)

No Unhallowed Hand

The Standard of Truth has been erected; no unhallowed hand can stop the work from progressing; persecutions may rage, mobs may combine, armies may assemble, calumny may defame, but the truth of God will go forth boldly, nobly, and independent, till it has penetrated every continent, visited every clime, swept every country, and sounded in every ear, till the purposes of God shall be accomplished, and the Great Jehovah shall say the work is done.

—Joseph Smith, 1842

To Nathan's surprise, the temple block was deserted. He looked around carefully. The Nauvoo Cemetery was east of the city a short distance, set amid a grove of scattered trees, but sometime before his death Joseph had designated a site near the temple as his place of burial. It was still early, but it was the Sabbath. He had assumed that people might come out early, before the worship services. When he came yesterday afternoon, to no great wonder he found more than a hundred people milling around the two freshly dug graves. He had turned on his heel and walked back to town. He didn't begrudge the people's being there, he just didn't want to be there with them. But now there was no one. Grateful, he walked through the opening in the rail fence, moving slowly now.

The grass was heavy with dew and he could feel its wetness quickly soaking through his pant legs as he walked toward the spot where the rich color of green was cut into two freshly spaded plots of black earth. His step slowed and he reached up and took off his hat. A sudden forlornness swept over him, as sharp as if it were actual physical pain. There were no grave markers on either end of the burial plots. Nothing said who was buried here beneath the Illinois sod. It was a bitter and ironic final footnote to the lives of Joseph and Hyrum Smith. Even with the brothers' deaths their enemies were not satisfied. Word had reached Nauvoo that some might try to get the head of the Mormon prophet for the reward promised for it in Missouri. Hoping that it was rumor, not daring to believe that it was only that, the Saints had not marked the graves.

He bent down at the one end of the nearest plot. It had rained last night and the soil was smooth and damp. He reached out with a finger and began to write.

Joseph Smith December 23, 1805—June 27, 1844
Hyrum Smith February 9, 1800—June 27, 1844

He looked at what he had written, absently rubbing the mud from his finger, then leaned forward again and wrote one additional line.

Prophets, Servants, Friends

He straightened slowly. That was it. Prophets, yes. Servants of the Lord, without question. But for Nathan Steed, it was all of that and so much more. They had been his friends.

Most of the twenty-some thousand people now in the Church knew Joseph only as their prophet. They knew only the public Joseph, the man who preached the powerful sermons in the East or West Grove, the man who was responsible for the Book of Mormon and the Doctrine and Covenants. Their grief was a public grief and was shared jointly by all the Saints. During the last two days, Nathan had joined in the public mourning during the viewing of the bodies and the subsequent funerals. Now he wished to spend some moments with his own private loss.

Nathan's relationship with Joseph and Hyrum Smith spanned seventeen years. In the spring of 1827, on the recommendation of their neighbor Martin Harris, Benjamin Steed hired the two Smith boys as day labor to help him clear his land. That was before there was a Book of Mormon, before the priesthood had been restored, before the Church had been organized. Nathan had wrestled stumps from the earth, plowed virgin fields, and pulled sticks together with Joseph and Hyrum. They had eaten together at the Steed table. They had become friends.

He looked away now. In his mind was the vivid image of a meadow, just off the road a mile or two south of the Steed farm. Nathan had been walking Joseph and Hyrum partway home. They stopped to rest. And then Joseph had begun, with Hyrum nodding solemn witness. He told of that morning seven years earlier when he had gone into a grove of trees to ask a simple question: Which of the churches is right? Nathan could remember, as clearly as though it had happened this very morning, his utter astonishment, his mind wanting to reject the enormity of what he was hearing but his heart telling him it was true.

There were so many memories. The night in the Smith home when Joseph returned from retrieving the plates from where he had hidden them in an old birch log, having a dislocated thumb from fighting off would-be attackers. There was that sunlit day when Oliver Cowdery and Nathan sat on the banks of the Susquehanna River in Harmony, Pennsylvania, and Oliver told him about the coming of John the Baptist. There was the Peter Whitmer cabin and the small group there to witness the restoration of the Church of Jesus Christ on the earth. He remembered sham trials in Colesville, mobs in Jackson County, the betrayal and arrest in Far West. The images, the voices, the memories marched like rank upon rank of soldiers in his mind. So much. So long. So treasured. And now they were dead.

He half turned, using the wet grass to wash the mud from his finger. In that first summer here in Nauvoo, during that terrible time when the ague was cutting through the Saints like the scythe of death itself, Joseph had risen from his sickbed and come to the home of Nathan and Lydia Steed. If he had not, their little Elizabeth Mary, whimpering and near death, would be gone too. Benjamin Steed would twice have been dead had it not been for Joseph's commanding power. What would the Steeds be, where would they have gone, had it not been for the lives of Joseph and Hyrum Smith? How many threads had been woven into the fabric of their friendship? How many bonds had forged what lay between them? This was his personal loss. A prophet, yes. But a friend like few men ever had.

He turned back, looking down at the crude letters in the damp earth. *Three days! Can it really be only three days now?* He shook his head. Now the memories were like the lash, tearing into flesh and leaving raw wounds. If only he had stayed. If only he and Stephen Markham had not left the jail for medicine, they would have been there. Perhaps two more in the bedroom would have been enough to stave off the mob. But they had not been there. They had come to Nauvoo for help, driven out of Carthage at the point of forty or more bayonets, their boots filling with blood from the stab wounds they had suffered.

And now he was here. And they were gone.

He reached out and gently tamped the earth with the toe of his boot, erasing the lines of tribute and leaving the two graves unmarked once again.

———————

"Can you just leave them here by my bed, Matthew?"

Matthew Steed stopped. The crutches he held in his hand swung gently back and forth. He looked at his wife, not quite able to conceal the sudden look of dismay that flashed across his face. Jenny gave a slight shake of her head.

Kathryn McIntire's Irish temper flared. She turned on her sister. "Jenny, I just want them here where I can see them. I know that I'm not ready for them yet."

Jenny's face pulled into a disapproving frown. "Like last week, right?"

Just a week ago, Jenny had been out in the main room of the house playing with little Betsy Jo. Matthew was away at the cabinet shop. There had been a tremendous crash from Kathryn's bedroom. When Jenny came running in, she found Kathryn on the floor beside her bed, holding one wrist and wincing in pain. Just behind her, the wheelchair was on its side, one wheel still spinning slowly. In spite of repeated warnings not to try and get out of bed by herself, she had gone ahead and nearly broken her arm.

Kathryn concentrated on Matthew, giving him a look of childlike innocence as she pointed to the chair near the head of her bed. "Come on, Matthew."

"Kathryn," Jenny started, her voice heavy with warning. "You are making progress, but you have to learn to be patient."

Kathryn's head jerked up. "Don't use that word."

Jenny blinked. "What?"

"Don't tell me to be patient, Jenny." There were sudden, hot tears. "I hate that word. I hate it."

"I'm sorry, Kathryn," Jenny said, instantly seeing her mistake.

There was not a flicker of response. Kathryn turned to Matthew as if he were alone in the room with her. She reached out and patted the chair. "I know I can't use them yet, but I want to be able to touch them. It will inspire me to heal more quickly."

Jenny McIntire Steed felt a stab of guilt. Two years ago last April, while out on a picnic with Jessica and the children, a bolt of lightning struck within a few feet of where Kathryn was standing. When she recovered consciousness three days later, she was paralyzed from the neck down. The paralysis was tragedy enough for someone who loved life as Kathryn did, but the humiliation of suddenly being totally dependent on others—for eating, bathing, even something as simple as turning over in bed—was a far greater tragedy in her eyes. She fought back fiercely. She simply refused to accept the idea that her condition might be permanent.

And miraculously, her situation did improve. Gradually, control over her hands and arms returned. Soon her upper body was back to nearly what it had been before. A few weeks after the tragedy, Matthew crafted a wheelchair for her in the cabinet shop. Thrilled with her new freedom, at first she had to be pushed everywhere. But that was not good enough. Soon she was strong enough to propel herself around, covering everything but the roughest ground without help. But that was as far as it had gone. She spent hours every day massaging her legs, lifting and bending them over and over, but there was no further lessening of the paralysis. Two years of waiting, and nothing more. No wonder she hated the word *patience*.

The crutches had been Kathryn's idea. They had all tried to talk her out of it. Even Joshua, who had been the most supportive in her battle against her handicap, saw that crutches required at least some control in the legs and feet. But she wouldn't listen to him either. And now, watching Kathryn's eyes, full of silent pleadings and proud determination, Jenny understood the need for hope, the importance of having something to challenge her further.

She laid a hand on Matthew's arm and nodded briefly. There was a quick, grateful smile from Kathryn as Matthew stepped forward and set the crutches against the chair. Unlike the single crutch Matthew had once carved for Joshua back in Missouri, this pair was a finely crafted set and finished professionally. As he had done with the wheelchair, Matthew used a pattern he found in an Eastern catalog. He had turned the wood on the lathe until each piece was perfectly round, then sanded them until they felt silky to the touch. The place where they fit under the arms was padded with layers of soft cotton cloth. He had just finished putting the padding on late the night before.

She reached out and touched the wood, letting her fingertips caress the polished surface. "Thank you, Matthew. They're beautiful."

He reached down and kissed her on the cheek. "You're most welcome. I hope I measured right. I made them a little long." He flashed a warm grin. "It's easier to take a little off than to add it back on again."

"I'm sure they'll be just fine."

Jenny leaned over and hugged her. "Are you sure you'll be all right alone?"

"Of course." She looked contrite. "I know I ought to go to worship services, but I just don't feel up to it today."

"That's fine. We'll be home shortly after noon. We'll come get you before we go over to Mother Steed's."

"Okay. Do you really think Jessica will come today?"

"That's what one family told Father Steed. The man said Solomon had been out checking on the schools, but planned to come today."

"I'm so anxious to see them. I'll bet little Miriam has grown a foot since we last saw them." She lay back against the pillow. "I just wish it were happier times that brought them."

"Yes," Jenny said, sudden tears springing to her eyes. Like thousands of other Latter-day Saints, Jessica and Solomon were coming to Nauvoo because they wanted to pay their last respects to their martyred leaders.

"Well," Matthew said, brightening a little, "I'm sure they'll be here this afternoon sometime. But we'll come get you before then."

"All right."

"Of course," Matthew went on, "Mother plans a big supper this afternoon. It will be the first time the whole family has been together for some time."

"Except for Carl and Melissa," Jenny said.

There was nothing to say to that. Upon learning that Carl's father was dying, Carl and Melissa had returned to Kirtland, Ohio, in March. Though his father had passed away a few weeks ago, in their letters there was no mention of returning to Nauvoo.

"Get Betsy Jo," Jenny said to Matthew. Then, as he left the room, she looked sternly at her sister, motioning toward the crutches. "You're not to be rushing things," she chided softly, "you hear me?"

Kathryn answered with equal softness. "I know what I can and can't do, Jenny."

Their eyes held each other for several moments; then finally Jenny nodded. "All right," she said. "We'll see you in a couple of hours."

Kathryn waited for a full twenty minutes just to make sure that they didn't return to get something they had forgotten, or that some other family member didn't stop to say hello, which they were in the habit of doing. But the house was quiet, and through the open windows she could hear nothing outside. Nauvoo had gone to worship services and the rest of the city was deserted.

She drew back the covers, reached down with both hands, and pulled her feet up, swinging them around over the side of the bed, grunting with the effort, talking to them as if they were naughty children who refused to listen to their parent. She had to stop for a moment when she was done and the first beads of perspiration started to form on her forehead. She sat there, feeling the warmth of the floor on her bare feet. At least she had that much. Someone had told her that sometimes with paralysis, one lost all feeling too. But thankfully, that was not the case with her. She had feeling, just absolutely no control of her body from the waist down.

She took a deep breath, steeling herself for the task ahead, then reached for the crutches and brought them to her. Today would be the first step to greater independence. She grimaced at the unintended play on words. *First step?* If you dragged feet and legs across the floor using crutches, did that qualify as a step? Then she nodded to herself. Maybe not to someone else, but it would be a major first step for her.

Sitting straight now, she pulled at her dress until it was down around her ankles again, then positioned the crutches under her arms. Gripping the hand braces tightly, she held them out straight. She smiled as she remembered the day Matthew had come in with a carpenter's ruler and measured her to see where the hand braces needed to go. He had made her stretch out so he could take the measurement from her armpits to the palms of her hands, and from her armpits to the bottom of her feet.

"I feel like you're measuring me for a coffin," she had quipped.

With great solemnity, Matthew shook his head. "We only do that for customers who have passed on," he said. "That way we get fewer complaints." She had giggled, and loved him all the more for being willing to tease her about it.

With crutches firmly in hand now, she leaned forward, positioning the tips on the floor (the tips had been wrapped with a thick padding of canvas so as to cover the polished wood and take a better grip to the floor's surface). The challenge immediately became evident. From a sitting position there was no way she could pull herself up using only her arms and upper body. Chiding herself for being so foolish, she set the crutches aside, slid sideways on the bed, then pulled herself onto the arm of the overstuffed chair beside her bed. Once again she had to stop, the effort momentarily exhausting her. Though it was barely ten-thirty now, the day was going to be a hot one and the house was quickly warming up. A droplet of sweat broke loose from her temple and trickled down the side of her cheek.

She twisted around and, using the back of the chair, worked herself up into a semi-standing position, her breath coming in short, hard gasps now. That effort alone was enough to start her body trembling. Her feet were planted firmly enough on the floor to help her keep her balance, but they couldn't respond if she started to wobble. Closing her eyes for a moment, she let her body adjust itself to this new, strange feeling. Then, biting her lip, she reached for the crutches.

Now came the hard part. Steadying herself with one hand, she put one crutch under her left arm. She shifted her weight, cautiously letting go of the chair. She wobbled a little but steadied. Then she took the second crutch. She nearly fell twice before she had both of them under her arms. Once again she rested for a moment. Now the sweat was pouring down her forehead and into her eyes, stinging them. She was barely aware of it. She was on her feet, standing, with no one holding her, with no one having lifted her to that position. The exultation was like a deep draught of cold water on a hot day. It gave her the strength she needed to make the next move.

With a quick breath she pushed off, leaving the safety of the chair. To her surprise, she found that maneuvering the crutches was simple enough. She would steady herself, make sure her feet were solidly on the floor, and then with a quick motion lift both crutches and move them forward an inch or two. Then all she had to do was lean her upper body forward, dragging the lower part of her after it. Once. Twice. Three times. She felt a burst of exhilaration. It was working! It would take weeks and weeks of practice to master it, she could sense that, but she was up. With no one else in the house. She was up!

Halfway across the room, she had to stop. Her first step! The pure joy of knowing she was moving, completely free of anyone's help, dizzied her and she nearly lost her balance. Leaning heavily on the crutches now, she took a deep breath, then another, grinning foolishly. Steadying herself, she reached up one hand to wipe away the sweat from her eyes. It was a mistake. The crutch beneath her slipped on the wooden floor and shot outwards. With a cry, she grabbed at it, which threw her body off balance.

So simple a thing, to shift one's weight to the other foot to stop from losing one's balance. But for Kathryn, it was like asking an infant to walk. Down she went, trying to throw out one hand to catch the fall. But her hand was still tangled in the crutch and she couldn't free it in time. She hit on her right shoulder, with the crutch half-beneath her body. She screamed out and rolled over to her back, writhing in agony, holding her shoulder. Tears of pain filled her eyes, but after a moment, they gave way to tears of frustration and hopelessness and despair. She rolled over onto her stomach, ignoring the searing pain in her shoulder, and began to sob uncontrollably.

It was shortly after noon when Jenny returned to the house. Matthew had taken Betsy Jo to his mother's to start helping with the cooking. Jenny went immediately into Kathryn's room. Her first glance was to the chair. With relief, she saw the crutches were exactly as they had left them. Kathryn looked a little pale, but was sitting up in bed, reading a book.

She looked up and smiled. "How was the worship service?"

"Good. The brethren talked to us about remaining calm and not seeking revenge for Joseph's death."

"Oh."

Jenny moved over to sit beside her. "Are you okay?" she asked, looking at her more closely.

"I'm fine. I . . . I'm still not feeling quite well, but I'll be all right."

Jenny placed a hand on her forehead. "You feel cold and clammy. Are you sure you're all right?"

"Yes. I'm fine. I am tired, though. Perhaps I'll sleep a little before going over to Mother Steed's."

Jenny nodded, still looking concerned.

Kathryn forced her brightest smile. "Did Jessica and Solomon come yet?"

"No, the family who told us they were coming said they couldn't leave before this morning, so it will be three or four o'clock before they get here, I imagine."

"It's too bad they had to miss the funeral yesterday."

"Yes, well, the man said that Solomon was out visiting the settlements when the word came. But anyway, they'll be here soon."

"Good. Will you come get me when they arrive?"

"Of course." She leaned forward a little. "Are you sure you are all right?"

"Yes. I'll sleep a little, and then I'll be fine."

Jenny stood, still reluctant, and kissed Kathryn on the cheek. "All right, we'll be back in a little while."

"Thank you for caring, Jenny."

Surprised, Jenny nodded, still eyeing her sister with suspicion. But after a moment, she turned and left the room, giving her a little wave of farewell.

———•———

Peter had come, book under his arm, about an hour before, to help Kathryn pass the time until Jessica's family arrived. When the door opened and Kathryn saw him standing there, she felt her heart drop. She hadn't expected this, didn't want it. Not today. The pain in her right side was growing with each passing hour. Nothing was broken—she had proven that during the agony of getting herself back to the bed and into it—but she was going to be one mass of black and blue on that right side. She had been lying here worrying about how she was going to explain all of that the next time Jenny helped her bathe. But the thought of having to smile and be pleasant to Peter when she hurt as keenly as she did was almost more than she could face.

But she did smile. She did manage a forced cheerfulness at his presence. She even was able to convince him she was thrilled that he had brought a book of Shakespeare to read to her. Normally she loved that. She loved to hear Peter's British voice, reading the great bard as though Peter himself had written the lines. She loved to watch the earnestness in his face, the light in his eyes. But not today. It was almost more effort than she could muster. She was so weary, so tired of it all.

Her eyes opened with a jerk when she realized that his voice had stopped. He was watching her, his eyes wide and filled with concern. He smiled now, a little embarrassed. "Would you like to rest, Kathryn? I shouldn't go on so."

She waved a hand and managed a soft laugh. "No, I wasn't sleeping. I was listening to your voice. I like to hear your voice, Peter."

"Thank you." He closed the book and set it on the bed beside her feet. He clasped his hands together in his lap and started to examine them closely. For a moment, she thought his acting this way might be because of her closing her eyes, but then she sensed it was something else. He was growing increasingly nervous even as she watched him. He shifted positions in his chair. His eyes rose to hers, then instantly darted away again when he saw she was looking at him.

"Do you have another appointment, Peter?" she finally asked with her characteristic bluntness.

That startled him. "No, why do you ask?"

"Well, it's like you can barely wait to get out of here."

His face flushed and he dropped his eyes to stare at his hands. "No, don't be silly."

"Then what is it?" she demanded, the irritation and anger at herself suddenly taking focus on him.

His shoulders lifted and fell as he took a quick breath. "Kathryn, I . . ."

"Yes?"

"I've been thinking about . . . well, about us."

She gaped at him. "Us?" she echoed dumbly.

"Yes, you and me."

She was too dumbfounded to know what to say.

His face was flaming all the brighter now, but his head came up. He swallowed hard twice, then plunged in. "I suppose this is not the most ideal time, but . . . Well, you know that we've always been good friends, Kathryn."

"Yes." She heard herself say it as though from a great distance. Waves of panic were washing over her. *No, Peter. Not today. On any other day this would be hard enough, but not today, Peter. Please! Please! Not now!*

"Well, my feelings are more than just friendship now, Kathryn. These past few months, I've come to realize that you mean a—"

"Peter?"

He looked up, surprised by the curtness in her voice. "Yes?"

"Don't!" she whispered. "Please don't."

His eyes were large and wounded. "But—"

"Peter, you are very sweet and I like you as a friend, but it could never be anything more than that for me. I just—" Her voice nearly broke and she reached out and touched his hand to cover herself. "I just don't care for you in that way. I never could."

"Oh."

She looked away, not able to bear the pain she had brought to his eyes. Then finally, very softly, she heard, "I understand."

"I'm sorry, Peter."

"No, it's all right. I appreciate you being honest."

She winced at that, and not because of the pain. Honesty was the last thing she was willing to give right now. "Can we still be friends?"

He looked up, as though he hadn't quite heard right. Then there was a sickly smile. "Yeah, sure. Who else would try to read Shakespeare to you?"

Tears sprang to her eyes. *Yes! Who else?* But Shakespeare was not enough. How fully she had proved that on this day. "Thank you, Peter. Thank you for being so understanding."

He stood. "Well, maybe I'd better go."

"Yes," she said softly. Her lips parted, wanting to say more, wanting to take away the hurt from his face, but she couldn't. She was as crippled in that regard as she was in her body.

He nodded, lifted his hand as if he was going to touch her cheek, then let it drop again. "Good-bye, Kathryn."

"Good-bye, Peter."

He nodded and left the room, walking very slowly. As the door shut quietly behind him, Kathryn turned her head toward the wall and began to weep.

Joshua leaned forward, his dark eyes earnest. "Look, I'm not being critical of the Church. I'm just telling you, Joseph Smith was the force that made the Church what it is. Joseph is gone now. All I'm saying is that we need to start thinking about what that means."

Matthew's Jenny was shaking her head even before he finished. "But that's exactly the point, Joshua. It's not 'The Church of Joseph Smith of Latter-day Saints.' It's 'The Church of Jesus Christ of Latter-day Saints.' We believe the Savior is the head of the Church and the real power that makes it live."

Nathan had to smile. Spunk. That was the word for this Irish girl whom his younger brother had married. She was so gentle and so sweet of disposition, but cross her—especially on something that related to the gospel—and she stood right up and let herself be heard.

Beside him, his own wife jumped in. "We all know what a loss this will be for us," Lydia said. "No one disagrees with you on that. Joseph was a remarkable man but—"

"Joseph was more than that," Joshua cut in. "I know this sounds odd coming from me, but Joseph was more than just remarkable. He was the kind of man that comes along once in a lifetime. Maybe not even that often. If it weren't for Joseph Smith, you would have no Church."

Jessica turned to him and smiled. "You are right, Joshua. Coming from you that does sound odd." They all laughed at that, Joshua included. Then immediately several started answering him, all speaking at once—Caroline, Derek, Solomon. Jenny again.

Jenny's sister, Kathryn, sat in her wheelchair, hands folded in her lap. She followed the conversation, but so far had said nothing. Sitting somewhat apart from the others, Peter was equally quiet, not looking at Kathryn at all. Nathan watched the two of them with wonder. The rest of the family hadn't noticed, but there was no mistaking it. Something had happened between Peter and Kathryn. He made a mental note to ask Lydia about it later.

He turned to watch the other members of the family. He was half-amused, half-astonished. Jessica and Solomon had finally arrived shortly after four o'clock. Immediately all the family gathered to Grandma and Grandpa Steed's home. Now it was dark. They were seated in the yard. Supper was over. The dishes were done. The three youngest—Caroline's Livvy, who was not even a month old yet, Jessica's Miriam, not quite a year, and Lydia's little Joseph, just a year—were asleep next door in one bedroom of Nathan's home. The window of that room was open so they could hear the babies if they cried. The rest of the children had gone down to Miller's pasture to play night games. The night was soft and warm around them. Here and there a firefly winked in the darkness. The harmony of crickets and cicadas provided a droning, barely noticed background for their conversation.

Nathan was amused because this was so like his family. Get supper done, get the children taken care of, then open up a discussion topic and go at it with quiet but friendly tenacity. This was their typical summer evening's activity. He was astonished because what they were witnessing at this moment was an amazing turnaround. Just four months ago, through the devious half-lies of Robert Foster, Joshua had been convinced that Joseph Smith had tried to take Olivia Steed, not yet seventeen, into plural marriage. Foster also claimed that he had seen Joseph kissing Olivia.

To describe Joshua's reaction as fury was to seriously understate the case. It was a towering, mindless rage—at the Church, at the family for being part of it, and most especially at Joseph Smith. Nothing penetrated through it. Not Caroline's explanations. Not Olivia's denials. Joshua had gone to Joseph and in an ugly confrontation threatened his life if he even so much as spoke to Olivia again. Joseph never did. Within four months of that confrontation, Olivia lay dead of a broken neck in the dusty streets of Warsaw. Two weeks later, Joseph was killed by a mob with painted faces.

So to hear Joshua defending Joseph Smith as he was now was truly an amazing turnaround. Part of that was the guilt. Nathan knew that. Joshua was devastated by the death of his daughter, but knowing that it was his anger and his blind refusal to listen to and accept the truth from his wife and daughter that had contributed to the tragedy was enough to jerk him up short, like a wild horse hitting the end of its first rope. But it was more than that. Joseph Smith had done a remarkable thing that night. When he learned of the accident, he came in the night to Warsaw. He came to the town where the people were howling for his blood. All of the so-called friends of Joshua, who had courted his favor when they thought he would turn against the Church, did not even so much as come to give their condolences. And Joseph, at great personal risk, came to help. And when there could have been just recrimination, when Joseph could so easily have reminded Joshua of his foolishness and of the fact that he had grossly misjudged Joseph, Joseph said nothing about that. He simply took Joshua in his arms and they wept together for the loss of Olivia.

There were many things for which Joshua Steed could be criticized, but loyalty to a trusted friend was not one of those. And now part of Joshua's mourning, part of this turning that they were witnessing, was Joshua's way of trying to make things right again, even though Joseph's death had cut short any attempt to do so with Joseph himself.

Nathan turned to look at Caroline. She had nearly lost her life that day too. A broken arm. A broken ankle. Many bruises, which were mostly gone now. She was recovering nicely, thanks to the blessing Joseph had given her that night, but she still tired easily. She half reclined on a lounge, and Nathan saw that she was not following the conversation. She was looking past the family, out into the darkness, intently, as if watching for someone. Her face was mostly in shadow, but suddenly it was as if it were brightly illuminated for him and he saw the inner sorrow that filled her soul. He looked away, embarrassed to have caught her in such a moment of naked vulnerability.

"Someone will take Joseph's place," Solomon Garrett was saying, pulling Nathan back to the conversation.

"Who?" Joshua demanded. "Hyrum—the most logical one—is dead with Joseph. Sidney Rigdon's in Pittsburgh. That's all three members of the First Presidency."

"What about Brigham?" Matthew said.

"Brigham's a fine man," Joshua shot right back, "but he's no Joseph Smith."

"No one is Joseph Smith," Mary Ann said quietly, "but that doesn't mean they can't lead the Church."

"Where is Brigham?" Joshua said, not wanting to directly disagree with his mother. "He's in the East. So is Heber Kimball and the Pratts and John Page and George Albert Smith."

"Joseph sent a letter before he died calling them back," Derek volunteered. "They'll be coming soon."

Joshua went right on as if Derek hadn't spoken. "John Taylor's a fine man, but he's critically wounded himself. It will be months before he will recover. Willard Richards is still in shock. I don't think he can take over." He stopped, pleased to see that his words were registering now. "You've got a crisis here. Nauvoo is in an uproar. Governor Ford is surely not going to step in and restore order. And you're without a leader."

On they went, Nathan only half listening again. He was thinking about Melissa and Carl now. Had Melissa had the baby yet? Were they going to stay in Kirtland now that Carl's father had died? How long would it take for news of Joseph's death to reach them?

Nathan looked up in surprise as someone laid a hand on his shoulder. He turned and saw it was his father.

"I'm going to go check on the babies. Want to come?"

There was something in Benjamin's eyes that alerted Nathan to the fact that his father had been watching him, had sensed his mood and his thoughts, and decided it was time to intervene. He laughed softly. "Yeah. I'd like that."

Benjamin and Nathan stood in the bedroom where little Joseph Steed normally slept alone. Now, however, a crib and a small mattress had also been brought in and the bedroom seemed almost crowded. Jessica's youngest, Miriam, was in the crib, her long dark hair spilling out across the mattress. On a small mattress in the corner, walled with pillows just in case she moved, was the youngest of the Steed clan. Livvy Caroline Steed—the child given the name of her older sister who had died just hours before her birth—was on her tummy, her face to the light, her tiny fists doubled up beside her head.

"It's a miracle we even have her, isn't it?" Benjamin said.

"Yes. Joshua is sure that what happened that day with Olivia was his punishment for his being foolish, but if Olivia's loss was a punishment, the birth of this little angel was a compensating gift."

"Caroline too," Benjamin murmured. "It's a miracle she wasn't killed. Joshua got a double gift that day in return for his loss."

"Yes."

They backed out of the room. As they walked toward the stairs, Benjamin slowed his step. "You went to the graves this morning."

It wasn't a question. Nathan turned in surprise.

There was a low chuckle. "I happened to be at the window as you left."

"So you're not sleeping much either."

A brief shake of his head gave Nathan the answer. In silence they went down the stairs and back into the main part of the house. It was dark. Through the open windows they could hear the family out in the yard next door. The conversation had turned from Joseph and Hyrum to the flooding of the Mississippi. Heavy late snows in the Rockies had now melted. That, coupled with almost constant rain for the last two weeks, had created a crisis. The Missouri River was flooding heavily. At St. Louis, where it joined the Mississippi, the waterfront docks were under-water. Thousands of acres of farmland were inundated. Now the high waters were backing upstream. Forty miles downstream, Quincy had been mostly evacuated. The people of Warsaw, just fifteen miles south of Nauvoo, were now moving to higher ground. The rapids at Keokuk were partially blocking the rising waters, but one had only to walk down to the river to see that if it continued, Nauvoo was going to be next. The current ran brown and sluggish and was filled with logs and other debris.

Benjamin stopped as they came to the sitting room. To Nathan's surprise, he turned into it rather than going back outside. He sat down with a weary sigh. Curious, Nathan moved into the room and sat down across from him. They sat that way for several minutes, half listening to the conversation in the yard next door, half lost in their own thoughts.

"You agree with Joshua?" Benjamin finally asked.

Nathan's head came up. "You mean about the Church disintegrating? Of course not."

"But in a way he's right, you know. What happens now will prove to be very important."

"Yes, I believe that. But what Jenny said was the perfect answer. This isn't the Church of Joseph Smith. If it were, then I wouldn't have much hope."

For several moments Benjamin watched him. In the darkness of the room it was hard for Nathan to read Benjamin's expression, but he sensed it was sobered, perhaps even grave. "It is still a crisis. Make no mistake of that. There's already talk begun."

"By whom?"

"More than one."

"What are they saying?"

"That Sidney Rigdon should come back and take over."

"No!" It came out as a soft explosion.

"Or that Brigham should do it. Joseph was using him more and more there toward the end. Or Heber. Or maybe someone completely new. I hear that one or two are even starting to wonder aloud if they may not be the chosen ones."

Disgust welled up. "Joseph is barely in the ground and already they're picking the bones."

"Not everyone. But a few." There was a long pause. "It's a natural concern, Nathan. And the speculation is only going to get worse until something is settled."

A sudden bleakness swept across Nathan. "I can't believe Joseph is really gone. As I stood there this morning, looking down at the graves, it didn't seem real. I felt like I would return to the city and find him and Hyrum stocking shelves at the store, or maybe Joseph out playing stickball with the boys. It was like I was looking at the graves of some strangers. I couldn't make myself believe they were really down there."

Benjamin leaned forward, hands on his knees, head down in thought. It lifted now and he gazed at Nathan for several seconds. "They're not," he finally said softly.

Startled, Nathan jerked forward. "What did you say?"

"I said they are not down there."

He was aghast. "What kind of a comment is that?"

Benjamin gazed out the window for a moment. When he turned back, he spoke in a low voice. "What I am about to tell you, you cannot tell anyone else. Not even Mary Ann knows. This isn't because I don't trust her, it's a protection to her."

"What?" Nathan asked in bewilderment. He couldn't fathom what his father was suggesting. He had seen the two gaping holes. He had listened to the funeral speech. He had seen the two coffins lowered into the ground. He had felt a sharp jolt with every shovelful of dirt rattling on the wooden boxes.

"Yesterday, do you remember how after the viewing of the bodies the people were asked to clear the Mansion House so the family could have a few final private moments with their husbands and fathers before the funeral?"

"Yes." He and Lydia had been among the small circle of close friends called in by the family on the night of the twenty-eighth to see Joseph and Hyrum after their bodies were prepared for burial. That was before the public viewing the next day, when thousands lined up to see them. Nathan hadn't gone on that day, but he knew that his father had been there at the last, when the family ended the viewing and paid their last respects to the loved ones.

"Did you know that some of Joseph's enemies have talked about getting his body, or at least his head, so they can take it to Missouri and collect a reward offered there for Joseph's return, dead or alive?"

Nathan blew out his breath in horrified disgust. "I heard that. Is it true?"

Benjamin nodded slowly, letting the implications of that sink in. "And it's a handsome sum too."

"But they killed him! Isn't that enough? Do the money-grubbers have to try to cash in on it as well?"

"I think it may go beyond just the reward money," said Benjamin. "Already rumors are starting that Joseph wasn't really killed, that he was only critically wounded. They're saying that some of us somehow got him out of town and that he's in hiding and recovering."

"But that's absurd."

"Of course it is. But some folks thrive on the absurd. Others are even saying that he's been resurrected and is back in Nauvoo." There was a soft burst of exasperation. "That might even be coming from a few of our own people." There was a slow shake of his head, as if this were still difficult for him to believe. "So, some of Joseph's most bitter enemies are saying the best way to put an end to the absurdity is to produce the head of Joseph Smith for all to see."

It was so ghastly, so incredibly horrible, that Nathan could barely grasp it.

Benjamin went on more slowly now. "Maybe it's nothing more than rumor, but we couldn't take that chance. As you know, for the public viewing, the bodies of Joseph and Hyrum were placed in two matching coffins, then put in wooden boxes that would protect the coffins from the surrounding earth."

"Yes."

"Well, yesterday, after everyone was asked to leave, in the utmost secrecy, the coffins were removed from the outer boxes and locked in a small corner bedroom."

He stopped, seeing Nathan's astonishment. He went on grimly. "We used bags of sand. We filled up the wooden boxes until they were about the same weight as the bodies. Then the lids were nailed shut."

"You mean—"

"Yes," Benjamin said quietly. "We carried the boxes out to the wagon and drove to the temple block for the service. All that was buried out there were boxes of sand. So you weren't standing at the place they were buried."

"But . . ." Nathan was having difficulty comprehending this.

"That's why I was awake when you left this morning. I was just getting ready for bed."

"Where did you bury them?"

"We waited until after midnight; then the same group who filled the boxes went back to the Mansion House. One man stood guard to make sure there was no one around. We took the bodies across to the Nauvoo House. We buried them in the basement."

Nathan's astonishment turned now to wonder, and it was mixed with a strong sense of relief. The Nauvoo House had been under construction for some time now. In recent months, construction on it had halted so that all efforts could be put on finishing the temple. The first floor of what was to be a grand hotel right next to the southern riverboat dock was nearly completed now, but the adjoining basement was still under construction and was only up to the first joists.

"We buried Joseph and Hyrum there in the basement. When we were done, we carefully smoothed the dirt back over the site. We spread wood chips and construction rubbish over the ground to hide any traces of the grave sites." There was a faint smile. "We needn't have bothered. Did you hear that storm in the night?"

"I did. It woke both Lydia and me up."

"It came just after we had finished burying them. By the time the rain stopped, there was no way anyone could tell that there were fresh graves there."

"I can't believe it." Nathan leaned back, identifying the relief for what it was now. "And yet I'm glad. I'm glad they're safe. It would be terrible if someone got to them."

"Emma wanted you to know. But no one else."

"I understand."

Benjamin began to massage his temples with the tips of his fingers. "Joseph and Hyrum are safe," he murmured. "Now comes the bigger question. What about the Church?"

———◆———

"How old is Sister Smith's boy, Grandma?"

Mary Ann Morgan Steed smiled down at her granddaughter. Savannah's head was tipped to one side, the red hair fiery in the morning sunlight, the wide, very adult eyes as blue as an alpine lake. "I'm not sure. Probably about thirty-five or so."

"But that's old, Grandma."

She chuckled. "I suppose when you're seven, it does seem old. When you're fifty-eight, it seems quite young actually."

"Then why do you call him a boy?"

"I should have said son, Savannah. Samuel is Mother Smith's son. He is not a boy."

"Why is he sick?"

"Because of what happened down in Carthage."

"When the men chased him?"

Mary Ann was surprised. "Yes. How did you know that?"

"Will told me."

"Oh."

"Why were those bad men chasing him, Grandma?"

For a moment, Mary Ann debated how much to tell this precocious little girl, but then decided that if she was hearing it around town, she might as well know the true story. "Samuel was living in Plymouth, which is quite a ways from here."

"Is it by where Aunt Jessica lives?"

"Yes, somewhat. It's a little more south and east than Ramus, but it's in that same area."

"Mama says I can go out and see Aunt Jessica sometime. I miss my cousins, now that they've gone home again."

"I know you do, sweetheart. You and the boys are good friends." Mary Ann missed Jessica too. They had stayed for over a week, but left yesterday. All the family hated to see them go again.

Savannah reached out and took her grandmother's hand, as though to help her instead of the other way around. They were walking along Water Street, toward Main Street, and they were taking what time they needed. "So," she said, reminding Mary Ann that she hadn't forgotten what the conversation was about. "He lived at Plymouth."

"Yes. Well, that's not far from Carthage, where Brother Joseph and Brother Hyrum were in jail. When Samuel learned that his brothers were being held there, he decided to go help them."

"Was this on the day they were killed, Grandma?"

"Yes. He didn't know it, but the mob had already gone to the jail to kill Joseph and Hyrum."

"That still makes me sad, Grandma."

"It makes us all very sad, Savannah."

"I pray for Brother Joseph every night."

"You do?"

"Yes, and Brother Hyrum too. I pray Heavenly Father will keep them with him now so no other bad men can hurt them."

"What a wonderful thing to pray for, Savannah." Mary Ann was touched by the sweet faith and assurance implied in that statement. "Anyway, as Samuel was coming toward Carthage, some of the very men who had killed Joseph and Hyrum were running away. They met Samuel on the road. When they learned he was a Smith too, they tried to kill him."

"No!" Savannah cried.

"Yes. They were very bad men. They shot at him, but they missed. Samuel spurred his horse away but they chased after him."

Savannah had stopped now and was looking up at Mary Ann, totally intent. "Did they catch him?"

"No. They chased him for a long time but he finally got away. But when he finally came to Nauvoo, he had a terrible pain in his side. He's been very sick ever since."

She thought about that. "And that's why we're going to see him?"

"We're not going to see Samuel, Savannah. I just want to drop in on Mother Smith and see how he is doing."

"Oh." She took Mary Ann's hand again and started walking.

That was all it took. Savannah was seven now, but from the time she had started talking she had been highly inquisitive. About every third sentence started with words like "Why?" or "How come?" or "What does that do?" or "Where does that come from?" She pestered anyone around her with a constant stream of demanding questions. But if she was given a satisfactory answer, that was the end of it for a time while her mind digested what she had learned. Then another round would soon begin.

Mary Ann reached up and pushed the sunbonnet back just a bit and wiped at her forehead. "It's going to be another hot one."

Savannah didn't seem to hear. She was still engrossed in her own thoughts. As they approached Main Street, Mary Ann moved toward the Mansion House, which was on the northeast corner of the intersection of Main and Water Streets. Suddenly it registered on Savannah that that was where they were going.

"Why are we going here, Grandma?"

"Because this is where Mother Smith is."

Savannah's face screwed up into a puzzled frown. "But Emily says Mother Smith has a house of her own."

Mary Ann opened the gate. "She did, dear, but then Father Smith and Don Carlos—that was her son—died and young Lucy got married and—"

"Why do they call her young Lucy?"

"Because Mother Smith's name is also Lucy, so they call her daughter young Lucy to distinguish her from her mother. Anyway, Brother Joseph and Sister Emma asked Mother Smith to move in with them some time ago and—"

"Do they call Mother Smith 'Old Lucy'?"

Mary Ann smiled. "No, dear, they don't."

"How come?"

Mary Ann shook her head. "Because 'Old Lucy' doesn't sound very flattering."

"Why not?"

"It just doesn't." They went through the gate and up on the porch. As Mary Ann reached for the door knocker, she saw Savannah's pursed lips. "What?"

"I don't think 'Young Lucy' is a very good name either. She's old too, isn't she?"

"Well, she's old enough to be married, but—"

"Nobody better call me young Savannah," she muttered darkly.

Mary Ann laughed aloud. "All right. I'll warn the family."

"And I'm not going to name my daughter Savannah either. I don't want them calling me Old Mother Steed."

Thoroughly amused now, Mary Ann kept her face serious. "After you marry, Savannah, your name won't be Steed anymore."

That stopped her short. "Why not?"

"Because you'll take your husband's name. Just like Jenny used to be Jenny McIntire, but now that she's married to Matthew she's Jenny Steed. And Aunt Rebecca used to be a Steed, but now her name is Ingalls because she married Derek. And Aunt Jessica changed her name to Garrett when she married Uncle Solomon."

Savannah stood still for a moment, letting that slide into the proper slots in her mind. Then something else occurred to her. "How come Matthew never calls Jenny 'Jennifer Jo' anymore?"

Mary Ann chuckled. The way that young mind worked was fascinating. "Because for a while there, when Will was fond of Jenny Pottsworth, we always had two Jennys around, so Matthew always called his Jenny 'Jennifer Jo.' But now that Jenny Pottsworth is married and lives across the river, Matthew slipped back to calling her Jenny like the rest of us do."

Savannah nodded. Still smiling, Mary Ann lifted the door knocker and rapped sharply.

"I'm going to marry Billy Carver."

"Oh?"

"Yeah. Except he tried to kiss me yesterday." There was deep disgust in her voice.

"Really?" Mary Ann said.

"Yes. Abner Kellogg dared him."

"And what did you do?"

"I hit him in the stomach."

"Oh dear. Billy or Abner?"

Savannah looked up, sensing that her grandmother might be teasing her now. Her eyes were filled with innocence and at the same time were so perfectly impish that Mary Ann had to resist the impulse to take her in her arms and hug her. "I hit Billy," she said in a matter-of-fact tone. "Abner ran home before I could get him too."

Mary Ann was still laughing when the door opened and young Joseph Smith III stood before them. His eyes narrowed slightly in the brightness; then he smiled quickly. "Good morning, Sister Steed."

"Good morning, Joseph." A shadow of pain momentarily darkened her face. Joseph would be twelve in the fall, and in only a couple of years would be the same age as his father when he had first gone into the grove to ask which church was right. It was like seeing the young Prophet Joseph standing before her. With an effort, she kept her eyes on his face and smiled pleasantly. "Is your grandmother up and about yet, Joseph?"

The grin broadened noticeably. "Grandma Smith is always the first one up at our house. Just a minute. I'll tell her you're here." Then, remembering his manners, he did a little bow in Savannah's direction. "Good morning."

"Good morning, Joseph."

"Come in and I'll go get her."

He saw them seated in the front parlor, then trotted upstairs. He had barely disappeared when two dark heads appeared around the corner of the hallway that led back to the kitchen. Savannah was up in an instant.

"Hi, Freddie," she called brightly. "Hello, Alexander."

"Hi, Savannah," they said in unison. The two boys stepped into full view, grinning shyly. Frederick, named for Frederick G. Williams, was a year older than Savannah. Alexander, named for Alexander Doniphan, the attorney who had so often befriended and defended Joseph and the Saints in Missouri, was a year younger. Savannah and Elizabeth Mary, Lydia's daughter, often accompanied their mothers here to see Emma, and the two girls had become fast friends with Emma's two sons.

"Can you play?" Alexander asked, glancing sideways at Mary Ann.

Savannah whirled. "Can I, Grandma? Can I?"

"I suppose. I don't know how long we will be, Savannah, so don't go far. And stay away from the river." The rising waters of a week ago were starting to subside, but the river's edge was still just a few feet below the yard of the Old Homestead across the street.

"Yes, Grandma." She was down the hallway as Freddie and Alexander led the way out the back. The door had barely shut when she heard Savannah give a whoop. "Watch yourselves, boys," Mary Ann murmured, "you're playing with a very lively filly there."

———•———

Lucy Mack Smith was born on the eighth of July, 1775. In one year she would turn seventy, Mary Ann thought, a rarity among women in these days when so many died before they reached forty. She was in her late sixties now, but her mind was as quick as that of a twenty-year-old. And she had the energy of a teenaged girl. But now, for the first time, she looked closer to her real age. And little wonder. A husband, three sons, a son-in-law, and two grandsons—all dead within the last three years. Two of the sons had been gunned down just ten days before at the hands of violent men. And now, with Samuel growing worse, another tragedy loomed over this woman.

As she spoke of Samuel and his worsening condition, the tragedy seemed written in every line of her face, the sorrow so ingrained in her that it filled her eyes with an enormous sadness. Mary Ann watched her with a growing sense of her own frustration. You could come and comfort, but what could be done to take away this kind of hurt?

"Do you know what, though?" Mother Smith suddenly said, as though sensing that Mary Ann was troubled.

"What?"

"I remembered something last night and it gave me great comfort."

"What was that?"

"You well remember that horrible time in Far West after Colonel Hinkle betrayed my sons into the hands of the Missourians."

Mary Ann felt a little shudder run through her. Benjamin had ended up in chains from that one as well. "I remember it well."

"You can imagine the shock and distress that Father Smith and I felt at the loss of our sons. Their enemies were threatening to shoot them at any moment. I was not allowed to even say a proper good-bye. We didn't know if we would ever see them again."

"How can any of us ever forget what you went through?"

"Well, for some time our house was filled with mourning and grief. We were at a loss as to what to do. But then, in the midst of my grief, I found solace which surpassed all earthly comfort."

Mary Ann leaned forward. "What?"

"I was filled with the Spirit of God, and by the gift of prophecy I received the following words: 'Let your heart be comforted concerning your children. They shall not be harmed by their enemies. And in five years from this time, Joseph will have power over his enemies.'"

Silence filled the room. Mary Ann watched the wrinkles smooth a little.

"That was in November, eighteen thirty-eight. The five years were up this last November."

Mary Ann nodded slowly. "No wonder you find solace in that promise," she murmured. "What a wonderful thing."

"Yes," Mother Smith said firmly, "the time has elapsed. The promise is fulfilled. Joseph and Hyrum are where no one can hurt them now, and they have triumphed over all their enemies." Her eyes dropped. "And if the Lord sees fit to take Samuel as well, how can I forbid him to unite these brothers again?"

"I understand how you feel," Mary Ann sighed. Then, after a moment, she added, "It's not fair, you know."

"What isn't fair?" Mother Smith asked in surprise.

"I come here to try and comfort you, and you end up comforting me."

There was a sad smile. "It is the Lord who comforts us both," she said, "and we can both be grateful for it."

They heard a noise and looked up. Young Joseph was standing at the entrance to the sitting room. "Grandma, Sister Jane is here."

"Jane?" Then her shoulders straightened. "Jane Manning?"

"Yes, Grandma."

"Oh, do show her in." Both of them stood as Joseph left, and then in a moment, he came back in with a young black woman in her mid-twenties.

"Mother Smith," the woman said, and opened her arms. They embraced, rocking back and forth slowly. "I'm just back from Burlington. I hear that Samuel is not well."

"No, Jane, not well at all."

"I tried to see Sister Emma before we left, but young Joseph said she was still too distraught for visitors. How is she doing?"

"Poor Emma. She has been devastated by the loss of Joseph. Hyrum's wife is greatly bereaved as well, but it has not laid her low in the same manner as it has Emma."

"Emma's being with child must surely be part of that," Mary Ann spoke up.

Jane Manning looked at her and smiled. "Good morning, Sister Steed. I should have known you would be here."

She came over and took Mary Ann's hands. "It is good to see you again, Jane," Mary Ann said. "I heard you and Angeline had gone off for a time."

"Yes, we went to visit family and have just returned. Then I heard about Samuel. That is terrible, just terrible. As if killing two of the Smith sons were not enough. And I wanted to come see Mother Smith as well." She smiled cheerfully. "I needed some cheering."

Mary Ann nodded knowingly. "I was just speaking to her about that, as a matter of fact."

Jane turned back to Joseph's mother. "I saw the boys outside. They seem to be doing well." She looked at Mary Ann for a moment. "And your granddaughter. She is going to be a beauty, isn't she?"

"Yes, quite. And I pity the man who marries her who doesn't have a very large sack filled with answers."

They all laughed at that as they sat down now. As Jane began to quiz Lucy about how things were going, Mary Ann sat back and watched. Jane Manning had been a servant girl at the Mansion House for several months during the previous winter.

Born a free black in Connecticut, she and her family had heard the gospel and then left to come out to Nauvoo with a group headed by one of the missionaries. Emma had told Caroline and Lydia that Jane's family had come with great difficulty, that when they got to Buffalo, New York, the steamship captain refused them passage because they were colored. Jane and her family had to part with the main group and ended up walking the whole distance. When they arrived, Joseph and Emma had taken them in—all nine of them—until they could find homes. A week later they had all found homes and work, except for Jane. Joseph and Emma invited her to stay on as a hired servant to help Emma with the housework and with the guests who frequently stayed at the Mansion House. Intelligent, cheerful, and a hard worker, she had not only been a great help with the work but also provided Emma and Mother Smith with pleasant companionship.

"So you are not working for Emma any longer?" Mary Ann asked.

Jane shook her head. "No, Emma and Brother Joseph were thinking about selling the Mansion House because it is so costly to run. That meant there was not enough for paying servants. Now with Joseph gone"—she shrugged—"I went to live with my mother."

"Oh," Mary Ann said, and sat back again. The effects of the death of Joseph were still rippling outward. Where would it stop?

As they walked back up Granger Street, Savannah walking quietly beside them but constantly looking up at Jane Manning, Mary Ann gave her a sideways look. "Jane, have you work?"

There was a slow shake of her head. "Not really. I've thought about going to Brother Robinson and asking him if there's work at the Mansion House, but I'm not sure it would be the same now. Emma is so forlorn, and with Brother Joseph gone . . ."

"Yes, I know. The Mansion House used to be one of the happiest places in all of Nauvoo. Now it breaks one's heart to even pass by it." Then she came back to her original point. "Let me start asking around, see if we can't find you something."

"That would be wonderful," Jane answered. "Thank you, Sister Steed."

"Call me Mary Ann, please."

"Sister Manning?"

Jane turned and looked down. "Yes, Savannah?"

"Why is your skin so brown?"

Mary Ann's mouth dropped open. "*Savannah!*"

Her eyes widened in surprise at the sharpness in her grandmother's voice. "What, Grandma?"

"You don't ask things like—"

Jane's hand went out, stopping her. "It's all right," she said. She slowed her step, looking at the young girl, whose face was filled with curious innocence. "Can I ask you a question first?"

"Sure."

"Why is your hair so red?"

That seemed like a fair question to Savannah and she answered immediately. "Mama says God gave it to me to make me pretty."

"And my Mama says God gave me brown skin to make me pretty."

"Oh." That seemed eminently reasonable. She nodded. "I think you're very pretty, Sister Manning."

Jane reared back a little, caught off guard by the open genuineness of the compliment. "Why, thank you, Savannah. What a nice thing to say."

"Do you think I'm pretty?"

Mary Ann winced, but Jane just hooted. "I think you're beautiful, Savannah. I think God did it just right when he gave you red hair."

"Thank you."

And then without thinking, Savannah reached up and took Jane's hand in her own as they walked on toward Steed Row.

Chapter Notes

The details of the secret burial of Joseph and Hyrum are given in the official history of the Church (see *HC* 6:628). Lucy Mack Smith, mother of the martyrs, tells about the reward that the Missourians were offering for Joseph's head (see *Mack Hist.*, p. 324).

That fall, as construction on the Nauvoo House progressed, the coffins were secretly exhumed again and buried across the street on the property of the Old Homestead, where Joseph and Emma had lived for most of their time in Nauvoo. The bodies were placed under the "spring house" near the river, but once again the site was kept secret. (See B. H. Roberts, *A Comprehensive History of The Church of Jesus Christ of Latter-day Saints*, Century I, 6 vols. [Salt Lake City: The Church of Jesus Christ of Latter-day Saints, 1930], 6:529.)

The story of Samuel Smith's attempt to reach his brothers, his own brush with the assassins, and his subsequent sickness are told by his mother and also in the official history of the Church (see *Mack Hist.*, pp. 324, 325; *HC* 7:110–11). Mother Smith's being told that in five years Joseph would have power over his enemies is also found in her history (see *Mack Hist.*, pp. 291, 325).

Caroline moved through the house awkwardly, feeling a growing sense of anxiety. One arm was in a sling. One foot had a splint on it. Both were the result of the accident in Warsaw a month earlier. She hobbled about with a cane in her good hand, steadying herself against a wall or a piece of furniture from time to time. She lit no lamp or candle. There was no need. The moon was nearly full, and enough light filtered in through the windows for her to see clearly that each succeeding room was empty. Where had he gone?

She stopped and looked around. She had been almost asleep when Joshua finally came to bed. That had been almost eleven. There had been problems down at the freight yard and he had worked through supper. But Joshua had settled down beside her and gone quickly to sleep, even beating her, since his coming to bed had brought her awake again.

She moved to the fireplace mantel and peered at the clock.

It was twenty-two minutes past three a.m. She turned. Surely he would have said something to her if he had decided to go back down to the office.

And then, through the window, she saw a movement. Peering through the curtain she saw Joshua's dark shape rocking slowly back and forth in the porch swing. With a rush of relief, she felt herself relax. For a moment, she debated about whether or not to let him know she was there, but then, wondering what had driven him out here, she made her way to the door and stepped outside.

He started and looked up in surprise. "Oh," he said softly, "I didn't mean to wake you."

"You didn't. How long have you been out here?"

"About an hour."

She heard a soft buzzing sound around her ear. "Aren't the mosquitoes eating you alive?"

"I guess I've got too tough a hide. They don't bother me much."

"Well, they love me. Can we go inside?"

He shrugged and stood. "Let's just go back to bed. I'm sorry that you had to get up."

"No, I'm awake now. Let's sit in the parlor. It's cool in there."

Joshua nodded and followed her into the room. She sat down on the sofa, but he took the chair across from it. She looked at him sharply, but he seemed not to be even aware of what he had done.

"Did you get the problem at the stables solved?"

"Not completely. I'm going to have to send one of the men to Peoria, I guess."

"Is that what woke you up, worrying about that?"

He shook his head and turned away so she couldn't see his face. She had a fleeting impression of great agony.

"Olivia?" she asked softly after a few moments.

He nodded.

Now she was glad it was dark, for the emotions rose up in her with a sudden, unexpectedly sharp surge and she found herself blinking quickly to stem the tears. In four days, it would be exactly one month. In a way it seemed unreal that so much time had passed. It seemed like only this morning, the horror of the wagon ride—her, heavy with child, hiding in the back under a tarp, hearing the voices of the men who were taunting Will, terror striking when the horses bolted, feeling the wagon box start to turn over, hearing the wheel beneath her snap like a dried stick. And yet in another way it was as though it had been years ago. It was as if she had not heard Olivia laughing with Savannah or Charles, or at the piano, filling the house with music, or arguing amiably with Will over some scripture they had been reading together. How could the sweetness of those memories fade so quickly? she asked herself. She bit her lip and wiped at her eyes with the back of one hand, trying to ignore the terrible ache inside her.

"This morning, a wagon came in from Chicago." He spoke in a low voice, barely above a whisper. She had to strain to hear him over the sound of the crickets outside. "It was that Knabe piano from New York that Jonathan Williams ordered a few months back." There was a sudden choking sound, and now his voice was strained and filled with anguish. "I never told you, but I was going to surprise Olivia and get her a Knabe for her seventeenth birthday."

Caroline got to her feet and hobbled over to stand beside him. Setting her cane against the chair, she leaned against him and laid a hand on his shoulder. He reached up and took it. "She had read all about them in a catalog," he went on. "They say they are the finest piano made in America."

"I know," she whispered. "She talked to me about it a lot, wondering if she ever dared ask you. How she would have loved it!"

He pulled his hand away. "Why is it that you don't hate me?" he suddenly burst out.

"Hate you?" She was astonished.

"Yes. If I hadn't been so pigheaded, if only I would have listened to her. To you! She could be here now and . . ." He couldn't finish and dropped his chin against his chest. "If only I had believed her."

"I read where a man once said that the two most terrible words in the world are 'if only.'" She reached down and took his hand again. She brought it and pressed it softly to her lips. "How can I hate you, Joshua? You were trying to protect Olivia from what you thought was a terrible thing."

"But if I would have listened. If I would just have believed her, Caroline," he cried. "She never lied to me. Not ever. If only I had believed her."

"And if only I had been up on the wagon seat with her," Caroline intoned in a dull voice. "If only we had gone another way out of town that day. If only I hadn't been so eager to leave and we had waited for dark." She squeezed his hand. "I have gone over it again and again, Joshua. 'If only' will not ever bring you comfort. It will only drive you mad."

There was a deep intake of breath, then a long, tortured sigh. "I know. But I can't stop. I can't stop the dreams."

"The dreams?"

"Yes." He pulled his hand free and lifted his head to look at her now. Gently he brought her around to sit on his lap so she didn't have to stand. His voice was wooden and lifeless, like a schoolboy reciting lessons which have been memorized but not learned. "Like tonight. Olivia and I are walking in a meadow. Everything is beautiful. We are laughing and talking. She picks me a bouquet of wildflowers. And then we come to a raging river. I can hear the boulders rumbling as they are pushed downstream. The rapids are swift and dangerous."

He paused. With his head up, he was facing the window, and the moonlight illuminated his face with a pale, delicate silver, smoothing the harsh angles, softening the twisted mouth, lessening the torture in his eyes.

"There is a narrow bridge, not much more than one log. I go across, then turn back. I—" Now he faltered and had to look away for a moment. But his head turned again and he went on relentlessly, lashing himself with every word. "I call for Olivia to come. She tells me she cannot make it, that she's afraid. I am angry. I tell her that even a child can cross. She shakes her head. She . . ."

Now Caroline could feel his breath coming more quickly, as though he were caught up in the nightmare all over again. She laid her head against his shoulder, not trying to stop the tears now from spilling over and running down the side of her face. His hand came up and he began to stroke her hair, very slowly, very gently.

"I am very angry now. I shout at her. I command her to come. She is crying, but I won't listen. Then . . ." He took a quick breath, then another. Now his voice was heavy and thick. "Then, about halfway across, her foot slips. She falls. It is suddenly like the river is a thousand feet below her. I can see her falling, over and over. But I can see her face clearly, even though she is growing smaller and smaller. And she cries out to me, reaching out a hand, as though I could catch her."

Caroline had to take a breath of her own to clear the constriction in her throat. "And what does she say?" she asked in a barely audible whisper.

" 'Why wouldn't you believe me, Papa? Why wouldn't you believe me?' "

They sat there together for a long time, neither speaking. Over and over Joshua's hand brushed softly against Caroline's hair. Finally, she spoke. "How long does it take to get a Knabe piano out here?"

His eyes widened slightly. "Two or three months, I would suppose."

"So you could have it here by November, in time for her birthday?"

He slowly nodded. "I think so."

Her shoulders lifted and pulled back slightly. "The Lord saw fit to take our Olivia home to him," she murmured. "But in return, he gave us another little Olivia. I want you to order that piano. And then, on what would have been Olivia's birthday, we will give it to Savannah and little Olivia as a gift from their older sister."

He began to nod slowly. "Yes," he said.

"And I will find a piano teacher for Savannah and start her on lessons."

"Immediately," he agreed.

He slipped his arms around her. Caroline looked into his face. "If Olivia thought that there would never be music in our house again, she would be very sad, I think."

Joshua's head came up fully now. "And she would never forgive me."

Caroline took his face in her free hand. "She has forgiven you for what happened, Joshua," she said with sudden fierceness. "Do you know that? She still lives, Joshua, and she does not blame you."

His head snapped up and his voice was suddenly sharp. "You believe that, Caroline. You believe that she still lives somewhere, but I don't know if I do or not." His voice dropped as suddenly as it had risen. "If I did, then maybe I could find some semblance of peace."

A great sadness came over her, but she said nothing further. She closed her eyes. It was almost a full minute before he spoke again, and then it was one brief, pain-filled sentence. "I shall write to the Knabe Piano Company first thing tomorrow."

———— • ————

Lydia stood on the porch, watching Nathan at the pump behind the house as he washed the dust from his face and neck. She carried thirteen-month-old Joseph in one arm, standing with her body bent slightly so as to carry the child's weight mostly on her hip. He straightened, wiping the water from his eyes but not bothering to dry his face with the small towel that hung on the pump handle.

"Did you get the survey finished?" she asked.

He nodded. "Mostly. Pa wants to remeasure the three lots that butt up against Brother Llewellyn's property on the east. He's not sure they are really equal. But we'll do that tomorrow. Mother wanted him to take her somewhere." He moved across the grass and onto the porch. As he did so, little Joseph raised his arms and began to grunt. Nathan smiled and took him from his mother. "Hello there, you little scamp. What have you been doing today?"

Joseph eyed his father gravely, as if to say, "Please don't ask, at least not in the presence of Mama."

Lydia pulled a face. "I found him sitting on top of the dish chest."

"What?" Nathan said, pulling back a little to look at his son, the pleasure showing in his eyes. "How did he manage that?"

"Pushed a stool over while I was in the bedroom. When I came out, he was sitting there just like he was the king of England or something."

"Well, you little character. You've barely been walking for three months and now you're climbing on things?"

"He is into everything now," Lydia moaned. "I can't turn my back on him for a minute."

Joseph started to squirm, his eyes fixed on something in the yard, so Nathan stepped off the porch again and let him down.

"Someone from Ramus brought a note from Jessica," Lydia said. "They got home safely that same day."

Nathan nodded. "Good. It was nice to have them here for that week. Jessica seems really happy."

"Very," Lydia agreed, coming down to stand beside him. "Solomon is just wonderful. I think she's happier than she has ever been, and she was very happy with John before he was killed."

"Yes, I think you're right. And there's no one who deserves it more."

As he went to look away, he saw a sardonic smile on Lydia's face. She was looking directly at him with a twinkle in her eyes.

"What?" he asked.

"Aren't you going to ask me about the other news?"

"What other news?"

"That young Joshua brought back from the store."

"I didn't know that he did."

"A wise husband is supposed to know these things."

"I haven't seen Joshua since I got home. What is it?"

"I don't think I'll tell you, since you weren't even interested enough to ask."

He threw up his hands. "I didn't know there was anything to ask about."

She laughed lightly, then went up and kissed him on the nose. "And you think that is an excuse?"

"Normally I would have thought so, but—"

"Parley's home."

For a moment the words didn't register. Then his face was infused with joy. "Parley Pratt?"

There was a mocking smile. "Just how many Parleys do you know?"

"Really? Parley here, in Nauvoo? When?"

"I guess he got in last night." She reached out and touched his arm, pleased that she should be the bearer of such news for him. "He came to the store, but of course neither of us was there. He told Joshua to have you come see him as soon as you returned home."

"Well, well," Nathan breathed. "Parley is back. That is good news."

"Go," she said, giving him a gentle push. "Knowing how you two like to talk, we'll not hold supper for you."

———

"Where were you when you heard the news?"

"Well, actually, I was nearly home. I didn't hear anything until the steamer I was on stopped at a landing in Wisconsin. Some of the passengers who joined us there brought news that Joseph and Hyrum were dead."

"Wisconsin?" Nathan echoed. "You were already coming home, then?"

Parley nodded solemnly, not explaining further. Parley Parker Pratt was born in 1807, which made him thirty-seven now. That was two years younger than Joseph Smith and two years senior to Nathan. He was built much like Heber C. Kimball—stout, heavily muscled from hard work—and he tended to roll slightly when he walked. His face was round, the dark eyes alert and always probing, and quick to light with good humor. His hair was almost black, thick around his ears and with a slight curl at the neck, but thinning rapidly on top. Normally he bore a look of immense energy and unabashed enjoyment of life. Now he looked tired. His mouth was drawn, the eyes filled with a deep weariness.

He rose from his chair and began to pace. "I was in the Boston area. A day or two before the twenty-seventh of June, I felt a strong prompting that I should return home. I had no idea why. I thought perhaps it might have something to do with my family. But I immediately started west."

"That was surely the Lord's doing," Nathan said.

"Yes, though I did not understand it at the time. But anyway, I was passing on a canal boat on the Erie Canal, near Utica, New York, when to my amazement, my brother William, being then on a mission in New York, happened, quite providentially, to take passage on the same boat. I was much pleased to see him again, and we spent some time telling each other about our labors. By now it was the afternoon of the twenty-seventh."

He took the poker that stood in its holder beside the cold fireplace and began to idly poke at the empty grate. "As we conversed together on the deck, a strange and solemn awe came over me, as if the powers of hell were let loose. I was so overwhelmed with sorrow I could hardly speak. I did not know what had come over me. After pacing the deck for some time in silence, I turned to William and exclaimed: 'Brother William, this is a dark hour! The powers of darkness seem to triumph, and the spirit of murder is abroad in the land. It controls the hearts of the American people, and a vast majority of them sanction the killing of the innocent.'"

He straightened, putting the poker back in its place, and turned to Nathan, who was watching him intently. Nathan had been with Parley on a mission to Canada. He knew of the spiritual depths in the man. But this was still an amazing story he was hearing.

"'My brother,' I said to William, 'let us keep silence and not open our mouths. If you have any pamphlets or books on the fulness of the gospel lock them up. Show them not. Neither open your mouth to the people. Let us observe an entire and solemn silence, for this is a dark day, and the hour of triumph for the powers of darkness.'"

"And this was in the afternoon?" Nathan asked in a low voice.

Parley's head moved up and down slowly. "I didn't take particular note of the time, but as near as I can judge, it was the same hour that the Carthage mob were shedding the blood of Joseph and Hyrum Smith and John Taylor, nearly a thousand miles to the west of where William and I then were."

Parley moved across the room and sat down beside Nathan again. "My brother bid me farewell somewhere in western New York, he being on his way to a conference in that quarter. I passed on to Buffalo, where I took steamer for Chicago. The steamer touched at a landing in Wisconsin, some fifty or sixty miles from Chicago, and here some new passengers came on board. They brought the news of the martyrdom. That was the first I knew of it, and then I understood what had happened on the canal boat that previous afternoon."

Nathan could only nod.

"It was horrible," Parley went on, his voice quite low now. "Great excitement prevailed on board the steamer. The people were filled with a spirit of exultation and triumph at this 'glorious' news. I could barely believe it. They received this news with much the same spirit as is generally shown on the receipt of the news of a great national victory in time of war. Knowing that I was a member of the Church and a member of the Twelve, many passengers gathered about me and tauntingly inquired what the Mormons would do now, seeing their prophet and leader was killed.

"To these taunts and questions I replied that we should continue our mission and spread to all the world the work Joseph had restored. I pointed out that nearly all the prophets and

Apostles who were in times of old had been killed and also the Savior of the world, yet their death did not alter the truth nor hinder its final triumph."

"And what did they answer to that?"

"Oh, some seemed moved by it. They began to inquire as to who would be the new leader and some even asked if it might be me. I disabused them of that notion, telling them that no man would rejoice in the death of the innocent for personal gain. This served as a sufficient rebuke, and all were silent."

"Well, you're here. I'll bet Elder Taylor and Elder Richards were pleased to see you."

"Yes, poor Willard. He's had the full burden of keeping things together here. I was shocked to see Elder Taylor. It is a miracle that he is alive."

"In more ways than one," Nathan agreed. "Lydia saw Leonora yesterday. She invited us to have supper with them in the next week or so. She said that Elder Taylor enjoys having someone to talk to."

"He does." Parley turned toward the window, looking through it to the city beyond. There was a soft sigh, and then he began to speak again. "There is more to my story, Nathan."

"Tell me," he replied.

"Landing in Chicago I found great excitement there as well. The press had issued extras announcing the triumph of the murderous mob in killing the Smiths. Yes, that's the word they used. Triumph. It chills the blood, doesn't it, to think that they could rejoice in such terrible deeds."

"The whole world seems to be rejoicing, Parley. Except for here. It has been almost two weeks now, and here there is still only sorrow."

"Yes. I knew that would be the case. And that brings me to the rest of my story. Leaving Chicago, I now hastened on to Peoria, and, staying overnight, I started the next day on foot across the country. During the two or three days I spent traveling between Chicago and Peoria, I felt so weighed down with sorrow and the powers of darkness that it was painful for me to converse or speak to anyone or even to try to eat or sleep. I really felt that if it had been my own family who had died and our beloved prophet been spared alive, I could have borne it, and the blow would have fallen on me with far less weight. For fourteen years I had loved Joseph with a warmth of affection indescribable. I had associated with him in private and in public, in travels and at home, in joy and sorrow, in honor and dishonor, in adversity of every kind. With him I had lain in dungeons and in chains; and with him I had triumphed over all our foes in Missouri and found deliverance for ourselves and people in Nauvoo, where we had reared this great city. But now he was gone, gone to the invisible world, and we and the Church of the Saints were left to mourn in sorrow and without the presence of our beloved founder and prophet.

"As I walked along over the plains of Illinois, lonely and solitary, my thoughts were somewhat as follows: 'I am now drawing near to the beloved city; in a day or two I shall be there. How shall I meet the sorrowing widows and orphans? How shall I meet the aged and widowed mother of these two martyrs? How shall I meet an entire community bowed down with grief and sorrow unutterable? What shall I say? How can I console and advise twenty-five thousand people who will throng about me in tears and, in the absence of the President of my quorum and the older members of the now presiding council, will ask counsel at my hands? Shall I tell them to fly to the wilderness and deserts? Or, shall I tell them to stay at home and take care of themselves, and continue to build the temple?' With these reflections, I walked onward, weighed down as it were unto death."

Nathan wanted to say something, to express in words the sorrow and numbing shock which had come over him, but he did not. He did not want to break into Parley's reverie, for that was what it was. He seemed barely conscious of Nathan's presence now.

The pain laced his face, deepening the lines, drawing the mouth tight. "When I could endure it no longer, I cried out aloud, saying: 'O Lord! in the name of Jesus Christ I pray thee, show me what these things mean, and what I shall say to thy people.'"

Finally he turned his head to look directly at Nathan. "And then it happened. On a sudden, the Spirit of God came upon me and filled my heart with joy and gladness indescribable. The spirit of revelation glowed in my bosom with as visible a warmth and gladness as if it were fire. The Spirit whispered unto me: 'Lift up your head and rejoice, for behold, it is well with my servants Joseph and Hyrum. My servant Joseph still holds the keys of my kingdom in this dispensation, and he shall stand in due time on the earth, in the flesh, and fulfill that to which he is appointed.'"

Without being aware that he had moved at all, Nathan had leaned forward, as though by his being closer the words could reach him more quickly.

"'Go!' whispered the Spirit, 'go and say unto my people in Nauvoo that they shall continue to pursue their daily duties and take care of themselves. They are to make no movement in Church government to reorganize or alter anything until the return of the remainder of the Quorum of the Twelve. But exhort them that they continue to build the house of the Lord which I have commanded them to build in Nauvoo.'"

He stopped. There wasn't a sound in the room. Even outside, the world seemed withdrawn beyond the reach of anything that might disturb this moment. Finally, Nathan released his breath, feeling the tension go with it. "That is what the Saints need to hear, Parley," he said softly. "That is exactly what they need to hear."

"Yes," Parley said, smiling now for the first time. "You can imagine what I felt when this happened. This information caused my bosom to burn with joy and gladness, and I was comforted above measure. All my sorrow seemed in a moment to be lifted as a burden from my back."

"It is wonderful counsel."

"I know. Then I must confess, I began to doubt again. The change in me was so sudden, I hardly dared to believe my senses. One minute there had been this terrible despair and hopelessness, the next indescribable joy. I began to wonder if it were really from the Lord. Therefore, I prayed the Lord to repeat to me the same things the second time so that, indeed, if it was of him and the truth, I might be sure of it so that I might really tell the Saints to stay in Nauvoo and continue to build the temple.

"And as I prayed thus, the same spirit burned in my bosom again, and the Spirit of the Lord repeated to me the same message once more, exactly the same all over again. I then went on my way rejoicing, arriving late yesterday afternoon."

"You must tell the people," Nathan exclaimed. "We need to hear what the Lord's will is for us now. There is much confusion, much speculation."

"I shall, Nathan. Brother Taylor and Brother Richards said exactly the same thing."

"Tell me when and where and the Steeds shall be present."

The round face softened into a sad smile. "I just learned this morning of Joshua's tragedy. I am very sorry, Nathan."

"Yes, it has been a difficult thing. But it has brought Joshua and Caroline back to us, at least for a time." Then he brightened. "You shall come and have supper with us tonight. Bring your family. We would be honored."

Parley reached across and clapped a hand on Nathan's shoulder. "No, it is we who shall be honored."

Chapter Notes

Parley P. Pratt's account of his experience at the time of the Martyrdom and on his return to Nauvoo is told here almost word for word as he wrote it in his history (see *Autobiography of Parley P. Pratt*, ed. Parley P. Pratt, Jr., Classics in Mormon Literature [Salt Lake City: Deseret Book Co., 1985], pp. 292–94).

When Melissa Rogers opened the door to Carl's office, he looked up in surprise, then stood up immediately. "Melissa, what are you doing outside on a day like this?"

"Hello, Carl."

He quickly went to her and helped her across the room to the chair in front of his desk. He helped her sit down, holding her arm carefully. With the baby only a week or two away now, she moved awkwardly, heavily, like an old woman with lumbago. As she got seated, he took a handkerchief from his pocket and handed it to her. Gratefully she took it and wiped at her face and neck, wishing she could somehow get at the trickles of sweat going down her back.

"It's much too hot for you to be out walking, Melissa," he said, his voice half-anxious, half-chiding. And then he peered more closely at her face. "What's wrong? Is it one of the children. Or Mother?"

She shook her head quickly. And then, not trusting her

voice, she opened her handbag and withdrew the folded newspaper and handed it to him.

Puzzled, he glanced at it, then back to her. "What?"

"Look at the front page."

Even as he started to unfold the newspaper he saw from the masthead that it was not their local weekly but one of the Cleveland papers. He also noted that it had yesterday's date—July 10, 1844. Then, as he opened it up fully, there was an involuntary gasp. The headline ran across the full width of the paper.

MORMON PROPHET SLAIN IN ILLINOIS.

He read swiftly, glancing up from time to time at Melissa. When he was through, he lowered the paper, folded it back up again, then walked over beside her. He let the paper slip from his fingers, then knelt down and took her into his arms. She turned her head to him and wept silently against his shoulder.

———•———

"You want to go home again, don't you?"

It was past nine o'clock, and the children were all asleep. They sat in the kitchen of Carl's mother's house, where they had stayed since returning to Kirtland in March. Marian Rogers had watched them quietly during supper, saying nothing, her eyes saying everything. It was very much like her that she had gone upstairs to read, leaving them alone to sort this out.

As Melissa watched Carl now, she could see the gentleness of his mother in his features, along with the hardheaded practicality of his father. Finally, a shadow of a smile touched her mouth. "Do you realize what you just asked me?" she queried.

"I asked you if you want to go—" He stopped. Then, softly, he finished his sentence. "Home."

She didn't push him further on it. "I can't imagine what it must be like," she murmured. "Joseph and Hyrum gone. I can hardly make myself believe it."

"I know. Your family must be in a state of terrible shock."

There were sudden tears. "I was thinking back as I came to see you today. Joseph and Hyrum came to our farm to help clear the land. I was just sixteen. One night we all went out to the barn. Joseph and Nathan pulled sticks." She reached up and brushed at her eyes with the back of her hand. "Joseph was much more than just the Prophet to us."

"I know."

"What will happen now?" It was as much a plea as a question.

He considered that, and finally just shook his head.

For a long time they sat there. The only sound in the house was the steady ticking of the grandfather clock in the hallway. Finally, he reached out and took her hand. "I've been a little concerned about the brickyards."

Her eyes widened slightly, but she said nothing.

"We couldn't leave until the baby is born."

Now she squeezed his hand back. "Carl, I won't ask you to take me back. If you feel like we should stay here, I'll not be saying anything more."

"I know." He was looking past her now, and though his face showed nothing, she knew he was thinking about his mother. The other Rogers sons were here in Kirtland with their children. She wouldn't be alone. But Carl—or Carlton, as she always called him—was Marian Rogers's favorite son. She tried to hide that, but they all knew it. Their return to Kirtland had meant a great deal to her. Having all of her grandchildren with her also meant a great deal to her.

"I'm not saying we'd stay there, Melissa."

"I understand."

"On the other hand, I've felt pretty useless here. Except for Mother, of course." There was an ironic smile. "I'm not sure they need another brickyard here in Kirtland."

"Probably not." It was a wonderful understatement. The Kirtland they knew from years past—bustling, growing rapidly with the torrent of Latter-day Saints pouring in—was no more. It was a quiet town again of two or three thousand. It was certainly not dying, but another brickyard? Hardly. She knew Carl had been somewhat frustrated since their return. He was just an added hand at the livery stable. David and William, his two younger brothers, had done a good job with the family business and it was growing, but it didn't need another family to support. And running the most prosperous brickyards in Nauvoo had been exhilarating as well as highly profitable for him.

He pulled his hand away and leaned back, his face thoughtful. "I'll go up and tell Mother. She knows that's what we're talking about."

"Are you sure, Carl? Really sure?"

"Are you?"

She looked at him for several seconds and then her eyes dropped. "Yes."

"And what about the plural marriage thing?"

She didn't look up. "I'm not going back for the Church, Carl. I'm going back for the family."

That seemed to satisfy him, and he stood up. He turned and looked toward the hall where the stairs began. There was a soft sigh; then his shoulders squared and he moved toward the doorway.

"Thank you, Carl," she said softly.

He turned back and smiled at her. "Are you sure that it's not me who should be thanking you?"

Her chin lifted and there was a sudden happiness in her eyes. She was remembering a spring day in 1831. She was on the banks of the Chagrin River, just behind the Newel K. Whitney store, when a redheaded young man had introduced himself to her and offered to carry her groceries home in his cart. "If it weren't for Joseph Smith, I would never have come to Kirtland," she murmured.

His smile was immediate and filled with the same memories. "Yes, we do owe him that, don't we?"

"And more," she said sadly.

"Yes, and more," he agreed. He then turned and went through the doorway, and she heard his steps going slowly up the stairs.

◆━◆

"I'll get it." Will rose from the table and went into the hall-way. Through the glass of the front door he could make out two dark shapes, one tall and broad, the other smaller and more slen-der. Above him, he heard the floor creak, and knew that his mother was moving toward the head of the stairs where she could listen to find out who it was.

He opened the door. There was no lamp lit in the hallway and the light from the sitting room was faint. For a moment he didn't recognize the two figures standing in the darkness. Then, as their faces registered, his mouth opened in stunned amaze-ment. "Mr. Samuelson!"

"Hello, Will," Walter Samuelson said gravely.

"Hello, Mr. Will Steed," Alice said, clearly amused at the expression on his face.

"Alice? Hello. What are you—" Then he remembered his manners. He stepped back, opening the door wider. "Won't you come in?"

They came through the door and stopped. "Is your father in?" Samuelson said.

But before Will could answer, there was the sound of hob-bling footsteps coming down the stairs, and then Caroline was there in the hall behind them. "Walter? Is that really you?"

"Hello, Caroline." He moved to her and took both of her hands. "We came the moment we heard the news. I'm so sorry, Caroline."

Alice was nodding, looking at Will. "Yes, we only learned of Olivia's accident a week or ten days ago. Papa wanted to come immediately. I insisted on coming with him."

"Thank you," said Will. "It's good to see you again."

Caroline came awkwardly forward and took Alice's hands. "How kind of you to come, Alice."

From behind her, Samuelson spoke. "As you know, Judith has been in poor health for some time now. She wanted to come as well, but . . ."

"We understand. You convey our best wishes to her. Your coming all the way from St. Louis is more than was required." She turned to Will. "Go fetch your father while the Samuelsons freshen up a little." Back to Samuelson. "Do you have luggage?"

Alice answered for her father. "We left it with a man at the steamer dock. He directed us how to find your house."

Will didn't wait for the command from his mother. "Father and I will pick it up and bring it here."

He touched Alice's arm. "It really is good to see you again, Alice. Perhaps tomorrow I can show you around Nauvoo."

"I would like that," she said warmly. "I've heard so much about it."

He bowed slightly, then moved around her and went out the door.

"So," Joshua began, once he and Walter Samuelson were comfortably seated in his office. "How bad is the flood damage?"

"Not terrible. We'll have to do some repairs on the warehouses." He shook his head. "The high-water mark was eight feet above flood level."

Joshua blew out his breath in a soft whistle. "Eight feet! We got some flooding here, but not anything like that."

"Fortunately, we had plenty of warning. I moved all of the cotton to some sheds up on the hill. We lost maybe a ton or so of wheat that we couldn't get out in time, but all in all, it wasn't bad."

"Thank you for taking care of things. I wanted to come but . . ."

Samuelson waved it away. "Your place was here with Caroline." He paused a moment, then asked, "Can I be honest with you, Joshua?"

They were sitting in Joshua's office at the freight yard east of town. Samuelson had suggested they go for a walk after breakfast, and sensing that there was more on Samuelson's mind than just offering condolences for Livvy's death, Joshua had brought him here, where they could speak privately without interruption.

Joshua's sharp look brought a quick grunt of apology from his business partner. "Of course I can be honest with you. We've always been honest with each other."

"That's why this partnership has lasted as long as it has, Walter. And I didn't think you had come all this way just to report on the flood damage."

The businessman from St. Louis reached inside his jacket pocket and pulled out two cigars. He started to offer one to Joshua, then remembered. "That's right," he said. "I keep forgetting you've quit these things."

Joshua pulled a face. "It's done wonders for my marriage."

As he put one of the cigars back in his pocket, Samuelson's mouth twisted into a rueful expression. "Judith keeps reminding me that it would do the same in my house should I ever decide to quit," he said. And then, as though in direct defiance of his wife's wishes, he pulled a small penknife out of his vest pocket and carefully cut one end off the cigar. He took out a match. Suddenly his hand froze in midair. He looked around guiltily. "I'm not going to get arrested or something for smoking in Nauvoo, am I?"

Joshua chortled. "Oh, you may get some strange looks, but other than that, I think you're safe."

"Good." He struck the match, held it to the tip of the cigar, and puffed until it glowed an orange red. He tipped back in his chair, blowing the smoke into the air, savoring the moment, his eyes narrowing as the smoke billowed around his face.

"So?" Joshua asked after a moment.

"What?"

"You were going to be honest with me, remember?"

"Oh, yes. That."

"So what is it?"

Samuelson took another deep draw on the cigar, then turned his head and blew the smoke to one side. To his surprise, Joshua found the smell of the smoke annoying. It had once been something he enjoyed, even just the smell of a cigar or pipe. But it had been several years now since he had last smoked one, and he didn't miss it anymore.

"You remember Clemson Harwood from Quincy?"

"Of course." Clemson was one of their jobbers and served as an important link in their shipping back and forth between Nauvoo and St. Louis.

"He was the one who brought the news of Olivia's death to St. Louis. It was a real shock."

"Yes." It came out more abruptly than he intended. They had gone over that at supper last night. He didn't want to talk about Olivia anymore.

"He told us how it all happened, why you were in Warsaw in the first place."

"Yes, so?"

Samuelson let the chair come down again, then took the cigar out of his mouth and set it on the ashtray that Joshua kept on one corner of his desk for his foreman. "Joshua, Alice and I would have been here four days sooner, but I stopped in Quincy and Warsaw and made some inquiries."

"Inquiries? About me?"

"No. About the situation."

"Oh."

"You're the one who's always saying a man needs to get the lay of the land before he sounds the call either to charge or to retreat."

"Yes." Joshua was trying not to show any irritation. This was a chapter in his life which he was not ready to discuss, and he particularly did not feel like having it analyzed for him.

His partner seemed to sense this and so began cautiously. "What is your assessment of what is going to happen here, now that Joe Smith is dead?"

"Joseph Smith," Joshua corrected him without thinking. "I think you'll see the Church gradually break up and fall apart." At Samuelson's dubious look, he pressed on earnestly, using some of the same arguments he had used with his family. "Joseph was the force that held this people together. Oh, they've got other leaders, all right, but no one with Joseph's vision, no one with his leadership ability or appeal."

"So what does that mean for Nauvoo? For you?"

He shrugged. "Nauvoo is a thriving city. I expect the Church will collapse of its own weight in a year or two, just kind of fade away. But the people will stay on and do whatever they're doing now. I think Nauvoo has real potential for the river trade."

"And you think the people who killed Joseph will be satisfied with that?"

"Why shouldn't they be?" He thought of Robert Foster and the Higbee brothers and John C. Bennett. The depth of their hatred for Joseph was substantial, but they had their wish now. Joseph was dead. He smiled, half to himself. What was it that Joseph had called them? Dough heads. That about summed it up. Full of hate and not two ounces of intelligence between the lot of them. "Joseph's gone," he concluded. "That's all they were after."

Samuelson shook his head gravely. "Joshua, I think you ought to give serious thought to moving your family to St. Louis."

Joshua hooted. "You're not serious!"

"I'm not just talking about Caroline and the children, Joshua. I mean your whole family. Your parents. Your brothers and sisters and their families." He was leaning forward, his eyes earnest, almost pleading. "The mills and the warehouses are doing well. We can find employment for all of them, houses for them. I've even been thinking about some new opportunities you and I might consider. I remember you said your brother Nathan has got some good business sense."

Joshua was shaking his head before Samuelson had finished the last sentence. "My family will never leave. Not now, anyway. There's a great feeling among the Mormons that now, of all times, they have to stick together."

"Will you just listen for a few minutes? I didn't just spend my time in the saloons in Quincy and Warsaw listening to the rabble. I have been questioning men that you and I know and trust. I've talked with the civic leaders, newspaper editors—"

"Like Thomas Sharp?" Joshua exploded in disgust.

"Among others," Samuelson admitted evenly.

"I hold that man responsible for Joseph's death as much as anyone."

"He would be pleased to hear you say that," Samuelson said dryly. Then again he asked the question. "Will you just listen for a few minutes?"

"All right," Joshua said reluctantly. If Walter had come this far and had concerns, the least Joshua could do was hear him out.

"Now, here's what they're saying. I know you think this whole thing is religiously motivated, that Joe Sm—Joseph Smith—was viewed as a fanatic and his teachings were not only blasphemous but dangerous. But it's much bigger than that, Joshua. I was told that your governor came to Nauvoo on the day of the killings. What's his name again?"

"Thomas Ford. Yes, you heard that right. He gave his word to Joseph and Hyrum that he wouldn't leave them there unprotected, then broke his promise and came here with the one militia which had enough honor to protect Joseph."

"Did you know that the plan was that he would be killed here?"

Joshua frowned. "You mean Joseph?"

"No, Governor Ford!"

"*What?*"

"Yes. The men responsible for the murders hate Governor Ford almost as much as they hated Joseph Smith. The plan was that he would be here in Nauvoo when word came that Joseph had been murdered. They were hoping that the Mormons would be so outraged, they would rise up and massacre the governor and his entire party."

Joshua's eyes narrowed. "Where'd you hear a crazy thing like that?"

"From men who know," came the even reply. He was pleased that the skepticism was now erased from Joshua's face. "As near as I can determine, what you have are three separate parties working here, Joshua. You have what I call the religionists.

These are the preachers and their congregations who hate the Mormons for what they claim to preach and teach. Then there are the politicians. And by this I don't just mean the ones running for office. The politicians are the ones to whom the political situation is important. And they see this huge voting block of Mormons as a direct threat to their goals. That's why Thomas Sharp created a whole anti-Mormon political party. And he's got Democrats and Whigs alike to support him. There are powerful forces at work here, Joshua."

"And the third group?"

Samuelson shook his head. "These are the most dangerous, and what's really frightening is that the other two groups—both the religionists and the politicians—are willing to use this third group to further their own ends."

"And they are?"

"The lawless," Samuelson said slowly. "According to my sources, there's a whole group of scoundrels—blacklegs, counterfeiters, horse thieves, murderers—who are being brought into this because they have no qualms about using violence to achieve their ends. Their motivation is clear. They see a city ripe for the plunder, and so they're willing to throw in with those who want to see the Mormons driven out of the state. They are violent. They have absolutely no scruples, and they can be very dangerous."

Joshua was thinking of Joseph Jackson, who had nearly shot Joseph Smith once. He was a known murderer, a violent and frightening man. And yet Robert Foster and Chauncey Higbee and others—all so-called stalwarts in the community—had created an alliance with Jackson because they knew he would do what they did not have the courage to do.

Joshua finally nodded. "I agree with you, Walter. There is reason for concern, but I think we can handle it."

Samuelson was clearly frustrated. "Joshua, listen to me. I didn't go around telling people who I was. I didn't mention my partnership with you. I just asked questions and listened. And I'm telling you, your name came up again and again. They thought you were going to be their ally, then you turned against them. You are not just some invisible man in a crowd here, Joshua. I'm telling you, it is a dangerous situation. You have got to leave."

Joshua just shook his head. "You saw Caroline last night and this morning. She's doing much better now, but she's still not well. And in her heart . . ." He shook his head slowly, sadly. "I insisted that we leave once, Walter, and it cost us our daughter's life. I could no more talk to Caroline about leaving right now than I could—" Suddenly his eyes narrowed. "Does Alice know any of this? Is she going to be talking to Will?"

"No. When I was in Warsaw I left her with friends or associates while I was investigating things. She thinks I was simply transacting business."

"Thank you. Thank you for not bringing this up in front of my family. You are a true friend, Walter."

The man of wealth and influence in St. Louis knew he had lost, but he had to make one last try. "Will you at least consider it, Joshua? Will you think about it? Keep your ear to the ground?"

"Yes, I will do that."

Samuelson leaned forward and stubbed his cigar out in the ashtray. "Joshua, you know I'd love to have you down in St. Louis with us. That would be wonderful. But I'm telling you all of this for your sake, not for ours."

"I know, and I appreciate it. But I'll be careful."

Samuelson looked down at his hands, unable to let it go completely. "I'm telling you, Joshua, it is not over. And if you and your family throw your lot in with the Mormons, there's going to be bad trouble. Bad trouble."

—◆—

"Oh, my!"

Will slowed to a halt, letting Alice go a step or two farther before she too stopped.

"It's huge! Papa said it would be no more than the size of a small store or something."

He laughed aloud. "A small store? Why would he say something like that?"

Alice Samuelson glanced at him momentarily; then her eyes were pulled back to the temple which dominated the bluff ahead of them. In the morning sunlight, the building gleamed grayish white, the walls looking more like marble than limestone. Against the deep blue eastern sky it did seem to loom much larger than it really was, like a full moon just as it rises above the horizon. She slowly shook her head, still staring at the temple, and he could tell she had already forgotten his question.

"Why did your father think it would be small?"

"Papa said building a temple was just another wild notion of Joseph Smith's and that the Mormons were nearly destitute. I didn't expect much more than a shack or a tin shanty or something. Can we go up there?"

"Yes. I thought you might like to see it."

"Oh, yes, Will. I would."

She hadn't turned to look at him. She was riveted to the spot, staring with openmouthed astonishment.

He suppressed a chuckle, took her elbow, and started forward. Alice and her father had come in after dark last night, and so he knew that she hadn't seen the temple. As they left the house, he deliberately walked on the east side of the street, close to the houses, so that they would block her view eastward. Any time they came to a break where the temple would be visible, he had peppered her with questions to keep her gaze drawn to him. It had worked superbly well. When they rounded the corner of Steed Row, turning east on Mulholland Street, it was as if the temple leaped out of nowhere and assaulted their eyes.

Since her arrival, Alice had been tossing off one gentle barb after another—about Nauvoo, about the Mormons, about their religion. Little things like, "I didn't know Nauvoo had a riverboat dock. I thought the captain would have to just toss us off as we steamed by." Or, "Were those really brick houses we passed coming here? What happened, did you run out of mud and sticks?" There was nothing malicious in it. It was her way of gently teasing him, breaking down the first awkwardness of being together again. But it had revealed her conception of Nauvoo as being a backwater river stop. He had laughed at the little digs—Alice always made him laugh—but inwardly he had vowed he would get back at her. Now he felt joyously triumphant. Where were all the glib comments now?

When they reached the temple site, they did not go inside the rail fencing. The stonecutters and the other workmen were already filling the air with the sounds of hammer and chisel, creaking winches, shouts of instruction, and the dozen other things that accompany a great building project such as this. So they simply stopped and leaned on the fence, Will saying nothing while her eyes ran slowly up the great expanse of wall before them.

He watched her out of the corner of his eye, pleased with the awestruck look on her face, the silence that the temple had wrought upon her. To his surprise, the image of Jenny Pottsworth—now Jenny Pottsworth Stokes—suddenly popped into his mind, and he found himself comparing Alice to her. With a quick flash of insight, he realized that if Alice knew he was doing that, she would not be flattered. Jenny had a natural beauty that caught a man's eye from across the street, or down the block. Long honey-colored hair, wide arresting eyes, a smile that melted a man like butter in the sunlight. Alice, who would be eighteen in December, was much different than that. The first time he had seen her down in St. Louis, he had thought her somewhat plain. She had been only fifteen then. She had worn her dark brown hair cut off squarely at the neck, and that, coupled with the slenderness of her body, made her seem a little boyish. Now she had let her hair grow longer and it spilled across her shoulders. It softened her face and made her look older. She had also grown another inch or two and now was taller than Jenny, being five foot four or five. And the boyishness was definitely gone. She had dark brown eyes that reminded Will of two bright buttons that danced with life. They could tease and cajole, plead or probe, rebuke or praise, all without a single word from her. Her nose was straight and nicely rounded, her chin firm, her mouth soft and given naturally to a smile that was slightly sardonic and yet warm and gentle at the same time.

With a touch of surprise he realized that he couldn't remember now exactly why he had thought her plain. She might find his comparing her to Jenny Pottsworth threatening, but in Will's mind, she came out quite nicely in the comparison. That was a surprise to him, because for so long he had thought of her only as a wonderful friend. From the moment Will first went to St. Louis with his father on business, Alice's parents got it into their heads that here was the future husband for their daughter. Will's father heartily agreed with that prospect and began to push Will as hard as they were pushing Alice. Gratefully, Alice had resisted their matchmaking as strongly as Will had done, and that had opened up the opportunity for their friendship. With Jenny he had always felt awkward, bumbling, like an adolescent in the presence of an older woman. With Alice he was completely comfortable, feeling free to say what came to his mind, not fearing to contradict her if they disagreed. Their friendship was completely uncomplicated and that was a treasure indeed. Yes, he decided again, Alice Samuelson would compare very favorably to Jenny Pottsworth.

She glanced at him, giving him a curious look, so he turned his head and looked at the temple. The walls towered above them. All but the last few courses of stone were done. Soon they would be placing the capitals on the pilasters, and then the roof would follow. For a time, during the disastrous events that followed the destruction of the *Nauvoo Expositor*, work on the temple had ceased. Now it was in full swing again.

"Well, what do you think?" he asked.

"It's wonderful, Will! Simply wonderful." She turned and pointed. "Is that the sun carved on those stones there?" She was pointing to where several large blocks of stone were lined up in a row.

"Yes, those are what we call the sun stones," Will answered. He turned and pointed to the nearest pilaster—the pillar-like divisions between each vertical row of windows. "These will be the capitals that go on the top of each pilaster."

"But there are so many of them," she said, clearly awed.

"Well, there are something like thirty pilasters around the temple, if I remember right, and there will be a sun stone on the top of each one."

"But why?"

He turned, pointing to the temple wall. "Look at the base of each pilaster."

"That looks like the moon."

"It is." He pointed in another direction, to where a group of smaller stones was also lined up in rows. "And those are star stones. They'll go above the sun stones."

"So the sun, the moon, and the stars."

He turned to face her squarely now. "As I remember, you and your family are Methodists, right?"

"Yes." She smiled. "Well, our pastor sometimes wonders if Papa is, he goes so seldom, but yes. Why do you ask?"

"I know what the Methodists and most other Christian churches teach about the afterlife. How many places are there you can go?"

"Heaven and hell."

"Doesn't that bother you a little?"

"Only hell," she said with a droll smile.

He chuckled at that. "No, I mean—" He stopped, and now memories of his mission in England came flooding back. This was something he had worked out in his own mind as he tried to talk to the people there. "Do you really want to know?" he asked.

She nodded firmly. "Of course."

He took her hand and led her across the street to a thick patch of grass. "Let's sit down."

When they were seated, facing each other, he started right in. "Let me use a simple analogy to show you what I mean. I'll simplify it to the point of being ridiculous, but that will help me make the point."

She looked shocked. "I've never known you to be ridiculous before, Will. I don't know if I can handle this."

He tried to frown at her, pretending severity, but couldn't hold it and laughed instead, shaking his head helplessly. This was what made their friendship so delightful. They were as at ease with each other as brother and sister. "Just listen, Miss Samuelson," he growled. "If you can stop poking fun at me for a minute or two, I'll continue."

"Sorry," she said meekly.

"All right. Let's suppose that whether you go to heaven or hell is determined by a set number of sins you commit in this life."

"It seems like the Bible says something similar to that."

"I know, but let's suppose that it was a very precise number. Let's suppose that to get into heaven you have to have less than . . . oh, let's say less than five hundred sins."

"Whoa!" she cried, "for us sinners, couldn't you raise the total a little higher than that?"

"Sorry, five hundred is the cutoff point." Smiling, he went on. "So if you have less than five hundred, it's heaven. Five hundred or more, it's hell, all right?"

"It's going to be crowded down there," she observed, nodding her head.

"Now, here's my point. Alice Samuelson has only ten sins and so it's a sure thing she'll make it through the gates of heaven."

She inclined her head slightly. "I like that. Thank you."

"But let's say that someone else—say, your father—has four hundred and ninety-nine sins."

She giggled a little. "I don't think you ought to share this analogy with my father."

"Remember, I told you I was being ridiculous to make my point. So, your father gets to go into heaven with you."

"Good."

"And Will Steed? Well, he has exactly five hundred sins, so he misses the mark and is sent to spend an eternity in hell."

"Perhaps there'll be visiting privileges and I could bring you a cool drink every hundred years or so."

"Come on, Alice," he said, laughing aloud, "this is serious theology here."

"Of course," she answered, instantly contrite. "I'm sorry."

"Do you think that's fair? That your father, with only one less sin than me, gets to go to heaven while I'm consigned to the lower regions? Or that someone with only a few sins goes to the same place as someone with quite a few?"

Now the teasing humor was gone from her eyes and she was considering his question. "In a way, I guess not. But there has to be a dividing point somewhere."

"Ah," he said, pleased to see he had her thinking now. "Or dividing *points*," he corrected her.

She leaned back a little, her eyes narrowing in thought. "Well," she finally said, speaking slowly and with a touch of tentativeness in her voice, "as long as God is making the judgment, then it would have to be fair, wouldn't it?"

"Of course, whatever God does is right," he agreed, "but we also know that God is a just God. Do you think that's just? That with all the diversity in human behavior he would have only two places to send us?"

"Well, I . . ." She shrugged. "If that's the way he set things up, then it has to be fair."

"Exactly the point. We don't believe that is the way God set things up. Joseph Smith once asked a question about whether that was the way things would be after we die, and learned some wonderful things."

"But heaven and hell are all the Bible talks about."

"I could show you some things in the Bible that might change your mind about that. For example, Paul taught the Corinthians that in the resurrection some will get celestial bodies and some will get terrestrial bodies. But that's not my point here. My point is that there are other possibilities."

As he paused for breath, she was watching him closely, head

cocked to one side, clearly amused by his earnestness. "Will, all I wanted to know was why you're putting sun stones on your temple."

"I know," he said sheepishly. "Mother says I always do this, get carried away. But believe it or not, I am trying to answer your question."

"Okay, go on, then."

He gave her a puzzled look. "'O.K.'? What does that mean?"

"Oh, haven't you heard that expression before? *Okay* means 'all right,' or 'that's correct.'"

"Where did you hear that?"

"Didn't you know? President Van Buren used it in the last presidential election campaign. I don't know how it got started, but *okay* means 'yes,' or 'all right,' or 'that's good.'"

"Oh." He smiled. "Okay." Then he got serious again. "One day while Joseph Smith was reading in the Bible, he was struck with the problem I've just described. He wondered how it could be just to send people to either heaven or hell. He went to the Lord in prayer and asked him about it. In answer, he was shown a vision of life after death, and he saw that there were different kingdoms, and that they differed in the glory each had."

"Different kingdoms?"

Now he leaned forward, the eagerness putting vibrancy into his words. "He saw that there are differing degrees of reward in the next life. And this is what Paul said too. Read the fifteenth chapter of First Corinthians some day. One kingdom is called the celestial degree—that is the highest degree, and people who are righteous go there. Another kingdom is called the terrestrial kingdom. This is not hell as we normally think of it. Good people go there, people who are decent and kind and honest, but who did not really care for religion. They may have been good, but they weren't valiant in their faith. The third place is called the telestial degree of glory, or the telestial kingdom. Here those that were the wicked while on the earth go—the liars and adulterers, whoremongers and murderers. But even within that kingdom, people differ, depending on how they lived here."

He was tempted to say more, but decided that was enough for one day. "Anyway, that's why the different stones on the temple. They represent those different degrees of glory. We believe that in the temple we will be given the ordinances that help us achieve the fulness of the celestial kingdom."

She didn't say anything for a long time, but let her eyes sweep across the great walls that towered above them. Finally, she looked at him, and to his surprise, he could see she was flustered a little. "Can I ask you a question about your religion?"

"Sure."

"Is it true that Joseph Smith taught that God expects a man to have more than one wife?"

The question was not totally unexpected, and he had thought a lot about how best to answer her if and when she asked it. "Not exactly," he responded.

"Not exactly?" she exclaimed. "What kind of an answer is that?"

"Well, the way you stated the question is not true. Joseph Smith did not teach that God expects every man to have more than one wife. But he has taught that having more than one wife, when God commands it, is not wrong."

The frown was so deep that Will wanted to reach out and touch the spot between her eyes that had furrowed into great wrinkles. Instead he went on quickly. "Do you remember what Paul once said to the Corinthians? He said, 'I have fed you with milk and not with meat because you are not able to bear it now.'"

"Well, thanks a lot," she said, for the first time sounding irritated.

"No, I don't mean it that way, Alice. I . . . I'm just saying that trying to understand whether or not Joseph was right in restoring the practice of plural marriage—I say 'restoring' because, as you know, the great prophets and patriarchs of the Old Testament had more than one wife. But anyway, starting with that question is like asking a young child to eat a steak. If you really want to know if Joseph was a prophet, there are other places to start."

She was still frowning at him, so he rushed on. "I'm really not trying to put you off, Alice, I'm just saying, if you really want to know about these things, even plural marriage, then start with something else."

"Like what?"

"Like reading the Book of Mormon. Like praying and asking God if the Church is true, if it really is his church."

She considered that, her eyes thoughtful.

Will wanted to close in, push her for a commitment, get her to accept a Book of Mormon. Suddenly, and inexplicably, he wanted that very much. But wisdom quietly whispered to wait. So he did.

"I'd like to think about it," she said after a time.

"Fair enough." He stood, took her by the hands, and pulled her to her feet. As she came up, she was facing him fully, her face close to his. As he looked down at her, he suddenly had a great urge to kiss her. It caught him so totally by surprise that he let go of her hands and fell back a step.

Alice's eyes widened. Then slowly that enigmatic smile of hers stole across her face. "Why, Will Steed," she exclaimed, "I do believe you're blushing."

That only flustered him all the more, and he just shook his head.

Now the smile broadened and her eyes were suddenly very soft. "I think that's the nicest thing you've ever said to me, Will."

"But I didn't say anything," he blurted.

"Exactly," she answered. Then, putting her arm through his, she moved toward the street. "What else do you have in this town of yours to show me?"

Chapter Notes

The situation in Hancock County as described here by Walter Samuelson is an accurate portrayal of what was happening in the aftermath of the martyrdom of Joseph and Hyrum (see HC 7:1–60).

There is probably no Americanism that passed so quickly into common use as the word *okay*. The first documented use of O.K. as an adjective was in 1839 in a Boston newspaper, which suggested that something was O.K., or "all correct." It was common practice of nineteenth-century humorists to deliberately misspell common words, and *O.K.* seems to have come from the misspelling of the phrase "all correct" as "oll korrect." The phrase might have passed into oblivion had it not been that in 1840 the Tammany Democratic Party of New York started "O.K. Clubs" to support Martin Van Buren, their candidate, who was nicknamed "Old Kinderhook," since he was born in Kinderhook, New York. The idea was that Old Kinderhook was O.K. or "oll korrect." Whatever its precise beginnings, the initials caught on in the minds of the public and quickly became the word *okay*, a common expression all across America. Eventually it became an almost universal expression and can be heard virtually in every country of the world today. (See *The Merriam-Webster New Book of Word Histories* [Springfield, Mass.: Merriam-Webster, 1991], pp. 329–30.)

They were walking east along Water Street, coming toward the intersection with Main Street. The evening air was warm but pleasant. The mosquitoes were out, but there was a breeze out of the west strong enough to keep them down to the point where they weren't unbearable.

Will pointed to the large log cabin that they were approaching on their right. "That's called the Homestead. That's where Joseph Smith lived when they first came to Nauvoo—or Commerce, as it was known then."

"Really," Alice said. "That's quite a nice home."

"Well, they added some of it after coming here. Joseph's mother lived with them for a time."

"And now they're in the—" She stopped, pointing toward the large two-story frame home on the opposite corner. "What do you call it?"

"The Mansion House."

"Yes, that is a beautiful home."

"Joseph planned it partially as a hotel. He had many visitors and guests."

"Lydia said that Emma has sold it."

"Actually, Joseph sold it to a man with the idea that he would rent some rooms back from him. But I heard the other day that Emma is thinking of moving out of the Mansion House and back to the Homestead again. She just doesn't have enough money to stay there."

They had reached the intersection now and stopped on the corner. To their left, directly east of the Homestead and south of the Mansion House, a large building was under construction. It sat right on the waterfront, just a few rods from the boat landing. "And what is that going to be?" Alice asked.

"We call that the Nauvoo House. It's going to be a hotel."

"A nice one."

"Yes." He smiled a little. "Us country bumpkins have managed to bring in one or two improvements."

She laughed softly, looking up at him. "I should never have teased you about Nauvoo."

"Why not? The scriptures say that pride goeth before destruction."

She slapped at him. "I beg your pardon." Then she sobered. "Actually, Will, I love Nauvoo. It's so open and airy. The streets are so wide and so straight. You always know exactly where you are. That's hardly what St. Louis is like."

"You think St. Louis is bad, you ought to see the cities in China or England."

"I would love to someday." And then she looked at him more closely. "Do you ever think about going to sea again?"

"Yes."

"Do you miss it?"

"Often."

"But?" She smiled, not wanting to pry into his personal feelings and yet wanting to know.

If he minded, he didn't show it. "But I think my destiny, my mission in life, if you will, lies elsewhere. Here, with my family and our people."

She nodded, noting the faraway look in his eyes and the touch of sadness around his mouth. After a moment, she spoke again. "I'm going to miss being here, Will."

He came back to her. "It's been wonderful to have you here this week. You'll have to tell your father to bring you with him the next time he comes."

"Or you could come down to St. Louis with your father," she said hopefully.

"I will."

After a moment, she looked back up at him. "Will?" she said shyly.

He looked down at her. "What?"

"I've decided I'd like to do what you suggested."

"What is that?"

"I'd like to read about your church."

His expression was so startled that she laughed aloud. "Well, is it that shocking?"

"No, but . . . I was just . . ." He had to stop, and she laughed the more at his confusion. "You never said anything more and I . . ." Now he got a sly smile. He turned away from her and fumbled around in his shirt. In a moment, he turned back. In his hand there was a Book of Mormon. He held it out to her. "This is for you."

She took it, looked at it, then gave him a strange look. "How did you know I would—"

"I didn't. I brought this along hoping I could find a way to ask you if you would consider taking it back with you."

Her head bobbed. "Thank you, Will. I will read it."

He took it back from her for a moment and opened it to the very end of the book. He held it up to the pale moonlight, and she could see he had bracketed one part of the page with a pen. "Read this first."

"All right." She took the book back and tried to see what it said, but the moon was down to less than three-quarters now and there was not enough light to see the words. "Thank you again." And then she had a thought. "Will, maybe it's better if you don't say anything about this to my father."

There was a soft hoot. "I hadn't planned on it." He took out a pocket watch and held it up to the light. "Well, I suppose I'd better get you back. I wouldn't want your father and mine to come looking for us."

She didn't move. "Thank you for a wonderful week, Will."

"Thank you for coming."

They stood there for a moment, awkwardly, and then Alice reached out and took his hand. "We'd better start back," she said.

"Yes," Will agreed, squeezing her hand and keeping it in his. "I suppose we'd better."

———————◆———————

Mary Ann was in the backyard of their home, taking down the clothes that she had washed and hung out this morning. She moved methodically, not minding the heat of the afternoon but also not moving too quickly. She took down a blouse, then pressed it against her face. She loved the smell of newly washed clothes, dried in the sun.

She half turned as she heard the gate at the front of the house give its customary creak. From here, the house blocked her view of the front yard, so she listened carefully as she folded the blouse to see if someone knocked on the front door or if it was just one of the grandchildren going in and out. To her surprise, a moment later Benjamin came around the house, followed closely by Nathan and Lydia. She laid the folded blouse in the basket, then turned to greet them. At the look on Lydia's face, she stopped.

Lydia came forward and took her hands. "Mother Steed, it's Samuel Smith."

She felt a sudden lurch, pain down deep inside her. "No," she whispered.

"Yes," Benjamin said, coming to put an arm around her shoulder. "He passed away earlier today."

She wanted to sink to the ground. Instead, she squeezed Lydia's hands. "We'd best go see Mother Smith," she said softly. "See if there's anything we can do to help."

"After all she has lost," Benjamin said, "now to lose another son."

Nathan raised his head slowly. "How much can one mother be expected to bear?"

"There it is! I see it! I see it!" Sarah Rogers started jumping up and down, pointing over the railing of the *Natchez Queen*. "That's Nauvoo, isn't it, Mama? Isn't it?"

Melissa smiled at her daughter. "Yes, Sarah, that's Nauvoo."

Sarah would be six in November, and usually her two older brothers—Caleb, who was nearly eight, and David, who was going on ten—didn't put much stock in anything she had to say. But now they pushed forward, in between their parents. "Where? Where?"

"On the hill. There. See it?"

Caleb squinted. It was barely past noon and the sun was high, glinting off the river and leaving the air gray blue with the haze. "I don't see anything," he said in disgust.

Carl leaned over and laid a hand on his son's shoulder. "Look, Caleb. See where the river turns to the left up ahead of us? That's where the city is."

Now young Carl moved up beside his brother. "Look a little to the right, Caleb. There's a low hill there. See the big white building?"

David started wiggling, his arm thrusting forward. "That's the temple, isn't it, Papa?"

"Yes, that's the temple."

"I see it!" Caleb chortled, looking at Sarah with begrudging respect.

"We'll be there in about twenty minutes," Melissa said. "You'd better go pack."

The three of them darted away, leaving only young Carl standing with his parents.

"Don't wake the baby!" Melissa called after them. "Papa and I will be there in a moment."

She moved closer to Carl and put her arm through his. "There it is," she murmured.

There was a slow nod, but no response beyond that.

"Papa?"

Carl turned to his namesake. "What, Carl?"

"Are we ever going to go back to Kirtland?"

One eyebrow came up. "Why do you ask?"

"I don't want to."

Melissa now turned, as surprised as Carl. Young Carl had turned twelve in April. Though he was much like his father in temperament—quiet, thoughtful, choosing his words with care— he was Melissa in every other way—dark hair, fine features, slim of body. He was getting his growth slowly and hadn't yet started into puberty, but he had always been mature in his thinking and in the way he assessed the world around him. "But why?" she asked.

"Because this is home," he said simply.

"Didn't you like being with Grandma Rogers?" his father asked.

"Yes. And I miss that part of our family already. But this is home."

"I know," Melissa whispered, looking up at Carl.

He held her glance for a minute, then looked at his son. "You go help your brothers and sister now, Carl."

"Yes, Papa." He gave one last glance out ahead of them, then turned and walked away.

"That was a strange thing for him to say," Melissa said when he was gone.

"Was it?"

She gave him an odd look, tilting her head slightly. "You don't think so?"

There was a short, silent laugh. "That's what I called it back in Kirtland, remember? Doesn't it feel that way to you too?" he asked.

"You know it does. I'm like the children. My heart is beating a little faster just seeing it out there ahead of us. I'm so excited to see the family again. They'll be so surprised."

"I'm glad you didn't write them. This should be fun."

She half turned, then stopped. "So, *are* we going to move back to Kirtland?"

There was a long moment when only the great swishing of the paddle wheel behind them could be heard. Then he slowly shook his head. "I don't think so. We'll have to go back and visit, of course, but . . . No, I don't think so. I think Carl's right. This is home."

"Yes." She started away, a sudden lightness in her heart, but she only went three or four steps before he spoke again.

"Melissa?"

"What?"

"I'll not be interested in having anything to do with the Church."

Her chin rose a little; she was not really surprised. "I know, Carl."

"You can do what you want. You know that."

"I do, and I thank you. But—" She looked away, biting at her lip, surprised at the sudden rise of emotion in her. "But until there's no more talk about plural marriage, I'll not be doing much with the Church either, Carl."

He watched her steadily, the sunlight off the water playing across the faint dusting of freckles on his cheeks, his green eyes grave and thoughtful. Finally, he nodded, clearly satisfied, then turned from the rail and took her hand. "Let's go pack, Mrs. Rogers. We're almost home."

Joshua and Will Steed were working in the large barn behind the stables. They used this barn as a warehouse for goods that either were being prepared for shipment or had come in by wagon and were waiting distribution. They had four men with them, and they were all loading sacks of barley onto a wagon that was destined for Montebello, south of Nauvoo. It was shortly before noon, and Joshua was eager to get the wagon on its way so it could reach its destination before nightfall. The lawless element which skulked around the river towns was growing more and more bold, and they had lost a wagonload of durable goods the previous week. The driver was still recovering from being pistol-whipped for trying to resist. So Will and Joshua had shed their coats and come out to help speed up the process.

The air in the barn was thick with dust, and they had necker-chiefs tied around their faces. They were hot, sweaty, dirty, and tired. It had been some time since Joshua had helped load a wagon, and he was puffing heavily enough that he was a bit embarrassed by it. In that disgusting way that youth have, Will worked in what looked like effortless ease. He too was sweating, but Joshua could hardly tell that he was breathing hard.

Will paused for a moment, grinning wickedly at his father. "Pa, maybe you shouldn't have backed out on the sale of the business."

Joshua just grunted and tossed another bag up on the wagon bed. In February, he had put the freight business up for sale when he had jerked his family out of Nauvoo in order to "save" Olivia from Joseph Smith and plural marriage. Then the potential buyers had been unable to raise enough capital. That had delayed their leaving Warsaw and, in a way, was directly responsible for the tragedy that followed. Even after Olivia's death, Joshua had been determined to sell and move to St. Louis, and found another group of buyers who acted interested. But the more he watched Caroline during her convalescence, the more he knew that if he tried to move his family out now, it would break her. So he had withdrawn the freight company from the market.

"If you had sold out," Will said, leaning against the back of the wagon, "you could be sitting in some office now. You'd be in a white shirt. It would be cool. Maybe one of the secretaries could bring you a tall glass of iced tea."

Joshua looked at the other men, who were smiling now too, though not too openly. "You know, after spending a week listening to you go on so, it's no wonder Alice looked so tired when she and her father finally went back home." He looked at the other men, who had stopped work now to listen, grinning at the interchange between father and son. "Maybe we'd best go to the office and have some iced tea and leave the rest of the job up to old Big Mouth here."

That brought a laugh from the men, but Will was unruffled. "Listening to you blowing like a winded horse, that might not be a bad idea. I'd hate to have to carry you home tonight."

"Look, you little pup—," Joshua started, ignoring the guffaws of the others. But just then the side door to the barn opened. Joshua's bookkeeper stuck his head in.

"Mr. Steed?"

"Yes?"

"There's a gentleman to see you."

"Who?" And then he knew it didn't matter who it was, they had to finish loading the wagon so it could get off. "Can you ask him to come back in about an hour?"

"I did that, sir. He said it's most urgent that he speak with you."

It always was, Joshua thought. He picked up another sack of barley and heaved it up on the load. "Did he give you a name?"

"Yes. He says his name is Bennett." The man had a strange look of distaste on his face. "Doctor John C. Bennett."

All four of Joshua's workers were Latter-day Saints, recent immigrants from England or the eastern United States looking for work in their new home. At the mention of the name of John C. Bennett they all swung around, anger darkening their faces.

"Bennett!" Will cried. "It can't be. He wouldn't dare."

The accountant nodded vigorously. "I don't know him, sir, but one of the others recognized him. It's him, Mr. Steed."

"I'll wager that he's riding a rail out of town by sundown," one of the men growled. There were angry mutters of agreement from the others. Joshua was still staring.

"What do you want me to tell him, Mr. Steed?"

That brought Joshua back. "Tell him I'll be right there," he said.

"I'm going with you, Pa," Will said immediately. He didn't wait for an answer. He took the neckerchief from off his face and wiped at his forehead with it even as he started for the door. For a moment, Joshua thought about calling him back, then shrugged it off. Maybe it was just as well to have company when he faced this man again.

Bennett was waiting in the office, seated in a chair. Joshua stopped for a moment, studying the man through the window. He had not seen them yet. He was dressed even more impeccably than normal, and Joshua saw immediately that the rumors were true. John C. Bennett had prospered considerably by writing a book and going on the lecture circuit to denounce Mormonism. His suit was well cut and clearly came from an excellent tailor. His shoes were city shoes and polished to a gleaming luster. He wore a white shirt with a silk cravat at the neck. A beaver-skin top hat sat on the desk. A cane with a brass tip and polished ebony head lay beside it. The hair, just starting to gray now, was slicked back and recently barbered. He looked every bit the wealthy New York businessman or Boston dandy.

Joshua frowned at Will, then opened the door. Bennett shot to his feet, all smiles. For a moment, Will thought he was going to cross the room, hand extended, as though greeting a brother not seen for long years. But when Bennett saw Will come in behind Joshua, the smile stiffened a little and he held his place.

"Joshua," he said, voice warm and welcoming, "how good to see you again!"

"Hello, John," Joshua responded in a cool voice. "This is a surprise."

"Thought it might be." He looked more closely at Will. "Will Steed, isn't it?"

Will nodded curtly but said nothing.

Bennett stepped back, the smile still unctuous, but strained now. "I heard about the tragic loss of your daughter, Joshua. I am truly sorry. I—"

"Don't!" Will said in a clipped, harsh tone. "Don't you even talk about Olivia. It's you and your kind that are responsible for her death."

Joshua reached back and laid a hand on his son's arm, still watching Bennett, who had drawn himself up, his face showing deep offense. "That's enough, Will," Joshua warned. Then to Bennett, "It does seem a little strange that you would come back here."

"Look," he said angrily, "Joseph and I had our differences. I felt obligated to oppose some of the things he taught, but—"

"You felt obligated to weave a tangle of outrageous lies and slanderous half-truths," Will said hotly.

Joshua swung on him. "Will, Doctor Bennett is well aware of your feelings. So am I. That's enough said. If you can't be polite, then excuse yourself and go back to loading the wagon."

Will stood there, his feet planted, his fists clenched, as though he were facing a possible attack, but finally there was a brief bob of his head. "All right."

"Thank you, Joshua," Bennett said. He turned and, without asking, returned to his chair. "There are things that I must discuss with you."

Joshua moved around and took the chair behind his desk. Will took one in the corner opposite Bennett.

"You have to believe me," Bennett said, hands out as if in supplication, "I deeply regret that in the heat of my embittered differences with Brother Joseph, I strayed into a severity of expression of which my cooler judgment would not approve."

There was a soft hoot of disgust from Will, but one sharp

look from Joshua stopped it there. Bennett half turned in his chair so that he could deliberately avoid Will's gaze. In his mind, there was only one other in the room now and that was Joshua. "You have to believe me, Joshua. I wanted to dethrone Joseph because I felt he was leading the Church astray, but I have never condoned or justified mob violence as the means of doing that."

Strangely enough, Joshua did believe him. Not that it proved much. Bennett had worked against Joseph in every other way. And Will was right. It was because of men like Bennett and the hatred they sowed that the opposition against the Mormon prophet exploded into open violence. He finally nodded, not responding one way or another.

Bennett reached inside his coat and withdrew an envelope. "You asked what I am doing here. Well, this partially explains it. I received this while in Louisville about mid-July." He leaned forward and tossed it onto the desk.

Joshua picked it up, opened it, and withdrew one sheet of paper. He unfolded it and looked at it. After a moment, he looked at Will. "It is dated June nineteenth from Carthage."

"June nineteenth?" Will said in surprise. "A week before the martyrdom?"

Joshua nodded absently, still looking at the sheet. He looked at Bennett as he spoke to Will. "There is no name. It is signed only as 'a brigadier general of the Illinois militia.'"

"Yes," Bennett said.

"'Dear General Bennett—,'" Joshua began. He had emphasized the word *general* with soft sarcasm and Bennett raised a deprecating hand.

"You must remember that I was quartermaster general for the state militia, appointed by the governor. This man also knew I was a general in the Nauvoo Legion."

"Who is it?" Joshua asked.

Bennett shook his head. "I have a pretty good idea, but the man obviously wanted to remain anonymous, so I feel I must honor his wishes. But read on."

"'Dear General Bennett. We need you very much in your

military capacity for our campaign against the Mormons. If you can and will come, start without a moment's delay, as things will come to a crisis in about eight or ten days.'"

Joshua looked up. If this was written on the nineteenth, it was exactly eight days before a mob stormed the Carthage Jail. He said nothing, but continued reading. "'Perhaps the committee will send this to you in Louisville by express. If so, come with the man who brings it to you. Come to me directly at either Carthage or Warsaw.' Then it's signed."

"I didn't come, Joshua. I didn't want to be part of that."

"Then why are you here now?" Will asked, his voice even and controlled.

Bennett answered, but not to Will. "When I heard the news of Joseph's tragic death, that changed everything. I knew that there would be many questions about who should lead the Church now."

"Surely you're not volunteering!" Will sneered.

"Will!" Joshua said, his voice crackling. "That is enough!"

Bennett finally gave Will a quick look, and it was filled with condescension and sly triumph. "Thank you, Joshua," he said smoothly. "No, of course I don't think I am the one to take over from Joseph. I have made my break with the Church. I still vehemently disagree with the direction that Joseph took the Church there at the last. No, the reason I came forward is because of something that happened while I was serving in the First Presidency."

"You were not in the First Presidency," Will corrected softly. "Joseph called you to act as an Assistant President while Sidney Rigdon was ill and could not function."

To Joshua's surprise, Bennett merely nodded. "That's correct. But Joseph treated me as though I were a full member of the Presidency. And it was while I was in that position that something of great importance happened." Again he reached in his pocket and withdrew another envelope. Joshua saw that it was sealed.

"What is that?" Will asked suspiciously.

"A revelation from Joseph Smith," Bennett retorted. There was no mistaking the triumph in his voice and his amusement at the reaction from both Joshua and Will.

"A revelation?" Will exclaimed.

"What kind of a revelation?" Joshua asked.

"Let me tell you first about how it came about. It was April seventh, eighteen forty-one, three years ago now. Joseph came to me and said that he had received a revelation. At that time, only Hyrum and I were functioning members of the Presidency. Elder Rigdon was quite ill, as Will has noted. But Joseph came to me. First he made me promise with the most solemn oath that I would never divulge, neither through friendship nor enmity, the secret he was about to communicate to me until after his death. If I were to proceed him in death, he said, then he would communicate the secret to another. Otherwise, I was under the most solemn oath. Then he handed me this sealed envelope."

He contemptuously ignored the skeptical look on Will's face. But Will wasn't the only one who found this to be just a bit too preposterous. Joshua couldn't help the smile that came as a response to Bennett's claim. "And I suppose that you have no idea what the envelope contains."

"Oh, no. I know exactly what it contains. Joseph told me."

"What?" both Will and Joshua asked together.

"Joseph made me swear to him with the most solemn oath that if he should die, I would hand this over to an authorized agent of the Church. It contains a revelation from the Lord about how to reorganize this church in the event that Joseph should die."

Both father and son just stared at him, mouths agape.

He smiled thinly. "That's right. And that's why I am here."

"And what does this supposed revelation say?" Will asked. He said it with cool detachment, but his eyes were hard and cold. Bennett flinched a little at the implacable bitterness there. Once again, he turned away, looking at Joshua. "Well, among other things," he said archly, like a child who has been insulted, "the Lord said that I had received the blessings of heaven"—he shot Will a withering glance—"and that I had been sealed up and should never fall."

"Well, so much for that promise," Will drawled.

"And that whosoever would bless me," Bennett went on quickly, his voice rising in warning, "should be blessed, *and . . .*" He paused for effect. "And whosoever should curse me should himself be cursed."

Will guffawed loudly, shaking his head. Joshua was too flabbergasted to try and rein Will in any longer. "And that is the message of the revelation, that you are approved of heaven?" Will made no attempt to hide his incredulity.

"Of course not," Bennett muttered. "That was just one sentence or two of it. A blessing for me, if you will. But the main part of the revelation gave instructions about Joseph's successor," he said. "It even named him." Then in a rush, at Will's look, he blurted it out. "Sidney Rigdon is to be appointed the prophet, seer, and revelator for the Church."

"Sidney Rigdon?" Will blurted.

"That's right!" Bennett shot right back. "William Marks and Brigham Young are to be his counselors. Not only is Rigdon to fill Joseph's position, but the revelation states that he is to be the king and imperial primate of the kingdom. He is to be assisted by princes, dukes, viceroys, and other nobles."

He leaned forward, his eyes blazing. "Go ahead and scoff if you like, young man, but Joseph told me the whole plan the Lord has in mind for reorganizing his church. He gave me the names of the men who were to fill the various positions and told me how the whole thing was to be done."

"Why you?" Joshua said. "Why not Brigham Young or one of the Twelve?"

"Because in my position as an Assistant President, and also as mayor of Nauvoo, I was charged with conferring the various degrees and organizing this Halcyon Order."

"Halcyon Order?" Joshua snapped, losing patience now. This was preposterous. He didn't much care what happened in the Church, but he knew Joseph Smith, and this was not how Joseph would have organized things. "What is that supposed to mean?"

"Halcyon means peaceful, happy, orderly. The halcyon was a mythical bird. When it landed on the seas, the waves were instantly calmed. This is what the kingdom shall become now. A Halcyon Order."

Joshua leaned back, searching Bennett's face carefully. "Just out of curiosity, why have you come to me? If Joseph told you to give it to the authorities of the Church, why aren't you telling this to John Taylor or Parley Pratt?"

"Does Sidney Rigdon know all this?" Will asked suddenly, before Bennett could answer. "You know, he's not here anymore."

"Of course I know," came the response. "I wrote to him in Pittsburgh. I was hoping he would arrive before me, but I expect him any day now."

"Why me?" Joshua pressed.

Bennett stood, picking up his hat from the desk. He dropped the sealed letter on Joshua's desk. "You have no vested interest in all of this, Joshua. I don't want anyone tampering with it. I would like you to read it first, so you know what it contains, but then give it to whomever you wish." Now his tone was lofty, imperious. "I have done my sacred duty. The rest is up to you."

"I don't want it," Joshua replied.

"I understand that you and Joseph were reconciled before his death. I think Joseph would expect that of you. This revelation came from him. It's the least you can do to make sure it gets into the right hands."

The former mayor of Nauvoo shrugged and moved to the door. "I didn't expect that I would be welcomed back here, Joshua, but I have always been one to follow the Lord's commandments." And with that, he stepped out the door and slammed it behind him.

———— ◆ ————

Mary Ann walked up to the small frame home that was being rented by the Manning family, and knocked on the door. After a moment, the door opened and Jane Manning was there. "Well," she said in surprise, "good morning, Mary Ann."

"Good morning, Jane. Do you have a moment I could speak with you?"

"Of course. Won't you come in?"

"It's so pleasant out here, can we just walk for a few minutes?"

Jane smiled and stepped out onto the porch. "Of course."

They walked out to the street, moving slowly. Mary Ann decided to plunge right in. "Jane, remember when I mentioned that I would look for work for you?"

"Yes."

"That was over three weeks ago. You probably thought I had forgotten."

Jane was clearly taken aback. "Well, actually . . ."

Mary Ann laughed. "At first I had no luck, but just last night I thought of a possibility."

The black woman was obviously touched. "You don't have to solve my problems, Mary Ann."

"I know, but I think this is perfect. But I wanted to talk with you first before proceeding."

"What is it?"

"You may have heard that my daughter Melissa and her family just returned from Kirtland a couple days ago."

"Yes, I did."

"Melissa's my older daughter. She had a baby on the fifteenth of July. She already has four young children. Just last night she and her husband, Carl, were talking about getting someone in to help out with the housework and to mind the children. Would that be of interest to you?"

"Yes, ma'am," Jane said enthusiastically. "We've been worried about making ends meet. Do you think they would have me?"

"With my recommendation," Mary Ann laughed, "they'll probably pay you double wages. If you'd like, we can stop in now and meet them. Then the three of you can talk and decide if this is something that will work out for everyone."

"That would be wonderful," Jane started, "but—"

Mary Ann went on smoothly. "It will be wonderful to have you as part of their family. Carl is a fine man and is prospering very much right now. As you may know, he owns the Rogers and Sons brickyards. I think having someone to help Melissa will greatly appeal to him."

"Let's see if your daughter finds me acceptable first," Jane murmured.

Mary Ann suddenly understood. "There is no need to worry about that," she said. "Not for one moment."

Jane suddenly felt at ease. If Melissa's mother was so openly accepting of her, perhaps the daughter would be as well. "Thank you, Mary Ann. Thank you for remembering."

———————

Parley P. Pratt was puffing heavily, obviously having come with some swiftness to the home of Benjamin Steed. He knocked briskly on the door, then stepped back, taking out a handkerchief to wipe his forehead. In a moment, Mary Ann came to the door.

"Elder Pratt, good afternoon."

"Good afternoon, Sister Mary Ann. Is Benjamin at home?"

"Yes, he and Nathan are in the kitchen working on some plats for their new property. Won't you come in?"

"Yes, thank you. I'm glad they're both here."

Benjamin and Nathan both looked up in surprise as Mary Ann ushered Parley into the kitchen. She started to back away, but the Apostle motioned for her to stay. "You may as well hear this too, Mary Ann. I have some disturbing news."

"What?" Benjamin asked, pushing the papers in front of him aside. "What's wrong?"

"You know that letter John Bennett gave to Joshua a couple of days ago?"

"Yes, what about it?"

"You know what it said about who should lead the Church?"

"Joshua didn't read it. Will took it to Elder Taylor unopened. But Bennett claimed it named Sidney Rigdon as the successor."

"That's right. That's what the letter said. Well, guess who arrived on the steamer today?"

Nathan started. "Sidney's here?"

"Yes, on the morning boat from Quincy."

"Here to humbly accept John C. Bennett's wondrous revelation?" Benjamin said with surprising bitterness.

Parley shook his head, his eyes clearly troubled. "He didn't get Bennett's letter. He came as soon as he got word that Joseph and Hyrum had been killed. He knew nothing about Bennett's supposed revelation."

"Well, that's something, at least," Nathan said.

"Not really," Parley said slowly.

"What do you mean?" Mary Ann asked, seeing the concern in his eyes.

"Well, according to what Sidney told Willard Richards, he's had his own revelation. He's to become the guardian of the Church."

Nathan slapped the table sharply, angrily. "What! He ran off to Pittsburgh just when things started getting dangerous here, and now he's back to claim the throne?"

"Yes. But only out of a sense of duty," Parley said with heavy sarcasm. He turned to Benjamin. "There's to be a short meeting this afternoon with some of the high priests. Can you and Nathan be there?"

"Of course. Where and when?"

"Four p.m. at Elder Richards's house."

"All right. We'll be there."

"Thank you." He tipped his head toward Mary Ann. "I'll be off and let others know. Good day." But as he reached the door he stopped and turned again. He was frowning deeply. "President Marks has invited Sidney to speak to the people at worship services tomorrow."

Benjamin straightened slowly. "Is that wise?" he asked.

"Do we have any choice? He is the only surviving member of the First Presidency. And President Marks is the stake president. He didn't really ask any of us." There was a weary sigh. "Besides, there are some people who are happy to hear that Sidney has returned."

There was a heavy silence as they considered all that that

meant. Finally, Benjamin stood, slowly, wearily, as if suddenly very tired. "It's begun, then," he said simply. "We knew it would, but now it's begun."

Nathan felt only anger. "The Prophet's dead and already the vultures are circling."

Parley nodded slowly. "Where are the rest of my brethren, the Twelve? There are four of us here now, but that is not sufficient for a quorum." He looked away, his voice stricken now. "The voice of the Lord told me to have the people wait for the Twelve before they acted. But where are they? How much longer must we wait?" He finally looked at the three Steeds, who watched him with great anxiety. "How much longer *can* we wait?"

Chapter Notes

The audacity of John C. Bennett as evidenced by his return to Nauvoo after the Martyrdom is a little known chapter in the history of the Church. After his public exposure and excommunication from the Church in 1842, he left Nauvoo to wage a bitter writing and lecturing campaign against the Church, covering much of the nation in the intervening two years. As described in volume 6 of this series, he tried to do enormous damage to the Church. It was astonishing enough that he would even dare return to Nauvoo, but that he would come claiming a personal revelation from Joseph shows the nature of the man. (See Andrew F. Smith, "The Saintly Scoundrel: The Life and Times of John Cook Bennett" [unpublished ms., Albany, N.Y., 1994], pp. 202–3.)

In an entry from Bennett's writings, he says he arrived in Nauvoo sometime in early August but gives no exact date. It had to be before the rest of the Twelve returned on 6 August, and it seems likely it was before Sidney Rigdon arrived, which was on 3 August (see HC 7:223). Thus, in the novel Bennett is shown as coming to Nauvoo on 1 August 1844.

Brigham Young and others who knew Joseph well said the purported revelation was written in Bennett's own handwriting. Evidently, Bennett took no active part in the succession crisis beyond the alleged revelation, probably because he knew how strongly the Saints resented him and he felt his support would only hurt Sidney Rigdon's chances. After the succession question was settled, Bennett left Nauvoo again and had no more significant interaction with the Church.

The roads were unbelievable—ruts deep enough in some places to hide the large wheels of the coach up to the hubs; ridges of mud that in the sun had turned hard as stone, enough to defy any set of springs ever put on a stagecoach; mud holes big enough and wide enough to look like small lakes, and deceptive enough to swallow a steam locomotive. The torrential rains during the latter part of June and the early part of July, which had caused so much flooding along the Mississippi River, were over now, but the effects of one of the wettest years in memory lingered on.

The five men traveling by stagecoach from Chicago to Galena, Illinois, a numbing journey of about a hundred and sixty miles, clung to the straps inside the coach as it rocked violently back and forth. They had left Chicago at seven a.m. the previous morning. That meant that so far they had endured thirty hours on the road, stopping only for a quick meal, a change of teams and drivers—or when the stage bogged down. Thirty hours of being viciously pummeled. Thirty long, jarring, jolting, lurching hours. And they were still about eighteen hours out from Galena.

Brigham Young turned to Heber C. Kimball, wedged in between him and Wilford Woodruff on the far side of the front-facing seat. "We should have just gone through Peoria, walked the whole way," he shouted. "That would have been heaven compared to this."

Kimball nodded grimly, holding himself up a little off the seat as he hung on to the strap so as to give his battered backside and legs some relief from the hammering they were taking. Galena was in the upper west corner of Illinois, actually even a little farther north than Chicago. The road snaked its way across the top of the state not far from its border with Wisconsin Territory. At Galena they would then turn south and go downriver to Nauvoo. All in all, coming this way was about a hundred miles farther than if they had angled straight southwest from Chicago through Peoria to Nauvoo. But distance was not the only consideration. Not only was there regular stage service between Chicago and Galena—which there was not from Peoria to Nauvoo—but Galena was only a short distance from the Mississippi River and a riverboat landing. A boat going downriver would save them a full day, maybe more.

Across from them, Orson Pratt and Lyman Wight leaned against each other, their heads bobbing and weaving like apples in a tub of water. Both had one hand through their respective straps; both were sound asleep. Brigham nudged Heber and inclined his head in their direction. "I think two of our brethren may have died sometime during the night."

Wilford Woodruff groaned. "Surely you are right, for no living man could sleep through this."

"It makes you question what the framers of the Declaration of Independence said, doesn't it?" Heber said.

"What's that?"

"That all men are created equal."

There was a low chuckle from Brigham. "I must admit that

right now I'm guilty of the sin of covetousness, and I—" He stopped as above them the driver gave a shout and the coach lurched to a shuddering stop.

Wight and Pratt came awake with a startled cry. "What is it?" Pratt asked, looking around wildly.

"Are we here?" Wight asked in bewilderment.

"Hardly," Brigham replied. He pulled the curtains back and tried to see what it was that had stopped them. There was nothing in view. "Time to get our poles, brethren," he said as he opened the door.

"You'd think the stage line would be paying us for this trip," Lyman Wight grumbled, "as many times as we've had to pry this thing out of the mud."

"Well," drawled Heber with a wry smile, "it sure beats sleeping."

As they climbed stiffly out of the coach, Brigham noted that they were not stuck in the mud or mired in water. The prairie grass looked soggy and almost marshy, but the road beneath the wheels, though it was dark and moist, was hard-packed and firm. "What's the—," he started to ask of the driver above him; then his eyes moved forward and there was no need to finish the question.

They had come to a low spot in the prairie, a long swale where the ground dipped, providing a gathering place for the rains to fill each spring. But this had not been just any spring, and the low spot had become a miniature swamp a hundred yards across and maybe a quarter of a mile in length. The road ran straight through the middle of it. The water was no more than a foot deep, and the coach, with its high wheels, should have been able to negotiate it without problem. But ten or fifteen yards ahead of where the stage had stopped the road was blocked by a wagon, mired up to its axles. Four men waded around it, trousers wet to the waist, bawling and yelling in some strange language at the three yoke of oxen hitched to the wagon. Across on the other side, several more wagons waited. A dozen more men and women shouted their encouragement to the ones in the water.

"Uh-oh," Heber said beside him. "They're really in there."

"No wonder," Lyman Wight said, pointing. "Look at how heavily that wagon is loaded."

Above them, the stage driver was swearing softly but steadily. His companion looked down at the passengers. "Norwegians," he said. "On their way to northern Iowa Territory, I'd guess."

That explained the strange language, Brigham thought, watching as the men took out their frustration on the animals. Two of them had whips and were laying it across the backs of the animals, shouting and yelling in incomprehensible syllables. Two more were at the back of the wagon, pushing and grunting. It did nothing to get the wagon moving. The oxen were bellowing, eyes rolling, crashing against one another to try and avoid the lash. When they did lunge forward against the traces the wagon didn't budge, and they fell back, panting and moaning.

"That's never going to move," Wight was saying to the two men above him on the coach's seat. "They're going to have to unload that wagon, take it out empty, then reload it."

The driver swore again, nodding. "Half a day at the least. As if we're not late enough already. Crazy Scandinavians." His voice dropped back into muttering, but now his words were no longer distinguishable.

"Can we get by it?" Wilford Woodruff asked.

The second man, sitting beside the driver, shook his head. "No. The road's barely wide enough for two wagons and they're square in the middle of it. We get off the roadbed and we'll sink so deep you'll be swimming inside the coach. And then we'll have to wait until Christmas, when it freezes up again, to get out of there."

"Is there a way to get around the swampy area?" Brigham asked, watching the Norwegian teamsters with obvious distaste for how they were treating their animals.

The driver shook his head in disgust. "Not without backtracking who knows how many miles. Look!" He waved his arm in a great circle. "Only a d—" He caught himself at Brigham's warning look. "Only a stupid fool would venture off the beaten track right now. The whole state of Illinois is one vast bog."

"So we're stuck?" Woodruff asked again.

"Until they get that wagon out of there," the driver's assistant replied, sitting back in his seat and pulling his hat down low over his eyes.

"They're not going to get that wagon to move even if they do unload it," Brigham said. "Look at them. The oxen are like frightened children." Suddenly he straightened. "I'm going to go talk to them."

Heber jerked up in surprise. "But you don't speak Nor—"

Brigham was already bent over pulling off his boots. He turned his head enough to give Heber a jaunty grin. "I know," he said, cutting off Heber's protest.

The driver climbed down now to stand beside Orson Pratt. He was half-amused, half-disgusted. Up on the coach's seat, the assistant had lifted his head enough to watch from beneath the brim of the hat.

Handing his boots to Heber for safekeeping, Brigham strode forward into the water. Swarms of gnats and mosquitoes rose in black clouds. In moments, Brigham's trouser legs were wet to his knees, and he moved with a sloshing, sucking sound through the muck and the water. The Norwegians saw him coming and stopped what they were doing. One of the oxen gave a low bellow, which sounded like a great sigh of relief. Brigham raised his hand briefly in greeting. There were cautious grunts in return. They were watching him warily, curiously, even a little resentfully, as if they had dealt too frequently with these brash Americans who felt like they could do anything and everything.

"Would you stand clear, please?" he said to the Norwegian who seemed to be their leader. Without waiting for an answer, Brigham took the whip from the man's hand and motioned for him to step back. He walked to the head of the first span of oxen. He stood there for a moment, letting the animals eye him warily. Then he began to speak to the animals, his voice low.

Heber moved forward slightly, peering at his friend.

"What's he doing?" the assistant driver said, sitting up straight now and staring ahead. "What's he saying?"

"Shhh!" Orson Pratt commanded. "Listen."

Brigham reached out and scratched beneath the wooden yoke on the neck of one of the oxen. It half closed its eyes, lowering the head in sudden contentment. And all the time, he kept talking to them. His voice carried clearly back to the others, but they could not understand a word he was saying. All six animals were watching him now. It was clear that they were calming down. The nervous stomping in the mud and water stopped, and their tails were no longer switching wildly back and forth.

"What's he saying?" the assistant driver asked again.

"He's speaking Norwegian to them," Pratt said in awe.

"No," the assistant corrected them. "That's not Norwegian. I know Norwegian when I hear it."

"Well, it sure isn't English," Lyman Wight retorted.

"Look!" Heber commanded.

Reaching out, Brigham took hold of the yoke on the first span. He said a few more words, then gave a sharp, "Hee yaw!" He pulled on the yoke, urging them forward. With the other hand he raised the whip and cracked it, but it was high above their heads. Now as though they were one, the oxen lunged forward. Lines tightened, singletrees snapped upward, coming out of the water with a muddy spray. At first there was nothing as the animals pawed and snorted, churning the water into a froth, finding little footing in the thick goo beneath their hooves. Brigham did not use the whip again. His voice rose now, crying out to them, urging them forward, still speaking words the watching men could not understand. The men in the water with Brigham stared in amazement for a moment or two; then their leader shouted and they ran around to the back of the wagon and began to push.

With a great sucking sound, the wagon started to move. There was a collective gasp, then a ragged cheer. The wheels were turning now, slowly, the rims coming up black and dripping. They moved forward, faster now. Brigham walked alongside the animals, shouting into their ears, waving his hand forward. The men pushing let go, not able to keep up now as the wagon rolled ahead more quickly. Forty feet, fifty feet. And then there was no longer a question. The wheels were flinging mud and water in a circular spray. The wagon was across the muddy slough and onto dry land again.

Without a word, Brigham waded back into the water to where the leader of the Norwegians stood, eyes agog, staring at his wagon. The Apostle handed him his whip and smiled.

"Thank you," the man said with a heavy accent. Brigham lifted one hand, then turned and started back across the swamp toward the coach. The driver walked to the edge of the water to wait for him. As Brigham reached him, he stuck out his hand. "Mister, I ain't never seen anything like that before in my life."

"Me neither," crowed the driver's assistant. "How'd you do that?"

Brigham just shrugged. "You want us in or out of the coach as you take her through?" he asked the driver.

"Probably best if we went across empty," the driver said, still looking at Brigham with undisguised awe.

"Shed your boots, brethren," Brigham said to his companions. "The water's warm." He slapped at the back of his neck. "There are enough mosquitoes to carry you across without getting your feet wet if you'll let them."

As the driver and his companion climbed back up onto the seat and gathered up the reins, Heber handed Brigham his boots, looking at him with wide eyes. "How *did* you do that?" he asked softly.

Again Brigham merely shrugged.

"When you said you were going to go talk to them, you meant the oxen?"

Brigham was trying not to smile, like a young boy who has just done a man's job but who doesn't want to talk about it lest he seem childish. "Figured talking to the animals would do more good than talking to the men."

"What were you saying?" Heber asked quietly. "It sounded like a completely different language."

On the Way Back to Nauvoo

Brigham just laughed and slapped at another mosquito buzzing around his ear. "Come on," he said. "I can't wait to get that stagecoach moving again. I'm going to follow Brother Orson's example and see if it will rock me to sleep."

On the morning of Sunday, August fourth, it was no surprise to anyone that the grove was spilling over with people fifteen minutes before worship services were supposed to start. Word of Sidney Rigdon's return had swept through Nauvoo and the surrounding communities like a hot summer wind. Word had also spread that President William Marks, president of the Nauvoo Stake and the man who presided over the worship services, had invited President Rigdon to address the Saints. That was news indeed, and everyone sensed that this was going to be a most significant meeting.

Not all of the Steeds were there. Caroline was doing well in her convalescence but still wasn't up to sitting through a two- or three-hour meeting. Surprisingly, Joshua came without her. He said it was because he didn't think Will could handle the three children alone, but everyone knew he was keenly interested in what was happening in the Church's leadership crisis.

To no one's surprise, Melissa and Carl did not come. Within a day of their return to Nauvoo five days earlier, they had specifically let the family know that they would no longer be attending worship services. Melissa later told her mother that that could change in the future, but for now they would stay at home. And so they had, in spite of the fact that Carl too was openly curious about what would happen.

The grove itself had long since been filled by the time they got there, and so they lined up their carriages and used them for shade. Many others had done the same thing. But hundreds sat beneath parasols, hats, or bonnets in the sun.

Lydia was looking around, nodding now and then to people she knew, when she suddenly rose up and waved. Nathan turned. George A. Smith was coming toward them. George A.

saw her waving and changed directions, his large bulk moving lightly around the clumps of people seated on the ground.

"Good morning," he said pleasantly, including all of the family in his greeting.

"Is Bathsheba not with you?" Rebecca asked.

"She's back with Emma and Mary Fielding and Mother Smith. They've asked the Twelve to sit up front, so she said she would stay back with the family."

"How did this morning's meeting with Brother Rigdon go?" Benjamin asked. Yesterday afternoon, in the meeting of high priests called by Willard Richards and Parley Pratt, it had been determined that what members of the Twelve there were in Nauvoo would request a meeting with President Rigdon before worship services began. They wanted a better idea of what he was going to say to the Saints.

There was an answering frown. George A.'s eyes shifted to the front of the grove where the stand was located. Several men, including Parley Pratt, Willard Richards, and Sidney Rigdon, were seated on the row of chairs on the stand. George A. was looking directly at Sidney. "He was over an hour late," he finally said.

"An hour!" Benjamin exclaimed with dismay. "But I thought you were meeting at eight-thirty."

"We were supposed to," the Apostle said tartly. "After waiting for an hour, Parley finally went looking for him. He found him engaged in meeting with a lawyer on personal business. By then it was too late for him to meet with us." Then, shrugging that aside, he straightened, pulling out his watch from his vest pocket. "Well, it's almost ten. I'd better get up there." He waved and moved away.

Emily Steed, Nathan's second child, now twelve and rapidly turning into a lovely young woman, called after him. "Are you going to speak today, Elder Smith?"

He looked back and shook his head. "Not today, Emily. I haven't been invited."

As he went on, Emily looked at her father. "I was hoping he would speak. I love it when Elder George A. speaks to us."

"So do I, dear," Lydia said.

"Yes," Nathan agreed. Then he leaned over toward his father. "So Sidney didn't show," Nathan grunted, his face clearly showing what he thought of that.

"No," Benjamin said shortly. "Convenient, eh?"

Then, before Nathan could answer, George A. reached the stand, shook hands briefly up and down the line, and sat down. Immediately President William Marks stood up. It was precisely ten a.m. This caught more than a few by surprise because often some of the leaders, including the stake president, had a tendency to wait until the last stragglers were seated and comfortable before starting the meeting. Some meetings started as much as half or three-quarters of an hour late.

The moment he stood, it was as if someone had thrown a blanket over the sound. In the almost instant quiet, the cry of a baby somewhere behind them sounded like the blast of a boat's whistle, but the parents quickly silenced the child and all was quiet. Every eye was on the stake president now and he seemed keenly aware of that. With no more than a sentence or two of greeting, he announced the hymn number, named the tune to which it would be sung, called on a brother to give the invocation, and sat down. The moment the prayer was finished, he shot to his feet again.

"Brothers and sisters," he said in a loud voice, "it is not news to most of you that yesterday President Sidney Rigdon, a counselor in the First Presidency, arrived in Nauvoo from Pittsburgh. This was a most pleasant surprise for all of us. As you know, the tragic deaths of our beloved prophet and patriarch left President Rigdon as the sole surviving member of the First Presidency." He half turned. "Welcome home, President Rigdon."

Rigdon inclined his head in recognition and smiled out at the people.

"He's the surviving member of the First Presidency only because we, the Saints, refused to follow Joseph's counsel," Nathan muttered under his breath.

Young Joshua turned and gave him a puzzled look. "What did you say, Pa?" he whispered.

Lydia poked Nathan, warning him with a silent shake of her head. But Nathan felt that this was an important lesson for his son to learn. Joshua had turned fifteen in May. He was a man now, doing a man's work at the store. He was also very perceptive when it came to spiritual things. "Don't you remember? Last October at conference Brother Joseph rejected Sidney as his counselor. He asked the Church not to sustain him. But the Saints wouldn't listen and sustained him anyway."

Joshua was shaking his head slowly. He half remembered the conference, particularly the part where charges were brought forward against President Rigdon, but he hadn't remembered that Joseph Smith specifically asked for the removal of his counselor. But Emily was nodding. "I remember," she said in a low voice. "I remember how disappointed Joseph seemed."

"Yes, he was," said Nathan. "Most of the people didn't know all that Sidney had done—or had not done," he added quickly.

"Shhh," Lydia whispered, noting that others around them were glancing with annoyance in their direction.

Suddenly Nathan, still thinking back to October, straightened, staring at President Marks. "It was President Marks who recommended that Sidney be retained," he said. "It was, I remember."

"Shhh," Lydia said again, trying to be stern, but he saw that she was looking toward the stand now with a different expression than before. After a moment, she turned back. "And now he's the one who's rushed forward with this meeting so President Rigdon can speak to us."

Benjamin, who was following all of this, said softly, "President Marks has always felt like Sidney was treated badly by Joseph."

Nathan nodded, his mouth tight. He did not like what was happening here. The Twelve were being completely bypassed.

"As you all know," President Marks was saying, "since the terrible loss of our beloved prophet and his brother we have been without a leader. We have been awaiting the return of the Twelve, but thus far there has been no word from President Young and the rest of them who are in the East. Now, providentially, President Rigdon, the last surviving member of the First Presidency, has returned to us. President Rigdon has had some remarkable experiences back in Pittsburgh which may have great bearing on our circumstances today. We shall now be pleased to have him address us."

Sidney Rigdon stood and stepped forward, tugging at his coat to make sure the front was straight. He paused, letting his eyes move slowly across the large throng of people. He seemed energized by the response he was seeing in the eyes of some of them. It was no question that many were relieved and pleased to have him back.

"You have to admit," Lydia whispered to Nathan now, forgetting her previous warning to be quiet, "he is a striking man."

"Yes," Nathan said immediately, "and a wonderful orator. One of the best in the Church."

They both turned back. Sidney was about thirty yards away from where they sat, but Nathan could see him clearly. Sidney was in his early fifties now but was holding his age well. His hairline had receded somewhat but his hair was still thick and wavy, though liberally streaked with gray. His face was thin, his dark eyes quick and perceptive, peering out from beneath equally dark brows. He had a patrician nose and a finely shaped mouth, though his lips, often pressed together as part of his sober demeanor, always seemed a bit thin to Nathan. He wore a full beard, but Greek style, with the chin and upper jawline shaved clean. The beard was thick as well and even more nearly gray than his hair.

As he began to speak, expressing the deep shock and sorrow he felt at the loss of his friend and brother Joseph Smith and dear Hyrum, his voice was rich and carried easily across the crowd. Before becoming a member of the Church, Sidney Rigdon had been a highly successful Campbellite preacher in Ohio, and he was, Nathan had to admit, one of the finest preachers in the Church. On many occasions Nathan had sat mesmerized before him. He spoke with power and held his audience well. But now there was a very different feeling.

For about ten minutes, Sidney rehearsed his association with Joseph Smith—his traveling to New York to meet the Prophet, his call to preach, his privilege to be present when many of the revelations had been given, the grandest of which was the vision of the degrees of glory. As he spoke, Nathan found himself caught up in the memories again. Sidney had been part of so much of those early days. Joseph had depended upon him heavily.

"As many of you remember," Sidney was saying, "in eighteen thirty-three I accompanied Brother Joseph on a mission to Upper Canada. That was in October. It was while we were on that mission that Joseph received a revelation from the Lord directing me to act as a 'spokesman' for Joseph and to the Church. That was the Lord's exact word, a 'spokesman.'" He paused for a moment to let that sink in. "That revelation is found in the Doctrine and Covenants today, and many of you have read it for yourselves."

Many heads were nodding, and there were a few murmured yeses and amens uttered audibly. Nathan shot Benjamin a quick look. This was not just Sidney reminiscing about the past any longer. There was a purpose in this recollection, and he did not like the feel of it. He bent over slightly and spoke directly into Lydia's ear. "There was also another revelation, given just three years ago, where the Lord told Sidney that he was to remain with the people if he was to have the Lord's blessings. Does going to Pittsburgh and abandoning Joseph at the most critical time of his life count as being obedient to that commandment? But I suppose that won't be mentioned."

Lydia was staring at him. "The Lord really told him that?" she asked.

Nathan nodded.

"Brethren and sisters," Sidney cried, his voice rising sharply, "we have lost Brother Joseph. The natural successor to our beloved prophet should have been Hyrum Smith, but we have lost him as well. What shall we do? Who shall lead the Church now?"

Again he paused, but there was not a sound now. Every head was turned toward him; every eye, except those of the smallest children, was fastened on his face.

"Brethren and sisters, I should like to take my text from the book of Isaiah. In the fifty-fifth chapter, verses eight and nine, the Lord declares, 'For my thoughts are not your thoughts, neither are your ways my ways, saith the Lord.' Think about that, brothers and sisters. The Lord does not do things in the way that we might do them. His ways are different than our ways. So it is today, as we try to decide what now must happen in the Church."

Again there was a long pause and he visibly straightened. The effect was to deepen the anticipation and the silence even more, if that was possible. Then he leaned forward. "And the Lord has made it clear what his way shall be at this time. And he has done so to me through a vision I had in Pittsburgh."

It was as if an audible shock hit the crowd, though later Nathan wasn't sure if he heard sounds or just felt the impact of Sidney's words on the congregation.

"Yes," he went on firmly. "When I learned of the death of Joseph, I inquired of the Lord, and the Lord opened up in vision what must happen now." He raised one hand high, as though pointing to the heavens. "It was a continuation of the same vision Joseph and I had while in Ohio concerning the different glories, or mansions, which are in our Father's house. I saw Brother Joseph there," he said, his voice thundering now; "he had ascended to heaven and he stood on the right hand of the Son of God."

Somewhere a woman cried out with audible joy, "Oh, yes!"

Sidney turned toward her and smiled. "It was wonderful. I saw Joseph there in the celestial kingdom, clothed with all the power, glory, might, majesty, and dominion of that kingdom. And I tell you now, that Joseph still continues to hold the keys of the kingdom, even though he has left us. He will continue to hold them throughout all eternity, and no man can take those keys from him. No man can ever take his place, neither build up the kingdom to any other creature or being but to Joseph Smith!"

"Hear! Hear!" a man cried. "Amen!" said several. Nathan had a sudden thought and turned to scan the crowd, looking for John C. Bennett. But if he was there, Nathan could not pick him out. As he thought about it, if Sidney had the slightest modicum of good sense, he would ask Bennett to stay back. Though there were many questions about Sidney's loyalties in the minds of the Saints, there was no question about Bennett's. Having Bennett on his side would only hinder Sidney's cause.

"Then how shall the Church be led?" Sidney shouted. "If Joseph holds all the keys and no man can take his place, how, then, shall we go? Again I remind you what the Lord has said: 'My thoughts are not your thoughts, neither are your ways my ways.' Here is the Lord's answer. Here is what I was told in that vision."

Nathan felt Emily brush against his shoulder and turned. She was looking at him with a troubled expression. "Do you think he really had a vision, Papa?"

Nathan reached out and took her hand. "I don't know, Emily. Let's listen; then we'll talk about it afterwards."

She nodded and they both turned back toward the stand.

"No one can take the place of Joseph," Sidney repeated, "so there must be a guardian appointed, a guardian who will build up the Church to Joseph. The Lord revealed to me that I am to be that man. Long ago I was appointed the 'spokesman' for the Church and to Joseph. I didn't fully understand what that meant. Now I do. I am the guardian, and I have come back to accept that role and position, even though it may put my life in danger.

"I am the identical man that the ancient prophets have written about, sung about, and rejoiced over. I am called to do the identical work that has been the theme of all the prophets of every generation. We are to prepare the world for the coming of Armageddon." Now one fist punched the air. "The time is fast approaching and we must be ready. The earth is about to be cleansed and we must be prepared."

Suddenly, into Nathan's mind flashed a scene from six years

earlier. It was in the public square at Far West. It was the Independence Day celebration, 1838. A newly erected flag pole—the "liberty pole"—stood in the center of the square, proudly flying the Stars and Stripes. Sidney Rigdon was chosen orator for the day and gave, in the same thundering pronouncements, a fiery speech. He exhorted the Saints to defend their liberties even to the death, sweeping off the enemies of God before them if necessary.

The talk was published and quickly swept across Missouri. It was a critical factor in galvanizing the opposition and gave the Missourians the fodder they needed to whip the people into a panic. A month following that speech, the Mormons were attacked as they tried to vote in Gallatin. Two months after that, the Mormon War was sweeping across western Missouri.

Nathan felt a little chill, now remembering something else. Ironically, two days following Sidney's call to arms, the liberty pole had been struck by lightning, leaving nothing but splinters. It had proven to be an omen of what was to come.

"I tell you now, brothers and sisters," Sidney was roaring, "the time is near at hand when you will see one hundred tons of metal per second thrown at the enemies of God. You will see blood flow as deep as the horses' bridles. I am going to fight a real and bloody battle with sword and with gun. I will fight the battles of the Lord. I will cross the Atlantic, encounter the forces of Queen Victoria, and overcome them. I will plant the America standard on English ground, and then march to the palace of her majesty and demand a portion of her riches and dominions."

Just to the left and behind them, Derek and Peter Ingalls sat together, Derek with Rebecca and their children, Peter sitting beside Kathryn McIntire's wheelchair. Nathan could not help stealing a glance at them. Derek and Peter were English. So were hundreds of others in the congregation. And in that quick glance he had his answer. This was not what they expected to hear. He could see the obvious discomfort on their faces and on the faces of many others, and not just the British Saints.

"If the queen refuses to give heed to our demands," Sidney was shouting, "I will take the little madam by the nose and lead her out, and she shall have no power to help herself. If I do not do this, the Lord never spake by mortal man."

He leaned back, his shoulders slumping. "That is all I have to say at the moment, my brothers and sisters. The times which are coming are such that we must not be without a leader. No one but Joseph has been called to lead us. But I have been called by the voice of the Lord to act as guardian until Joseph himself descends as a mighty angel and takes the reins of the kingdom himself. Thank you."

He turned and sat down, leaving the congregation to stare at him, a few in open admiration, but most in stunned and bewildered amazement.

Chapter Notes

Brigham Young, Orson Hyde, and Wilford Woodruff were in Boston on the day of the Martyrdom. A conference of the Church was scheduled there for 29 June, and seven members of the Twelve attended that conference (see HC 7:149). Though they split up again following that meeting, after word reached them of the Martyrdom on 9 July, Brigham Young, along with Heber C. Kimball, Wilford Woodruff, Lyman Wight, and Orson Pratt were eventually able to link up together and head for Nauvoo. They traveled by railway, boat, stagecoach, and buggy, reaching Nauvoo on 6 August. The story of Brigham's remarkable experience with the oxen is found in the official history of the Church (see HC 7:224). There were two other people in the stagecoach besides the five Apostles, but for purposes of the novel they are not included here.

The meeting held on 4 August is briefly described in the official history of the Church (see HC 7:224–25). Fuller accounts of Sidney's "vision" and of his claims to the guardianship, as well as his fiery call for battle, are given in other sources, including an 1845 speech by Orson Hyde to a group of high priests in Nauvoo (see *Speech of Orson Hyde, Delivered Before the High Priests*

Quorum, in Nauvoo, April 27th, 1845, Upon the Course and Conduct of Mr. Sidney Rigdon, and Upon the Merits of His Claims to the Presidency of the Church of Jesus Christ of Latter-day Saints [Liverpool: James and Woodburn, 1845], pp. 11–16). Though Elder Hyde specifically places some of Sidney's remarks (e.g., the mention of battles and going to Queen Victoria) in the context of a 1 September 1844 talk that Sidney gave just before returning to Pennsylvania, other sources mention material of this same nature in both the 4 August and the 1 September speeches.

The scripture cited by Sidney in which he is named as "spokesman" is now D&C 100:9, 11. The revelation cited by Nathan in which Sidney is told to stay with the people is now D&C 124:104–5.

I just should have gone," Caroline said forlornly. "I was feeling quite well this morning. I wish I had been with you."

Joshua, who was standing behind her chair, bent down and kissed her on the cheek. "It was beastly hot by the afternoon meeting. It would have been too much for you. Besides, even though you've got that splint off your ankle now, it's better if you're not on it too much yet."

Normally they would have been at Father and Mother Steed's house, their usual tradition for a Sabbath evening, but in the past four days Carl and Melissa had worked hard to get their house opened up again and ready to live in. With Jane Manning's help, they had finished the previous evening and Melissa had insisted they use their Sunday evening get-together as a formal house-warming party, even though both she and Carl suspected the main topic of conversation would be the meeting held earlier in the day. Also contrary to the norm, it was adults only tonight. The older children were scattered among the houses tending their brothers and sisters, or their cousins in the case of those with younger children only.

Caroline turned her head, looking up at Joshua. "You really think Brother Rigdon swayed the people?" she asked.

There was no hesitation. "Absolutely. He's a master with a crowd. I thought they were going to applaud him when he finally sat down this morning. Probably would have if it hadn't been a church service."

Four or five of them stirred at once in response to that, but it was Kathryn McIntire who jumped in first. "I don't think so," she said. "At first, when he was talking about his vision, I could tell some people were really impressed. But then he started in on all that blood and gore stuff."

"Yes," Jenny said, even before her sister had finished. "And all that about England. That was awful."

Derek hooted at that. "Now, that tells you something, Caroline," he said. "When even the Irish are offended by what he said about the British monarch, you can be sure it wasn't well received."

"Come on," Joshua said, surprised at this reaction. "Sure, it was a little fiery, but that's Sidney's style. And some people like what he said. They think the English have been due for a come-uppance for some time now."

"Well, I don't think he made much of an impression on the English who were present," Lydia suggested. "Which, by the way, is no small number."

"You wouldn't understand, Joshua," Matthew said. "When Derek and I were in England, I was really surprised to find out how strongly the people feel about their royalty. And Queen Victoria is one of the most popular of the royals, as they call them, in several generations. Even the poorest of the common people love her. If Brother Rigdon had made those kind of statements in London—calling her a 'little madam,' promising to lead her around by the nose—he wouldn't have had the chance to finish his speech, I can tell you that."

"You jolly well better believe it," Derek said. "Though Peter and I now consider ourselves dyed-in-the-wool Americans, I felt my blood boiling a little this morning."

Joshua moved around and sat down on the floor beside Caroline. He was smiling tolerantly. "I'm not saying that I agreed with what he said. I'm just saying that I think he swayed a lot of people there today."

"But tell me about the afternoon meeting," Caroline said. "Nathan said there was quite a disagreement between President Marks and the Twelve."

Joshua looked at his brother. "You explain what happened, Nathan. You know all the people better than I do."

Nathan nodded. "Well, Sidney's claims during the morning service stirred up considerable controversy, as Joshua has already indicated. But in the afternoon service, he was not scheduled to speak again. Charles C. Rich, a member of the Nauvoo Stake high council, was speaking to us. All of a sudden, President Marks stood up and stepped forward."

"While Brother Rich was speaking?" Caroline asked in surprise.

"Yes, right in the middle of his talk."

"Just before that happened," Rebecca volunteered, "I saw Brother Rigdon lean over and say something to President Marks. That's when he got up."

"What did he say?"

Nathan was shaking his head, his mouth tightening with a touch of anger. "President Marks said that he had an announcement for the congregation. So right there, in the middle of Brother Rich's talk, he announced that on Thursday there will be a public meeting held for the purpose of choosing a guardian for the Church."

"No!" Caroline cried.

"Yes," Joshua answered. "And those were his words. 'For the purpose of choosing a guardian.' Since Sidney had already pronounced that he had been called to be the guardian, there was no question but what Marks was saying the meeting would be held to sustain Sidney Rigdon."

"Exactly," Nathan agreed, "and everyone knew it."

"Can he do that? Did he even ask the Twelve?"

"Yes and no." Nathan's frown deepened. "The announcement triggered a lively debate. A Brother Grover, whom I don't know, proposed that the meeting be delayed until there had been more time to examine Rigdon's revelation. He spoke for a lot of people. There was a lot of agitation by then."

Benjamin picked it up now. "President Marks tried to calm things by telling us that Brother Rigdon had suggested the meeting be held on Tuesday, just day after tomorrow, but Marks had determined it would be on Thursday instead."

"I talked with William Clayton afterwards," Nathan added, "and—"

"Who is he?" Melissa asked.

"Brother Clayton is one of the clerks for the Church," Nathan answered. "Anyway, he told me he was dissatisfied with the hurried manner in which this was being done. He is suggesting they wait until the remainder of the Twelve return."

Caroline was shaking her head. "And all of this was right in the worship service."

"Yes," Nathan replied. "First President Marks got up. Then Sidney stood too."

"I think by then," Mary Ann said dryly, "there wasn't much of a spirit of either worship or service."

That brought a laugh from all of them, and several murmurs of agreement.

"So," Carl prompted Nathan, following along closely with the report. "Sidney Rigdon got up. Then what?"

"Sidney told us he was some distance from his family and was anxious to return to them. He asked if the people had anything for him to do; otherwise he would be on his way back to Pittsburgh, as there were thousands and tens of thousands there who would receive him."

"In Pittsburgh?" Carl asked dubiously. "Do you have a lot of members in Pittsburgh?"

Nathan laughed. "A hundred maybe. Perhaps less."

"Then . . . ?"

Nathan shrugged. "I'm just telling you what he said. Anyway, in spite of the protests, President Marks said the meeting for Thursday would stand. We will meet to appoint a guardian for the Church."

"President Marks has always been a strong supporter of Sidney Rigdon," Benjamin said. "And he's not particularly fond of Brigham Young. There's no question as to who he wants to see take over here."

"So," Carl concluded, "back to Caroline's question. Is Sidney Rigdon going to carry the day?"

"No!" Nathan said flatly, even as Joshua was nodding.

"Who, then?" Melissa asked. "Willard Richards?"

"Willard's a fine man," Nathan said, "but I don't think the people think of him as the one to lead the Church."

That brought Lydia's head around. She gave him a quizzical look. He went on. "I don't think Parley can do it, not George A. either, as much as we personally care for these brethren."

"Are you agreeing with Joshua, then?" Caroline asked him. She looked as surprised as Lydia by his stance.

"Yes, I am, I guess."

"See there?" Joshua crowed. "If Nathan and I agree on something, it has to be right."

"You think Sidney ought to lead the Church?" Jenny said incredulously.

"No!" Nathan said sharply. "Absolutely not. But that wasn't what Joshua was—"

"That's right," Joshua broke in. "I wasn't suggesting that he *should* lead the Church. I was only saying that after today, I think he *will* lead the Church."

Nathan laughed. "I knew it was too good to be true. No, if that's what you meant, I don't agree with you."

They all laughed at that. To an outside observer, Joshua and Nathan seemed always to be disagreeing with each other on various matters. To the family, this was evidence of the depths of their relationship. Though poles apart in their thinking and beliefs, they spoke freely with one another without fear of offense or misunderstanding.

"No, all I was saying was that I agree with Joshua's assessment of the impact that Sidney had on the people today. I think he did influence some minds. Obviously, President Marks has his made up."

Now Benjamin jumped in and likewise caught them by surprise. "If you took a vote tonight, I think it would be Sidney Rigdon as guardian of the Church."

"I agree!" Joshua said triumphantly.

"But, Grandpa," Will exploded, "don't you think that would be wrong?"

"I certainly do. At least, I think it's wrong to do it this way. It's like Sidney wants to get it done before people have a chance to really think about it."

Nathan was nodding emphatically. "And before the Twelve get here to talk to people and change their minds."

"The people are hungry for an end to this," Benjamin said. "It's been almost six weeks now. There are still a dozen rumors that our enemies are trying to marshal arms against us. The upcoming elections have everyone stirred up. If the anti-Mormon candidates win, it could mean disaster for us. You can feel the fear and tension in the air. It is not the time to be without a head. The people want someone to lead them. Someone strong, decisive, proven. Sidney, at least on the surface, fits that description."

"But you don't think he's the one?" Carl asked.

"No, I don't."

"He's opposed to plural marriage," Melissa said suddenly. "I heard that he and Joseph disagreed strongly over that question."

That brought a long silence to the room. No one looked at Melissa, who was watching her father, her eyes almost pleading.

"That's true, Melissa," Benjamin finally said. "Sidney would probably set aside the teaching of plural marriage."

She said nothing. She didn't have to. It hung in the air like some invisible presence, the words that she had not spoken: "Then I would vote for Sidney Rigdon."

Finally, feeling pressured by the silence, Melissa spoke again. "Sidney has done a lot of wonderful things for the Church. Joseph himself said some wonderful things about him."

"He also refused to support Joseph in a time of crisis," Nathan said, keeping his voice gentle. "He was sympathetic to John C. Bennett during that whole mess. Don't you remember? That's why Joseph wanted to release Sidney from the Presidency. John C. Bennett wrote to Sidney after he left Nauvoo. He was trying to find a way to get Joseph back into Missouri so his enemies there could get their hands on him. Sidney said nothing to Joseph about the letter. Orson Pratt finally told Joseph."

Matthew had sat quietly through it all, listening, nodding occasionally, but mostly thinking about what was said. "The Savior said that the way you tell a true prophet from a false one is by their fruits. If you'll remember, when we came out of Missouri and started gathering at Quincy, Sidney told us that we shouldn't do that. He said that we had to scatter to be safe. We had to stay apart so as not to offend the non-Mormons." Now he looked at Melissa. "If we had followed him back then, there would be no Nauvoo right now."

"I—" Melissa stopped. She did remember Sidney's posture back then, and thought of Nauvoo and all that it now held. It was a telling point.

"And he left Joseph when the situation started getting dangerous," Nathan jumped in. "I'm sorry, but I can't just forget that."

"I heard that Joseph asked him to leave," Carl said, "so he wouldn't be killed. Just like he tried to get Hyrum to leave so he would be safe."

"Yeah," Nathan shot back, more hotly than he intended, "that's Sidney's story. But even if that's true, isn't it interesting? Sidney went to Pittsburgh. Hyrum went to Carthage."

Suddenly Mary Ann spoke up. She spoke to Carl. "Does it look like Jane Manning is going to work out?"

For a moment there was bewildered silence. It was totally unrelated to anything they had been talking about. Then several began to grin. Benjamin was chuckling softly. This was Grandma's role in these family gatherings. She usually said little in the discussions, but she listened—not just to the words, but to the feelings as well. And if things started down the wrong path, she was the monitor that pulled them back.

"She is going to work out wonderfully well," Melissa said, smiling and understanding what was going on as clearly as Benjamin did. "I invited her to be here tonight, but Sunday is her day off and she wanted to be with her family."

"The children adore her," Carl said. "Thank you for suggesting her, Mother Steed. She's going to work out just fine."

Mary Ann nodded in satisfaction. "Now, I'd like to say one more thing."

Every eye was on her. Nathan dropped his head a little, expecting a rebuke. He was the one who had let his emotions get away with him a little.

Instead, she smiled sweetly and asked, "How about some bread and milk?"

They all laughed at that, relieved that she had done her work again. Melissa looked to her gratefully. "I would like that," she said softly.

As they began to rise, Will had to make one last shot. "So," he said, "come Thursday, will the Saints vote for Sidney Rigdon to be their guardian or not?"

It was a sobering question, and they fell silent as they considered it. Finally it was Nathan who spoke. "There's one last thing to consider. Think about what Sidney said today. What he claimed the Lord told him. What did he say he was told to do about the Church?"

"To be the guardian?" Derek ventured.

"No, that's what Sidney is to *be*. But what did he say he was to *do* as guardian?"

"He is to build the Church up to Joseph," Matthew answered.

"Yes. Exactly. He said it twice. That he was called to build up the Church to Joseph."

"Yes. So?" Joshua queried. "I thought that was a wise move on his part. It says to the Saints that he's not in this for himself."

Nathan looked around at his family, first to Lydia, then to his mother, and finally stopped at his father. "Suppose Joseph were here and you asked him what his successor was supposed to do. What do you think Joseph would say? Would he say that the man who was called to replace him was supposed to build up the Church to Joseph Smith?"

There were instant expressions of discovery and understanding. "No," said Jenny slowly. "That's not what he would say."

"What would he say?" Nathan asked softly.

"He would say that whoever follows is to build up the Church to Jesus Christ, not Joseph Smith."

"Exactly," Nathan said. "Exactly the point."

As they left the room and went into the kitchen, Nathan lingered until Carl and Melissa came up beside him. With a warm smile, he put his arm around his sister and pulled her against his shoulder. She looked up in surprise.

"We may disagree about Sidney Rigdon, little sister," he murmured, "but I want you to know how happy we all are to have you back in Nauvoo."

She seemed startled, and then there was an instant sheen of tears in her eyes. "Thank you, Nathan," she whispered, as she leaned against him.

He reached down and kissed her cheek. "We missed you," he said, his voice husky. He released her and looked at Carl. "Welcome home."

Matthew and Jenny Steed and Kathryn McIntire were gathered around a kerosene lamp reading passages from the Book of Mormon, specifically the account of the Savior's visit to the peoples living in America. Betsy Jo was asleep in her crib down the hall and they read in soft voices, even though it took a great deal to wake Betsy Jo up once she fell asleep. The windows were open, and a soft breeze off the river was stirring the curtains in gentle motions. The house had been unbearably hot during the afternoon, but with the breeze, it had become quite pleasant now. Through the open windows they could hear the sound of the crickets or an occasional barking dog. Now and then the soft murmur of voices would pass—someone out for an evening's stroll—or they would hear the clop-clop of a horse's hooves as a rider went by, moving up or down Granger Street.

In her wheelchair, Kathryn was reading, her hair falling softly around her cheeks, her head bent slightly to better catch the light falling on the book. "'And when he had said these words, he wept, and the multitude bear record of it, and he took their little children, one by one, and blessed them, and prayed unto the Father for them. And when he had done this he wept again.'"

Kathryn stopped and looked at Jenny and Matthew. "I just can't imagine what that must have been like," she said quietly. "Can you imagine the Savior taking Betsy Jo and Savannah and Sarah and little Joseph—" She had to stop as the image of each of the children filled her mind. "And taking them in his arms and blessing them," she finished, her voice breaking a little.

Jenny reached up and brushed at the corner of her eye with the back of her hand. "This is my favorite passage in all the Book of Mormon. When I try to think what it must have been like for the parents to watch that happen with their children, I always start to cry."

Kathryn nodded and lifted the book again. "'And he spake unto the multitude, and saith unto them, behold your little ones. And as they looked to behold, they cast their eyes towards heaven, and they saw the heavens open, and they saw angels descending out of heaven as it were, in the midst of fire; and they came down and encircled those little ones about, and they were encircled about with fire; and the angels did minister unto them.'"

She stopped and silence filled the room. Each was trying to picture that glorious event so many centuries before.

"What must it have been like to be there?" Matthew finally said in a low whisper.

"Incredibly wonderful," Jenny said.

Kathryn could only nod.

And then, through the window, they heard the sound of a carriage going by. "Whoa!" someone called, and the carriage came to a halt in the street in front of their house. There was a murmur of voices, the sound of the carriage door opening and shutting again, the creak of springs. Then one voice spoke just loudly enough to be heard above the others.

"You go on, brethren. I can make my way home from here."

Matthew stiffened as though he had been jabbed with a sharpened stick. He was staring at the window, dumbfounded.

From outside, the first voice spoke to the horse, and over the sound of the carriage starting to move again there were calls of farewell. Then clearly now, more loudly, the first voice spoke again. "We'll meet in the morning in council. At Brother Taylor's house."

Matthew was on his feet, gaping at the window and the dark beyond it. "That's Brigham!" he cried in a hoarse whisper. He swung around to Jenny and Kathryn. "That's Brigham's voice," he said.

"But—," Jenny started.

Matthew didn't hear her. He was across the room, pulling open the door. Even as he did so there was the sound of heavy steps on the porch. "Brigham!" Matthew cried. "It *is* you!"

There was the chief Apostle standing at the door, a knapsack over his shoulder, looking very tired and rumpled, but grinning as though he were a miner who had just struck a vein of pure silver. "Hello, Matthew."

Matthew flung the door open and threw his arms around the older man. They grabbed one another and pounded each other on the back. "I can't believe it," Matthew said over and over. "You're home."

Jenny was on her feet now, and Kathryn wheeled her chair around to face the door.

Brigham saw them over Matthew's shoulder and pulled free. "And here are two of my favorite people," he exclaimed. In three great steps he was across the room and swept Jenny up into his arms, swinging her around and around. Then he dropped to one knee, taking Kathryn's hands in his. "Dear, sweet Kathryn. How are you?"

"I'm wonderful," she said, still a little dazed. "But how—"

"We just arrived at the north landing. Came down the river from Galena."

"Oh, Brigham!" Jenny said. "You don't know how glad we are to have you back."

"And the others of the Twelve?" Matthew said, realizing with Jenny's words just what this meant for Nauvoo.

"There are five of us—Wilford, Heber, Orson Pratt, Lyman Wight, and myself. We came as quickly as we could."

"Won't you sit down?" Jenny said, motioning toward a chair.

"No, no! I saw your light and just wanted to stop and say hello to my partner. I haven't been home yet. We just arrived, not twenty minutes ago."

"And just in the nick of time," Matthew said. "Sidney Rigdon's here, saying that he should lead the Church. There's much confusion."

A quick frown momentarily crossed the Apostle's face. "We heard. That's why the Twelve will gather tomorrow. I understand there's to be a big meeting on Thursday."

Kathryn answered him. "Yes. Sidney wanted it for today, but there were protests and so President Marks said it would be—" Suddenly her eyes grew wide. "If it had been today, you wouldn't have been here."

He nodded, as though he had already considered that. "Well, we are here. Everything's going to be fine." He turned back around to Matthew. "I also hear that my partner is running the finest woodworking and cabinet shop in all of Hancock County."

Matthew flushed a little under Brigham's open look of admiration. "Well, business has been good and—"

Reaching out with both hands, Brigham grasped Matthew's shoulders and shook him gently. "How can I ever thank you, dear friend? I'm afraid affairs in the kingdom haven't left me much time to be a good business partner."

"It's fine. Things are going well."

"Thank you," Brigham said again, his voice husky now. "Thank you, Brother Matthew." Then he stepped back. "Well, as you can imagine, I am most anxious to see Mary Ann and the children again. I shall be off. But I just had to stop and say hello to three of my dearest friends. It is so good to see you all again."

And then he was gone as quickly as he had come, leaving the three of them to stare at each other in wonder.

"Brigham's back," Matthew finally said, grinning happily. He swung around. "I've got to go tell Nathan and Pa. They won't believe it."

———————

Under date of August sixth, 1844, Elder Wilford Woodruff recorded the following in his journal: "We arrived in the city of Nauvoo at 8 o'clock in the evening at the upper stone house. We were hailed with joy by all the citizens we met. I accompanied the Quorum of the Twelve to their families, after which I was conveyed to my own and truly felt to rejoice to once more embrace my wife and children. I spent the night at home with my family. Thus it is with me. I have not spent but one summer either at home or with the Church for the last 10 years, as my lot has been all the day long in the vineyard. I go and come from year to year. . . . When we landed in the city, there was a deep gloom seemed to rest over the city of Nauvoo which we never experienced before."

By morning, news that five more members of the Twelve had returned, including Brigham Young, President of the Quorum, did much to dispel that gloom. The Twelve were back. This is what the people had been told to wait for. Now a decision could be made. This was more than simple good fortune. Many saw the clear hand of Providence in the return of the Twelve at this particular juncture.

The next morning, Wednesday, August seventh, eight men came to the home of John Taylor. For the first time in months, a majority of the Twelve were together to meet in council. Brigham Young, Heber C. Kimball, Parley P. Pratt, Orson Pratt, Willard Richards, Wilford Woodruff, George A. Smith, and Lyman Wight—all assembled together at the home of the wounded Apostle. William Smith, John Page, and Orson Hyde had not yet returned. But there were nine Apostles present. Three-fourths of the Quorum. A clear majority. It was enough. It was a time of sorrowing for the loss of their beloved Joseph and Hyrum. It was a time of rejoicing that they were together again. It was a time for action. With the meeting called by President Marks scheduled for the next day, they could not delay.

"Brother Brigham is going to let President Marks go ahead with the meeting tomorrow," Benjamin said, reaching out to take his wife's hands.

"He is? Is that wise? They have barely had time to assess the situation."

"I know, but Brigham told me Sidney is now claiming that it's only meant to be a prayer meeting. And think what it will mean if they try to cancel it. First of all, it is President Marks who called the meeting. I think if Brigham asks him to cancel it, he will refuse. Second, if they do cancel, it will look as though the Twelve are afraid of Sidney's power."

"So what will they do?"

"The Twelve have called for a meeting of the stake high council and the high priests quorum. It will be held at four o'clock this afternoon at the Seventies Hall."

"But I didn't think the hall was finished yet."

"No, but it is close enough. There won't be benches, but it is still a good place to meet."

"So you and Nathan will be going."

"Yes, and a lot more. Brigham has sent out runners to spread the word across the city."

The moment President Marks, president of the Nauvoo Stake, finished his prayer and sat down, Brigham Young stood and came to the pulpit. The hall was jammed to capacity. Every temporary bench was filled, and men stood three and four deep around the perimeter of the hall. Great solemnity was the prevailing mood. There had been little talking as they assembled and waited for the appointed hour. Benjamin and Nathan Steed sat near the center. Nathan looked at his father and smiled as Brigham stood. The crisis was not yet over, but the Twelve were here. It would be all right now.

"Brethren," Brigham began, "as you know, President Sidney Rigdon has recently returned to Nauvoo. Many of you have already heard him speak about a vision and revelation he has received which has to do with the leadership of the Church. Unfortunately, only a few of the Twelve were here to hear that statement. Therefore, I should like to call on President Rigdon now to speak to us and to put forth his claims."

There was a stir and many men looked at each other in surprise. They hadn't expected Brigham to turn the podium over to Brother Rigdon. Sidney nodded and stood, waiting for Brigham to be seated again before he moved to the pulpit.

He stood there for a moment, calm and dignified, though it surely must have created some anxiety within him. "Brethren, the object of my mission was to visit the Saints and offer myself to them as a guardian. As I said on Sunday, I had a vision at Pittsburgh, on June twenty-seventh. I did not know at that time that it was the very day that our beloved Joseph was slain. This vision was presented to my mind not as an open vision, but rather a continuation of the vision mentioned in the book of Doctrine and Covenants, the one having to do with the three degrees of glory."

Benjamin turned and looked at Nathan. That was not quite how he had expressed it at the Sunday meeting. He had not said anything about it not being an open vision. Nathan nodded, understanding exactly what his father was thinking, and they both turned back to the front.

"In that vision, it was shown to me that this church must be built up to Joseph, and that all the blessings we receive must come through him. I have been previously ordained as spokesman to Joseph. In the vision I was told that I must come to Nauvoo and see that the Church is governed in a proper manner. Joseph sustains the same relationship to this church as he has always done. No man can be the successor of Joseph.

"The kingdom is to be built up to Jesus Christ through Joseph. There must be revelation still. The martyred prophet is still the head of this church. Every quorum should stand as you stood in your washings and consecrations. I have been consecrated a spokesman to Joseph, and I was commanded to speak for him. The Church is not disorganized, though our head is gone."

He stopped, letting the men have a moment to consider his words. As Nathan looked around, he saw one or two heads nodding, but for the most part the expression on the faces of the brethren was unreadable. They were listening, and listening with attentiveness. But they were not committing themselves—at least not visibly—one way or the other.

"We may have a diversity of feelings on this matter. I have been called to be a spokesman unto Joseph, and I want to build up the Church unto him. And if the people want to sustain me in this position, I want it upon the principle that every individual shall acknowledge it for himself. I propose to be a guardian to the people. In this I have discharged my duty and done what God has commanded me, and the people can please themselves whether they accept me or not."

His head came up slightly as he looked around. Then he nodded briefly and said, "Thank you," and sat down again.

Brigham rose slowly, his face grave. He looked tired, and it struck Nathan that it had not been even twenty-four hours since their return. There had been no time to rest after weeks of difficult travel. And it showed on his face. He came to the pulpit, laid his hands upon it, and leaned forward.

"My beloved brethren, I would like to make my position very clear. I do not care who leads the Church, even though it were Ann Lee."

He paused to enjoy the quick look of surprise and then the immediate grins that followed. Ann Lee had been the leader of the United Society of Believers—or "Shakers," as they were commonly called—in the late 1700s. The Shakers believed in communal property, condemned marriage as a lower order of life, and refused to eat pork (some abstaining from all meats). They taught that the second coming of Christ had already taken place but that he had returned in the form of a woman, namely Ann Lee. Back in Kirtland, the Shakers had been influential, and some members of the Church found their teachings attractive. A revelation in the Doctrine and Covenants had been given by the Lord to refute their teachings. Brigham couldn't have chosen a more unlikely name to put forth as to the kind of person who should lead the Church.

"That's right," Brigham affirmed, "even though it were Ann Lee." Now he raised his right hand, stabbing at the air to emphasize his words. "There is only one thing I must know, and that is what God says about it. If God were to bring Ann Lee back and say she is to lead the Church, I would accept that. But there is something else you must consider. As President of the Quorum, I have the keys and the means of obtaining the mind of God on the subject.

"I know there are those in our midst who will seek the lives of the Twelve as they did the lives of Joseph and Hyrum. I know that we still have enemies around us. But we in the Twelve shall ordain others and give them the fulness of the priesthood so that if we are killed the fulness of the priesthood may remain. Brethren, I tell you now that Joseph conferred upon our heads all the keys and powers belonging to the apostleship which he himself held before he was taken away. And no man or set of men can get between Joseph and the Twelve in this world or in the world to come. How often has Joseph said to the Twelve, 'I have laid the foundation and you must build thereon, for upon your shoulders the kingdom rests'?"

Nathan felt a little thrill. Now heads all around him were nodding up and down. This is what they needed—a firm, bold declaration of where the keys and power were. Here was a clear reminder of what Joseph had planned in case of his death.

"Brethren, you need to know that the Twelve, as a quorum, will not be permitted to tarry here long. They will go abroad and bear off the kingdom to the nations of the earth." Now his voice rose sharply. "And we will baptize the people faster than mobs can kill them off. I would like, were it my privilege, to take my valise and travel and preach till we had a people gathered who would be true. My private feelings would be to let the affairs of men and women alone, only go and preach and baptize them into the kingdom of God. But my private feelings do not matter. Whatever duty God places upon me, in his strength I intend to fulfill it."

He turned and glanced at Sidney Rigdon, then at the Twelve who were behind him. When he turned back, his face was suddenly at peace. "As you know, President Marks has called for a prayer meeting to be held tomorrow. President Rigdon has privately told some of the Twelve that it is not his intent to have the Church vote tomorrow on whether or not to choose a guardian. He tells us it is to be only a prayer meeting and interchange of thought and feeling, and will provide a chance for us to warm each other's hearts."

It was said with a level voice, and there was not the slightest touch of either sarcasm or irony in how he said it. But there were few who didn't see it as the highly ironical statement that it was. No more than a prayer meeting? Hardly.

Brigham went on in a softer voice now. "The prayer meeting will be held, but I want to see this people, with the various quorums of the priesthood, assembled together in special conference next Tuesday at 10 a.m."

Several heads came up at that, including Nathan's. Seated by quorums? That meant a solemn assembly. That meant far more than a prayer meeting or even a normal worship service. Was Brigham going to call for resolution to the question then? Did he want to—

"Brethren, that is my recommendation. All in favor show by the raise of the right hand."

Every hand in the hall came up, some with a swift jerk, others slowly, still showing how surprised they were by Brigham's decisiveness.

Brigham gave a curt nod. "Thank you. We shall now be dismissed until tomorrow morning."

And he sat down. After a moment, amid the buzz that erupted in the hall, President Marks stood up and, looking a little dazed himself, called on one of the brethren to give the benediction.

Chapter Notes

The return of five members of the Twelve just two days before the meeting called by President Marks and the events of the following day, including the address by Sidney Rigdon and the response by Brigham Young, are chronicled in the history of the Church (see HC 7:225–30).

As noted here, President Marks's decision to move the meeting from Tuesday, 6 August, to Thursday, 8 August, proved to be providential, as Brigham and the other members of the Twelve returned home on the evening of 6 August, the very day that the Tuesday meeting would have been held (see CHFT, p. 289).

Nathan lay on his back in the grass, his eyes closed, pretending sleep. The sound of five thousand voices came at him from every direction, filling the air with a low, continuous hum, like the distant crashing of waves against the shore, or the sound of a rushing river heard through a thick forest. Blended in with the others, though closer, were the individual voices of his family. He could easily have focused on any one voice or set of voices and heard what they were saying—Benjamin and Carl talking about the brickyard; Mary Ann, Lydia, Caroline, and Rebecca speaking about Sidney Rigdon's morning address; Matthew and Jenny playing "hide the thimble" with several of the children; Peter telling Kathryn about the latest edition of the *Nauvoo Neighbor*. But he did not focus on what they were saying. He was lost in his own thoughts, closing his eyes and his ears to what was around him so he could sort it out.

They were not down at the grove below the bluff where the Saints often gathered; that was nowhere near a large enough assembly area for the huge crowd that had come that morning. Instead, they were in another grove in a large field east of the temple. This was where the meeting that all of Nauvoo had been waiting for had finally commenced.

The meeting had started out pretty much as expected, but turned out in the end to be quite dramatic. President Marks, Sidney Rigdon, and a few other leaders were seated on the stand at the head of the vast congregation. Brigham Young was not to be seen. President Marks turned the pulpit over to Sidney Rigdon immediately after the opening hymn and prayer. There had been a stiff wind blowing directly into Sidney's face, and it was difficult to hear him. So he had stopped, walked around to the opposite side of the crowd, climbed up into the back of a wagon, and continued, letting the wind now carry his words to the people, who turned around to face him.

He had spoken for an hour and a half, exhorting the Saints to accept him as the "guardian" of the Church. An hour and a half! Nathan had always felt impressed with Sidney Rigdon's oratory skills, but this morning it had been more of a harangue, an interminable droning that had no power. At first, Nathan thought it just might be his own feelings, but when he had looked around at the crowd, it was obvious from their reaction that they saw little power there either. And while this had been billed as a prayer meeting only, it was clear that Sidney was making his pitch for the guardianship, probably worried now that the Twelve were back in town. Near the end of his speech, at about eleven-thirty, Nathan started to worry that President Marks might call for a vote and not wait for next Tuesday's solemn assembly.

He should have known that Brigham Young wouldn't let things get away from him so easily. The people being turned in the opposite direction from the stand now, hardly anyone noticed that Brigham came to the meeting shortly after Sidney moved to the wagon. Brigham came without fanfare and took the seat on the stand vacated by Sidney Rigdon. It was when Sidney finished that the surprise took place. Brigham stood immediately and began to speak, startling everyone. They swung back around in surprise, pleased that he had come. But he spoke only briefly. He dismissed the meeting, noting that he was calling upon the Saints to reassemble, being seated by quorums, at two p.m. The Twelve had decided not to wait until next week for the solemn assembly that would bring this question to closure.

That announcement had caught some families off guard. They had not come prepared for an afternoon session, and they immediately went down into the city to secure food and drink. Benjamin, with his usual wisdom, had told the family he was sure they would not finish in the morning session, and so they had brought several picnic baskets filled with food and jugs of milk wrapped in thick towels to keep them cool. Though they had not expected a full two and a half hours of break time, they decided to stay where they were so they would not lose their place, which was just a few rods from the stand. So they had settled in for a leisurely wait, enjoying the time they had to be together.

No one had stayed home. Not today. Even Caroline had insisted, over Joshua's protests, that she was not going to miss this meeting. Though she still had a noticeable limp and favored the arm that had been broken, she was not about to stay home. Too much rested on what would happen here this day. Like everyone else, she sensed that this would prove to be a historic meeting. Carl and Melissa had even brought their children, though Melissa continued to declare that it didn't matter much to her whether Rigdon or someone else was chosen to succeed Joseph Smith. Jane Manning was with them to help care for little Mary Melissa, now just three weeks old.

Nathan opened his eyes and turned his head. Jane held the baby in her arms and was speaking softly to Sarah. This was a good thing his mother had done, he thought. This black woman's quiet and unobtrusive yet very strong faith was exactly what was needed in the Rogers household right now.

He felt a touch on his arm and looked up. Lydia was sitting beside him, looking down at him with a smile. She reached out and touched a spot between his eyes, rubbing it softly. "You have such a frown," she teased him. "Are you thinking about Brother Rigdon again?"

He laughed in spite of himself and sat up. "No, actually I was thinking about Jane."

"That's no reason to frown," she said.

"I know. I guess it was Melissa and Carl who caused the frown. But I'm glad Jane is there now."

"Yes, she's just right for them."

He looked around. "Who's got the baby?"

"Young Joshua. Who always has the baby?"

"He loves Joseph a great deal," Nathan agreed.

Lydia turned her head and looked toward the stand. The Twelve were starting to arrive now. President Marks and Sidney Rigdon weren't there yet, but it was almost time. In ten minutes, the meeting would begin, and then all of their questions would be answered. "If Sidney is not chosen," she asked, looking back at Nathan now, "what do you think he'll do?"

"Go back to Pittsburgh with his tail between his legs." And then even as he said it, he shook his head. "No. I don't think he'll accept it. I think he'll try to get others to support him."

Joshua, lying down just a few feet away, sat up. He had heard Lydia's question. "I think Nathan's right," he said. "You mark my words. I don't know how much they'll decide here today, but when it is all over, and the dust has settled, this church is going to be split right down the middle. There'll be two churches then—Sidney's church and Brigham's church. Maybe others, for that matter. You've already got that church that Wilson and William Law and the Fosters started."

"And that's what you came to see?" Nathan said sourly. "You're here to watch the great breakup?"

"Nathan," Joshua said softly, "believe it or not, that makes me very sad. I don't want to see that happen. But it's like I told you before. Joseph was the power that held you together. Now Joseph is gone."

Caroline pulled herself up into a sitting position with some effort. She held a parasol over her head to shade her from the sun. She was looking at her husband with sudden understanding. "So that's it."

"What's it?"

"If that's how you see the Church, it's no wonder that you're not interested in becoming a member. It's just the work of men to you, isn't it?"

He shrugged. "I know how you all feel. And I suppose I hope you're right. But I also know human nature." He looked around at the vast assembly. "And I know what I see here today." He turned back to Nathan. "When this is over—tonight, I mean—I'd like to talk to the family about something."

"The family?" Caroline asked in surprise.

Nathan was likewise a little taken aback by that. "About what?"

"About moving." He took Caroline's hand quickly as her eyes flew open in astonishment. "Not just us. The whole family. All of us. Carl and Melissa. Matthew and Jenny. Nathan and Lydia. Maybe it's time to think about starting anew somewhere and—" He stopped, realizing that his timing was terrible. "Look, let's suppose Sidney does take over. Even if it's just a portion of the Church. How long before his call for blood up to the bridle bits brings out every anti-Mormon in the state against you? It won't matter one bit whether you agree with him or not."

"I—"

It was as if Joshua read his thoughts perfectly. "I was there in Far West that day too, remember. We know what Sidney's fiery rhetoric caused." Now he was very somber. "I just think we need to talk about the future, Nathan. Times are changing. They're going to change even more. We need to talk about what that means for the family."

Nathan was noncommittal. "Let's wait and see what happens."

"If Sidney wins, will you at least consider it?" Joshua persisted.

For a long moment their eyes held, and then Nathan slowly nodded. "If Sidney wins, yes, I'll consider it."

———•———

Joshua looked around, smiling to himself. He and Carl were the only men now with the family. There were a few other adult males around them, but they were like an occasional island in an ocean of women and children. He smiled because he saw the curious looks they were getting. He also smiled because a moment before, someone had whispered, "Who is that?" and there came the hushed response, "That's Joshua Steed." "Oh," said the first, as though that explained everything.

The great majority of the men in the congregation were now seated in half circles around the podium and stand. In response to Brigham's request that the brethren sit by quorums for the meeting, on the stand were the Quorum of the Twelve and the high council. Circling around them were the high priests, then the seventies, then the elders, and finally the quorums of the Aaronic Priesthood. From there the required order ended. The rest of the audience spread out behind them—women and children were the biggest group, but there were also the few men who were not yet priesthood holders or those, such as himself and Carl, who were the reprobate nonmembers.

Benjamin and Nathan had tried to explain to him and Carl about the seating arrangement and how this constituted a solemn assembly and what that meant. Joshua had at first brushed that idea aside and credited Brigham with nothing more than cheap posturing, a visible way to reassert the fact that he was in charge and to blunt Sidney Rigdon's influence. Now, as he looked around, he wasn't so sure. There was a certain solemnity to the whole proceedings that Joshua had not seen before in previous worship services.

When the song and prayer were done, Brigham immediately stood and moved to the podium. He was dressed in a white shirt with ruffles at the neck and a long coat with tails. He stood erect and dignified. The sun caught his hair, emphasizing the slight reddish tint to it. Though too far away to see his eyes clearly, Joshua could picture them—gray blue and filled with humor, or dark and threatening when he was angry. Brigham was two or three inches shorter than Joseph had been, and had a tendency at times to be stoop-shouldered, making him seem even less tall than he was. Brigham was a capable leader. He had proven that while Joseph was in Liberty Jail and he and the Twelve had led the people out of Missouri. But he was no Joseph Smith. And the only hope for keeping the Church together was to find another Joseph Smith. In Joshua's mind, there was not the slightest question about that.

Brigham stood there for several moments, letting the last murmurings die away to total and complete silence. Even the soft breeze that had been rustling through the limbs of the trees above them seemed to have stopped in anticipation of what was about to happen.

"Attention all!" Brigham called out. His voice was firm and loud, carrying clearly across the heads of the group before him. "This congregation makes me think of the days of King Benjamin in the Book of Mormon, the multitude being so great that all could not hear. I know it is a warm summer day. I know that you have already been here for a long time. But I request the brethren not to have any feelings against being convened again this afternoon, for it is necessary. We want you all to be still and give attention, that all may hear. Let none complain because of the situation of the congregation, we will do the best we can."

Joshua felt Caroline stir beside him. Her eyes were fastened on Brigham and she leaned forward attentively. He looked around. His mother and Rebecca and Jenny and Melissa and even the older children were in the same posture. Brigham was asking for their undivided attention. It was an unnecessary request. He already had it.

"For the first time in my life," Brigham went on, "for the first time in your lives, for the first time in the kingdom of God in this century, without a prophet at our head, do I step forth to act in my calling in connection with the Quorum of the Twelve. We are Apostles of Jesus Christ unto this generation—Apostles whom God has called by revelation through the Prophet Joseph. We are ordained and anointed to bear off the keys of the kingdom of God in all the world.

"This people have hitherto walked by sight and not by faith. You have had the Prophet in your midst. Do you all understand? You have walked by sight and without much pleading to the Lord to know whether things were right or not. Heretofore you have had a prophet as the mouth of the Lord to speak to you, but he has sealed his testimony with his blood, and now, for the first time, are you called to walk by faith, not by sight.

"The first position I take in behalf of the Twelve and the people is to ask a few questions. Here is what I wish to ask the Latter-day Saints: Do you as individuals at this time want to choose a prophet or a guardian? Inasmuch as our prophet and patriarch are taken from our midst, do you want someone to guard, to guide and lead you through this world into the kingdom of God, or not? All that want some person to be a guardian, a spokesman or something else, signify it by raising the right hand."

Carl gave Joshua a startled look and Joshua returned it. Sidney had put forth his case for an hour and a half this morning. It had been a long and often lifeless address, unusual for Sidney Rigdon. Joshua had simply assumed that Brigham would take time to do the same. Yet he was barely a minute into his address and here he was asking for a vote on Sidney's proposal. He lifted his head and scanned across the congregation. Not a single hand was up. The people weren't ready to make that commitment, at least not yet.

Brigham nodded slowly, clearly pleased. "When I came to this stand I had peculiar feelings and impressions. The faces of this people seem to say, we want a shepherd to guide and lead us through this world. All that want to draw away a party from the Church after them, let them do it if they can, *but they will not prosper!*" He thundered out the last five words, causing some people to jump in surprise. "If any man thinks he has influence among this people to lead away a party, let him try it, and he will find out that there is power with the Apostles which will carry them off victorious through all the world, and it is they who will build up and defend the church and kingdom of God."

Joshua was shaking his head, half in astonishment, half in admiration. This was no rhetorical contest to let the people be swayed by one speech or another. This was a direct frontal assault on Sidney Rigdon's position.

"What do the people want?" Brigham cried. "I feel as though I wanted the privilege to weep and mourn for Joseph and Hyrum for thirty days at least. Then I would have been better prepared to rise up, shake myself, and tell the people what the Lord wants of them. My heart is too full of mourning to launch forth into business transactions or to deal with the organization of the Church. But there is no choice. I feel compelled this day to step forth in the discharge of those duties God has placed upon me as President of the Quorum of the Twelve."

He paused, letting his eyes sweep across the crowd. They seemed to take in every living soul before him, as though he were asking the question to each one individually and waiting for an answer.

"I now wish to speak about the organization of The Church of Jesus Christ of Latter-day Saints. If the Church is organized, and I know that you want to know how it should be organized, I will tell you. I know your feelings. Do you want me to tell your feelings?" He half turned and motioned to where Sidney Rigdon was seated. "Here is President Rigdon, who was counselor to Joseph. He says he has been appointed as the spokesman for Joseph and should act as guardian. But I ask you, brothers and sisters, where are Joseph and Hyrum now? They are gone beyond the veil, and if Elder Rigdon wants to act as Joseph's counselor, he must go beyond the veil where he is."

"Whew!" Joshua said softly. "That's not pulling any punches."

"Shhh!" Caroline said without turning her head.

Brigham let his previous words sink in for a few moments before going on. "There has been much said about President Rigdon being President of the Church and leading the people, being the head, and so on. Brother Rigdon has come sixteen hundred miles to tell you what he wants to do for you. And if the people want President Rigdon to lead them, they may have him.

But I say unto you that the Quorum of the Twelve have the keys of the kingdom of God in all the world. I tell you that the Twelve are appointed by the finger of God. Here is Brigham. Have his knees ever faltered? Have his lips ever quivered?"

A slight movement near the stand caught Joshua's eye. Sidney Rigdon had lowered his head and was staring at the ground. If there was one thing Sidney Rigdon could not honestly say, it was that his knees had never faltered.

"Here is Heber and the rest of the Twelve, an independent body who have the keys of the priesthood—the keys of the kingdom of God to deliver to all the world. Those keys were given to us by Brother Joseph. This is true, so help me God!" He stopped, those piercing eyes sweeping across the faces of the people like a burning wind. "The Twelve stand next to Joseph and are as the First Presidency of the Church. I do not know whether my enemies will take my life or not, and I do not care, for I want to be with the man I love."

Then, in an instant, his head lifted higher, his voice rose until it was like the roar of a lion. "*You* cannot fill the office of a prophet, seer, and revelator. God must do this. You are like children without a father and sheep without a shepherd. You must not appoint any man at our head. If you should, the Twelve must ordain him. If you want some other man or men to lead you, take them and we, the Twelve, will go our own way to build up the kingdom in all the world.

"I know who are Joseph's friends and who are his enemies. I know where the keys of the kingdom are and where they will eternally be. *You* cannot call a man to be a prophet. *You* cannot take Elder Rigdon and place him above the Twelve. If so, he must be ordained by them. I tell you there is an overanxiety to hurry matters here. You as a people cannot take just any man and put him at the head. You would scatter the Saints to the four winds, you would sever the priesthood. So long as we remain as we are, the heavenly Head is in constant cooperation with us; and if you go out of that course, God will have nothing to do with you."

Once again he turned and looked at Sidney Rigdon. Rigdon did not look up. Finally, Brigham turned back slowly. He straightened to his full height, letting his gaze sweep across the huge assembly before him. Now his voice rang like a blacksmith's hammer striking on hot steel. "I again repeat," he thundered, not with anger, but with absolute confidence that almost approached serenity, "no man can stand at our head, except God reveals it from the heavens. Do you want a spokesman? Elder Rigdon claims to be spokesman to the Prophet. Very well, he was. But can he now act in that office? If he wants now to be a spokesman to the Prophet, he must go to the other side of the veil, for that is where the Prophet is.

"Does this Church want things organized as God organized them? Or do you want to clip the power of the priesthood and let those who have the keys of the priesthood go off somewhere where the people will hear them and build up the kingdom in all the world?"

Joshua, fully intent now on the drama playing out before his eyes, was suddenly startled by Caroline's hand shooting out and grabbing at his arm. He turned, but to his surprise she was not looking at him. She was leaning forward, chin thrust out, her eyes wide and filled with astonishment, her body straining as though against invisible bonds.

"What?" he said, alarmed by the sudden intensity he saw in her face.

If she heard him, she gave no sign. Every muscle in her body seemed focused on the stand and the figure that stood there. It was as though, for her, Brigham Young and Caroline Steed were suddenly the only two people in existence and if she took her eyes from him he would disappear and leave her totally alone.

"If there is a spokesman," Brigham's voice cried, "if he is a king and priest as Sidney claims, then let him go and build up a kingdom unto himself. That is his right and it is the right of many here. But I tell you, the Twelve are at the head of this church. *They are the head!*"

Caroline's fingers were digging into the flesh of Joshua's arm through the fabric of his sleeve, hurting him a little. "Joshua, it's Joseph!"

He gaped at her. "What?" he cried.

"Look, it's Joseph!"

He straightened, lifting his head, swinging it around to see what it was that had caught her eye. But her eyes were fixed on Brigham Young. There was nothing else to see. He turned back to her. The sight of her face stunned him. The very intensity of it was almost frightening to him.

"Caroline!" He took her hand, pulled it firmly, trying to break the spell, trying to make her turn away. She did not move or turn her head. For her, he was not there at that moment.

Suddenly, Mary Ann was beside them, reaching out for Caroline. "Caroline!" she whispered, giving Joshua a frightened look. "What's the matter?"

Caroline turned now, looking at Mary Ann with such radiant joy in her eyes that Joshua fell back a little. "Look, Mother Steed, it's Joseph. It's Joseph speaking to us. Brigham appears to be Joseph."

"What?" Joshua cried aloud.

But his mother had turned to look where Caroline was pointing. There was an audible gasp. "Oh, Caroline!" she exclaimed. "It *is* Joseph!"

Whirling to see, feeling cold chills coursing up and down his back, too dumbfounded to respond, Joshua turned too. All he saw was Brigham Young standing there at the pulpit, speaking to the people.

"Now," the Apostle cried, "if you want Sidney Rigdon or William Law to lead you, or anybody else, you are welcome to them. But I tell you, in the name of the Lord, that no man can put another between the Twelve and the Prophet Joseph. Why? Because Joseph has committed into our hands the keys of the kingdom in this last dispensation. I will ask you," he said, his voice suddenly dropping in loudness but still carrying across the air as though he spoke through a trumpet. "I ask you, who has stood next to Joseph and Hyrum? I have, and I will stand next to him. We have a head, *and that head is the apostleship!*"

Still feeling that prickling sensation, Joshua was about to turn back to his wife and his mother to see what madness had gripped them, when his eye was caught by another movement. Up ahead of him, a woman's arm had shot out and she was pointing. She whispered in great urgency to an older daughter who sat beside her. There was that same look of stunned astonishment, and then a blazing, awestruck look of pure joy on both women's faces. He heard a soft cry.

To his left, Rebecca was on her knees, clutching five-year-old Christopher on both shoulders. She spun him around to face Brigham. "Look, Christopher!" she said in a fierce whisper. "Look! It's Joseph. Do you see him?"

Without being conscious of it, Joshua held his breath, straining to see Christopher's face. He was squinting in fierce concentration. Then suddenly his eyebrows shot up, the eyes widened perceptibly. "It is, Mama! It is Brother Joseph!"

It was as if a whirlwind had dropped out of the sky and stirred up the congregation gathered there near the temple. Brigham was speaking, but all across the congregation—in the quorums of the priesthood, in the audience of women and children—people were staring, pointing, whispering in stunned amazement. Up near the stand a man had leaped to his feet and stood gaping up at Brigham.

Behind him he heard Kathryn's voice. "Jenny! Jenny! Do you hear it? It is Joseph speaking to us."

"Yes!" It came as half cry of ecstasy, half sob of amazement. "It is the voice of Joseph."

Joshua whirled now, angry and confused and frustrated all at once. "What are you talking about?" he hissed fiercely to Caroline. "It's Brigham. Brigham Young." He looked to Carl and Melissa. Carl's expression told Joshua that he was experiencing exactly the same confusion as he was. Melissa looked around at the people around her with quick, jerky movements of her head.

She seemed bewildered, almost a little frightened. And then she turned back toward the stand and froze, her eyes flying open. "Ohhh," she said in a low gasp of astonishment.

And then, as though a thunderclap had sounded out of clear sky, or lightning had struck within a few feet of him, Joshua stiffened, rocking back. He raised one hand and swept it across his eyes, as though that might bring him back to reality. But it was not his eyes that were betraying him. It was his ears. He leaned forward, blinked, blinked again, staring across the five or six rods that separated them from where Brigham was standing. It was still Brigham Young he was staring at, of that there was no question.

But the voice!

"No man has a right to counsel the Twelve but Joseph Smith," Brigham was saying.

Without being aware of it, Joshua rose to his knees, peering forward. It was Brigham Young he saw, standing there speaking to them. But it was not Brigham who was speaking! It was no longer the voice that was high-pitched and powerful, filled with passion and ringing conviction. It was a deep voice now—resonant, full of love, gentle, powerful, compelling. It was the voice that Joshua Steed had last heard just a few days before the martyrdom. It was the voice that told him to stay in Nauvoo and care for Caroline. It was the voice that forgave Joshua Steed for his blind anger and thanked him for his friendship.

It was the voice of Joseph Smith!

"I do not ask you to take my counsel or advice alone," the voice said evenly now, "but every one of you must act for yourselves. If Brother Rigdon is the person you want to lead you, vote for him. But don't vote for him unless you intend to follow him and support him as you did Joseph. Do not vote unless you mean to take his counsel hereafter."

From somewhere far off Joshua was aware that someone was shaking his shoulder. He turned. Carl was kneeling by his side. "Joshua! What's the matter?"

He shook his head, brushing the query aside, not wanting to break his concentration.

"And I would say the same for the Twelve. Don't make a covenant to support the Twelve unless you intend to abide by their counsel. And if they do not counsel you as you please, don't turn round and oppose them. I want every man, before he enters into a covenant, to know what he is going to do. But I am asking you. We want to know if this people will support the priesthood in the name of Israel's God. If you say you will, do so."

Joshua felt another hand, this time on his arm, this time gentle and caressing. "Do you hear it, Joshua?" Caroline was saying to him, as though from across a large room. He just looked at her, his eyes searching hers. He turned back as the voice continued.

"The Twelve have the power now—the seventies, the elders, and all of you can have power to go and build up the kingdom in the name of Israel's God. I tell you, Nauvoo will not hold all the people that will come into the kingdom."

Joshua reeled again, his jaw going instantly slack. The voice of Joseph was gone. It was as if a completely strange voice had taken over now. And then he realized that it was Brigham once again. It was not a stranger's voice. It was simply the voice of Brigham again.

"We want to build the temple," Brigham was saying, "so as to get our endowment. And if we do our best and Satan will not let us build it, then we will go into the wilderness and there we will receive the endowment, for we will receive an endowment one way or the other."

As shocking as it was to have the voice of Brigham back again, even more totally astounding to Joshua was the sharpness of his disappointment. It was as though Joseph's voice had electrified him, soothed him, made things right again. Now it was gone, as swiftly as it had come. And something deep within Joshua had gone with it.

"Will you abide our counsel?" Brigham cried. "I will ask you as quorums, Do you want Brother Rigdon to stand forward as your leader, your guide, your spokesman?"

Suddenly, Sidney Rigdon waved a hand and said something that only the nearest could hear. Brigham turned, bent half-down toward the First Counselor. Again something was said which Joshua could not hear. Brigham nodded and turned back to the congregation.

"President Rigdon wants me to bring up the other question first, and that is: Does the Church want and is it their only desire to sustain the Twelve as the First Presidency of this people? Here are the Apostles. If the Church wants the Twelve to stand as the head of this kingdom in all the world, to stand next to Joseph, to walk up into their calling, and to hold the keys of this kingdom, every man, every woman, every quorum is now put in order, and you are now the sole controllers of it. We shall call for a vote."

He paused, standing erect and still, as calm and unruffled as any man could possibly be. Now all the whispering, all the awestruck mumbles and cries stopped. Not a sound disturbed the silence. To the west of them, the walls of the temple gleamed pale and majestic, as though watching over what was about to happen. Then at last Brigham spoke.

"All that are in favor of this, in all the congregation of the Saints, manifest it by holding up the right hand."

As one single member of one vast body, thousands of hands shot upward. Men, women, children—it was like looking at a small forest miraculously sprung into instant existence. Brigham seemed to visibly swell with joy and relief.

"And those," he said, with the greatest of solemnity, "that do not want the Twelve to preside, lift up your hands in like manner."

Now every head in the congregation swiveled, searching the audience for any sign of movement, any one hand raised to the sky. There was not one. Nowhere. Not one.

Though without any audible sound, it was as if a great collective sigh of release swept through the crowd. The moment had come. The decision was now made.

"Brethren and sisters," Brigham said, his voice husky now with emotion, "with the vote being clearly unanimous, this supersedes the other question about guardianship. There is no need to try that by the vote of the quorums. Thank you."

Joshua saw Sidney Rigdon, seated on the stand, fold his hands in his lap. Sidney's shoulders slumped. His head went down. It was over.

Chapter Notes

On 8 August 1844, two meetings were held in a grove of trees east of the partially completed Nauvoo Temple. Sidney Rigdon spoke for an hour and a half in the morning meeting, putting forth his cause that he should be appointed to lead the Church as spokesman and guardian. Brigham then dismissed the meeting and announced that they would gather again at two p.m. for a solemn assembly. The words of Brigham's address are taken from the extensive transcript found in the history of the Church (see HC 7:231–42). Amasa Lyman, an Apostle but not of the Quorum of the Twelve, and Parley P. Pratt of the Twelve also spoke at the afternoon meeting, each speaking in favor of sustaining the Twelve. Brigham invited Sidney to speak, but he said he could not speak and asked that W. W. Phelps speak for him. Brother Phelps, who had been tireless in helping John Taylor and Willard Richards run the affairs of the Church after the Martyrdom, rose and spoke, but he too exhorted the people to accept the Twelve as their head. (See HC 7:236–39.) Those speeches and much else of what Brigham said are omitted here for the purposes of the novel.

It is not clear at exactly what point during Brigham's speech the miraculous transformation took place, but unquestionably it had happened by the time he called for the vote. Several sources place the transformation in the morning meeting when Brigham first stood up. The official history suggests it happened in the afternoon meeting. The author chose to follow that placement, though he recognizes it may have happened earlier.

Here, in the people's own words, are some of the testimonies borne about that day:

George Q. Cannon, seventeen at the time and later to be a counselor in the First Presidency, said: "If Joseph had risen from the dead and again spoken in their hearing, the effect could not have been more startling than it was to many present at that meeting, it was the voice of Joseph himself; and not only was it the voice of Joseph which was heard, but it seemed in the eyes of the people as if it were the very person of Joseph which stood before them. A more wonderful and miraculous event than was wrought that day in the presence of that congregation, we never heard of. The Lord gave His people a testimony that left no room for doubt as to who was the man chosen to lead them. . . . On that occasion Brigham Young seemed to be transformed, and a change such as that we read of in the scriptures, as happening to the Prophet Elisha, when Elijah was translated in his presence, seemed to have taken place with him. The mantle of the Prophet Joseph had been left for Brigham. . . . The people said one to another: 'The spirit of Joseph rests on Brigham'; they knew that he was the man chosen to lead them and they honored him accordingly." (Cited in Kate B. Carter, comp., *Heart Throbs of the West* [Salt Lake City: Daughters of Utah Pioneers, 1943], 4:420.)

Wilford Woodruff described the event as follows: "If I had not seen him with my own eyes, there is no one that could have convinced me that it was not Joseph Smith, and anyone can testify to this who was acquainted with these two men" (*Deseret Evening News*, 12 March 1892; cited in HC 7:236).

Benjamin F. Johnson, who was twenty-six at the time, said: "As soon as he [Brigham Young] spoke I jumped upon my feet, for in every possible degree it was Joseph's voice, and his person, in look, attitude, dress and appearance was Joseph himself, personified; and I knew in a moment the spirit and mantle of Joseph was upon him" (cited in *CHFT*, p. 291).

Zina Huntington, then a young woman of twenty-three, recalled: "President Young was speaking. It was the voice of Joseph Smith—not that of Brigham Young. His very person was changed. . . . I closed my eyes. I could have exclaimed, I know that is Joseph Smith's voice! Yet I knew he had gone. But the same spirit was with the people." (Cited in *CHFT*, p. 292.)

Mosiah Hancock, the young boy who ran barefoot across the Mississippi River ice as it broke up around him (see volume 4 of this series, pp. 577–78), was fourteen in August 1844. He said of that day: "Although only a boy, I saw the mantle of the Prophet Joseph rest on Brigham Young; and he arose lion-like to the occasion, and led the people forth" (as cited in *American Moses*, p. 115).

It should be noted that there is no known account by a nonmember who experienced anything unusual. Having Joshua there and having him hear what he does is a device used for purposes of the novel.

Once the vote was taken and it was clearly established in the minds of the people that the Twelve would lead the Church, Brigham called for a vote on several other important items of business. He asked if it was the will of the congregation that they be tithed as they had hitherto been, so that the temple could be completed. The vote was unanimous. He asked if the congregation would support the Twelve in carrying out missionary work throughout the world. The vote was unanimous. He asked if the Twelve could dictate the finances and other business affairs of the Church. The vote was unanimous. With the death of Hyrum Smith, the Saints were left without a Patriarch to the Church. Brigham reaffirmed that this right belonged to Joseph's family and that it should have gone to Samuel Smith. But since Samuel had died for the cause as well, Brigham proposed that the Church leave it to the Twelve to determine which of the Smiths it should be. The vote in the affirmative was unanimous. (See HC 7:241–42.)

Whe they reached Steed Row, only Carl and Melissa went right to their home, taking Jane Manning and the children with them. Will, Peter, and young Joshua took the carriages away to unhitch the horses and turn them loose in the pasture. The rest stood around, reluctant to part company, wanting to talk about what they had experienced, and yet still so overwhelmed by it that they weren't sure they could talk about it. On the way home from the grove, there had been nothing more than whispered conversations between couples sitting together. There was no general discussion among the family, partly out of respect for Carl and Melissa, who were visibly disturbed over what had happened at the meeting. Now finally, with Carl and Melissa gone, Lydia asked the question that was burning in each of their minds. "Did you see it?" She was looking at Benjamin, but it was clear she was asking it of the others as well.

There was a long silence. Nathan saw that Joshua leaned forward slightly, his lips parted, his eyes not moving from his father's face. Then Benjamin slowly shook his head. "I saw and heard Brigham Young give a powerful address," he said in a low voice. "But that was all."

There was no comment from Joshua, but he straightened again, the tension ebbing out of his body. His expression had not changed, but Nathan could sense his relief.

"I saw it, Grandpa!" Savannah said, moving up to stand beside Benjamin.

"Did you?" he said, putting a hand on her shoulder and smiling. There was the briefest of glances back at Joshua, who had stiffened all over again. "What did you see, Savannah? Tell me about it."

The blue eyes were large and lighter than the summer sky above them. The red hair, now darkening more toward the shade of her mother's, fell back across her shoulders as she tipped her head to one side, her brows knitting together in concentration. "It was . . . I don't know how to say it, Grandpa. One minute I was watching President Young and then . . ." She frowned, as though trying to recapture it completely in her mind before going on. "And then it was Brother Joseph. I knew it really wasn't, but Brother Brigham looked just like Brother Joseph."

Five-year-old Christopher pulled free from Rebecca's hand and trotted over to his cousin. "I saw it, Vanna," he said proudly. "I saw Brother Joseph too."

"So did I," Lydia's Emily said. She was twelve now and more a young woman than a child any longer. "I couldn't believe my eyes."

Joshua ignored the others. He was looking directly at his daughter. "Savannah?"

She looked up at him. "Yes, Papa?"

"Are you sure you just didn't hear what your mama was saying? Sometimes when things happen around us, we want to see the same thing that others are seeing and—"

"Savannah wasn't sitting by me," Caroline said softly. "If you remember, she was sitting with Emily and Will and young Joshua."

"Yes, Papa," Savannah said. "I wasn't sitting by Mama."

He didn't turn to look at his wife, but there was the briefest flash of annoyance before he smiled at Savannah. "Oh, that's right. But tell me, who saw this . . . who saw it first? Did Emily tell you what she was seeing?"

Emily and Savannah looked at each other. They had sensed an edge to Joshua's question, and Emily looked suddenly uncertain. Lydia smiled and nodded at her. "It's all right, Emily. Try to remember for Uncle Joshua. Did you see that President Young looked like Brother Joseph first or did Savannah?"

Again the two girls looked at each other, this time trying to remember. After a moment, Savannah said, "I think you did, Emily. Remember? You grabbed Joshua's arm and told him to look. I asked you what you saw and you told me."

"Yes, that's right," Emily said. "I saw it first."

Joshua nodded, clearly satisfied. "Thank you, Emily." He said nothing more, but for the adults, at least, he didn't need to.

"Pa," Matthew said, "Jenny and Kathryn both saw it happen. I didn't see anything. Like you. What does that mean? Is it because I didn't have enough faith?"

"I hope not," Benjamin said with exaggerated horror, bringing a laugh from the others. Then more seriously he added, "I don't know why, Matthew. It just seems to be that some saw it and some did not."

With that, everyone started talking at once. Lydia turned to Nathan. "You're sure?" she whispered. "You saw and heard nothing extraordinary?"

He shook his head. "I always told you that you were the more spiritual of the two of us."

Now it was her turn to shake her head and she did so vigorously. "You know that's not true."

"Maybe it was because I didn't need a miracle to know that Brigham and the Twelve are the ones to lead us." But even as he said it, he was shaking his head. "No, that's not it either. You didn't have any question about whether Sidney should direct us, did you?"

"None."

His shoulders lifted and fell. "I don't know, Lydia. I honestly don't know." And then he saw that while Joshua had moved over to stand beside Caroline, he was watching the two of them curiously and Nathan knew he had been listening. He drew in a breath. "So Joshua, let me ask you a question."

Instantly all talking ceased and every eye turned to Nathan. He saw it in his family's eyes; every adult here was dying to ask Joshua the question they were asking of each other, but no one had dared do it until now. Nathan could see the gladness in their eyes that he was going to do it for them. And then he saw something else. Joshua had gone very still and his eyes were blank, as if a curtain had been pulled across them from behind. In the split second it took for all of that to register in Nathan's mind, he also saw the open warning on Caroline's face: *No, Nathan. Not now.*

He smiled easily, grateful as another question came to his mind. "So, Joshua, do you still think Sidney Rigdon will lead a significant number of Saints off with him?"

Joshua seemed momentarily taken aback. Clearly he had expected the other question. He leaned back, trying to hide his relief. A thoughtful look came across his face. "No, Nathan. You were right and I was wrong. If the people had voted last Sunday, it would be Guardian Sidney Rigdon right now. But Brigham handled it beautifully today."

Nathan smiled briefly at Caroline, to let her know he understood her mouthed "Thank you," then settled back to listen. He had invited Joshua onto safer ground, and Joshua had planted both feet firmly there and planned to stay there for a time.

"I don't know how long it will take Sidney to realize that," Joshua went on, more warmly now, "but he is through. What Brigham did today was brilliant. Absolutely brilliant. The crisis is over. You can feel it in the air. Oh, there'll be a few dissenters, I'm sure. And you can bet there may be others who try to challenge Brigham, but no, the crisis is over."

———•———

It was nearly ten o'clock when Joshua stepped through the front gate of Carl and Melissa's yard and moved quietly up the walk. There was only one light on in the house, and through the open window he could see Melissa bent over some kind of sewing she was doing. She was alone in the room. There was a soft grunt of satisfaction, and he moved to the door and knocked softly. In a moment she was there, looking up in surprise at him.

He held out the book he had in his hand. "Hi," he said. Then more sheepishly, "I've been going to return this book on breeding horses to Carl for almost a month now. I thought I'd better do it before I forget again."

She laughed lightly and pulled the door open for him. "Joshua, there are two people you should never try to lie to. Caroline and me. We both know you too well."

He stepped inside and set the book on the narrow table standing there. "Well, I *have* been meaning to bring it back."

"I know. I'm just teasing. Come in."

He looked toward the stairs and she laughed again. "Carl's asleep. He's taking a wagonload of bricks down to Yelrome early in the morning. We can talk."

On impulse he took her in his arms and hugged her for a moment. He remembered the years of their growing up, and especially those last years when he and his father had started to act like two aging roosters trying to prove who was king of the barnyard. Always Melissa had understood the fires within him, the things that drove him so hard. "Thanks," was all he said.

They moved back into the room where she had been sitting and sat down together on the couch. She half turned so she could see him as they talked. "Caroline wanted to come too, but she was quite tired tonight."

"It was a long day."

"Yes." He was watching her closely, seeing the pain tightening the muscles around her mouth, the confusion in her eyes.

"Melissa?"

"Yes." She only partially turned back towards him.

"We've always been honest with each other."

There was a faint smile. "Well, almost always."

His surprise was evident.

Now she chuckled. "Do you remember that day you got in so much trouble with Mama for eating her freshly baked gooseberry pie?"

"Yes." His surprise had deepened noticeably. Then suddenly his eyebrows shot up. "That was you?" he cried.

She blushed. "Me and Emma Jean Thornton. We took it out in the barn and ate the whole thing."

He frowned deeply. "I tried to blame it on the dog, but Mama always said the dog might lick the pie plate clean, but he wouldn't have put it back up on the window sill."

"That was kind of foolish, all right," she said, her eyes warm now with the memory.

"Pa made me clean the chicken coop all by myself for that," he growled. Then he laughed in wonder. "And that was you? All these years and you never said."

"I'd forgotten about it until you said how we are always honest with each other."

He nodded slowly, feeling the warmth of their friendship as well as their family love. "So, will you be honest with me now?"

"I'd rather not," she said, any humor suddenly gone now.

"What happened there today?" he asked, ignoring her stricken look. "Did you . . . I mean, when Brigham was talking, did . . ." He blew out his breath. "Well, did you?"

She stood and went over to the chair where she had been sitting. She reached out and touched the material she had been working on. Joshua could see the thread and needle but couldn't discern what it was she was sewing. Finally she turned around.

"I saw him, Joshua."

He went very still. "You saw who?" he finally asked.

"I saw Joseph."

"Melissa, I—"

"I did, Joshua. It wasn't just my imagination. I was looking at Brigham and suddenly it was Joseph. Just as plain as when he used to speak to us."

"It couldn't be!" he snapped. "Melissa! Think about it. Suddenly people were crying out, pointing. It was a highly charged moment. The people wanted some kind of a sign. It was the power of suggestion. Did Caroline or Lydia tell you what they were seeing?"

Her smile was sad but filled with love. "I've tried all that, Joshua. I've told myself the same thing all day. Maybe it was my imagination. Maybe the sun was in my eyes. Maybe . . . maybe a hundred other things."

He bent forward, staring at the floor. "It can't be, Melissa. It just cannot be. Maybe you just wanted it to be."

There was a soft, bitter hoot of laughter. "Joshua, Sidney Rigdon is against plural marriage. Brigham Young believes with all his heart that it is from God. He already has another wife. Maybe more. You think I wanted a sign that Brigham is the one to lead us?"

He lifted his head and saw in her eyes the agony she was feeling. He stood and walked slowly to her. She turned her back on him, tears suddenly welling up that she did not want him to see. He took her by the shoulders. "Does Carl know?"

There was a quick shake of her head.

"Are you going to tell him?"

Again, her head went back and forth. "I don't think so."

"Did he . . . ?"

"No. Nothing. He knew something strange was happening. As you could tell coming home, he is quite bothered by it all. He wouldn't talk about it." She turned around to face him now. "And frankly, I'm glad. I don't want to talk about it."

"What's strange," Joshua began, almost musing now, "when this whole thing with plural marriage started, and Carl and I and Nathan were starting to investigate it, Carl was far less troubled by the whole idea than I was. He was so logical about it. He didn't believe that it had been given to Joseph by God, but he could see that Abraham and others had practiced it in the Old Testament." He stopped, remembering how maddening it had been that Carl wasn't as infuriated by it all as he was. "What changed him, Melissa? He is so absolutely against it now."

"I did," she said simply. At the look in his eyes, she went on quickly. "When he saw how it upset me, even the very thought of him having another woman as his wife . . ." She had to look away again. "I think I would die, Joshua. And I'm not just saying that. If Carl ever took another wife, I think I would just lie down and die of a broken heart. Seeing that, he really turned against it."

He left her and walked back to the sofa, but he didn't sit down. He looked at her. "Then what does that mean, Melissa? If you think you saw Joseph today, then what? Does that mean you believe God wants Brigham to lead the Church? And if so, what about how God feels about plural marriage?"

Her lower lip was trembling slightly, barely visible in the soft lamplight. But there was no mistaking the glistening in her eyes. "It doesn't change how I feel, Joshua," she said in a low whisper. "It should, but—" A shudder ran through her body. "Even if I knew for absolutely sure that it was God's will, it wouldn't change how I feel about it."

He nodded, wishing now that he hadn't come. "I'm sorry, Melissa. I didn't mean to pry. I just . . . Well, I'd better get back. Caroline said she might wait up for me."

As he started to the door she remained motionless. When he reached the hallway he stopped and looked back.

"We've always been honest with each other, Joshua," she said softly, not only repeating his words but also using the same tone of voice.

He laughed. "Not always, as I learned tonight."

"Did you see anything today, Joshua?"

He didn't move. It was as if someone had shot off a cannon beside him and his ears were ringing so loudly that he hadn't heard. Then, as though someone from outside of himself was making his body move, he slowly shook his head.

"I saw you," she said, coming toward him now. "I saw you go rigid and then straighten up. You saw something!"

"I . . ." For several moments, mind racing, he searched for the right words. Then he shook his head, this time with an attempt at firmness. "I didn't see Brigham turn into Joseph Smith," he said, with more sharpness than he intended. "If that's what you mean, the answer is no. I didn't see anything."

With a quick, humorless smile he stepped to her, bent down, and kissed her on the cheek. "How come you and me ended up in this family, Melissa?" he said. Then, without waiting for an answer, he turned and walked out into the night.

———————

By the time Joshua returned home the house was dark. He stopped on the porch and removed his boots, then went inside, moving carefully so as not to make any noise. As he moved through the entryway, past the arched opening into the main parlor, Caroline spoke. "I'm in here."

Surprised, he set his boots down and went in to join her. "I thought you'd gone to bed," he said, bending down to kiss her.

"I told you I'd wait up."

"Yes."

"How is Melissa?"

There was no moon outside tonight, but they always kept a lamp burning in the hallway upstairs for the children, and it put enough light in the house that he could see her face dimly. He peered at her in the near darkness, then chuckled. "You women. A man doesn't stand much of a chance against your intuition, does he?"

Caroline reached out and took his hand. "Returning the book was a pretty thin excuse."

"That's what Melissa said too," he replied.

"Was Carl there?"

"No, he'd gone to bed."

"So?"

"So what?" It was feigned ignorance and obviously so.

There was no response, but he could feel her reproachful look even if he couldn't fully see it. He sighed softly. "She is very troubled."

"Because . . . ?" she prompted.

"Because she thinks she saw it too."

For several seconds Caroline considered that, then softly asked, "I assume that by 'it' you mean the transformation of Brigham Young?"

His head bobbed once curtly.

"Was that the way that Melissa put it, that she *thinks* she saw it?"

He started slightly at that, only now realizing that he had used that word. He finally had to shake his head. "No."

There was a soft murmur, an expression of sorrow and empathy and concern all at once. "No wonder she's troubled."

"Sidney Rigdon would have made things easier for her."

"I know."

Then, wanting to change the subject, he snapped his fingers. "By the way, George Galloway came by the stables this evening. Guess who he saw heading for the boat dock with his valise in hand?"

"Who?"

"John C. Bennett."

Caroline slowly nodded. "So he knows it's over."

"Evidently. There's the old saying about rats and sinking ships. I think after today, Bennett knows that Rigdon's ship is sinking."

"Good. I'm glad he's gone. He is an evil man."

They fell silent, and after a few moments, Joshua straightened. "Well," he said, pulling on her hand to bring her up, "you must be exhausted."

She didn't respond. She kept his hand, but didn't rise. "I am. But I wouldn't have missed this day for the world. Thank you for taking me."

"You're welcome. I'm glad I was there." At that moment Joshua wanted to turn to her, to ask her exactly what it was she thought she had experienced today. He wanted to probe, to question, to challenge her assumptions, to dissect and analyze the whole experience—because of all the family, Caroline was the most troublesome to him. First, he had absolute confidence in her honesty. Second, she had been the first. He might be able to explain away Savannah and Christopher as having been influenced by the others, but Caroline had been first. No one had told her what to look for, what she should be seeing. But somehow he couldn't bring himself to do it. He was not sure he wanted to hear what he was fairly certain she would say.

"Joshua?"

He tensed inwardly. "What?"

"Tell me about today."

He found that his breath had caught momentarily. He forced himself to let it out, and then answered with studied casualness. "What about today?"

That won him a second look of reproach. She wasn't going to let him play that game with her. He straightened, remembering his words to Melissa. "Well," he grunted, "I didn't see Brigham Young turn into Joseph Smith, if that's what you mean."

"*Was* that what I meant?" she asked sardonically.

"I don't know, Caroline, what did you mean?"

"I asked you to tell me about today."

"Well, Pa was right. Brigham Young did speak with great power. Aside from all of the other, that alone was enough to convince the people that he should lead them. I've never seen Sidney Rigdon so lifeless and dull. It was—" He stopped. He had almost said "remarkable." "It was unusual," he finished, knowing how lamely it came out.

She waited, watching him steadily. He began to squirm a little under the directness of her gaze. Then finally she shook her head slowly. "Why you, do you suppose?"

His head came up quickly. "Why me what?"

Caroline reached out with her other hand so that she held

his hand with both of hers. "Joshua, I won't force you to tell me anything, but I was sitting right beside you, remember? Something happened to you today."

"I saw nothing," he said sullenly.

"I know that you *saw* nothing," she said, repeating the one word with soft emphasis to let him know that she saw through his little ruse. Then it was as if he were no longer there and she was speaking to herself. "But why you? Father Steed neither saw nor heard anything unusual. Nathan. Rebecca. They didn't either. And they have never faltered in their faith. So why me and why you? It is strange."

And then, before he could answer—if he had wanted to answer—she stood. "I really am very tired, Joshua. Let's go to bed."

"All right."

They moved across the darkened room and into the hallway. Now the pale illumination from the lamp above shed more light on them. As they reached the stairs, Caroline stopped and turned to face him again. "Joshua?"

He sighed wearily. He was *not* going to say anything more about today. "Caroline, I don't want to—"

She lifted a hand and touched his lips, cutting him off. "Did you mean what you said to Nathan today? Do you really think the crisis is over?"

"Yes. Sidney is through."

"Then can we stop talking about leaving Nauvoo?"

It was her eyes that cut off his retort and kept him still. By "crisis" he assumed she meant the leadership crisis and he had answered accordingly. The other was another matter altogether. Walter Samuelson mentioned it in almost every letter he sent. His sources from Quincy and Warsaw were reporting that the opposition was intensifying, deepening, consolidating. He had some wonderful business opportunities for the family in St. Louis. Every day they delayed increased their danger. Joshua didn't feel the sense of urgency that his partner did, but he knew that the death of Joseph had not satisfied his enemies. His mouth opened slightly but then shut again. There was so much weariness there on her face, in her eyes, in the way her body seemed to droop, and he knew it was more than just the result of a long and tiring day. With Olivia's fatal accident and her own brush with death, Caroline's physical and emotional reserves were drained. She needed something to hold on to.

Finally he nodded. "All right," he said softly.

He saw the flicker of concern and knew that she knew what he was thinking. But it was enough, what he had said, and he also saw her instant gratitude. "Thank you, Joshua."

He slipped his arm around her waist and started up the stairs, helping her, feeling her lean against him as though the effort of climbing was too much for her all of a sudden.

She didn't speak again until she was in bed, propped up against her pillows, watching him fold up his shirt. When he finally turned and saw her watching him with those large green eyes, he stopped. "What?" he asked.

"What are you thinking about? You are frowning something horrible."

He chuckled. He had not been aware that his thoughts were showing so clearly on his face.

"Come on. Be honest now."

"I was thinking that I need to go to St. Louis. Walter has had to deal with all that flood damage by himself and—" He stopped, surprised by the smile on her face.

"I know you have to go, Joshua. And I know why you haven't dared leave me before now. But I'll be all right now. I really am doing much better."

He set the shirt on the top of the dresser. "Will is pretty good at taking care of you. If it weren't for—"

"Take Will with you, Joshua."

He turned, startled.

"I have your family. There is more help around than I can accept. Take Will with you."

"But why?"

She gave him a pitying look.

His eyes widened. "You mean Alice?"

"I mean Alice."

He reared back, his face wreathed with sudden pleasure. "Do you think something is developing there?"

"I think it has potential."

His eyes narrowed. "How can you tell? They've been such friends for so long, I didn't notice any difference when she was here."

She laughed. "That's why you married me."

He came over to the bed, reached down, and kissed her. "I didn't know just how smart I was that day I asked you," he murmured.

She kissed him back. "I did," she said with a wise smile.

He shook his head in wonder. Then he straightened, his mind going back to his original question. "You're sure you'll be all right?"

"I'll be fine. You take Will and go. Everything is going to be fine now."

———◆———

Will waited until he could stand it no longer. They were walking along Front Street, the street that ran alongside the bank of the Missouri River, a block or two before it joined the Mississippi. As soon as dinner was over, Alice had suggested that they come down here so Will could see with his own eyes the extent of the damage done by the great flood of two months previous. As they walked along, she pointed out this and that, chatting gaily, obviously happy to be in his presence. But now he could bear it no more.

"Alice?"

"Yes?"

"Have you started reading the Book of Mormon yet?"

Her step slowed and her chin dropped slightly, so he couldn't see her eyes. "Yes," she finally said.

"And?" he asked, half holding his breath.

She glanced at him briefly, then suddenly turned, pointing. "Look! There're the Baker warehouses," she said. "Old Mr. Baker wouldn't believe Papa. He moved his cotton to the loft and said it would be fine. Papa says he lost almost half a million dollars' worth of raw cotton."

Will had fallen a step behind her. He was staring after her. Had she not heard?

But as they moved forward, she went on as if he hadn't spoken. She darted here and there, rattling off facts about the greatest flood in St. Louis history—how many acres of farmland were ruined, the number of cattle that were drowned, the smell that filled the air, the businesses that had been damaged.

He listened, his mind only half on it. Clearly she had sidestepped his question and didn't want to answer it. He felt a deep gloom settle in on him. This was not a good sign.

Suddenly she dropped back and grabbed his hand. "Oh, come, Will! You must see this. They just put this up."

"What?"

She pulled him over to the side of the street, near a three-story warehouse and office building. There, beside one corner, was a stone monument, towering upwards eight or ten feet above the street. As they approached, he could see that letters had been chiseled into it.

"What is this?"

She didn't answer but pulled him around to the front of it. The inscription was simple. About two feet above Will's head a line had been cut into the stone across the width of the monument. Below it were the words: "High Water June 27, 1844."

"Oh," Will said, understanding now.

"Yes," Alice said eagerly. "That shows how high the water got. Eight feet above flood stage."

"No wonder," he said softly. Eight feet! How did you protect your cotton—or anything else, for that matter—from something eight feet above flood stage? He half closed his eyes, trying to imagine what this whole district must have been like.

"It was awful," Alice said, subdued now. "They're still not sure how many people died. There were riverboats up on the banks, like they had been pulled there by some angry giant of a child. Some buildings just collapsed from the pressure of the water."

Will leaned forward, peering at the inscription again. "June twenty-seventh?" he asked.

"Yes. That was the day it reached its highest point."

"Do you know what day June twenty-seventh is?"

She shook her head, puzzled. "No."

"It is the day that Joseph and Hyrum Smith were killed at Carthage."

"Hmm," she said, digesting that. "So?"

He shrugged. "Nothing. It's just an interesting coincidence. On the very day that the world made its ultimate rejection of the Lord's prophet—an act that would cause many Missourians to rejoice—you were undergoing a tragedy of your own down here."

"Are you saying that God caused this as a punishment?"

"No," he said quickly, wishing now he had said nothing. "I don't think God works that way. I was just struck by the oddity of it, that was all."

That seemed to satisfy her. She looked up at the sky. The sun had set now and evening was coming on quickly. "Maybe we'd better go," she suggested. "Front Street isn't the best place to be after dark."

"Okay."

She looked up and grinned at him. "So you like my word, do you?"

"Yep. I use it all the time now. Is that okay?"

"That's okay!" she said, laughing. And they turned around and started back the way they had come. They went about a block, when Alice glanced up at him, and then away again. "Will?"

"What?"

"I want to do this on my own."

That took him by surprise. "You want to do what on your own?"

"Find out about your church."

She ignored his astonished look and hurried on. "I don't want you asking me questions." There was a quick, impish grin. "If *I* have questions, I'll ask you, but I don't want you asking me how I'm doing. When I'm ready, one way or the other, I'll tell you. Fair enough?"

He was stunned. So she *had* heard his earlier question. And now here was her answer. "Of course," he finally said.

"Good." And with that it was as if the subject were totally forgotten again.

Chapter Notes

Though it was actually put in place a few months later than shown in the novel, there was a stone monument erected on Front Street in St. Louis commemorating the high-water mark of the great flood of 1844, which occurred on 27 June (see HC 7:316).

Chapter Ten

With the death of Joseph and Hyrum Smith, the enemies of the Church assumed that they had pulled the linchpin on the Church. The "Mormon problem" was solved. As news of the internal dispute over who should be the next leader leaked out, the anti-Mormons rejoiced. Surely this was the first sign of the foundation cracking. Even when Brigham Young—"Brigham who?" they scoffed—took over the reins, it did not raise their anxieties much. Whatever else they might have said about him, however strongly they may have hated him, no one disputed the fact that Joseph Smith was a powerful leader, and with his death the power was gone.

But such was not the case. Since the organization of the Quorum of the Twelve in 1835, Joseph had been grooming the Apostles for leadership, giving them more and more responsibility and greater and greater voice in the kingdom. Then, in an extraordinary council meeting held in March of 1844, the Prophet conferred the keys of the kingdom on the Twelve and specifically told them they were now empowered to lead the Church.

Many years later, President Wilford Woodruff, speaking of that meeting, said: "I remember the last speech that he [Joseph Smith] ever gave us before his death. It was before we started upon our mission to the East. He stood upon his feet some three hours. The room was filled as with consuming fire, his face was as clear as amber, and he was clothed upon by the power of God. He laid before us our duty. He laid before us the fullness of this great work of God; and in his remarks to us he said: 'I have had sealed upon my head every key, every power, every principle of life and salvation that God has ever given to any man who ever lived upon the face of the earth. And these principles and this Priesthood and power belong to this great and last dispensation which the God of Heaven has set His hand to establish in the earth. Now,' said he, addressing the Twelve, 'I have sealed upon your heads every key, every power, and every principle which the Lord has sealed upon my head.' . . .

"After addressing us in this manner he said: 'I tell you, the burden of this kingdom now rests upon your shoulders; you have got to bear it off in all the world, and if you don't do it you will be damned.'"

How little did they comprehend on that day that the time for the exercise of those keys would come so swiftly! They went east thinking they were going to help foster Joseph's candidacy for president of the United States. In actuality, Joseph sent them away so they would escape what lay ahead. During July and August of 1844, they returned to Nauvoo one by one or in small groups. They came home thinking to mourn their beloved Joseph. Instead, they found others already there clamoring for the crown.

In the days following the meeting in which Brigham and the Twelve were sustained to lead the Church, the Quorum met together often. They immediately began to exercise their leadership and to put in order the organization of the Church. Bishops Newel K. Whitney and George Miller were appointed to the office of trustee-in-trust for the Church so the Twelve could be relieved of demanding day-to-day supervision of the financial affairs of the Church. Individual members of the Twelve were given specific responsibilities. Wilford Woodruff was sent back to England to preside over the work there. Parley P. Pratt was asked to go to New York City and serve as president, publisher, and emigrant agent for the Church in the East. Lyman Wight went to Texas to look for a possible site for resettlement of the Church, an assignment given to him by Joseph before his death. John Taylor, still recovering from his wounds, was reassigned as editor of the *Times and Seasons* and later the *Nauvoo Neighbor* as well. Willard Richards stayed on as Church historian and recorder. Amasa Lyman was sustained as an Apostle once again. William Smith, one of the Twelve and the last surviving son of Joseph Smith, Sr., was appointed as Patriarch to the Church.

Other organizational changes were made so as to better administer a rapidly growing Church. The seventies were organized into quorums and seven presidents were called to preside over them. The United States and Canada were divided into Church districts, and it was decided that high priests would be called to preside over them. Aaronic Priesthood holders, which in the early days of the Church were mostly adult males, were brought into action as well. In Nauvoo and the other settlements around it, the teachers quorums were admonished to visit the homes of the Saints and to watch over the Church as had been outlined in the revelation given on the day the Church was organized. Deacons were asked to help the bishops in caring for the poor.

Not everyone was satisfied with the way things had gone on August eighth. Just as there had been during Joseph's life, there were opposing forces here too. Sidney Rigdon publicly accepted the vote of that day, but privately he was bitter and angry. Quietly he tried to undermine the leadership of Brigham Young. When he continued to maintain that his authority was superior to that of the Twelve, he was excommunicated on the eighth of September, one month to the day following his failed attempt to become guardian of the Church.

Others ever so humbly stepped up to claim they were the chosen one. A short time after the August eighth meeting, a man by the name of James J. Strang came forward. He had been baptized by Joseph Smith a few months before his death. Now Strang claimed he had a letter from Joseph which appointed him as Joseph's successor and which designated Voree, Wisconsin, as the gathering place for the Saints. Brigham and the Twelve stamped the letter as a blatant forgery and counseled Strang to withdraw his claims. Bright, proud, charismatic, he refused and started to sway others to follow his lead. He too was excommunicated.

As August passed and September came and went, things began at last to settle into a calmer and steadier course.

For the Steed family, it looked for a time as though things would do the same for them. They had experienced their own turmoil. Now a more stable and normal pattern of living seemed in the offing.

In late August, Rebecca and Derek made a joint announcement with Matthew and Jenny. In the late spring of 1842, the two women had given birth to babies—Rebecca a boy, and Jenny a girl—just eleven days apart. Now they announced that they would be giving Mary Ann and Benjamin two more grandchildren in the early spring, again within a few weeks of each other. If all went well, the two new ones would be the twenty-third and twenty-fourth living grandchildren. In early September, while visiting from Ramus, Jessica and Solomon Garrett announced that Jessica would make it number twenty-five in early to mid-April.

With Brigham's new role as leading officer in the Church, he virtually had to abandon his partnership with Matthew in the carpentry and cabinet shop. Ever more skilled in his woodworking expertise, Matthew expanded the shop once, then a second time as the growth in Nauvoo continued unchecked. He hired a second full-time apprentice and then a third and a fourth.

Carl also benefitted from the continuing building boom. He

ran the brick kilns from dawn to dark six days a week and still could not keep pace with demand. Neither he nor Melissa attended worship services anymore, though they did not stop Jane Manning from taking the children each Sunday. The women of the clan made no more attempts to convince Melissa that plural marriage was a principle revealed from God. "We'll just show Melissa that we love her no matter how she feels," Mary Ann said to the others one day, a few weeks after Carl and Melissa had returned. "Hopefully her heart will soften as time passes. But if not, well, she's still our Melissa and that doesn't change how we feel about her."

In a similar fashion, Joshua determined that he would say no more to Caroline about leaving Nauvoo. But that didn't change his mind about the need to do so. In September, just as things were settling down again for the Saints, Levi Williams, of Green Plains, just south of Warsaw, called for a great "wolf hunt." Williams was one of the men who had led the mob from Warsaw that had stormed the Carthage Jail and killed Joseph and Hyrum. Since wolves were now an extreme rarity in this section of the country, there was little question in anyone's mind but what the call was nothing more than a thinly disguised excuse to ride against the Mormons. Nevertheless, it was advertised in many newspapers throughout Hancock County and stirred up considerable excitement.

Stung by statewide criticism that it was his lack of forceful leadership that had allowed the deaths of the two Smith brothers, Governor Thomas Ford reacted with uncharacteristic swiftness. He sent a contingent of state militia to Warsaw with instructions to stay through the winter and keep the peace. The wolf hunt fizzled out almost as quickly as it had begun.

But all of this only convinced Joshua more strongly than ever that Samuelson was right. It was going to be only a matter of time before this whole thing exploded, and Nauvoo would be right in the middle of it. Quietly, not even articulating his strategy to Will, he began some long-range preparations. He and Will made additional trips downriver to St. Louis. Twice Samuelson came to Nauvoo, bringing Alice with him both times. It was a simple plan and, as was typical of most of Joshua's dealings, profitable as well. New business enterprises were undertaken in St. Louis, each one carefully chosen with the idea that eventually a family member could come into it and find employment. The two partners bought a struggling construction company and aggressively went after the booming St. Louis building market. They added the subsidiary businesses that were needed to handle both commercial and residential building projects—a sawmill to process the great rafts of lumber coming down from Joshua's Wisconsin pineries operation; a brickyard, chosen only after careful consultation with Carl; a foundry; a milling shop.

As for Alice and Will, she was true to her word. As the months went on, she said nothing more about the Church or her investigation of it. Will knew that when she was in Nauvoo she peppered other family members, particularly the women, with questions. But she never asked him anything, nor did she give him any indications of her feelings. Though it drove him to distraction, he kept his word to her as well and never once pushed her for details.

On the third day of October, 1844, a huge wooden crate arrived at the south riverboat dock with Joshua Steed's name on it. It was the Knabe piano he had ordered three months before. Though Olivia's birthday wasn't until November third, they decided not to wait. It was unpacked and assembled, to the great celebration of the family, and set up in Caroline's parlor. The old piano was given to Nathan and Lydia, who started Emily on piano lessons at the same time that Caroline started Savannah. On the front of the piano, above the ivory keys, Joshua placed a small engraved metal plaque. It read simply:

In memory of Olivia Mendenhall Steed
November 3, 1827, to June 13, 1844
Happy Birthday, Livvy!

Five days later, on Tuesday morning, October eighth, the third day of October's conference meetings, any thoughts that the Steeds' family life was going to be normal ended once and for all.

———•———

It had been a wonderful conference thus far. The questions that had divided the Saints about who would follow in the footsteps of Joseph were behind them. The call for the "wolf hunt" had been put down with dispatch because for once the state government was acting like a state government. Things were calm, though certainly not amiable. The Church was moving forward and organizing itself to cope with the continuing growth. Benjamin considered all of those as good omens.

Brigham had spoken, of course, and taken most of Sunday morning's meeting. To everyone's surprise, John Taylor spoke to the afternoon assembly. It was his first public address since being gunned down at Carthage. He still carried some of the remnants of the balls that had struck him in his body. He was pale and still down by fifteen pounds or more, but he spoke with power and authority. More than one pair of eyes—male and female—shed tears that day, touched by what they saw before them.

Monday was devoted to business. The authorities were sustained—the local stake and quorum authorities as well as the Twelve and the Presiding Bishopric. Then Parley Pratt and Heber Kimball addressed the congregation. Brigham had concluded the meeting, startling everyone near the end of his speech when he began to talk about those who had fallen as martyrs. At first, Benjamin had thought he was simply reaffirming the fact that Joseph had not fallen before his time. He reminded the congregation of that day when Joseph and Hyrum had been arrested at Far West. As they were loaded in a wagon, some of the Missouri militia rushed forward, snapping their pistols and trying to shoot them. But it was not Joseph's time to go, he reminded them. Every gun had misfired that day.

"The Lord never let a prophet fall on the earth until he had accomplished his work," Brigham went on. "And the Lord did not take Joseph until he had finished his work, and it is the greatest blessing to Joseph and Hyrum God could bestow to take them away, for they had suffered enough."

Then suddenly he had brought every adult head in the congregation up with a snap.

"They are not the only martyrs that will have to die for the truth," he cried. "There are men before me today who will be martyrs, and who will have to seal their testimony with their blood."

Benjamin did not remember much of what was said after that. He had been so struck by the words that nothing else registered. He looked around again even now—at his own family, at the Twelve, at the various other leaders. And some of those would die for their testimony? That was enough to sober any man.

This morning they had assembled for the third day of meetings. Benjamin could tell the crowd had lightened somewhat. Many from outlying areas, such as Solomon and his family, had to return to the last of the harvest or to other occupations. But there were still several thousand gathered together for the last day. John Taylor had just finished speaking about some new economic policies to be inaugurated in Nauvoo. As he finished, Heber C. Kimball stood up.

"Brethren and sisters, President Young will speak to us shortly, but I have a matter of business first. As you know, the call of the seventy is to take the gospel into all the world. The elders are to watch over the Church, the high priests to administer in all spiritual things. But it is the role of the seventy to carry the word to the world and proclaim the gospel. There is much to do in that regard, brethren, and the number of our seventies is limited. We have sent elders and priests out as missionaries, but primarily this should be the work of the seventies. Elder George A. Smith, therefore, has a proposal."

George A. Smith, a large man by any standards, was soon up and out of his chair and standing beside his fellow Apostle. "Brothers and sisters, I would like to propose that all men who are currently in the elders quorum who are under the age of thirty-five be ordained into the seventies, assuming they are in good standing, are worthy, and will accept the calling."

"Second the motion," someone cried.

"All in favor?" Heber asked. Hands came up all over the place, though now the crowd had erupted in a low rumble of sound.

Matthew and Jenny, sitting beside Kathryn in her wheelchair, looked at each other in surprise. Matthew was an elder. He was currently twenty-four years old. He qualified. Derek and Rebecca were staring at each other as well. Derek was an elder. He would turn twenty-seven next week. He would become a seventy. Will and Peter sat beside each other. Peter was still only a priest and a member of the Aaronic Priesthood, but Will had been made an elder prior to his mission to England. He was twenty now. He qualified. With one quick motion, seconded and sustained, the Steeds had just gained three seventies in the family.

The question was unspoken but clear on their faces. The seventies were called to do missionary service. Usually that happened in the fall, when the harvest was in and winter kept many men basically unemployed for the next five or six months. Now they had three seventies. Rebecca dropped her head, not wanting Derek to see her sudden tears. Jenny reached out and took Matthew's hand. They looked at each other for a long time. Caroline tried to catch Will's eye, but he was staring off into space, probably thinking about Alice and what this now meant for them.

Benjamin watched it all, feeling a sudden exhilaration, and yet at the same time a pang of sorrow. The exhilaration came from thinking about members of the family going into the missionary labor again. Nathan in Toronto. Derek and Matthew and Will in England. What a blessing all of those had been to the family! His sorrow came from knowing that he would not be part of it. It was eleven years ago now that he had been baptized. For eleven years he had longed for the opportunity to go out and be a missionary. For eleven years, the Lord evidently had not felt like he could provide that kind of service to the kingdom. Oh, Joseph had tried to dissuade him from having those feelings, telling him that Benjamin's services were needed elsewhere—on the Kirtland Temple building committee, helping lay out Nauvoo. It was not that Benjamin doubted what he said. It was not that he resented the service he had given. It was just that he had not ever been a missionary. And now his son and son-in-law and his grandson might get that privilege. And once again, he would be left here, a graying old man, keeping the kingdom together but not doing much to expand its reach.

Heber C. Kimball sat down and Brigham stood. He looked around the congregation, nodding in satisfaction. "Brethren," he said, looking from face to face at those who held the priesthood. "We have another organizational matter to attend to. As you know, shortly after our return from the East, and after we were sustained by your hand, we announced that the United States would be divided into districts, based on the congressional districts, and that we would send out high priests to preside over those branches and to build up the Church."

Benjamin's head came up.

"We have eighty-five names of high priests here. We would now like to extend those calls as follows."

Benjamin was suddenly all ears. He was a high priest. The call to the seventies had just passed him by, but he was a *high* priest. A short distance away, Benjamin saw Lydia stiffen. Nathan was a high priest too, and suddenly Benjamin realized what such a call would mean for them and their young family. Earlier he had heard Brigham explain that this branch presidency was not to be some short-term call. "The design," he had said, "is not to go out for six months and then return, but to go and settle down. Take your families and tarry there until the temple is built. Then come and get your endowments, and then you can return and build up stakes there as large as what we have in Nauvoo."

For Benjamin and Mary Ann that would mean leaving the family. And that would be painful somewhat. But for Nathan and Lydia, it would mean taking five children; it would mean leaving the store, their primary source of income.

He felt Mary Ann's hand take his arm as Brigham opened a large sheet of paper and squinted down at it. He didn't dare look at her. He was barely breathing.

"David Evans. Abraham O. Smoot. Edson Whipple."

Benjamin was straining, almost flinching at every name. That the list was not alphabetical was the first thing he noted. So there was no relaxing until they got to the S's. But then he felt a stab of disappointment. He knew all three men. David Evans was about forty, as was Whipple. Smoot was about thirty. It wasn't a surprise. These men were in their prime. And he was fifty-nine now. Fifty-nine!

"Harvey Green. J. S. Fullmer."

He knew neither of those two, so that didn't help, except to confirm that this was not an alphabetical list. He turned to look at Mary Ann. "You don't think . . . ?" she started, but he shook his head. "Nathan," he responded. "I'll bet they call Nathan."

They both turned back. Brigham was reading the name of each man slowly, in a loud, ringing voice. It seemed to Benjamin that he was pausing for thirty or forty seconds between every name. And then he became aware of the sounds around him, the reactions as the voice intoned each name. There were soft "aahs," or the quick intake of breath.

"D. B. Huntington."

The Huntingtons were sitting just two or three rows ahead of them. Benjamin heard a gasp, then saw Sister Huntington's shoulders slump.

Brigham didn't seem to notice the cries of either dismay or elation rising all around him now. "Lorenzo Snow. William Snow. Noah Packard. Elijah Fordham. Franklin D. Richards."

Mary Ann turned to look at Lydia. Her head was down, her hands clasped tightly together. Her eyes were not closed but just stared downward, registering every name with dread. And then

Mary Ann saw her lips moving and realized that Lydia was counting. There were eighty-five names, Brigham said. With every one that passed, Nathan's chances went down.

Brigham was well past forty names now, and Nathan Steed was still uncalled. Mary Ann turned back to Benjamin, watching him closely now, feeling his hope, hurting with his growing despair. He wanted it so badly. Not the position, but the opportunity to feel like he was of service. And yet, like Lydia, she felt a sense of dread. It would be wonderful in one way, but oh, what it would mean for her! To leave the family. To be gone when Rebecca and Jenny and Jessica all had their babies. To miss the baptisms, the birthdays. She felt a sudden pain. Christmas around the piano at Joshua's house. If Benjamin got his wish, they would not be here at Christmas.

When it finally came, she nearly missed it. She was listening to the names with such intensity that for a moment it sounded like the name of a stranger.

"E. T. Benson. *Benjamin Steed.* Shadrach Roundy. E. D. Woolley."

The family gasped and jerked around to stare at Benjamin, who was thunderstruck. And then, seeing their eyes upon him, he let a slow grin steal across his face. He was shaking his head and beaming like a young boy.

Any dread Mary Ann felt was swept away in that instant. The look was of such supernal joy that, for now, she felt only his pleasure, only his vast relief. Later she could think about what it would mean to her.

But Lydia's ordeal was not over. Mary Ann turned to agonize with her. She was counting aloud now, in a whisper, but audibly enough that Mary Ann could hear her words. "Eighty-one. Eighty-two." Her fingers were digging into Nathan's arm.

"Titus Billings."

"Eighty-three."

"Harvey Olumstead."

"Eighty-four."

Brigham looked up, and smiled. "And finally, Daniel Stanton."

A great whoosh of air went out of Lydia and Nathan at the same time. They looked at each other and Lydia slowly released her grip on him. Then they too grinned, but it was a smile of relief and not exultation.

———•———

That night Brigham came. He came to Benjamin's home, but he had sent word ahead with Matthew. He asked for others to come there as well. And so they did. Nathan and Lydia. Derek and Rebecca. Matthew and Jenny. During the hours before his coming, they speculated on what this might mean. Perhaps more high priests were to be added to the list. Maybe it was a call for missionary work for Nathan as well. That was almost certainly why Matthew and Derek were told to come. Lydia's agony began in earnest all over again. This time it was shared by Jenny and Rebecca.

Once he arrived, there was little delay in getting to what he had on his mind. Brigham was heavily occupied now with leading the Church and, particularly after a conference, he didn't have a lot of time for idle talk.

"Benjamin," he began, "I watched your face today as I read your name. Can I take that as a yes to your calling?"

"Yes, Brother Brigham," he said joyfully, still reeling a little from the wonder of it all.

Brigham gave Mary Ann a querying look.

"You know the answer is yes, President," she said immediately.

"And I know what that will mean to you, dear Mary Ann. Thank you."

"Have you decided where we shall be asked to go?" she asked.

He nodded. "I'd like Benjamin to preside in Nashville."

"Nashville!" Nathan exclaimed.

"Yippee!" Matthew yelped, slapping his father on the back. "Nashville, imagine that."

Brigham waited until the congratulations were through. "I

know it will take a while to get your affairs in order, but as soon as you can, we'd ask you to depart. It won't be long before the ice is on the river, and then you'll have to wait until spring or go overland."

"We've talked about it this afternoon," Benjamin said, looking at Mary Ann for confirmation. "We think we can be ready in about a week."

She nodded firmly.

"Good." Now Brigham turned to Nathan and Lydia. Though neither of them moved, the tension in Lydia was obvious. Her eyes were fastened on Brigham's, as if he were about to give her the secret to everlasting life. "You may have wondered if you were going to be called as well, Nathan."

"When you said it would be high priests, I did," he admitted.

"Your name was put forward, but I took it off the list."

Lydia jerked forward a little, her eyes widening even more than they already were.

Brigham chuckled softly. "With your father going, this family is going to need someone at the head. That will be your role until your parents can return."

"You mean here?" Lydia blurted. "You want us to stay here?"

Brigham laughed aloud. "Unless you'd like Nathan to try and keep track of things from St. Louis or somewhere."

Her face colored and she gave a soft, self-deprecating laugh. "I'm sorry, President. You know that we would go anywhere you asked."

"I do. But . . . ?" he prompted.

The smile burst from her like the late afternoon sun suddenly striking the waters on a lake. "But I'm so glad we don't have to go right now."

"I know." He swung around to the other two couples. "Unfortunately, the news is not so good for you two sisters."

Rebecca and Jenny both looked at him steadily. "We expected no less, President Young," Jenny finally said. "And we shall support Matthew and Derek in whatever you require of them."

"I know that too," he said in a low voice. "And that means

a great deal to me." Then he straightened, looking at the two men. "I saw the missionary service you two gave while in England. You have proven yourselves as able emissaries for the Lord."

Rebecca sagged a little as she heard the mention of England. If Brigham noted it, he gave no sign.

"Can we serve together again?" Derek asked.

"Of course."

They both smiled at that.

"When and where?" Jenny asked in a tiny voice.

"And for how long?" Rebecca added.

"Well," Brigham said, frowning slightly, "after the determination was made to call these two young men, I heard that both of you are with child. Is that correct?"

"Yes," Mary Ann answered for them as they both blushed a little and ducked their heads. "Both are due about the middle of March."

"Then I shall have them back to you before that." He turned to Matthew and Derek. "I should like you to leave as soon as possible. Your field of labor shall be in the state of Arkansas."

Again he waited while the others reacted to that. Then he looked at Matthew. "You must feel as though I'm trying to destroy your efforts to make a go of the cabinet shop. First I leave you to run it by yourself, now I send you away as well."

"It will be all right. I have some excellent help now."

"I know," Brigham said wryly. "I checked that out first."

"What about the others?" Derek spoke up. "Will? Peter?"

"No, I think we've taken enough from this family for now. Actually, Peter's name was considered to accompany you two, or perhaps some other missionaries, but John Taylor howled like he'd been shot all over again. He says that without Peter at the newspaper office, the whole thing would collapse. And Will? Well, all things considered—his father, his mother's health—I think it's best to wait for a time."

He stood, taking his hat in hand. "Well, I'd best be off. I have others I must see."

They all stood and moved with him to the door.

"Thank you, Brother Brigham," Mary Ann said. "Thank you for taking the time to come and tell us this personally."

"No thanks are necessary. The Twelve are making most of the other calls, but I told them I had to see the Steeds myself." He stopped, looking first at Mary Ann and then to Benjamin. "Do you know what I would give," he said, his voice suddenly gruff, "if I had a hundred families like you? A thousand? Why, we'd have the world converted by Christmas and be welcoming back the city of Enoch by New Year's Day."

He clasped Benjamin's hand, shook it once with great fervor, waved to the others, and walked out the door, leaving the Steeds to assess what had just happened to them.

———◆———

That same night, less than half an hour after Jenny and Matthew had returned home with the news, there was a soft knock on Kathryn's door. She looked up from her journal. "Come in."

It was Jenny. She stepped inside the bedroom and shut the door behind her. "Peter's here," she said.

"Oh. Tell him he can come in."

But Jenny didn't move. "Kathryn?"

She looked up, suddenly wary. Was this going to be another sisterly lecture? Three times now Jenny had caught her trying to move about on the crutches and had given her stern rebukes. The crutches now hung in the armoire, where she could get them only if someone helped her. And Jenny and Matthew had both noted the sudden drop in Peter's visits to the house. Jenny had pumped her unmercifully to know what had happened. When Kathryn had finally told her what she had done and why, Jenny was furious with her. And now she had that look in her eyes again. "What?" Kathryn said shortly.

"Peter wanted badly to go on a mission," Jenny said, ignoring the tartness in Kathryn's voice.

"So?"

"John Taylor thinks his mission is here, helping with the paper."

"So do I. What Peter does there is very important."

"But staying here doesn't solve his problem."

"What problem?"

"You."

"Jenny, don't start again on that."

"I'm not starting anything," she shot right back. "I'm just telling you. Peter has to stay. I know how you feel, Kathryn, in spite of all you say. I know you don't want to hurt him."

"I don't," she admitted meekly.

"So just stop it."

"I can't," she whispered.

"Yes, you can," Jenny said, more kindly now. "I'm not saying you have to give him any hope that you will change your mind. That's your decision. But you can stop treating him like *he* is the problem."

Then, without waiting for an answer, she turned and walked to the door. She opened it and looked out. "Come in, Peter. She's ready."

As Jenny left the room, Peter came in, hat in one hand, a small book in the other. For a moment Kathryn was afraid it might be the book that he wrote his poems in, but then she saw, with relief, that it was not.

"Hello, Kathryn."

"Good evening, Peter. Come, sit down."

"I can only stay for a few minutes."

"Because of you or because of me?" she asked.

His eyes got that startled look, like a deer that has just seen a sudden movement in the forest. Kathryn had a way of doing that to him, and she felt a wave of shame.

"I . . . I'm not sure what you mean."

"Just sit down, Peter," she said, reaching across and patting the chair beside her bed. "Pull the chair around so I can see you."

He did so, setting the hat and book on the small table

behind the chair. She watched him settle in, feeling a deep pain as she studied the features that she knew so well. As usual, one lock of his thick dark hair had fallen down over his forehead, and, as usual, he reached up and brushed it back with ink-stained fingers, barely conscious of what he was doing. His eyes, pale blue and seemingly open into the depths of his soul, were gentle, inquisitive, filled with the caring he had for her. His features, which Derek said he had inherited from their mother, were smooth and fine, making him look more like he was eighteen years old than twenty. She wanted to close her eyes, for she had every detail, every tiny line and wrinkle and every faint freckle memorized.

Growing uncomfortable under her gaze, he leaned forward. "I guess you heard about Matthew and Derek," he said tentatively.

"I did. Does that make you sad?"

"In a way."

"But in another way it should make you feel very good."

"Why?"

She gave him an incredulous look. "You have an Apostle of the Lord who says that what you're doing here is more important than going out to serve a mission and you ask why?"

He shrugged. "Elder Taylor is very kind."

"Elder Taylor is very wise," she corrected him.

He sat quietly, clearly uncomfortable under her penetrating gaze. She knew Jenny was right. She had been punishing Peter for her own frustrations. Now she wasn't sure what to do about it. Then, realizing that she knew only one way to go about it, she took a quick breath. "Peter, I didn't mean to hurt you."

He gulped, looking more cornered than ever. "What?"

"When I stopped you from . . . well, from saying what you were going to say that day. It was not a good day for me and . . . Well, what I mean is . . . I'm sorry."

"It's all right. I think I understand."

She slapped angrily at the covers of the bed. "Peter, stop

being so nice. Why don't you just tell me that I acted like a spoiled brat, that I treated you abominably, and that I ought to have my bottom spanked?"

He was gaping at her, and then a strange look stole into his eyes. "Well," he started very slowly, "sometimes I do think you ought to have your bottom spanked."

She blinked, then blinked again. "I beg your pardon," she said, not in protest, but in complete shock.

"Well," he grinned sheepishly, "you asked." He reached up and pushed back the lock of hair again.

Leaning back against the pillows, eyeing him as though he were a complete stranger, she spoke slowly. "Say that again. I'm not sure I heard you right."

"I said I think there are times that you ought to have your bottom spanked." Pleased by the new respect he saw in her eyes, he decided to go further. "Not that it would do any good."

"Peter Ingalls!" she cried in dismay, but smiling broadly as she did so.

"Well," he said, "you act like I don't know one thing about what's going on here. Well, you're wrong. I do understand. I think I know how you feel about me, and I think I know why you keep pushing me away."

Now it was her that was starting to squirm. This was pushing in too close to her vulnerability. And as usual, her defense was anger. "I'm not sure you do," she snapped.

He bristled right back. "Well, if I don't, it sure isn't your fault. You've been so honest and open with me, sharing everything about how you feel."

She felt her face burning. "I think you'd better go, Peter."

"Oh no. No you don't. Not this time." He stood, too agitated to remain seated anymore. "I've been thinking about this all afternoon. I should be overjoyed that I didn't get a call to be a missionary today. I should be happy that I get to stay where I can see you, be close to you. Instead, I've never been more disappointed."

He swung around, then swung instantly back. "Do you know

why I came tonight? To tell you that I'm going to John Taylor tomorrow and telling him I don't care about the paper anymore. I'm going to beg him to let me go with Derek and Matthew."

She was staring at him now, half in horror, half in numbed shock. "You don't mean that," she whispered.

"I do mean it, Kathryn!" He started pacing back and forth; then, on impulse, he spun around and stalked to her armoire. Jerking the doors open, he reached inside. When he turned, he was holding one of her crutches. "You think I care one minute that you have to use these?"

She turned her face toward the wall. "I can't use those, Peter. I can't even stand up on them."

He jammed it back in the armoire. "I don't care! But what I can't bear are those other crutches you keep using." He tapped his head. "The ones up here, Kathryn. Those are the crutches you use all the time—self-pity, anger, rejection of me."

She was without a response. His words lashed at her like cords; but that he was saying them to her, that he felt such anger of his own, struck her dumb. Was this what she had done to her quiet, gentle Peter?

"Do you remember that poem I once wrote for you, right after the accident?"

She still held her journal in her hands. She opened it to the back and withdrew a folded piece of paper and waved it at him. She nodded, not trusting her voice.

He came back across the room. The anger was gone now. All that was left was pleading. "Do you remember the last few stanzas?"

Remember them? She had memorized them long ago, and hardly a day passed without her reciting them in her mind. She put the paper back in her journal and set it on the bed. Her head came up. There were no tears, only a firm determination to get through it without breaking.

" 'What bars of earthly form—,' " she began softly, " ' Steel or iron, wind or storm—Can bind to earth my boundless heart; Stopping me from pushing back the night? My freedom lies within—Only sorrow, only sin—' " She had to stop and take a breath before she could go on. "'Only sorrow, only sin—Can clip my inner wings; And bind me tight.'"

There was a long silence, and then, in a bare whisper, "'Shackles of my own are all that stay my flight.'"

He came back over and sat down, heavily, wearily, resignedly. "I'm sorry, Kathryn. I didn't come here to say all that."

She nodded, her face calm now. She turned her head, looking at the small table. "You brought a book?"

There was a short, mirthless laugh. "Yes."

"Read it to me."

His head came up slightly. "Now?"

"Yes."

"All of it?"

She nodded again, her eyes misting now.

Looking a little befuddled, he turned and got the book and opened it. "It's a book of poetry by an English poet, Robert Browning. It's called *Pippa Passes*." He looked up again. "It's a long narrative poem."

"Read it to me."

And then as he opened the book and turned to the first page, she spoke quietly. "Peter. I don't want you to get your hopes up. I don't know if I can ever change how I feel about—" She faltered momentarily. "About the future. But I would like you to read to me again."

For a long, long time—what almost seemed like five minutes to her—he scanned her face, probed her eyes, searched her soul, and then he finally nodded slowly. "I would like that too," he said. And then with a smile, he flipped some pages. "I'll come back and read from the first in a minute, but there's one line here that I've got to read to you."

"All right."

She watched him, loving how his brow puckered ever so slightly as he concentrated. And then he had it. He looked up. "Just two lines, but I think they are particularly appropriate right now."

"Read them to me."

He didn't look down. Like her, he had these committed to memory. "'God's in his heaven,'" he said, very softly, "'All's right with the world!'"

Ten days later, on the afternoon of October seventeenth, over thirty weeping family members gathered at the boat dock at the south end of Main Street. With heavy hearts, the Steeds watched their father and mother, grandfather and grandmother, walk up the gangplank onto the *Golden Dawn*, a medium-sized riverboat out of Memphis, Tennessee. Benjamin and Mary Ann would travel by boat down to where the Ohio River joined the Mississippi at Cairo (which the locals pronounced "Karo"), Illinois. They were accompanied by Derek and Matthew, who would continue downriver as far as Memphis, then strike off by land for Little Rock.

As the great whistle blew and the boat backed away from the dock, Jenny and Rebecca stood side by side, both showing their coming motherhood, both holding the hands of young children who would now be without their fathers for the next four months. Only when the boat finally disappeared around a bend in the river did they and the children stop waving and turn to go back to their homes.

Chapter Notes

A good summary of this period of time in the Church's history is found in *CHFT*, pp. 293–307, and in *American Moses*, pp. 117–24.

The remarks of Wilford Woodruff concerning the March 1844 meeting with Joseph are quoted exactly as given (cited in *CHFT*, p. 294).

Amasa Lyman was re-sustained to the apostleship on 12 August 1844. He had been called as an Apostle in 1842 when Orson Pratt became embittered and was dropped from the Quorum. When Elder Pratt repented and was reinstated, Elder Lyman dropped out of the Quorum, and Joseph Smith took him into the First Presidency, though he was not considered a counselor in the same sense as were Hyrum Smith and Sidney Rigdon. At Joseph's death, the First Presidency was dissolved. Brigham then presented Elder Lyman's name to the Church to become an Apostle again. However, since that would make thirteen Apostles, Elder Lyman was not made a member of the Quorum of the Twelve until there was a later vacancy. (See HC 7:295; Deseret News 1993–1994 Church Almanac [Salt Lake City: Deseret News, 1992], p. 51; CHFT, p. 292.)

After his excommunication in September, Sidney Rigdon moved back to Pittsburgh and in the spring of 1845 started a "Church of Christ" with apostles, prophets, priests, and kings. He published a newspaper for a time and drew a small group of supporters. By 1847, his organization had mostly disintegrated. Sidney held on to a few followers for the next thirty years and finally died in obscurity in New York State.

William Marks continued to support Sidney's claims of leadership after the 8 August meeting. At the October 1844 conference, the Saints refused to sustain him as president of the Nauvoo Stake any longer and he was released from that position. (See HC 7:296.) He aligned himself with Rigdon's movement for a time, but later became disillusioned and followed the Strangite movement. Finally, he became part of the group that formed the Reorganized Church of Jesus Christ of Latter Day Saints.

James J. Strang, a man of strong and persuasive personality, eventually won over three former Apostles: William E. McLellin, John E. Page, and William Smith. McLellin had been excommunicated in 1838; Smith, in 1845; and Page, in 1846. For a time Strang was also supported by Martin Harris and William Marks, former president of the Nauvoo Stake. In 1849, Strang located his colony on an island in Lake Michigan and pronounced himself as "king of the kingdom." In 1856, Strang was murdered by a disaffected member of his group and the Strangite movement collapsed. (See CHFT, pp. 294–95.)

William Smith was sustained as Patriarch to the Church in October 1844, but for a variety of reasons his ordination was delayed until May 1845. Still a member of the Quorum of the Twelve, he gave some patriarchal blessings but then began to put forth his own claims to be Church leader. He was excommunicated in October 1845. He followed James Strang for a brief time, then began to put forth the idea that Joseph Smith III, the oldest son of Joseph, was the rightful successor to his father. Since Joseph III was still but a boy, William offered to be "guardian and president pro tem" until young Joseph was of age. (See CHFT, p. 295.) For a number of years William vacillated between the Church in Utah and the Reorganized Church, eventually joining the latter organization in 1878.

Rebecca Ingalls was bundled up tightly in coat, muffler, rubber galoshes—a recent innovation from the East that had become very popular in Nauvoo—and mittens. The galoshes proved more helpful for warmth than for wet, as the temperature was barely in the mid-twenties this morning and the streets and sidewalks were frozen hard. It was only the tenth day of December, 1844, but already they had had several major snowstorms and severe cold. It was starting off to be a hard winter. A wind was blowing straight out of the north and cut through even the thickest layer of clothing. She shivered, watching the wind snatch the vapor of her breath away, and she walked more quickly along.

As she approached the small house of Mary Fielding Smith and Mercy Fielding Thompson, she shook her head. What a sad change for these two widowed sisters! When Joseph and Emma moved from the Homestead into the Mansion House in the fall of 1843, Hyrum moved his family into the Homestead. By then his family included Mercy Thompson and her one child as well as Mary and their own children. After the death of his brother-in-law Robert Thompson, and under a direct commandment from the Lord through Joseph, Hyrum had taken Mercy Thompson as his second wife.

The Homestead, quite roomy now with the additions Joseph had added over the past several years, was a wonderful blessing to the family, especially when Hyrum was killed and left the two sisters widowed. Then, just a few weeks ago, Emma, facing her own financial problems, decided to rent out the Mansion House to President Marks and move back into the Homestead. So the two sisters and their children had to go. Now they lived in this small house with barely enough room to turn around in.

Rebecca remembered clearly the day that the two Fielding sisters came to Kirtland with their brother Joseph Fielding. Since Nathan had been with Parley Pratt in Toronto and had been instrumental in helping bring the family into the Church, along with John and Leonora Taylor, the Canadians came to visit the Steeds. Though Mary was almost seventeen years Rebecca's senior, the two had almost instantly become close friends, and that friendship had endured until now.

Rebecca went through the gate and up to the door and knocked, pulling off her mittens after doing so. Almost immediately the door opened and Mary was smiling warmly at her. "Oh, Rebecca, how good to see you! Come in, come in."

———

They sat near the small metal stove in one corner of the only sitting room, sipping warm herbal tea. Off in the back room, Rebecca could hear the children playing some sort of game. She smiled. The house might be small and the firewood barely adequate to keep it heated, but there was plenty of warmth and happiness in this house.

"So," Mary asked, "have you heard from Derek yet?"

"Yes, just two days ago. They wrote about two weeks before that. They have arrived in Little Rock and found a small shed behind the home of a member of the Church where they can stay rent free. He said they will have to work for a week or two to get sufficient funds to see them through the winter, but they have already started holding meetings." She sipped her tea. "It's still too early to tell what kind of success they will have."

"Are you doing all right?" Mercy asked.

Rebecca nodded. How like these two good women. Here they were, widowed on a permanent basis, not just for four months, living in a home a third the size of Rebecca's, and they were asking if *she* was getting along all right. She put the cup back in the saucer and looked at the two of them. "The children are still struggling a little. Last night, after we had said prayers, I noticed that little Benjamin was crying. When I asked him why, he asked two questions. 'Where is Papa?' was the first. When I explained that Papa was a missionary in Arkansas, that seemed to satisfy him. His next question was, 'When can I see Grandma Steed?' I'm afraid that then I started to cry too because I had to tell him that we didn't know for sure how soon Grandma would return."

Mary shook her head sadly. "When you're only two years old, it's hard to understand such things." She looked deliberately at the roundness of Rebecca's belly. "Are you all right?"

Rebecca laid a hand on her stomach, remembering when, with her second pregnancy, she first realized that things were different than they had been when she had carried Christopher. Finally in concern she had gone to see John C. Bennett, who was a doctor, setting off a whole chain of events that were not happy memories for her. "Yes," she said gratefully, "everything's fine this time."

"And how are your parents doing?" Mercy asked. "They made it to Nashville all right?"

"Oh, yes. We've had two letters from Mama now. She says Papa is reveling in the work. That's the word she used. She said she has never seen him derive so much satisfaction from what he's doing."

"That's wonderful," Mary said. "Your father is such a good man. I just love him. I would love to be in his branch."

Now Rebecca decided to change the subject away from her and the family. She had already inquired about how the two sisters were getting along, so she asked another question. "Tell me, Mercy, what is this I hear about the penny fund?"

Mercy, the younger of the two, and in her mid-thirties now, leaned back, smiling with pleasure. "You heard about President Young's request?"

"Only briefly. Tell me."

"Well, you remember how this whole thing came about, don't you?"

"I do. I remember Hyrum making the announcement at the Christmas party last year."

"It was a direct answer to prayer, you know. I watched how hard Hyrum and the brethren were working to complete the temple and I wanted to know what I could do as a sister. And then the answer came, clear as the ringing of a bell. 'Get the sisters to contribute one cent per week to the temple fund.'" Her eyes had softened with the memory. "One cent per week isn't much—just barely more than fifty cents per year, but I knew that if we could get all the sisters to contribute, we could perhaps get enough to help purchase window glass and nails for the roof, two of the commodities that we cannot make ourselves."

"It was a wonderful idea," Rebecca said enthusiastically. "Mary told me the other day that you have collected five or six hundred dollars."

"Closer to six hundred, I think. We have a large bag"— Mercy held out her arms to demonstrate—"a very large bag of pennies now."

"And heavy," Mary came in. "We had to find a place in that pile of bricks out back to hide it."

"So tell me about President Young," said Rebecca.

"Well," Mercy went on, thoughtful now, "about ten days ago, President Young wrote to us. He said the Church was facing a serious financial crisis. There were some notes coming due for land held in the name of the trustees-in-trust for the Church.

Thirty-one hundred dollars was needed within ninety days as payment on the notes."

"Whew!" Rebecca exclaimed. "Over three thousand dollars!" In a society that was not rich in cash, that was a small fortune.

"Yes, but one-third of that amount was needed immediately or the title holders were threatening to foreclose on the property."

Now Mary came in again. "Brigham said the land is worth some ten to fifteen thousand dollars, so to lose it would be a major blow to the Church."

"But the Church simply does not have a thousand dollars in cash right now," Mercy went on, nodding, "and so they were on the verge of foreclosure. Then Brigham remembered the penny fund. He asked if we would be willing to turn the pennies over to the Twelve to pay off the note. By spring, when they will need the money for the windows and the nails, they will be able to pay it back, he said. But the real crisis was now."

"And so you agreed?"

"Of course. We were very pleased that our little penny fund might prove to be a way to save the Church a lot of money."

"I should say," Rebecca echoed.

"I thought it was wonderful of the Twelve to ask," Mary said. "I mean, in a way, it is the Church's money, not ours, and they could have just taken it. But Brigham made it clear that it was only a request and we could say no if we wanted."

"So it's done?"

"Yes. They found the other four hundred dollars somewhere else and made the first payment. Brigham told me yesterday that he is confident they can raise the rest of it in time now."

"That is wonderful news. You must feel very proud."

Mercy smiled. "Well, as Hyrum once told us, in the scriptures pride is always considered a sin. But when God wants to talk about how he feels about his Son, he says, 'This is my Beloved Son, *in whom I am well pleased.*'" She smiled shyly, almost like a young girl. "I suppose it would be all right if Mary and I said that we are well pleased with what happened."

They fell silent for a few moments as they finished their tea. Rebecca set it aside and murmured contentedly, "That tastes so good. It is miserably cold outside today."

"I notice that there's ice running in the river already," Mercy said. "It must be very cold up north."

They nodded at that, and then Rebecca asked another question, a question that was one of the main reasons she had come. "How is Emma doing?"

Mary and Mercy looked at each other, shaking their heads. "Not very good," Mary said sadly.

"And the baby, little David Hyrum?"

"I'm afraid he is going to be a sickly child," Mercy murmured. "He is not in any danger, mind you, but neither is he a strong and healthy baby."

"One more burden for her to bear," Rebecca said.

"Yes, but at least it wasn't another silent child," said Mercy. "The fear of that weighed heavily on her mind, as you know."

"And to have to face it without Joseph," Mary broke in. "Poor Emma."

Rebecca hesitated for a moment, then went on. "Do you think she and Brother Brigham will be able to reconcile matters?"

Again there came that dual shaking of the heads.

"Lydia spends two or three days a week now with Emma and says that Emma grows more bold in expressing her strong feelings about President Young. She fears that the rift between them grows deeper and deeper."

"We are greatly concerned too," Mary said.

Rebecca drew a quick breath. "One of the reasons I have come is that Lydia wants to know how to best help Emma. She wants to try and understand the whole situation so that as she speaks with her, she will better know what to say. She wanted to come herself this morning and talk to you. There is too much gossip in the city and she does not want to base her actions on gossip. But unfortunately, Elizabeth Mary had bad croup last night and is still struggling to overcome it this morning, and so

Lydia dared not leave her. She asked if I would represent her concerns to you and see if you might help."

Again the two sisters looked at each other, and a brief nod passed between them. "We hope she can help," Mary said. "We have tried, but have learned that it only raises Emma's resentment. Where she and Lydia are so close, perhaps that is the answer."

"One of the main problems," Mercy explained, "is that Emma feels that Brigham and the other Apostles did not come immediately to see her and pay their condolences when they arrived back in Nauvoo last August."

"But Matthew says they did go to see her."

"Yes, but only after some time had passed."

"We understand why," Mary interjected quickly. "As you know, the very moment Brigham and the other four stepped off the boat, they were caught up in the crisis with Sidney Rigdon. The Twelve barely had a chance to get a full night's sleep before Brigham had them in council trying to determine what was to be done. President Marks had already set the meeting to call for a vote on Brother Rigdon's guardianship."

"I know," Mercy sighed. "And to be honest, Emma was not reluctant to express her feelings about who should replace Joseph. She was clearly in favor of it being either President Rigdon or else President Marks."

"A lot of people took unfair advantage of her, I think," Mary added. "She was the widow of the Prophet and had great influence. So men who wanted to take over the reins sought her support as they jockeyed for position. Claims were made publicly by them that I'm not sure Emma ever said privately."

Rebecca nodded. "As you know, Matthew is very close to Brother Brigham, and Brigham was upset by what was going on. He felt strongly that this was not Emma's choice, nor anyone else's, for that matter. This was the Lord's decision." She took in a deep breath. "There's something else," she said slowly. "Matthew shared this with Lydia and me when we told him that we planned to speak to you today. We've not spoken about it to anyone else, but I think it is an important factor."

"What?" they both asked together.

"Matthew says Brigham wonders what would have happened if Emma had not sent that letter across the river, begging Joseph not to flee to the West but to come back and face his accusers."

"Yes," Mary said very quietly, and there were just the tiniest lines of bitterness now around her mouth. "Joseph and Hyrum would have been gone by that afternoon otherwise. The letter was one thing, but then when the men who brought the letter called Joseph and Hyrum cowards . . ." She shook her head slowly. "Who knows how things might have been different?"

"Well, in Brigham's mind, that decision to return sealed their fate." Then Rebecca sighed. This was such a twisted and complicated problem. "Lydia attributes much of all this to Emma's emotional state. She has seen so much tragedy in the last few years—the horror of Far West and Joseph's imprison- ment, little Don Carlos dying, then shortly after that giving birth to a silent child."

"No question about it," Mary said, the bitterness gone as quickly as it had come. "She was terribly frightened to think she might have to face another birth alone."

They were quiet now for a time, each lost in her own thoughts of tragedy and how slim were the hinges upon which it swung.

Finally, Mercy straightened, looking at Rebecca. "What has happened most recently is the deep disagreement over the prop- erties of the Church and Joseph's own private properties. This is what is widening the rift between Emma and Brigham now. And these are complicated questions, Rebecca. I am glad that I am not the one to have to sort them out. One can see justice on both sides of the issue. For Brigham's part, he believes that while some things were put in the name of Joseph Smith, that was done only because Joseph was the trustee-in-trust for the Church. For example, many tithing funds went toward the pur- chase of land or the construction of certain buildings, including the Mansion House. Therefore, in Brother Brigham's mind, they clearly belong to the Church. Emma, on the other hand, claims that these things were done by Joseph for his family."

"And," Mary said, "Emma has one strong point. She often worked alongside Joseph in certain endeavors in order to make them a success. For example, look how many hours she spent getting the store built and stocked. Joseph was there sometimes, but with his duties, she was the one who basically ran it. And at the Mansion House, she took in boarders, cooking and washing for them. Is she not entitled, then, to some remuneration or part title to these properties?"

"So that's it," Rebecca said. "Lydia said that Emma keeps making comments about Brigham trying to rob her."

Mary nodded. "Even Brother Brigham agrees that the line between personal and Church ownership was rarely, if ever, clearly drawn by Joseph. Particularly galling to Brigham," she went on, "is Emma's insistence that the sacred manuscripts—particularly the notes from Joseph's work on translating the Bible—belong to her and not to the Church. In Brigham's mind, this is one area where there should be no question. But as you know, during those terrible days in Far West, at great risk to herself, Emma preserved those manuscripts by carrying them about beneath her skirts. When she fled from Missouri to Illinois, she even carried them across the frozen Mississippi with four children hanging on to her. So in her mind, they were Joseph's private property, and by saving them she earned full rights to them."

"That is a difficult question," Rebecca said softly, not sure exactly how she would rule on that if it were put to her. Finally she looked at her two friends. "Thank you. That will help Lydia as she tries to help Emma."

"Tell her we appreciate her concern very much," Mercy responded.

"How is Mother Smith taking all of this?" Rebecca asked.

"Mother Smith is Mother Smith," Mary answered with a warm smile. "She is strong, wise, caring. She tries to negotiate peace between all of us."

"Does she side with Emma or Brigham?"

"She is careful to try and not to appear to take sides," Mary replied, "but there is no question but what she believes Brigham and the Twelve are the ones to lead the Church. I suspect Joseph said enough to her before he died that she knows Brigham's claim that the Twelve hold the keys is correct."

"And the Twelve have been wonderful to her and to us," Mercy added. "They have announced that they are building Mother Smith a home of her own. Brigham also has given her unlimited use of one of the carriages that belong to the Church. She is obviously getting older now, but she is still the wonderful, tireless, ever-cheerful Mother Smith. What a dear woman! What an inspiration to all of us!"

"What dear women you all are!" Rebecca exclaimed. "I was counting the other day. With you two, and the wives of Samuel and Don Carlos, and, of course, Mother Smith and Emma, there are six widows now in the Smith family. And numerous fatherless children as well. And yet you go on in faith and good cheer." There was a sudden shininess in Rebecca's eyes. "You are all an inspiration to the rest of us. How can I complain about having Derek gone for only four months when I know what each of you faces?"

Chapter Notes

The story of how the penny fund started by the Fielding sisters in the winter of 1843 was used to stave off a financial crisis for the Church is told in Mary Fielding Smith's biography (see Don Cecil Corbett, *Mary Fielding Smith: Daughter of Britain* [Salt Lake City: Deseret Book Co., 1966], pp. 177–78).

For a thorough discussion on the conflict between Emma and Brigham, see *American Moses*, pp. 117–18.

Emma never did surrender the manuscript of Joseph's work on the Bible to the Twelve. This work is known now by the RLDS Church as the "Inspired

Version" of the Bible and by the LDS Church as the "Joseph Smith Translation" of the Bible. Emma married Lewis Bidamon, a non-Mormon, in December 1847 and lived with him until her death in 1879. At her death, the manuscript passed to the Reorganized Church through Joseph Smith III, who was the first president and prophet of that church. That manuscript is still held by the Reorganized Church today.

In a similar manner, the properties which belonged to Joseph's family—namely, the Homestead, the Red Brick Store, the Mansion House, and the Nauvoo House—eventually became the property of the Reorganized Church. These buildings—with the exception of the Nauvoo House, which is not open to the public—are preserved and maintained in an excellent fashion and are available to visitors today. Most of the other restored sites in Nauvoo are the property of The Church of Jesus Christ of Latter-day Saints.

Lucy Mack Smith turned sixty-nine less than two weeks after her two sons were killed in Carthage. She remained faithful to the Church throughout her life and publicly declared that she was satisfied with how the Twelve were carrying out its affairs.

Matthew Steed was cold. The rain had stopped now, but there was a stiffening breeze blowing out of the west straight into their faces. The rain had not been heavy enough to soak them through, but he could feel the damp clamminess even down to his long johns. He pulled his coat more tightly around him, letting his eyes sweep the thick forest and undergrowth around them. They were in a range of mountains known as the Ouachitas, a range south of the Ozarks. There was not even a flicker of a light to break the darkness on every side. They could barely see the wagon track they were following, and had it not been for the break it made through the thickness of the forest on either side they could easily have lost it.

"How cold do you suppose it is?" he finally asked, simply to break the monotonous silence.

Derek looked up. The stubble of his beard in the darkness made him look as if he had only half a face, two eyes and a nose hanging there eerily, without chin or neck or body. There was a slight movement in the darkness as he shrugged. "Forty degrees, maybe forty-two."

"Is it possible to freeze to death when it isn't really freezing?"

"Yeah," was all Derek said.

"Thanks." Matthew trudged on, suddenly filled with gloom. He hadn't asked because he didn't know. There were plenty of stories about men caught out in the cold who had died of exposure when the temperature was warmer than this. If the body's core got too cold, a wonderful sense of warmth and euphoria swept over you, and if it was not fought vigorously, you would just lie down and die. He knew that there was a very good chance of that happening tonight if they didn't find shelter soon. During a break in the clouds earlier that day, they had seen a dusting of snow on some of the higher ridges. It was going to be cold tonight.

"They said that Caddo Gap was only fifteen miles or so from Bonnerdale," Derek muttered. "It feels like we've come twice that."

Matthew didn't say anything. There was no need to. In the past nearly four months, the two missionaries had learned that if the people of Arkansas knew anything about the Mormons, they had mostly learned it from their neighbors to the north, the Missourians. That was like asking a Democrat to give you an honest opinion about a Whig. Though the woman in Bonnerdale had seemed cordial enough, she clearly wanted no part of the Mormon missionaries. Perhaps she had lied to them about Caddo Gap. Perhaps she had sent them off on some nameless road that led to nowhere.

Instantly he pushed that thought away, angry at himself. It was not a heavily traveled road, but neither was it giving out. They had not passed anyone since before dark, but with the weather and the temperature being what they were, it was not surprising that people were not out and about.

His mind next tried to evaluate the wisdom of coming out this way, but once again he pushed the thought aside. It had been a week ago—February tenth—that John Taylor's letter arrived general delivery at the post office in Little Rock. The Twelve were releasing them from their mission, they were informed. They should continue on no later than the first of March and then return home. It had been tempting to both of them to just start homeward then, but when someone told them there were two or three families of Mormons in a small town up in the mountains, they reluctantly determined to try and find them as their last official act as missionaries. So here they were, moving farther and farther away from any hope of a warm fire and food.

They walked on in silence, the gloom of the night now made worse by the despondency they both were feeling. After five full minutes, Derek cleared his throat. "Matthew, have you ever wondered why the Savior asked missionaries to go without purse or scrip?"

Matthew turned his head curiously. "Can't say that I have. Why?"

"No, I want you to think about it. Joshua offered to pay our way and send us money when we needed it. What would we have missed if we had accepted his offer?"

There was a soft, rueful laugh. "We would have missed being cold and hungry. We wouldn't have boots with newspapers in them to plug the holes in the bottom. We could have had a nice room, a warm bed, breakfast each morning."

Over Derek's nodding he went on, warming to the question now. "Uh, let's see. What else? Oh yeah. We wouldn't have gotten to spend the night in that jail in Searcy because we didn't have any money and couldn't prove we weren't vagrants. Have I missed anything?"

Derek grunted. "How about that moldy bread and clabbered milk we had last night?"

"That's right. We would never have been able to buy something like that with money."

"So why would the Lord want us to do it this way?"

After a long pause came the answer from Matthew. "I once heard a rumor that there is a direct relationship between being cold and hungry and being humble."

There was a half laugh, filled with longing. "I think you're right, and I can't ever remember being quite so humble as right at this moment."

"Same here." Then Matthew got more serious. "We've been together too long, Brother Ingalls, sir, for me not to know that you've got something else on your mind with that question. What is it?"

"What time do you suppose it is?" Derek said, looking up at the sky above, only barely discernible from the land around them. The sky was overcast and no stars were visible.

"I don't know. Nine-thirty. Maybe ten o'clock. Why?"

"How much longer do you think there's gonna be people up with a lamp on this far out away from nowhere?"

There was a long silence; then in a low voice Matthew responded. "We could be passing by houses all the time right now and not even know it."

"Yeah," Derek said glumly. "That's what I was thinking. And that could go on until morning. So, what I'm wondering is, are we humble enough yet?"

Matthew stopped, understanding now. "I'm feeling pretty humble, actually."

"Humble enough to stop and ask the Lord for his help?"

"At least that humble."

Without a word they both turned off the road to the weed-choked shoulder. They dropped to their knees, shoulder to shoulder, and in a moment, Derek began to pray.

Fifteen minutes later, as they stumbled along, shivering in the darkness, Matthew's hand shot out and grabbed Derek's arm. "Look!" he said, pointing off to their left.

"What?"

"Watch! Through the trees. 'Bout a hundred yards off."

"Yes." The one word was spoken in a long, drawn-out sigh of

relief. A flicker of light glimmered momentarily, then disappeared again as the wind blew branches across their view. Then it was there again. Derek gripped Matthew's arm. "Yes, I see it too."

"We're much obliged, ma'am. That was a fine breakfast."

The woman turned from the stone fireplace and looked at the two missionaries sitting at her table. "You're welcome. Wish we had a bed for you too, but we're simple folk here."

"Believe me, ma'am," Matthew said, and he said it with deep fervor, "your barn was an answer to a prayer. I can't think of a finer night's sleep I've had since we left home."

That seemed to please her. She looked to be in her early forties, but judging from the ages of her seven children, and knowing that the hill-country people typically married quite early, she was maybe thirty-two or thirty-three, possibly less than that.

"We are truly grateful," Derek said, standing now and reaching for his hat. "As the Lord says in the Bible, 'And whosoever shall give a cup of cold water to my little ones shall in no wise lose their reward.'"

There was a sad smile that briefly played around her mouth. "We can use all the blessings we can get," she finally said.

Derek smiled at the children, lined up in a row along one wall, oldest to youngest. They were ragged, thin, smudged with grime that bespoke long weeks between baths. Their eyes watched the two strangers with great solemnity. "Bye, y'all," Derek said with a smile.

The oldest raised one hand and waved briefly. The others did not stir.

"Ma'am," Matthew said, standing now too. "We've come out this way trying to find Caddo Gap. Are we far from it?"

"About two miles." She pointed.

"Oh, good. So—" And then suddenly it registered which way her hand was pointing. "It's that way?"

For the first time she laughed. It was a pleasant sound, like hearing the first bird on a beautiful morning. "You passed it in the night."

"Really?" Derek said. "Is there a sign on the road? We were watching real close."

"Yep!"

At that the children started to giggle.

"What?" Matthew asked, suspecting he and Derek were being teased now.

The oldest boy, still chortling, said, "There's a sign, all right, but it's been knocked down now for nigh onto a year."

"Arrow points right to Caddo Gap," the mother said, still enjoying their little joke.

The two missionaries exchanged looks and then Derek had another idea. "Ma'am, we came out looking for a couple of families we were told about. Name of Webster and Scadlock. You wouldn't know them by any chance?"

"Know them both."

"Could you tell us how to find either one of them?"

"Find one, find them both. They live just a stone's throw away from each other."

"Oh. Could you tell us how to get there, please?"

She wiped her hands on her apron. "Go back out to the road. Keep moving north. Go two sees and a holler and you'll find a path that leads off to the right into the woods. Goes right to the Scadlock place."

Matthew looked puzzled. The "holler" was no problem. In this country, a holler was a hollow or a small valley. "Two 'sees,' ma'am," he asked politely, "what does that mean?"

She looked a little surprised. "When you get to the road, go to the next ridge. From there, look as far as you can see down the road to the next ridge. That will be one see. Go to the second ridge. Look down the road again as far as you can see."

Matthew was nodding. "That'll be two sees, I take it."

"Yep. Then go to the next holler and you're there."

"Much obliged, ma'am," Derek said, suppressing a grin.

"You preachers?" she suddenly asked, catching them both by surprise.

"Yes," Derek replied.

"Mormons?"

For some reason Derek felt a little chill. "Yes, ma'am."

"Best be careful, then," she said. "Circuit rider went through here day before yesterday. Said two men might be coming. Warned folks about you."

"I see," Derek responded, keeping his face impassive.

"Scadlocks and Websters Mormons?" she asked, startling them again.

"That's what we heard, ma'am," Matthew answered after a moment.

"'Tain't no more," she said shortly.

"What do you mean?" Derek asked.

"Heard Pulsipher Scadlock was madder than a hound dog stepping in a hornet's nest when he came home from a trip one day and found his missus had become a Mormon."

"Oh." Again the two men exchanged looks, this time with evident dismay.

"Best watch your step. Scadlock's got a mean temper. 'Specially when he's been nipping at his own moonshine."

"Much obliged, ma'am," Derek said once again, only this time it came out with more genuine gratitude than before. "We'll be careful."

———— ◆ ————

Two sees and a holler proved to be about three miles farther on from where they had stayed the night. The rain was gone now and the sky clear. By nine o'clock, they took off their jackets and walked along in their shirtsleeves. As they reached the bottom of the small, narrow valley after the second "see," Matthew stopped and pointed. Ahead about thirty yards there was a footpath going off to the right. "That must be it," he said.

Derek nodded and they walked on until they reached it. There was nothing more than a slight track where the grass had been trampled down into bare dirt. It couldn't have taken even the smallest cart, let alone a wagon. The dirt, peppered clean by last night's rain, showed only one set of tracks from an unshod horse. There was no sign, no markings of any kind. Derek studied it for a moment, looked up and down the road, and when he saw nothing else, he nodded. "Let's go find out."

The first house—or better, the first shanty—was about a quarter of a mile through the trees. It was set near the far edge of a clearing that was maybe fifty yards across in either direction. Matthew and Derek stopped near the edge of the trees to take stock of what lay before them. The house—no more than one or two rooms—was on brick stilts which lifted it about a foot and a half above the ground. The walls were of clapboard and rough-cut lumber, patched here and there with newer-looking pieces of board. One of the two windows had glass. The other was covered with a cloth. From a tin chimney that seemed more like a stick jammed into a hole in the roof rose a wisp of white smoke. A small garden patch, filled with the first of the season's weeds and a few stalks from last year's corn patch, was partly visible behind the house. To the right of that was the outhouse, door partly open, and a small rabbit hutch or chicken pen farther on from there. A sow pig with three little ones was rooting in the grass behind the garden, and a half dozen chickens scratched and pecked in the hardened ground directly around the house.

"Scadlocks' or Websters'?" Matthew murmured, ignoring a sudden prickling sensation along the back of his neck.

Derek didn't answer. He just started forward, striding out with purpose. A little shamed by Derek's forcefulness, Matthew fell into step beside him. As they approached within the last few yards, Derek stopped and raised one hand to his mouth. "Hello the house!" The chickens looked up for a moment, then went on as before. Derek looked at Matthew and then went the rest of the way and up onto the porch. He knocked on the door. It was open a crack and creaked wider under Derek's blows. Matthew stopped at the step, listening. There was not a sound. Derek pulled the door shut again and knocked a second time. Again there was nothing.

He turned. "They had bacon for breakfast," he said, smiling thinly.

If it was meant to calm Matthew's nervousness it didn't work. He had smelled it too. The sweet aroma of frying bacon was heavy in the air. Someone had been in the house not many minutes before. They walked around back and watched the pigs for a moment. Everything here was perfectly normal except that there were no people. Derek pointed past the garden. Another path led into the trees. "Maybe they went to call on their neighbors," he said and started off.

The second house, no more than another five or six hundred yards through the hardwood forest, was nearly identical to the first. The only visible difference was a corral with a brown and white milk cow in it; the rest looked the same, even down to the smoke curling lazily from the chimney. This time Matthew took the lead and went to the door. He knocked once, twice, and then a third time. There was no response.

As Matthew stepped off the porch, Derek sighed. "Do you get the feeling they knew we were coming?"

"Yeah," Matthew muttered, "and I don't like it."

"Maybe they've gone into town or something," Derek volunteered. It came out lamely and they both knew it. Matthew looked around. Someone had cut some long grass and dumped it into the corral where the cow munched on it contentedly. Once again, the grass was fresh enough to show that it hadn't been cut very long ago.

"So what now?" Matthew's head was swinging back and forth, searching the trees, looking for any sign of the families who inhabited this desolate part of the Ouachitas.

"It's a long ways to walk for nothing," Derek finally answered. "I wish we could at least talk to them, let them know that someone from the Church was interested in them."

"I suppose we could go back to town and ask around." There was a brief grimace. "Assuming we can find the town."

"Good idea. Then at least we can leave word that we were here." Derek swung around and started back the way they had come. Gladly, Matthew fell in behind him. They had gone only about ten or fifteen yards back into the forest when a low voice called to them out of the brush. "Hey, mister!"

They both stopped dead, peering into the undergrowth whence the sound had come. There was a rustling of leaves, and then a young boy, maybe eight or nine, was standing there, half-hidden in the foliage.

"Hello," Derek said, taking a step forward. Instantly the boy disappeared again. "Wait!" he cried after the boy. "I won't hurt you."

A moment later the boy was there again, poised like a deer, ready to bolt at the slightest sign of danger. "Good morning," Matthew said, smiling warmly. "Are you one of the Websters?"

"Listen!" the boy said, ignoring the question. "Ma sent me to give you a message."

Derek lowered himself into a crouch, moving slowly so as not to spook the boy again. "A message?"

"Yes!" He leaned forward slightly, so they could see the young face more clearly. He was towheaded with ruddy cheeks. His chest was rising and falling and suddenly Matthew knew that it was not from having run hard. The boy was badly frightened. That sent the chills racing up and down Matthew's back now.

"My ma knows who you are. She thanks you for coming. But you are in danger. Big danger. My . . . Mr. Scadlock is out looking for you. He's told everybody round about that you've come looking to find you more wives. He's whipping up the folks to git you and git you good."

"That's not true—," Matthew started, but the boy cut him off with an urgent wave of his hand.

"You'd better go. Ma says to stay off the road. Don't go back through town. Just git. Hole up. Move at night. Hurry!"

Even as his clipped words registered in their minds, he turned and was gone.

"Wait!" Matthew cried.

From the same direction as the brief sound of bushes rustling they heard a faint, "Ya best hurry," and then nothing but the silence of the forest.

For a moment, they stared at each other. "So what do we do now?" Matthew finally asked in a hushed whisper.

Derek hesitated only for a moment. "Did you see his eyes? The boy is terrified. Sister Webster—or maybe it's Sister Scadlock—just took a tremendous risk to try and warn us. So I think his advice is good. I think we'd best hurry."

"I don't know if it's a good idea to stay so close to the road," Derek said in a low voice. They were stopped amid the trees, and Matthew moved carefully off to the left just far enough to see if they were still parallel to the road.

Matthew came back to join him. "We get off into the forest very far and we may never find our way out again. The road is our map back to Bonnerdale."

Derek grunted, accepting that. Though there was only three years' difference in their ages, from the beginning, by mutual agreement, Derek had assumed the leadership role of this missionary companionship. But Derek had spent all of his early years in a city where the landmarks around you were clear and precise. Put him out in the open or in thick trees such as this and his sense of direction was notoriously bad. Without comment from either, as they had left the two deserted homesteads Matthew moved ahead and took the lead. Twice they had smelled smoke and made a wide circle to avoid whoever or whatever was making it. Once they heard a wagon rattle past on the road and they dropped to the ground, hearts pounding, until it was gone again.

"What do you think?" Derek asked as they started off again now. "Are we going to have rain again tonight?"

Matthew peered up at the sky, sniffing at the air. The sunny skies of morning were long since gone now, and in the last hour the overcast was definitely thickening and growing darker. "Is there mud in the Mississippi?" was his answer.

"No way we're going to make Bonnerdale tonight, is there?"

There was a slow shake of his head. "Staying off the road has cut our progress in half at least. Besides, Bonnerdale may not be a wise move. No, my friend, I think we're due for a wet night in the forest."

"I was afraid you'd say something like that. I was—"

He stopped as Matthew whirled around, holding up his hand for silence. His head was cocked to one side and he was listening intently.

"What?" Derek hissed. "What is it?"

"Listen!" came the urgent command.

And then Derek heard it too. It was a long way off, but there was no mistaking the sound. He felt his knees go weak and suddenly he was licking his lips. "Dogs?" he asked, not wanting to believe what he was hearing.

Matthew nodded grimly. "Hunting dogs." He grabbed his knapsack and threw it over his shoulder. "Let's go." He swung left, pushing through the brush, heading straight for the road.

"Where are you going?" Derek asked in surprise.

"They're letting the dogs run, so likely they're on horseback. That means we've got to make better time. The road is our only chance now."

"The road?" Derek cried. "But we can't outrun dogs and horses."

Matthew was grim. "You better pray we can find a creek and mighty fast."

Derek said nothing more, at least not out loud. They settled into a steady trot, trying to listen for their pursuers, trying to convince themselves the sound was not growing louder. Fortunately they were coming out of the hills and the road was mostly downhill. And equally fortunate, they were in excellent physical shape. They had been away from home now since

October. For almost four months they had spent most of their days walking—sometimes as much as twenty or twenty-five miles a day. Their feet were tough and their bodies lean and hard.

It was nearly ten minutes later when Matthew leaned forward, peering down the road. "There!" he said, pointing to where a plank bridge was visible about a hundred yards ahead of them.

"It's about time," Derek grunted.

The stream was not a large one, maybe three or four feet across and a foot or two deep. The planks were rough-hewn and nailed with spikes to two logs.

"All right," Matthew said, plunging into the water on the upstream side of the bridge without hesitation. He kicked some water up onto the bank. "Let's let them see where we went in." He kicked again. "All right, come on."

Derek needed no urging. He stepped into the creek and felt the shock of the cold water instantly filling his boots.

"Brush against some of the bushes," Matthew said, reaching out to drag his hands through some willows. "Not too much. Just enough for the dogs to pick it up."

Derek looked at him as though he were mad, but knew that Matthew had the better sense of what to do now than he did. Splashing wildly, they jogged upstream about two hundred yards. Finally Matthew stopped, breathing heavily. He held his breath, listening. Derek did the same. The sound of the baying was distinctly clearer now.

"I'd say they're fifteen, maybe twenty minutes behind us now," Matthew guessed. "All right. Back downstream again. When we reach the bridge, we'll go under it. Don't touch anything after that. Stay right in the middle of the stream. No splashing. We've got to make them think we went up this way." He jerked his thumb over his shoulder.

Derek's bewilderment was now admiration. He followed Matthew back to the bridge, moving much more carefully now. When they were a few yards from the plank covering, Matthew dropped to his belly and let the stream carry him beneath the bridge. Derek did the same. Even if their pursuers were up the road only a short distance, they couldn't have seen them cross beneath it. Matthew let the water carry them well into the forest again before he stood up. "All right," he said, shivering, "be careful not to splash. Be careful not to touch the underbrush." He looked up at the sky. "It'll be dark in another hour. Even with the dogs, finding us at night will be a challenge."

Derek just nodded and fell in behind him as he started off again.

Matthew's plan was really quite ingenious, given the circumstances of going up against dogs and against men on horseback. There was only one drawback. They did not know the countryside. Matthew was so intent on staying to the center of the creek, not brushing against the bushes and tree limbs, and listening for any sounds of pursuit, all at the same time, that he didn't pay much attention to which direction they were going. Had he been able to look on a map, he could have seen that the creek they had chosen made a long, lazy half circle and eventually doubled back on itself to cross under the road again.

They trudged along more slowly now, growing more and more tired with every step. In spite of their exertions, their bodies shook violently. Utterly soaked, their clothes did little to keep out the deepening chill of the air. And each time they had to go low to get under a bush or low-hanging branch, they immersed themselves in the icy water again. Their feet felt like stumps of ice. Internally, it was a different matter indeed. It was as if every part of their bodies was on fire. Their hips ached from the effort of dragging their feet through the water, fighting to keep their balance on the mossy rocks or patches of clutching mud. Their lungs burned, and Matthew could already feel the first touches of pleurisy, that deep aching hurt in the bottom of the lungs that often follows extreme exertion.

Then suddenly Matthew stopped, holding up his hand.

There was an audible gasp of dismay. Derek peered around him. About twenty yards ahead of them the trees opened up. And there was the road and another bridge. For a moment, they gaped at it, not comprehending.

"Matthew?"

Matthew shook his hand at him. He half turned, finger to his lips. "I think we've circled back to the road," he finally said in a low voice.

"No!" Derek cried softly. "That can't be."

"Listen! The dogs have stopped barking."

Suddenly a dark shape stepped out from behind a tree. A long-barreled rifle was pointing directly at Matthew's chest. "Ain't no need for dogs now," said a man's voice with a staccato burst of laughter.

Pulsipher Scadlock was the undisputed leader of the group. By the time he and the other two men had them securely tied, three more men appeared. These had the dogs, and Matthew instantly understood Scadlock's strategy and begrudgingly had to admit it was brilliant. He had not been fooled for one moment by the upstream gambit, so he and two more rode straight down the road to the next bridge to wait. Meanwhile, the other three followed the creek with the now silenced dogs just to make sure their game hadn't forsaken the creek and taken to the forest again. The bitter taste of defeat was so strong in Matthew's mouth that he wanted to gag. They had done their best and their best hadn't been good enough.

Scadlock tied the hands of his prisoners behind their backs, then tied their legs to separate trees. He warned them not to speak to each other, and then set about making a fire—no mean feat, since a light rain had started again. By the time the three men with the dogs arrived, the others had a frying pan on the fire cooking large slabs of ham. Round loaves of bread were brought out and broken into chunks, and a large earthenware jug was uncorked and started around the circle. The men were rough men of the backcountry—worn clothes, ragged beards, matted hair, foul mouths, crooked or rotted teeth, faces hard and angular, eyes like those of a circling band of coyotes. As the liquor began to warm them up, the fireside became a scene of joviality and raucous laughter. It was as though the prisoners had been completely forgotten.

Derek was shivering violently beneath his bonds. His clothes were still soaked. If he moved his legs, the water squished inside his boots. It wasn't going to be as cold as the night before, but it would be cold enough. He looked to where Matthew was, and saw that his body was shaking as violently as his own. "They leave us here very much longer," Derek whispered, "and they won't have to worry about what to do with us."

It was as if Scadlock had the ears of a cat. He jerked around, swept up a fist-sized rock, and hurled it at Derek. "I said no talking!" he barked.

Derek jerked his head to one side and the rock bounced off the tree trunk above him with a solid thud. If it had hit him . . . He shuddered. Matthew, watching him, gave a quick shake of his head.

One of the men tossed a piece of meat through the air to where the half dozen dogs lay on the ground near the horses. In an instant the dogs were at each other, snarling, snapping, fighting furiously for the morsel. The men roared with laughter. After a moment, one of the dogs came slinking to the fire to see if there was more. The man who had thrown the meat, one of the younger of the group, swore and gave the animal a hard kick, sending it yelping away. That brought another roar from the group.

And that seemed to bring Scadlock back to the task at hand. Muttering something under his breath, he stood up. He looked toward Derek and Matthew. "It's getting late boys. The missus will be wondering how the 'squirrel hunt' went." He pronounced the two words with exaggerated seriousness.

There was another burst of laughter, as if he had made some enormous joke. The rest stood now and moved closer to Scadlock.

That is, all except for one. Matthew saw that the man who had first accosted them still sat on his haunches, staring into the fire.

"Come on, Webster," Scadlock snarled. "You're not going soft on us now, are you?"

The man called Webster got to his feet, shaking his head. "What's your plan, Pulse?"

The big man jerked his head at the one nearest him. "Get the rope."

That brought startled looks from several of the men. Webster just stared at his neighbor but said nothing. Scadlock strode over to where Matthew and Derek were tied. "Untie their legs," he commanded. Two men sprang to obey, and in a moment dragged the prisoners to their feet, a man at each elbow, partly restraining them, partly holding them up, as they were having difficulty standing with their legs and feet so numb. In a moment, the man returned from the horses with a large coil of rope.

Scadlock was looking up at the trees around him. Finally, he found what he was looking for—a stout horizontal branch where there was sufficient space for a horse to stand beneath it. He pointed. "There. That will do." The man with the rope didn't move. Scadlock swore loudly. "Don't just stand there, tie a noose in the end of that rope."

Now the men around him fell silent. The hunt was over, the funning was done. Find their prey, thrash them soundly, maybe even play with them a little to scare them real good. That had been their expectation. But it was clear that Scadlock wasn't playing at anything. He was far too determined for the rest of them to be comfortable now.

The youngest man—a boy of no more than sixteen or seventeen—looked at Scadlock, then away quickly. Another man was staring at his feet, pushing the dirt and leaves around with the toe of his boot. Webster hung back, watching closely, waiting to see what the others said. Finally one of them cleared his throat. "You didn't say nothing about no hanging, Scadlock."

Scadlock didn't even turn. "What'd you think," he asked in

contempt, "that we'd give these whoremongers a pat on the cheek and let them go? You heard what the circuit rider said. They've been seducing women all the way from Memphis to Little Rock. They left a fourteen-year-old girl in Bonnerdale in a family way."

"That's a lie," Matthew said quietly.

Scadlock whirled with the agility of a cat and swung. The back of his hand caught Matthew full across the face, snapping his head back with a sharp crack. "You calling me a liar?" he screamed into Matthew's face.

When Matthew straightened again, a trickle of blood was coming out of his nose. His chin came up slowly. "No, sir, I am calling the man who told you that a liar."

Again the beefy arm swung and there was the thud of flesh on flesh. Derek leaped forward to stand between the two of them, half dragging with him the two men who held him by the arms. Scadlock cocked his fist back, ready to strike again. Derek looked at him calmly. "I can prove that the man was lying to you."

Scadlock's fist tightened, but Webster spoke quickly. "How?"

Gratefully, Derek turned toward the man who he was almost positive had once been a Mormon. "We only came to Bonnerdale day before yesterday. Knowing how fast news travels around up here, you know that's true. So how could we have gotten a girl in a family way when it takes two months to even know if a girl is in a family way?"

The men surrounding them looked at each other, and Derek could tell his point was made. No one spoke. Every eye was on Scadlock. His arm slowly lowered and he seemed to relax. Derek took a quick breath. "Mr. Scadlock, we are just a couple of missionaries from—"

The blow came so quickly that Derek didn't have time to even steel himself. The massive fist buried itself up to the wrist in his solar plexus. With an explosion of air, Derek gasped and dropped to his knees, his mouth working frantically, his eyes nearly popping out. The bearded man didn't even look down at him. "Get this slug out of the way!" he snarled.

The two men grabbed Derek's arms and dragged him backwards, letting him drop to the ground where he coiled into a ball, gasping and wheezing and fighting for breath, the struggle made all the worse by the fact that his arms were tied behind his back.

"Now," the leader said, jutting his face up next to Matthew's, "who was that you were calling a liar?" Matthew said nothing, but neither did he drop his eyes. He looked steadily into the beady roundness of Pulsipher Scadlock's bloodshot and rheumy eyes.

"Now, you listen, boy, I'm going to ask you some questions. I'm only going to ask them once. And you'd better try real hard to make me like your answers, you hear?"

"I hear you," Matthew said evenly.

"What are you doing here in Caddo Gap country?"

"Like my brother-in-law said, we are missionaries from Nauvoo, Illinois, for The Church of—"

This time it was a slap with the flat of his palm. But it still cracked like a pistol shot in the stillness of the night around them. "I didn't ask you *what* you are, mister! I asked you what you are doing *here* in Caddo Gap country."

The marks of the beefy fingers left sharp pink outlines on Matthew's cheeks. He licked his lower lip. "We were told there were some members of our church who lived up this way."

"Names?"

Matthew hesitated for a moment, but knew that it wouldn't take much of this kind of interrogation to leave him blind or without some of his teeth. "Scadlock and Webster."

There was a low grunt. "And when you found them, then what?"

"We just wanted to see how they were doing, let them know that the Church still cared about them. Actually, my brother-in-law and I are ready to go back to Illinois. This was going to be our last place to visit and—"

Crack! His head was flung to one side and his ears were instantly ringing.

"Then what?" Scadlock roared again.

Matthew wanted to shake his head, make the stinging and the ringing go away, get his mind working again. "We just wanted to see how they were doing," he started again, his words slurring slightly now. He jerked away, but not fast enough. The blow caught him alongside the head.

"You came looking for wives for Joe Smith, didn't ya?" Scadlock screamed into his face. "You came looking for women."

Matthew shook his head and the hand came up again.

"Leave him alone," Derek cried, still curled up on the ground. "Joseph Smith is dead. Haven't you heard?"

Swearing loudly, Scadlock swung around, took three steps, and kicked out. The toe of his boot caught Derek just below the knee, squarely on the shinbone. Derek screamed in agony, writhing on the ground. "You don't hear very well, preacher boy!" Scadlock breathed, panting heavily. He looked at one of the men. "If he speaks again, put a ball through his head."

Webster stepped forward. "Pulse, I know you're angry, but—"

One look from Scadlock and Webster's mouth clamped shut again. The big man stepped back to Matthew and grabbed him by the front of his shirt. "You married, boy?"

"Yes, sir."

He looked around, grinning suddenly. It was more frightening than his anger. "Did you hear that, boys? He called me sir. These Mormons are learning a little respect now, aren't they?" His head jerked back around to face Matthew. "Children?"

"A little girl that's two. Another one coming next month."

"Aah," Scadlock said, all honey and molasses now. "Ain't that nice?" Then instantly his voice was hard again. "How many wives?"

"One, sir."

"*Liar!*" The roar was almost like being struck again. "How many wives you got, boy?"

"One, sir. Her name is Jennifer Jo Steed."

"And how many does your friend here have?"

"One. She's my sister, and—"

"So that's it?" he said curiously, as though just having heard an interesting piece of gossip down at the local saloon. Then in a flash his voice was all ice and steel again. "So it's not for old Joe Smith? You're out looking to find more wives for yourselves, is that it?"

Matthew didn't even bother to answer. His hands were still tied behind his back, so he tensed for the next blow, but to his surprise Scadlock stepped back. "Tell you what, Mr.—What was your name again, boy?"

"Steed. Matthew Steed."

"Tell you what, Mr. Matthew Steed, I'm going to do a little preaching of my own here for a minute." He stepped over and took the coiled rope from the man who had fetched it from the horse. Suddenly Matthew felt like he was going to be sick. One end of it was tied in a typical hangman's noose. Barely looking at what he was doing, Scadlock began fondling the loop, his fingers caressing the knot gently. Finally he turned to the boy. "Get me a horse, Willie Boy."

"Pa, I—"

"Did you not hear me, boy?" he asked, the menace like that of a coiled prairie rattlesnake.

Willie jumped, nearly tripping over himself as he raced to obey.

The man called Webster was looking at the ground. "Pulse, I want no part of a lynching." A couple of the other men were shaking their heads too.

Scadlock never turned his head in Webster's direction. "You better watch yourself, John. We start lynching us some Mormons here tonight and we just might think that you're still one of them."

"I came with you to drive these two out," Webster said. "I'm quit of the Church. You know that. So is your wife and my wife. That's done and over. But I didn't come out to start killing people, no matter who they are."

"Yeah, come on, Scadlock," the man directly behind Webster

said uneasily, "we can have some fun with them. Give them a good whipping, but . . ."

Scadlock ignored the man and stepped up to Matthew. He sized him up for a moment, calmly adjusted the size of the loop a bit, then slipped it over Matthew's head. His boy came walking up with one of the horses, saddle still on.

"Get him up there, Willie. Caleb, give him a hand."

They lifted Matthew bodily off the ground and pushed him up into the saddle. Scadlock took the horse's bridle and led him to the tree that he had previously picked out. With one flip of his arm, the rope sailed up and over the branch above Matthew's head. Scadlock caught the end of it easily and took in the slack.

"Now, Mr. Steed, you listen real good and you just might go on back home to Illinois with your neck size still the same. You understand me?"

Matthew, against his will, had lifted his eyes to the tree above him to see the sturdiness of the branch. Now he forced himself to look down at his tormentor. In spite of the cold air and the faint mist of rain, he was perspiring heavily.

"I said, do you understand me?" Scadlock shouted, jerking on the rope enough that it pulled at Matthew's neck, the rough hemp scraping the skin.

"I do."

"Good. Now, tell me, what church do you belong to?"

"The Church of Jesus Christ of Latter-day Saints."

That brought a puzzled look from the men around Scadlock. "You said they was Mormons," one of them called to Scadlock.

The big man's mouth twisted. "What does that mean?" he said to Matthew. "Are you a Mormon or ain't you?"

Matthew, his mouth dry, his heart thudding, nodded. "Yes, I am a Mormon."

There was a short laugh. "That's too bad. How would you like to change your religion?"

His eyes widened, for now he understood where this was going. "At the end of a rope or of my own free will and choice?"

That brought a guffaw from Scadlock. "End of a rope is quicker than listening to some preacher. What do you say?"

Matthew thought of this morning after the boy had warned them and then left so abruptly. He thought of finding the woman's house and barn the night before in the middle of a dark, cold night. He remembered how many times the Lord had answered their prayers since they left Nauvoo. And most of all, he remembered Joseph and Hyrum Smith lying dead in Carthage, Illinois. And suddenly he was at peace. "What do I say? I say what the Apostle Paul said. I say that I am not ashamed of the gospel of Jesus Christ, for it is the power of God unto salvation. Yes, sir. I am a Mormon and plan to stay a Mormon until the day I die."

Scadlock's hand pulled on the rope, tightening it again around Matthew's neck, making him stand in the stirrups to stop from choking. "Am I to take that as a turndown of my invitation?" he hissed.

"Come on, Pulse," Webster called in a low voice. "This has gone far enough."

Scadlock's head snapped around, and his voice crackled with anger. "Shut up, John, or you're next!" He wrapped the rope around his left hand, once, twice, and then gripped the end of it firmly in his right hand as well. It was a way to be sure it didn't slip through his hands when the weight hit it. "I'll be asking you only once more," Scadlock said to Matthew, his voice barely a whisper now. "You tell me you're not a Mormon anymore, and you can climb down off that horse. We'll have a few snorts of whiskey together, then you and your friend here are on your way. But as the good Lord is my witness, if you don't, you're going to be swinging by your Adam's apple in about ten seconds. What do you say, Mr. Matthew Steed?"

Matthew closed his eyes. The men thought it was in fear. In reality, he was searching his mind to see if he could remember the scripture from the Second Epistle to Timothy he had first memorized in England. After a moment his eyes opened and he looked straight into the eyes of Pulsipher Scadlock and began once again to quote the words of Paul. "'I am now ready to be offered, and the time of my departure is at hand. I have fought a good fight. I have finished my course. I have kept the faith. Henceforth there is laid up for me a crown of righteousness, which the Lord shall give me at the last day.'" He took a breath and squared his shoulders. "I won't deny what I know to be true, Mr. Scadlock. You're going to have to kill me." He let his eyes sweep from man to man. "And may God have mercy on all of your souls."

For what seemed like a full minute, there was not a sound in the small grove of trees. Finally, Scadlock shook his head with sadness. "This pains me, boy, believe it or not. I've got to hand it to ya, ya got grit." He looked around. The men couldn't meet his glaring challenge. One by one their eyes dropped or they turned their heads. There was a snort of disgust and Scadlock turned back to the horse. He took a step forward, preparing to strike the animal across the rump.

Several things happened all at once then. "Giddyap!" Matthew shouted. At the same instant, he drove his heels into the horse's flanks. The horse, which seemed to sense that something was up and was standing fully alert, leaped forward like a startled antelope. Caught completely off guard, Scadlock barely had time to raise his hands. The bearded Mormon-hater screamed as the full weight of Matthew's body hit the rope and snapped it taut across the tree limb. Scadlock's arms were jerked violently forward, nearly yanking him off his feet. For one instant, Matthew swung wildly back and forth, gasping and croaking. Then Scadlock couldn't hold it. The rope pulled free of his hands, whipping across the bare flesh of his palms. He screamed again. The rope flew free and Matthew crashed to the ground.

At the same moment, Derek, who had been completely forgotten in the final tense moments, scrambled up into a half crouch. Then he launched himself in a hobbling sprint for Scadlock. His hands were tied too, but he lowered his right shoulder and drove with all his power straight into Scadlock's abdomen. It didn't have quite the same effect as being hit by a fist, but Scadlock was staring at the palms of his hands, now bloody from the rope's burning power, and he didn't see Derek coming. He went down hard, gasping and retching.

John Webster and the other men were stupefied, and it took them a moment to react before they dove for their rifles. But Webster was the quickest. He came up with his first and leveled it at the bellies of the other men. "Leave 'em, boys. Leave 'em there." They straightened slowly, raising their hands. Behind him, Scadlock was grunting and gasping, getting back up to his knees. Webster half turned to watch. The big man looked momentarily bewildered; then he saw Derek, head down and panting heavily, and Matthew squirming on the ground, the rope coiled around him. Then he saw Webster with his rifle, and something inside him snapped. With a cry like that of a mother grizzly bear cut off from her cubs, he was up on his feet and lumbering toward his neighbor, cursing and swearing in an incomprehensible stream.

Webster didn't move. He didn't swing the muzzle of the rifle around to face Scadlock or raise it to defend himself. "Watch out!" Derek cried as Scadlock hurtled forward.

But Webster knew exactly what he was doing. As Scadlock launched himself, Webster moved back one step, swung the butt of the rifle, and caught Scadlock directly behind the ear with it. There was a great thud as Matthew's would-be executioner hit the ground and slid a few inches facedown in the mud.

"Pa!" his son cried, and ran to drop beside him. At the same time, Derek ran to Matthew and backed up to him, trying to take the noose up and over his head with his tied hands. There was already a bright red welt, two inches wide, all around Matthew's neck.

Webster stepped away, looking at the men now. "All right, boys. You said you're not interested in a lynching any more than I am. So this is over right now. Caleb, go cut those two men free."

There were slow nods, almost a visible relief. One of them pulled out a knife and went to Derek and Matthew. Another

"I Won't Deny What I Know to Be True"

man was staring at the bulky figure on the ground before them. "What are you going to do, John?"

"I'll wait here for Pulse to wake up. The rest of you take the dogs and go on home."

"He'll kill you!" Willie said, but curiously it was not said with anger. There was genuine concern for John Webster's safety.

Webster shook his head. "Once the liquor wears off he'll be manageable." There was a rueful grin. "He'll want to fight, but I can handle that."

Free now, Derek helped Matthew to his feet and Caleb cut his hands loose as well. "What about us?"

Webster considered only for a moment. "Did you mean what you said about leaving Arkansas? Going home?"

"Yes. This was the last thing we planned to do." There was a momentary, humorless smile. "Probably not our best idea."

"Take that horse," Webster said, pointing to the one Matthew had been on, "and mine—the pinto there. You can leave them in Bonnerdale at the general store. Then git on out of here."

The missionaries nodded wearily. "Thank you."

Webster's face was very somber. "We know you meant well, coming out here to see us and all, but we're quit of the Church now. It's best you not come back."

There were grunts and angry nods from a couple of the men. Had Webster taken the missionaries in warmly, he might have had a rebellion. But if they were leaving the state, well then . . .

Matthew walked slowly to the horse. He took the reins and led it back as Derek got the pinto from where it was tied. As they swung up into the saddles, Matthew looked down. "Was that your boy who came to warn us this morning?"

Webster looked puzzled and shook his head. Willie Scadlock stood up, still looking down at his father. "No, that was my brother. Ma sent him."

Matthew nodded. "May God bless her for her goodness."

Derek looked down at the man with the rifle. "And God bless you, John Webster."

There was a curt nod; then Webster turned and walked over to kneel down beside Pulsipher Scadlock. "Get some water from the creek, Willie," he said. He did not look up as Matthew and Derek rode back out to the road and turned south toward Bonnerdale.

———•———

"How's your neck?"

Without thinking, Matthew turned to look at Derek and winced as he did so. The welt around his neck had turned into an ugly mass of bruised and scraped flesh. It looked like some kind of horrible clerical collar. But Matthew forced a smile. "I think it's stretched an inch or two. Jennifer Jo's going to have to go up on tiptoes to kiss me now."

Derek chuckled. "What ever made you spur your horse that way?"

Matthew sobered. "I don't know. It was just a flash of thought. Suddenly I realized that Scadlock had made a mistake. He should have tied the rope to something solid or gotten on another horse and wrapped it round the saddle horn. He's a big man, but I'm near to a hundred seventy-five pounds myself, I'd say. I just suddenly pictured that much weight hitting the end of the rope and knew that he couldn't hold it, especially if he wasn't ready for it." He shook his head. "It takes longer to describe it now than it took for it all to come clearly into my mind."

Derek said nothing. There was no need to. They rode on for several more minutes before Matthew spoke again. "When we get back to Little Rock, I'd like to start home."

"I think it's time," Derek said. "Seems like we wore out our welcome here."

By the time Derek and Matthew returned to Little Rock and closed out their affairs and started home, it was the twentieth of February. It took them three more days to cover the one hundred and forty miles to Memphis, where they caught a riverboat. Two days later they disembarked at St. Louis. The ice running in the Mississippi farther north was starting to come in big enough chunks that it could tear a hole in the keel. Anxious now to return before their babies were born, they walked, rode, hitched rides with freight wagons or local farmers, and spent as little time eating and sleeping as they could possibly get by with. It was roughly a hundred and eighty miles from St. Louis to Nauvoo, an eight- to ten-day trip overland. They made it in seven. Late in the afternoon of March fourth, slogging along in a drizzling cold rain, Derek Ingalls and Matthew Steed returned to Nauvoo, having been gone four months, two weeks, and two days, and having traveled approximately fifteen hundred miles, the better part of that on foot.

The fortune that had smiled upon them so often during that time, and especially on the day they were pursued by Pulsipher Scadlock, continued to smile down upon them. Neither Rebecca nor Jenny had given birth by the time they arrived. It was barely five days later, on March ninth, 1845, that Rebecca Steed Ingalls gave birth to a squalling little girl whom they immediately named Leah Rebecca Ingalls. One week later, almost exactly to the hour, on March sixteenth, 1845, Jennifer Jo McIntire Steed brought forth another little girl. After some considerable debate, they named her Emmeline Steed, for Jenny's grandmother back in Ireland.

About three weeks later, just after midnight on the sixth of April, the fifteenth anniversary of the organization of the Church, Jessica Garrett gave birth to a whopping boy. They named him Solomon Clinton Garrett—Solomon for his father, and Clinton for Jessica's father, who had died two years before in Independence, Missouri, not having seen his daughter since she had fled Jackson County some eleven years previously.

In all three cases, the babies were healthy and strong. In the case of Jessica, having the baby healthy and strong brought a collective sigh of relief throughout the family. Jessica was just two months shy of her forty-first birthday when she gave birth. This would almost certainly be her last child. It was a joy to know it would also be without any problems.

In all three cases, when the letters arrived in Nashville from the new parents, Mary Ann waited until Benjamin was gone somewhere, or asleep, and then she wept because she could not see and hold her newest grandchildren.

On the twentieth of March, 1845, Savannah Steed, the first-born child of Joshua Steed and Caroline Mendenhall Steed, turned eight years old. When her father asked her, some days in advance, what she wanted for her birthday, she answered without hesitation. "To be baptized."

Joshua merely laughed and brushed it aside. When she

refused to give him any other answer, he finally bought her a beautiful little gray Shetland pony with a finely tooled saddle and matching bridle. That worked its magic for over a month and she said nothing more. But as May came and the river ice disappeared, many children—and, in some cases, new converts—who had waited through the winter went down to the spot near the ferry dock and were baptized into the Church. That did it. Though the pony was loved and dearly treasured, Savannah now realized she had been bought off.

And life became miserable for Joshua.

————•◦•————

"Papa?"

Joshua was at the small blacksmith shop they kept on the premises of his freight yard, helping prepare a horse for shoeing. He was bent over, the left front leg of the horse pulled up and held between his knees while he clipped around the edge of the overgrown hoof so it would take the shoe. At the sound of her voice, he jerked up, letting the horse's leg slip out of his hands. "Savannah, what are you doing here?"

"I want to talk with you, Papa."

"You what?"

"I need to talk with you, Papa."

He shook his head, as the blacksmith stopped to watch. The man, a grandfather of fifteen, smiled and waved. "Good morning, Savannah."

"Good morning, Brother Meyers."

"Savannah, how did you get here?" Joshua asked her.

"I walked."

"By yourself?"

"Yes. Mama couldn't come."

He threw up his hands. "Did she know you were coming?"

Savannah looked away, suddenly interested in the bellows that Brother Meyers had started to pump again. "What does that do?" she asked.

"Savannah!"

"Yes, Papa?"

"Does your mother know you're here?"

"She does now."

"What do you mean by that?"

"I wrote a note."

The blacksmith guffawed, then at Joshua's look quickly turned around and began to select a pre-hammered shoe that would be closest to what they would need.

"You get yourself home right now, young lady."

The dark red curls bounced vigorously as she shook her head. "I need to talk with you, Papa."

He stepped back to the horse, turning his back on her, and picked up the front leg again. "I know what you want to talk about, and the answer is no. I'm busy, Savannah. I can't talk." He picked up the clippers again and started in on the hoof where he had left off.

She stepped closer. "Ew! Doesn't that hurt him?"

He didn't look up. "Savannah, I mean it."

She looked up at the horse's face, as if she hadn't heard him. She watched intently as the clippers snipped off another piece of hoof. "Why doesn't it hurt him?" she asked of the blacksmith this time.

"Because the hoof is much like our fingernails," he said, "only much thicker, of course. Does it hurt when you cut your fingernails?"

"I don't cut them. I always chew them off."

Joshua just shook his head as Meyers hooted. The blacksmith brought the shoe over and laid it against the horse's foot as Joshua set the clippers aside. The shoe was too round and it extended past the edge of the freshly clipped hoof. Meyers took a pair of tongs, put the shoe in the pincers, and shoved it into the glowing coals.

"What are you doing that for?"

"Watch, and I'll show you."

Joshua had to smile. This wasn't just her way of stalling. Whatever it was she had come to talk to him about—as if he didn't know—was forgotten for the moment as she watched with fascination something she didn't understand.

"The bellows pump more air into the fire," Meyers explained, pumping the bellows with one hand and adjusting the placement of the shoe in the fire with the other. "That makes the fire get very, very hot and this gets the iron in the shoe very hot. When the iron gets hot enough, then its softer and I can hammer it into shape. Watch."

After waiting another minute, he withdrew the shoe, which was now glowing cherry red.

"Oh," Savannah gasped in amazement.

Meyers swung around to the big anvil, picked up a two-pound sledgehammer, and began to tap the shoe firmly, sending off hot sparks.

"Won't it burn the horse?" she asked, her eyes wide.

"Nope." He hit it again, held it up for scrutiny, pounded on the edge a couple more times, then turned and thrust the shoe into a tub of water. There was a fierce, momentary sizzle, and a wisp of steam rose from the water. After a brief pause, he withdrew the shoe and walked back to the horse. Joshua lifted its foot again. The fit was better this time, but still not sufficient. Back into the fire the shoe went.

"All right, Savannah, you've seen how he does it. Now, off with you. Your mother will be worried."

"Papa, I want to be baptized."

He sighed wearily. "Savannah, I've told you and I've told you. When you are a little older and can understand things better, then if you want to join the Church like Olivia and Will did, I won't say anything. But until then, no. For the hundredth time, the answer is no."

"But, Papa, I am old enough. I'm accounterable."

He cocked his head slightly. "You're what?"

"I'm accounterable."

Meyers was watching, smiling again. "I think the word you want is *accountable*, Savannah."

"Yeah, that's it. Accountable."

"And just what is that supposed to mean?" said Joshua.

"It means that when I turned eight years old, Heavenly Father said I was accounter— accountable."

"I know that, Savannah, but do you even know what it means?"

She rose up, her face offended. "Of course I do. It means I'm old enough to know right and wrong."

Meyers, a convert to the Church from Connecticut, decided to help. "The revelations say that a child is innocent and not capable of sin until they become accountable at the age of eight. That's why we don't baptize a person before then. Savannah is exactly right. Accountability means a person is old enough to start realizing the difference between what is right and what is wrong."

Joshua merely grunted, looking at Savannah. "If you know right and wrong, how come you left home and came all the way across town without telling your mother?"

If he had thought to trip her up with that logic, he was mistaken. "Because being baptized is the right thing to do. Even Mama believes that."

"No, Savannah. When you're older, maybe. But now, the answer is no. I'm not going to say it again. Now, go home."

"Why does my Heavenly Father think I'm old enough to be baptized and you don't?" she shot right back at him.

Meyers nearly dropped the tongs and the shoe along with it. He had to stifle a laugh when Joshua shot him a withering look. He turned back to the fire, saying, just loud enough for Joshua to hear, "Sounds like a pretty good question to me."

"Savannah," Joshua said, walking to her and taking her by the shoulders, "I'm losing patience now. I've given you my answer. And I've asked you to go home. Now, I want you to mind me."

Now her face crumpled and she began to cry. "Please, Papa. Please let me be baptized."

"That's not going to work either, young lady." He turned her around, gave her an affectionate swat across the bottom, then shoved her gently in the direction of the gate. "Go home, Savannah. I mean it."

She walked away, not in dejection but in defiance. Her shoulders were squared, her head high. "I'm going to be baptized, Papa," she called over her shoulder. "You'll see. You can't make me not be baptized."

———•——•———

It was past noon when the door to the freight office opened and Caroline stepped in. Joshua looked up in surprise. "Hello."

She looked around, her face anxious. "Where is Savannah?"

He set the pen down slowly. "You mean she's not with you?"

"No." She held up her hand. A wrinkled piece of paper was in it. "She left me a note saying she had come down here. She was supposed to be over at Melissa's with Sarah. Jane Manning was going to help them make doll clothes."

Joshua stood and came around the desk, his face now showing worry. "She *was* here, pestering me about being baptized. But I sent her home over two hours ago."

Caroline's hand came up to her face. "Two hours?"

"Yes, at least. Did you check at the other cousins'?"

"I asked them, but they all said they hadn't seen her this morning."

He went to the coatrack behind the door and took down his jacket. "I'll come with you."

———•——•———

Darkness had come almost an hour before. Caroline sat at the kitchen table, her eyes red and puffy, her face pale, staring out the window into the night. She jumped as she heard the front door open, and was instantly on her feet. By the time she reached the doorway, Will was striding down the hall toward her. "Emily found her," he said. "She's all right."

"I didn't think of it before," Emily said to her aunt and uncle as they walked toward the barn Nathan and Lydia had built on the back of their property. "We were playing hide-and-seek last summer. One night we couldn't find her and Elizabeth Mary. Finally we all had to beg them to come out and show us where they were."

Joshua nodded grimly. Caroline reached out and laid a hand on her shoulder. The rest of the family stopped at the door of the barn, hugging themselves against the evening's chill. Joshua, Caroline, and Emily went inside, Joshua holding the lamp up high so they could see better.

For the last seven hours, all Steed family activities had come to a halt—the store had been closed, the brickyard and the freighting businesses were left to foremen, the cabinet shop locked and shuttered as Matthew brought his workmen with him to help. Cousins scattered, spreading out from Steed Row in every direction, calling out, lifting every bush and weed, looking behind every fence, going into every shed, outhouse, barn, icehouse and root cellar. Soon more than a dozen neighbors were in on the search as well. With every passing hour, the fear grew. It was early May now, and while the day had been sunny and warm, once the sun went down it turned quite cool. Savannah had worn neither sweater nor wrap of any kind.

Emily led the way across the main part of the barn to a corner stable. Nathan and Lydia had only one cow and one horse, so this stable was not used for animals. It was used for storage of old equipment, tools, and lumber. Emily opened the door to the stable and pointed. Joshua saw immediately where someone had crawled through the dust into a narrow opening under the accumulated junk.

Going up on tiptoe, Emily whispered into Joshua's ear. "She's in there. I heard her moving."

"Thank you, Emily," Caroline said.

Emily nodded, turned around, and left.

Joshua dropped to his knees, set the lamp down to one side, careful to put it on a bare spot on the floor, then called out softly. "Savannah. It's Papa. Are you in there?"

There was a muffled response.

"Come on out, Savannah. Mama is here too. We're not angry with you."

There was no further response. He stood and began lifting the items off the pile and setting them aside. After a moment, he moved one large plank, then retrieved the lamp and held it high. Savannah sat in the far corner of the makeshift hut, huddled in a little ball, hugging herself and shivering noticeably. "Savannah?"

She looked up. "Yes, Papa?" In the lamplight they could see that her teeth were chattering.

Caroline stepped forward. "Oh, Savannah. You're safe."

Joshua motioned, his face gentle. "Come on out, sweetheart. It's all right. I'm not angry with you."

There was a tiny whimper; then she crawled slowly out. He reached out and helped her through the narrow entry. When he took her into his arms, he could feel the trembling in her slender body. He took off his coat and wrapped it around her. It went down to her ankles and made her look like a little girl again.

Caroline threw her arms around her. "Oh, Savannah. You had us frightened to death. What were you doing?" she asked, holding her against her body and rocking her back and forth.

"Papa said I couldn't be baptized. I was going to stay in there until he said I could."

"Didn't you hear us calling for you?" Joshua asked. "We've been looking for you for hours and hours."

Her head bobbed up and down. "I heard Uncle Nathan. Then later I heard Will."

"Then why didn't you—"

Caroline shook her head at him and he stopped.

"Come on, Savannah," Caroline said. "Let's go home. We'll get you a hot bath and some supper. You must be starving."

When Joshua came out into the hall, he was shaking his head. Caroline had to suppress a smile. Through the open door she had heard it all. Now that Savannah was warm and full and in her own bed, the battle was on all over again.

"She is *so* stubborn!" he whispered, taking Caroline's elbow and starting toward their own bedroom.

Caroline just looked up at him and smiled sweetly.

"Oh no!" he said. "Don't you give me that look. She doesn't get that from me."

"Not totally."

There was half a smile. "So you're willing to take a little of the credit?"

"No, I was thinking that you and Benjamin have given her about equal shares." There was a soft, affectionate laugh. "She is so much like the both of you."

"She says she is 'accounterable,'" he moaned. "She doesn't even know how to say it."

"But she knows what it means," Caroline answered quietly.

He made no comment to that. They moved into their bedroom and closed the door. "She says if I don't let her be baptized, she'll run away again."

"I heard."

"If she tries that again, I'll tan her bottom."

"Yes, I heard that too. Do you think that will convince her?"

He stopped, turned, and looked at her, his frown deep and formidable. "I'm not going to say yes, Caroline."

"Why?"

"Because she's not old enough."

Caroline sniffed in amusement. "She's old enough to hide successfully for seven hours from three or four dozen people."

"That has nothing to do with it."

She didn't challenge him on that. "I don't have to tell you that Savannah is a very unusual child. She's already reading two grades past her age. Jessica couldn't believe it when she was here at Christmas. Sister Anderson, her piano teacher, says she has learned more in seven months than her other students do in two years." She paused for a moment or two. "And the fact that we have spoiled her shamelessly, doted on her like she was ten years older than she is, hasn't helped."

"You mean *I* have doted on her."

"So have I," Caroline answered. "We all have. She's bright, she's darling, she's the apple of her grandfather's eye. And she has a mind and heart all her own." She looked straight at him. "And if you ask me, I think all of that is proof that she is accountable."

"Maybe when she's older," he said stubbornly.

She wiggled down under the covers. "All right," she said. "But I hope you don't think it's over."

"Caroline, I want you to make it clear to her that she is not to run away again."

"I will, Joshua. I'm just telling you, knowing Savannah, this isn't over yet."

———•———

Savannah sat at the table, her back straight and stiff, staring at the wall, ignoring the others. Caroline looked at Joshua for a moment, rolled her eyes, then turned to her daughter. "Savannah, eat your breakfast."

"I'm not going to eat today."

Joshua slammed his fork down. "Oh no you don't, young lady. You'll not be starting something like that."

"Will you let me baptized?"

"No. You have my answer and there'll be no more funny stuff."

"Pa, I—"

Joshua swung around to Will, his eyes dark and filled with warning. Will met his gaze and then finally shrugged. "This sure feels familiar," he muttered, but said nothing more.

Turning back to Savannah, Joshua was fighting for patience.

"Savannah, either you will eat your breakfast or you will go to your room and stay there until you are ready to come down and eat. Do you hear me?" He swung on Caroline. "I want you to leave her plate here until it's gone."

Savannah stood up. She lifted her head and sniffed in disdain at the food, every inch the martyr now. "Good day, Papa," she said loftily. "I shall be in my room."

"Savannah!" Joshua warned, but she turned around and marched out. He looked at Will and five-year-old Charles, who watched the drama with wide eyes. "There'll be no sneaking her food, now, you hear me?"

"Yes, Papa," Charles said meekly. Will merely nodded.

He stood, leaving his plate unfinished. "I've got work to do," he said shortly, and then he too left the room.

Will looked at his mother, but she just shook her head.

———•———

It was just after sundown when Will and Joshua returned from the freight yard. As they came into the kitchen, Joshua saw the plate of food sitting there untouched. Caroline, at the stove, had turned and was watching his eyes. Charles, setting the table around the cold, greasy plate, stopped, watching his father gravely. Even little Livvy, not yet a year old, watched him from her high chair.

"She hasn't been down all day," Caroline said.

"No other food?"

She shook her head. "Charles felt so bad for her—you know how tenderhearted he is—that he snuck some bread and jam up to her this afternoon. Savannah refused to touch it."

Charles ducked his head, expecting a rebuke, but Joshua didn't even look at him. He just let out his breath in a long, weary sigh. "I don't know about that girl."

"Well, I do," Caroline said.

"What is that supposed to mean?"

"Savannah was in that horrid place yesterday for seven hours,

Joshua. You know how she hates spiders and bugs, and yet she stayed in there for seven hours. She was cold, she was frightened—it must have been pitch black. Any other child would have given up after two or three hours. But not Savannah. I am convinced that she would have stayed there all night if we hadn't found her."

"So?"

"So she's not eating, Joshua. I can't make her. I know you think I am supporting her in this, but I am not. I tried to talk to her today. I tried to reason with her. I told her perhaps if she waits a year it would be better. She won't hear of it."

"Let her go through the night without food and she'll be ready to compromise."

Will just shook his head, remembering the confrontations between father and son in Wisconsin.

Flaring, Joshua whirled on him. "Have you got something to say, Will?"

"I do," he said evenly. "What you are after is not compromise. It's capitulation."

"This is not your affair."

"Oh? Somehow I thought Savannah was my sister."

Joshua turned away and stomped out to go and wash up. Ten minutes later, the Steed family sat down to supper, with one chair empty. It was a quiet affair. The only conversation took place between Caroline and Livvy as Caroline fed her dinner.

***

Joshua came home again at noon. As he stepped into the parlor and saw Caroline, he didn't even have to ask. She just shook her head slowly.

He swore softly under his breath, the exasperation showing clearly on his face.

Caroline stood. "She is listless and without energy, Joshua. She's starting to worry me."

"So what do we do?"

Caroline looked grim. "I don't care how you do it or what

you say, but this is between you and her. You go up there, and you somehow find a way to compromise. The battle of the titans is over."

He stood there for almost a minute; then, when she refused to lower her gaze, he nodded and turned around and went upstairs.

At the sound of the door opening, Savannah, lying on her bed, staring up at the ceiling, took one look, then turned to face the wall.

He moved over and sat down on the bed beside her. He laid a hand on her shoulder. She jerked it away. "Savannah, we need to talk. This can't go on."

"Will you let me be baptized?" she demanded, still staring at the wall.

"Look, if you'll just wait until you're nine or ten, then if you still want to, I'll let you."

"Heavenly Father said we are to be baptized when we're eight."

"Not all people are baptized then. Your mother, Will, Olivia— they were all older when they were baptized."

"They weren't children when they knew about the Church."

He reached out and gently turned her over to face him. "Savannah, I'm doing this for your own good. I want you to be sure you know . . ."

He let it trail off, her look telling him how ridiculous that sounded to her. He sat back, frowning down at her, wanting to take this stubborn little redhead in his arms and just hold her, and yet so infuriated with her that he also felt like putting her across his knee.

She sat up now, her face earnest, the light blue eyes filled with pleading. "Papa, I know you don't like the Church and that you think I don't know what's right. But I do, Papa. If you let me be baptized, I'll be the best girl you've ever seen. I won't give you any trouble. I won't fight with Charles anymore. I'll make my bed every day and do the dishes for Mama without whining."

That so startled him that he laughed aloud. She hated the dishes above all else and worked out elaborate schemes to avoid doing them. "It really means that much to you?"

"Oh, yes, Papa. I want to be baptized so much. Please, Papa! Please!"

He watched her, remembering the night she was born, remembering when Caroline had put her into his arms and asked what they should name her. He had called her Savannah because it was in Savannah, Georgia, home of Caroline Mendenhall, that Joshua had found his life again. And this little imp, this maddening, exasperating, frustrating little redheaded imp was a major part of that new life.

"Suppose I said that I would consider saying yes if you will wait at least until the first of June. That will give you a chance to prove to me that you really will be better. Then, if you still want to, I'll say yes."

"The first of June?" she said tentatively.

"Yes. That's just three weeks. Three more weeks to see if you really mean what you say."

She threw her arms around him, nearly choking him. "Oh, yes, Papa. Yes."

"You'll have to show me that this really is the best thing for you."

"I will, Papa. I will."

He pulled her arms loose and took her into his arms. "I'm sorry, Savannah. I'm sorry we had to fight."

"Me too, Papa, but I want to be baptized so badly."

"I can see that." He straightened. "Well, let's go down and tell your mother. She's waiting to see how the two fighting bulls came out."

Nauvoo, June 10, 1845

Dear Mama and Papa,

Surprise! I am writing the family letter this month instead of
Lydia. I have promised myself to do it for some time, but with the
press of business—both in keeping the store running properly and
trying to develop our latest plat into building lots—my time has
been taken up.

The family is fine. I'm sure Savannah has written to you by
now, but she was baptized in the Mississippi River on the 2nd of
this month by Will. Joshua seems resigned to the fact, and in a
way he is even pleased. Her promise to be the best girl he could
ever imagine has not been an empty one. Even since her baptism, she continues to shine as an example of what a young
Christian ought to be. There was a grand turnout, including
Brigham Young, Heber C. Kimball, and John Taylor. Alice and
her father also happened to be here, and we watched Alice with

great interest. She seemed fascinated by the story of Savannah's determination, but still says nothing about her own feelings. Her father has learned that Will gave her a Book of Mormon last fall and is very angry. Fortunately, her decision to keep Will completely out of things in her quest for answers allowed him to honestly say he has not been trying to sway her mind. Will she or won't she be baptized? Right now, I personally think it is doubtful, but Lydia disagrees.

Things in Nauvoo are peaceful for the moment, though they do not bode well for us. I must say, however, that we are coping with the changes more successfully than I would have guessed. In previous letters, various family members have told you about the repeal of the Nauvoo Charter last January. The antis finally got their way and stripped us of our right to civil government. Our enemies have achieved their goal, which is to leave us without power or means of defending ourselves. How ironic! How like the thinking of politicians! Their major complaint and their justification for the repeal of the charter was that we were not controlling the lawless element among us—a shameless lie! But even if it were true, what do they do? They take away the very powers required to maintain law and order.

As you can imagine, for the lawless and the predators, news of the repeal was like waving a banner saying, "Here are the helpless Saints! They have no more civil powers. Come and prey upon them at your leisure! Plunder as you please!" And for a time that was the result. Ruffians swept in and worked all kinds of mischief. It was not uncommon to have a party from one of the riverboats come into the city, work their deviltry, then leave again by nightfall. They knew full well that we had no power to stop them.

However, before you become too discouraged with this news, let me assure you that all is not hopeless. As you know, Brother Brigham has never been one to be daunted by adverse circumstances. As he himself says, if the Saints were to be sent to hell by their enemies, we would turn the devil and his angels out of it, dig ditches and canals to irrigate it, and quickly turn it into a garden paradise. This is what we are doing now. We are making the best of a bad situation.

President Young determined to use the organization of the Church to fill the need which our state government refuses to grant us. This is how it works. The whole city has been organized into sectors. Groups of about twelve men, which we call "quorums of deacons," patrol the city both day and night. In each quorum, one man is chosen as the "bishop" and he is in charge of his group. These are not true quorums, nor are the leaders really bishops. They are not based on what priesthood a man holds, but for convenience that is what they are called.

It has become an interim militia or police force. The city is divided into blocks, and a "deacon" is posted on virtually every corner. But, you ask, what good is this if there is no legal power for them to act? This is the brilliance of Brother Brigham's plan. I think Hosea Stout, our chief of police, had much to do with it as well. First of all, those who think they can come into the city at will now find that they are being watched on every hand. Any suspicious behavior is reported immediately to the leaders. This alone deters them from much of their mischief.

But there is something more. I refer to what has come to be called the "whistling and whittling brigade." Here is how it works. The young men and boys play an important role here. When a stranger comes into town, particularly a questionable-looking stranger who can give no valid reason for being here, a group of fifteen or twenty boys quickly gather around him. They have long hickory sticks and large jackknives. As they gather around the stranger, they take out their knives and begin whittling on the sticks. All the time they whistle a tune together. They never say a word. They ask no questions of the stranger and make no answer when he demands to know what they want. They are too young and small to strike individually, and too many collectively to strike back at. When they descend on a hapless stranger they hang around the man like fleas on a dog until in exasperation he finally leaves town.

It is amazing. I have watched the most hardened men give

way in the face of this silent but eerie treatment. Sometimes it goes on for hours, sometimes days. Eventually the unwanted stranger gets the message and is more than happy to leave. The whistling and whittling brigade follows him right to the boat dock or to the borders of our city. It has worked wonders and our city is mostly safe again. Crime has all but ceased, for there is not a place in the city that is not under the watchful care of someone at all times.

Young Joshua and I serve in one of these "quorums," as do Peter and Will. Most surprising, Joshua and Carl have both volunteered and serve together in another quorum. I suppose it is not surprising, for they both consider themselves fully as citizens of Nauvoo and this is a city concern. Carl also sends young Carl to be part of the whistling and whittling brigade. David is but eleven, and generally they want boys who are twelve and older, but Carl says that when he turns twelve, if the problem still exists, David will join his brother as well.

Oh, by the way, at April conference, Brigham proposed that we change the name of the city. I suppose that's partly in response to the repeal of the charter and partly because he feels it would be an appropriate tribute. But it is now official. We voted to change the name of the city to "the City of Joseph."

The long-awaited trial of the men responsible for the deaths of Joseph and Hyrum was held last month. There were nine men indicted altogether, but four fled the county. The other five, prominent citizens all, including our longtime nemesis, Thomas Sharp, have sworn they would never be convicted. Swaggering, arrogant, and contemptuous, they openly brag that they were the ones responsible. But they were finally brought to trial, some eleven months after the terrible deed.

What a sham! When the trial opened it became evident what kind of "justice" would be sought. The jury was made up totally of non-Mormons. Witnesses brought forth by the prosecution offered openly contradictory testimony. And get this. The defense attorneys argued that Joseph Smith was killed in response to the popular will of the people, the implication being that no specific person or group could be held responsible. The trial lasted for a week, and at its conclusion, all were acquitted. Surprised?

Actually, this trial was for the assassination of Joseph only. A separate trial for the murder of Hyrum Smith is scheduled for later this month, but we have little hope that it will turn out any differently.

For those who were watching the affairs in western Illinois closely, here was another sign which was easily read. <u>Act as you will against the Mormons. There will be no legal action against you.</u> That is a sobering thought to us. Joshua still talks now and then of trying to leave Nauvoo, but I think he is resigned to the fact that this is our home.

One last thing to share, then I will close. In April, Governor Ford wrote a letter to Brigham Young, who let me copy down some of it. Among other things Ford said: "Your religion is new, and it surprises the people as any great novelty in religion generally does. They cannot rise above the prejudices excited by such novelty. . . . I would suggest a matter in confidence. California now offers a field for the prettiest enterprise that has been undertaken in modern time. . . . Why would it not be a pretty operation for your people to go out there, take possession of and conquer a portion of the vacant country, and establish an independent government of your own subject only to the laws of nations?"

The invitation is put in friendly terms, but the message is clear. In the governor's eyes, there is no place for us here. That is no surprise, and Brother Brigham continues what Brother Joseph started, and that is a search for a place in the West where we can be safe. Over the past few months, the Twelve have spent a lot of time studying the journals of fur trappers and reports of government exploration expeditions. Of particular importance are the journals of John C. Fremont, an army man who has led several expeditions of exploration in Oregon Territory and California. They have also been reading newspaper articles written by those who have traveled to the West.

Right now both Texas, which as you know is now an independent nation, and Vancouver Island, which is just off the Pacific Coast and is part of Oregon Country, are being seriously considered as potential sites for colonies of Saints. Somewhere near the headwaters of the Colorado has also been talked about. But Brigham sees none of those as suitable for the massive numbers of Saints that would have to be relocated. Perhaps those locations could take smaller colonies, but in his mind they cannot be the center place. So far, one particular place in what they call the Great Basin seems like it might fit our needs. It is called the Valley of the Great Salt Lake because evidently there is a vast inland sea, a salty sea, there.

However, for all the talk and investigation, Brigham is still adamant about not leaving until the temple is completed. This is the Lord's commandment and we cannot ignore it. He says if we go into the wilderness before we get our endowments, we will fail. Talk now is that we shall dedicate the temple next April conference, a little less than a year from now, and then leave immediately thereafter.

Incidentally, Derek and Matthew and Will—all of whom have labored in England—were delighted to learn that in response to requests from the British Saints as to what they could do for the temple, in addition to sending money, Brigham suggested that perhaps they might wish to furnish a bell that would be hung in the steeple of the temple. We expect they will answer by sending a bell of some size in time for the dedication.

As the summer moves on, work on the temple progresses rapidly. Work on a stone wall—eight feet high and five feet thick at the base—that will surround the temple block has begun. The glaziers are ready to begin installing the glass in the windows. The shingles are nearly all on, the tower raised, and work on the dome will start in a month or so. The joiners are now at work finishing off the inside. It will be a great monument to the faith of our people, who have built it in their poverty, even as we make plans to abandon it.

One bit of good news. Brigham plans to have all the high priests who are out presiding over branches come back to Nauvoo to be endowed. That means we will get to see you both, at least for a time, then. We are most anxious for that day.

Well, enough for now. We all send our love. You are in our prayers. All in all, things are well with us. We hope they are the same for you.

Nathan

One other note: Lydia reminds me to tell you another piece of good news. As you know, a few months ago, Jane Manning left Carl's employ and went to live in Brigham Young's household. Carl and Melissa and the children were heartbroken because she has been so wonderful. But with the press of Church affairs, Brigham is often gone from the home and his Mary Ann needed help much more than Carl and Melissa did, though I doubt that the Youngs can pay her as well. Anyway, we just learned that she is going to wed. There is another member of the Church here who is also a free Negro. He has been courting her for some time and finally asked for her hand from Brigham. She accepted. We are very pleased for her. She is a wonderful woman and a good friend to all of us.

———•———

Even though it was the first day of September, there was no break in the blistering heat that held Nauvoo in its grip and that had done so for the past several days. The grass, the leaves, the flowers, even the animals in the fields—everything seemed wilted and drained by the high humidity and blazing sun. The last two nights had seen dazzling displays of thunder and lightning, but produced no more than a few drops of rain. Throughout the city, tempers were short, energy was low, activities were held to the barest necessities. Conversations—desultory and limpid— invariably turned to longing speculation as to when the first cooler days of autumn would come.

Caroline Steed and the children had come outside right after breakfast, determined to root out the grass and weeds from the flower gardens that lined the front of the house while the gardens were still in the shade. They worked for an hour and finally quit. She let Savannah and Charles go with their cousins to the store for candy as a reward for their efforts. Now she and Livvy sat in the shade of the front porch. Livvy, fifteen months old now, played with the kitten Joshua had brought home from the stables three days before. She knew there were a dozen things that needed to be done, but the thoughts of going inside the sweltering house were unbearable to her. So she sat here beside her daughter, doing nothing but rocking back and forth and making sure Livvy didn't smother the kitten with her love.

The sound of a carriage coming up the street from the south brought her head up. Not surprisingly, she recognized it immediately. It was a carriage from the Johnsons' livery stable, the one that typically went down to the boat dock to see if there were passengers arriving who needed transport to various destinations in the city. The sight did not surprise her, because fifteen minutes before she had heard the three blasts of the whistle of a steamboat announcing that it was arriving at the dock at the south end of Main Street. As the carriage approached, she lifted a hand to wave to Ben Johnson, the young man who always drove the carriage for his father. To her surprise, the carriage pulled up in front of her gate.

"Mornin', Sister Steed."

Caroline stopped rocking. "Mornin', Ben."

"Brought you a visitor." He jumped down and opened the carriage door. There was a rustle of skirts, the flash of a bonnet, and then Alice Samuelson stepped down. Caroline was on her feet and moving down the walk, the surprise evident on her face. "Why, Alice," she exclaimed, "what a pleasant surprise!"

Alice smiled at her, fumbled in her purse until she found a coin, and paid the boy. He walked around to the back of the carriage, got a valise and a smaller case down, set them inside the gate, then climbed up and drove off with a final wave. Caroline held the gate open wide as Alice picked up the cases and moved toward her. On the porch, Livvy was standing, the kitten forgotten, watching her mother and the new arrival.

Setting the two cases down, Alice gave Caroline a quick hug. "How good to see you again," Caroline said. Then suddenly she looked a little dismayed. "Oh, I hope your father didn't go to the freight office. Joshua isn't there. He and Will have gone upriver to Galena to meet a raft of lumber coming down from the lumber mills. They won't be back for three or four more days."

"I know," Alice responded, blushing slightly. "Will told me in his last letter that he would be gone now." At Caroline's look of surprise, she laughed softly. "Actually, I didn't want Will around this time."

"Really?" Caroline said cautiously.

"And I'm alone. My father did not come with me."

There was no helping it. Caroline was genuinely startled. "Alone?"

"Yes." Avoiding her eyes, Alice turned and looked to Livvy. "Hello, Livvy."

Livvy didn't move, but just watched the newcomer with wide, appraising eyes.

"Can't you say hello to Alice, Livvy?" Caroline said. "You remember Alice. She read stories to you the last time she was here."

There was a faint smile; then Livvy reached down and scooped up the kitten and held it out to her. The kitten began to mew as it dangled from her hands.

Alice walked forward and took the cat. "Is this your kitten, Livvy?" She began to stroke it gently. "What a pretty kitten. Does it have a name?"

Livvy's head moved back and forth with great soberness. Caroline laughed. "It's just 'Kitty' for now."

Alice handed the kitten back and turned to Caroline. "Mrs. Steed, I—"

"Oh, Alice, it's Caroline. Please!"

"Caroline, I know this seems a little strange, and I wanted to write to you, but—" She bit her lip, her eyes dropping. "But would it be possible for me to stay with you for a few days?"

"But of course." And then, looking at her more closely, she asked, "Is there anything wrong, Alice?"

Her head came up again. "No, not really." She laughed briefly, a laugh designed to cover a feeling of awkwardness. "Well, Papa is pretty upset with me for coming up here alone. But no."

Caroline considered that only for a moment, then reached out and laid a hand on Alice's arm. Warmly now she said, "I would be pleased to have your company, Alice. Let's get your things inside. You must be exhausted."

Alice didn't move. "Mrs.—Caroline, I . . ."

Caroline saw the concern and worry in the young woman's eyes. "What?"

"Did you know that Will gave me a Book of Mormon?"

"Yes," Caroline said slowly. "Have you been reading it?"

"I have. I have read it all now."

"And?"

"That's why I'm here. I want to decide about the Church once and for all." Now it came out it in a rush. "Sometimes I think I know it's true, then . . . other times I'm not sure. But I want to know. I would like to talk with Jenny and Rebecca and Lydia." She blushed a little. "I know that I've surely asked enough questions of all of you over the past months, but this time I want more than just information about the Church. I want to know how you feel, how you came to know."

Taken completely by surprise, pleased, delighted, at a loss for words, Caroline found herself merely nodding.

Now Alice was looking away, to the left, to the house that stood next to where they were, on the north side of Joshua and Caroline's place. "I know that Melissa feels differently about things," she said cautiously. "Will has told me all of that. I would like to talk to her too."

Caroline smiled warmly now. "If you are serious about this, Alice, you need to talk to Melissa too. And Carl. They'll have a different perspective, but they'll be honest with you." Her mouth took on a rueful expression. "When Joshua gets back, you won't have to ask to talk to him. If he finds out you're thinking about joining the Church, you'll get an earful." And then she couldn't help but ask the next question. "Does your father know all this?"

Alice bit her lip again, her eyes darkening. "I think he suspects. He doesn't want to think about it. He'll be furious if I decide to become a Mormon." She looked away and there was a sudden shininess in her eyes. "Really furious. But he finally relented because he thinks I want to see Will again. At least that's what he tells himself."

Caroline put an arm around her. "And do you want to see Will again?" she asked gently.

Alice sighed. "I don't know. Yes. Of course I do." Her face twisted in frustration. "And yet I am glad he's not here. I want to do this on my own. I know how he feels. Now I need to know how the rest of you feel."

"I understand."

"Besides," she said, with a trace of wistfulness, "I don't know if Will would ever be able to think of me as more than a friend."

At that, Caroline reached out and picked up Alice's bags. There was a twinkle in her eye. "Oh, I think there's an outside chance that Will already thinks of you as more than a friend."

Alice's eyes became very big. "Really?"

"Really," Caroline said. "And I can't think of anything that would please Joshua and me more than that."

⸻◦⸻

Alice Samuelson and Jenny Steed walked eastward along Mulholland Street. It was quarter past five in the afternoon and the air was insufferably hot. Both wore bonnets and Alice carried a parasol, but they still moved along slowly. Jenny carried a small picnic basket filled with sandwiches and tomatoes from the garden to take to Matthew. Brigham was pushing the workers at the temple at full speed now, wanting to enclose and finish enough rooms that they could start administering the endowment in a couple of months. As a skilled carpenter, Matthew was pressed into service now three days each week. They would work until dark, so Jenny was taking supper to him.

True to her word, for the past two days Alice had spent most of her time with the women of the Steed family. First it was Rebecca, then Lydia, and finally an afternoon with Melissa. Each night she and Caroline talked late. This morning she had come right after breakfast and spent the day with Jenny and Kathryn. When Jenny mentioned that she had to take food up to Matthew, Alice begged to go. She loved the majestic building that dominated the bluffs on the eastern side of the city. Jenny put the baby down for a nap and left three-year-old Betsy Jo playing dolls with Kathryn.

"What is it?" Alice asked as they moved along. "What is it about this place that I love so much, even more than I love St. Louis?"

Jenny laughed. "Well, not ever having been to St. Louis, I can't say. Will tells us that St. Louis is a pretty wonderful place too."

"It is. And we live in one of the prettiest parts of town. But this . . ." She flung out an arm. A little embarrassed by her enthusiasm, she let her arm drop.

After a moment, Alice looked sideways at Jenny. How comfortable she felt with this wonderful girl with the faint dusting of freckles on her face and a touch of Irish lilt in her speech. Alice would turn nineteen in December. A month following that, Jenny would be twenty-four. That made Jenny closest to her in age of all the Steed wives. And Kathryn was only nine months older than Alice. So while she felt perfectly comfortable with Caroline now, as well as Lydia and the others, Alice felt the closest to these two sisters. She loved Jenny's sweet and gentle disposition, which was laced with a good dose of good-natured but very firm spunk. She felt enormous admiration for Kathryn's quiet courage in the face of personal tragedy and for her droll wit that was constantly catching her by surprise.

"Can I ask you a question, Jenny?"

"Of course."

"How old were you when you joined the Church?"

If Jenny was surprised, she gave no sign. "I was baptized five days after my seventeenth birthday."

"That's when your mother and Kathryn were too?"

"Yes. We were all baptized together."

"Were you . . ." She colored slightly, but went on, her eyes probing Jenny's. "Did you join the Church just because your mother was joining?"

Jenny shook her head. "No. In fact, I was the first to know the Church was true. Matthew gave me a Book of Mormon and I read it. I convinced Mama and Kathryn to read it."

"Oh."

"You've been reading the Book of Mormon too, haven't you?"

"Yes, like you I got mine as a gift, from Will."

"You'd better watch out, then," Jenny teased. "Look what happened to me when I accepted Matthew's gift."

Now Alice's color deepened. "I . . ." Her lashes lowered and her cheeks were absolutely flaming now. "I wouldn't mind it if it did," she said.

Jenny reached out and slipped an arm around her waist. "And we would be absolutely delighted."

"Really?"

"Yes, really. Our whole family adores you. And Joshua—why, he would do the Virginia reel on the top of a team of horses if he thought you and Will would marry."

Alice smiled happily. "I know. He tells me that straight out. And Caroline has been wonderful too."

"Just be patient, and things will develop as the Lord wishes." And then when Alice merely nodded, Jenny went on. "Now that you've read the Book of Mormon, how do you feel about it?"

"Well, some parts I don't understand very well. But I like how often it teaches about Jesus and also how it teaches what he wants us to do."

"Have you come to the part where Jesus comes down and visits the people?"

"Yes, I've finished the book now. I thought that part was lovely."

"But you don't know if it's true?"

That made her eyebrows narrow. "Well, I don't feel that it's not true. That's what Papa keeps telling me. That it's a fraud. That it is of the devil. I don't believe that."

"Then that's an important start."

"Will won't marry me if I'm not a member of your church, will he?"

That one caught Jenny by surprise and she hesitated for a moment. "I don't know, Alice. He feels very strongly about the Church. Has he told you about the struggle he had when he was trying to decide whether or not to become a Mormon?"

"Yes. He also told me about Jenny Pottsworth. We met her at the ferry dock while I was here on my last visit. Will told me how angry it made him when she told him she wouldn't marry him unless he joined the Church, and how furious it made his father. So he's been very strong about me making up my own mind. In fact, we never talk about it. I asked him not to."

"Yes, he told Matthew. You know that we'd all love to see you join, but *you* need to know that it's true for yourself."

"Carl and Melissa don't want me to join."

Jenny stopped dead. "Is that what they said?"

There was a slow nod. "Carl did. Straight out. He said that the Church has many good things about it, but it's full of tomfoolery, what with all this about plural marriage."

"And what did Melissa say?" Jenny asked, half holding her breath.

Alice sighed. "She didn't put it that strongly. At least not until I asked her."

"You asked her if you should join the Church?"

"Actually, I asked if she believed the Church was true."

"And?"

"She said she once did. Now she wasn't sure anymore. She still believes much of it—the Book of Mormon, that Joseph was once a prophet, but . . ." She shrugged.

Jenny sighed. The family had collectively held its breath when Alice had spent the previous evening at Carl and Melissa's home for supper. And yet Alice had come to ask questions, and they felt she needed to ask them of whomever she wished.

"She talked a lot about what happened when she first learned that Joseph was teaching plural marriage. She said how it really upset her. And how it turned Carl against the Church."

"Yes, it hit Melissa very hard."

"But not you?"

They had started to walk again, and though her step momentarily slowed, Jenny did not turn to look at Alice. She was staring out ahead of them now, to the looming mass of the temple. "It would be less than the truth if I said the thought of Matthew taking a second wife doesn't bother me. A lot! But I believe that God gave the commandment to Joseph, and while I may not fully understand it, if it comes from God, then I have faith that it must be for a wise purpose. I hope that Matthew is never asked to live it. I really hope for that. But if it comes . . ." There was a quick shrug, and then a forced smile. "Well, I'll ask God to strengthen me."

"What do you mean you hope Matthew is never asked to live it? I thought sooner or later every man had to have more than one wife."

"Good heavens, no," Jenny laughed in surprise. "Right now there are only a very few. And Brother Brigham once told Matthew that he never foresees the day when every man will be asked to have more than one wife."

"Hmm, that's not the impression I got from Melissa. When Carl went up to put Mary Melissa to bed, Melissa told me straight out that's why she doesn't want Carl to join the Church. She doesn't want him to have to live it."

"I know."

"And then she started to cry," Alice continued.

"But that's not the question for me," Jenny said. "The real question is, is plural marriage something the Lord asked his people to do? There are lots of things God may ask of us that I don't like to do."

"Hmm," Alice said. She hadn't looked at it from that perspective. "Wouldn't it be wonderful if we got to choose what commandments we had to live?"

"Not really," Jenny answered immediately.

That caught Alice off guard. She had been speaking it in jest.

"We believe God gives us laws and commandments to bless us," Jenny explained. "They aren't something that keeps us from having a good time. They are meant to bring us happiness."

Alice had to look away, blinking quickly to push back the tears that sprang to her eyes.

Jenny was startled by her reaction. "I'm sorry, did I say something that offends you?"

"No," Alice answered in a husky voice. "I just wondered . . ." The tears spilled over her eyelids and started down her cheeks. "Can I be happy if I lose my family?"

"What?" Jenny blurted.

"My father says if I join the Mormons, I am no longer welcome in his home."

There was a soft gasp of astonishment.

"Even my mother, who almost always takes my side, thinks it is a terrible mistake. She stands by my father."

"Oh, Alice." Jenny slipped one arm around her. Then after a moment, she had a thought. "Have you told Lydia this?"

"What?"

"About your father?"

"No, why?"

"I want you to go over there tonight and tell her."

"But why?"

"Because Lydia's father had even stronger feelings against the Church than yours does. You need to hear her story."

And with that she gave Alice's hand a quick pat, then pulled free. "We'd best hurry. When Matthew's been working all day long, he gets very hungry. And we've just been dawdling along. I wouldn't want him to bark at us for being too late."

Alice laughed merrily at that image. "I think Matthew's bark would not be much more frightening than that of a chipmunk."

"I agree," Jenny said with a smile, "but you mustn't let him know that we know that."

<hr />

They sat on the ground east of the temple. They had come to get out of the sun, but in the half an hour since Matthew had come outside to eat his supper, the sky had become overcast. The air was still hot and heavy. It felt like a storm was coming. That was not surprising. There had been dry lightning storms the previous three evenings.

The food was gone. Jenny and Alice sat on the grass with their backs up against a large stone that was left over from the stonecutter's work. Matthew lay flat, his head in Jenny's lap. His eyes were closed and she ran her fingers slowly through his hair.

"So, Alice," Matthew said, without opening his eyes, "are you getting all your questions answered?"

"Yes. Everyone in the family has been wonderful."

"How did it go with Melissa and Carl last night?" he asked easily.

Alice laughed. "It was fine."

He cracked an eye open. "What is so funny?"

"Your family. Everyone was worried about me asking questions of Carl and Melissa, but no one tried to dissuade me."

"Oh," Matthew grunted, and his eye closed again. "Of course we wouldn't. We are all—"

From behind them, there was a low rumble of thunder. It was loud enough that they felt a slight trembling beneath their bodies. Matthew sat up, turning his head. Jenny had gone very still. In a moment, they heard it again, this time much farther away. Instantly, Matthew was on his feet and pulled Jenny up. He strode to the side of the building and looked to the west. "Uh-oh!" he muttered.

Jenny and Alice followed, and when Jenny cleared the building and looked to the sky, one hand flew to her mouth. Above them the sky was covered with thick overcast, but it held no immediate threat of rain. Out to the west, over the plains of

Iowa, it was a very different scene indeed. Huge black thunderheads were massing together, bumping up against one another like battering rams lining up for an assault on the gates of hell itself. Forked lightning flashed downward and again the low rumble was heard.

Matthew took her by the elbow and moved her forward a little. "You'd better go, Jenny. Quickly. Leave the basket. I'll bring it when I've finished work."

"Yes." She jerked her head toward Alice. "We have to go, Alice."

As they hurried back out to the street, Alice had to half run to keep up. "What is it?" she said. "What's wrong?"

Jenny lifted a hand to point. Even as she did so, the lightning flashed, flickering like the tongue of some great serpent. It flared again, more brightly than before. "One, two, three," she started beneath her breath. She got to fourteen before the thunder shook the sky, making the air around them seem to shudder.

Alice didn't need to ask what that meant. Every five seconds meant the lightning had struck about a mile away. Fourteen seconds meant less than three miles, barely across the river. A dark veil hung from beneath the great cumulus clouds, almost black as night and more thick than a heavy fog. It was pouring not far across the river, and the storm was moving visibly toward them.

"This could be a bad one, Jenny," Alice said with some foreboding. "Perhaps it would be better for us to stay here at the temple."

"Kathryn," Jenny said with a sharp shake of her head. "I've got to get back and be with Kathryn."

"Kathryn? But why?"

Jenny's mouth was tight. "Since her accident, lightning and thunderstorms terrify her. Especially if she's alone."

Chapter Notes

The response of the Church to the repeal of the Nauvoo Charter, including the "whistling and whittling brigade," is described in several places (see

CHFT, pp. 299–300; *American Moses,* pp. 122–23; Thurmon Dean Moody, "Nauvoo's Whistling and Whittling Brigade," *BYU Studies* 15 [Summer 1975]: 480–90).

The trial for the murder of Hyrum Smith was scheduled for 24 June 1845, but the prosecuting attorney didn't bother to show up and so it was never held.

Governor Ford's letter of "invitation" for the Saints to leave the state is recorded in the official history of the Church (see *HC* 7:398). Before his death, Joseph Smith was planning to find a place of refuge for the Saints somewhere in the Rocky Mountains. During the months following the Martyrdom, the Twelve never wavered in their determination to carry out that plan. Lyman Wight, a member of the Twelve, had been sent to Texas by Joseph Smith to explore the possibilities of establishing a colony there. Rather than exploring, however, he established a permanent settlement and called on the Church to come to Texas. When the Twelve asked the Wight group to return to join the main body of Saints, the independent-minded Wight refused. After several tries at reconciliation, he eventually was excommunicated in 1848. (See *CHFT,* p. 305.)

The ongoing progress of the temple construction is reported at various times in the official history (see *HC* 7:358, 385–86, 388–89, 401, 407–8, 417–18, 430–31). The British Saints did respond to President Young's suggestion and sent a bell for the temple steeple. It weighed over fifteen hundred pounds. When the Saints left for the West, the bell was taken down and carried across the plains. (See *Encyclopedia of Mormonism,* s.v. "Nauvoo Temple.") The "Nauvoo Bell," as it came to be called, now sits on Temple Square in Salt Lake City.

One of the best indicators of how strongly Brigham Young felt about completing the temple, even though he knew they would abandon it shortly thereafter, is found in a talk he gave on 18 August 1844, just ten days after he and the Twelve were sustained to lead the Church. He said: "There seems to be a disposition by many to leave Nauvoo and go into the wilderness or somewhere else. . . .

". . . If we should go to the wilderness and ask the Lord to give us an endowment, he might ask us, saying, Did I not give you rock in Nauvoo to build the Temple with? Yes. Did I not through my providence furnish men to quarry and cut the stone and prepare it for the building? Yes. Did I not give you means to build the Temple there? Yes. Very well, had you died in Nauvoo, on the walls of the Temple, or in your fields, I would have taken you to myself and raised up men to officiate for you, and you would have enjoyed the highest glory. . . .

"Such may go away but I want to have the faithful stay here to build the Temple and settle the city." (*HC* 7:256, 257.)

Kathryn McIntire felt the icy fingers of dread start clutching at her chest a full ten minutes before she heard the first rumblings of thunder. Her hair felt the first prickly sensations of static electricity in the air. Her body seemed to sense that something was changing. She was sitting in her wheelchair, still playing dollhouse with Betsy Jo. Her head came up, and she listened—no, it was more like she felt the air around her, sensing it as a wild animal senses danger long before the first scent of the wolf is in the wind.

Without a word to her niece, she turned the chair and wheeled it to the window that looked out to the northwest. When Carl and Melissa built their second house, a larger two-story structure, Jenny and Matthew moved into their first house. It was on the east side of Granger Street at the corner with Mulholland. Because there was no building on the opposite corner, Kathryn's view was unlimited, and she could see that the sky was much darker out across the river than it was above her. She returned, saying nothing, but her mind was now only partially on the make-believe conversation Betsy Jo was creating.

When the first low rumble came she whirled and rolled to the window again. Now she saw what Jenny and Alice had seen from the bluffs. She pulled her chair around again. "Betsy Jo, will you go shut the doors to the house?"

Betsy Jo, three now, and looking very much like her father, except for the thick dotting of freckles across her cheeks and nose, looked up in surprise. "Why, Kathryn? It's hot."

She fought to keep her voice from betraying any sign of concern. "There may be a storm coming. We'd better shut the doors." Without waiting for a response, she turned, gave one last look at the gathering clouds, and pulled the window shut. She reached up and pulled the drapes shut as well. While she rolled from window to window and shut each one, Betsy Jo went to the front door and closed it. As Betsy Jo went to the back door to check it, another clap of distant thunder rattled the windows softly. Kathryn gripped the arms of her wheelchair to stop her hands from trembling. A moment later there was a faint flash. She visibly jumped, keeping her eyes from clamping shut only by a huge effort of will.

"Aunt Kathryn," Betsy Jo said, her eyes filled with concern, "what's the matter? Why is it so dark?"

Her fingers dug into the wood of her chair as she forced herself to smile. "I pulled all the drapes, Betsy Jo. If the wind blows we don't want the rain to come in."

She looked puzzled, but Kathryn didn't feel like trying to explain. "Let's go in the bedroom now. It's about time for Emmeline to wake up."

"All right," Betsy Jo said cheerfully. "Can I bring Molly?" She picked up her doll.

"Of course," Kathryn said. She swallowed to combat the sudden constriction in her throat. She swallowed again. Her heart was pounding like that of a rabbit cornered by a hound. As Betsy Jo trooped past her and into the hall that led to the bedroom, Kathryn closed her eyes. *Oh, please, Father. Let this pass by me. Let me be strong.*

The last few nights had seen a series of dry thunderstorms that shook the ground and blazed across the sky. They had left her trembling and pale, even with Jenny and Matthew there beside her to help steady her. About two weeks before, a man walking along Parley Street, just a few blocks from where she now was, had been struck by lightning and killed. It was a grim contradiction to what everyone—including herself—kept saying in order to try and allay her fears. Her reserves of strength, both physically and emotionally, had been tapped too often. She was trembling visibly now.

She jumped slightly as she saw that Betsy Jo was watching her with large grave eyes. "Kathryn? Come on!"

"Yes, dear," she said with a flick of her hand. "You go in and I'll be right there." As Betsy Jo complied, there was another flash of lightning, brighter this time, barely dimmed by the drawn curtains. She dropped her head into her hands, her body shaking violently now. "Jenny!" she whispered desperately. "Hurry! Oh, please! Hurry!"

Matthew caught up with them just as they reached the bottom of the bluff. The wind had started now. In a matter of three or four minutes, it had gone from the first stirrings of a breeze to stiff, noticeably colder blasts that tore at their clothes. Matthew's head was uncovered. He had either left his hat back at the temple or lost it as he raced down the hill after the two women. Either way, he paid it no mind. To Jenny's surprised look he only said, "This is going to be a bad one. I'll come with you."

She nodded grimly, and they hurried on. There was no question about his assessment. The leading edge of the storm was just a mile or two away now, coming out of the northwest. The whole western horizon looked as if it had been draped with a filmy black curtain. They could still see some of the buildings of Montrose, Iowa, across the river, but beyond that, the prairie was taking a terrific pounding with what promised to be torrential rain. Lightning crackled and shot downwards every two or three seconds now, and the cracks of thunder followed one right after another.

By the time they were off the bluff and to Durphy Street, the wind was hardening, blowing straight into their faces, making them bend into it. It tore at their clothes, at the trees and bushes, stirring up clouds of dust and debris. Alice's bonnet was snatched off her head, and was saved only because she had tied it beneath her chin. The dresses of the two women were pressed against their bodies, like sails, and made walking an effort.

As they crossed Partridge Street, the first rain started to fall—huge, slashing drops that splattered like eggs on the dusty street. "You run ahead, Matthew," Jenny yelled into the wind. "Kathryn will be terrified."

Matthew shook his head quickly. He had already considered that. Though he said nothing, his eye kept searching the western sky. The blackness was so deep, the huge masses of clouds scudding rapidly even as he watched, that he half expected at any moment to see the dark clouds start to coalesce, curling round and round even as they started to drop toward the ground and become that most dreaded of all sights, the funnel cloud of a tornado. He dared not leave the two women alone in something like that. "We'll find shelter first. Then I'll go."

As if the sluice in a dam had suddenly been pulled, the skies opened and the rain poured down, whipped into great sheets in front of them. In seconds they were soaked to the skin. Water poured from the roofs of nearby buildings. What had been thick dust just moments before was now a river of thick, gooey mud that stuck to their feet like binder's glue. They were half running, half stumbling now, fighting the rain and mud, struggling against the tearing wind, raising their hands up to their eyes to keep the rain from blinding them.

Less than a minute later, the first of the white pellets came streaking out of the sky. Almost before they could comprehend what had happened, the sheets of water turned to curtains of hail. The ground danced as though it were suddenly alive, the pellets bouncing like popcorn kernels on a hot griddle. The roar of the wind and thunder was now joined by the steady rattle of hail. There was a blinding flash, followed almost instantly by a thunderous crack that nearly knocked them off their feet.

Jenny gasped and nearly tripped, but Matthew scooped her up and steadied her. He raised one arm to try and cover her head. "Carl's brickyard is just ahead. We'll go there."

"Ow!" Alice cried, throwing her hands above her head. Matthew winced too as his arms were suddenly peppered with stinging blows. The hail was no longer just snow pellets but hard little ice balls, about the size of a pea. It was as though a thousand little devils were cracking tiny whips on the surface of their skin. Matthew looked up, trying to see how far they were. And then he saw the round dark shape off to their right. "There!" he cried, pointing. "We're here! Take cover!"

"No!" cried Jenny. "We've got to get home. Kathryn will be—" Her words were cut off by a cry of pain. A larger hailstone struck her directly on the bridge of her nose. One hand flew up to grasp the spot. Tears of pain sprang to her eyes. When she withdrew her hand, her nose was bleeding from a shallow scratch.

"Run!" Matthew exclaimed, taking Alice by one hand and Jenny by the other. There was no protest on Jenny's part now. It was as though the gods above had emptied their buckets of the pea-sized gravel and had gone to the next larger size. Hailstones the size of marbles were drumming around them now, cutting leaves from the trees above them, turning the puddles into violent, churning cauldrons. Already the ground was whitening with a layer of summer "snow." Every blow stung sharply now, even through their clothing.

They ducked behind the shelter of the nearest brick kiln, but it provided only marginal protection. A few feet away was one of the drying sheds. The hail on the wood shingles sounded like the roar of a great waterfall. Matthew reached it in three great leaps, threw open the door, and dragged the two women inside.

They leaned over, gasping for breath, water streaming from their hair down into their faces. Alice's bonnet hung around her neck like a child's washrag. Jenny's was gone completely. Matthew was standing at the door, staring out in dumbfounded amazement. "Look!" he commanded.

The women came to stand beside him. What he was looking at was hailstones the size of hen's eggs. Now it was not the rattle of a hundred drummers on the roof but that of a thousand rifles blasting off all at once. Limbs were stripped from the trees and whipped away by the wind. Across the street, through the hail, a cornfield looked as though it were being shredded by invisible hands. Above the roar he heard the terrified neighing of a horse.

He moved forward a little, putting one hand above his head. "You stay here," he said to Jenny. "Don't leave until it stops." But before he could move, there was a sharp crash behind them. They whirled to see one of the windows along the north end of the building shatter and spray glass along the floor. *Crack!* A second window exploded inward, followed by a large hailstone which bounced off the low counter and onto the floor.

"No, Matthew!" Jenny cried, turning back to grab his arm. "You can't go out in this."

Matthew started to pull away, then looked at the devastation being wreaked all around them. He stepped back, staring out at the storm. "What about Kathryn?" he asked.

Jenny just looked away, shaking her head.

———•———

"I'm scared, Kathryn," Betsy Jo whined, burying her head against Kathryn's shoulder. Outside, the storm was raging. The almost constant crash of thunder now was virtually drowned out by the roar of the hail on the roof.

Kathryn didn't dare touch Betsy Jo with her hands. They were shaking so badly she was afraid it would frighten her all the more. "I know," she said, "I know. It's all right, Betsy Jo. It won't hurt us. It's just loud and noisy."

She turned again to the trundle bed, steeling herself to reach down and pick up the baby, who was wide awake and starting to whimper. There was a sharp crack and then the sound of shattering glass. Betsy Jo screamed in terror. Kathryn jerked up so violently she nearly turned the wheelchair over. Instantly the curtains were dancing wildly and a blast of cold, wet air swept through the room. The baby started to shriek.

Kathryn threw her arms around her body, hugging herself fiercely to try and regain control. Tears streamed down her cheeks and she wanted to fall to the floor and roll under the bed. She forced herself to straighten. "It's all right! It's all right!" she stammered. She had to shout to make herself heard over the tremendous noise of the storm. "Help me get the baby up, Betsy Jo! Come on, help me!" She didn't realize that she was sobbing, walking the very edge of hysteria herself.

But the sharpness of her voice was enough to pull Betsy Jo out of her own terror. She stepped up to the bed and together they leaned over and lifted the baby up and put her into Kathryn's lap. It was almost more than Kathryn could do to hold little Emmeline on her lap, her body was shaking so badly.

Though it was still an hour or so from sunset, the house was as dark as though it were eventide. Suddenly, every room in the house was lit brightly by a terrible flash. Instantly there was a tremendous blast of sound and the house shook from rafter to root cellar. Betsy Jo dropped to her knees, screaming at the top of her little-girl lungs. Her face was contorted and twisted in sheer terror. But Kathryn couldn't help her. She was clutching the baby, fighting her own blind panic, and it was taking every effort of will not to drop the baby and throw her hands over her eyes. "Help me, Jenny!" she cried, her voice sounding much like that of Betsy Jo's. "Please, Jenny! Please!"

In the next room the front door crashed open. Kathryn started, thinking the wind had blown the door open. There was another blinding flash and she clamped her eyes shut tightly, fighting to stop from screaming out herself. One more paralyzing flash and she would be undone, leaving these two children to fend for themselves.

She opened her eyes again and gave a little cry. There in the doorway to her bedroom stood Peter. He was soaked to the skin, his shirt stuck to his chest as if it had been dipped in paste. His hair was wildly disheveled and dripping water. His boots looked twice their normal size, so plastered with mud were they. In three leaps he was across the room and dropping to his knees beside her. He put his arms around her. "It's all right, Kathryn. I'm here. I'm here."

She stared at him as though he were an apparition; then, with a racking sob, she threw one arm out to him. "Peter! Oh, Peter!"

"It's all right. It's all right," he soothed. "I'm here now. Everything is all right." He moved around the chair and scooped up Betsy Jo. "It's me, little Betsy Boo! It's Peter."

Peter came to the house to read to Kathryn or just to visit two or three times a week now. He and Betsy Jo were the best of friends. At three now, she wouldn't stand for the nickname she had been given as a child—except from Peter. With a look of pure joy, she threw her arms around his neck and thrust her face against his shoulder.

"Are you all right?" Peter asked, reaching out with one hand to lay it over Kathryn's trembling arm.

"The window," she started, pointing numbly, wanting to act as though there was at least some semblance of control still left in her.

"I know. The hail broke several windows at the printing office too. But it's all right. I'm here now."

And then for the first time, she really looked at him. There was a small cut just below his left eye. Another one on his forehead. A third lower on the opposite cheek. The blood had been half washed away, but a fresh trickle was starting down his cheek. And then she looked down and gasped. His arm looked as though he had thrust it into a rosebush. There were half a dozen cuts, all bleeding and mingling with the wetness of his arm.

"Peter, what happened?" And then her mouth opened wide as she answered her own question. "The hail?"

He nodded. "I've never seen anything like it," he murmured. "It's like running through a shower of rocks."

Understanding slowly dawned. "You came for me?" she said in awe.

He nodded, then smiled, stroking Betsy Jo's hair now, whispering softly into her ear. The great shudders of relief were lessening now and she was no longer crying. Finally he looked at Kathryn. "I saw Matthew this morning on his way to the temple. He told me Jenny was going to bring him supper. I was at the printing office and suddenly I wondered if you were alone."

She jumped visibly again as another flash of lightning, followed by another thunderous crack, shook the house. He moved closer to her, pulling Betsy Jo with him. Smiling, he put one arm around her, putting his body against her leg so as to help brace the baby too. "It's all right, Kathryn," he said. "I'm here."

She closed her eyes, her body sagging back against the seat. "Yes," she murmured softly. "Yes."

"I can't believe it," Will said, shaking his head. "Pa and I must have seen thirty or forty windows broken out, and that was just coming here from the northern landing."

"The boat captain nearly ran aground," Joshua said with a nod. "For a while there, we couldn't see ten yards ahead of us. The river looked like it was boiling."

"I believe it," Matthew said. "For a time there, I could barely see the ground."

They all nodded, each remembering with a trace of horror the storm that had swept over them just a couple of hours before. They sat in Matthew and Jenny's main room, filling every chair and bench. Though it was smaller than the other houses, by common consent everyone came here because they knew that with the heavy mud and the street littered with debris it would be hard for Kathryn to maneuver her wheelchair. They gathered naturally, without any specific call to do so. They were here to discuss the damage and make plans for correcting it. To their great surprise and relief, they had barely gathered, when Joshua and Will had arrived, returning from their trip to Galena a day earlier than expected.

And so began the reports of the damage. Every house had windows shattered and shingles gone. Carl had lost a whole run of bricks when several inches of water flooded one of his drying sheds. Derek's cornfield was little more than a forest of stubs and shredded stalks. His watermelons and cantaloupe looked like they had been blasted with buckshot. At the dry goods store, the two north-facing windows had both been blown in, and a room full of barley and wheat had been flooded. A cabinet, finished except for receiving its stain and varnish and which had taken Matthew over a month to construct, was sitting directly under one of the windows at the cabinet shop that had been blown out. It was now sodden and terribly warped.

"Let's just hope the rain has stopped for now," Derek spoke up. "We need some time to get those roofs patched up again before more comes."

Joshua grimaced. "I'll bet there is damage at the freight yard. I just hope the men had sense enough to get the stock in."

"They did," Peter spoke up. "I walked down there just before dark to check on things."

"You did?" Joshua asked in surprise.

"Yes. The stock was all inside the stables and the men said your warehouse lost a few shingles, but that's all. You don't have windows, so nothing seems to have been flooded."

"Well, thank you, Peter," Joshua said, completely surprised by that. Kathryn too was giving him a strange look.

Matthew was looking at Peter oddly as well. "You had a busy night tonight, didn't you?"

He shrugged and looked away.

Joshua reached out and took Caroline's hand. "I was going to go check on things later tonight, but I'll take Peter's word on it that everything's all right."

"What about the rafts of lumber?" Nathan asked. "Will they be all right?"

"I think so," Joshua answered. "They're probably a day, maybe a day and a half behind us. The storm may have missed them completely."

"Normally," Will added, "they tie up on shore if a storm is coming. I think they'll be all right."

"And are you taking the lumber on down to St. Louis?" Alice asked. She spoke to Joshua, but it was Will who was getting the sidelong glances.

Will smiled. "Pa thinks we can sell off about a third of it here. Frenchie will take the rest on down to your father."

"So you won't be going?" Alice blurted. There was no mistaking the open pleasure in her voice, and several smiled, including Joshua.

Will shook his head firmly. "Nope. I'm here to stay for a time."

"Frenchie?" Nathan broke in. "So Jean Claude is still your foreman up there?"

"Aye," Joshua said, "and there's not a better man in all the pineries either."

"Yes," Nathan said softly. "He's a good man."

Will turned to Alice. "It was Jean Claude and Nathan who pulled me from the river up there. They saved my life."

Caroline shuddered slightly. "Please, don't talk about that. I had nightmares for months after I learned what happened. I can't bear to think about it."

"Is he still a Mormon?" Lydia asked.

Joshua pulled a face. "Frenchie? Yes, and converting half the camp as well." But it was said without rancor.

"Really?" Nathan exclaimed with open pleasure.

Will laughed at his father. "He's converted four others. That's hardly half the camp." Still smiling, Will went on. "In truth, he could convert the whole territory of Wisconsin and baptize them Mormons, and Pa wouldn't do much. He's too valuable. If he loses Jean Claude, he'll have to go up there himself again."

"Perhaps we ought to send your father back up with Jean Claude, Will," Kathryn said with a straight face. "Maybe the Frenchman could get him baptized as well."

For a moment everyone looked startled, none less than Joshua, then several laughed. Joshua turned and gave the girl in the wheelchair a fierce look. She smiled coyly at him. Of all the family, only Kathryn dared tease Joshua about the Church.

Jenny was delighted with her sister's boldness and clapped her hands. "I say we take a vote. How many want to send Joshua up to Wisconsin for the winter so he can find religion?"

Every hand shot up, including Caroline's. Then, to everyone's surprise, Joshua turned to Alice. "My greatest fear is that one of these nights a member of the family is going to creep into my bedroom, knock me over the head with a truncheon, and drag me down to the river. I'll be baptized and a holder of the priesthood before I even wake up."

There was a moment of stunned astonishment. Joshua was joking about being baptized?

To everyone's further amazement, Carl jumped in too. "I lock my door and post a watch every night, just in case," he suggested evenly to Joshua. For one long moment, there was shocked silence as everyone stared at Carl and Joshua. Then Carl grinned shyly and the room exploded with laughter. Carl too? That *was* a healthy sign. Even Melissa was laughing.

"Actually, Joshua locks our door too," Caroline said mischievously, "but if you let me know when you're coming, I'll see that it's open." That really brought a roar from the family as Joshua yelped in protest.

Alice waited for things to subside, and then tentatively spoke up, looking at Will as she did so. "Well, if someone will just knock on my door, they won't have to drag me at all."

For a moment Will's expression was that of disbelief; then he lit up as though a lamp had just been turned onto his face. "Are you saying that . . ." He reared back a little, not daring to believe.

She nodded.

"What?" Joshua asked suspiciously. "What are you saying?"

"I'm saying I've made up my mind. I am going to be baptized."

The room went totally silent. This was no longer just speaking in jest, and Joshua's face had lost all humor now. He repeated his question. "What are you saying, Alice?"

Alice had not said what she did on mere impulse. She had been waiting for the right moment, and she guessed what the reaction from Will's father would be. She was ready for his question. "I came up here to find out for myself, Mr. Steed." Her head was up and her eyes steady. She did not flinch from his perturbed glare. "And don't be thinking your family has pushed me into it. This is my decision, and my decision alone."

Will was out of his chair, standing before her, staring down at her in wonder. "You mean it?" he blurted. "You really want to be baptized?"

"Yes, I do."

"Your father will be livid," Joshua said, shaking his head. "You just can't come up here alone and make a decision like that. You have to talk to your father."

"I have talked with my father. I am quite clear on where he stands."

He whirled on Caroline. "I could have guessed."

Again to everyone's surprise, Carl spoke up. "Actually, it was not Caroline's doing, Joshua. Of all of us, she has been the most circumspect in not trying to sway Alice's feelings."

"You too?" Joshua cried, feeling betrayed. "You support this too, Carl?"

"No, I don't," he answered evenly. "As a matter of fact, Melissa and I tried to convince her that she should not be baptized. If anyone's been preaching at her, trying to change her mind, it's been us." He smiled at Alice warmly. "Obviously we failed. But it really is her decision, Joshua. Not yours. Not her father's."

Alice smiled back at Carl. "Thank you, Mr. Rogers."

Carl pulled a face. "Really, Alice, since you're going to be part of the family, you've got to stop calling us Mr. Steed and Mr. Rogers."

Alice gasped a little and went a deep crimson. Melissa looked at her husband sternly. But Carl was in a strange mood, it seemed. He ignored his wife, ignored Joshua's glowering countenance, and turned to Will. "Well, it's no secret, is it, Will? Don't you love this girl?"

Alice dropped her head, not daring to meet Will's eyes, absolutely mortified.

Will looked down at her, then went down on one knee to face her. "I'm glad you asked that, Carl, because the answer is yes. I love Alice Samuelson, and I'm glad she's here, because on the way here from Galena I decided I was going to sail right on down to St. Louis and ask her father for her hand in marriage."

As the whole family erupted with applause and cries of congratulations, Alice's head came up slowly. Her eyes were wide and shining with disbelieving joy. Will leaned forward, took her face in his hands, and kissed her gently. "That is, assuming Miss Samuelson approves."

That was enough to even put Joshua's dismay at her announcement of baptism aside. He jumped to his feet and strode across to them. "You really mean it?" he said, clapping Will on the shoulder.

"I do."

Caroline was up too. By the time she reached Alice, Alice was up and walked right into her arms. "Welcome to our family, Alice." Caroline pulled back and smiled at her. "I told you I thought there might be something to wait around for."

Now the others crowded in, pounding Will on the back, grasping their hands, hugging Alice, and shedding a few tears of joy together.

When things finally settled down a little, Kathryn suddenly started slapping the arm of her wheelchair with the flat of her hand to get everyone's attention. As they quieted and turned to her, she held up both hands. "In light of this wonderful announcement, there is a request I would like to make of this couple."

"What?" Will asked, standing beside Alice, and turning to face Kathryn.

Now the room was all but still. "I know this is a lot to ask of two people who are so much in love, but I'm wondering if you might consider postponing your wedding somewhat."

There were soft cries of surprise and dismay. "Postponing it?" Will asked with a puzzled expression. "What for? I mean, we haven't even set a date yet." He laughed. "Alice is still trying to get her breath here."

That won him a round of good-natured laughter all around.

"Actually," Kathryn said, very sober now, "I was wondering if you might postpone it long enough to plan a double wedding."

For several seconds it didn't register. A puzzled look was on every face. "Double wedding?" Lydia finally said. And then her eyes flew open and her hand went up to her mouth. "You, Kathryn?"

Suddenly she was as red as Alice had been a moment before. "Yes—that is, if I can get Peter here to propose to me, like Will just did to Alice."

Every eye turned to Peter but he didn't see them. Thunderstruck, he gaped at Kathryn.

It was Matthew who reacted first. He reached out, grabbed Peter by the arm, and propelled him toward Kathryn's chair. "Are you daft, man? The lady just asked you for a proposal of marriage."

Peter took two steps forward, haltingly. His gaze was fixed on Kathryn's face, still in complete astonishment.

Rebecca handed the baby to Derek and got to her feet. She picked up where Matthew left off, taking Peter by the hand and leading him to Kathryn's chair. "Go down on one knee like Will did," she whispered. "That was a very nice touch."

He did, only slowly, still dazed. Kathryn was laughing at him now, and crying at the same time. "You really mean it?" he stammered.

"Yes, Peter."

"But . . . but why?"

"Why?" Joshua said softly, grinning widely. "You have to ask why at a time like this?"

But Kathryn knew exactly what he meant. She reached out and touched his bare arm, covered now with angry red cuts and scratches. She caressed it gently with her fingertips. "Because you came," she murmured.

Five days later and some thirty miles southeast, Solomon Garrett came in from putting his horse in the barn. As he entered the back door, Jessica and the children were all waiting for him at the end of the hall. He smiled at the expectant look on their faces. "Well, what have we here?"

Jessica held up the letter she was holding. "This came today. It's from Lydia."

"Oh? And how are things in the City of Joseph?"

Jessica smiled. Out of habit almost everyone still called it Nauvoo, but since last April conference when the name had been officially changed to the City of Joseph, her husband never slipped. It was always the City of Joseph.

"Can I tell him, Mama?" young John cried out. "Please?"

"I want to. I want to," Mark chimed in.

"No, I get to," Luke said with finality. "I brought the letter home from the postmaster."

Little Miriam, now just two, stuck her hand in the air and started dancing up and down, even though she had no idea what she was vying for. Solomon laughed and scooped her up in his arms. "This must be very good news," he said to Jessica.

She nodded happily. "The best, Solomon. The very best."

"Papa?"

"Yes, John."

"Can we go to Nauvoo and see Alice and Kathryn get married?"

They were at the supper table now. John barely waited for the blessing on the food to be said before making his request. Solomon nodded. "Of course. We wouldn't miss that."

Jessica smiled at her son, the only child she had borne with John Griffith before he was killed at Haun's Mill. "Kathryn has asked Rachel to be one of her bridesmaids. Do you know what that means, John?"

"No."

"Well, it means that—" She stopped, realizing that what she was about to say wouldn't make much sense to a seven-year-old. "Actually, it is someone who is there at the wedding who . . ." She shook her head. "How do you explain what a bridesmaid is?"

Rachel turned to her brother. "It's someone who dresses up in their prettiest dress and stands by Kathryn when she's being married so she'll have someone to share in her joy."

"Oh." That made sense.

"When will the wedding be?" Mark asked.

Now Jessica spoke up. "They didn't say. Alice wants to be baptized first, and she is going to write to her parents and tell them. It will take a couple of weeks to get their reply."

"That kind of surprised me," Solomon said. "I would have thought Alice would go back to St. Louis to tell her parents about the baptism and the wedding."

"Reading between the lines," Jessica answered, "I think she wants to break it to them by letter first and see what they say."

"That may be the wisest move if Joshua is right about how her father's going to react."

"Do you have to be baptized before you can get married, Mama?" Mark asked.

She laughed. "No. Alice just wants to, that's all."

Solomon had a thought. "If Mother and Father Steed come home in a month or two to get their endowments, as President Young has said, I'll bet they'll wait until they're back."

"Of course they will," Jessica said. "I hadn't even thought about that yet."

"When will that be, Papa?" Rachel said, looking disappointed.

"Not until late October, or perhaps early November."

"Then we can't go see them until then?" The disappointment was heavy.

Solomon looked at Jessica, who smiled, then nodded. "Oh," he answered, "I think this news is so good, we should go over and see the family right away. What do you think?"

That won him an instant chorus of acclamation. "Oh, yes, Papa. Yes."

"When could we go?" Rachel cried.

Jessica watched the excitement that swept around the table, not wanting to douse their enthusiasm. "Remember, school is scheduled to begin in two weeks. And your father is going to leave in a few days to see how the common schools are coming along."

Solomon decided to rescue Rachel. "I'll tell you what. Today is the eighth of September. I leave on the tenth, but I'll be back on the thirteenth, or the fourteenth at the latest. Then we can leave the following day. How's that?"

"How long can we stay?" Luke demanded to know.

"Four or five days." Then, at the look on Jessica's face, he added, "Starting school a little late will be all right. How many of your students are going to complain at that?"

"Oh, Mama, can we?" Rachel said, turning to Jessica. Her eyes were shining with excitement.

Jessica laughed. "Your father is the best judge of these things."

"Yea!" Mark shouted. He started doing a little wiggle-dance right in place in his chair. "We're going to Nauvoo! We're going to Nauvoo!"

As they settled down to eating again, Jessica looked at her husband. "Where all do you plan to go?"

"I'll go straight to Yelrome because that will likely take me the longest time. Father Morley is anxious to have their common school get started on the right foot and he has many questions.

Then I'll slip on up to Green Plains before starting back. I don't think Bear Creek is ready, but I'll talk to them on the way."

A look of concern had darkened Jessica's eyes. "You're not going into Warsaw, are you?"

"No. Not this time."

"Good. And you'll not be stopping in Carthage?"

"Nope. Just passing through it on my way there and on my way back home."

Her face smoothed again. Nothing more needed to be said, especially not in front of the children. There were many places in Hancock County where one could find anti-Mormon sentiment, but Warsaw and Carthage were the two centers. It was not by chance that Joseph and Hyrum had been killed in Carthage by a mob mostly made up of Warsaw militia. And things were stirring again. Since his acquittal the previous spring for the murders of Joseph and Hyrum, Thomas Sharp, editor of the *Warsaw Signal*, had been whipping up the anti-Mormon sentiment again. Only now he was getting more and more popular support.

"Pa?" Mark said, setting his fork down. "Is it true that Yelrome is named after Brother Morley, only spelled backwards?"

"Of course it's true," Luke answered for his father.

"Yes, son," Solomon agreed. "Yelrome was settled by Father Morley, and so his people decided to call it Yelrome, which is his name spelled backwards."

Mark's face screwed up in puzzlement. "But it doesn't work."

"What doesn't work?"

"Yelrome spelled backwards is E-more-ly, not Morley."

"They added the *e* to make it Yel-*rome* and not Yel-*rum*," Solomon explained.

"Oh." Mark thought about it. "That's kinda dumb. Why not do it right?"

Luke shook his head. "Because Yel-*rum* is dumb!"

"Hush, Luke," Jessica said gently. "Don't you be talking that way to your brother. Now, you all finish up supper. Rachel and I have to start getting the textbooks ready."

Chapter Notes

Nauvoo is known to have had severe thunderstorms at this time. On 20 August 1845, a man was struck by lightning and killed in Nauvoo (see *HC* 7:436). Thomas Bullock, who often recorded comments on the weather in his journal, wrote an entry under the date of 3 September, the same date depicted in the novel: "The most terrific hail storm I ever saw came on. Thunder awful, lightning tremendous. The hail fell, and lumps of ice two inches in circumference smashed 26 panes in my house, cut the corn into ribbons, leveled every thing else in the garden. It came from the N. West and lasted about 3 quarters of an hour." The following day he wrote that virtually every glass window in Nauvoo that fronted the north was smashed. (See "Journal of Thomas Bullock," pp. 15–17.)

Thomas Sharp had the eyes of a hawk—bright, glittering, taking everything in with intense, darting glances; then, fixing on their prey, they would become like two rounded pieces of glowing obsidian. His nose was large and hooked, his mouth tight and drawn down, all of which further added to the impression of a raptor on the hunt.

He sat at the front of the single large room at the Green Plains schoolhouse. It was jammed with men. They lined the walls and spilled outside. Some stood at the open windows peering in. Most of them he knew. Most of the crowd was either from here in Green Plains or from Warsaw, six miles to the northwest. There were a few from Carthage and other surrounding settlements. But even the ones he couldn't have identified by name were familiar faces. More important, named or unnamed, the faces were hard, bitter, angry. In that one thing the crowd was as one—they hated Mormons and were willing to do something about it. When the time was right, they could be molded for his purposes, but for now Sharp was content to listen and watch.

Colonel Levi Williams and Frank Worrell were the ones doing the talking at the moment. Or rather they were shouting. Ostensibly, the meeting was called to discuss protecting their property rights from encroachment by the Mormons. But it was quickly turning into an anti-Mormon rally. Sharp watched Williams harangue the crowd. This was the colonel's town. As he railed at them, he kept calling on men by name. "Abner, you've been wronged by the Mormons, haven't you?" "James, wasn't it you that had a cow stolen by a couple of Mormon boys?" "Walter, are you ready to have the Mormons steal away your property rights?" And so on. He was working them well, with Frank Worrell chipping in from time to time.

Sharp was patient because he understood people. It was always like this. It took time to get a crowd going. It took some doing to ratchet them down to the point where they were ready to act and not just bellow. And for that, Worrell and Williams made a good team. They were highly popular—almost adulated—by the men. Both had played a central role in the killing of the Smith brothers the year before. A lot of men bragged about going after Joseph Smith, but Levi Williams had been one of the leaders of the men who stormed the jail. There were whispers that he had been the one who actually fired the shot that killed Joseph Smith, but Sharp had questions about that.

Frank Worrell had been in command of the squad of Carthage Greys who were supposedly charged to protect the Mormon prisoners. He and his men conveniently "fled" when the mob with painted faces came running down the street. He too was a hero in their eyes.

Yes, thought Sharp, these two were good for doing what had to be done tonight. Then, when the mood was right, the brighter mind and the sharper tongue would take over. He smiled at his own unintended pun. The Sharp-er tongue. Not a bad description. The men who descended on Carthage Jail may have looked upon Levi Williams as a leader, but it had been the Thomas Sharp speech given a few miles west of the county seat that had put the steel in their backbones and sent them racing off to storm the jail. And before that, it had been the editorials of Thomas Sharp that fanned the flames of resentment to the point where the whole county was howling for the blood of Joe Smith. Yes, he thought, Williams and Worrell might have been there to smell the gunpowder on that day of 27 June 1844, but it was the Sharp tongue that made it all possible.

He gave them another ten minutes, then slowly rose to his feet. Instantly the roar dropped off. He moved forward and laid a hand on Frank Worrell's arm. Flushed with excitement, breathing hard from shouting at the crowd, Worrell immediately nodded and sat down. Levi Williams took only one moment to speak further to the upturned faces. "Friends, neighbors, we are here tonight to cope with a very real danger to our community. If there has been one man who from the beginning has clearly seen that danger and helped us cope with it, it is our own distinguished Thomas Sharp, from Warsaw. Let's hear it for Mr. Sharp now." And then he sat down.

The crowd went wild, whistling, roaring, shouting, stamping their feet until the small building shook. Sharp smiled, holding up his hands in acceptance of their adulation. *They're ready now,* he thought as his hawk's eyes swept from man to man. *Yes, they're ready.*

He stood there for almost a full minute, letting the men have their way, letting the roar roll around him. Then finally he raised his arms higher, signaling for a suspension of the noise. Gradually they gave him what he wanted and the room was quiet again. He looked around, letting his eyes move from one face to another, pausing long enough for them to know he had seen who they were and acknowledged their presence. Then he took a deep breath and began.

"Thank you!" he called loudly, wanting even those outside to hear him clearly. "Thank you for coming in this hour of crisis." Suddenly he slapped the speaking stand hard with the flat of his hand. "For this is an hour of grave crisis. Do you not agree?"

"Yes!" It was ragged, because they had not expected it, but it was affirmation.

"The Mormons threaten everything we hold dear here in Hancock County, don't they?"

"Yes!"

"Do you not agree that for over a year now we have been patient in waiting for the state to do something about this problem?"

Now they were in rhythm with him and the answers came as one voice. "Yes!"

"Has the state done one thing to help us solve this problem?"

"No!"

"Oh," he said with heavy sarcasm, "I disagree. Our namby-pamby governor sent out the state militia last fall, as you remember. To stop the Mormons? No! To disarm the Nauvoo Legion? No! For what, then? To harass us, that's what. To prevent us from doing what every citizen has a right to do, and that is to protect our rights. Isn't that true?" he cried.

"Yes!"

"Where are the Mormons now? Were they broken up after Joe Smith died?"

"No!"

"Have they left the state as they told us they were going to?"

"No!" With each answer the sound grew louder and more angry. The rafters above them seemed to tremble now.

"Are they growing stronger with every passing day?"

"Yes!"

"Are we going to stand for that kind of deceit and treachery?"

"No! No! No!"

He stood and watched them shaking their fists at him, as though he were the enemy now. This was good. They had been angry before. Now they were approaching genuine rage.

Up came his hands again, cutting off the sound. "Who, then, is willing to march with us to put these Mormons out of the state once and for all?"

There was a response, but suddenly the unanimity was gone.

"What was that?" Sharp roared at them. "I didn't hear your answer. How many are willing to take up arms? Right now! Here! Tonight! Come on, let me hear it."

Several cried out, shaking their fists, but others were looking around with some concern. It was one thing to bellow yes at the top of your lungs, another to get a rifle and ride against the Mormons. For all that they were hated, no one underestimated their combined strength.

"What about the Nauvoo Legion?" someone in the back yelled.

Sharp swung on him, his eyes like molten fire, but he could not tell who it was. "The Nauvoo Legion has been disbanded."

"That's not what we hear," another man grumbled, half under his breath but loud enough for most to hear. "Maybe they ain't legal anymore, but there are still four thousand of them out there waiting for us."

Sharp knew they had just reached a critical point—a point that, fortunately, had not been totally unforeseen by him. "My friends, my friends," he soothed, "I am not talking about marching on Nauvoo. The Mormons are too strong for us there, I'll grant you that. But that's not what we're talking about here."

Williams was on his feet now, his mouth pulled back so that he had the look of a wolf sizing up a downed stag. "We don't have to march nineteen miles to Nauvoo to find Mormons," he shouted. "There's a whole settlement of them just six miles from here."

Now the men were looking at each other in surprise.

"Yes!" he bellowed. "I'm talking about the Morley Settlement. I'm talking about Lima, just a few miles beyond that. How many of the Nauvoo Legion are there down there, I ask you?"

"Not enough to stop the Warsaw militia!" a voice shouted, and Sharp noted with satisfaction that it was the same man who had first cried out about the Nauvoo Legion. As Williams kept hollering at them, whipping them with his contempt, Sharp turned and gave Worrell a questioning look. Worrell kept his face impassive but gave one brief nod. "Do it!" Sharp commanded softly. "Now's the time." Worrell nodded, stood, and slipped out the side door.

"Citizens," Sharp cut in, taking the podium back from Williams, "everywhere you look now there are Mormons. The Morley Settlement, Lima, Ramus, Plymouth. I tell you, they're taking over the county. They keep it up and soon none of us will have any property rights. They're like the tentacles of some great octopus, reaching out in every direction, taking our lands, corrupting our political processes, taking over what is legitimately ours. Are we going to stand for that?"

"No!"

"We have a new sheriff in Hancock County, one Jacob Backenstos."

A chorus of boos and jeers greeted the mention of that name.

"If ever there was a Jack Mormon, Backenstos is it. I ask you, how did a man like Backenstos, a Mormon-lover, ever get elected sheriff?"

"Because the Mormons put him in!" a man exclaimed.

"That's right!" Sharp said, pounding his fist against the stand. "And we let them. We are the ones who have let them get so strong. We are the ones who let them keep moving in all around us. How many others—Mormons or Jack Mormons—are going to be telling us how to live? Is that what you want?"

He turned his head. Worrell had come back in and was standing by the side door. When he caught Sharp's eye, he nodded once.

Sharp turned back to the crowd. Now it was pandemonium. Some were shouting no. Others were shaking their fists. Some were cursing the name of their new sheriff.

"Then I say we start here," Sharp yelled. "Let's get out there and teach these Mormons a lesson. We can't attack them in Nauvoo, but we can go after these other settlements. If we drive all the outlying Mormons into Nauvoo, then maybe the state will help us drive them from Illinois. I say let our answer to them be with powder and ball."

He stopped, noting again that at the mention of violence some still seemed to shrink back.

"Who's with me now?" he cried. "Who will—"

Blam! A window at the back of the room shattered, spraying glass over several seated beneath it. *Blam! Blam! Blam!* Three more rifle shots cracked out. A second window exploded. A ball lodged in the ceiling and dust and plaster rained down. Men screamed and dove for cover. Those nearest the door bolted blindly, smashing into those who couldn't see into the room and weren't sure what was happening. Men pulled the benches over the top of them to hide. The noise was deafening, the panic complete.

Moving with some speed, but certainly not in a panic, Sharp dropped to a crouch and scuttled backwards to where Williams and Worrell were likewise hunched over. Like Sharp, they seemed calm. They certainly were not scrambling for cover. "We're under attack," Sharp noted dryly.

Worrell was grinning. "Must be those crazy Mormons."

Sharp laughed softly. "Agreed. Why don't you take some men and go after them?"

Worrell was up immediately, waving his hands. "It's the Mormons! It's the Mormons! After them!" He rushed forward, shoving men roughly out of his way. Half a dozen men leaped to their feet and rushed out after him.

He was gone seven or eight minutes. By the time he returned, order had been restored, though no one had returned to the seats by the windows. Worrell came striding in with three men behind him.

"Who was it?" "Did you find them?" "Did you get them?" came the shouts as he came back into the schoolroom.

He shook his head in disgust. "It was two riders. They got away. Headed south."

"South!" Sharp roared, bringing every head back around to look at him. "The Morley Settlement. They're from the Morley Settlement."

Now the answering cry was ugly, frightening, totally united.

"Powder and ball!" Sharp cried. "Tomorrow I want the word to go out across the whole area. Gather every man with a rifle. Tomorrow afternoon we ride against Yelrome. Let's get them! Let's teach those Mormons they can't frighten honest men!"

———•———

Solomon Garrett was whistling softly as he rode along the road that led south to Yelrome. It was a beautiful late afternoon. The terrible storm of the week before seemed to have ended the last spell of hot weather. The days had become pleasant and the nights were starting to take on the first touch of coolness. He looked to the west. The sun was just approaching the western horizon and had turned the high wispy trails of clouds gold and would soon turn them again into fiery reds and oranges. There was a light breeze out of the west which stirred the cornstalks and wheat fields that stretched out on either side of him. Ahead somewhere an unseen meadowlark was putting heart and soul into a song praising the ending of another day. Solomon leaned back in his saddle, feeling a great contentment.

Things in Bear Creek had gone better than expected, and it looked like by October they might get their first common school under way. He would be in Morley Settlement in another ten minutes or so—he could already see the first buildings out ahead of him now—and Father Morley always set an ample table. Morley's daughter Cordelia had been teaching school there since '41. Last spring she'd had twenty-one students. He would try to convince her to become the teacher for the common school. He thought he had a good chance of doing so. That meant he would return earlier than expected and that he and the family could leave immediately for the City of Joseph.

He stood up in the stirrups for a moment, stretching his legs and twisting his body back and forth to unkink his muscles. Though he rode the horse often and was toughened to the saddle, he'd started out this morning just after six, and taken only a two-hour stop at Bear Creek. That meant about ten hours in the saddle, and his backside was getting tender, and the rest of his body was starting to protest as well.

As he lowered himself back down again, the ears of his mare suddenly cocked forward and she turned her head around, as though trying to see back down the road they had just traversed.

Curious now, Solomon turned in the saddle and peered back. About a mile behind him, there was a T in the road that was the junction between Green Plains and Warsaw to the west, Bear Creek and Carthage to the east, and Yelrome to the south. He had come from the east and taken the left turn for Yelrome just a quarter of an hour before. At that time, the road had been completely empty. Now suddenly it was filled with a large cloud of dust and what looked like riders in the midst of it.

Solomon reached down and unbuckled his right saddlebag. In a moment he had in his hand the spyglass he always carried with him. His mother had given it to him on the day he first started teaching school some ten years before. He took it everywhere with him when he was out on his circuits, because he loved to watch a soaring hawk or eagle or catch a deer or a fox or a badger. It took him a moment to focus, but then he jerked forward a little. There were now thirty or forty riders visible and more coming from the west at every moment. As he peered through the glass, he felt the hair on the back of his head start to prickle a little. Even at this distance, he could see their rifles—some held across their laps, others pointing in the air.

Still they came. They had their horses in that easy trot that eats up the miles without tiring the animals terribly. He watched in astonishment, absently counting. Fifty, sixty, seventy. On they came, a whole column of horsemen. There were no carriages, no wagons, no buggies. They were all men, and all were on horseback. And all armed!

Solomon started to put the spyglass back into its case, when he froze in place. The lead horseman had just wheeled to Solomon's right, turning off the road. He jerked the glass up again. The others were following. For a moment, he felt great relief. They were no longer coming at him. But then his brow furrowed. Where were they going? There was no side road between here and the junction. He thought quickly, remembering. A ways back he had passed a lane that led through corn and wheat fields to a farmhouse. There was also a new-looking barn, a shed or two, some corrals. Behind the outbuildings, the first of the grain harvest was stacked in neat bundles, waiting to be threshed. At the time he passed it, Solomon had wondered if it might be a Latter-day Saint family who had homesteaded there.

Once again he went up in the stirrups, only this time standing on the tips of his toes to get as much height as possible. He brought the spyglass up. Yes! Over the fields of green he could make out the shingled roof of the barn, the stovepipe chimney of the house. He also could see heads bobbing up and down above the corn. That was where the riders were going. Unable to shake the deep uneasiness twisting down inside him, he sat back down again, chewing on his lip, wondering.

And then he jerked forward, startling the horse, and nearly unsettling himself. There was a faint popping sound. Rifles! Pistols! From this distance they sounded like a child's toy, but he knew better. Up came the spyglass again. And then in horror he saw a faint wisp of white smoke rising in the sky. It was not coming from the chimney. It was back farther, behind the house, behind the barn. Even as he watched, the wisp thickened and turned more gray. In moments a narrow pillar of smoke was towering upward.

"The grain stacks!" he gasped, realizing what he was watching. As if to confirm his words, a second column, and then a third, went billowing upward. Through the magnification of the spyglass, his eye caught a movement. A tiny point of orange arched upwards, tumbling over and over. He stared, then sucked in his breath again. It was a torch, trailing a tiny wisp of black smoke. He watched in horror as it dropped onto the roof of the barn.

He didn't need to watch any more. He jammed the spyglass back in the saddlebag, wheeled the horse around so she faced back toward Yelrome again, and put spurs to her. "Go, girl!" he shouted. "Go!"

Brother Isaac Morley was nearly sixty now. His hair was white, his face deeply lined. He had been one of the first of the converts in Kirtland when the missionaries came through there in the latter part of 1830 and early 1831. The Morley farm had been the center for much Church activity during the ensuing years. For nine years Father Morley had been a counselor to Bishop Edward Partridge. He had fled to Missouri when the apostates drove the Saints out of Kirtland, and he had helped found Far West. Except for the very first years of the Restoration, he had been part of virtually every major event associated with the Church's history.

Now he was all business. "So what are the latest reports?"

Besides Sister Morley and one of their daughters, there were three other Yelrome residents in Morley's kitchen. One, Solomon knew well. That was Brother Solomon Hancock. The other two men, Walter Cox and Edwin Whiting, were counselors in the branch presidency to Brother Morley.

Brother Cox stepped forward. "So far there have been only two reported burnings—Brother Durfee's grain stacks and his house and barn, and the house of John Edmondson. Once the mob rode away, Brother Durfee and his family were able to put out the flames before too much damage was done. Brother Edmondson sustained greater loss."

"Where is the mob now?"

Brother Whiting shrugged. "There are a lot of antis in Lima. Some of the mob seem to be holing up with them for the night. Some may have gone back to Green Plains."

"Maybe it's over," Brother Cox suggested.

Solomon shook his head. "There are two or three hundred men mounted and armed. They may have gone to roost for the night, but it isn't over. They're looking for battle."

Solomon Hancock nodded. "I'm afraid Brother Garrett is right."

"Watchmen?" Morley asked.

"Posted everywhere. If they reappear, we'll know about it immediately."

"We also sent a fast rider north to tell President Young," Brother Cox added. "He left immediately, while the mob was still milling around south of town, so we assume he won't run into any trouble. He should be in Nauvoo within the hour."

"Do you know what's ironic?" Isaac Morley asked quietly. Suddenly, he looked much older than his sixty years. Each of the other men watched him. "We were going to leave tomorrow."

Solomon nodded. That explained why there were boxes all around and piles of folded linen and clothing. Since Solomon was the only one who was not from here and didn't know the story, Morley spoke to him directly. "Last February there was some trouble with the antis. Colonel Williams again. I slipped away and rode to Nauvoo to tell President Young. He sent me back, but he counseled me to get my family, make Brother Hancock here the branch president, and move to Nauvoo."

He shook his head, staring now into the dead fireplace. "But I decided I had to get things ready first. I've got a business here. I employ twelve men in my cooper's shop."

Solomon nodded. Isaac Morley's barrels were renowned for being some of the best made in all of western Illinois. He had a brisk business selling them down at Quincy for the river trade.

"There's the granary, the livestock, my crops. I decided if I could just get things in order first . . ." He looked away. "Tomorrow. We planned to leave tomorrow."

"We *are* leaving tomorrow," his wife said firmly. "First thing, we are packing the wagon and following President Young's counsel."

He brightened a little at that. "Yes," he said, looking at her gratefully. "Yes, tomorrow. Good." His shoulders lifted and fell. "Well, I suppose there's nothing more to do now than wait. Keep our guard up. Be prepared for whatever tomorrow shall bring."

They all nodded at that. The gentle old man turned to Solomon. "Will you stand with us, Brother Garrett? We know this isn't your problem, but we need every man we can muster."

There was no hesitation. "Of course. If the mob heads north for the other settlements, I'll have to go for my family, but I don't think that's their intent." His mouth pulled down. "At least not yet. So I shall stay here with you and see it through."

"Thank you."

He gave a short, mirthless laugh. "And I thought I was coming down here to talk about schools."

They were up early. Sister Morley fixed them a quick breakfast, and then Father Morley called for a short meeting with the leading brethren of the town. There were eight or ten present. As they gathered, grim faced, in the yard in front of the cooper shop, Solomon Garrett saw that while there was determination in their eyes, there was also a great sense of foreboding. One or two carried rifles, but for the most part the Saints had no weapons. And if they had, they were not sure if they were expected to use them or not.

Morley waited until the last of the men had come in, and then raised one hand for silence. "Brethren, thank you for coming."

There were solemn nods all around.

"Last night a mob attacked and burned two homes of our brethren. Perhaps they will be back today. We have sent to President Young for counsel. Until then we need to be wise—on our guard and yet wise in our response. We know what happened in Missouri. We do not want another Haun's Mill here."

He motioned for Brother Solomon Hancock to step up beside him.

"Brethren, though it is a time of peril, I feel that I must leave you. This is not out of fear, but out of determination to accept the counsel of one of God's servants, which I should have done some time ago."

There was no surprise at that, and Solomon Garrett realized that Father Morley's situation was known to all.

"I shall be loading the wagons with my furniture and goods this morning and leaving you. As you know, President Young has designated Brother Hancock to be the new branch president." He laid a hand on Hancock's shoulder. "I need not tell you that you are in good hands with Brother Hancock."

There were smiles and nods from the assembly. Hancock was as well respected as Morley.

"All right, brethren," Morley concluded. "Let's be alert. Go about your work. Remember to stay calm. This is not a time for hotheadedness. We must—"

"Look!"

They spun around. One of the brethren at the back of the group was staring northward, pointing.

Solomon felt his stomach drop. Once again a column of smoke was rising into the sky a mile or so to the north of them.

"It's Durfee's place," someone cried. "They've fired Durfee's place again."

The shock was deep and profound. It instantly dispelled any hope that last night's raids were a minor skirmish and that the mob was satisfied.

"Listen!" Brother Hancock commanded. In the silence that followed, they could hear the faint popping that signaled the sound of rifles.

"Oh, dear Lord," one of the men breathed, "watch over our brother and his family."

"Shall we ride out to help?" someone asked.

Father Morley was staring at the smoke, the sickness of his heart written clearly in the lines of his face. "No," he finally said, "that's what the mob will be hoping for. Just pray that the Durfees will be all right. You'd better see to your own homes, brethren."

"And you'd better get your things loaded, Isaac," Brother Hancock said firmly. "You must leave before they come here."

"Yes," he said, half-dazed. "Yes."

And then as they turned round and started to disperse, there was another cry. "No!"

As one, they gaped across the fields to the south. A pall of smoke filled the sky to the south of them. This was not one isolated column, but fire after fire.

"It's Lima!" someone shouted. "They're burning Lima!"

"Heaven help us!" Sister Morley cried softly.

Solomon turned and ran for the barn where his horse was stabled. A moment later he returned with his spyglass. With a great hollowness inside him, he raised it to his eye. It was hard to tell how many fires there were, for one pillar of smoke seemed to blend with another. After a moment, he lowered the glass and looked at Father Morley and Solomon Hancock. He shook his head. "I'd say seven or eight homes. Maybe more."

He heard the soft gasps and the low murmurs of shock, but no one said anything. They were too horrified by what lay before their eyes.

"Rider coming!"

They swung around as one. Lima was another settlement made up largely of Mormons which lay about three miles to the south of Yelrome. As they looked, they saw a solitary horseman, coming at a hard run up the road that led to Lima. They watched in silence as the rider approached the Morley farm and finally pulled into the yard and reined up hard. He was off the horse and running to Father Morley. "They're burning Lima, Father Morley," he shouted.

He was a young man, maybe eighteen or nineteen. He wore no hat. His face was flushed with excitement, his eyes wide and frightened. Brother Hancock went to him immediately. "John, how bad is it?"

He brushed a hand over his eyes. "Bad, Brother Hancock. They've set fire to eight homes now." He looked south, then looked away again. "They came in just after sunrise. There must be a hundred of them. Levi Williams is their leader."

"Williams?" Father Morley cried. "This is not good."

"They made us come out of our houses. Men. Women. Children. They drove everyone outside. Some are barefoot or in nightclothes. It made no difference. Ma is real sick right now, but that didn't matter either. They drove us outside at the point of a rifle. They carried our stuff out of the house and set it in the yard. Then they stuffed the corners of the house with straw and set it on fire."

He had to stop for a moment, swallowing hard. "Our house is gone. Our sheds are burning. As soon as they left to go to the next place, Pa sent me to warn you."

Father Morley reached out and placed his hand on the young man's shoulder. "Thank you, John. Go back to your father. Tell the people not to fight them. That's what they're hoping for. They'll gun us down like ducks in a pond." He turned to the other men. "It's begun," he said softly. "Brethren, I suggest you return to your homes and prepare for the worst."

Chapter Notes

At this time in the Church's history, the term *Jack Mormon* referred to nonmembers who were either friendly with the Mormons or sympathetic to the Mormon cause. Jacob Backenstos, a well-known Jack Mormon, was elected sheriff of Hancock County largely with the support of the Mormon vote in August of 1845. Thus he was bitterly hated by the anti-Mormons (which, incidentally, was their name for themselves).

There was a meeting held on 9 September in Green Plains, Hancock County. Green Plains was six miles southeast of Warsaw, which is about fifteen miles south of Nauvoo. Yelrome, or the Morley Settlement, was about five or six miles south of Green Plains. Levi Williams, one of the most bitter and violent of the antis, lived in Green Plains and was at the meeting. No specific mention is made in the records as to whether Thomas Sharp was there, but his role as shown here is true to his character, his motives, and his leadership role. (See Thomas Gregg, *History of Hancock County, Illinois* [Chicago: Chas. C. Chapman and Co., 1880], p. 340; *CHFT*, p. 301; *Edmund Durfee*, pp. 14–15.)

As shown here, the meeting was fired upon, which the crowd took to be an attack by the Mormons. This precipitated the march the next day against Yelrome. Governor Ford, who was no friend to the Mormons, later said in his history of Illinois that "some persons of their own number," meaning of the number of the mob, and not Mormons, fired the shots into the meeting (Thomas Ford, *A History of Illinois* [1854; reprint, Chicago: Lakeside Press, 1946], 2:293–94.)

They had about two-thirds of the furniture out of the house and into the waiting wagons by nine o'clock. Though the morning was still cool and the air fresh, Solomon was sweating heavily. They were working as swiftly as possible. An uneasy silence lay over all of them as they kept glancing to the south where the smoke was dying now but still clearly evident. Ten minutes before, to everyone's great relief, Edmund Durfee and his family arrived and came to report to Father Morley. The good news was that they were all safe. The house and barn they had saved last night were total losses, but none of them had been harmed. That was the good news. The news that sent a shiver through everyone was the report that the mob had fired on the family—including the children!—as they scurried for safety. The night before, the riders shot only in the air to intimidate the Durfees. They were obviously deeply shaken. Brother Hancock took them to his home, where they could rest and be safe for a time. Those that stayed to help Father Morley dug in with renewed energy.

Ten minutes later, as they were loading one of the last large pieces of furniture onto the wagon, once again the cry of "Riders coming!" jerked everyone's head up. Instinctively they all moved in closer to each other, because this was not just someone coming to report. A band of horsemen, fifty or sixty strong at least, were cantering down the road toward them. Every man had a rifle out of its scabbard and held at the ready.

Isaac Morley glanced at Solomon. The horsemen had reached the lane that led to the Morley farm and were turning in. "The lead rider is Levi Williams," he said grimly. "Murderer of the Prophet."

The riders trotted up, horses blowing, bridles jingling, stirring up clouds of dust in the yard. A dozen or so had large burlap bags tied to their saddle horns. Solomon could see that they were stuffed with straw. They immediately spread out into a circle surrounding the wagons and the Mormons who stood by them.

"Well, well, well," Williams said with a sneer. "Old Father Morley. Just what is going on here? You planning to take a trip?"

Morley stepped forward, his head up, his eyes calm now. "Hello, Williams." He inclined his head briefly toward the south. "I thought you might be behind all this."

Levi Williams was a big man, going somewhat to paunch now, but with broad shoulders and thick torso. His face was hard, blunt, brutal. There was no life in his eyes, though they glittered with dark anticipation. He shoved his rifle back in its scabbard and swung down. His men did not follow suit. The rifles lay easily across their legs now, but every muzzle was pointing in the direction of the men around the wagons. Williams moved to the lead wagon and walked around it slowly. When he made the circle he came back to Father Morley. "I asked you a question, Morley. You taking a trip somewhere?"

"I am moving my family to Nauvoo, as directed."

"As directed?"

"Yes. I was asked to move there by Brigham Young."

"Smart move on his part," Williams said with an insolent grin.

"Look," Brother Hancock said, stepping forward. "We haven't done you any harm. Why are you doing this?" He looked around at the men, recognizing some of them. "You. You're from Lima. How can you do this to your neighbors? They haven't done anything to you."

Williams looked incredulous, then grinned up at his men. "He asked you boys a question. Could it be because you don't like your neighbors? Could that be it?"

There was a burst of laughter, raucous and crude.

"What do you want?" Morley asked.

Now there was a sudden hardness to Williams's jaw. "Why, we want to help you on your way." He turned his head. "You men. Get in there and get the rest of that furniture out of the house. These brethren look tired."

As four men dismounted and ran into the house, Williams turned and looked toward the large shed that housed Isaac Morley's cooper shop. "It seems to me that a man who's moving to Nauvoo might be burdened down with worry if he were to leave too much behind."

Morley jerked forward a step. "No, not the cooper shop. I employ twelve men there. It's their livelihood."

"Now, ain't that a shame," came the snarling reply. Williams jerked a thumb at some more of his men. Five more swung down, this time those with the burlap bags. Without waiting for further instructions, they darted toward the cooper shop. In moments they were stuffing huge handfuls of straw into every crack and cranny.

"Seems to me," Williams said with a wolfish grin, "that if something were to happen to your cooper's shop, those twelve men might no longer have a livelihood. Then they just might have to move to Nauvoo along with you. And wouldn't that be a shame." He jerked his head at another man. "Burn it to the ground."

"No!" cried Sister Morley, lurching forward, her hands outstretched, imploring. Her husband grabbed her and pulled her back. The man got down, took a short length of tree limb from a saddlebag, and started fumbling in his pocket. The end of the tree limb had burlap wrapped around it and it smelled strongly of kerosene. In a moment, he withdrew a match, struck it on the leather of his saddle, and lit the torch. With a war whoop he was off and touching the flames to the straw.

Sister Morley closed her eyes and turned to bury her face against her husband's chest. Now more men were getting down with their bags. They moved swiftly. Others stayed astride their horses and jammed straw up under the eaves and in the higher cracks of the house.

Sister Morley turned, weeping now. "Please. Not my house. We're leaving. There's no need to burn it."

But the forced joviality in Williams was gone now. His expression was stony, his body rigid and unbending. He watched as the men finished their work. The cooper shop was ablaze now, and the torch man came running to start on the house.

"No!"

Solomon jerked around. One of the men who had been helping them load the wagons was staring at the cooper shop, his mouth working. "No! Not the shop!"

He suddenly darted away, racing for the shed.

"Brother Hallett!" Father Morley shouted. "Come back!"

"Get him!" Williams bellowed. Half a dozen rifles jerked up and there was a deafening roar as one after another fired. Clark Hallett darted back and forth, like a bantam rooster trying to escape the chicken hawk. Spurts of dust were kicking up all around him. Without hesitation he plunged through the door of the shop, grabbing at a sack that was not yet burning. He disappeared into the smoke, beating at the flames, shouting wildly.

Williams swore, jerked a pistol from his belt, and took aim at the shadowy figure barely glimpsed through the smoke and the fire. Without a sound, and with no conscious thought behind the action, Solomon Garrett launched himself at Levi Williams. His shoulder caught him squarely in the back, knocking him sprawling. His mistake was that he did nothing more. He wasn't trying to fight Williams, only stop the senseless shooting at Clark Hallett. But two of the men who had carried the furniture out of the house leaped on Solomon, clubbing him to the ground with their rifle butts.

Burnings at Yelrome

Williams got slowly to his feet, breathing hard. He came over to where the two men stood over Solomon, their rifles pointed at his chest. "Hold!" he said. He stepped closer, looking down at Solomon. Solomon was on his back. There was a deep cut over his eye and blood was streaming out of it. His nose was bleeding and his lower lip was also cut. He tried to stir and winced in pain, grasping at his ribs. Williams bent over him, peering more closely at him.

"Who are you?" he demanded. "You're not from here." He turned his head to Morley. "Is this a new family? Who is this?"

Solomon heard the crackling of fire and felt the heat beating against his face now. The house was burning furiously and the flames were already eating into the roof. Isaac Morley deliberately did not look at it. He was staring at Solomon, debating what to do.

Solomon saw instantly where this could lead. This was no time for bravado. "My name is Solomon Garrett. I'm from Ramus. I am the supervisor of common schools for Hancock County. I came here to talk about opening a common school."

"You a Mormon?" Williams sneered.

Solomon licked his lower lip, then nodded. "I am."

"Want us to kill him, Colonel?" one of the men who had beaten him said hungrily. His muzzle moved up slightly to point at Solomon's head.

Not moving a muscle, Solomon continued to stare into the eyes of Colonel Levi Williams, knowing that he was only seconds from possible death.

After a moment, Williams finally straightened. He waved the men back, his eyes never leaving Solomon's face. "Mr. Garrett, this is your lucky day. Let me tell you why." He glanced for a brief moment at Father Morley, then at Brother Hancock. "And you all listen and listen good to this. We know we aren't strong enough to raise an army to go against Nauvoo. So our intent is to do just what we're doing here. Move in on your settlements. Burn your houses. Shoot your livestock. Spoil your crops. You won't have any choice. All of you will be like wise old

Father Morley here and will flee to Nauvoo for protection. When others see that it's working—that we are driving the Mormons out—then there'll be enough support to get the state and the federal governments behind us, and we will drive you from the state."

Triumph was heavy in his voice now. "Do you understand what I'm saying, Mr. Garrett?"

Solomon sat up, trying not to gasp with the pain. "Yes," he said.

"Do you? You tell me what I'm saying, then."

"You want me to go back to Ramus and spread the word among the other settlements. Convince them to move into Nauvoo immediately."

Williams looked at his fellow mobocrats with mock astonishment. "Well, I declare. This man must be a schoolteacher. He's smart as a brand-new twenty-dollar gold piece." The feral look was instantly back. He reached out with one foot and pushed softly at Solomon's chest with the toe of his boot. "I wouldn't leave until tomorrow, Mormon. The roads won't be safe today. But then you'd better get. You go on back home and spread the word. Tell 'em in Bear Creek. Tell 'em in Plymouth. Tell 'em in Ramus. You tell 'em we're coming."

Williams turned. The cooper shop was a mass of flames. The house was fully engulfed by the fire now. Giving one last contemptuous look at Solomon, and then at Isaac Morley, he walked to his horse and swung up into the saddle. It was as if the Mormons had ceased to exist for him. He looked only at his men. "Come on," he snapped. "We've got work to do."

———◆———

It was a little past noon of the next day. They met inside one of the small sheds on the Morley property that had survived the fire. There were twenty or twenty-five of them—men, women, and a few children. They had come here because they assumed it would be safe. If they met where a house was still standing, it would put them all in danger. The Morley homestead was now nothing more than a smouldering set of ruins.

Above them, the sky was overcast and the rain that had started during the night was still falling. The air had turned noticeably cooler, and one needed a coat if one was to be out in it for any length of time. Behind them, the rain fell softly on the cold and blackened heaps of burnt timbers and charred logs. The acrid, biting smoke that had stung their eyes and choked their throats yesterday was gone now, at least from the Morley farm.

What hadn't changed much in the last twenty-four hours was the situation. Less than gunshot range away, the mob was gathered in the yard of another member's house. They could hear them shouting and yelling, firing off an occasional rifle. Great black pillars of smoke rose upward. Those who watched were almost past shock now. This had become such a common sight it was as though they could not assimilate any more horror or generate any more revulsion. All that was said were things like: "It's Brother Whiting's chair shop." "That must be Azariah Tuttle's house." "It's the Cox place." At sundown the day before, when the mobbers had retreated to Lima to spend a second night with the antis who lived there, the count of destroyed homes and buildings stood at twenty-nine. With their return this morning, the count was approaching forty and still climbing.

The Morleys were gone. Once it was clear that no amount of effort would save the house or the cooper shop, there was little point in staying. Solomon slept under their wagons with them— hardly the warm hospitality he had been planning on, Solomon thought wryly. They rose at dawn to salvage what little had survived the fire. By eight o'clock they were on their way north. As near as Solomon had been able to tell, they had not looked back even once.

Solomon raised his head and came back to the meeting. Brother Hancock was at the front of the shed, talking quietly with the men, getting their reports, trying to assess the extent of the damage. Solomon stood near the back of the shed, leaning against the wall. He held his side gingerly, careful not to move too quickly. He also held very still to try to minimize the blinding ache in his head. His left eye—the one just below where he had been cut on his forehead—was a mass of black and blue and nearly swollen shut. His lips were puffy and cracked. There was another bruise on his right cheek.

But that did not make him unique in this group. Many of the faces around him were blackened with soot. There were angry red burns visible on arms and hands and faces. One man's face was more battered than his own. But more frightening were the evidences of a different kind—the shattered looks, the haunted eyes, the hopeless faces. Women wore nightdresses under men's shirts or ill-fitting dresses borrowed from others. Two or three were barefoot. Others wore men's boots. It was mute witness to the hatred of the men under Levi Williams's command. Time after time families were driven out of their homes at the point of a rifle. They were not allowed to grab a wrap or a coat. Sick children, pregnant women, aged parents—it mattered not. Out into the rain they went and then were forced to watch as their houses were put to the torch.

Just behind him, Edmund Durfee and his family sat huddled on the floor. The older children were listening, but Durfee himself seemed not to be aware of anything around him. He was staring vacantly at the ceiling of the shed. Was it any wonder? Solomon thought. Twice they had come to his home. Twice they had left it afire. The first time Durfee and his family fought to save it. The second time they had barely escaped with their lives.

Someone at the window called out and they all turned to see where he was pointing. A solitary rider was coming up the street, the horse walking slowly. The rider's head kept moving back and forth as though he had come to a town where he no longer recognized any of the familiar landmarks. President Hancock strode over to the window and peered out. A broad smile broke across his face. "It's Charles," he exclaimed. "Charles is back from President Young." He turned and ran outside, waving his arms and calling softly.

"It's his son," one woman said to Solomon. "He sent his own son to report to Nauvoo."

They waited until Charles and his father entered back into the shed. There were calls of hello and urgent questions about what he had found out. But to those Brother Hancock held up his hand. It held a letter. "It's a letter from President Young. Charles brought it down with him."

A great sense of relief passed over the group. Their plight was known in Nauvoo. Even though the mob was still just a few hundred yards away, still on the rampage, still burning their homes and businesses, they were no longer alone. It was a badly needed ray of hope.

Brother Hancock opened the letter and scanned it quickly. He nodded in quick satisfaction, then lifted it higher and began to read aloud. "It's dated this morning, September twelfth."

Charles, who was about twenty or twenty-one, nodded. "The President dictated it in my presence, then gave it to me about nine o'clock."

"It's addressed to me," Brother Hancock said, then started to read slowly and distinctly. "'Dear Brother: We have received your communication of last eve and have taken it into consideration in council. We have decided that it is wisdom for you to remove the women and children from Yelrome as fast as you can with what teams you have got, and we will send you more as fast as we can.'"

That brought murmurs of satisfaction and relief from the whole group, but more especially from the women.

"'We ask that you not only remove the women and children but your grain also. Let all the brethren stay there and keep "bachelor's hall" and watch the movements of the mob. The object of our enemies is to get opposition enough to raise popular excitement, but we think it best to let them burn up our houses while we take care of our families and grain. Let the sheriff of Hancock County attend to the mob, and let us see whether he and the Jack Mormons, so-called, the friends of law and order, will calmly sit down and watch the funeral processions of

Illinois liberty. If so, they will all fall under the same condemnation. At a future day our course will be plain. Be calm and patient till all things are ready. What is a little property compared with the properties and lives of a great people, and the house and ordinances on which the salvation of that people depend?

"'You will employ the best scribe you have, or half a dozen of them, if necessary, to pen minutely all the movements of the enemy and friends, what houses are burned, by whom, at what hour, who were present, and who saw them do it, etc., even every particular, and forward us a daily copy, if opportunity permits.'"

He stopped and looked up. "It is signed by Brigham Young, President, and written by W. Richards, Clerk." He let that sink in for several moments, then bowed his head slightly. "This is good news, brothers and sisters. Help is on the way. We have to organize ourselves, decide who should go first on the wagons we have here and who should wait for the others."

A man off to one side raised his hand. Solomon saw that it was Walter Cox, one of Hancock's counselors. Cox had lost his home the previous afternoon. The branch president nodded in his direction, "Yes, Brother Cox?"

"Shall we proceed with our letter to the mobbers, then?"

Hancock started to nod, then stopped. "Brothers and sisters, we have been meeting in council as your branch presidency. We have a proposal. We propose that we send a note to Williams. We shall offer to leave Yelrome, selling our deeded lands and all the improvements thereon to the locals for as low a price as could be reasonably expected. We shall ask only that we be allowed to keep our livestock and the crops currently on our premises. For that we shall take in trade oxen, beef cattle, cows, sheep, horses, wagons, or other such things as shall help us remove to Nauvoo. We shall appoint a committee of brethren who will act as agents for us to negotiate with the settlers."

To Solomon's surprise, there were no cries of dismay, no shouts of protest. These people had been terrorized and they seemed to sense that this was not happenstance. It would not simply go away. So far, there had been no loss of life—a blessing indeed!—but how long would that last? And what were land and buildings compared to that? There was a deep, sorrowful silence, but no one was protesting.

Charles Hancock spoke up then. "President Young told me to emphasize that we should try to sell our property and come to Nauvoo. He said to tell the mob to burn all the bedbugs that they wish and we shall not hinder them."

There were a few wan smiles at that. In a settlement like this where most of the mattresses were made of straw ticking, warfare with the bedbugs was a fact of life. Now hundreds of straw mattresses had been consumed, along with their tiny unwanted occupants.

The branch president looked around. "As your presidency, we feel this is a way to defuse the crisis we now find ourselves in. All of you who feel you can support this action, will you show it by raising your hand?"

There was no need to look around or count. Every hand in the room was up. Hancock nodded in satisfaction. "We shall appoint a committee and draft the letter immediately. Go to your homes. Get the sisters and the children ready to leave. Stay away from the mob. Don't provoke them any more than they already are." He paused, then nodded one last time. "All right. There is much to do."

As they came out of the shed and slipped back to their homes—such as was left of them—Brother Hancock came over to Solomon. "When shall you start back?" he asked.

"Immediately."

A look of concern filled his eyes as he searched Solomon's battered face, but finally he looked away. When there were no options, it made making a decision easier. "Go saddle up. I'll have Sister Hancock fix you something to eat on the way."

———•———

Will Steed came racing up onto the porch of the Steed Family Dry Goods and General Store and burst through the door. Nathan was behind the counter with young Joshua taking inventory. Emily was in a chair in the corner, straightening out the thread and needle box. With the light rain, few people were out, and the store at the moment was empty of customers. "Nathan! You have to come. Brother Brigham's called a meeting of all the brethren at the Seventies Hall."

"What is it?"

"The reports are true!" Will cried, bending over slightly to catch his breath. "They're burning out our people in Yelrome and Lima."

"How bad?" Nathan asked, setting down the box of buttons he had been counting.

"Bad! More than forty homes have been burned so far."

Nathan blanched. "Forty!"

"Yes. You heard that Charles Hancock rode back with a letter from Brother Brigham yesterday. Well, President Hancock sent back another report with another rider. It came in last night. There are about three hundred men. Levi Williams is at their head. Frank Worrell and Thomas Sharp are part of it too."

"Williams?" Nathan sagged back a little. This was the worst possible news. He untied his apron and tossed it at a peg, not caring that it missed and slid to the floor. He turned. "Joshua, you watch the store. Emily, go tell Mama to get some food ready."

"Savannah is already telling everyone at home," said Will.

"What about your father? Does he know?"

"Yes. Brigham sent someone to the freight yards to see how many wagons we can spare."

"Then let's go."

Nathan, Joshua, Will, Matthew, Derek, Peter, and Carl all stood in a group just outside the fine brick building located on the northeast corner of Parley and Bain Streets. These were the men of the Steed clan, ranging in age from Joshua's thirty-eight years to Will and Peter's twenty-one years. Normally, they would have been presided over by Benjamin, patriarch to the family, but Benjamin was presiding over things in Nashville, Tennessee. Though it was a crisis for the Church, there had not been the slightest hesitation in Carl or Joshua. Families were victims of a tragedy. It didn't matter that the tragedy was related to their religion. It was the Steed way.

The meeting was over and many of the men were already walking swiftly up the street, headed for their homes and barns, but as they had come out of the meeting, Joshua had motioned to the others to come together, apart a little from the rest. Now he was speaking earnestly.

"I'm telling you, Nathan, it's not going to stop at Yelrome. This is what Walter Samuelson's been trying to tell us all along. Now it's happening. We've got to go get Jessica and Solomon and bring them here."

"I'm not disagreeing with you, Joshua," Nathan said. "All I'm saying is that it hasn't spread yet. Those people down south need every wagon we can spare right now. When we get them back safely, then we can go after Jessica."

"And what if you're wrong?" he shot back.

Nathan was patient. "If I was wrong, we would have had reports by now. So far it's only in the south part of the county."

"Between Joshua and me," Carl spoke up, the first he'd done so since they came out, "we can spare two wagons to go to Ramus and still send what Brigham is asking for."

"Can we?" Matthew asked, supporting Nathan on this one. "Brother Brigham wants us to bring as much grain back as possible. If people from all the outlying settlements come in, we'll need every bushel we can get. How do we know how many wagons it will take?"

Nathan was nodding vigorously, but before he could speak, President Young, Heber C. Kimball, and John Taylor came out the door of the Seventies Hall. When Brigham saw them, he immediately came over. The other two Apostles came with him. President Young was grim. He looked at Joshua. "Thank you for pledging your teams, Joshua. They are desperately needed."

"We're glad to help."

"And you too, Carl. You both could stand back and say this isn't your problem, but you didn't. And we appreciate it."

Nathan had a sudden thought. "Ask Brother Brigham, Joshua. If he agrees with you, I'll not say another word."

Joshua was caught off guard by that and his brow furrowed as he considered it.

"Ask me what?"

Joshua took a quick breath. "As you know, Jessica and Solomon Garrett live out in Ramus. We . . . I think this trouble down south is going to spread. Carl and I would like to take a couple of wagons and go bring Jessica and her family into Nauvoo. We'd still send other wagons south, of course."

"And I said there is no danger to the other settlements yet and we need every wagon we can spare to go south," Nathan explained.

Brigham looked thoughtful and he pulled at his lower lip. He glanced at his companions, but they said nothing. Finally, he looked directly at Joshua. "I cannot tell you what to do, especially when it involves a family member."

"I know," Joshua said, surprised and pleased that Brigham, who certainly was not hesitant to speak his mind, wasn't going to make some hard declaration. "But we'd like to know what you think."

"All right. Let me say a couple of things, then you can decide. First"—he was looking at Nathan now—"in a way Joshua is right. There is danger." He motioned toward his brethren. "We in the Twelve have already decided to send out a call to all the Saints to come into the City of Joseph as soon as they possibly can."

He held up his hand as Joshua started to crow a little bit to Nathan. "However, that danger is not immediate. And the problem in the Morley Settlement is urgent. We have forty or more families without homes. The weather is turning cold. The mob is still on the rampage, though we believe they have about exhausted their spleen at this point. Can we get by without those two wagons? Of course. Will two more wagons be of value to us? Most definitely."

Carl spoke now. "And you feel that if we wait, Jessica and her family won't be in any immediate danger?"

That was a difficult question and Brigham did not take it lightly. He turned to Heber, then to John Taylor. "Brethren, if you disagree with me, please speak your mind." Then he looked back to Carl. "No, I don't think the eastern settlements are in danger yet. I feel they will be all right until you return. You may go to Yelrome with a calm heart."

"You're really going to ask everyone to come into Nauvoo?" Matthew asked, a little dazed by the enormity of what he had just heard.

"Yes. It's no secret. We plan to go west in the spring. We were hoping that our enemies would leave us in peace until then, allow us time to finish the temple, but we were not planning on it. We have already started stockpiling grain. If we bring everyone in here, not only will it keep them safe, but it will show the antis that we mean what we say about leaving."

"You're telling us that if we go to Yelrome, there'll be no trouble in Ramus?" Joshua asked, still not convinced.

Brigham shook his head slowly. "I cannot tell you what I do not know, only what I feel, Joshua. And I told you what I feel. Now you must make up your mind. Just know that if you choose to send wagons to Ramus, we will still be very grateful for whatever you and Carl can send south."

With that, he straightened and motioned to his brethren. "Well, we have much to do. By tomorrow or the next day, I think we're going to have several hundred people to house and feed. Good day, gentlemen, and again, thank you for your help."

The three of them started away, but about ten paces was all the farther they got. Brigham turned back. "Brethren, you might be interested to know that as part of the call to gather here for safety, we're going to ask all the high priests we sent out to return home as well, and to bring as many Saints as possible with them."

Nathan was bowled over by that comment. "Do you mean . . . ?" he started.

Brigham laughed softly. "Yes. We'll be asking your mother and father to return to the City of Joseph as soon as possible." Then he waved briefly and he and the other Apostles continued on their way.

"Well, well," Carl said. "That is good news."

"The women will be pleased to hear that," Derek agreed.

Nathan looked at Joshua. "So? What is your decision about the wagons?"

"You still think we ought to go south with everything, don't you?"

Nathan shook his head. "I told you I would accept whatever Brother Brigham said. Brigham said it was your decision. I agree. Whatever you feel is best, I'll support it."

Joshua looked at Carl. "Well?" he asked.

Carl took off his hat and rubbed his hand through his hair. Finally he put it back on, and shrugged. "I'm willing to go south first. But I'd like to have Lydia or Melissa or someone write Jessica a letter and tell them we'll be there for them in a few days. We'll need to open up their house and get it ready for occupancy again."

Joshua looked at Will. "It's your freight business too. What do you say?"

"I say go south."

He made up his mind. "All right, south it is. We'll leave first thing in the morning." As Nathan visibly relaxed, Joshua lifted a finger and pointed it directly at him. "But on one condition, Nathan. Once we get this business done and get Jessica and Solomon here from Ramus, then we're going to talk about what happens next. We're going to talk about the family leaving Nauvoo."

A look of great sadness descended on Nathan's face, and he turned and looked out across the fields and houses of the City of Joseph. "We know we're leaving Nauvoo, Joshua."

"I'm not talking about some colony out in the Rocky Mountains. I'm talking about finding a safe haven, a place like St. Louis, where we won't have to worry about being hated and driven out every time you stick your plow in the ground."

Nathan's eyes were downcast, his mouth in a slight frown. "I know what you've been doing in St. Louis, Joshua—working it out so we'll all have a place to go and something to do to make a living—and we're very grateful for that. You have always been completely generous in your willingness to help the family. But St. Louis is not the answer for us, Joshua."

Joshua's eyes darkened, but Nathan went on quickly before he could retort. "But you are right. We need a family council. And we need to talk about what the future holds for us. As soon as we get this business settled, we'll do as you say."

Chapter Notes

The attack on the Yelrome settlement, or Morley Town, as it was also called, started in the late afternoon of the tenth of September, 1845. The next morning, the riders returned and nearly forty homes and other buildings were set on fire. That continued heavily through the twelfth and sporadically after that. Before it was through, over a hundred homes would be burned. The details depicted here, including the names of the Saints in Yelrome, are accurate. (See HC 7:439–43; *Edmund Durfee*, pp. 14–18.)

One source says the rider sent back from Nauvoo with Brigham's letter was James H. Woodland. Another says Charles Hancock, son of Solomon Hancock, was the one who brought it back. It may be that both men were sent to Nauvoo and that both returned with messages at different times.

Clark Hallett, the man who ran into the cooper shop to try and save it, was feared killed. Fortunately, he escaped through another door unhurt.

It was early morning on the sixteenth of September, three days following the start of the shuttle of wagons to Yelrome to bring back the Saints there. The sun was not yet up. However, a half dozen roosters could be heard crowing heartily, proving that it soon would be. Lydia came out of the bedroom and moved sleepily down the hall toward the kitchen. She still wore her nightdress and her feet were bare. Her dark hair was tousled and there were faint wrinkles on one cheek where she had lain on it while sleeping.

Nathan looked around as he heard her footsteps and turned from the stove. "Good morning." He walked over and put his arms around her waist, kissing her firmly on the nose.

"You're up already?" she murmured, kissing him back, then laying her head against his chest and closing her eyes again.

"Yes."

"What time was it when you came to bed?"

"About eleven."

That brought her head up. "And you're up so soon? Why?"

He bent his head again and kissed her softly, this time on the lips. "I'm going back again this morning."

She pulled away from him, the dismay evident on her face. "No, Nathan! You've been gone three days."

He took her hand and pulled her toward the table. "Come on. Sit down and I'll explain."

As she followed him, she saw the frying pan on the stove and the eggs and potatoes that he was cooking there. "Oh, Nathan. You should have gotten me up."

"No. I thought I'd eat first and then come in to tell you. You seemed really tired last night."

She looked a little sheepish. "I remember you coming in, but I don't remember much else. Josiah and Joseph were upset because their papa wasn't there to say prayers with them and tell them a Book of Mormon story. They were up until past ten."

"Oh, dear," he said.

She pushed him down into a chair and then moved to the stove and began to stir the potatoes. "I remember asking you if there was any trouble." There was an embarrassed smile. "I don't remember you answering me."

He laughed. "I did, but when I asked you a question about ten seconds later, there was no answer and I knew I'd lost you."

"I'm sorry."

"Don't be. Joshua and Emily said you didn't sleep much the night before either."

"I never do when you're not here. I'm just like the little ones, I guess." She walked to the cupboard and got a plate. In a moment she had the eggs and potatoes on it and came over to the table and sat down beside him. "So tell me. How did it go? Why do you have to go back again?"

"Well," he said as he started in on the food, "I assume Carl told you why I didn't come back with the first group."

She nodded. "He said you were just a few miles south of town here when you met another group of wagons going back to Yelrome."

"Yes. They were short on men to help load the grain, so . . ." He shrugged. "Anyway, we got back with that second group about nine last night. Brother Brigham was waiting for us and had places for them to stay. By the time we got them delivered around to their hosts, it was past ten."

"So were there problems?"

"Not really. As we came into Yelrome a second time, Williams and a small group of his so-called militia were starting to burn another house on the outskirts of town. When they saw the wagons coming and that we had about thirty or forty men, they scattered like ducks before the fox. So much for their great courage."

"And why is it you have to go back? This will be your third trip."

"There are a few people left who were too sick to travel." And then his shoulders lifted and fell. "Because President Young asked me to," he said simply.

She nodded. It wasn't a happy answer, but it was answer enough.

"Porter Rockwell and Return Redden will be going too."

She reached out and laid a hand on his. "I'm sorry, Nathan. Here we are, safe and warm, eating good food, with our children asleep upstairs. How can I resent you going to help?"

He took her hand and squeezed it gently. "I know. Yelrome is unbelievable. Everywhere you look there are blackened hulks of buildings, cornfields trampled, cows and pigs shot and left to rot. It's terrible." He leaned back, brightening somewhat. "We decided to leave early so we can get back tonight. Then it will be over."

She shook her head slowly. "President Young got a letter last night from Backenstos."

"The sheriff?"

"Yes. He told Brigham that he had tried to raise a posse to stop the burnings, to get enough law-abiding citizens together to establish peace again, but he couldn't do it. Now the citizens are furious with him for even trying. He asked President Young to immediately hold two thousand well-armed men in readiness. He says that if we are not willing to defend our lives and property that he—Sheriff Backenstos—won't be able to convince those we call Jack Mormons to rise up in our defense."

As he let the implications of that sink in, without comment the fear showed in Lydia's eyes. "Oh, Nathan," she said in a low voice. "Will it ever end?"

"We're better prepared now than we ever were in Far West. We'll be all right. By the way, what did Joshua and Carl decide about going to Ramus and getting Jessica?"

"Oh, that's right. You don't know. Jessica and Solomon arrived yesterday afternoon."

He was dumbfounded. "What? But how could Joshua—"

"Joshua didn't go after them. Solomon was in Yelrome four days ago. He got there just as this began."

"No! None of those I talked to at Yelrome mentioned he was there. Was he hurt?"

"They beat him up a little. He has a terrible black eye. But not really. He went right home, packed up their goods, and came here. He hadn't even heard that President Young was calling everyone in. They're staying in your parent's home until we can get their house opened up again."

He heaved a great sigh of relief. "Oh, I'm so glad to hear that. I've been worrying about them." He wiped his mouth and pushed his chair back. "Well, I'd better get going."

"Yes," Lydia said in a near whisper. "Please hurry, Nathan. And be careful."

He half stood, stretching across the table to kiss her again. A crooked little grin twisted his face.

"What?" she asked, looking at him closely.

"I love you best in the mornings."

She blushed a little, and one hand went up to her hair. "Like this?" she exclaimed.

"Yes. Exactly like that." And then he came around the table and brought her to her feet and took her in his arms. "I love you, Lydia McBride."

"No, Lydia *Steed*," she corrected him. "I am yours, Nathan. I am totally, joyously, lovingly yours. And don't you ever forget it."

He kissed her, hard now and lingering. "I won't. There's not a day that goes by that I don't thank the Lord for this wonderful miracle in my life."

"Hurry, Nathan. I want you out of that place once and for all."

To Nathan's surprise, when he went out to the barn to saddle his horse, Joshua was waiting for him.

"Good morning, little brother."

"Well, what brings you out so early?"

"Heard you were headed south one more time."

"How'd you hear that?"

He shrugged. "Want some company?"

"Sure." They went inside the barn. Nathan got the saddle, while Joshua led the horse out. "Lydia just told me about Solomon and Jessica coming."

"Yeah. How about that?"

Nathan repressed a grin and threw the saddle up on the horse.

Joshua watched him with a dour look. "You're going to bust if you don't say it," he growled.

"Say what?"

" 'I told you so.' That we didn't need to go get them."

Nathan gave him his most innocent look. "I don't know what you're talking about," he said.

Orrin Porter Rockwell in some ways looked like a wild man of the mountains. Nathan watched him as he led to the small brook the team which was pulling the wagon and let the horses drink. Rockwell's mustache and beard were thick and straight, the beard coming down now to three or four inches below his chin. His hair was thin on the top of his head, but from the sides the hair grew long and with a natural curl to it. And long meant more than the usual neck-length hair that many men wore. It was as long as a woman's, falling in thick bunches over his shoulder and partway down his back.

"Have you ever cut your hair since that night at Christmas when you broke in on Joseph's party?" Nathan suddenly asked.

Porter looked up in surprise and then smiled. "Nope! Were you there that night?"

"I was. That was quite a stir you created."

They were stopped at a small brook near the old railroad crossing about three miles north and east of Warsaw. They had met at Return Jackson Redden's place at seven a.m., but by the time they got a wagon and team and the necessary supplies, it was almost eight before they left Nauvoo. Now it was ten-thirty and time to let the horses rest a little. Joshua still sat astride his horse, though it was drinking at the brook with the others. Joshua's head would lift from time to time and sweep the surrounding countryside. This was not by assignment, but by unspoken agreement. This close to Warsaw, all four of them were a little nervous, especially in light of the events of the past few days. They would bypass the actual town, but if there were still some of Levi Williams's militia out, they wanted to know it as soon as possible.

Return Redden was on the wagon seat, holding the reins of the team loosely. A former private detective and bodyguard to Joseph Smith, Brother Redden was as competent a man as Porter Rockwell. He looked down at Porter. "What stir was that, Port?"

Porter looked up and shrugged. "Nathan's talking about the night I arrived in Nauvoo after getting out of prison in Missouri. I ended up walking in on Brother Joseph's big Christmas party at the Mansion House." There was a droll smile. "They thought I was a Missourian and tried to throw me out."

"So what is this about cutting your hair?" Joshua asked. He hadn't been at the Christmas party that night, but he remembered Nathan telling them about it.

"May I tell him, Port?" asked Nathan.

"Just keep it simple," Porter said amiably.

Nathan laughed, knowing that that was Porter's way of saying yes but don't make too big a deal out of it. For all Porter Rockwell's fearsome reputation, and his looks which seemed to support it, he was really quite pleasant of personality. He was soft-spoken and not given to garrulousness. He said what was on his mind when he felt it important but otherwise didn't say much.

"Well," Nathan began, "when Porter crashed the door, walking right past the marshal, everyone panicked. You've got to remember, he had been in jail for nine months."

"And on the road for almost two weeks getting out of Missouri," Porter added.

"His clothes were tattered and filthy. He had a hat low over his face. No one knew that he had been released from jail. So, like I said, he created quite a stir. But he didn't scare Joseph. Joseph grabbed him by the arms and pinned them to his sides. Then Porter began to laugh and Joseph finally recognized him."

"Joseph and I go way back, you know," Porter inserted. "Our farm was just down the road from the Smith farm in Manchester Township south of Palmyra."

"I didn't know that," Joshua said in surprise.

And then Nathan remembered that Joshua had left Palmyra before the Church was organized and therefore didn't know who was part of that early history. And since the Steeds lived north of Palmyra, they didn't know many of the people down around Joseph's family farm.

"Yep," Porter said. "I knew Brother Joseph before he ever walked into that grove of trees and came out a prophet."

"But what does all this have to do with you cutting your hair?" Redden asked.

"Well," Porter answered, "it was at that party that Joseph told me if I wore my hair long and was faithful, my enemies would never have power over me. They would not be able to take my life."

"Really?" Redden blurted. "He actually said that?"

"Yes."

"When was this?" Joshua demanded.

"Christmas Day, 1843. Almost two years ago now."

Joshua was eyeing him strangely. "And you haven't cut your hair since?"

Porter shot him a look that made Joshua flinch a little. It was answer enough. Then Porter straightened and walked around to the wagon. "Well, we'd best be going. We've jawed here long enough."

The others nodded. Nathan took the reins of his horse and pulled her head up, getting ready to mount. Porter put a foot on the hub of the wagon wheel, ready to swing up. It was at that moment that Joshua stiffened in his saddle. He was staring at something to the south of them. "Someone's coming!" he hissed.

In three steps, Rockwell made it around to the back of the wagon and grabbed his rifle from its holster. "Get down!" he commanded.

Neither Joshua nor Return Redden needed further prodding. Both were down behind the wagon in a hurry, Joshua pulling his rifle from its leather case as he did so. Nathan didn't own a rifle, but he had a pistol, and now he laid his hand on the butt of it, feeling glad that he was not unarmed.

About a quarter of a mile away, a buggy was coming toward them. The horse was running hard and they could see the buggy bounce wildly, its back end fishtailing back and forth, threatening to overturn.

"Someone's put a burr in his back pocket," Redden commented, squinting to see better.

"Look!" Porter said, pointing off to the west. "Someone's after him."

He was right. Coming just as hard toward them was a band of eight or ten men on horseback, angling toward the road where the four of them now were waiting. They were coming fast too, their horses stretched out in a hard run, trying to cut the buggy off.

The buggy was close enough now that they could see the man inside. He had a buggy whip and was lashing at his horse, all the time his head jerking around to gauge the oncoming speed of his pursuers. Even from this distance—down to about a hundred yards now—it was clear that they were watching a very frightened man in a race for his life.

"I don't like the look of this," Nathan murmured. He drew his pistol out of his belt and made sure it was at the ready.

Porter Rockwell suddenly cried out, pointing toward the oncoming buggy. "I think that's Jacob Backenstos."

"The sheriff?" Redden asked.

"Yes. I'm sure that's him."

As they watched, the buggy careened to one side as it took a slight curve in the road, spewing mud and dirt from off the outer wheels. Suddenly the sheriff spotted the wagon and the four men up ahead of him. Waving frantically he shouted something and whipped the horse all the more. Behind him, the riders were closing the distance fast and were now just a couple of hundred yards away themselves. At that same moment, they also saw the wagon and the four men waiting by the crossing. Startled, the lead rider threw up his hand and cried out. There was a melee of horses and riders as they pulled up hard, trying not to crash into one another.

The buggy splashed across the narrow creek where the road forded it and wheeled in behind Rockwell's group. The horse's eyes were wild and frightened, its neck covered with the lather of its sweat. Flecks of foam dripped from the two sides of the bit between its teeth. Backenstos, pistol in hand, was out of the buggy and running towards them before it even came to a halt. There was an immense relief on his face now. "Rockwell!" he gasped. "Am I glad to see you!"

"What is it, Sheriff? Who is that after you?"

He had to bend over slightly. His chest was rising and falling like a blacksmith's bellows. "Men from Warsaw!" His words came out between huge gulps of air. "They're determined to kill me. I command you in the name of the state to protect me."

Porter and the others turned to peer at the riders, who were now milling around in confusion as they tried to determine what to do. Porter and his companions all had the same thought: this was the same group of men who had been burning out the Saints. Rockwell's mouth was tight. "We *will* protect you. We have two rifles here and about fifty rounds."

"Thank the Lord," Backenstos breathed. "I thought they had me."

"What's going on?" Joshua demanded. "Why are they after you?"

Backenstos removed his hat and wiped at his brow with the sleeve of his jacket. "A mob drove me out of Carthage yesterday afternoon. They were so enraged at me for trying to raise a posse to stop the burnings. I finally went to Warsaw last night."

"That's not the safest place for someone who's viewed as a Jack Mormon," Joshua observed dryly.

The sheriff didn't answer for a moment. His eyes were fixed on the group of riders, who, for the moment at least, were not coming any closer. Then he looked at Joshua. "I thought I had friends there. But by this morning, word got out that I was there. It was worse than in Carthage. I wasn't sure I was going to get out alive. I finally prevailed upon one of the leading citizens to escort me out of town. He didn't want to—he hates the Mormons more than anyone—but fortunately, he didn't believe in killing sheriffs either."

He stopped, rubbing at his eyes with the heels of his hands. "He rode with me about a mile out of town, then warned me that if I saw any riders, I'd better run for it, because there were deep plans laid to kill me. A few minutes later, I saw this group on the next road over from me, so I took off. I was far enough ahead of them, I thought I could outrun them. But then they found a road that would cut across my track." He shook his head. "I thought they had me."

"They're coming!" Nathan cried in a low voice.

All heads jerked around toward the riders. They were advancing, but at a cautious walk. One man was out ahead of the others. He had a pistol in his hand. They came forward about fifty yards, then stopped again. The leader raised his hand to his mouth. "You there! At the wagon! Who are you?"

Backenstos stood up and cupped his hands to his mouth. "They are my deputies, sir. I just deputized them. Now, turn around and go home."

There was a low muttering cry but it was indistinguishable as to words. They started moving again. Porter Rockwell leaned forward, resting the rifle on the side of the wagon box, taking aim at the man.

"All we want is Backenstos," the leader yelled. "Go away and you won't be harmed."

"It's over," Backenstos shouted back. "Go home."

"All we want is Backenstos. Whoever the rest of you are, just turn and walk away and you won't get hurt."

"I think they're Mormons," someone cried out. He started to curse. "Backenstos has found him some stinking Mormons to help him."

The leader of the riders pulled his rifle out of the saddle holster. The others followed suit. "Get away from him, Mormons, or we'll gun you down like dogs." And with that he started forward again, still coming slowly, but coming nevertheless.

"Don't do it!" the sheriff yelled, his voice touched with desperation now.

They didn't stop. The five men behind the wagon watched as the riders came closer. Seventy-five yards. Fifty yards. Forty yards.

"Fire!" Backenstos yelled into Rockwell's ear.

Porter Rockwell had been sighting on the spot where the lead rider's belt buckle would be. He took a quick breath, let part of it out, then squeezed the trigger. The blast of the rifle made Nathan jump and there was the instant smell of gunpowder.

Forty yards away, the man leading the charge was blown from his saddle as if by some unseen puff of wind. The pistol went flying from his hand as he went head over heels over the rump of his horse and hit the ground with a thud that was clearly heard by all.

That did it. Screaming, cursing, swearing, the other men

jerked their horses around and raced away, leaving the body of their leader sprawled in the muddy roadway, facedown, not moving.

———◆———

"You're positive it was Frank Worrell?" the sheriff asked, standing now to stare at the body about forty yards from where they were.

Porter Rockwell and Nathan nodded at the same instant. Both had walked out to see who it was that Porter had shot.

Porter thought it might be Worrell, but Nathan was sure. Fifteen months before, Nathan had been in Carthage with Joseph and Hyrum Smith. He had seen Frank Worrell face-to-face. "Yes," he said to Backenstos. "It's Frank Worrell."

Backenstos sighed, clearly troubled, and yet angry too. "Well, Worrell has been one of the ringleaders in all of this."

"I am sorry that a man has died here today," Porter said in a low voice, "but with Frank Worrell, there is some justice in having him come to this kind of an end."

"And you're sure he's dead?" Joshua asked. He too was grim. He didn't blame anyone. He had been ready to fire on the riders too, but Porter's single well-fired shot had eliminated the need. But Frank Worrell! He knew the name as well. It would send a fire through the ranks of the antis. They had a martyr now too.

A half an hour had passed. The four Mormons and the sheriff of Hancock County were still there by the brook, crouched down behind the wagon, watching to see what might happen. They did not dare go forward for fear that the men they had spooked might sneak back to ambush them.

Then Redden straightened. "Here comes someone."

They moved closer together, all of them behind the protective cover of the wagon box. A lone rider appeared coming up the narrow road that led to Worrell's body. A moment later, a wagon pulled by two mules appeared behind him. They watched closely, looking for others. There were none to be seen. Both rider and wagon came on slowly.

Nathan saw that the rider was waving something back and forth. "He's carrying a white flag," he said to the others.

Rockwell had the rifle cradled in his arm, and for a moment Nathan thought he would drop into the shooter's crouch again and prepare for action. But he straightened fully now, then set his rifle in the wagon bed. He lifted both arms high. "We'll not be disturbing you," he shouted. "You are free to come and get your man."

There was no response except that the three men came on until they reached the body. All were clearly frightened. Their heads kept jerking in the direction of the sheriff and his "deputies." But when it was clear that the five men by the crossing were not going to try and stop them, the man on the horse and the second man in the wagon got down. One took Worrell's arms, the other his legs. In a moment, they had him in the wagon. In a few moments, the wagon was backed around and started west again. The white flag was tossed aside, and finally the road was empty.

Without a word, Porter Rockwell climbed up onto the wagon seat. Return Redden followed. Joshua and Nathan untied their horses and mounted. Jacob Backenstos went to his buggy. He patted the horse and rubbed its now dry neck softly. Then he too climbed up. He looked to his four benefactors. "Much obliged, friends. Go with care."

"We will. Thank you for what you're trying to do," Redden answered back.

Porter clucked at the horses and snapped the reins. The wagon started off. Joshua watched them for a moment, not moving, then looked at Nathan. "You know what this means, don't you?"

Nathan felt the unhappiness all the way through him. "Yes."

Grim-faced, Joshua said nothing more. He kicked his heels gently into the horse's flanks and started after the wagon. After a moment, Nathan fell in behind him.

———•———

Caroline looked up as the door opened. It was almost nine-thirty, and normally she would have been in bed by now. Though fifteen months had passed since the accident, she still found that she tired easily. But like Lydia, whose lamp still could be seen in the window across the street, Caroline had determined she would not be going to bed until her man returned safely.

She set the book aside. "I'm in here," she called, rising to greet him. They met in the hallway and she threw her arms around him. "Oh, Joshua, I am so glad to have you back."

He bent down and kissed her lightly. "I'm glad to be home."

She caught the tone of his voice and gave him a closer look. "Did everything go okay today?"

"We brought back the last three families."

His evasiveness only raised her concerns higher. "What's the matter, Joshua?"

He looked around. "Are the children all asleep?"

"Well, except for Will and Alice. Jenny and Matthew invited them to supper with Peter and Kathryn to talk about wedding plans. They shouldn't be too much longer."

"Oh. Maybe I'll run over and get them."

She took his arm and pulled him back around as he turned away. "Joshua? What is it? What's wrong?"

He sighed, his eyes hooded and weary, realizing that the news couldn't wait until morning. "There was some trouble today. On the way down."

Her fingers tightened on his arm. "What?"

"Some of the antis were chasing Sheriff Backenstos."

"Sheriff Backenstos? But why?"

"He tried to raise a posse to stop the burnings."

"What happened?"

"He saw us and asked us to help him. Deputized us, actually." He was looking past her now, remembering.

"And?" she prompted.

"And when the men after him wouldn't stop, he commanded us to fire. Porter Rockwell shot and killed their leader."

One hand flew to her mouth. "Oh, no!"

"Yes. Frank Worrell."

The name sounded familiar to Caroline, but she didn't know it well enough that it meant anything.

"It couldn't have happened to a much nicer guy," he said sarcastically, "but it's not good, Caroline. They took his body back to Warsaw." He didn't have to say any more than that. If anyone on earth knew about the virulence of the hatred that resided in Warsaw, it was Caroline Steed.

"I don't know what's going to happen," he said after a moment of watching her carefully, "but there will almost certainly be a backlash. And I can't risk having Alice get caught up in the middle of it. Walter will get word of this in two or three days and be worried sick." He stopped. "I guess Alice didn't hear from her father today?"

Now it was Caroline who sighed. "No. I asked her about it and she admitted that she never sent the letter she wrote to him. She was too afraid of what he's going to say."

He threw up his hands. "You mean he doesn't even know any of this yet?"

"No. Even Will was surprised."

That made up his mind. "I'm sorry, Caroline. I hate to leave you again so soon, especially when there may be trouble brewing. But they'll not dare come against Nauvoo. They've only got enough courage to hit the isolated settlements. But we're catching the first boat out of here tomorrow. I'll take Alice down there and—"

"No, you—meaning you and Will—will take her down there. Will had already made up his mind that he needs to go to St. Louis and talk to Walter personally."

"He is going to be absolutely furious."

"That's why Will needs to go too, Joshua."

He considered that for only a moment. "Yes, you're right. He's got to face it sooner or later. It may as well be sooner. The only thing in their favor is that Judith is going to be ecstatic when she learns they've decided to marry." Then he groaned softly. "But Walter! Oh my, when he learns she wants to be a Mormon, I don't know what he'll do."

"What can he do? She's of age."

"He'll cut her off, that's what he'll do. He's a reasonable man, but he thinks this whole Mormon thing is an abomination. He's already threatened her, told her that if she even thinks about becoming a Mormon he'll not have her in his house. Then what will she do?"

"She'll become part of *our* family," Caroline answered steadily. "If she loses her father and mother, she will gain a father-in-law and mother-in-law." She gave him a hard look. "Or do you plan to reject her as well?"

"You know better than that."

"Do I?"

"Yes. You know I think Alice is a wonderful girl. I think she will make Will a very good wife."

"And the fact that she's being baptized?"

"You were baptized. Will was baptized." There was a doleful grin. "I suppose one more Mormon in the family won't make that much difference."

"Then help her, Joshua. Alice loves her parents very much, but especially her father. If Walter forces her to choose between him and Will and the Church, it will be terrible. For her and for him."

He was shaking his head even as she spoke. "Caroline, Walter thinks that by taking a hard line, it will make her change her mind. In other words, he thinks that if she has to choose, she'll not choose the Church. It's going to be hard to convince him otherwise."

"Joshua, do you know what finally helped Alice decide? It was Lydia."

"Lydia?"

"Yes. Jenny told her that Lydia had faced a similar experience when she was trying to decide whether or not to marry

Nathan. That night Alice went over and spent a long time talking with Lydia. I don't know what Lydia told her, but it was after that that she made up her mind."

"Is that really fair?" he said, a little peeved.

"I don't know," she answered honestly. "You and Carl talked your heads off to try and convince her not to be baptized. Melissa shared all of her reservations about plural marriage. Is that really fair? Why do you who are opposed to her joining get to say what you want and Lydia doesn't?"

He sighed, and then finally smiled. "You'd think, after nine years of marriage, I would have learned that debating with you is like wrestling with a Brahma bull. It's not very often I come out the winner."

She looked up sweetly at him. "Was that your way of saying, 'Yes, Caroline, you are right about what I just said'?"

"Yes, Caroline. Do you have to keep rubbing my nose in it?"

"No," she answered contritely. She took him by the hand and led him back into the sitting room. She sat down on the sofa and patted the cushion beside her. "Joshua?"

"What?" He sat down beside her.

"I would like to say something to you. I want you to listen. I will tell you how I feel. I will tell you what I would hope will happen when you get to St. Louis. But then I will trust you to do what's best."

He started to smile, about to make another teasing remark, but the look in her eyes changed his mind and he finally just nodded. "All right."

"I mean it. You know Walter best. You know your son. You know Alice. You'll need to take all of that into consideration. But you need to understand and believe something yourself."

"All right, I'm listening."

She was watching him carefully. "What I'm telling you is this. Alice talked to Lydia. Lydia told her about the terrible time that she had with her parents. Alice is fully aware that her parents may reject her. The fact that she decided to go ahead and be baptized means that she has decided that if she has to choose, it will not be to stay with her parents."

She stopped, wanting him to think about that.

Finally he nodded. "Yes, I see that."

She leaned forward, elbows on her knees, hands gripped together, staring across the room at the opposite wall. Her face was twisting, tormented now. From the side, he saw just a hint of the sudden tremor in her lower lip. The change was so sudden, so dramatic, that it caught him off guard.

"What's the matter, Caroline?"

"Joshua, it was fifteen months ago that we lost our Olivia."

He started at that. That was not what he had expected. "Yes?" he said cautiously.

"I know how badly you miss her, even now, after all this time."

His voice was low now, and very soft. "I do. I think about her every day."

"So do I." She sat back and looked up at him fully. There were tears in her eyes now. "You weren't Olivia's natural father, Joshua. But that didn't matter, did it? Before long, Will and Olivia were as much your children as mine. Olivia loved you very much, Joshua."

"I know." It came out hoarse and strained, and he had to look away, blinking quickly at the burning in his own eyes.

She turned back to stare at the wall. There was a long silence, and then, "Alice is only a year older than Olivia would have been now."

His eyes widened a little. He hadn't thought of Alice in that way.

"I know she can never take Olivia's place. Not even our little Livvy can do that. But . . ." Now the tremor had crept into her voice. "I would very much like having an older daughter again, Joshua. I would like that very much."

He reached out and began to rub her back very softly and slowly. He leaned over and brushed her shoulder with his lips, then laid his head against it.

"Help her, Joshua. Walter has so much respect for you. He trusts your judgment. Help Alice so that it won't be such a terrible cost for her to choose Will and become a Mormon." Now she turned her body so that she faced him squarely. "If you do that, Alice will come to love you like Olivia came to love you. That's what I want you to think about tomorrow as you start downriver with Alice and Will."

Chapter Notes

On receiving word of the tragedy in Yelrome and its surrounding areas, Brigham immediately called on the brethren to send wagons south to get the people and their goods, including their grain. One hundred thirty-four wagons were pledged and left soon after the call. (See HC 7:442–43.)

The story of Joseph's prophecy about Porter Rockwell's hair is told in Richard Lloyd Dewey, *Porter Rockwell: A Biography* (New York: Paramount Books, 1986), p. 77.

The story of Jacob Backenstos's having to flee for his life and calling on the Mormons to save him, including Porter Rockwell's killing Frank Worrell, is told here as it is reported in the official history of the Church, with the obvious addition of Joshua and Nathan Steed to the scene (see HC 7:446–47).

Thuy were at the riverboat landing at the south end of Main Street. There was a substantial throng of people, all saying their farewells. The arriving passengers had disembarked and were gone. Now it was time for those headed south to get aboard.

Though Joshua and Will would be gone for only a few days, and though they expected that Alice would soon return to the City of Joseph, with one exception all of the family had come to see them off. It was their unspoken way of letting Alice know she had another family now, no matter what happened in St. Louis. The exception was Carl and Melissa. That was not by choice. Carl was having some serious problems with his number one kiln at the brickyard, and Mary Melissa, their youngest, had been fighting a bad case of the shakes for the past day and a half, and Melissa did not dare leave her. But the rest, including all of the children, had come down to say good-bye.

Once she had finished giving Alice a good hug and wishing Will a quiet but fervent "Good luck," Kathryn McIntire rolled her wheelchair out of the way. When she saw Joshua was also standing back, watching the family say their good-byes, she pushed herself over beside him.

"Hi," she said.

He looked around, then gave her an immediate answering smile. "Hello, Katydid."

She chuckled softly. One night at the beginning of the summer, they had been over at his house, out in the yard. The katydids had started their noisy chorus, and Joshua said it sounded just like her when she was trying to get Matthew and Jenny to let her try out the crutches or something. Since then, it had been his nickname for her.

She looked over and watched Alice for a moment. "Is it going to be awful?" she asked, looking back up at Joshua.

He shook his head slowly. "I don't know. Walter Samuelson is a strong-minded man. And Mormonism turns his blood cold."

"Sounds like someone else I once knew," she said evenly.

He jerked up at that, then instantly grinned. "Wouldn't be anyone I know, by chance?"

"Oh, no," she said with mock gravity.

"So, I guess you wouldn't consider changing your mind?"

"About what?"

"Why don't we let Peter marry Alice and then you could marry Will?" he asked gravely, though his eyes were twinkling a little.

Now she laughed aloud, tipping her head back, letting her hair fall across her shoulders. He had always teased her about having Will marry her. And what touched her about it was that he really meant it—not the actual marriage, but that he would have her gladly as his daughter-in-law. She gave him a measured look, matching his solemnity in tone. "I told you once. If I could get Will's father to join the Church, I might be tempted."

"Almost thou persuadest me."

Her eyes widened in shock. "Joshua Steed quoting scripture?"

He looked horrified. "Was that scripture?"

"Yes," she answered merrily. "It was King Agrippa's answer to the Apostle Paul. He said, 'Almost thou persuadest me to be a Christian.'"

"Swear that you won't tell anyone," he said, pretending to be totally cowed now.

She laughed again. "Uncle Joshua, I sure hope you can be at the wedding, because you make me laugh."

He pulled a face. "When you're getting married, you're not supposed to need someone to make you laugh."

She slapped playfully at him. "You know what I mean. You're—" To her surprise, she had to stop. Suddenly her eyes were burning and her throat had tightened into a knot. "You're the only one who really understands me and why I've been so difficult to live with this past while."

If she was surprised at her reaction, she was all the more so at his. He stared at her for a moment, then had to look away. "Thank you," he finally mumbled. Then, gratefully, above their heads, the steam whistle on the riverboat let out a long blast, causing everyone on the dock to jump. It let off a second blast, signaling that the boat was getting ready to depart.

He picked up his valise as Savannah came running up. "It's time to go, Papa."

"I know. Go get Alice and Will." As she darted away, on impulse Joshua bent down and kissed Kathryn on the cheek. "See you, Katydid."

"See you, Uncle Hardhead."

He laughed and started away, but she grabbed his hand. "It will be all right," she promised. "If Mr. Samuelson won't listen to reason, tell him that you'll no longer be his partner."

He hooted at that. "Why don't I just push him in the river?"

"That was my next suggestion," she replied with an impish smile.

———◆———

As the family moved up and away from the boat landing and approached the intersection of Water and Granger Streets, Nathan decided the opportunity was a good one. The children were already out ahead of the adults, calling to each other and playing a running game of tag. The four oldest—young Joshua, Emily, Rachel, and Luke—were hanging back, liking the feeling that they were adults now and not children any longer. That was good too, he thought. He wanted the older ones to be part of this. "I have something I'd like to say to all of you," he said without preamble.

The conversations stopped and they looked at him in surprise. Lydia gave him a querying look, but he just smiled. He raised a hand to his mouth and called. "Mark? Savannah?"

The two oldest of the remaining children looked back.

"We're going to rest for a minute here," Nathan called. "You can go on, but will you make sure the younger ones stay out of the road if a wagon comes?"

"Yes, Uncle Nathan." Then, delighted to be freed from the assumed restraint, the children broke into a ragged run, whooping and hollering as they went.

"Savannah!" Caroline cried. "Watch Livvy!"

"Yes, Mama," came the reply.

"Elizabeth Mary!" Lydia called. "You take Joseph by the hand."

"Yes, Mother."

In a moment, they were gone. Nathan motioned toward the shade of a large oak tree. "Let's stop here."

Openly curious now, they gathered in beneath the tree in a half circle facing him. Jenny whispered something to Lydia, but she shrugged, as puzzled as the rest of them.

For a moment, Nathan didn't speak. He was collecting his thoughts, trying to decide how best to start. Then he decided that hitting it square on was perhaps the best way.

"What I am about to say I wanted to say when certain of our family were not here—Joshua, Melissa, and Carl." He held up one hand quickly. "Not that it's a secret, but . . . well, you'll see why in a moment."

That certainly caught their attention, and they watched him closely now.

"I think it was wonderful that we could all come down to see

Alice off today. It's our way of lending our faith to hers, giving more strength to her and Will. And unfortunately, I'm afraid they are going to need everything they can get. So I have a suggestion."

"What is it, Papa?" Emily asked.

She was standing beside him, looking up at him.

"I was reading in the Book of Mormon early this morning. I came across a passage in Alma that talked about how the Church should care for one another. It says something like this: 'The children of God were commanded to gather together oft and to join in fasting and mighty prayer in behalf of the welfare of the souls of those who knew not God.'"

Now Lydia understood, and spoke softly. "Like Walter and Judith Samuelson?"

"Yes."

"A wonderful idea, Nathan," Jenny said, looking at Matthew, who was nodding.

"They should be arriving in St. Louis day after tomorrow," said Nathan. "I'd like to propose that we start after our lunch meal. We'll skip dinner tonight, fast tomorrow, then all meet at our house tomorrow night for supper. We'll have a family prayer before we break the fast." He turned to Lydia. "Is that all right?"

"Of course. I think it's a wonderful idea."

"What about Melissa?" Kathryn asked.

"I'll tell Melissa and Carl. They may not be pleased that Alice is joining the Church, but they both feel strongly that Alice is right for Will and they don't want her to lose her family."

"Yes," Lydia said. "I'll go with you to tell Melissa."

"Good," Nathan said, pleased that they had caught the spirit of what he was proposing. He looked at the four youth. "You older children can join with us too. Your faith is just as strong, if not stronger, than ours."

"I would like that," Rachel said. The others nodded as well.

"Thank you, Nathan, for suggesting this," Caroline said, obviously touched.

"There's something else," he said, more hesitantly now.

"What?" Solomon Garrett asked.

Nathan inhaled deeply, then let it out in a long, slow sigh. "I think we all know that we are rapidly approaching a major family crisis."

"A crisis?" Jessica asked. Some of the others looked bewildered, but Caroline was slowly nodding her head.

"Yes." He was very somber now, the weight of what he was about to say resting heavily on him. "In light of what has recently happened, I don't think there is any question about whether we will be leaving Nauvoo now. Come spring, Brigham is going to take us west to the Rocky Mountains. It's September now. So in six months, our lives will change forever."

Now they understood, and the reality of it was terribly sobering. Nathan looked at Matthew and Jenny. "Is there any question in your mind about whether or not you will go?"

Matthew seemed surprised. "None," he answered right back.

Jenny shook her head as she slipped an arm through his. "No."

He turned. "Derek? Rebecca?"

They too moved closer together. "No, no question."

He looked at Jessica and Solomon. They shook their heads.

Now he looked at Kathryn and at Peter, who stood behind her wheelchair. "It will be the most difficult for you," Nathan said quietly. "Will you go?"

"Of course," Kathryn said without hesitation. She patted the wheels. "I'll just hook up a yoke of oxen to this thing, and I'll be fine."

Finally he turned to Caroline. Her eyes were shining and she was looking past him. He couldn't bear to ask her. He didn't have to. Here there was no surety. Here there was no answer. He looked around the circle. "And Melissa and Carl? Do you think they will go?"

No one spoke, but from their expressions it was clear that most would have answered with no.

"And this time, we won't just be moving from Kirtland to Nauvoo. We're talking more than twelve hundred miles, with no riverboats, no railways, no stage lines, not even any major roads. Once we leave, it's very unlikely that we will ever come back, at least not for a long time."

"You all know what Joshua wants," Caroline said softly now. "He knows it's coming too. As soon as he returns, he wants a family meeting to try and persuade us all to move to St. Louis."

"That's why I wanted to talk about it now," Nathan answered gravely. "In a way, I'm glad that he had to take Alice back. It will give us time to think about how we're going to deal with this."

"But how can we not go?" Matthew exclaimed.

"That's just it," Caroline responded. "What Joshua still doesn't understand is that this isn't just following after Brigham Young, or Heber C. Kimball. This is answering the call of the Lord. And unfortunately, the Lord isn't asking us to go to St. Louis." Now the tears spilled over and started down her cheeks. "Do you think Will and Alice will hesitate to go?"

Matthew shook his head. "Not one minute."

She bit her lip. "I know."

"What can we do, Papa?" Nathan turned to his daughter. To his surprise, Emily was crying now too. "We can't leave Aunt Caroline. Or Aunt Melissa. We can't just leave them."

Lydia was watching Caroline closely. "What *will* you do?" she asked, feeling her sister-in-law's pain.

Caroline's head dropped and she looked at the ground. "I don't know. He'll never go west. And then what's my choice? Follow the Lord or stay with my husband?"

Nathan put an arm around his daughter and pulled her against his shoulder. "I'd like to try and answer Emily's question." He blew out his breath, wanting so much to be able to say this right. "In the scriptures, we are often taught that there are times when our prayers need to be combined with fasting, that there are certain problems of such difficulty, such magnitude, that a special effort is needed to get an answer."

"Like getting Lydia McBride to join the Church," Lydia half whispered. "If it hadn't been for Nathan's fasting, I wouldn't be here."

"That's how Mama finally got Papa to sell the farm and go to Ohio," Rebecca spoke up. "Remember?"

"Yes," Nathan exclaimed, "that's exactly what I'm talking about. I think that what we have here is a problem of great magnitude. We know the Lord won't force anyone to be what they don't want to be. But we also know that he can soften hearts, change feelings. Isn't the greatest miracle of all the changing of the human heart? Isn't that worth whatever effort it takes on our part to see if that will happen?"

"A family fast for Joshua?" Matthew asked.

"No, a family fast for our family," Nathan corrected him. "I am proposing that we start a fast tonight for Alice and Will. And then I am suggesting that after that, once a week, we have a fast for our family, that we fast and pray that we can stay together, that somehow the Lord will help us work out this impossible situation." He paused, his voice filled with emotion. "That's what I am suggesting."

Walter Samuelson slammed his fist against the tabletop, accidentally hitting the corner of his ashtray. Cigar butts and ashes went flying across the glass top. He swore bitterly, then looked at Will. "No! Absolutely not. I will not give my permission for you to marry Alice, and I will not allow her to become a Mormon. That is final. Discussion over, Will!"

"But, Mr. Samuelson, I—"

"I said no!" he roared. "Do you hear me, Will? No!"

Will was calm. He did not flinch under the barrage of words nor the heat of Samuelson's anger. "Sir, begging your pardon, but Alice is eighteen years of age. She will be nineteen in December. She was hoping for your blessing. She does not need your permission."

"Will!" Joshua cut in sharply as Samuelson turned a bright red and looked as if he would choke. "That's enough."

With that same calm equanimity, Will looked at Joshua. "I'm sorry, Father, but I'm not going to pretend that Walter's opposition is going to change things when it's not. Alice and I plan to marry. If we cannot get his permission, we shall do without his blessing as well."

And with that, he turned around and walked out of the office, ignoring the spluttering sounds coming from behind him.

Samuelson swore again. Joshua shook his head. So much for all of his carefully rehearsed dialogues on the way down here. "Walter," he began.

His partner didn't look up, just waved him off.

"Walter, look, we need to talk about this."

His head shot up. "No, Joshua, *we* don't need to talk. You and Will need to talk. I've said my last word on this. If you want to do some good, you go talk to your son."

———————•———————

He caught up with Will just outside the main door of the warehouse. To Joshua's surprise, Will had not turned up the street toward Alice's house, but down the street, toward the river. Joshua ran quickly to catch up, and then fell in step beside him. Will glanced at him but said nothing.

They walked along in silence for better than five minutes, down to the great river with its long wharves, its chugging river-boats, and warehouse after warehouse filled with huge stacks of cotton, bales of wool, mountains of lumber, sweet-smelling spices from the Orient, and a hundred other samplings of the commerce of the world. Finally, at one of the piers Will slowed his step. There was no riverboat docked there at present, so he stepped over the chain that kept the wagons and carriages out and walked out to the end of the dock. He sat down, his legs dangling over the edge, staring down at the swirling waters below them. Joshua sat down beside him and leaned back on his hands.

For almost another full minute they didn't speak; then Joshua cleared his throat. Will turned his head and looked at him fully, as if this was no more than what he had expected.

"Will you listen to me for a minute or two without getting angry?" Joshua asked.

Will shrugged easily. "I'm not at all angry, Pa. Not at you. Not at Alice's father."

"Will, taking that kind of stance isn't going to help."

"What kind of stance is that, Pa?"

"Saying that you and Alice are going to do what you want to do no matter what Walter says. It will only make him dig in his heels all the deeper."

"And what do you think I should say to him?"

"I—" He stopped for a minute. "I don't know. But being so confrontational isn't helping your cause at all."

"I didn't think I was pleading *my* cause, Pa."

"Well, it's certainly not going to help Alice."

"I wasn't pleading Alice's cause either."

"Then just what were you doing? Being stubborn?" And then to take the bite out of his words, he smiled. "Like your father?"

"I was trying to help Walter see what *his* best alternative is."

Joshua couldn't help but laugh. "You what?"

"That's right. There are only two alternatives here. He can give his permission, even if he doesn't approve, and make the best of the situation. If that's the case, Alice will be baptized, we'll be married. Oh, there will be a little strain, but at least the family will stay together." Will shrugged again, still quite untroubled. "Or he can utterly refuse, fight us at every step. Alice will still be baptized, we will still be married, and the family will be torn apart. So isn't the first the better alternative?"

Joshua just stared at him, remembering Will's unbendable determination to be baptized and the conflict it had generated between them.

"I know what he's thinking," Will went on. "He's thinking that if he is angry enough and threatens to throw her out, it will change her mind. But it won't, Pa. I am telling you, she knows what she wants to do, and even if it comes to the other, she is not going to change her mind. So, the sooner Walter comes to accept that, the better choice he will be able to make."

"And you think it's that simple?" Joshua asked in amazement, not hiding his irritation.

Will half turned, looking behind them to where a small slab of board was nailed above the entrance to the wharf. He nodded toward it. "Do you know why I came here, Pa?"

Joshua looked around, not sure what Will was looking at. "No. Why?"

"This is pier number seventeen."

"So?"

"That sign there was the only thing I could see from the coal bin they locked me in," he said softly. "Pier number seventeen."

"Coal bin? Locked you—" And then understanding came. It had been here in St. Louis that Will had been kidnapped and sold to a riverboat captain, who then took him to New Orleans and sold him off to a packet ship captain. He slowly nodded.

"It was not a wonderful time, Pa. I thought you were dead. I had stolen money from Mama in Savannah, then run away, with her not knowing where I was. I had a broken wrist. I had just seen two men gunned down and killed because of my stupidity." He laughed in soft self-mockery. "I was fourteen and I was going to solve everything."

"You were trying to make things right, Will."

"I was a fool, Pa. Why I'm not dead, I don't know. I was very nearly killed."

"I know."

"After Charlie dragged me down here and sold me to the boat captain, they locked me in the coal bin. The only light I had was from one small crack in the outside wall. In the morning, before we left St. Louis, I peeked out of that crack. The only thing I could see was that sign there. Pier number seventeen." He looked at his father now. "It wasn't much, but it was all I had. I knew I was still in St. Louis, and for a few hours it gave me hope."

Joshua said nothing. Will had told him about that terrible time when he had come back to Missouri seeking to avenge what he thought was his father's death, but he had never before shared these details.

"You know what, Pa? For a long time, especially after I was

sold to that sea captain, I was terribly bitter. Life had dealt with me in some pretty awful ways. I fought back. I tried to run away. Nothing worked. It only made things worse for me."

"I can't believe that you came through it as well as you did."

"Do you know why I did?"

"No."

"Because one day I realized that reality was reality. I was on a sailing ship in the Caribbean. My family thought I was dead. There was no way to escape. Whether I liked it or not, that was reality. When I finally realized that, and accepted it, that's when things began to turn around."

"Hmm." Joshua was looking at his son with new respect and admiration, starting now to understand what he had been saying previously.

"It's pier seventeen all over again, Pa. Walter can either accept reality and make the best of it, or he can not accept reality and make the worst of it. That's what he needs to see, Pa. That's what you need to help him understand. That's why I said that I'm not trying to plead my cause, or Alice's cause. It's *his* cause. It is the best for him and for his wife."

Joshua gave his son a long, appraising look, then slowly nodded. He had not fully believed it until now, but now he saw it clearly. And Will was right. That didn't mean he agreed with him, but he could see he was right.

Will had a sudden thought. "Pa, suppose this were a business venture and not a family matter. Then what would you say to him?"

Joshua leaned back, remembering that first day in Savannah when he had stepped off the boat and been greeted by a cocky, swaggering twelve-year-old who offered guide services to the city. He shook his head. What a pivotal meeting that had turned out to be! He came back to the present. "A business deal? I'm not sure what you mean."

"Suppose you and Walter were talking about a business deal here and not a family matter. Let's say that you have a failing business. You don't like it; in fact, you desperately do not want it to fail. But you have tried everything. Nothing works. The reality is, it's going to fail. What would you tell him to do?"

Joshua's mouth opened and then shut again as he thought about that. It took him only a second or two to know the answer. "I would tell him to cut his losses."

"Meaning?"

"If you really can't turn it around, then throwing more money at it is not the answer. So you cut your losses. You get out before you lose any more. You stop throwing good money after bad."

"In other words," Will said softly, "once you accept reality, you try to make the best of it."

"Yes." Joshua sighed. "It's very hard, though. Especially if you have a huge investment in it. It's hard to finally say, there's nothing more we can do."

"That's Walter's problem, Pa. I know he and Judith have a huge investment in Alice, but they're going to throw it all away if they're not careful. Somehow, he's got to see that."

For a long time, Joshua was silent.

"You don't know this," Will said, bringing him back to the present, "but I come down here almost every time we are in St. Louis."

"You do?"

"Yes. It reminds me of some important things about life, about myself. And I always end up saying a prayer before I leave, thanking my Heavenly Father for taking a foolish, immature fourteen-year-old and watching over him until he could grow up a little."

"Why didn't you ever tell me all this?"

"It wasn't the right time."

"And now it is?"

Will nodded slowly. "I hope so."

Joshua stood up. He stared across the river to the Illinois side, thinking paradoxically of Nauvoo and home. He was filled with a sudden longing to be there, to talk to Caroline about the remarkable young man she had raised. Will got to his feet and came to stand beside him.

"I don't think right now is a good time," Joshua said.

"A good time for what?"

"For trying to talk to Walter."

Will smiled sadly. "Probably not."

"But we will tonight."

"We?" Will said in surprise. "I don't think that is a good idea. Really."

After a pause, Joshua's head bobbed up and down once. "Perhaps you're right." He took a breath. "All right, Will. I'm not making any promises, but I'll talk to him. To them. I think Judith needs to hear this too."

"I agree. Thank you, Father."

They started back up the wharf, toward the street. As they stepped over the chain, Joshua turned and looked back. "How big was the coal bin?" he asked.

Surprised, Will thought for a moment. "Oh, maybe five feet by ten feet. Why?"

"I was just wondering. Normally, the best schoolrooms are larger than that."

———— ✦ ————

Alice turned over and sat up the moment the door opened. The light from the hallway put the figure in her doorway in shadow, but she recognized the bulky outline of her father immediately. "Papa?"

"Are you still awake?"

"Yes."

He came in, walking slowly. For a moment he stood over her, looking down at her, his face still in shadows and unreadable. She slid over and patted the bed. He hesitated, and then sat down beside her.

"What is it, Papa?"

He looked away, and now the light from the open doorway fell on the profile of his face and she could partially see his for-lorn expression. She wanted to reach out and touch him, but she wasn't sure it was what he needed right now. So she waited.

"What did you and Will do tonight?" he asked.

"We went for a walk down by the river."

"To pier seventeen?"

Alice started a little. "Yes. How did you know?"

"A wild guess," he said dryly. "Had he ever taken you there before?"

"Yes, but he never told me why before."

"Oh." There was a long silence, and then, "Is he right?"

She didn't have to ask what he meant. She knew full well the emotion behind that question. She took a deep breath. "Yes, Papa."

"Is there nothing your mother and I can do to change your mind?"

She hesitated, wanting so badly to say what had to be said, but also wanting to say it in the right way. "Can I ask you a question before I answer?"

"Of course."

"Grandpa Wilson was not happy when you asked him for Mama's hand, was he?"

He turned and she could see his frown. "That's not fair, Alice."

She laughed softly. "I've been holding this argument back for just the right time."

"I expected you would have used it before now." He sighed. "But no, he wasn't happy."

"Why?"

"Because he was this big wealthy plantation owner, and I was the son of a cotton factor. A very successful cotton factor, but a cotton factor nevertheless. But"—he raised a finger and shook it at her with some vigor—"although he wasn't happy, he did not forbid it."

"And if he had?"

He sighed again. "I don't know what your mother would have done."

"I would have gone with you to St. Louis."

They both turned as Judith Samuelson stepped into the room. She came over and sat down beside her husband.

"You would?" he said in wonder.

"I would have gone with you anywhere," she smiled. "You were so bold, so impetuous, so determined to go on your own and make a fortune. Yes, anywhere."

Walter reached out and took her hand and squeezed it. Then Judith turned to Alice and her face was stern now. "But I was not talking about going off after some wild religion, abandoning everything I believed in."

Alice's first impulse was to cry out against that. She was not abandoning what she believed in. Instead, for the first time, she felt that the things she believed in had taken on a more complete meaning now. But instead she turned to her father. "Is Will so horrible as all that, Papa?"

"Well, no . . . you know how we feel about Will. It's just this Mormon thing."

"Mama has never met any of the rest of the Steeds, but you have, Papa. Are they such horrible people?"

"Well, no, but . . ."

"No buts, Papa. Are they or aren't they?"

"No," he finally admitted. "They are fine folk."

She said nothing more.

"So," her father asked, "back to the original question. Is there nothing Mother and I can do to change your mind?"

She looked at both of them and tears welled up. If only they knew how dearly she loved them! But she slowly shook her head.

"What if we say yes to the marriage?" her mother asked. "Would you consider waiting for a time to become a Mormon?"

She started to shake her head again, but her mother went on quickly. "If once you're married you still feel like this is what you must do, then . . ." She looked away. "We'll say nothing more."

"Mother, I know you think I am joining the Church only because of Will, but it's so much more than—"

Her father cut in quickly. "It's easy to fool yourself, Alice. What's wrong with Mother's suggestion? Once you're married, if you still feel the same, then we'll not say anything more."

Alice leaned forward, wrapping her arms around her knees.

Was that a reasonable compromise? Here they were offering reconciliation, and her spirit was soaring with that prospect. She wouldn't have to lose them. There wouldn't be this terrible, final severance. Could she bend a little? Would Will be disappointed in her? The questions tumbled over and over in her mind. And then she saw her father's eyes, the hope and pleading in them, and she knew what it meant for him to have bent this far.

Finally she looked up. "All right, Papa. I'll do this. You think it was just my being up in Nauvoo, under the influence of his family. But you're wrong. I'll not be baptized right now. If we wait for Will's grandparents to return from Nashville, it will be late October, or even the first of November, before we can be married. I'll wait until then. You can do everything in your power to try and convince me I am wrong. But if you haven't been able to change my mind by then, I will be baptized before I marry Will. Is that fair enough?"

Her father drew in his breath, but his wife quickly laid a hand on his arm. "That's a compromise, Walter."

Finally he sighed. "All right, but you must promise to listen to what we have to say. I'd also like you to talk to the parson."

Alice nodded quickly, for the first time her hopes rising that there might be a way out of this terrible impasse.

"Now, there's one more thing."

Her heart dropped. "What, Papa?"

"I know that a woman needs to go with her husband, wherever that may be."

She felt a sudden tug of anxiety. "Yes, Papa?"

"I know that Will wants to take you back to Nauvoo." He almost said, "And then he wants to take you to the Rocky Mountains with the rest of the Mormons," but he resisted it, as much for Judith's sake as for Alice's. He took a quick breath. "You know that I've wanted Will to come here and work with me in the business."

Her eyes were downcast. "Yes, Papa."

"It's not like that is such a terrible thing, is it? He'll be handsomely paid. Then your mama will have you close for a time."

"I don't know if I can ask that of him, Papa."

"I'm not asking for a permanent commitment. But will you give it a chance just until spring? Then if he still wants to go back to his family, we'll not stand in your way."

She searched his face. Is this why he was such a successful businessman? He knew when to compromise, but only enough to win, not enough to make serious concessions. The hope in Alice had died. Will had no interest in running her father's businesses. He had no desire to stay in St. Louis. On the other hand, it would be nice for her. The thoughts of leaving her family had weighed on her heavily.

"Will you at least talk to him about it?" her mother asked. "Please, Alice? Just until spring?"

Finally she nodded, not meeting their gaze. "I'll talk to him in the morning."

"Good." Her father stood, then bent down and kissed her on the top of her head. "If he will agree to that, there'll be no more opposition from us."

"All right, Papa. I'll talk to him."

He straightened and snapped his fingers. "I have an idea." He swung around to his wife. "It's not fair to ask Will to be married here without all of his family. Yet if we go to Nauvoo, our family and friends will miss it." He reached down, put a finger under his wife's chin, and lifted her head. "We'll bring the whole Steed family down here."

Both mother and daughter gaped at him, dumbfounded.

"Yes," he rushed on. "I'll charter a boat. We'll have the wedding here, but we'll bring the whole family. Everyone! That way you can be married with Kathryn and Peter. Their family will not miss anything. And Mother will get her wish to see her daughter married properly."

Alice was spinning a little. "Are you sure, Papa?"

"Yes, yes!" He started to pace, his mind racing. "That's the answer."

"I'll bet you Joshua would want to help with the cost," Judith suggested.

"And I'll let him," Walter growled. "After all, he's the one who convinced me to give in to all of this." He turned to Alice. "What do you think?"

She was still half-dazed. "I . . . If Will thinks it's okay, then that would be wonderful."

"We'll ask him first thing in the morning."

***

As Walter Samuelson undressed and prepared for bed, Judith watched him in the mirror. She was brushing out her hair with long, even strokes, but her eyes were on him. He turned, saw that she was watching him, and stopped. "What?"

"I thought you were going to talk to her about going west."

There was a quick shake of his head. "I thought about it."

"Walter, I can't bear the thoughts of her going that far away, into a trackless wilderness. I can't!"

"I know." He came over to stand behind her, and put his hands on her shoulders. "It will be all right."

"How can you say that?" she cried. "Even Joshua says there is little doubt now about the Mormons leaving Illinois."

"Undoubtedly they will," he agreed. "But that's not the point."

"What is the point?"

"I'm fifty-four now, Judith. I'm getting tired. There are things I'd like to do, new places I'd like to see."

She turned around to stare up at him. "What are you saying?"

"I think it's time to think about retiring, Judith."

She was flabbergasted. "Retiring?"

"Yes." A slow smile stole over his face. "I'm going to use these next few months to let Will start taking over. Eventually— let's say two or three years—he'll have it all. We'll have the income to do whatever we want, and he will become a very wealthy and successful young man."

"I . . ." She shook her head. He had not said one word about any of this to her before.

"I don't want him knowing my plans right now, Mother, but give me six months and I'll convince him that he can be a

millionaire by the time he is thirty." There was a soft laugh and
he squeezed her shoulders lightly. "Once he understands that, I
don't think we need to be worrying about him taking Alice anywhere. Do you?"

For a long time Will was silent. He stared out the window
across the city, his brow furrowed. Finally, without turning to
her, he asked, "What do you think, Alice?"

"I think I want to be with you. If that is here, that would be
wonderful in a way. If it is in Nauvoo, that would be wonderful
in another way."

"And what if it is somewhere in the West?"

"So you believe it too," she said, not with any bitterness, but
with just a touch of sadness.

"Believe what?"

"That the only reason I'm joining the Church is because of
you."

He was instantly sorry. "No, Alice. I don't. Of all people, I
know what you've gone through. I'm sorry if I sounded like I feel
that way."

"Then isn't that answer enough? If I am going to be a Latter-
day Saint, and if Brigham Young says the Saints are to gather in
the West somewhere, then I want to be with the Saints. I would
feel that way even if we weren't getting married."

He moved closer to her, brushing his shoulder against hers.
"How come all those times I was here, I thought you were just a
good friend? How come I never thought of you as someone I
would come to love?"

A tiny smile was playing around the corners of her mouth. "I
could say something about diminished mental capacity or lack of
good judgment, but wisdom dictates that I don't."

He took her by the shoulders and shook her gently. "You're
pretty cocky for a woman who's here asking me for favors." And
then he sobered. "Did you know back then?"

She laughed softly at his earnestness. "Not right at first. Like you, I was glad to have it just be a friendship. Your father and my father were trying so hard to get us together."

"I know. It was awful."

"But I knew long before you did," she murmured, her eyes softening. "And I was afraid for a long time that you might never come to know."

He kissed her softly. "Like you say, diminished mental capacity." Then he sighed, let her go, and turned back to the window. "So back to the question at hand."

"Will, we made our decision. We said we would do what was best for us no matter what my parents said. So if you say no to my father and we go back to Nauvoo, I will support you completely."

"I know you will, and I love you for that. But . . ."

He fell silent, his face furrowing as he considered what it would mean. She waited patiently, wanting him to sort it out completely before deciding.

Suddenly he straightened. "I'll do it."

"You will?" she asked in surprise.

"Yes. We also decided we would make every effort we could so that you didn't have to break with your family. Six months working with your father is not a terrible price to pay."

Her voice caught and she could only take his hand.

"Really," he said. "If we do go west, this will be your last chance to be with your family. Maybe for a long time. And besides, earning some handsome wages in the meantime will be very helpful for us too."

"You would do that for me?" she finally managed.

"And for them." There was a sudden grin. "Contrary to what your father thinks, I am not totally without understanding of their feelings in this whole situation." Then, as he began to consider what this decision would mean, he had a thought. "I can't just stay here for the next six months, however. I have to go back to Nauvoo. I didn't bring anything but one valise."

"I hadn't thought about that."

Now his mind began to race. "Look, if we are going to spend the next six months here with your family, what if you go back with me until the wedding?"

"To Nauvoo?" she said in surprise.

"Yes. I'd like to have some time with my family. And Grandma and Grandpa Steed should be coming home anytime now. I want to see them before I go off for six months. If you come back with me now, we could be with my family for a time, then we can come back all together for the wedding."

Alice bit her lip, thinking. "I like the idea, but Mama will want me here to get ready for the wedding—get the dress, all the other things that have to happen."

"All right. What if we just go for a couple of weeks? Then we'll come back and you'll have a couple of weeks here. Surely your parents can't object to that. Not if I'm willing to leave my family."

She was nodding slowly now. "Mama will be disappointed. She's already talking about going shopping today, but . . ."

He snapped his fingers. "All right, so we wait a few days before we leave. Today is the twenty-second. General conference starts in about two weeks, on the fifth of October—that's a Sunday. What if we let my father go on back? We will stay here for another week, and then leave. We could still make it back in time for conference. It's going to be held in the temple, Alice. Imagine that. The first meeting in the temple. I'd really like to be there for that."

"Oh, so would I."

He grinned, looking suddenly mischievous. "I don't suppose we need to talk a lot about that with your folks. But we could go up to Nauvoo for two or three weeks, then come back down here the final week before the wedding so you and your mother can finish the preparations. Your folks ought to be willing to accept that."

"When they learn that you are willing to stay and work with Papa until spring," Alice responded eagerly, "they're going to be so happy, they'll agree to anything. Let's go talk to them about it right now."

As they both stood, Alice suddenly threw her arms around Will. "Thank you, Will. This will mean so much to them."

He put his arms around her and held her tightly. After a moment, he started to chuckle.

"What?"

"If I keep this up, people might start thinking that I'm not as absolutely impossible to get along with as they thought. That could come as quite a shock to both my father and yours."

Whence a kettle of stew hangs for a long time above a bed of coals, it simmers. But stir the coals in any way, or add wood to the fire, and the simmering quickly becomes a rolling boil. For the fifteen months following the martyrdom of Joseph Smith and his brother Hyrum, the pot of anti-Mormon sentiment had mostly simmered. The state took action immediately after the murders and sent the militia to Hancock County to keep things in check. That fall, the courts handed down indictments on nine men accused of being responsible for the killings. Then, by the spring of 1845, things started to change. The state militia went home; the men tried for the murder of Joseph Smith were acquitted handily. The antis had been given a clear signal. The state and the courts might make a lot of noise about the rights of Mormons, but when it came right down to it, nothing much really happened. And since the Mormon Church had not collapsed of its own weight after Joseph Smith's death, as everyone had predicted it would, this general lack of support for the Mormons was good news indeed to the Church's enemies.

Thomas Sharp and others started throwing more wood on the fire again. The simmering hatred turned to open violence, and the natural result was the raid on the Morley Settlement. But that was not the end of it. Frank Worrell's death was like piling even more logs on the fire. To no one's surprise, the kettle boiled over.

On September twenty-second, 1845, just six days following the killing, a meeting was called in Quincy, about forty miles south of Nauvoo. Ironically, Quincy was the very city that had so warmly welcomed the exiled Saints as they fled from Missouri in the harsh winter of 1838–39. It had a reputation for moderation and tolerance. This only added to the irony of the petition the Quincy committee drafted and delivered to the Church leaders.

The gist of their resolutions was simple. The Mormons had already given some indication that they were willing to leave Illinois and find someplace else to locate. That was such a nice solution. And the Mormons should have no doubts as to the impending disaster in Hancock County if something was not done. So the committee urged Church leaders to communicate in writing, as soon as possible, the intentions of the Mormon people relative to leaving the state.

In an article published not long after the meeting in Quincy, the editor of the *Quincy Whig* opined that it was the Mormons' "duty to obey the public will, and leave the state as speedily as possible." Almost anywhere else in the Union, this would have been branded as an unusual definition of *duty*—abandon your homes, forget your constitutional rights, ignore the fact that you are the wronged party. Just leave, please.

When the Twelve received the petition from the Quincy committee, not only did President Young see the handwriting on the wall, but, like Daniel of old, he interpreted it accurately. After meeting in council, the Church leaders decided that there was no hope of a lawful and just settlement. On September twenty-fourth, a response was drafted, and the next day it was given to the Quincy committee. Signed by Brigham Young, the Twelve's answer read, in part:

"Whereas, it is our desire, and ever has been, to live in peace with all men, so far as we can, without sacrificing the right of worshipping God according to the dictates of our own consciences, which privilege is guaranteed to us by the Constitution of these United States;

"And, whereas, we have, time and again, and again, been driven from our peaceful homes, and our women and children been obliged to exist on the prairies, in the forests, on the roads, and in tents, in the dead of winter, suffering all manner of hardships, even to death itself . . . ;

"And, whereas, it is now so late in the season that it is impossible for us, as a people, to remove this fall, without causing a repetition of like sufferings; . . .

"And, whereas, we desire peace above all other earthly blessings—

"Therefore, we would say to the committee above mentioned and to the governor, and all the authorities and people of Illinois, and the surrounding states and territories, that we propose to leave this county next spring, for some point so remote, that there will not need to be a difficulty with the people and ourselves."

The Church leaders did outline some propositions that needed to be observed if the removal was to be accomplished, including the following: that there be no more depredations against the Mormons, and that the citizens of Hancock and the surrounding counties help the Mormons sell their property at a fair market value. The document concluded with the leaders stating "that it is a mistaken idea that we 'have proposed to remove in six months;' for that would be so early in the spring, that grass might not grow nor water run, both of which would be necessary for our removal, but we propose to use our influence, to have no more seed time nor harvest among our people in this county, after gathering our present crops."

Once the Quincy committee had their answer from President Young, it didn't take them long to hold another meeting and, after some deliberations, draw up yet another set of resolutions. In these they declared, among other things, that the major point of the Mormons' letter—namely, that the Saints were formally promising to leave the state—was acceptable. However, certain points needed to be clearly stated. With great cries of offended pride, the committee rejected the idea that the citizens of Hancock County were in any way responsible for the depredations which the Mormons had experienced. Moreover, while they did agree that they would do everything in their power "to prevent the occurrence of anything which might operate against" the Mormons' removal, they wanted it clearly understood that the citizens of Illinois were under no obligation to help the Saints dispose of their properties.

Heaven forbid that they should help the Mormons become exiles!

The Quincy committee's resolutions reached Nauvoo early in October, just prior to general conference.

Meanwhile, the stance taken by Thomas Ford, governor of the state, gave little or no comfort to the Saints. At about this time in the fall of 1845, a four-man commission, appointed by Ford to help resolve matters between the Mormons and the other inhabitants of Illinois, was in contact, both in person and by letter, with Church leaders. A dispatch from the governor to the leader of this commission made the governor's position clear. "I wish you to say to the Mormons for me," wrote the governor, "that I regret very much, that so much excitement and hatred against them should exist in the public mind. Nevertheless, it is due to truth to say that the public mind everywhere is so decidedly hostile to them that public opinion is not inclined to do them justice. . . . Under these circumstances, I fear that they will never be able to live in peace with their neighbors of Hancock and the surrounding counties. There is no legal power in the state to compel them to leave, and no such power will be exercised during my administration.

"The spirit of the people, however, is up and the signs are very evident that an attempt will be made by the surrounding counties to drive them out. . . . Those who may think it wrong to drive out the Mormons cannot be made to fight in their defense, and indeed the people of the state will never tolerate the expense of frequent military expeditions to defend them."

There it was, clothed in typical political obfuscation. The state will not actually drive the Mormons out, but neither can it—or better, will it—use its powers to stop others from doing so. Such expressions were as good as an engraved invitation to the likes of Thomas Sharp and Levi Williams.

As the time for the Church's general conference approached, then, the Saints were unquestionably feeling the heat of state-wide anti-Mormon sentiment. Yet another anti-Mormon gathering was held on October first and second, this time in Carthage, involving people from nine counties, with Hancock County being excluded since it was embroiled in the current difficulty.

To no one's surprise, the events and communications of the past few weeks would make this general conference of the Church significantly different than others which had been held in the past.

In the end, Joshua decided to stay on in St. Louis for the additional week and return with Alice and Will. They arrived in Nauvoo on the afternoon of Friday, October third. It was only later that evening, after the family had been gathered, after Walter Samuelson's proposal to bring all the family to St. Louis had been announced, and after the children—set into a dither by such incredible news as a family trip downriver—had finally settled down, that Joshua was able to quietly take Nathan aside and get to the subject that was on his mind.

"I heard about the Quincy committee while we were coming upriver," he began without preamble.

"Yes."

"Is it true that Brigham has capitulated?"

"Capitulated?" Nathan said with a touch of irritation. "That's an interesting choice of words."

Joshua shook his head. "I'm not trying to argue about what he's doing. Is it true? Has he agreed to leave the state?"

"Yes. Brigham has formally announced that we will be leaving in the spring."

Joshua's shoulders lifted and fell. That had been the rumor. He was certain it had some basis in truth. "Then I'd say we'd better call that family council you promised."

Nathan looked around the crowded room. "Like tonight?" he asked dryly.

"No, of course not. But tomorrow."

"Look, Joshua," Nathan answered, "I'm not trying to fight you. I completely agree with you. It's time. But I'm sure that leaving the state will be the focus of much of the conference. That starts on Sunday. What if we waited until that is over? Then we'll have a much better feel for what is going to happen—how soon, what will be expected of us, and so on."

After a moment's consideration of that, Joshua bobbed his head up and down once. "Fair enough."

———— • ————

Nashville, Tennessee, October 4th, 1845

Dear Family—

This will be a very short note. Two days ago we got the letter from the Twelve calling us home. We received that with mixed emotions. This has been a wonderful experience both for your father and for me. But at the same time, I have not slept for the last two nights. I am too excited at the thoughts of being with our family again.

We are sending this express in hopes that it will reach you before we do. We will go by light craft down the Cumberland River to the Ohio. There we have booked passage on a regular scheduled steamer which goes all the way up the Mississippi to Galena, Illinois. This means we can travel all the way home via boat, unless the weather turns cold and the river fills with ice.

The boat is the "Pittsburgh Palace." Though there may be

delays (or swifter passage than anticipated), the captain estimates arrival in Galena no later than October 21st to 24th. That would bring us to Nauvoo around the 18th to the 21st of the same month.

Get the house open and ready for us. Break out the pie pans. We are coming home!

All my love,
Mary Ann

Though he had originally planned to go to conference to hear for himself what was going to be said, Joshua changed his mind about attending the first session. On Saturday, Matthew went to Brigham's home to visit on a matter, and Brigham told him that Sunday's meetings would be devoted to dedicating the portion of the temple that was now completed, and to talks on the temple and other general gospel themes. The Monday morning session would be the sustaining of the Church authorities and officers. Not until Monday afternoon would the focus turn to the move west. Since that and that alone interested Joshua, he declined to go to anything before that. To no one's surprise, Carl and Melissa said they would not even attend on Monday afternoon. The move west would not affect them; therefore there was no need to go.

On Sunday morning, Will and Alice walked up to the temple early with Peter and Kathryn. Will and Peter took turns pushing Kathryn's wheelchair up the low rise that led to the top of the bluffs. They arrived shortly after eight o'clock. The furniture for the temple was not finished as yet, so temporary chairs and benches were set up in the great assembly room of the temple. Not knowing what that would mean for a person in a wheelchair, Kathryn wanted to be there in plenty of time to make suitable arrangements for herself. They found a place near the center row of benches and spread themselves out across two rows to save places for the rest of the family, who came about half an hour later.

It was a good thing they had come early, for by nine o'clock the assembly room was totally filled, and any standing room was taken as well. The room was hushed and yet a quiet hum of excitement filled the great hall. To be in the temple, even though it was not yet completed, had stirred the hearts of the people. Many, perhaps even as much as half or more of the congregation, had come into the Church since 1837. They had never seen the Kirtland Temple, never sat in an assembly hall such as this. In Nauvoo, worship services were held in the homes of the Saints. Joint meetings of any size were held out in the open—weather permitting—generally in large groves of trees either in or near the city where the people could be sheltered from the sun. During the winter months, such general meetings were rarely held.

So it was little wonder that many of those who sat inside the great hall on this day were touched with a sense of awe and gratitude. At last they had a building, and what a magnificent building it was! It was a temple, a house of the Lord. There was not much in America, even in the large eastern cities, to compare with this. It was surpassed only by some of the great cathedrals of Europe.

Alice sat beside Will near the end of the bench, still close to Kathryn and Peter. She slipped her arm through his and he turned to look at her. "Thank you," she said softly.

"For what?"

"For making sure I was here today."

He smiled and squeezed her arm. "Thank you for being here."

Kathryn reached across Peter and touched Alice's arm. "Oh, yes, Alice, we are so glad you are here."

Then before she could respond, Brigham Young stood and moved to the great pulpit that stood at the head of the room. Immediately the sound died away and all eyes turned to him.

For what seemed like an eternity to Alice, President Young stood there without speaking. She had seen him once or twice before, but never at such close range. She was surprised that he was no taller than he was. He had seemed like such a towering fig-ure before. But it was his face that drew her. He let his eyes sweep across the congregation. Then they slowly rose, taking in the great, towering walls, the pulpit at the far end of the room behind them, the beautiful arched windows, the exquisitely carved doors, the lamps hung from the ceilings or ensconced on the walls. His eyes were glistening, his lips pressed tight together to stop them from trembling, and she saw his Adam's apple bob several times as he swallowed to try and keep in control. Finally, his eyes dropped again to look at the people and he leaned forward.

"My brothers and sisters, I am deeply touched by this sight. We sit here today, in the house of the Lord, having come to wor-ship him and offer thanks. Why am I so moved by this sight? Because I know that it is only through the indefatigable exer-tions, unceasing industry, and heaven-blessed labors of this people—labors given in the midst of trials, tribulations, poverty, and worldly obstacles—that we gather here in this sacred place this day. Some of that sacrifice, some of that tribulation, has been solemnized by the ultimate sacrifice, even that of death, to make this possible. And now here we are, about five thousand strong, gathered in this room and outside, having the inexpressible joy and gratification to be meeting for the first time here in the City of Joseph in the house of the Lord."

He had to stop for a moment, and one hand stole up to brush at the corner of his eye. "I know what this means, brothers and sisters. I know that it is only from the widows' mites given by many, and tithing rising into the millions of dollars, that we have been able to see raised here a temple, where the children of the kingdom could come together and praise the Lord."

There was a long pause before he went on. "It certainly affords us all a holy satisfaction to think that since the sixth of April, eighteen forty-one, when the first stone was laid, amidst the most straitened of circumstances, The Church of Jesus Christ of Latter-day Saints has witnessed their bread cast upon waters, or, to put it in another way, their obedience to the command-ments of the Lord, appear in the tangible form of a temple."

As he continued, his gaze swept around the great building once more. "We see here today a temple that is entirely enclosed, with the windows in, with temporary floors, pulpits, and seats to accommodate so many persons preparatory to our general conference. I know this building is not complete, but we are making every effort to move the work forward. Even though we shall leave it in the spring, we shall leave it completed, and it shall be a monument to our determination to fulfill God's requirement of us. Our hope is to dedicate this building in its entirety on April sixth next, but in the meantime, I should like to dedicate the portion that is now complete, in preparation for our holding conference herein."

He bowed his head and instantly all the congregation did the same.

Alice was so swept up in the power of Brigham's words that she didn't think to close her eyes. She watched him in fascination, then turned to look at the people around her. His words, simple and brief, droned in her mind, but it was filled with other thoughts as well. As Brigham spoke to the Lord about the sacrifice of the Saints and their offering up, in liberality and in faith, their labors, their efforts, and their money in order to have this temple built, she looked down the row in both directions and she felt her heart swell. If the Steed family was not a perfect example of what President Young was telling the Lord in this prayer of dedication, then she could not think of any family that was a better example.

Finally, she let her eyes stop on Will's face. His head was bowed, his arms folded, his eyes softly closed. Instantly tears sprang to her eyes. How she loved this man! She could scarcely believe that he loved her in turn. Was this what had brought her to the Church? Yes, she answered almost immediately. There was little question of that. If it weren't for her love for him, she might not even know about the Mormon faith. He had brought her to the point of inquiry. But was he the reason she had decided to *join* the Church?

As she considered that, suddenly words seemed to fill her

mind. *I know for myself.* Her eyes widened as she thought about what she had just said to herself. And then she nodded, understanding now. This was her answer. Will had brought her to want to know. But it wasn't just for Will that she had made the decision. *Yes!* Her eyes were exultant now. *I do know for myself.* With tears streaming down her face, she lowered her head and closed her eyes.

As she did so, Brigham Young was just completing his dedicatory prayer. "O Lord, with humble hearts, and in the name of thy Beloved Son, we dedicate this house—and ourselves—to thee. Amen."

Amen! Alice cried inwardly. *Amen and amen!*

As the heads came up and the sound of hundreds of people slightly stirring filled the room, Brigham looked around in satisfaction. "Brethren and sisters, we should now like to devote the rest of this day to offering up the gratitude of our hearts. We shall render thanks for the privilege of worshipping God within this edifice, whose beauty and workmanship will compare with any house of worship in America, and whose motto is 'Holiness to the Lord.' We have called upon several of the brethren to speak to us on that theme and shall now ask them to come forward."

Alice hung back slightly as the family made their way down the road that led from the bluff and the temple site back to the main part of Nauvoo. Will was talking earnestly with Matthew and Peter about the day's activities, but in a moment or two he noticed that she was no longer with him and he fell back to be beside her.

She slowed her step even more, so that in a moment, they were some fifteen or twenty feet behind the rest. "Will?"

"Yes?"

"I think I have made a mistake."

His head came around with a sharp snap. "What?" And then there was that quick, boyish grin that she so loved. "You're not going to try and back out on the marriage, are you?"

She clasped his hand quickly. "Absolutely not."

"Then what mistake?"

"In telling my father I would wait for a while to be baptized."

He stopped in midstride, pulling her to a halt beside him.

She nodded firmly. "I mean it, Will. As I listened to President Young and the other brethren today, I felt very strongly that I shouldn't wait. I'm doing it just to please Mama and Papa. Shouldn't I be more concerned about pleasing my Heavenly Father?"

To her surprise, Will did not answer her at once. She felt a stab of uncertainty. "Do you think I'm wrong?"

"Of course not," he said, moving forward again, but very slowly. "To want to please God is a wonderful thing. It's just that . . . well, I'm not sure that Heavenly Father is displeased with our wanting to keep your family happy too. And if you are baptized now, they'll think this was all a trick just to get you away from St. Louis so we could do it."

"I know," she said glumly. "But Papa will try to talk me out of it whenever I decide to do it."

"I know," Will said, "but all you did was commit to waiting until just before we are married. And that's less than a month now." They started walking again, Will deep in thought. Finally his head came up and he looked at her. "What if we do this? As soon as you and I return to St. Louis, we'll tell your parents that you are not going to wait any longer. Then I'll baptize you immediately. They may not be happy about that, but at least they couldn't accuse us of sneaking behind their backs."

She brightened instantly. "Oh, yes, Will. That would do it, wouldn't it? It's only two more weeks before we go back. I can wait that long." She went up on tiptoes and kissed him quickly on the cheek. "Thank you, Will. That's our answer, isn't it?"

———◆———

The morning session on Monday, October sixth, was devoted wholly to the sustaining of Church authorities and officers and conducting other business. The only things of unexpected note came during the sustaining of the Twelve. In the order of their seniority, each member of the Quorum was sustained. When it was William Smith's turn, Elder Orson Pratt rose and objected, observing that William Smith was an aspiring man and that he was working to undermine the legal Presidency of the Church in order to occupy the place himself. When the vote was called for, William Smith was unanimously rejected. When his name was put forth to be sustained as Patriarch to the Church, again the congregation unanimously refused to sustain him.

Lyman Wight, another member of the Twelve, was still in Texas with his colony. He had refused to heed the call of the Twelve to come back. Someone proposed that he be rejected as well, but Heber Kimball noted that the Twelve were waiting for a response to their last letter and recommended that further action be postponed until they saw what Elder Wight's answer would be. The congregation accepted that recommendation and voted accordingly.

Finally, the business session was completed, the two-hour midday break also passed, and at two o'clock the next session began. By that time, the atmosphere in the temple assembly room was charged with excitement and anticipation. This was what everyone had been waiting for. It was time to have their questions answered.

Caroline had saved a place for Joshua to join her, and he squeezed in between her and Savannah just as the choir began singing the opening hymn, "The Prodigal Son." Elder John Taylor then read a list of sick persons and offered an invocation on the meeting and a plea that the sick would be healed. The choir sang another number, after which Elder Taylor called Parley P. Pratt to the stand.

Nathan leaned forward, listening intently. He noted that most others, including Joshua, did the same. Nathan was not greatly surprised that his friend had been asked to be the first speaker. Two days before, he and Lydia had spent the evening with Parley and his wife. Parley told them that he had been asked to address the Saints on preparing for their journey.

As Parley walked slowly to the stand, unfolding a sheaf of papers, Nathan reached out and took Lydia's hand. She looked at him and smiled wanly. This was it, her face said. They all knew they were going, but today would finalize it, make it official. Somehow the very reality of it made it all the more disconcerting.

Parley reached the pulpit, laid the papers on it, then grasped it firmly with both hands. "My brothers and sisters," he began loudly, "I should like to speak to you for a few moments on the subject of our present situation and of our future prospects."

There was a low, almost inaudible murmur in the crowd.

"As you know, a few days ago, in response to a specific request of a committee of upstanding citizens in Quincy"—the word *upstanding* was spoken with soft sarcasm—"we, as a church, formally declared our intention to cease from planting winter wheat or any other crops for next season and to leave Nauvoo as soon as the weather turns warm. As of now, we plan to dedicate the remainder of this magnificent building at April conference next, on the sixth of that month to be precise, and then leave shortly thereafter.

"Obviously, that shall take considerable preparation on our part," Parley continued. "You don't move some ten to fifteen thousand people across a vast inland wilderness without careful and extensive planning. With only six months before our departure, we must begin that preparation now. Not tomorrow. Not after Christmas. Now!"

He lifted the sheaf of papers. "I have been asked by the Twelve to do some figuring so as to give you an idea of what will be required. Each family must be prepared. The Church cannot simply take this huge body of people under their wings and somehow waft them to the Rocky Mountains. It will take every person, every family, every head of household starting to prepare now. You must be ready come spring to leave our beautiful city and sustain yourselves in the wilderness. Therefore, I give you the following list of requirements. Do not feel as though you have to remember everything I am about to say. We are in the process of printing up this list so that all may have it."

Now not a sound could be heard in the assembly hall of the temple.

Parley looked at his sheet and began to read: "'Requirements of Each Family of Five for the Journey Across the Plains.'" He paused, letting that sink in for a moment. "Each family consisting of five persons will require the following." He glanced at his list from time to time, but was clearly citing much of it from memory. "One good, strong wagon, well covered; three good yoke of oxen between the ages of four and ten. Mules or horses can be used, but oxen are preferred. Two or more cows. One or more good beeves; some sheep if they have them."

He stopped and looked around. Many were nodding. The wagon was the basis for everything else. One could walk a thousand miles, but one didn't carry a four- or five-month supply of food and goods on his back.

Parley's finger moved down the page as he read on. "Still thinking in terms of a family of five. You will need one thousand pounds of flour or other breadstuff and good sacks to put it in. One bushel of beans. One hundred pounds of sugar. One good musket or rifle to each man. One pound of powder and three pounds of lead, or perhaps more. Two pounds of tea; five pounds of coffee. Twenty-five pounds of salt. A few pounds of dried beef, or bacon, as they choose."

A *thousand pounds of flour*, Nathan thought in dismay. For city folk, especially those who had recently arrived with nothing more than the clothes they wore, that was no small requirement. And yet, a family of five would go through a lot of food in the months it would take before they reached their new home.

"Now, as for other equipment. For each two families, a good tent and some furniture to put in it." Parley got a wry smile. "Brethren and sisters, we're talking about cots and perhaps a wash basin here, not sofas and pianofortes."

That brought a hearty laugh from the crowd and a reduction in the tension that had been building with the intimidating reality of the list he was reading. He lifted the paper again.

"From ten to fifty pounds of seed to a family. And from

twenty-five to one hundred pounds of farming or other tools. Clothing and bedding to each family of five persons not to exceed five hundred pounds."

Somewhere behind him, someone groaned. It sounded like the voice of a young woman, and that brought a second round of laughter. What Parley had just stated meant that on average, each person could take a hundred pounds of personal belongings. It sounded like a lot, but in most cases it would be a pitifully small portion of their total goods.

"One or more sets of saw and gristmill irons to each company of one hundred families," Parley intoned. "Cooking utensils to consist of a bake-kettle, frying pan, coffee pot, tin cups, plates, and forks, spoons, pans, and so forth. But remember, a few items will serve you well on the trail. A few goods to trade with the Indians. A little iron and steel, a few pounds of nails."

He stopped and took a breath, and Nathan glanced at Joshua. He was nodding slowly in approval. When Joshua saw Nathan looking at him, he leaned over. "He's been careful. I think it's a pretty good list."

"Yes," Nathan agreed.

"If you will consider all that I have read," Parley began again, "that means that each wagon will be loaded at the start of the journey with about one ton of goods—not counting the family members. With the people, it will be about twenty-eight hundred pounds per wagon. For this reason, as you can see, people will be encouraged to walk when possible, to save the teams." He paused, but there was nothing but a few nods. "A few horses will be necessary for each company. Also a few cannon and ammunition for the same. There is also added two sets of pulley blocks and rope for crossing rivers to each company of a hundred families. Two ferryboats to each company. One keg of alcohol of five gallons for each two families. Ten pounds of dried apples for each family. Five pounds of dried peaches. Twenty pounds of dried pumpkin. Two pounds of black pepper. One pound of cayenne. One-half pound mustard. Twelve nutmegs. One fish seine for each company. Hooks and lines for each family."

He laid the papers down finally, took off his spectacles, and wiped them with his handkerchief. "I estimate that if a family were to start with nothing except their own personal clothing and bed stuff, outfitting themselves as herein described will cost about two hundred fifty to three hundred dollars."

That did bring several low moans. In a cash-poor society like Nauvoo, two hundred fifty dollars was a considerable sum. Now Nathan saw Joshua shaking his head. "I think he's low," he whispered.

"This that I have read will require considerable sacrifice on the part of most of us," Parley continued, "and so I would like to say just a word or two on that subject. I don't know how this list of requirements has struck you, but I couldn't help but think of how little it represents of what I have acquired since coming to this place some six years ago. We have, all of us, put in a great amount of expense and labor so that we could purchase lands, build houses, erect this beautiful temple. Now we shall walk away from it all. We might ask ourselves, why is it that after all we have done we are called to leave it? I would answer that, as our beloved Prophet Joseph taught us in the School of the Prophets, the people of God have always been required to make sacrifices. It is how we demonstrate our faith.

"And I say to you, my brothers and sisters, if we have a sacrifice to make, then I am in favor of its being something worthy of the people of God. We do not want to leave a desolate place behind, a place that will be a reproach to us, but something that will be a monument to our industry, our diligence, and our virtue. And I say to you, Nauvoo is such a place.

"I tell you," Parley suddenly thundered, startling several, "there is no sacrifice required at the hands of the people of God but what it shall be rewarded to them an hundredfold, in time or eternity. That is the promise of God, and God's promises are sure.

"We know that the great work of God must be on the increase and grow greater. As a people we must enlarge—in numbers and in our borders. We cannot always live in one city, nor in one county. Nor can we always wear the yoke that our enemies would place on our necks. We are modern Israel, God's chosen people, and Israel must be the head and not the tail. The Lord designs to lead us to a wider field of action, where there will be more room for the Saints to grow and increase, and where there will be no one to say that we are crowding them in. We need a place where there is room to enjoy the pure principles of liberty and equal rights."

A slight movement caught Nathan's eye and he turned again to Joshua. To his astonishment, Joshua Steed was nodding in agreement. He sat back on his bench, staring up at Parley, and he was nodding his agreement. And then, on reflection, Nathan was not surprised so much. That concept of separation would make sense to Joshua. Get away from your enemies. Find a place where you were free to do what you wished. Yes, that would appeal to Joshua.

The Apostle leaned forward on the pulpit now, his eyes fiery and filled with power. "One small nursery may produce many thousands of fruit trees while they are small. But as soon as those trees expand towards maturity, they must needs be transplanted in order to have room to grow and produce their natural fruits. It is so with us. We want a country where we have room to expand, and to use all our energies and all the enterprise and talents of a numerous, intelligent, and growing people."

He took a deep breath. "In short, I tell you that we are called to find a place of our own where we will be free to fulfill the destiny the Lord has promised. And I rejoice, my brothers and sisters, I rejoice that the time has finally come." He picked up the list and shook it at them. "I rejoice that we are now being called upon to prepare ourselves to go forth and meet our destiny. Oh, may we only be worthy of what the Lord sees fit to place upon our shoulders!"

Chapter Notes

Fuller accounts of the doings of the Quincy committee, the mass meetings held by the anti-Mormons, the various resolutions, and the response from the Church can be found in B. H. Roberts, *A Comprehensive History of The Church of Jesus Christ of Latter-day Saints, Century I*, 6 vols. (Salt Lake City: The Church of Jesus Christ of Latter-day Saints, 1930), 2:504–20 (see also HC 7:447–53).

The minutes of the general conference for October 1845, including Brigham's introductory address, his dedicating the temple, the business of sustaining the officers, and the remarks of Parley P. Pratt, are found in the official history of the Church (see HC 7:456–64). The conference minutes do not say that during the session Elder Parley Pratt read the list of things required of a family for the journey west. We do know, however, that Parley was asked to calculate what the requirements for a family would be. The full list, used here in his speech, was included in the official history under date of 4 October, just the day before the conference began (see HC 7:447, 454–55), so the assumption is that it was shared with the Saints at about this same time.

For more information on the apostasy of William Smith, see the chapter notes at the end of chapter 10 herein.

Modern Church members find the inclusion of tea, coffee, and alcohol on the list of supplies for the journey westward somewhat surprising. In the official history no justification is given for any of these. The five gallons of alcohol for each two families suggests this was medicinal, much like our own rubbing alcohol, and not some form of liquor. As for the tea and coffee, the *Encyclopedia of Mormonism* gives this explanation: "Compliance with [the Word of Wisdom's] teachings was sporadic from the late 1830s until the early years of the twentieth century. The Church encouraged leaders to be an example to the people in abstaining from alcohol, tobacco, tea, and coffee; but no binding Church policy was articulated during this time." (S.v. "Word of Wisdom.")

On Wednesday night, the night of October eighth, 1845, the night following the last day of general conference, they gathered together at Nathan's home. There were no children. Even the three babies, Jenny's, Rebecca's, and Jessica's—two at seven months and one at six months—were nursed and left at home with older siblings or cousins. This would not be a night when the Steeds gathered together for light conversation or gentle laughter. This was the long-awaited Steed family council, a council to deal with the most pressing family crisis the Steeds had ever faced.

That they came to Nathan and Lydia's home was not surprising. Brigham had told Nathan he was leaving him home to become spiritual head of the family in Benjamin's absence. Most did not know that. Nathan had not ever said anything about it. But whether they knew it or not, they sensed the reality of it, and seemed pleased that someone was taking that role for Benjamin.

Lydia watched her husband as he greeted each couple and ushered them into their sitting room. He had taken Benjamin's role, she suddenly realized, not because Brigham had said he should, but because he was the most like Benjamin. He *was* the spiritual leader of the family now. Even Joshua, who, as the oldest, might have felt that it was his place to lead out, accepted Nathan's leadership as though it were the natural order of things. Benjamin and Mary Ann were expected back in the next three weeks or so, assuming they had received Brigham's letter. What would happen then? Lydia wondered. Would Nathan step back again? Possibly, but she didn't think so. But either way, until then the family accepted Nathan's role and were glad for it.

And then as she too greeted each of them and ushered them into the sitting room, Lydia felt a peculiar mixing of sorrow and joy down inside her. How she loved these people! She was not related by blood to any one of them, but how dear they had become to her! She looked around, wanting to burst out with an exclamation of joy, and yet wanting to cry at the same moment.

Here were Matthew and Jenny, as much in love today as they had been on the day they were married four years before. Beside them on one side sat Derek. Derek—raised in the slums of Preston, England, grown up in the great cotton mills of Great Britain—was now a gentleman farmer of great depth and wisdom. He and Rebecca, with their three children, were a quiet but solid cornerstone of the family. On the other side, seated in matching hard-back chairs, sat Jessica and Solomon Garrett. Sweet, quiet Jessica, who had endured so much—a divorce, being driven from Jackson County in the midst of a bitter winter, a second marriage which ended tragically at Haun's Mill, then exile to Nauvoo. How wonderful that she had found Solomon, who was so wise and gentle and caring. How right that she should now have found such complete happiness.

Directly across from them were the two young couples—Kathryn and Peter, Will and Alice. Both had recently come to love through markedly different paths. But love they had found. Soon they would be married and take their place in the family circle.

And then a strange thought struck her. Not one of the four were Steeds by blood. Will, Caroline's oldest, was Joshua's stepson. Peter, Derek's brother, came into the family first as guest, then as friend, and finally as an adopted son. Kathryn and Jenny had come in with their Irish mother and been all but adopted by Jessica when Nancy McIntire had died. And finally there was Alice, truly an outsider in one way, and yet so much a part of the family in another. Lydia never thought of any of them as anything but family, as everyone else was family.

Carl and Melissa and Joshua and Caroline came in together at the last. Somehow, in Lydia's reflective mood, that seemed appropriate, for here would be the greatest source of tears, the greatest challenge to the family's unity, the point for which this council would need the greatest counsel.

Lydia pulled out of her thoughts as they found chairs and Nathan moved to the front of the room. She went to the chair beside him and sat down. Nathan let his eyes go around the room, letting the quiet settle in upon them more completely before beginning. Finally, he cleared his throat. "I think we all know that we are facing a crisis for the family," he began. "I'd like, therefore, to suggest that we begin our family council with a petition to the Lord for his help as we wrestle with the issue at hand." He looked at Joshua. "Would that be all right with you, Joshua?"

"Of course."

"Carl?"

"I think we need it."

Nathan nodded, looking around again, debating about whom to call. Then his eyes came back to Carl. "Carl? Would you offer that prayer for us?"

Carl was so startled that he visibly jumped a little. "Me?" He was not the only one who was looking surprised. Melissa looked dazed for a moment.

"Yes. You may not be a churchgoing man, but we all know you are a God-fearing one. I know that you and Melissa pray in your family. This isn't just a Mormon question, Carl, it's a family problem. We need a family prayer."

Melissa reached out and laid her hand on Carl's arm. When he turned to look at her, she nodded silently at him.

"All right," he finally agreed. He lowered his head, closing his eyes. The rest followed suit. "Our Father who art in heaven, hallowed be thy name." There was a long pause. "O God, we come to you in prayer. We come to ask for your help. We care very much for this family. We know that our family is a great blessing. Now we face a real problem. Circumstances are combining to split us apart. We do not want that to happen. Help us to know what is best."

There was another long pause, and in the silence, Nathan heard Melissa sniff softly.

"O Lord," Carl went on after a moment, "we want to do what is right. We want to be good. Help us now to know how we best can do that. In Jesus' name, amen."

There was a choked cry, and as Lydia opened her eyes, she saw Carl put his arms around Melissa and hold her tightly. Lydia found her own eyes stinging, and saw that several others were near tears too.

Nathan slowly straightened. "Thank you, Carl," he said softly. "I think you have prayed what is in all of our hearts."

"Yes," Matthew murmured. Several others were nodding.

Carl inclined his head briefly. "I appreciate your recognizing that if Melissa and I choose not to go, it doesn't mean we are turning our back on God or on the family."

"No one thinks that, Carl," Lydia responded.

"I know, and we appreciate that."

"But that is the issue before us, isn't it?" Nathan said, his voice still filled with gravity. "I think we all recognize now, after what was said in conference, that come next spring the Church will be leaving Nauvoo. And this time it won't be going just a couple of hundred miles. We are going who knows how far. And that is not all. We are going into the wilderness. There are no railroads, no stage service, no canal boats or river steamers there. Mail service, if any, will be extremely limited. For all intents and purposes, the separation will be total and, for a time at least, quite permanent."

Every eye was upon him, and every face registered the reality of what he was saying.

"I think we all know where each of us stands, but I'd like to have it formally noted. Perhaps not all of us have made a decision yet, and that's fine, but I'd like each couple to say what that decision is if they have decided." He turned and looked down at his wife.

She looked at him for several seconds, then turned to the others. "Yesterday, after the afternoon meeting, I happened to be talking to Newel Knight and his wife, Lydia. I asked them what they thought, now that our going was certain. Sister Knight looked right at me and, without the slightest hesitation, said this: 'There's nothing to discuss. Our place is with the kingdom of God. We shall set about immediately to make preparations to leave.'"

Lydia's head came up now and she looked steadily at the family that she loved so dearly. "That's how we feel. The kingdom of God is going west. Nathan and I will be part of it as long as they'll have us."

Nathan reached out and laid his hand on her shoulder and squeezed it gently. Then he turned to Solomon and Jessica. "Let's just go right around the room."

"We're going west with the Saints," Jessica murmured.

Solomon nodded gravely. "Yes."

Nathan nodded and turned to Matthew and Jenny.

"Going," they said together.

Next was Derek and Rebecca. There was no hesitation there either. "We'll be going," Derek said in a clear, calm voice.

With a deep breath, Nathan looked at Melissa and Carl. Melissa's head dropped. "Not going," Carl said slowly.

"Will you be returning to Kirtland?" Nathan asked.

Melissa's head came up and her eyes were shining. "No. This is home now. For us and the children."

"That's good," Nathan said, and he genuinely meant it. Nauvoo was six hundred miles closer to the West than Kirtland was. "I think once the main body of the Church leaves, things will be all right here."

"Yes," was all Carl said.

Now Nathan was looking at the young couples. Peter glanced at Kathryn. They had discussed this at some length earlier today, knowing what the purpose of the family council was to be. "It won't be without challenge," Kathryn said with some sadness, "but yes, we will be going."

Will and Alice took each other's hands. "As you know," Will said, "I've committed to work for Walter Samuelson until spring. But we'll be back then and we will be going with you."

Nathan saw Joshua's deep frown, but said nothing. He hadn't meant them to be last, but Joshua and Caroline had taken the end chairs. Now every eye turned to them. Caroline was looking at her hands, which were folded tightly in her lap. Joshua was watching her carefully, but she didn't look up and so he finally turned to Nathan. "As you might guess, we haven't decided for sure, but we're thinking of going to St. Louis."

Now Caroline's head did come up. "We?" she asked in a faint whisper. And then, mindful that all were listening, but needing to say it anyway, she went on. "I'm not saying that I won't go with you, Joshua, but it is *you* that is thinking of St. Louis, not me."

It was as if all the others in the room were forgotten. Since he and Will and Alice had returned from St. Louis, Joshua had tried to talk with Caroline about this question. Each time it ended either in impasse or tears or both. He spoke to her softly. "I don't think it's wise to stay here in Nauvoo, Caroline."

"I don't want to stay here."

"And I don't want to take my family off into the wilderness and risk their lives."

"I know it is not just my decision, Joshua," she answered right back. "But if it were, my answer would be to go."

"And my answer would be to go to St. Louis."

"So?" she said sadly. "Do you have the final say?"

"No, you know I'm not saying that. But do you?"

She shook her head, then looked at Nathan. She was near tears now. "As you can see, the Joshua Steed family has not yet decided what to do."

"I understand. And that's fine. For those of us who are going, we must begin preparations immediately. We all heard the list of what each family must bring. Peter was able to get us a copy of it from the print shop. So we have it before us. We have food to gather, equipment to make or buy, property to sell."

Kathryn's head came up. Her eyes filled with anguish as a thought struck her. "Steed Row will no longer be Steed Row, will it?"

That hit them all hard, Nathan no less than the others. He had to swallow once. "No," he said softly, "Steed Row will soon be only a memory."

"That makes me want to cry," Jenny said, her face looking like she was going to. "There have been so many happy times here."

"And what if you can't sell?" Carl asked.

There was a long silence, and then Derek answered for all of them. He shrugged. "Our place is with the kingdom of God."

Carl cleared his throat and looked around. "I don't need to tell you that I am not sympathetic to your beliefs. We all know that. But I will say this. I don't blame you for leaving. In fact, I believe it is the best thing for you to do. Brigham is right in saying that you are never going to have peace here." He took a quick breath. "I am not a rich man, but I would like to buy Derek's land from him."

Derek jerked up, but no more swiftly than Melissa did. She was staring at her husband.

"And"—Carl was looking at Matthew now—"I would like to purchase the cabinet shop as well." There was a quick, embarrassed smile. "I've always thought that having a brickyard and a cabinet shop in the same family might have some advantages."

Melissa was dumbfounded. So were the rest of them.

"We don't expect that, Carl," Lydia finally said.

"You are going to need a lot of money to get everyone ready," came the answer. "I don't have a lot, enough for a down payment, maybe, but it will be enough to help you get outfitted. Then I will send the balance to wherever you end up. I will make sure you get a fair price."

"You know I'll also help with whatever it takes to get ready," Joshua spoke up.

Nathan turned. "Joshua, you and Carl have always been willing to help the family, and that means a lot to us. But if we can just get a fair price for what we've got here, then we'll be fine."

"No, listen. If we go to St. Louis—" He looked at Caroline quickly, then away. "Or whatever we decide—I'll be selling the freight business here. Before I do that, though, I'll just give you whatever wagons and teams you need."

"That would be a major head start for us," Solomon said.

"What about your property in Ramus?" Matthew asked.

"It's up for sale. I have a man representing my interests there. So far I've been offered two hundred dollars."

"Two hundred dollars?" Carl cried. "That's an outrage. With your house and the school and the land you've got, it's worth three or four thousand if it's worth a dime."

"I hardly think this is a seller's market," Solomon remarked dryly and with no touch of bitterness. "I'll wait a while, but two hundred may be the best I can get."

The reality of that sobered them all. "Well," Nathan said after a moment, "I guess that settles it. Except for Joshua and Caroline, we all know what choice we've made. For those of us who have decided to go, I'd like to suggest we continue this meeting and start laying out a plan on how to prepare." He looked to Carl and Melissa, then to Joshua and Caroline. "You are welcome to stay if you'd like, but if you'd rather not, we'll understand."

Carl rose immediately. "I think we'll get back to the children." He pulled Melissa up.

Joshua rose too, but Caroline didn't stir. "Do you mind if I stay and listen, Joshua?"

He frowned momentarily, then shook his head. "Not if you want."

"I do."

To her surprise, he sat back down again.

As Carl and Melissa said their good-byes and started for the door, Melissa stopped and gave Nathan a quick hug. "Thank you," she whispered into his ear. "Thank you for not making us feel like we are awful for not coming with you."

He put his arms around her and held her. They stood that way for several moments, brother and sister, knowing all that had been decided tonight and what it would mean for them. "We will miss you, Melissa," he whispered back. "We'll miss you something terrible."

She nodded, her eyes wet again, then quickly turned and followed Carl out the door.

———— ◆ ————

Joshua was currying a team of sorrel Belgians that had come in the previous night on a run from Springfield. With the recent rains the roads were rutted and muddy, and the horses showed it. It had been too late to do anything more than unharness them and give them each a bucket of grain, so this morning Joshua had come to the stable to clean them up. When his stable boys showed up and found their boss already there doing their work, they were greatly chagrined and tried to take over, but he waved them off and sent them out to do other things.

He finished the first horse, gave her an affectionate slap on the rump, and led her back to her stall. As he brought the second one out and tied her to the post, the door to the stable opened and a figure stepped inside. Joshua turned, expecting more of his help, but was surprised to see it was Nathan.

"Good morning."

"Mornin'." Joshua was standing there, currycomb in hand, watching his brother approach.

Nathan smiled. "You can close your mouth now, Joshua. Is it so shocking that I would come out to see you?"

"It's pretty early," Joshua said, recovering a little. He moved around the horse and began working on her neck. The animal lowered its head a little, her skin rippling with pleasure under the firm hand of her owner.

Nathan walked over to the bench, found a brush, and moved

to the opposite side of the horse. His arm moved back and forth in long, methodical strokes now too. They worked together like that in silence for almost five minutes, smoothing the hair, brushing out the caked mud, untangling clods of dirt and cockleburs from the tail and mane.

By the time they reached the withers, Joshua could look directly at Nathan over the mare's back. "So are you going to tell me, or are you going to make me guess? You've obviously got something on your mind."

Nathan shrugged. "I didn't sleep much last night."

There was a soft hoot. "Couldn't happen to a more deserving man."

"Joshua, I'm not the cause of the problem. All I'm trying to do is to get us to start talking about this decision, face it so we can do something about it."

Joshua stopped the steady stroking and looked at his brother. "I know that, Nathan. I guess I don't like being made to face it." A quick shadow passed across his face. "It doesn't help."

There was a slow nod, then Nathan went back to brushing the horse.

"At least Carl and Melissa have committed themselves," Joshua said after a few moments.

"Yeah. That kind of surprised me. The last I talked to Carl he was still agonizing over what they were going to do."

"No, not over what they were going to do, only about how to break it to the family. You gave him that opportunity and he took it."

"Mother will be heartbroken," Nathan noted softly. "And Papa too. Melissa has always had a special way with him."

"I know, and thank heavens. She's the one who kept Pa and me from going at each other more than once in those long-ago years."

"Yes." Now Nathan lowered the brush and looked at Joshua steadily. "And what are you and Caroline going to do, Joshua? How are you going to resolve this?"

Joshua shook his head brusquely. This was the very thing that had gotten him out of bed long before dawn and brought him to the stables to give him a chance to think. "I don't know, Nathan. I truly don't know."

Nathan said nothing, but continued to watch him. Now Joshua stopped as well and leaned against the horse, staring at Nathan. "You know," he said pointedly, "I've made some pretty significant compromises lately."

"Yes, you have."

"I accepted Will's decision to be baptized. I gave Caroline my blessing to join the Church. And Savannah, I gave her permission too."

"I thought that was more of a surrender than a permission," Nathan drawled laconically.

Joshua laughed in spite of himself. "I think you're right." Then the smile faded. "But Will and Alice too, Nathan. I did my best to convince Walter to give in and accept what is."

"I know you did. Will told me. And Alice told Lydia what that means to her. What *you* mean to her."

"She did?"

"Yes."

Joshua stepped back, cleaning the hair from the currycomb's teeth. "Anyway, back to my point. I've given in a lot for the family lately. Isn't it about my turn to have something go my way?"

Nathan sighed. "Is that how it's done?"

"Is that how what is done?"

"Making decisions in a marriage? You take turns?"

Joshua's mouth hardened a little.

"I'm not trying to say you're wrong, Joshua. I'm asking a fundamental question. When a man and a woman are poles apart on something this significant, how do they decide what to do? Is taking turns the way to do that?"

"It's one way," he said stubbornly.

"And if the situation were reversed," Nathan went on in a quiet voice, "if it were Caroline who had made all of those compromises, and she said it was your turn to compromise now, would taking turns be an acceptable solution for you? Would you agree to go west because it was your turn to let her decide?"

Joshua went down on one knee and began to work on the mare's legs. After a moment, Nathan did the same, looking at him under the horse. When Joshua looked up, he was frowning. "You know what, little brother? Sometimes you are a pain in the neck."

Nathan chuckled. "You only say that when you know I'm right."

"Well, I don't like your point," he grumbled. "And being right only makes it worse."

Now Nathan was very quiet. "Caroline has made some compromises too, Joshua. She went your way once."

Joshua's head jerked up. His eyes were filled with instant pain. It was almost as if he were staring right through Nathan.

Glad now that he hadn't added what he had been tempted to say—that Caroline had gone to Warsaw at Joshua's insistence, and that it had cost Olivia her life—Nathan waited, watching his brother's face. It was over a year now, but it was clear that the ache had not eased much.

"Look, Joshua," Nathan went on in a low voice, "I didn't come to try and tell you what to do. I know how difficult this is for you and Caroline, and I thought you might want to talk about it."

There was a brief nod; then Joshua stood and walked around the horse, seeing how she looked. Satisfied, he took the halter rope and led her back to the stall. "Want to get some oats?" he finally asked.

Nathan went to the barrel, retrieved a bucket of oats, and spread the oats evenly down the feeding trough. As the horses began to snuffle them up, Nathan returned the bucket. Then they both moved to a bench and sat back against it.

"So what *do* we do, Nathan?" Joshua asked. "I don't see any compromise on this one."

"Not an obvious one," Nathan agreed.

"It's not just that I'm against the Church, Nathan. It means moving my family out into the wilderness. It means a thousand miles across who knows what kind of country. There'll be Indians, wild animals, dysentery, cholera. I've got a baby who's not even two yet." He stopped, realizing that Nathan had a child just one year older, and that Lydia was with child again. If there were reasons for being concerned, Nathan's were equal to if not greater than his.

"I don't think that's the real reason you don't want to go."

There was a quick flash of irritation. "You think taking care of my family isn't a good reason?"

"Of course it is." He decided to let it go at that. "There is another possible solution," he said, not turning.

"What?" Then Joshua snorted. "Join the Church? No thank you."

"I'm not talking about joining the Church."

"Then what?"

"Accepting what you know to be true."

"And what's that?" Joshua snapped at him.

"You know that there's something to this work that you can't explain. You know there is a power here that you don't want to think about."

"Do I?" Joshua shot up. "Sorry, Nathan. I know you're all filled with testimony and conviction, but leave me out of it."

"You should never have lived," Nathan said quietly.

That rocked him back a little. "What?"

"When they brought you to our house that night in Far West, with a hole in your back, and a bigger hole in your stomach where the ball came out, you were so close to death, we didn't think you'd make it through the night."

Joshua was watching him closely, still breathing hard from his anger, but silenced for the moment.

"And to put you on a travois and drag you over rough terrain for twenty-five miles. It was insane. You should have been dead before we got you out of the house."

"But you blessed me with the priesthood." It was meant to be a sneer, but it came out with a touch of wonder in it as well.

"Yes, we did." He waited for a moment. "And you lived."

"I'm strong. I was younger then."

"Of course," Nathan agreed amiably. "And it wasn't a year later that you sat in Pa's house and watched Joseph Smith command our father in the name of Christ to get off his deathbed and be well. You saw it, Joshua! And just hours before, you were saying your last good-byes to him. Was there any question in your mind that Pa was dying? Any question at all?"

Joshua didn't answer. He stared at Nathan with great, haunted eyes.

"I didn't think so. And yet with one single command from Joseph, he rose and went with you across the river. Then Joseph went to our house and blessed our Elizabeth Mary. She was dying too. You know that. I know that. And yet she was immediately healed."

Nathan's voice was barely above a whisper now. "You went across the river with Joseph that day," he pressed on with relentless softness. "You were there in that room with Elijah Fordham. You saw him raised from his bed, Joshua. You yourself said you thought he was dead. And yet now he lives because Joseph Smith commanded him to. How do you explain that, Joshua? Tell me. I want to know. How do you explain what you have witnessed with your own eyes?"

There was a long silence, then a slow shake of his head. "I don't know how to explain it." Then once again he started to fight back. "But if it is God's hand in all of this, like you say, then why did Joseph and Hyrum have to die? Why didn't God protect them?"

"Because God has his own purposes. Joseph said over and over in those last months that his work was through. You heard him. Even the Savior himself had to die when his work was finished."

Joshua shook his head, half-angry, half-bewildered.

"What did you see that day in the meeting when Brigham was speaking to us?" Nathan suddenly asked.

Joshua jumped as though he had been stung by the flick of a buggy whip. "What meeting?" he temporized.

Nathan gave him a look of patient weariness.

"I didn't see anything."

"All right. You didn't *see* anything. So what happened? Something happened to you. I was watching, Joshua. Caroline was watching. What was it?"

Joshua's head dropped. "I . . . I thought I heard Joseph's voice."

"You *thought?*" Nathan bore in.

"It may have been a trick of the mind," he began.

"And Caroline? Was she tricked too? And Lydia? Or maybe they're all lying to you. What about Christopher, Joshua? He was five years old, and yet he suddenly saw Joseph Smith talking to the crowd instead of Brigham Young. Was he trying to trick you too? Did Derek and Rebecca put him up to that so he could deceive you?"

"Now you're being ridiculous."

"Am I? Hundreds of people experienced what you experienced that day, Joshua. They either saw or heard something miraculous. These are good people. Decent people. What was it? Some form of mass hysteria? Some gigantic hoax that Brigham foisted on the people?"

"What did *you* see that day? What did Pa see?"

Nathan shook his head slowly. "It's not like you to dodge the truth, Joshua."

"I'm not dodging anything. I want to know what happened to you that day."

"Nothing."

"So how do you explain that?"

Nathan just looked at him and shook his head again. "It won't work, Joshua."

"What?"

"Dodging the issue by trying to focus on me. What does it matter what happened or didn't happen to me? How do you explain what happened to you?"

"I don't have to explain it," came the reply. He was suddenly angry again.

"No, you don't *want* to explain it," Nathan shot right back. His voice rose to meet the intensity of Joshua's, but there was no anger, no loss of temper. He had thought about this a great deal all through the night and had determined that he was not going to let his brother simply sidestep the issue because it made him uncomfortable. "And do you know why you don't want to?"

Joshua was suddenly tired of it all. He shook his head wearily. "No, little brother. Why don't you just tell me?"

Nathan dropped his hands to his side. "I don't need to." He turned and started toward the door of the stable. He stopped as he reached it, and turned back. "I think this is the first time in my life I have ever seen Joshua Steed refuse to deal with reality, no matter how unpleasant it may be to him."

"This is not my reality!" Joshua shouted hoarsely. "It's yours. All this talk of God and miracles. It's your explanation, not mine."

"All right. I'm not asking you to accept my explanation— God, faith, prayer, priesthood. Give me yours, Joshua. But give me something. Don't just stand there and refuse to answer because you know you will be convicted by your own words."

"I don't have to account to you."

"No, you don't," Nathan agreed. "But you're fast approaching the day when you have to make a choice, Joshua. Then there will be an accounting of some kind, whether you like it or not."

"Then it's my problem, isn't it?"

Nathan's head came up, his face lined with weariness and surrender. "For some time, Joshua, the Lord has been trying to tell you something. Just how many tellings is it going to take?"

"It's my problem," Joshua said again stubbornly.

"Oh, how much simpler it would be if that were really true."

Caroline was in the backyard, hanging out the wash she and Savannah had finished earlier that morning. She looked up in surprise as Nathan walked around the house and raised one hand in greeting. "Good morning."

"Hello, Nathan." She gave him a strange look. "Business at the store that bad?"

He laughed. "I am very fortunate in that I have not only a wife but two children who actually like running a store." Then he sobered. "To be honest, I spent the last hour down at the stable currying horses."

"Our stable?"

"Yes." He motioned toward the porch and the two chairs sitting there. It was a cool morning, but the sun was bright and shining directly onto the porch. "Have you got a minute?"

"Of course." She pinned Savannah's petticoat to the line, wiped her hands on her apron, then followed him to the back porch. Before sitting down, she turned her chair so she could face him more squarely. "Did it do any good?" she asked, once they were settled.

His eyes widened momentarily that she should have guessed; then he pulled a face. "Well, it got him mad at me again. But that's no surprise."

"He knows you're just trying to keep the family together, Nathan."

"No, it's more than that. He knows I'm trying to get him to face things he doesn't want to face."

She said nothing, just leaned back in the chair and closed her eyes, feeling the sun on her face and liking it. He watched her absently, running through his conversation with Joshua again in his head. He had been quite discouraged walking back from the freight yards. Then, as he rounded Parley Street, it had come to him. It came with such swiftness and such clarity, that he had been quite excited with the idea. Now he was not nearly as certain about the wisdom of it.

She opened her eyes. "What are we going to do, Nathan?" she asked in a small, forlorn voice.

"I have no right to counsel you, Caroline."

Something in his voice made her sit up. "But . . . ?"

"I have a recommendation."

"I'm listening."

"I had a thought as I was walking back. I'm not saying you ought to do it, I'm just saying I'd like you to think about it."

She smoothed the apron in her lap, considering what that really meant. "All right."

"Let me ask you three questions," he started.

"Go ahead."

"First question. Do you believe Joshua loves you?"

"Of course."

"Really loves you?"

She hesitated this time, but only to give his question honest consideration. Her answer was still the same. "Without doubt."

"Good. Second question. Do you think that at heart he wants what is best for you and the children?"

That took her longer, but after a moment, she nodded again. "Definitely for the children."

"But not for you?"

"Well, he wants what he *thinks* is best for me. But he doesn't understand how important the Church is to me."

He started to raise a third finger, but she cut him off. "No, that's not fair. Joshua does understand in one way, it's just that . . . well, I don't know. The Church doesn't mean anything to Joshua, so he can't *really* understand what I'm feeling inside. Does that make sense to you?"

"Yes, it does. Okay, third question. If you don't go west with us, do you think you would put the salvation of yourself and your children in jeopardy?"

That took her aback and she looked puzzled. "In jeopardy?"

"Yes. Do you think you would lose your standing with God if you don't go?"

Her brows puckered as she thought about that. "Well, I truly believe that it is God's will that we go west. By we, I mean as a church. But no, I suppose that if we don't go—especially if the reason was to keep our family together—that would not displease God."

He took a deep breath. "So trust Joshua, Caroline."

Her eyes lifted and widened. "What?"

"Trust him!"

"You mean let him make the decision?" she scoffed. "We'll go to St. Louis."

"I'm not sure you will."

"So the man gets to make the decision," she said, a trace of bitterness hardening her voice. "Is that what you're saying?"

"Do you think that's what I believe?" he answered softly.

After a moment she shook her head. "No, I've watched how you and Lydia work. It's wonderful, Nathan."

He stood up and began to pace back and forth as he spoke. "Right now, Joshua is so determined to talk you out of going west that he's not really thinking about what is the right thing to do. If you believe that he loves you and that he wants what is best for you and the children, then trust him. Tell him you really believe that he will make the right choice for your family."

She started to speak, but he held up one hand quickly. "However, you can only say that if you really do believe it."

She formed a steeple with her fingers, watching them closely as she made sure each finger lined up precisely with the other. "And you think this may be the solution?" she finally asked dubiously.

He threw up his hands. "I don't know," he cried. "I think so. You know Joshua better than I do. You know how stubborn he can be. He digs in to make his point, sometimes even after he's forgotten what the point is."

She laughed. "I think you know him pretty well."

"That's why he and Pa used to have such frightful battles. Half the time they couldn't remember what the battle was all about. When you get like that, the battle becomes the thing that drives you. All I am saying is, don't give him battle and see what happens."

She blew out her breath in a low whistle. "You're not asking much, are you?"

He sat down again, leaning forward earnestly. "And what

frightens me is that I have no right to say it, Caroline. It's easy for me to hand out advice. I don't have to live with the consequences."

For a long time she was silent, her eyes half-closed as she watched him. Finally, she straightened, and then she too leaned forward so she was looking directly at him. "Can I ask you a question, Nathan?"

"Of course."

"The family has been fasting every week now in order to get an answer to this whole problem."

"Yes."

"Do you think this"—she threw out one hand—"this thought of yours is the result of that?"

That caught him completely off guard. He rocked back in his chair a little. "I . . . I hadn't thought about it in that way."

"You said the thought came to you while you were coming back from the freight yards."

"Yes."

"Suddenly? Out of nowhere?"

"Well, yes. Kind of." But then he shook his head immediately, seeing where this was leading. "No, Caroline. I can't say it was from the Lord. You should only do this if *you* feel good about it."

"Can you say it *wasn't* from the Lord?"

He thought about that. "No, but—"

"If it's from the Lord, I should be able to have him confirm it to me too, shouldn't I?"

There was instant relief on his face. "Yes, of course."

"Then I will think about it, Nathan." Her face softened. "Thank you. This really isn't your burden."

"That's what Joshua tried to say too," he answered quietly.

She nodded, then reached out and touched his hand briefly. "Well, thank you."

He stood again and stepped off the porch. He gave her a jaunty grin. "Well, the store awaits."

She laughed. "When you get to wherever it is the Church is going, are you going to be a storekeeper again?"

The grin slowly faded. "I don't know. Hadn't thought about it."

She smiled warmly at him. "You don't have to be, Nathan. You can be whatever you want to be."

"Joshua?"

He looked up from the newspaper.

"Do you think it is your right as the man to make this decision for us?"

The paper lowered slowly. "By this decision, I assume you mean—"

She waved her hand at him impatiently. "Of course."

He looked suspicious now as he turned the question over in his mind, wondering what had brought this out of the blue, looking for any hidden traps. "Well," he began cautiously, "I think I have a responsibility as the head of the house to watch over the family, but not without consulting you."

She could see the relief in his eyes as he realized that was a good answer. "And if we cannot agree?" she asked.

"Then we talk until we do."

"And you won't just declare it to be so, whatever it is you think we ought to do?"

"If I was willing to do that, we could have solved this problem some time ago," he quipped.

She looked a little surprised. "Yes, I suppose that's true." She stood abruptly and walked over to him. To his surprise, she leaned down and kissed him. "I appreciate the fact that you haven't done that."

He laid the paper down in his lap, clearly perplexed. "What is this about, Caroline?"

"Oh," she said airily, "I was just thinking about it today." Then she grew more serious. "If I thought you were going to make me do what you want without really considering what I want, I would fight you every step of the way, Joshua. But I know you are not that way."

His bewilderment was only deepening. "So?"

"So I want you to know that I trust you. I'm going to stop talking about what I feel is best. You already know that. I am going to trust you to decide."

Now his brows narrowed suspiciously. "Is this a trick?"

She laughed, then reached down and took the paper, tossing it aside. She sat down in his lap, pulling his arms around her neck. "Yes. It's a trick to get you to hold me."

"That I can do," he said, enfolding her now in his arms.

She laid her head against his shoulder.

"You really mean it?" he said after a moment. "About trusting me?"

"I do." She kissed him softly. "I really do, Joshua. I know you want what is best for all of us."

"Yes," he said slowly. "I do." He drew back a little, staring at her in wonder. "What brought all this on?"

She shrugged that off. "I've been thinking about it all day." She kissed him again, and now he kissed her back, pulling her fully into his embrace. Suddenly a noise from the hallway jerked them apart. They looked up to see Savannah, Charles, and little Livvy standing there in the lamplight, staring at them with wide eyes.

Caroline blushed furiously and started to get up, but Joshua, laughing, held her down. "Hello, children," he said. "Can we help you?"

"Will you read us a story, Daddy?" Charles, now almost six, asked tentatively.

But Savannah shook her head. Her eyes were wise and motherly. "No, Charles. Mama and Daddy are loving each other. I'd better read the story tonight."

Chapter Twenty-Two

Young Joshua Steed lifted the spyglass that he had borrowed from his Uncle Solomon Garrett and focused it on the steamboat that had rounded the bend about a mile downriver. He did so lazily and without hope. This was his fourth day here, sitting on a point of land that jutted out into the river about five miles south of Nauvoo. He would ride out in the morning, sit there through the long day, then ride home again at dark. It was easy duty and it beat the frantic pace of preparation going on back at home, but Joshua, who had turned fourteen in May, did not like enforced inactivity. He much preferred having something to do, even if it was hot and sweaty and dusty work. But his father had been adamant. He didn't trust any of the other male cousins, all of whom were younger than Joshua, and none of the adults could be spared.

It was the twentieth of October. The letter from his grandparents, which had arrived five days before, said they thought the time of their arrival would be somewhere between the eighteenth and the twenty-first. But the family was taking no chances and started the vigil on the seventeenth. They would keep him coming until the twenty-fourth, a thought which filled him with dread.

He found the boat in the spyglass, adjusted the focus slightly, then leaned forward, elbows on his knees. Though nearly as tall as Nathan now, he was still long and lanky and not filled out like his father, so he had to wiggle his legs a little to find a comfortable position. It was still much too far away to see the nameplate, but he could tell it was a single rear-paddle steamer. It was spurting out great streams of black smoke from twin smokestacks on each side of the boat. That meant twin boilers and explained why it was making such good time against the current.

He lowered the spyglass and sat back against the trunk of the tree that provided him a backrest. At first he had started counting the boats that passed upriver to help pass the time. That was too infrequent to be interesting, so he added those going downriver as well, keeping the ratio between the two in his head. Two up, three down. Six up, nine down. But by yesterday afternoon he had tired of that and lost count. This one would be the tenth or eleventh boat going upriver. Almost twice that many were going downriver, an indicator of how late the river season was growing.

He waited five more minutes. Now the *swish-swish* of the great paddles was filling the air, and the boat was just two to three hundred yards downriver from him. He straightened and lifted the spyglass again. It took him a minute to find the nameplate—the boat was painted a bright red and white, with black smokestacks and blue paddle wheels. But then he had it, just back of the prow.

He stiffened, jerking forward. He pulled away from the spyglass, blinked his eyes to clear them, then brought them up again. There was no mistaking it. In large black letters against the white background it was plain to read. *Pittsburgh Palace*.

Joshua leaped to his feet, stuffing the spyglass back into its case, and sprinted for his horse. In a moment he was back out on the road to Nauvoo, leaning forward in the saddle, urging the horse into a hard lope.

———————•:•———————

As the *Pittsburgh Palace* nosed gently up against the dock on South Main Street, Mary Ann scanned the crowd anxiously, looking for a familiar face. It was not a large crowd—maybe two dozen at most—and the task was not a hard one. Her face fell and she came back down off her tiptoes shaking her head.

"They probably didn't get our letter," Benjamin said, strangely feeling almost as sharply disappointed as Mary Ann.

"I was afraid they wouldn't." She reached down and picked up her valise as the crew jumped onto the dock and secured the boat to thick wooden pillars. In a moment, they heard the creak of the gangplank being lowered and joined the few passengers who moved toward it.

As they stepped off the dock and started up Main Street, Benjamin looked to their left at the house there. It was a two-story wooden home, originally made of logs but with some frame additions on the back and side. It was the Homestead, the original home of Joseph and Emma Smith in Nauvoo. "I wonder how Emma's doing," he said.

Mary Ann just shook her head. "From what the children have said, I—" She stopped. Directly across the street to the east was the Nauvoo House, Joseph Smith's planned hotel for the incoming riverboat traffic. It was still under construction and there were two workers on the upper story. But what had stopped her was the man who had stepped out from behind the rear wall. It was Joshua.

"Hello, Mother."

With a little gasp, she dropped the valise and ran into his arms, throwing herself the last few feet and almost knocking him over. "Joshua! Joshua!"

He picked her up as easily as if she were a child and swung her around and around. Finally he set her down and kissed her soundly on the cheek. "Welcome home, Mother!"

By then Benjamin had come over to join them. Mary Ann stepped back and father and son moved into each other's embrace, hugging each other tightly and pounding each other on the back. "Hello, Pa."

"Joshua, it is so good to see you."

"It is so good to have you back."

Mary Ann looked around. "Where are Caroline and the children? And the rest of the family?"

"Well, that's a long story. Come on," he said, taking her valise with one hand and her elbow with the other. "Let me go over here and get my things, and then I'll explain."

They moved across the street to the Nauvoo House, and he stepped around the corner of the building whence he had appeared. He motioned for them to follow. "Come here. I want to show you something."

As they came around the corner, both stopped dead. The east wall of the Nauvoo House was a long one and made of brick. There, lined up in a perfectly ordered row—not by age but by size—were Mary Ann's twenty-five living grandchildren. Will was the tallest at the far end. And then, like steps coming down from the attic, they went one by one down to Carl and Melissa's little one-year-old Mary Melissa, who was the shortest. The only exception were the three babies who had been born earlier in the spring—babies which their grandparents had never seen—who were held by older brothers and sisters. Each grandchild was dressed in his or her Sunday best. All were grinning as if they were going to split their faces wide open if they held the smiles for one more second.

"Oh, my!" Mary Ann exclaimed, her hands coming up to her mouth.

"Surprise!" Joshua said softly. And with that, from around the far end of the big house, the adults stepped out now too, smiling just as broadly and happily as their children.

Mary Ann just stood there, rooted to the spot, tears instantly springing to her eyes and spilling over. She had borne ten children. Her oldest, a girl, had died a few hours after birth. Three, including twin girls, had been silent children, never drawing a breath. A boy born between the stillbirths had died at age four. But the rest of her five children had grown to adulthood and now were married and had families of their own. And every one of them was here now to greet her and Benjamin. Along the way they had picked up four foster children—Derek and Peter Ingalls and Kathryn and Jennifer Jo McIntire. Now here they all were— sons, daughters, sons-in-law, daughters-in-law, and enough grandchildren to fill a wall.

With a cry of inexpressible joy, she dropped to her knees, unmindful of the wet earth, and held out her arms. "Well," she said hoarsely, "don't just stand there. Grandpa and I haven't had a really good hug in over a year."

The younger children let out a shriek, and in seconds Benjamin and Mary Ann were swarmed under as their family came to welcome them home.

———————

As Alice and Will walked slowly southward along Granger Street, a tiny breeze sprung up, blowing off the river. Alice gave a little shiver and pulled her coat more tightly around her. It was barely four in the afternoon and the sun still had two hours before it would set, but the wind was blowing out of the west and had a distinct coolness to it. It held the promise of frost by morning. It was the twentieth day of October, and the last signs of autumn were everywhere evident. Off to their right, a field was covered with orange polka dots, the last of the pumpkins waiting to be harvested. Just behind the rail fence on the other side of the road, dry brown cornstalks, some of the few that had survived the great hailstorm of early September, rattled softly in the breeze.

"And you have no idea what this is about?" Alice asked with some nervousness, even though she had previously asked the same question of Will three times.

"None."

"Are you sure the messenger asked me to come too?"

He reached inside his jacket and retrieved a folded paper. He opened it to show Savannah's neatly lettered hand. "'President Brigham Young wants Will and Alice to come to his home this afternoon at four o'clock. It will take only about half an hour.'"

She sighed. He had only read that to her half a dozen times. "Oh, Will, you must think me an absolute ninny, but I just can't figure what President Young wants with both of us."

"Maybe he's heard about your decision to be baptized and wants to counsel you on the matter."

"Do you think so? Would the President of the Quorum of the Twelve take time to do that with someone he doesn't even know?"

"He is the President of the Quorum, and he is very busy," Will agreed, "but he is also close to our family." Then he had another thought. "Maybe he wants to be the one to marry us."

"How could he? Would he come to St. Louis?"

He laughed and put his arm around her waist. "Alice, I don't know what it is. I'm just plain guessing." Then he looked up. They were approaching Kimball Street, and Brigham Young's fine two-story red brick home was in sight. "Well, it won't be long now."

Brigham was in the small study at the back of his house, working at a desk filled with papers. He had his boots off and woolen socks on. As his oldest daughter knocked softly and opened the door, he turned, squinting in the dimming light. Instantly he rose and padded over to greet the two people who stood behind her.

"So this is the famous Alice Samuelson that Matthew speaks so highly of?" he said, smiling warmly as he took Alice's hand.

"How do you do?" Alice said, giving a slight curtsy.

"I'm very pleased to meet you, Sister Samuelson." He inclined his head slightly. "I understand that you are to be baptized soon, so may I call you Sister Samuelson?"

"Of course."

The Apostle turned to Will and gripped his hand firmly, pumping it up and down. "Ah, Will. I was thinking about you earlier. Do you remember that day we spent some time together on the open deck of that ship?"

"I remember it as though it were yesterday." He turned to Alice. "We were coming back from England. There had been a terrible storm. The ship was pitching and yawing violently all night long, throwing people about like rubber balls. Everyone was sick. Then the Twelve gathered together in the hold and said a prayer. In a short time, the storm was gone and the sea was like a plate of polished china."

Brigham sighed again, taking Alice's hand and moving her forward toward one of the chairs. "Can't say as I miss the sea. For an old New York woodsman and glazier like myself, having something solid under your feet means a lot."

"I have never sailed on a ship," Alice ventured, "but I get nervous even on the riverboats thinking about how much water there is beneath my feet."

"Exactly," Brigham said fervently. "Exactly my sentiments. Well, you two young people, sit down. I appreciate you coming. I almost came to your house, but I thought it best if we were alone."

"We were glad to come," Will inserted quickly.

"Good." The President sat down across the desk from them and leaned forward. His blue-gray eyes sized them up quickly, and then he leaned back. "Tell me your plans, you two. I understand from Matthew that there's to be a double wedding in St. Louis."

"Yes," Will explained. "Alice's father has graciously offered to bring the whole family down to St. Louis on a riverboat. Kathryn and Peter will be married at the same time as we are. Alice and I will leave day after tomorrow to go back. The rest of the family will come down in time to be there on the first of November."

"Will Nathan be marrying you?"

"We thought so at first, but now Grandpa Steed will."

Brigham came forward with a jerk. "Is your grandfather home now?"

"Oh, yes. They arrived just after noon today."

"Wonderful! Wonderful! I was hoping they would make it home in a timely manner." He rubbed his hands together with genuine pleasure. "Tell your grandfather and grandmother to come see me, will you? Not tonight, of course. They must be exhausted. But tomorrow. They don't need an appointment."

"I shall tell them," Will answered, pleased to be the bearer of such news.

The smile slowly faded and Brigham's lips pursed together, as if he had felt a sudden pain. Then he shook his head slowly. "That makes this all the more difficult." A deep gloom seemed to settle over him. "Sister Samuelson, I understand your father is not pleased with the idea of your becoming a Mormon, that there is some fear that if you join the Church he might sever your relationship entirely."

"Yes," said Alice, "but I am pleased to say that both he and my mother have relented. Will and I will be staying in St. Louis until spring, and that helped immensely. I think my father hopes that by then we will change our minds about going west."

"But you don't think you will?"

"Absolutely not," Will said quickly. "We want to go where the Church goes." Alice nodded firmly to let Brigham know that Will spoke for her too.

This time the sigh seemed to come from the bottom of his soul. "Very, very difficult," Brigham muttered to himself.

Will was tempted to blurt out and ask him what he was talking about, but he resisted, and together, holding hands, he and Alice waited for President Young to speak.

Finally, Brigham looked up. "Will, does the name Sam Brannan mean anything to you?"

He thought for a moment. "Yes. I remember Elder Parley Pratt talking about him with Nathan. Isn't he one of the presiding elders in New York City?"

"Yes."

And then Will snapped his fingers. "And wasn't he one of those that were sent back here under charges of apostasy?"

"Yes, last spring. He and William Smith and George Adams were accused of teaching all sorts of false doctrine and raising havoc in the Church back there. They were all disfellowshipped. William and George had been sent back here to Nauvoo, but Brother Brannan was still in New York. Parley Pratt, who was presiding there, sent Brother Brannan back to clear his name. Fortunately, Samuel seemed not to be the primary instigator of the troubles. He convinced the Twelve to reinstate him and went back to New York. He still serves there, so far faithfully."

"Oh," Will said, not exactly sure why he had been asked about the man.

Brigham was lost in thought. Silence hung in the air for several moments; then he looked up, seeming to have made up his mind. "We—meaning the Twelve—have determined that Samuel Brannan's the man to try a bold experiment."

"What's that?"

"We feel strongly that we need to explore going to the Rocky Mountains by sea," Brigham replied. At Will's amazed look, he nodded vigorously. "Think of it, Will. If we go overland, we are severely limited in what we can carry in our wagons. Tools for farming, industry, gristmills, sawmills—all of that kind of stuff is far too heavy to cart in a wagon. But by sea! Ah, there would be virtually no limit to what we can take. We have a printing press in New York, for example. They print the *Messenger* there. Think what it would take to get a printing press across the plains. But by ship it would be a simple task."

No one needed to talk Will Steed into the advantages of sending cargo by ship rather than by wagon. "I think that's a wonderful idea, President Young."

"Do you?" he asked eagerly. "You have a great savvy for ocean travel, Will. Do you really think it is a good idea?"

"I do." Now Will understood his purpose in being there. He knew the sailing trade and knew it well. There weren't many Latter-day Saints who could say that.

"They would sail to Cape Horn," explained Brigham, "all the way around South America, and put in at San Francisco Bay in Upper California, which, as you know, belongs to Mexico. Then, no matter where we eventually stop, they wouldn't be far from us. Our people and tools would already be there waiting for us."

Alice was trying to picture a voyage that would go all the way around South America. "How long would it take?" she asked.

"About six months," Will answered promptly. He had never sailed that route, but he had talked to many who had.

"It would be important to start soon," Brigham mused. "With the seasons in the south being the opposite of ours, June and July will be their winter months, the worst for sailing."

"True," Will said. "What are you thinking?"

"I've written to Elder Brannan and asked him to see if he could get a group ready to leave by early to mid-January."

"Perfect!" Will exclaimed. "So you're going to do it for sure?"

"Yes."

To Will's surprise, Brigham still seemed troubled. "It's a long journey, President Young," he said enthusiastically, "but if you get the right ship and crew, it shouldn't be any problem. They would be to California by June or July."

"And we hope to be to our new home somewhere not long after that."

"Then it sounds like a wonderful solution to me."

"Will?"

"Yes?"

"I would like you to go with them."

If a boulder had dropped from the sky and hit Will in the chest he couldn't have been more dumbfounded. He just stared at the Apostle, his jaw slack. Alice gasped audibly.

"That's right, Will. We think Elder Brannan will do us the job we need, but we're still a little nervous about him, after what happened. And to have someone with your knowledge of ships and the sea there in New York as he gets ready to sail . . . I know you're young, but we just don't have that many sailors in the Church. I think your advice would be invaluable to him and to us."

"You want Will to go to New York?" Alice asked in a tiny voice.

Brigham smiled. "No, my dear, I want *you and Will* to go to New York. And then I want you to sail with Brannan to California." He laughed at the expression on their faces. "I think this qualifies as catching you off guard."

Will just shook his head, still speechless. Alice looked as though she hadn't understood his words.

Now the humor completely disappeared. "It isn't often a call from the Lord requires so much of two people. I suppose I could send just Will. Then you'd have to wait a year to be married. That would please your folks, I suppose. But no, what I am asking is even worse than that."

"Worse than being apart for a year?" Alice cried. "What could be worse than that?"

Brigham moved slowly, tiredly, as he leaned forward on his elbows. "If you accept this calling—together, I mean—then you will have to leave immediately. You must be in New York no later than the first of December if you are going to be of any use in the planning of the voyage."

"Immediately?" Will stammered. "I don't understand."

"If you leave in the next couple of days you can go to Chicago and catch a steamboat before the Great Lakes freeze. That will be the fastest."

"But that means . . . ," Alice started, her voice quavering.

Brigham's head dropped lower. "It means that you cannot wait until the first of November to be married. It means that Will can't stay in St. Louis working until next spring to please your father." He put his hands over his eyes, rubbing at the lids slowly with his fingertips. "It means that you will have to tell your parents that you are going to California and may never see them again."

———◆———

They sat on the cold planking of the ferryboat dock, their feet dangling within inches of the water. It was quarter of five now, and the sun was dropping lower in the sky. With the sun in their eyes it was hard to make out the buildings of Zarahemla and Montrose across the river on the Iowa side. Will had picked up a stick as they walked along and now poked it absently into the water, writing letters on the "tablet" of the water that instantly swirled away.

"Tell me, Will."

He wrote a quick B for *Brigham*. "I was just thinking about something President Young said right there at the last."

"What?"

"He said that it wasn't often that a call from the Lord requires so much of two people."

"Yes, and . . . ?"

"It was the fall of eighteen thirty-nine. I was still sailing then and hadn't returned to my family, but Derek and Matthew have told me the whole story. As you know, they went to England with the Twelve. Anyway, the Church had been in Nauvoo only a few months by then. Brigham and Heber had very simple homes—Brigham's family lived in some abandoned military barracks, and Heber's in a log shanty. The ague had been terrible all summer. When it came time to leave, Brigham, who was living across over there"—he gestured toward the opposite bank—"was so sick he couldn't even walk the thirty or so rods from his house to the river. A neighbor had to help him. Someone rowed him across to here, but he was so weak, they put him to bed at Heber's place."

Alice had turned to watch him, her face somber in the glow of the sun.

"His wife had just given birth to a baby girl a few days before, but when she learned that Brigham was across the river and sick, she came across to care for him. Everyone in the home was so sick that Heber's four-year-old son had to fetch the water for them. Four days later, the two brethren determined that they had to start. They were both still so weak they had to be helped up into the wagon. Just as they were driving out of the yard, Brother Heber turned to Brigham and said, 'This is no way to leave our families. Let's rise up and give them a cheer.'"

Now Will's voice had gone very soft. "So they staggered to their feet, lifted their hats, and cried, 'Hurrah! Hurrah for Israel!' In a moment, their wives stumbled to the door. 'Good-bye, and God bless you,' they called out in return." There was a long silence; then he tossed the stick into the river and turned to Alice. "They were gone for almost two years."

"So Brigham knows what he's asking, doesn't he?" Alice said after a long moment.

"Yes. What we are facing is pretty tough, Alice. But the call didn't come from someone who doesn't understand."

"Will, do you believe this call is from the Lord?"

"I do," Will answered without hesitation.

"So do I. Then is there any question about whether or not we should do it?"

His head moved back and forth slowly.

She felt her chin drop until it touched her chest. Hot tears spilled over and scalded her cheeks as they trickled downward. "How are we ever going to tell my father?" she said mournfully. "Even if I were to write them and tell them that I had been baptized here, and that we got married here, that would be terrible enough. But then to tell them I'm going to California and may never see them again? How can I write that to them?"

"May I ask you some questions, Alice?"

"Yes."

"Do you want to postpone our marriage?"

Her head came up sharply. "No!"

"Do you want to get married and then stay with your folks while I go?"

"No!" It came out with equal force.

"Do you want to get married and have me go to New York while you go west with Brigham and the Church?"

"No, I want to be with you, Will." Suddenly there was hurt in her eyes. "Do you want me with you?"

He reached over and seized her by the shoulders. "I have been sick to my stomach ever since we left Brigham's house just thinking about having to leave you behind."

Lifting a fist, she shook it beneath his nose. "It's a good thing you answered that correctly," she said. Then she sighed and slid closer to him, snuggling up against him. "Then the only question is what to do now."

Will was thinking furiously, trying to sort it all out. Finally he voiced his first conclusion. "If we are determined to answer this call, then are we agreed that there is no way that we can make your parents happy?"

"None. But how can I write them—"

He shook his head firmly. "No, that would not be right. They will see this as betrayal enough. The least we can do is tell them in person."

"But how?"

His mind was racing now. "We do have to leave immediately, but what if we went by way of St. Louis and not Chicago? I'll bet we could stop there for a day or two, then go on up the Ohio a long ways before it freezes over. I think we could make New York by December first."

"But Mother won't have any warning. She's planning on the wedding being November first. And we can't wait that long."

He took both of her hands and turned her toward him. "We'll baptize you tomorrow morning, and be married tomorrow night. Then we'll leave on Thursday morning for St. Louis."

Her eyes flew open. "Tomorrow?" she echoed numbly.

"Yes. I know it's soon, but it's better to do it here than in St. Louis. Then we can just tell them that it's done." And then he started to shake his head. "No, I guess you're right. It's a crazy idea."

Now it was Alice who was gripping his hands. "No, Will. You're right. Peter and Kathryn will probably not want to do it so quickly, so it will be just us. But yes. I'll become a member of the Church in the morning, and your wife in the afternoon." She felt the tears well up. "Then when I see Mama and Papa . . ." She stopped, looking away.

Will pulled her into his arms. "We could go to St. Louis first and tell them. Then we could be married there. At least your mother could be there." He reached out and wiped at the wet spot on her cheek. "And you would have your wedding dress."

"Will, we are going to St. Louis for one reason and one reason only. I feel I owe it to my parents to tell them directly rather than writing a letter. But I have no illusions. It is going to be ugly. It will be—" Her voice caught and she bit her lip. "It will be the end for me and them." Finally, she looked up at him. "No, Will, your family is the only family I have now. I want to be married here. Especially now that your grandparents are back."

A thousand questions tumbled through his mind, but he knew they were of no consequence. Where would the marriage take place? What would his mother say? His father! What would Alice wear? Whom would they invite? What about food? Those were the luxuries that time provided. They seemed so trivial all of a sudden. "Yes. Tomorrow. It will be a new life for you, and a new life for the both of us."

She slumped against him and began to cry softly. They sat that way for almost five minutes, he holding her, she weeping quietly, neither of them speaking further. Finally, Alice pulled free of him and stood up. She took him by both hands and helped him to his feet. "Let's go tell Brother Brigham," she said. "I think he's waiting for our answer. And then we'd better go tell your family."

———•———

Brigham Young gave Alice and Will an hour with Will's family before he came to the house to see what he could do to help lessen the damage. Evidently, Will had told his parents that Brigham would be coming, because when he knocked, Joshua came to the door, nodded curtly, and stepped back without a word but motioned him in. Brigham took a deep breath, took off his hat, and entered. Will and Alice were not there, and Brigham decided that was good. Just he and the parents. It would be best that way. He took out his watch and glanced at it as he followed Joshua down the hallway. It was barely six o'clock in the evening.

------ ∗ ------

Joshua listened to it all without comment—Brigham's explanation of how the call had come, why the timing of it was so urgent, and how he fully understood the implications of what he was asking of this young couple. It took most of the willpower he had, but Joshua said nothing through it all. Caroline nodded and murmured in two or three places, but said nothing else either. She looked very tired. However, Joshua sensed that she felt weary because she knew how upset he was, not because Will and Alice's decision terribly upset her.

When Brigham finally finished, he sat back, sobered and waiting.

"I suppose you're not here to ask our permission?" Joshua asked evenly, after a moment.

"Will is twenty-one years old," Caroline whispered.

There was a quick flash of irritation; then his face went blank again. "I know that," he said without looking at her. On the surface his patience was seemingly endless, but underneath, he felt like a rope that was stretched to the point that each strand was breaking and unraveling with increasing speed. "But I want to hear it from him."

Brigham didn't move.

"Are you asking my permission?" Joshua demanded.

There was a slow shake of his head. "Joshua, I know this is very difficult, but this is a call from the Lord and—"

One hand shot up. "Let's just leave the Lord out of this. I know what you believe. I know that Will and most of the rest of my family believe it too. But I don't, and there's no point in trying to convince me."

Caroline cleared her throat. "Joshua, I know you're upset, but—"

"No, Caroline! I'm sick and tired of the Church always taking and taking from my family. And each time they do, they have the gall to suggest that I have no say in the matter at all. So don't talk religion. Don't talk God. Let's just talk about what's right and what's fair."

"Good enough," Brigham said tartly. "You want it straight. Here it is. I and the other members of the Twelve have been given a task to do, Joshua Steed. It's the task of moving thousands of people into the wilderness to a place we've never been or never seen. I didn't ask for this task. Neither did any other members of the Twelve. No one has checked with me to see if it happens to be a convenient time for my family to leave our home and go into exile." He sat back, his chest rising and falling. "You want to swap stories about what's fair and what's not? Fine. I'm ready when you are."

Joshua was clearly caught off guard by the suddenness of Brigham's offensive.

"You don't want to talk about the Lord? All right. I happen to believe that we are doing God's will in this matter, and I am hoping for his blessing. But I'll tell you this, Joshua. I don't plan to waltz out there into the wilderness and wait for the Lord to rain down manna upon us. I believe the Lord expects us to prepare ourselves, and that is what I mean to do."

Caroline watched him with wide eyes, a touch of awe showing on her face. This was a Brigham none of them had seen before.

"You find Will's call a personal inconvenience? Well, I beg your pardon. Why don't you go complain to Colonel Levi Williams or Thomas Sharp? Why don't you tell them that their plundering and looting has created a situation that is causing you problems? Why don't you lodge a complaint with those fine citizens down in Quincy or Governor Ford, who refuses to lift one hand to protect us?"

Stung, Joshua finally reacted. "Look, I'm not saying I don't understand the challenges you have but—"

"No, you look, Joshua. I'm sorry about having to call Will at a time like this. You don't believe that, but I truly am. I wept this afternoon thinking about the choice I just laid on the shoulders of those two young people. Oh, how I wish to heaven they could have their marriage and go to St. Louis and keep Alice's father smiling through it all. I wish I could tell them to run along and wait until spring so everything could work out more smoothly. But I don't have a choice in the matter, Joshua. If I can establish an outpost in California, I can save lives. If I can get food and tools and equipment on site before we arrive, then I stand a chance of making this work. And like it or not, that means calling on you and your family to sacrifice."

He sat back, his mouth tight, his eyes hard with challenge. No one spoke. Caroline watched Joshua closely. She knew she was on precarious ground, but she had something that had been on her mind now for several days. She leaned forward. "Just before the martyrdom, you were ready to go west with Joseph, Joshua. Why?"

Brigham reared back a little. "Is that true?"

Caroline nodded. "Joseph felt that if he could escape, it would solve the problem."

"Yes, yes," Brigham said impatiently. "I know all that."

"Well, Joseph asked Nathan and Joshua to go with him."

"And you were ready to go?" Brigham asked Joshua.

"Yes," Joshua admitted.

"Why?" Caroline asked, thoroughly puzzled. "Why were you ready then, and yet now you are so against it?"

"You know why."

"Because you felt that you owed Joseph a great debt when he came for us at Warsaw."

He looked down at the floor. "I did," he said softly.

"But it was more than that, Joshua. When you told me, I couldn't believe it. Remember? I asked you if that meant that when Joseph found a place for us, you meant to go with him permanently." She was pinning him tightly with her eyes now. "You didn't say no, Joshua."

"That was then. This is now."

Now Brigham stirred. "You are a man of plainness and honesty, Joshua Steed. I have always admired that in you. So I'm going to ask you straight out. If Joseph were still alive and leading this exodus, would you go with him?"

Joshua shot a look at Caroline, then turned back to Brigham. "I . . . I honestly don't know," he said after a moment.

Brigham smiled sadly. "Can't say as I blame you. I'd go with Joseph in the blink of an eye. But following Brigham Young? It gives one cause to think, doesn't it?"

"It's not that, Brigham," Joshua said. "This is not about you."

"I know," he shot right back. "That's what I wish I could make you see. It's not about me. It's not about you. It's about something so great, so grand, so incredibly wonderful, that even I can scarcely believe we're part of it. Doesn't that fire your blood, Joshua? Think of it! You've been a pioneer. You went to Independence, a godless place if ever there was one," he added with a quick grin, "and you made a business for yourself. You made a difference.

"Well, think about this. We're going into the wilderness to start a new civilization. We're not talking about just moving into some frontier town here and turning it civilized. We're talking about scratching a civilization from the dust, yanking it out of the sagebrush by its ears and setting it on its feet. Doesn't that do anything for you, Joshua? To be part of something like that? Something that will really make a difference? For you? For your family?"

After a moment, Joshua shook his head begrudgingly. "I've got to hand it to you, Brigham. I'm the one who's losing a son here, and not only will you not offer me even the thinnest slice of an apology, but the next thing I know, you're recruiting me to go along with him."

That broke the tension and Brigham and Caroline laughed, relieved that Joshua had not exploded.

"Brother Heber always said I should have been a snake oil salesman." Then the grin died away again. "Joshua, three years ago, Joseph got a letter from the editor of the *Chicago Democrat*, a Mr. John Wentworth by name, asking for information about the Church. Joseph wrote back to him, told him all about the Church. But one of the things he said was this. 'The standard of truth has been erected, and no unhallowed hand can stop the work from progressing. Armies may rage, persecution may follow, calumny may defame, but the truth of God will go forth boldly and nobly until it has penetrated every continent, visited every clime, swept every country, and sounded in every ear. It will not stop until the purposes of God are accomplished and the great Jehovah shall say to us, the work is done!'"

Now his voice quivered with excitement, his eyes burned with intensity. "That's what we're offering here, Joshua. Those men with their painted faces stormed Carthage Jail and thought they had stopped the work. Levi Williams and his torch riders burned out a hundred of our homes and thought they'd broken the back of Mormonism. Well, what an enormous shock this will be to them! They're driving us from the state, thinking that will end it. But give us ten years. Fifteen years! And then even a man as blind as Thomas Sharp will know that no unhallowed hand can stop this work.

"You may not want to put your hand to the work. All right. I honor your right to make that choice. I wish I could help you see what is afire in Will's heart. In Alice's heart. Then you wouldn't be angry about this, you would be envious."

"We made a promise to Walter Samuelson," Joshua said, wanting to get back to the original issue. "He will never understand this. He will see it as a direct betrayal, and blame the Church for it. Wouldn't you, under the circumstances?"

"I would. That's what makes me sickest about this whole thing. I wish there was time to sort it out. I wish there was time to let Will and Alice go through with their plans and keep her parents happy. But there is not. I didn't plan it that way. No one bothered to ask me if there was a more convenient time to bring this about."

He stood and picked up his hat. "I'm sorry, Joshua. I truly am."

For several long seconds, Joshua stared into the Apostle's face. Then finally he nodded. "I believe you. Thank you for taking time to come and talk with us."

"No Unhallowed Hand Can Stop This Work"

"Does that mean the wedding will go on tomorrow?" Caroline asked, holding her breath.

"Is there any way I could stop it?" he retorted, the bitterness edging back into his voice again.

"Yes," she said softly. "You can say no and there will be no wedding. Will and Alice will be married somewhere else and we won't be there to see it."

She was right. He knew she was right, and that was part of what was so maddening. This was how it always seemed to be. Circumstances brought on by this whole thing with Mormonism drove him into corners where there was no choice but to surrender and give in.

"Come with us, Joshua," Brigham urged. "Become part of this. You could offer so much."

He shook his head. "It's not my cause, Brigham. I'm sorry."

Brigham shrugged. "Destiny doesn't force herself into any man's pocket, Joshua. You've got to hold out your hands to catch it." He turned to Caroline. "Thank you for letting me come. Tell Will and Alice I will be there whenever they decide to hold the marriage."

She looked quickly at Joshua. "Now that we know we're going ahead, the women are going to meet and make plans. Peter and Kathryn have determined that if Will and Alice are married, they will be too. We'll let you know. But the baptism will be first thing in the morning, down near the ferry dock."

"I'll be there." He looked back at Joshua. "I can see myself out. Good evening."

Mary Ann rapped her spoon on the table sharply. In a moment, the buzz of women's voices died down and all faces turned to her.

"The Steed family women's council is hereby called to order," she intoned solemnly, looking around the room. There were ten of them in all in addition to her. Jessica Garrett was the oldest. Then came Caroline and Lydia, just three years' difference in age. Melissa was next, followed by Rebecca and Jenny. Of the single ones, Alice sat in a chair beside Kathryn—these two being the focus of the meeting, of course. Rachel and Emily, the only two granddaughters old enough to be part of the council, flanked them on either side, both still dreamy eyed with the thoughts of a double wedding.

"We have before us a challenge the likes of which we have never faced before," Mary Ann went on, keeping her expression serious but unable to hide the sparkle in her eye. "We have fed the poor, sheltered the widowed, clothed the orphaned. We have started our own linsey-woolsey industry, grown fruit and vegetables, milked cows, churned cream, sold butter. We have made quilts, knitted mittens, sewn clothes and curtains for the temple, and now, most recently, have become tent makers extraordinaire."

"Hear, hear!" Jessica said.

"But never have we had quite the task that is set before us now."

Alice raised her hand. "Mother Steed, I know that I am to blame for all of this. To get a wedding ready in one day would be hard enough, but two weddings? We don't expect you to try to—"

"Out of order! Out of order!" Lydia cried out, laughing.

"Agreed," Mary Ann said, giving Alice a stern look. "Miss Alice Samuelson will only speak when she is called upon."

"But—," Kathryn began.

"Out of order!" Jenny sang out, poking at her sister.

"The two young women in question," Mary Ann warned, shaking her finger at both of them, "will please contain themselves until they are asked to respond." She looked at Kathryn. "We have only one question for Miss McIntire. Do you wish to be married on the morrow with your soon-to-be sister-in-law?"

Kathryn colored and ducked her head. "Well, Peter is still trying to recover his breath, but yes."

"Good!" Emily cried triumphantly. "Doing a double wedding makes it all the more challenging."

"Now," Mary Ann said, trying not to smile, "I would like to see how the council feels about this situation. Is there anyone here who thinks that one day is insufficient time for the Steed family women to pull off a fantastic wedding?"

"No!" Rachel and Emily shouted together. The rest shook their heads emphatically.

"Is there anyone here who thinks this task is too big for our council to handle properly?"

"No!" they all shouted back at her, warming to the game now.

"Then," Mary Ann said primly, looking at the two laughing brides-to-be, "are there any further questions?"

Alice started to raise her hand again, but Mary Ann slapped the table sharply. "I didn't think there would be. All in favor of going to work right now to make this the best double wedding in the history of the United States, if not the world, raise your hand."

Again she didn't give any time for a response. "Motion carries. The floor will now entertain proposals for how we proceed."

Laughing in delight now, hardly believing that this was the quiet and thoughtful missionary mother who had come home from Nashville, several of them shot their hands up. She pointed at Caroline. "Sister Steed."

"As prospective mother-in-law to Miss Samuelson, I would like to volunteer for the assignment to provide Alice with her wedding dress."

Jenny's hand jerked up. "And as sister to the other bride-to-be, I get to do Kathryn's." She pulled a face. "Besides, I'm the only one who can handle her when she gets difficult—which is all too frequent. But please, don't let Peter know that, at least not until after the wedding." She jumped back, barely escaping Kathryn's playful slap. "See what I mean?" she said ominously. "Anyway, I claim the privilege of providing a wedding dress for Kathryn."

"I'll do the pies!" Melissa called out.

"We can't take that old red rooster with us on the trail anyway," Rebecca said. "I'll make chicken and dumplings."

Off they went now, chattering like a group of schoolgirls, making assignments, ticking off lists of things that would need to be done, naming people who would be invited and others who could help.

Rachel Garrett, who was only five years younger than Alice, leaned over. When Jessica had come home and announced that Alice and Will were going to be married right away, Rachel had asked her mother a lot of questions about what this decision would mean to the couple. Jessica had not tried to soften the realities of what Will and Alice would face when they told Alice's parents about their decision. Now Rachel took Alice's hand in hers. "You'll have to get used to the Steeds," she said with warm affection and not a little pride, "we're really quite bossy."

Alice laughed, but her eyes were shining with happiness. "I see that."

"It will be all right," Rachel said, squeezing her hand. "You have another family now."

"I know," Alice whispered. "And I am so glad."

———•———

It was not yet eight a.m. when there was a soft knock on the door. The women gathered around Kathryn and Alice in Mary Ann's parlor looked up as the door was pushed open. Benjamin stuck his head in. "I understand it's bad luck for the grooms to see their brides. How about the grandfather-in-law?"

Mary Ann waved him in. "Normally," she smiled, "that's even worse luck, but since you're going to marry these two, I think it will be all right."

"Oh, yes, Father Steed," Kathryn called. "Come in."

As he walked across the room, Mary Ann motioned to the others. "We're done here anyway," she said. "We'll go across to Joshua's house and make sure everything is ready."

Without a word, Lydia, Melissa, Jessica, Rebecca, and Jenny all gathered up their things and followed Mary Ann silently out the door, shutting it behind them.

Alice watched them, a little surprised at how swiftly they had gone. Then suddenly she understood. She turned to Benjamin and smiled warmly. "What have you and Mother Steed been cooking up?" she asked.

"Who, us?" he asked innocently. Then he shook his head. "I just came from Joshua's house. You can thank someone that the weather is nice, because we already have more people than the house can hold."

"We do?" Kathryn asked.

"Yes. I'd say there's over a hundred at least, not counting family. They are waiting to accompany us to the river for the baptism."

"A hundred!" Alice gasped. "But . . ."

He grinned. "We Steeds don't take days and days to get the word out. Twelve hours' notice is more than sufficient." He got a chair, brought it over, and set it beside Kathryn's wheelchair and motioned for Alice to sit. As she did so, he retrieved another chair and set it down a few feet in front of the two of them. Then he made one last trip. The sitting room in Benjamin and Mary Ann's home had been turned into the brides's preparation room. He moved to the lamp table in the corner, the one that sat beside his favorite chair, and he took the Bible from it, then came back over and sat down.

For several moments, he looked at the book, rubbing his fingers lightly over the black leather cover. Finally, his head came up. His face was soft, the wrinkles around his eyes and mouth deepening with the love that filled his heart. "There are some things I wanted to say to you two while we're alone and before we start this very hectic day." He laughed softly. "I thought I'd better do it where no one but you can see me getting all weepy-like."

Instantly he knew he had made a mistake, because even as he spoke, tears sprang to his eyes. And just as quickly, both Alice and Kathryn were blinking back their own tears. He swallowed quickly, and then went on in a voice strained by his attempts to stop it from breaking. "I don't need to tell you that in every single respect, Mary Ann and I consider you as our own flesh and blood. So do the rest of the family."

They both nodded, not trusting their voices either.

"Kathryn has been part of the family now for several years. Alice has become one of us just in the last few months. But you are family. You are . . ." He stopped again, and finally shook his head. "You are family."

He straightened, cleared his throat, brushed quickly at the corner of one eye with the back of his hand. "Now, if you'll forgive an old man, I have a couple of things I'd like to say. First, to Kathryn."

She nodded, leaning forward slightly, surprised at how the joy inside her could actually make her hurt when she tried to hold it in.

"There are times when life makes you wonder. Things happen—terrible things sometimes—and you start to question why God allows it. When tragedy strikes we often come to one of two conclusions. We decide that we must have done something very wrong and God is punishing us, or that he isn't pleased with us—"

Kathryn was nodding gravely.

"Or we want to blame God for letting it happen."

"I did that too," she said slowly. "Sometimes I wanted to shake my fist at the heavens and demand to know why. Why me?"

"I understand. But the way you have handled it has been a wonderful example to all of us, Kathryn."

She shook her head, flushing a little under the directness of his praise. "I'm not much of an example," she murmured.

"Oh, but you are, Kathryn," Alice exclaimed. "You were one of the main reasons why I decided I wanted to become a member of the Church."

Kathryn turned to her in wonder. "Really?"

"Yes. Someday I hope my faith will be as strong as yours."

"If only you knew," she murmured. "I'm a long ways from perfection."

Benjamin chuckled. "I've noticed that too. Which brings me to what I want to say to you, Kathryn."

She pulled a deep frown. "Uh-oh."

He smiled at her. It was brief and fleeting, for he was quite serious now. "When I marry you and Peter in a few minutes, I'm going to use one word several times. It is the word *cherish*. Cherish is more than love. It is a stronger, deeper feeling. When you cherish something, it becomes a treasure to you, more important than almost anything else."

"Yes?" She looked a little puzzled now.

"I am going to charge both you and Peter to cherish one another. And frankly, I'm worried about you and cherishing."

"But I love, Peter, Father Steed. I love him very much."

"Oh, I'm not worried about you cherishing Peter. I'm worried about you letting Peter cherish you."

She sat back in her wheelchair, thoroughly bewildered now.

"I understand why you don't want to be a burden to him, Kathryn. I would feel exactly the same way. I would hate having to be dependent on others."

Now she began to see where he was going with this. She nodded slowly. "That has been the hardest part of all."

"I know. And now, because you are his wife, Peter has a responsibility for you. If he truly cherishes you, which I know he does, then he will want to help you carry that burden, lighten it for you, take it away when he can. He will want to do things for you, worry about you, make things easier for you."

"But is that always best?" she cried. "If I let him do everything for me, I won't get better."

"I told him that. I told him he's got to be careful and not dote on you."

Both Kathryn and Alice were surprised by that. "You talked to Peter?" Kathryn asked.

He nodded. "Just before I came over here."

"Will too?" Alice asked.

He laughed. "Of course. Did you think I would only pick on the women?" He leaned forward, deeply earnest now. "Let him cherish you, Kathryn. If he doesn't, I'm going to box his ears. And if you don't let him, then I'll have to box yours too."

"Yes, Father Steed," she said meekly.

"Good." He turned. "Now it's your turn, Alice."

"Yes, Father Steed."

"You come with a different kind of burden. It's not physical, but it can be just as crippling. You are feeling terribly guilty right now, aren't you?"

Her eyes dropped and she nodded numbly.

"I wish I could take that away from you just as I wish I could take Kathryn's handicap away from her, but I can't. Only you can do that. So I want you to listen to me and listen very closely."

She looked up and forced a smile through the tears. "Did Will get this counsel too?"

"In a way, but in a different form." Again there was a flicker of a smile. "I told him that he'd better treat you like a queen or I'd box his ears as well."

That won him a little warmer smile. "He already does, Father Steed."

"I know. But now you listen to this." He lifted the Bible and shook it gently at her. "One of the Ten Commandments is that we should honor our father and our mother. And rightly so. It is a great debt we owe to them. Your parents especially deserve that because they have been so good to you."

"Yes," she said in a small voice. "So good."

"But the same God who gave that commandment also said something very important to Adam. After creating Eve and bringing her to Adam he said: 'Therefore shall a man leave his father and his mother, and shall cleave unto his wife: and they shall be one flesh.'"

Her head came up slowly as the import of those words hit her.

"Yes, Alice, it is part of the Lord's plan that we honor our parents. But equally important—no, sometimes even more important—is another commandment. There comes a time in the life of each person when they have to leave their first family and start a family of their own. Hopefully, the parents are glad when that happens. But if they are not, it still has to happen."

She said nothing, but she was watching him intently, as if she were afraid she might miss even one word. Her tears had stopped now.

"You and Will know that the Lord is pleased with your union. And you know that joining the Church is not wrong. So while the hurt will always be with you, don't let guilt over this cripple you. What you are doing is pleasing to your Heavenly Father. I testify to you that that is true. *What you are doing is right.*"

After a long time she slowly began to nod. "Thank you, Father Steed. I needed to hear that right now."

"What your parents have not, and probably will not, consider is that we too are going to have to say good-bye to two of our family. Joshua and Caroline are going to say good-bye to their son and a brand new daughter-in-law. That is hard for us as well. But we at least understand why it has to be so. We all hope and pray that some day your earthly parents will come to understand and be pleased as well. That's what happened to Lydia. It took years, but before her father died, Nathan had become like the son he had never had."

"I told myself that all through the night," she whispered.

He reached for the Bible in his lap and opened it. "There's one more thing I want to say. And this comes from the Savior himself." He thumbed through it until he found his place. "It's in the book of Matthew. The Savior had been talking about rich men and how difficult it would be for them to enter into heaven. Something about what he said struck the Apostle Peter and he asked the Savior a question. 'What about us?'"

Now he opened the book wide and lifted it slightly so he could read it. "Here is the Savior's answer: 'Every one that hath forsaken houses, or brethren, or sisters—'" He stopped, looking directly at Alice now. "'*Or father, or mother—*'"

The tears rose up and spilled over her lids, trickling down her cheeks.

"'—or father, or mother, or wife, or children, or lands, for my name's sake, shall receive an hundredfold, and shall inherit everlasting life.'"

He shut the book and set it aside. Now he too wept, and he was no longer ashamed. Kathryn was holding Alice's hand tightly and crying with the two of them as well.

"Here you two are," Benjamin went on, "each with your own set of challenges, each with your own test of faith. And yet you have not wavered. You are truly daughters of our Heavenly Father. How privileged Mother Steed and I feel to have you belong to our family!"

Then he straightened perceptibly and his voice rang out

with conviction. "And I feel strongly impressed to tell you that your children and your grandchildren and your great-grand-children shall rise up and honor your names and call themselves blessed to be born of such women as you."

———◆———

They went to Mrs. Willard's Dress Shop straight from the baptismal site, Alice's hair still wet. They arrived at eight-forty-five, hoping that Sister Willard might be there early, which she was. The dresses they found were simple both in line and fab-ric—white cotton, gently scooped neckline, half sleeve, full skirt gathered at the waist. There were two of them, almost identical, both marked at half price. That was partly because they were summer dresses; and it was partly because the Willards would be leaving Nauvoo come spring too, and white dresses were not high on the list of items that would be taken across the plains. Jenny had traded a plain but sturdy oak chest Matthew had made for her the year before and thrown in a dollar fifty cents to make up the difference. Caroline bargained for Alice's dress with twenty-five pounds of sugar from the store, something that was a needed commodity and much in demand.

The moment the purchases were completed, the women descended on Lydia's store. They hung a Closed sign on the door, pulled down the blinds, and then proceeded to help themselves freely to the dwindling supply of goods on the shelves. They took bows and ribbon, lace and trim. Lydia had set aside a small box of white buttons some months before, thinking they might someday come in handy for a wedding dress. By ten o'clock, they had transformed the two dresses into simple but elegant wedding gowns and had them fitted on Kathryn and Alice.

Once she was convinced that the makeover was well toward satisfactory completion, Mary Ann left the store and went home to see to the clothing for the two men. Will was relatively simple. Matthew—or more accurately, Jenny—had saved the wedding clothes which he had received as a gift from Joshua. They were all neatly folded in a box and placed in the attic and still in excellent shape. Nathan and Derek pointedly reminded Matthew that this was the case only because Matthew's waist had grown under Jenny's tutelage until he could no longer wear the trousers. Will, still being unmarried and uncoddled, was slim enough in the waist that he could have worn a size smaller if necessary. The long coat and the shirt presented a different problem, however. Fortunately, both Matthew and Will were about the same height, both being about six feet tall, but Will had his father's broad shoulders, whereas Matthew was more slender like his mother. The jacket would be tight, Mary Ann decided, but if she moved the two buttons over half an inch and warned Will sternly not to get too exuberant in hugging Alice when it was all over, they would be all right.

Peter presented a different problem. He had a coat he wore for Sunday worship services. He had purchased it four years earlier and it was starting to show signs of aging, but it would have to do. Off went young Joshua, Emily, Rachel, Mark, and Luke to see what they could find in the way of trousers. Solomon was too large, by several sizes. Derek had always been thicker through the body than his younger brother and could not help. Joshua had several fine suits of clothing, but he was even taller than Solomon.

So they went to see Carl Rogers. He was the closest in height to Peter, but not close enough. His legs were a good two inches longer than Peter's, and fifteen years of marriage had added enough to his waistline that Peter could have turned around inside the trousers comfortably. Yet it was still possible to make them work. By then the other women had finished the dresses, and they all came over to Derek's house and swarmed around Peter. The trouser legs were cuffed, the back of the waist gathered in and pinned heavily. Thank heavens for long coats! Carl's shirt was more easily altered. A neighbor furnished a white silk cravat that set off Peter's jacket very nicely. Joshua brought forth a set of boots—with rags stuffed in the toes—and the ensemble was complete.

Now as the four prospective wedding candidates greeted their guests, Mary Ann studied them with satisfaction. It was all right. Actually, considering they had not started until this morning after the baptism, it was downright miraculous. They looked very handsome, the four of them—three standing, and Kathryn in her chair. The girls looked like angels in their white dresses; Will and Peter looked more like members of one of the leading quorums of the Church than two very young and very happy bridegrooms.

"I think we did all right," she said, leaning over to whisper in Benjamin's ear.

He was thinking the same thing, only he wasn't looking at the prospective wedding partners. He was taking the measure of the tables of food that lined the fence along one side of Joshua's backyard. There were pies and cakes, puddings, cookies, buns, sweet rolls, and loaves of freshly baked bread. There were jars of jellies, jams, and preserves. There were pickled beets, pickled cucumbers, pickled pumpkin, and pickled pigs' feet. And as if that wasn't enough, in the Steed houses up and down the street, pots and pans of corn, potatoes, fried chicken, gravy, carrots, parsnips, turnips, chicken and dumplings, and half a dozen other dishes sat on the backs of stoves, kept hot until the moment of serving.

The weather could not have been better, considering that it was the twenty-first day of October. The air was cool and had been quite chilly for the baptism, but now in the late afternoon the sun had warmed it into the low sixties and it was most pleasant. The number of guests had now risen to almost two hundred, counting the family members, and the backyard was crowded and noisy. That many people would consume most of what he saw before him, that he knew. The children were already eyeing it hungrily, while suspicious parents gave them stern warning glances to keep them at bay. But considering the circumstances under which they now labored, this was something to behold. This was largesse out of poverty, generosity out of want. He was deeply touched.

"Yes," he said to his wife. "I think you did it right."

"Oh, look!" Mary Ann exclaimed.

Benjamin turned. Brigham Young was just coming around the house. He was accompanied by Parley Pratt, Heber Kimball, John Taylor, Willard Richards, Amasa Lyman, and George A. Smith. He could hardly believe his eyes. Every member of the Quorum of Twelve who was currently in Nauvoo was here. That was a singular honor indeed.

He took Mary Ann's arm. "Let's go say hello." His voice was low and filled with emotion. "I think it is time to begin."

They placed the two couples directly in front of the small covered arbor that Caroline kept in her backyard. The vines were leafless now but it was still the best backdrop. Kathryn insisted that she stand for the ceremony itself and had gone to crutches now. She was accompanied by Jenny as her matron of honor. Derek stood beside Peter as best man. Joshua stood beside Will as his best man and Caroline was matron of honor for Alice. On both sides of the arbor, all of the girl grandchildren—dressed in their finest long dresses—stood side by side, tallest to shortest moving from the center out. The boys, much to their relief, were spared such doings and were allowed to be the official "greeters," mingling with the crowd or just watching.

Benjamin stood in front of this rather large entourage, Bible and some written notes in hand and appropriately frocked in a long-tailed brown coat and fawn-colored trousers. The crowd, with the family members taking the first row, pushed in behind them so they could hear clearly.

Benjamin held up one hand and the crowd quickly quieted. "We have had prayer. We have sung a hymn. I think most of you have had a chance to greet these wonderful young people. Now it is time to begin." He let his eyes move across the faces of the four who watched him eagerly. "I suppose the first order of business is to determine which of these two couples is the most eager to be married."

There was good-natured laughter from all around him.

"This is a dilemma. I was afraid that if I chose to marry Peter and Kathryn first, Kathryn might think I was favoring her because she is on crutches." He winked at her. "Knowing how she likes to be coddled, I decided I might get my ears boxed if I tried that."

More laughter. Kathryn let it die, then spoke calmly. "I would never box your ears, Father Steed. But I might have been tempted to put some green gooseberries in your next gooseberry pie." That really brought a chuckle from the crowd, and Benjamin too.

"Will and Alice are the most urgent," he went on easily. "We've got to get them onto a boat tomorrow and sent off to St. Louis. But then, what difference would fifteen minutes one way or the other make?"

Will was nodding. "I think it should be Peter and Kathryn first."

"And we think it should be Will and Alice first," Kathryn retorted. "If it weren't for them, we wouldn't be getting married this soon." She smiled wickedly. "And had we delayed much longer, Peter might have changed his mind."

They roared at the shocked look that crossed Peter's face. Benjamin turned and held up his hands helplessly. "See what I mean? A real dilemma."

Now he turned back to face them. "So, after some thought, and after conferring with President Young"—he turned and Brigham inclined his head to confirm that—"we have determined that there is no reason why we cannot marry you both at the same time."

"Ah!" came the cry from the crowd. Mary Ann seemed at first startled, then smiled. That would be wonderful.

"Make no mistake. We shall perform two separate marriages. Everything we do in the Church is done for individuals. We baptize only one person at a time. We do endowments for one person at a time. When the Savior came to the Nephites here in America, he let each person come one by one to feel the wounds in his hands and feet, even though there were more than two thousand of them. So we shall perform two separate marriages." He smiled ruefully. "Wouldn't want anyone to think that we were marrying the four of you all to each other. People already think the Mormons are strange enough."

Brigham laughed aloud. "That would start a few heads a-wagging," he said loudly. The crowd was enjoying this immensely, and laughter filled the air once more.

"So," Benjamin went on. "We shall marry you separately, but at the same time." He smiled at his candidates. "I hope that is sufficiently confusing." But then all levity died away in him and he became very sober. "As you know, the Prophet Joseph Smith restored the keys for celestial marriage, making it possible for a man and a woman to be sealed together by the power of the priesthood for all eternity."

They all four nodded. They had already talked about this and knew that Benjamin was speaking mostly for the benefit of the other children in the family.

"The Twelve still hold those keys today, because Joseph bestowed them upon them. However, this is a sacred ordinance and must await the time when the temple is completed sufficiently for the sealings to be performed there." Again he turned and looked at Brigham.

Brigham stepped forward. "Father Steed is exactly right," he said, loud enough for all to hear. "Brother Joseph performed this ordinance for a few people prior to his death, but he instructed us that the rest must wait until it can be done in the house of the Lord. This is one of the reasons that we press forward with the work on the temple with such urgency. Unfortunately, Will and Alice will not be here when the temple is completed. But rest assured that as soon as we reach our new home, we shall build other temples so this work can progress. They will not be deprived of this great blessing due to their faithfulness in answering a call."

He stepped back as many heads nodded. Benjamin murmured a thank you, then looked back at the two couples again.

"However, as a holder of the priesthood, I am authorized to perform this marriage for time. And though we are not in a temple, the covenants you make with each other here today are also very sacred in the sight of God."

All four of them nodded gravely.

"All right. I think it is time for us to proceed." He pulled his shoulders back and straightened to his full height. "I would like the two couples to turn so that you are facing each other as I perform the marriage. You are not making a covenant with me. You are making a covenant with each other."

Kathryn swung around on her crutches to face Peter. Alice and Will likewise turned in toward each other.

"William Donovan Mendenhall Steed," Benjamin said clearly, "will you take Alice Samuelson by the right hand?"

He did so.

"And you, Peter Ingalls, please take Kathryn Marie McIntire by the right hand."

They did so too, Kathryn planting the right crutch firmly before letting go of it with her hand.

"I remind the four of you that what we undertake here is done under the will of God. He it was who married the first man and woman on earth, and he has ordained marriage as being one of the highest orders of his kingdom. Only as a man and a woman come together and strive to become one can they find a fulness of joy and happiness. As God himself declared in the Garden of Eden: 'It is not good for man to be alone.'

"Since Will is older by about six weeks than Peter, we shall begin with you." He took a breath and now his voice became more sonorous, as though he were speaking from a pulpit. "Do you, William Donovan Mendenhall Steed, take this woman who stands before you, even Alice Samuelson, to be your wife, legally and lawfully wed? Do you hereby covenant and promise with her, in front of God and all of these witnesses gathered around you, that you will love her and cherish her as though she were your own flesh? Do you covenant to care for her in whatever circumstances you may find yourselves; that you will stand by her and strengthen her, whether that be in health or sickness, youth or old age, joy or sorrow, times of prosperity or times of poverty?"

He paused. Will was looking deep into Alice's eyes, and the love that passed between them was almost tangible. He spoke loudly and clearly. "Yes, I do solemnly covenant."

"And do you, Alice Samuelson, give yourself to William Donovan Mendenhall Steed, to be his wife and take him to be your husband, legally and lawfully wed? Do you covenant and promise to love and cherish him above all others, including those of your own family? Do you covenant to care for him in whatever circumstances you may find yourselves, whether that be in sickness or in health, in youth or old age, in joy or sorrow, in prosperity or poverty?"

"Yes." It rang like one sweet tone of a bell.

Benjamin turned slightly. "Do you, Peter Ingalls, take Kathryn Marie McIntire to be your wife, legally and lawfully wed? Do you hereby covenant and promise, in front of God and all of these who have come to witness this marriage, that you do love her and that you will cherish her as though she were your own flesh? Do you covenant that you will care for her in whatever circumstances life may bring upon you? Do you covenant to stand by her and strengthen her, both in health and in sickness, youth and old age, joy and sorrow, times of plenty and times of want?"

"Yes." Peter was so overcome with happiness that his voice cracked and it came out little more than a croak. As everyone smiled, he blushed deeply, cleared his throat, and then boomed out, "Yes. I do so covenant."

"And do you, Kathryn Marie McIntire, give yourself wholly to Peter Ingalls to be his wife, and take him to be your legally and lawfully wedded husband? Do you solemnly covenant and promise to love and cherish him above all others? Do you promise to stand by his side as his helpmeet and care for him in whatever circumstances you may find yourselves, whether they be joyous or sad, healthy or well, in youth or old age, in times of prosperity and success as well as times of poverty?"

Kathryn was no longer aware of the crutches that bore her

up. She looked at the face of the man she loved, and spoke softly. "I promise I will do that forever and ever."

Benjamin nodded. "Then I, Benjamin Steed, by authority of the holy priesthood which has been vested in me, and with the permission of the authorities of The Church of Jesus Christ of Latter-day Saints, do pronounce you, Peter Ingalls and Kathryn Marie McIntire, husband and wife, this day legally and lawfully wed in the sight of God and in the eyes of the world. And I do pronounce you, William Donovan Mendenhall Steed and Alice Samuelson, husband and wife, this day legally and lawfully wed in the sight of God and before all the world.

"I do charge the both of you to remember that if you honor and sustain the covenants you have made with each other this day and strive to cherish one another and to love your partner and companion above all others except for God, then God will greatly bless your union and bring you untold happiness and joy."

He stopped for a moment, lowering the Bible and his notes, tucking them under his arm. A sweet and tender smile now softened his mouth. "As a seal and a witness to each other, and to those of us who have come here to witness this joyous occasion, you may now kiss each other as husbands and wives."

Chapter Notes

The scripture Benjamin cites to Alice about forsaking father and mother is found in Matthew 19:29.

Once the decision to go west was officially made and shared with the Saints in the October conference, the enormous task of preparing to leave began. In a matter of days, Nauvoo was transformed. The same prodigious energies and boundless determination that turned the swamps of Commerce into beautiful Nauvoo were now turned to the preparations required to move a whole people into the wilderness. Nauvoo became one vast workshop. Homes, businesses, barns, sheds—virtually every available building in the city became a shop for the manufacture of the items needed to take thousands of people across the plains. Day and night the ring of the blacksmith's anvil sounded through the city. One could not pass down the street without hearing the sound of the hammer and saw, the whir of spinning wheels, or the clickety-clack of looms.

To purchase a new, ready-made wagon—particularly when the demand skyrocketed as it did immediately following conference—could cost a family as much as a hundred dollars, an impossible amount of cash for most families. But they could make their own for a fraction of that cost. Off went men to various parts of the state or surrounding territories to cut lumber. The hardwoods required for the axles and wheels and other critical moving parts had to be purchased outright. Wood for the wagon boxes was cut green, brought to Nauvoo, and dried in heated drying sheds. The hardwood was boiled in great vats of salt water to soften it to the point where it could be curled into the shapes needed for hubs and for the felloe timbers, the outer part of the wheel into which the spokes were inserted.

Men with teams were sent off in other directions to procure the iron needed to make the axle thimbles, the bushings, the steel "tires" that went around the outside of the wheels, the clevises, bolts, endgate rods, and the hundred other iron pieces that were needed to make a serviceable wagon. Blacksmiths, coopers, wheelwrights, carpenters, joiners—artisans of every kind were pressed into service and worked from early morning until long into the night.

Nor were the women any less serviceable to the cause. In addition to the making of wagon covers and tents, there was grain, beans, dried fruit, and various seeds to be bagged and prepared for the journey. Clothing and bedding sufficient to withstand the rigors of outdoor living and the winters of the Rocky Mountain regions were required of every household. Then there was the food. The women dried squash, pumpkins, and fruits. They made pickles and vinegar, ground corn into meal, bagged potatoes and carrots and turnips.

Children of all ages became the day laborers for the massive effort. They worked alongside their fathers and mothers, doing whatever was required. They ran errands, spun linen, carded wool, planed wood, chopped firewood for the drying sheds or to keep the vats of water boiling.

The organizational structure was honed and perfected. Companies designed to accommodate a hundred families were first contemplated, but this proved to be too unwieldy and that number was cut in half. A company captain was called by the

Twelve, and individual families were assigned to the various companies. Each company was encouraged to meet together and plan how to best accomplish the work, share their resources, help the less able, procure the tools and equipment each company was required to bring. Within each company there were further divisions—captains of tens to watch over smaller groups of families; a commissary officer who would procure and distribute food along the way; a treasurer; wranglers to help manage the livestock; guards and "pioneers" who would watch for danger, scout out the trail, make roads and bridges or find the best stream crossings.

And all of this was done while trying desperately to sell off their property and trade unneeded items for absolute necessities. People from a hundred miles around flocked in to what amounted to "a sheriff's sale," where goods are sold at ridiculously low prices to recoup money from a debtor. For all the people's hatred of the Mormons and what they believed, everyone knew of their reputation for industry and enterprise. Nauvoo and the surrounding settlements were juicy plums ripe for the picking, and they came in like a flock of squabbling, squawking geese to peck it clean.

To no one's surprise, none of the buyers were willing to pay top dollar, or even half of what things were worth. Fully developed farms of fifty and sixty acres sold for a hundred dollars and a team of oxen. Homes went for twenty cents on the dollar, and sometimes not that. John D. Lee would later recount his experience: "My large house, costing me $8,000, I was offered $800 for. My fanaticism would not allow me to take that for it. I locked it up, selling only one stove out of it, for which I received eight yards of cloth. The building with its twenty-seven rooms, I turned over to the committee [a group of the brethren left behind to sell off property], to be sold to help the poor away. The committee informed afterwards that they sold the house for $12.50."

The Steed family fared better than many. First of all, they were a large and tightly knit clan. There were six family units planning to join the exodus—Benjamin and Mary Ann, Jessica and Solomon, Nathan and Lydia, Derek and Rebecca, Peter and Kathryn, Matthew and Jenny. They were all assigned to the same company. Nathan told Brigham that they were trying to persuade Joshua and Caroline to join them and asked that space in the company be held for them. Brigham agreed and recommended they simply form their own company of ten. If Joshua went, they would have seven families, with a total of fourteen adults and nineteen children—twenty, if one counted Lydia's baby that would be born in the spring. If by some miracle they ever talked Carl and Melissa into joining them, it would make eight families and twenty-four children.

Another reason why the Steeds fared better than others was that they were some of Nauvoo's more prosperous citizens. Thanks to Joshua's earlier financial help and their own industry and cooperative spirit, they had done well for themselves. They did not have large cash reserves, but they had more than most. They were not absolutely dependent upon the sale of their homes or property in order to finance their preparations. In addition to that, several of the family enterprises were naturally suited to the task of preparation. Matthew's cabinet shop became the new Steed "wagon factory." Joshua's blacksmith shop at the freight yard meant they didn't have to wait for the huge backlogs in the commercial blacksmith shops around town. The Steed Family Dry Goods and General Store gave them natural access to many of the personal items that were on the list, such as spices, cloth, tools, and so on. Added to that was Joshua's extensive network of commercial contacts built up over a decade of hauling freight and running a cotton mill in St. Louis. Items that could not be had even at outrageous prices by others, Joshua was able to procure for the family at semi-reasonable prices. Even Carl's brickyards proved to be an indirect blessing to the family. With the decision to move, construction of new homes all but stopped in Nauvoo, which sharply curtailed the market for bricks. Carl closed one of his drying sheds and gave it over to the family. Half became the "sewing shop" for the women; the other half was used to store the food and growing stack of supplies they were gathering. In addition, with slight adaptation, one of the brick kilns was converted into an oven for drying the lumber procured for the construction of their wagons.

At the October conference, the Twelve proposed ending the printing of the *Nauvoo Neighbor* and that the *Times and Seasons* be printed on a more limited basis until the end of the current year. The money used for paper and mailing was needed for far more critical purchases. That meant Peter's time at the printing office dropped by more than half. Once the double wedding was over and Will and Alice left for St. Louis, Peter and Kathryn became the recorders, treasurers, accountants, and clerks for their family company.

So as October closed out and November came in, the hum of activity filled the air all across the city. Over all, there lay a mood of sadness that the Saints had to leave their beloved City of Joseph. But there was also a growing air of anticipation. They were going west to find a new home. They would find a place where they could live without the constant persecution of their neighbors. Until then, they would try to make life as normal as possible.

Emily Steed stood at the small mirror in her bedroom, peering at the image before her. "Rachel?"

Her cousin was sprawled across the bed, watching her with large, solemn eyes. "Yes?"

"Do you think I look like I'm sixteen?"

Rachel smiled. She would be fourteen in January. Emily had turned thirteen on July fifth, just four months earlier. Both were maturing now, starting to look like young women and not just girls, but Emily was definitely ahead of Rachel in that regard. Though slender and supple, her body was filling out, making her waist look all the more tiny. Her eyes were large and dark—the color of rich saddle leather—and shaded by enormous black lashes. Her hair, now down past her shoulders, was thick and black and lustrous. Emily's features, striking enough to draw comment since the time she was a little girl, were growing even more attractive now as she made the transformation to young womanhood. Rachel watched her, feeling a touch of envy, wondering what it would be like to be so naturally beautiful.

"Well?" Emily said, turning and putting her hands on her hips.

"Well what?" Rachel asked, startled out of her reverie.

"Do I look like I could be sixteen? The other day Papa told Mama that it made him sad because I look like I'm sixteen."

"Why would that make him sad?"

There was a sigh, evidence of great suffering. "Because he doesn't want me to grow up, I suppose." Her lower lip jutted out slightly. "You're not going to answer me, are you?"

Sitting up, Rachel laughed. "No, Emily, I don't think you look like you're sixteen. Fifteen and a half maybe, but not sixteen."

"Really?" Emily asked eagerly, turning back to survey herself again.

"Really," Rachel assured her. Though Rachel felt quite the inferior to Emily when it came to physical attractiveness, there was no strain between the two cousins because of it. First of all, while Emily was keenly aware of her beauty and enjoyed the effect that it had on young men, Nathan and Lydia had gone to some lengths to stress that beauty was a gift from God and therefore not a basis for pride or conceit. Emily not only accepted that idea, she believed it. She had never once acted as though she saw herself as superior to Rachel in any way.

In reality—and this would have shocked Rachel greatly if she knew it—Emily carried a bit of envy for Rachel. Rachel was beloved by everyone in the family and by all who knew her. Taller than Emily by almost two inches—one of the primary reasons for the envy—Rachel had a quiet loveliness of her own that made her stand out from other young women. Her hair, medium brown and never cut, hung almost to her waist and glowed in the light like aged honey. Near the end, it curled naturally into gentle ringlets. Her skin was as smooth as expensive porcelain, setting off the large blue eyes. These were darker than one might expect, like the deep blue of lake water on a summer day. And where Emily was vivacious, full of life, impetuous, and daring, Rachel was more reflective, slower to judge, more mature in her outlook. Those differences, and the mutual envy and respect they held for each other, made them closer than many sisters and the best of friends.

Emily turned back around. "Well, are you ready?"

Rachel didn't move. "Are you sure we've been invited?"

"Of course," Emily said airily. "Vilate and Helen Mar asked me just this afternoon."

"But—"

"They specifically asked me to be sure and bring you." She reached out and took Rachel's hands and pulled her up. "I swear."

Rachel's shoulders lifted and fell. The thoughts of this evening excited and frightened her at the same time. These weren't just any girls they were going to be with. Vilate Young was the daughter of President Young. Helen Mar Kimball was the daughter of Heber C. Kimball, the chief Apostle behind President Young. Others would also be children of prominent Church leaders. She managed a smile. "Is Joshua coming?"

Emily frowned. "No. He has guard duty tonight. He wanted to." There was suddenly a mischievous grin. "Mary Beth Sanders is going to be very disappointed."

Rachel considered that for a moment, then squared her shoulders, as though steeling herself to face something difficult. "All right," she sighed.

Emily laughed. "It will be fun, you watch," she said. Then on impulse, she threw her arms around her cousin. "I know this isn't a happy time for our people, Rachel, but I'm so glad your family has come to live in Nauvoo now. When you were in Ramus, I missed you so."

At that, Rachel could nod without reservation. She enjoyed Ramus, particularly the role she had in helping her mother with the school. And her mother's marriage to Solomon Garrett had proven to be a wonderful blessing for all of them. But Nauvoo was so alive compared to those small outlying settlements. And then to have the family too—she was glad they would spend their last months here and not out there.

"I just love Uncle Solomon," Emily said, as if sensing her thoughts. "He has made your mother so happy."

"Yes," Rachel said softly. "And us too. He is very good to us." Her chin dropped slightly and her cheeks colored momentarily. "He is going to legally adopt us before we leave in the spring."

Emily clapped her hands. "Really? That's wonderful, Rachel!"

"Yes."

Stepping back, Emily was suddenly sober. "So now it will be Rachel Garrett."

"Yes."

"And when you're married, just think of it. You'll have four last names. First you were a Steed, and then a Griffith. Now you will be a Garrett." She paused for a moment, impishness in her eyes. "And someday, you'll be Mrs. Barnett."

Rachel's cheeks went instantly crimson and Emily laughed aloud. On a visit to Nauvoo some months before, Solomon Garrett had stopped at the Browning gunsmith shop to have a pistol fixed. Afterwards, chortling triumphantly, and to Rachel's complete mortification, Mark and Luke had told everyone that one of the boys working in the shop had talked with Rachel the whole time, inquiring after her name and seeming quite disappointed when he learned she was not from Nauvoo.

"What shall we call you then?" Emily mused, thoroughly enjoying Rachel's discomfiture. She struck an exaggerated pose. "Good morning," she said in a deep voice, "and how are you, Sister Rachel Steed Griffith Garrett Barnett?"

Rachel slapped at her playfully. And then, face flaming, she added shyly, "Sister Barnett will be just fine."

Emily rocked back a little, shocked by such candor. "Rachel Garrett!" she exclaimed.

"Come on," Rachel said, pleased to have taken Emily by surprise for once, "we'd better go."

As they started out the door, Emily got suddenly very serious. "Do you ever think of Uncle Joshua as your natural father anymore, Rachel?"

Rachel was startled. "No, not really."

"He tries not to show it, but you can tell he treats you differently than the other cousins."

"I don't think so. I never really knew him as my father, you know. I was very small when . . . when Mother left him."

"I know."

"Mother never tried to hide it from me, but she told me once that it would be easier for her, easier for Joshua, and easier for me if we just forgot the past and let things take a different course now. So to me, he's just Uncle Joshua."

"Mama says it was Joshua who sent Solomon to see Aunt Jessica's school. He was hoping they might fall in love."

"I know. My mother says that too."

"It is *so* romantic," Emily said dreamily. "I wish I had all those wonderful things in my life." She twirled around, her eyes half-closed. "Emily Steed"—she fluttered her eyelids—"Eberhardt."

Rachel just laughed. "Oh, Emily, you're so silly. Now, come on, let's go or we'll be late. And Charles Eberhardt won't like that one little bit."

As they came down the stairs, Nathan and Lydia were in the sitting room with two of their other children. Lydia looked up, then stood immediately. She went to the two girls and gave them an appraising look. "You both look lovely," she said.

Nathan was grinning. "Rachel, try to keep a rein on Emily for us, will you?"

"Ah!" Emily grunted in dismay. "I think it should be the other way around. You should have heard what your niece just said."

"What?"

Horrified, Rachel gave her a sharp look. Emily just laughed and shook her head. "Maybe later, Papa." She moved in and kissed him on the cheek, then bent down to two-year-old little Joseph, who was sitting at his father's feet, playing with some wooden blocks. "Bye, Joseph. Will you give Emmy a kiss?"

He dropped the blocks, stood, and gave her a resounding hug and a sloppy kiss on the cheek. Elizabeth Mary, a precocious seven now, was reading a book. She smiled at her sister. "Bye, Emmy."

"Bye, Elizabeth Mary." She looked around. "Where's Josiah?"

"Sleeping over at Christopher and young Benjamin's house," Lydia answered. She gave Emily one last hug. "You two have fun, now."

"We will, Mama."

As they left a moment later, Nathan looked to his wife. "Well, they seem excited enough."

"But of course," Lydia said wisely. "Don't you know what this is all about?"

"A get-together with some of the girls?"

"Yes," she said, smiling. "At the Young house."

"I thought they were going to be outside. The weather's nice enough."

Lydia gave him a patient look. "It will be outside. Don't you know which men stand guard outside the home of Brigham Young?"

Now Nathan's head came up. "John Kay," he said slowly.

"And Howard Egan," she added.

"I see," he said, understanding finally dawning. "So that's it?"

"The young people love both of those men. Howard is a great one for telling stories. He'll have the whole circle of them laughing until their sides hurt."

"And Kay—isn't he the one who sings?"

"Yes. He has a wonderful baritone voice. They all love to hear him." Now she laughed merrily. "In fact, I taught him a song the other day when he came in the store."

Nathan turned and gave her a quizzical look. "You did? Which one?"

"'Barbara Allen.'"

"Ah!" It came out in a soft expression of surprise and pleasure.

"I think he'll sing it to them tonight."

"But John Kay and Howard Egan are married."

She shook her head patiently. "Howard and John only provide the excuse for the young people to get together. It's being together that they like." She turned away from him to look out the window. The sound of girls laughing came in softly through the glass. "The one Emily is all agog over is Charles Eberhardt. She's a young woman now, Nathan. There are some girls in the city who are getting married at fourteen, you know."

He snorted in disgust. "Not with the encouragement of the Church leaders."

"Oh, I know, and I don't want Emily to be thinking about it for two or three years yet, but it's good for them to be out among the young people. And Rachel too. Did you see how radiant she looked?"

"Yes," he agreed. "She has become a beautiful young woman."

She laughed softly. "The other night when they were all together, Heber's boy William hitched up a wagon. They all climbed aboard and then persuaded John Kay to take them for a ride in the moonlight."

There was a noticeable frown. "While he was on guard duty?"

"Oh, it was all right," Lydia said with a touch of reproach for his stuffiness. "Emily said that all they did was go around the block over and over so that each time they would pass Brigham's gate, John could see that all was in order."

"I see."

"They had so much fun. That's why Emily wanted to take Rachel tonight."

Nathan did not miss the irony. The enemies of the Church had succeeded in having the Nauvoo Charter revoked. Others would gladly take advantage of that loss and try to plunder the Saints. And so John Kay and Howard Egan provided entertainment while they stood guard duty, and the young people came to gather around them. His own son, now fourteen and a half, was somewhere else in the city. Would there be young people coming to spend time with him as well? It was sad in a way, and yet it was somehow encouraging at the same time.

He stood now and went over to stand beside his wife, who was looking out the window again. "They are not burdened down with the same concerns that us old folks have, are they?" he said.

"No, and I'm glad."

He nodded and slipped his arms around her. "Me too." After a moment, he turned her around to face him. "Will you sing for me?"

Her eyebrows shot up. "Here? Now?"

"Yes."

She looked at her two children playing in the room around them. "Not here," she said, embarrassed.

"Why not? I would like my children to know what it was that made their father fall in love." He kissed her. "I'd like them to know how he saw this beautiful slip of a young girl, dancing among the apple blossoms one spring, singing the beautiful 'Barbara Allen.'"

She laid her head against his shoulder. "That was just day before yesterday, wasn't it?" she murmured, with just a tinge of sadness.

He buried his face in her hair, kissing the top of her head. "I was thinking it was just this morning." And then he added softly, "I shall have that picture in my mind for as long as I live. Thank you for these fifteen years, Lydia McBride. Thank you for having that farmer's boy who was such a dunce."

She looked up at him and put her arms around his neck. "You know what makes me feel bad?"

"What?"

"That you knew before I did."

"Knew what?"

"How much we were going to love each other." She went up on her toes and gave him a long, lingering kiss. Elizabeth Mary, who had been watching the two of them out of the corner of her eye, started to giggle. "Look, Joseph! Mama's kissing Papa!"

They clapped their hands and squealed with joy, but neither Lydia nor Nathan seemed to hear them.

———•———

Joshua looked up as Caroline opened the door of the freight office and stepped inside. There was a brief draft of cold air and the papers on his desk stirred a little. Before he could even say hello, she held up an envelope in her gloved hand. "This just arrived at the post office."

"From Will and Alice?"

She shook her head. "No, from Walter Samuelson."

He pushed the accounts book aside and stood. "I'm surprised we haven't heard before this. It's been almost three weeks since they left here."

He walked around the desk and she held out the envelope for him. "Did you read it?" he asked.

"No. It is addressed only to you."

Frowning, he looked at the address. The handwriting was firm and bold and unmistakably that of his business partner. Turning it over, he slipped a finger under the flap and tore it open. He took out the paper. Caroline saw that it was only one sheet and had only a few lines of writing. Joshua read it, grunted, then handed it over to her.

It was dated November sixth, five days before.

Joshua—

Imperative we meet. Will be at Riverside Hotel in Quincy on nights of November 13, 14, 15.

Samuelson

Caroline handed it back to Joshua. "I suppose he wants to discuss the situation with Will and Alice, don't you?"

"Hardly. You read Will's letter."

"Yes," she murmured. The heartrending letter written by Will had come about ten days after they left Nauvoo. It was posted just before he and Alice caught a steamer for Cairo, where they would then try to transfer to a boat going up the Ohio River. The meeting with Alice's parents had been even uglier than they feared, Will explained. Judith Samuelson had gasped when Will told them that Alice had been baptized. Walter had gone a deep, mottled red. But when they then told them that they had also been married, that they were even then on their way to New York to catch a ship that would sail to California around the tip of South America, Judith Samuelson had fainted and gone into a state of shock. She was still in her bed at the time Will had written.

Samuelson's rage had been staggering. Deadly grim, he had driven them from his home that very night, refusing to let them stay under his roof after such a betrayal. They had finally found a seedy hotel down on the riverfront. The next morning a curt note arrived. It was a simple but unmistakable ultimatum. If Alice so chose, her father would find a lawyer and bring him round to have the marriage annulled immediately. Will Steed would be sent packing, to New York or back to Nauvoo, it mattered not to them. Otherwise, that same lawyer would redraw the family will. There would be no inheritance in the future and no help of any kind in the meantime, no matter how desperate Alice's condition might become. The family would be instructed under pain of losing their own inheritance to make no further contact of any kind with her. For all intents and purposes, it would be as though she had died.

Will had expected no less, but the savagery of the rejection shook him deeply. Alice was shattered, but held firm. Two days later they left St. Louis on the *Carl Henry*, bound for Cairo. They left without either of them seeing Alice's parents or any other family members again.

Joshua turned and tossed the letter onto the stack of papers, bringing Caroline back to the present. "Let me see who's free to drive me down to Quincy; then I'll come home with you and pack some things."

"Could you tell me which room Mr. Samuelson is in?"

The clerk looked up from the register. "He's in room fourteen, Mr. Steed. But I saw him in the dining room about a quarter of an—" He looked past Joshua. "Oh, here he is now."

Joshua turned. Walter Samuelson was coming across the small lobby of the hotel. "Hello, Walter."

"Joshua." The greeting was icy and detached. "I saw you come in."

"We just arrived," he said smiling, forcing joviality. "What's for supper?"

"If you don't mind, I'd like us to speak together first. In my room." Without waiting for an answer, he turned to the clerk. "Will you see that Mr. Steed's bag is put in his room?"

"Of course." The man handed Joshua a key. "You'll be in room six."

"Thank you. My driver is putting the carriage away at the livery stable. When he comes in, will you tell him to go ahead and have supper without me?"

The clerk glanced at the register again. "That's Mr. Warren?"

"Yes."

"I will. He'll be in room seven, which is adjacent to yours."

"Thank you."

Samuelson was already walking to the stairs, his gait measured, his back stiff. Joshua pocketed the key and followed after him, shaking his head. Perhaps it was just as well. Let Samuelson get it off his chest; then they could go down and have supper together to smooth things out again.

To his surprise, when Walter turned the key and opened the door to his room, two men inside the room stood immediately. Both were men he had never seen before, and that was a little strange, since he knew most of the men the two of them employed. Without a word, the St. Louis businessman gave them a curt nod and they immediately got their hats and left the room. As the bigger of the two brushed past him, Joshua caught a glimpse of the butt of a pistol stuck in his belt beneath the jacket he wore.

As they shut the door, Joshua looked at his longtime friend and partner. "You're traveling with body guards now, Walter?" he said with a touch of a smile. "Am I that intimidating?"

There was no answering smile, not even so much as a grunt.

"Look, Walter," Joshua began, wanting to see if he could salvage something from what was about to happen. "This whole thing with Alice and Will came as a huge shock to me too. I was as angry as you are when I learned what they planned to do."

Walter's head came up slowly. "If you were as angry as I was, the marriage would have been in St. Louis and your son would now be working for me instead of being on his way to California."

Joshua moved over to the overstuffed chair in one corner of the room and sat down heavily. "Walter, Will is twenty-one. Alice will be nineteen next month. They're adults now. Neither you nor I can tell them what to do. Lord knows I tried. I even spoke with Brigham Young."

Walter, still standing in the center of the room, lowered his head into his shoulders, as though he were either preparing to charge or getting ready to be attacked. "Joshua, I am no longer interested in sharing a business partnership with you."

Joshua shot out of the chair. "*What?*"

"It's over, Joshua."

"I . . ." He spun away, then whirled instantly back. "Look, Walter, I know you're upset by all of this, but this is not my fault."

"Perhaps not. Perhaps you could not have prevented it. But you didn't even try. Not really. So I am holding you and Caroline, and especially your family, responsible. And I am no longer interested in being in partnership with you."

Joshua was aghast, not believing what he was hearing. "You're throwing away over ten years of our lives together because I couldn't make Alice do what you yourself could not make her do?" He fought down the anger. "Come on, Walter. This is insane."

Walter didn't answer, but walked around the bed to the far side of the room. There were three pieces of luggage there. He leaned down and with some effort picked up a small trunk, about the size of a square hatbox. Coming back around, he set it on the end of the bed, undid the padlock with a small key on his watch chain, and threw the lid back.

Joshua gaped. The trunk was stuffed with wads of money. As

he stared at them, he saw they were twenty- and fifty-dollar bank notes. He moved forward a step. "What is this?"

"We once talked about you selling me your half of the cotton warehouse and mill. Here is twenty-five thousand dollars. That is more than a fair price, I might add."

Now Joshua felt his face burning. "We talked about it, Walter. That's all. We just talked about it."

Walter met his gaze evenly. "Well, I felt that based on previous conversations, you would have no objection to selling out now. Here is the payment. I have some papers for you to sign." He walked to the desk and picked up a sheaf of papers. "Incidentally, that is why I hired the two men. They will stand guard outside your room tonight. After that, keeping the money safe will be your responsibility."

"Come on, man!" Joshua cried hoarsely. "Get a hold of yourself. Alice is gone but that doesn't overturn ten years of friendship."

"Are you saying you refuse to sell to me?" came the quiet, stubborn reply.

Joshua walked to the window, dazed to the point of nearly being speechless. Then a thought struck him. "And what about my interest in our other businesses—the construction company, the lumberyard? Did you buy me out on those too?" he said, jeering now.

"No. We never discussed selling those businesses, and so I have no right to assume you wanted out."

"Well, now, that's downright decent of you, Walter," he said, feeling the control on his temper slipping fast. "I guess you—"

"So I have sold *my* interest in each of the companies you mentioned."

Joshua rocked back as though struck. "You what!"

"I have sold out, Joshua. Half of everything is still yours, but the other half now belongs to the Barber brothers."

It was as if he had been kicked in the stomach. "Ben Barber and that slimy little brother of his?" he cried.

There was a frosty nod. "As you know, they've been after one or the other of us for a long time to sell. Judith is still very ill—thanks to your son and his influence on my daughter. So I'm taking my wife back home, to New Orleans. We are leaving St. Louis immediately after I return. Therefore I have liquidated all of my assets." He thrust the sheaf of papers at Joshua. "I'm sorry, Joshua."

"Sorry!" he cried. "You've just put me in partnership with two of the sleaziest, conniving thieves in St. Louis and all you can say is you're sorry?"

Walter was unmoved. He stood there, feet planted, shoulders squared, his face like obsidian. "In the winter of '38 and '39, your wife and family came to me, Joshua. They thought you were dead. They had two very bad men after them. I helped them, Joshua. Even though it put me at risk, I helped them. I found them a place to stay. I gave them money, and helped them make their way out of St. Louis undetected."

"You gave them my money!" Joshua retorted angrily.

Walter's eyes flickered dangerously. "I never touched one dime of your money, Joshua. I used my own. And I spent a considerable amount putting out a search for Will when he suddenly disappeared."

Backing down, Joshua was apologetic. "You're right, Walter. I'm sorry. I know you stood by my family at a terrible time. I thank you for that, but—"

"I expected that you would do the same for me, Joshua."

He threw up his hands. "I tried! I have opposed Alice's interest in the Church all along. When Brigham Young called them to go to New York, I fought him on it. I told Will he was making a terrible mistake. I tried, Walter."

"I didn't just *try* to help your family back then," came the soft and bitter answer. "I did it. I figured it was the least I could do for a friend and partner."

"Walter, you can't do this. You know what Ben Barber will do. He'll strip out every asset, sell off whatever he can get his hands on. He's done it to every company he's bought."

There was a weary sigh now. "I looked for other buyers,

Joshua. Believe it or not, I did. I am not trying to ruin you. But no one else had that kind of cash on hand. And Judith is very ill. I have to leave now before the river closes for the winter."

"So you sold me out."

Samuelson flinched but went on doggedly. "The sales are not final until the twentieth of this month. I would suggest you get to St. Louis and do what you can to protect your interest."

"The twentieth?" Joshua roared. "That's less than a week from now."

"I suggest you go straight from here."

As the enormity of what this meant hit Joshua, he thrust his face into Walter's. "You can't do this! This is rape, Walter. Why don't you just torch the businesses? At least there would be some honor in that."

"Honor?" Walter cried in fury, rising to his full height now. "You dare to talk to me of honor? You made a commitment, Joshua. When you left here we had a deal. Alice would wait to be baptized. They would be married here. Will would stay for at least six months. I was willing to put out a lot of money so your family could come. What about honoring that?"

Joshua's voice dropped and he was pleading now. "Circumstances changed, Walter. Be reasonable, man! Will didn't know Brigham was going to ask him to do this."

"He said he would come back," came the clipped reply. "He said he wouldn't take our Alice away. Not yet. You should have made him keep his word, Joshua."

"This is not my fault!" Joshua shouted, his face just inches from Walter's now.

The door flung open and the big man thrust his head in. "You okay, Mr. Samuelson?"

Walter waved him out again. "I'm fine. Leave us, please." Then, even as the door shut again, he turned back to face Joshua's wrath. "If I felt like you had even tried, Joshua, maybe it would be different. If you had even tried to stop them." Once again he shoved the papers at Joshua.

Darkly furious, dizzy with the shock of this revelation, Joshua stared at the papers for several seconds. Then he snatched them out of Samuelson's hands, stalked over to the desk, took the pen there, and signed the last page with a vicious stroke. He turned and flung the papers at his former partner. "There," he snarled. "You have your signature."

Walter didn't make a move toward them.

Feeling sick, wanting to shake Walter like a rag doll to make him understand, Joshua walked to the bed, slammed the lid on the trunk of bills, and picked it up.

Walter reached for the watch chain and unhooked the key from it. He stepped forward and held it out. Joshua just stared at it. Finally, with a shrug, Walter leaned forward to tuck the key into Joshua's vest pocket. Joshua slapped his hand away. "You think you can buy yourself a clean conscience with a key and a padlock?" he said incredulously. "No thank you." He picked up the chest and started for the door.

"Joshua?"

He stopped but did not turn around to look at him.

"You need to know something. I feel I owe you this much."

"You don't owe me anything," he hissed.

"You need to know that the people in Warsaw know you were there that day that Frank Worrell got shot."

That jerked him around. For a moment it didn't register. "What?"

"They know, Joshua." Walter's shoulders slumped a little now. "They already hated you for turning your back on them, for becoming a Mormon-lover. But now? My sources tell me they're out to make you pay, Joshua. You were part of killing one of their own."

"I didn't fire a shot."

"It doesn't matter. You were there. You stood with the Mormons."

"Frank Worrell was a swamp rat."

There was a brief nod. "I won't argue that. But his fellow swamp rats are determined to have justice. Be careful, Joshua."

Joshua just shook his head. "Good-bye, Walter."

"Good-bye, Joshua. I'm sorry it had to come to this."

"I can tell," he sneered.

As he came out into the hall, shutting the door behind him, the two men waiting there stepped back deferentially, then fell into step behind him. Joshua gripped the trunk by one handle, let it drop to his side, and reached inside his coat. He whipped out a small pistol and whirled to face them. "I don't need any help, boys. You understand me?"

The big one raised his hands, backing up. The other one's eyes were bulging as he stared at the gun in Joshua's hand.

"Have it your way, Mr. Steed," the big one muttered. "We're just following orders."

Without a word, Joshua slipped the pistol away, took the chest by both handles, and started down the hallway again. Behind him, he heard Samuelson's door open and sensed that he had stepped out to watch. Joshua didn't turn around, slow his step, or utter another word.

Chapter Notes

The transformation of Nauvoo into "one vast workshop" and the huge task of preparing to leave the city are described in various sources (for example, see HC 7:535–36; Andrew Karl Larson, *Erastus Snow: The Life of a Missionary and Pioneer for the Early Mormon Church* [Salt Lake City: University of Utah Press, 1971], pp. 101–3). The statement from John D. Lee on the sale of his home is quoted in Larson, *Erastus Snow*, p. 102.

During much of 1845, the young men of the City of Joseph often stood watch along with the older men. Heber C. Kimball's daughter, Helen Mar Kimball Whitney, gives us the description of how the young people gathered around John Kay and Howard Egan, who were assigned to stand watch at Brigham Young's house, for singing and storytelling (see *Women of Nauvoo*, pp. 142–43).

It was quarter of eight the next morning when Joshua walked quietly down the hotel hallway to room fourteen. Though he knew there would be other guests still sleeping, he rapped sharply on the door and stepped back. There was no sound from inside. After a moment, he rapped again, louder this time. He leaned forward, his ear to the door, listening. There wasn't a sound. He tried the door latch. It was locked. Swearing softly under his breath, he turned and strode down the hallway.

As he came down the stairs and moved across the lobby, the clerk, an older man than the one from the night before, came out of the back room. "Good morning."

"Have you seen Mr. Walter Samuelson this morning?"

The man's head bobbed. "Mr. Samuelson checked out just after dawn, Mr. Steed. He said he was returning to St. Louis."

Joshua's mouth opened, then clamped shut again. "Is there a boat leaving today?"

"No, sir. He left by carriage."

So that was that, Joshua thought. Samuelson had made sure there would be no further discussion, no further chance for negotiations.

The man brightened. "But those two men that were with him are still here. They could tell you more. They're in the dining room having breakfast."

"Thank you." He started away.

"In fact, they're with your driver."

Joshua stopped and turned back slowly. "Mr. Warren?"

"Yes. I saw them in there together not five minutes ago."

For several seconds, Joshua stood there, letting that sink in. Then he turned and went back to the desk. "Could you figure up my bill?" he said.

The man looked a little surprised but nodded. "Of course, Mr. Steed. I understand you had no supper last night, so it's four dollars."

Joshua reached inside his coat and withdrew his wallet. He took out two ten-dollar bills and laid them on the counter. The clerk's eyes widened a little as he watched Joshua's hands.

"I'd like some extra service."

"Of course, Mr. Steed. Whatever you say."

"I'm going up to my room and pack my things. Is there a back door to the hotel?"

"Yes, sir."

"Good. I want you to get me some food." He turned and glanced toward the dining room, feeling an urgency now. "Not anything fancy. Bring it to my room. But no one is to know. Understood?"

"Yes, sir. And that's all?"

"No. If Mr. Warren inquires after me, you tell him that you assume I am still asleep."

There was a slow, knowing nod. "Yes, sir." His hand reached out and took the two bills. They disappeared quickly into his pocket.

"Do you have a boy who can help me with my things to the livery stable?"

"Yes. I'll send him up with the food." The man's eyes were conspiratorial now. "It'll be best if I'm here at the desk in case Mr. Warren comes out."

"Good." Joshua turned and took a couple of steps toward the stairs, then turned back. "Do you know if Mr. Samuelson talked to his two men this morning at all?"

"No, sir. He was gone long before they came down."

"Are they from around here?"

"Only for the past few weeks. Came off a riverboat." There was obvious distaste in his eyes. "Mr. Samuelson hired them yesterday when he arrived."

"Thank you." He turned and went up the stairs.

———•———

Cranfield Warren strode up to the livery stable office and yanked open the door. The proprietor looked up. "Mornin'."

"I need that carriage we brought in last night made ready."

One eyebrow came up. "But Mr. Steed was already here."

"*What?*" Warren swore. "He's gone?"

"Yes, sir. 'Bout an hour ago."

He swore again and left, slamming the door behind him. The man rose up a little, watching his retreat through the window. Warren walked to where two men waited on horseback. They conferred for a moment, angrily; then Warren spun around and came back toward the office. The man sat back down and busied himself with his books. After a moment, the door jerked open again.

"I need the fastest horse you got," Warren snapped. "And make it quick."

———•———

Normally the forty miles from Nauvoo to Quincy took about a day and a half. It could be done in one day, but it made for a long ride and was hard on a horse that had to pull even a light carriage that far. Joshua had considered taking another route back, knowing that he was going to be pursued, but he had immediately rejected the idea. Everything had to appear perfectly normal.

They caught up to him about ten o'clock. He saw the three riders about a mile back, coming hard. He was tempted to reach for his pistol and lay it on the seat beside him, but he resisted that too. He just rode on, letting the horse have its head, until the three men came thundering up.

He reined up, looking surprised. "Warren! There you are."

"Thanks for leaving without me, Steed."

Joshua smiled blandly. "I knocked on your door. There was no answer. I thought maybe you'd had a little too much at the tavern last night. That's been known to happen before."

"So you just left me?"

"I have to get back to Nauvoo and get my things," he said. "I'm going to have to make an urgent trip to St. Louis." His voice went suddenly hard. "I don't have time to be out looking for some drunken sot." He turned his head and looked at the other two men. "Don't tell me Mr. Samuelson has changed his mind and wants to talk some more," he said coldly. "Sorry, not interested."

The big man's eyes narrowed. Then suddenly his hand came up. It was filled with a revolver which pointed at Joshua's chest. "No, actually, it's Billy and me and your Mr. Warren here who want to talk with you. Please get down."

Joshua looked sharply at his driver. "What is this, Warren?"

The second man had a pistol out too. "Out of the carriage, Steed!"

Warren licked his lips, nervous now. "You'd best get down, Mr. Steed."

Joshua shook his head. "Oh, so it's *Mister* Steed now, is it?" But he climbed down from the buggy.

"Hands up," the big man commanded. "Warren, get his pistol."

As Warren came up behind Joshua and took the pistol from his inside jacket pocket, the smaller man named Billy jumped off his horse and strode to the carriage. He leaned over the side, peering into the rear seat where Joshua's luggage was visible.

There was a moment's silence, then he swore. "It's not here, Dan." He pawed around a little, then turned, looking sharply disappointed. "There's no chest."

"Ah," Joshua said softly, "so that's it."

The man called Dan swung down from his horse and stalked to the buggy. The single valise Joshua had brought with him from Nauvoo was jerked out and slammed down to the ground. In seconds, the big man had it open and was pawing through the clothing and other articles inside. He stood, kicking at it savagely. "Nothing!" he exclaimed. Suddenly he had an idea. He moved to the back of the buggy where there was a large pouch for carrying baggage. He thrust his hand in it. It was empty.

"How big of a cut does Samuelson give you for this?" Joshua asked when the man came back to face him.

There was a snort of disgust. "That old fool! If you hadn't showed up so quickly, there would have been no chest to give you when you came."

"They weren't expecting us till today," Warren grunted, as much to himself as to Joshua.

Joshua said nothing but felt a tremendous relief. Walter Samuelson's bitterness had virtually devastated Joshua's financial situation, but had Samuelson been part of this it would have been a terrible thing indeed.

"Where is it?" the man called Dan asked tightly.

Joshua looked bland. "You mean the chest?" He shrugged. "I told the banker he could keep it. Once the money was gone, I had no further use for it."

"The bank?" Warren cried in dismay. "You took it to the bank?"

There was contempt in Joshua's eyes. "Good heavens, man! You think I'm fool enough to drive around with twenty-five thousand dollars in cash?"

Billy groaned and rolled his eyes. "Twenty-five thousand! Is that how much there was?"

The big man was watching Joshua narrowly. "The bank wasn't open before you left this morning."

Joshua scoffed openly at him. "Warren, how many times have I done business with the bank down here?"

"Dozens."

"Has old Mr. Barker ever opened the bank for me after hours?"

Warren's face fell. He looked at his two partners. "Barker would keep the bank open all night if Mr. Steed here asked him to."

Dan swore, the bitterness like fire in his eyes. "We should've just done it last night," he muttered. "We just should have done it."

Joshua smiled wickedly. "Seems like there's an old saying about striking while the iron is hot."

He jumped back, but not quickly enough. The big man swung his fist and drove it into Joshua's stomach. He gasped and dropped to his knees, retching.

"You know," Dan said, mimicking Joshua's jaunty tone, "I don't like you very much." He leaned over and snatched Joshua's wallet from the inside of his coat. Joshua was gasping frantically for air and made no move to stop him. Dan opened the wallet, withdrew a wad of bills, and counted quickly. "Sixty-eight dollars," he said in disgust. "It could have been twenty-five thousand, and we get a lousy sixty-eight dollars."

He swung around, clubbing downward with the butt of his pistol. There was a soft thud and Joshua went down face first into the dirt without a cry. "I don't like you at all," Dan said, breathing heavily now.

He shoved the money into his trouser pocket and jerked his thumb at Billy. "Cut his horse loose. We can't have him coming back to town before we've cleared out."

Warren had watched all that had transpired in stunned astonishment. Now, as Billy started unhitching the horse, Dan swung on him, raising the pistol. "What are you staring at?"

"I . . ." He backed up a step. "Nothing. I was just—"

"Tell you what, Warren," the big man said, his voice low with menace now. "Billy and me don't cotton to the idea of having you around these parts to be talking about what's happened here today. And knowing this man's reputation"—he reached out and gave Joshua a shove with the toe of his boot—"if I were you, I'd not want to be anywhere he will ever find you either."

Warren may not have been one of the world's brighter lights, but he didn't need more explanation than that. He backed up farther, his eyes fixed on the muzzle of Dan's pistol. Then, reaching his horse, he turned and swung up in the saddle. In a moment, he was racing away to the south, leaving a trail of dust in his wake.

Dan watched as Billy finished loosing Joshua's horse from the buggy. He slapped its rump hard, sending it speeding off, then came back to join his partner. For a moment they stood together, looking down at the still figure lying in the road. "Sixty-eight dollars!" Dan muttered. "Sixty-eight lousy, stinking dollars!" He kicked out viciously, driving his boot into Joshua's ribs. The body jerked, but there was no response.

"Come on," Dan snarled. "We'd best be making tracks before someone comes along."

Joshua jerked awake as the pain in his head stabbed into his consciousness. "Easy!" a voice commanded. "Take it easy."

He opened his eyes. Above him, a man peered into his eyes.

Joshua tried to turn and gasped as another lancing pain shot through his side.

"You've been hurt," the man's voice said. "Just lie easy."

Joshua rolled his head. He saw a horse, and then another carriage. Not his own. A woman watched with anxious eyes. Two children in the seat behind her looked frightened.

"Help me up," Joshua said, trying to rise, gasping through clenched teeth.

The man moved around, got his hands beneath Joshua's arms, and pulled him up to a sitting position, dragging him back enough to prop him up against the wheel of his own buggy.

"What happened?" the man asked, coming around again to face him.

Joshua looked around at the upturned valise and the clothing and personal items scattered across the road. "Three men.
They jumped me. Took my wallet."

The man nodded grimly. "We'd better get you into town.
Ursa's just about a mile north of here."

"No," Joshua said sharply. Then more softly he went on. "I'd
better stay here with the carriage. But if you could send someone
back with a horse. Maybe a doctor if there's one nearby."

"Your head is bleeding," the woman called.

He reached up, gingerly touching the lump on the back of
his head. His fingers came away sticky. He reached inside his
pocket, wincing with every movement, and withdrew his handkerchief. He folded it, then pressed it over the wound. "I'll be all
right. Just send someone back."

The man considered further protest, then nodded, sensing
Joshua's determination. "We'll have someone back in half an
hour. No more. Are you sure?"

"Yes. Thank you for stopping."

"All right." The man walked back to his buggy and climbed
up. He took the reins, waved briefly, then drove off. The heads
of the children pivoted, their eyes wide and grave as they moved
away.

Joshua waited until they were two or three hundred yards
down the road; then he rolled away from the wheel, easing his
body down again, groaning as he did so. He was on his back now,
looking up at the underside of the carriage. He stared for a
moment, then closed his eyes. It was still there—the thick
packet which he had wrapped tightly in two of his shirts and
then secured, using the sleeves of the outer shirt, firmly to the
bottom of the buggy.

It was still there.

"What in the world did he hit you with?" Willard Richards
probed gently at Joshua's ribs, watching him wince out of the
corner of his eye.

"The toe of his boot, I suspect," Joshua said dryly. "Actually, I wasn't awake at the time."

Caroline leaned forward, her eyes dark with anxiety. "You can't see it, Joshua, but you've got a bruise the size of a dinner plate."

"Does it hurt, Papa?" Savannah asked gravely.

"Only if I breathe." He smiled to reassure her. "It's a little tender, but I'm going to be all right."

"The head is going to be all right," Richards said, "but I think you've got a broken rib. Maybe two." Willard Richards had been a pharmacist and practicing physician at the time of his conversion near Boston, but he rarely practiced any longer, being caught up in the press of his role as an Apostle and as a clerk to Brigham Young and the Twelve. He was also Church historian. But when Brigham had learned that Joshua Steed had arrived in Nauvoo, driven by a hired man from south Hancock County, he immediately sent Willard over to help.

"Oh, Joshua," Mary Ann said. "I can't believe this has happened."

Benjamin raised his head. "You can't be going to St. Louis."

"I don't have any choice. I'm probably already too late."

"Joshua," Caroline started. She stopped at his look.

"If I give the Barber brothers free rein down there, I'll have nothing within six months' time. Nothing! That's their specialty."

"Then I'm going with you," Nathan said evenly.

"No!" He started to chop his hand downward, wanting to cut off the debate, but the movement sent a jolt through him and he gasped softly. "No, Nathan," he said more slowly. "You are needed here. Every one of you is needed here. There's too much work to do."

"We finished the first wagon," Benjamin said. "Started on the second."

"Great," Joshua growled, "and you only need six. Why are you so stubborn? Why won't you just take some of my wagons?"

"Because," his father answered patiently—they had gone over this half a dozen times or more—"you have a freight yard to run. It's a little hard to carry freight on your back."

"I'll be fine."

"So will we," Mary Ann said right back. "There are others who will need help much more than we will. If you have extra wagons, sell them to them."

He just shook his head. "Well, that only means it is all the more important that Nathan stay here and help. So that's settled."

"It is settled," Nathan retorted. "I'm ready whenever you want to go."

Doctor Richards cut in before Joshua could protest. "Sit up straight. If you're fool enough to go running off, then I'd better wrap your chest." He reached for a bolt of light cotton cloth Nathan had brought from the store.

Joshua straightened, fighting to keep his face from showing the pain. Caroline reached out and took his hands. "Please, Joshua. Won't you wait for just a day or two?"

He shook his head. "I'm already about a week too late. Just because the sale won't be final for five more days doesn't mean Ben Barber hasn't already started his maneuverings."

"I can't believe Walter did this to you," she murmured, near tears.

There was no more rancor in him. "He's pretty bitter. Thinks that it was me who betrayed him."

"But to risk everything you've worked for down there," Lydia cried, "just to get even with you."

"No, he's worried about Judith. He's been talking about selling out and retiring for about a year now. I just gave him a good excuse for doing it." At that, Joshua looked at Nathan. "Did you get that other matter taken care of?"

Nathan nodded.

"You put it where I told you?"

"Yes. I think you're right. It's a perfect place. It will be safe."

"Tell me when it hurts." Joshua had his arms raised and Doctor Richards had wrapped the first layer around his chest. Now he was cinching it up. "I want it firm, but not too tight."

"There," Joshua said, wincing in spite of himself. "That's good."

"I think I'd better go with you two," Benjamin said. "Maybe

Derek too. You can't be carrying that amount of cash around alone. We've already learned the dangers of that."

"No one's going to know I'm carrying it this time," he retorted.

"Why can't you just leave it where it is, if it's safe?" Lydia asked.

Joshua sighed. "Because all those bank notes are drawn on St. Louis banks. They're not exactly worthless up here, but you all know how skittish people are about accepting paper money, especially when it's paper issued by some bank they've never heard of." He shook his head again. "No, the sooner I'm down there and get it changed into specie, the better I like it."

Benjamin snorted. "And you're going to carry twenty-five thousand dollars in gold and silver back with you?"

Willard Richards's head came up at the naming of the amount, but he said nothing.

Benjamin barely noticed. "That's only—" He calculated quickly, the largest of all minted coins being worth ten dollars. "A minimum of twenty-five hundred coins. That should only weigh several hundred pounds and fill a huge chest. No one will ever notice."

"I'll use some of our employees down there. Men I can trust. We'll keep it well guarded."

"And this is my son that is supposed to have such wonderful business sense?" Benjamin snorted.

"I'm going," Joshua said flatly. "And that's that."

"And I'm going with you," Nathan said, with the same finality. "Keep arguing with me and I'm going to kick you in the ribs again."

Suddenly Caroline had a thought. "St. Louis is no longer an option, is it?"

Joshua turned. "What do you mean?"

"You thought we should move to St. Louis when the family leaves. Now . . ."

It said something about the turmoil he had been in for the past twenty-four hours that this implication had never hit him. He rocked back a little, pulling the cloth out of Doctor Richards's hands.

"Steady," the Apostle chided. "I'm almost done."

Joshua held Caroline's gaze for a moment or two, then looked away. "I don't know what it means," he mumbled.

Elder Richards took the pair of scissors and cut the cloth off. There were now several layers wrapped around Joshua's mid-section. "Hold this, please," he said to Caroline, motioning to where his fingers held the seam up against Joshua's body. As she did so, he reached for a small can of straight pins and began to fasten the edge of the cloth to the main portion of it. He glanced up at Nathan. "Did you watch how I did this?"

"Yes."

"Good." Then at Joshua's look his face went stern. "You can't be wrapping yourself, Joshua, so you may as well get used to the idea that Nathan will be with you. And you'd better be careful about doing too much tossing and turning or you are going to feel like you're sleeping with a porcupine."

Finished, he stepped back and surveyed his handiwork. "I think that will do it." He lifted a finger and shook it in Joshua's face. "I don't care how urgent things are, you're not leaving here before tomorrow. Understood?"

He didn't wait for an answer, just looked at Caroline. "I've got some rope if you need to tie him down for a while."

She smiled. "Thank you, Brother Richards. We really appreciate it."

He nodded, then glared at Joshua. "You hear me? Tomorrow at the very earliest."

"Yes, sir," Joshua said meekly.

As Willard Richards left, Joshua turned to Nathan. "We'll be making a stop in Quincy on the way down. I'm going to use three hundred dollars of that money to post me a reward for three particular men. And I'll double it if whoever catches them brings them back to me first."

Nathan's mouth opened to say something, then he just shook his head. This was not the time to talk about the foolishness of revenge.

———•———

They came in through the fence in pairs, moving slowly so as not to startle the horses in the corral. There was a heavy overcast, and neither moon nor stars gave any light. They were no more than shapes, blobs of slightly more intense blackness moving in a sea of blackness.

If it had been two or three years earlier, they would never have made it. Originally, Joshua's freight company had been in the southwestern part of Nauvoo, out by the river, near the intersection of Sidney and Marion Streets. But as the population soared and land within the city limits became more and more valuable, Joshua sold his land there and bought a large parcel of land out east of town not far from the temple. He built new stables, new barns, and eventually a new freight office, expanding his operation enormously. So had this silent group of men tried to make their way into the city to the old location, they would have been easily detected. The streets were still being patrolled at night by Brigham's organization of "bishops" and "deacons." Virtually every corner had a watch posted. But this far east of town there were no patrols, no watch set. And those that came knew this before they ever set out.

Leaving their horses tethered in a thick grove of trees a quarter of a mile away from their objective, they moved swiftly and silently along the dirt road that led to the Steed and Sons Freight and Portage Company.

The lead pair waited at the watering trough, peering into the night, straining to hear the slightest noise above the sound of the horses. Suddenly the leader had an idea. He reached out and rapped his knuckles on the thin layer of ice which covered the surface of the trough. "Pull the plug on this thing," he whispered.

His partner jerked up in surprise, but instantly he saw the genius of the idea. Sooner or later someone was going to sound the alarm. Why leave them with a ready-made supply of water? He groped in the darkness along the end of the trough that was opposite the pump, found the wooden plug there, and wrestled it out with both hands. There was a flash of a smile as water gushed out onto the frozen ground.

By the time the trough was empty, there were more pairs—twelve of them in all. The smell of kerosene was heavy in the air. Their leader clapped his hands quietly to get their attention. "All right," he whispered. "You know what to do. Two men to the smaller buildings. Two on each end of the barn and the stables. And don't just be tossing in the torch and running away. No one leaves until you're sure your building is completely in flames. Is that clear?"

There were soft grunts of assent.

"And no one lights their torch until you see mine. I'll be at the freight office. Everything gets started at once before someone can sound the alarm. Once the fires are going good, there's gonna be plenty of light, so keep your faces covered. We'll meet back at the horses."

"What about the animals inside the buildings?" someone asked.

After a moment of silence, there was a gruff, "What about them?"

There was a low whistle in the darkness. "We're just going to let them burn?"

"What are you so squeamish about all of a sudden?" another voiced hissed softly. "You weren't above shooting down those Mormon cows in Yelrome."

There was no reply to that. Then a third voice spoke up. "What about the horses here? There must be eight or ten head in the corral."

"Good thinking," grunted the leader. "Abner. Go open the corral gate. But don't shoo them out. They'll scatter wide enough once things get a little hotter around here." As the man beside him started to move, he reached and grabbed him, holding him still for a moment. He looked around. "I'll give you all five minutes to get into place and get your kerosene spread real good. Remember, no one lights until you see my torch."

He grinned wolfishly at them in the darkness. "This one's for Frank Worrell, boys, so let's do it right."

———•———

John Kay and Howard Egan walked slowly back and forth along the walk in front of Brigham Young's house. Each wore a heavy coat, gloves, a scarf wrapped around his face and ears, and two pairs of heavy woolen socks. But they still hugged themselves against the cold or beat at their bodies with flailing arms. It was an hour before dawn, and the coldest part of the night.

"Feel like singing?" Kay asked.

Howard watched his breath float slowly upward on the crisp air. "Anything to pass the time," he agreed. "What shall we sing?"

Kay chuckled softly. "How about, 'Awake, my soul, and with the sun, thy daily course of duty run'?"

Egan hooted softly. "Assuming we ever see the sun again." Then he quoted the next two lines. "'Shake off dull sloth, and early rise to pay thy morning sacrifice.'" He shook his head ruefully. "We've got the 'early rise' part down now, I think. Does being out here in the cold qualify as a morning sacrifice?"

John Kay, whose nature was naturally playful, was warming to his idea now. "Or how about we do, 'From Greenland's Icy Mountains,' only we'll change the words to 'On Nauvoo's Icy Plains'?" The man who loved to sing clapped his hands. "Or we could sing more loudly and start out with, 'Mortals, awake!'"

"Yes!" Egan exulted. "At the top of our lungs. Why should everyone else be—" He stopped, suddenly gaping.

"What?" said Kay, seeing his partner stiffen.

Egan lifted his arm, pointing to the northeast. "Look!"

Kay turned, and with a sudden chill that had nothing to do with the temperature, he stared at the orange glow lighting the underside of the low clouds, throwing the temple into sharp relief. "Oh, no!" Kay exclaimed. "Fire! It's the temple!"

Egan shook his head. "No, not the temple. Look! It's beyond that. Farther out."

From down the block they heard someone yelling. Then from the opposite direction another cry. The guards at other corners had seen it too. Even as they watched, the glow seemed to brighten.

Kay sprang into action. "Wake the President. I'll start hammering on doors. This is not some little bonfire, Howard. This is major."

———•———

Joshua came awake with a jerk and cried out as the pain jabbed into his side. Caroline was already up on one elbow. It was her shaking his shoulder that had brought him out of sleep. "Joshua, listen!"

He moaned as he rolled over slightly and sat up. "What?" But then he heard it too. Outside, men were shouting and calling to one another. He heard pounding. Someone was battering at a door across the street, probably his father's. He went rigid as he realized what the voices were crying. "Fire! Fire! We've got a fire!"

Carefully now, he threw back the covers and swung out of bed. Grunting with the pain, he hobbled over to the window. Their bedroom was on the back of the house and the window looked to the east. Joshua pulled back the curtain as Caroline moved up beside him. There was a sharp intake of breath. It was as if some hellish dawn had preempted nature. The eastern sky was brightly lit, the underside of the clouds pulsing with oranges and yellows which threw everything into sharp relief.

"Oh, Joshua," Caroline whispered. "What could it be?"

He shook his head slowly, not daring to speak what had jumped into his mind. "I don't know, Caroline." He turned, reaching for his trousers that hung over the back of a chair. "Go get Pa and Nathan. And Carl. Wake them all. Whatever it is, they're going to need every man we can find to fight it."

———•———

By sunrise, all efforts to fight the blaze were abandoned. The horrible shrieking cries of horses and mules and the frantic bellowing of oxen were silenced now. Hundreds of people stood on the far side of the street that fronted the freight yard, watching the roaring inferno—or rather six roaring infernos—with upraised hands to shield their eyes from the blistering heat. Joshua stood at the front of the crowd, staring vacantly at the sight before him, one arm holding Caroline tightly against him. The rest of the family were arrayed behind them in a half circle. No one spoke now. The enormity of what they saw before them shocked them all into silence.

Then all heads came up. There was a terrible screeching sound as the rafters of the largest warehouse began to twist and buckle. It was like watching a living thing gripped in its final death throes. The main beam that ran the length of the roof was tilting precariously now. The rafters clung to it, valiantly trying to hold it up against the dreaded flames. But then in one tremendous crash it gave way and collapsed inward. A huge tower of smoke, peppered with a million brilliant sparks of fire, surged upward, like some volcano blowing away its top to open up a crater to the sky.

Caroline's shoulders slumped. She sagged against Joshua and, for the first time, started to cry.

Nathan, standing off to the side just behind them, felt a tap on the shoulder. It was Carl. He held a gallon can, square and with a handle on the top. The cap was gone. Without a word, he handed it to Nathan. Nathan knew instantly what it was. It reeked of kerosene.

Joshua saw the movement out of the corner of his eye and turned. Carl, seeing that Joshua was watching them, spoke softly, but in a voice tight with shock and outrage. "This wasn't an accident, Joshua."

"I never thought it was," came the wooden reply.

There were just the three of them now. Joshua and his father stood back as Nathan took the grubbing hoe he carried and moved carefully into the smouldering pile of ashes that had once been the tack shed attached to the main stable.

"It was a good, strong steel box," Benjamin murmured. "I think you should be all right."

Joshua said nothing.

"Where was it?"

"Buried in a hole beneath the floorboards."

"Then hopefully . . ." But Benjamin stopped. In what had been the wagon shed they had already seen brass fittings melted into twisted puddles, so intense had been the heat.

Nathan moved gingerly, avoiding hot spots, one arm up across his face to block out the acrid smoke and the terrible smell of burnt hair and flesh. He stopped, looking around, trying to orient himself, then began to pull at the ruins with the hoe.

It took him only five minutes. There was a dull metallic clank, and then he started pulling back the charred timbers. Joshua and Benjamin moved forward swiftly. Then they stopped, staring in shock. Whether the lid had buckled with the heat and twisted open, or whether the bills inside had gotten so hot they burst into flames spontaneously, they didn't know and it didn't really matter much. All that mattered was that the cover to the metal strongbox was twisted grotesquely. As Nathan lifted the charred box up with the blade of the hoe, they could see that inside there were a few ashes remaining of what had once been twenty-five thousand dollars in St. Louis bank notes.

Joshua, face as pale as a dawning sky, turned away, holding one arm across his bandaged side, and stared blankly at the ground before him.

"How bad?" Carl asked.

Joshua shrugged, staring out the window into the darkness of the night. There were only five of the family in Joshua and Caroline's house. The rest of the family had stayed back for now, caring for their children throughout the day and letting Benjamin and Mary Ann, Nathan and Lydia, and Carl offer what comfort they could now that it was over.

After a moment, when it became clear that Joshua was not going to respond, Nathan answered for him. "Thirty-one horses, mules, or oxen dead, near as we can count. So far they've rounded up three of the horses that were set free. We're hoping to find the rest, but who knows? All the buildings are totally gone, of course."

"Wagons?"

"Everything in the shed was destroyed. Twenty-one in all. Five of those parked outside were set afire. Maybe one or two are salvageable."

"But I've got three out on the road somewhere," Joshua said with a sarcastic bark. "So we should be all right."

Caroline, sitting beside him, laid a hand on his. He barely noticed.

"If this were summer," Nathan explained, "it would be the other way around. Twenty-six wagons and teams would have been out on the road and only three or so in here."

"In the one warehouse, I had approximately fifteen thousand dollars' worth of dry goods slated to go to Fort Leavenworth," Joshua said without emotion. "We were going to load it up and ship it out tomorrow." Then came another dry and bitter laugh. "I'm not sure what I'll get out of that now. What's charcoal selling for nowadays?"

Mary Ann gave a little murmur of pain. "You have always been so generous in helping the family, Joshua. You know we'll stand with you now."

His head came up. "Right. When you're using every dime and every spare board and nail to get yourselves ready for spring."

"We'll do whatever has to be done," Nathan said quietly, and all nodded their affirmation of that.

"Do you think—," Lydia started. She hesitated, the thought almost too horrible to put into words. "Do you think Walter . . . ?"

Joshua shook his head. "No. Walter told me that our friends in Warsaw learned that I was there the day Worrell was shot. He warned me that they were going to try something." The pain and anger on his face twisted his mouth downward. "Oh, no, Walter's way of burning me out was much more gentle than this."

"Don't you think this might change his mind?" Mary Ann asked.

"It wouldn't matter if it did or didn't," Joshua said harshly. "The partnership between Joshua Steed and Walter Samuelson is over." He half turned in his chair, looking up at Nathan. "Getting down to St. Louis now is imperative, Nathan. Those other businesses are all I have left. If I lose them to the Barber boys, we'll be without anything."

"I understand."

"I'm going alone. Ribs or no ribs."

For a long moment, the two brothers stared at each other, something passing between them, then finally Nathan nodded. "All right."

Caroline grabbed at Joshua's arm. "I don't want you going alone, Joshua. Now that the river's closed, you'll have to travel right past Warsaw. And with your ribs stove in like they are, you're in no shape to be trying to get away if someone comes after you."

The two brothers looked at each other, Nathan's eyes questioning. Joshua finally nodded. "Tell her, Nathan," Joshua finally said.

"Tell me what?"

Nathan sighed, glancing sideways at Lydia. She had not heard this as yet either. "We saw Elder Taylor as we were coming home tonight. There is some bad news."

Lydia's mouth tightened. "What?"

"Do you remember Solomon talking about Edmund Durfee? His was the first settlement hit by the mobs down in Yelrome."

"Yes," said Caroline. "Didn't they come back the second day and burn him out again?"

"That's the one," Nathan said.

Lydia spoke up. "The Durfees have been in the store several times. Father Durfee asked if we might give him credit for a time, until he could gather in some of his crops. I said yes, of course."

Nathan looked away, his countenance darkening. The Durfees had also been one of the families that he and Joshua had brought back as part of the rescue effort of the Morley Settlement. Edmund Durfee was a man of great faith who had come into the Church early in its history.

"Yesterday," he began slowly, "Brother Durfee and some of his family went back to Yelrome to get a load of their grain. I saw him before he left, and he said that they would be safe because the state militia have been down there making sure that there are no more incidents. But evidently, our trusty militia left earlier in the day to visit friends. That was all it took. The Durfees dug some potatoes and got a load of wheat, then went to bed last night. They were staying at Solomon Hancock's place—the boys out in the barn, and Father Durfee in the house. They were planning to leave first thing this morning."

Lydia's eyes had gone very round. "No," she said.

Nathan just nodded. "About eleven o'clock, the boys heard a noise and looked outside. The mob had come in and set fire to some of the unthreshed grain. There was a wind blowing and the flames were moving in the direction of the barn. The boys ran and woke up their father and Brother Hancock."

"They thought the mob had fled," Benjamin spoke up. He had been there when John Taylor had given the report. "They looked around but could see no one, so they started fighting the fire and taking the horses and cows out of the stable."

"Suddenly," Nathan went on, "a man stepped out from behind a tree and fired one shot at Brother Hancock. They heard a shrill whistle and suddenly fifteen or twenty men who had been hiding behind the log fence stood up and started shooting. Everyone scattered, of course." He looked down at his hands. "But Father Durfee was struck in the throat and killed instantly."

"Oh, no!" Mary Ann gasped.

"Yes," Joshua said, grim as death now. "They found out later that one of the mob bet another one a gallon of whiskey that he couldn't hit the old man."

"I can't believe it," Lydia whispered in horror. "How old was he?"

"About the same age as me," Benjamin answered.

Joshua turned to Caroline now. "I think those cowards from Warsaw have done all that they're going to do to me," he said, "but I'm not taking any chances and leaving you here alone."

"We want you and the children to move in with us until Joshua comes back," Nathan explained.

Caroline just looked at Nathan, barely comprehending what was being suggested. Finally, she turned to her husband. "And you're going to go to St. Louis in spite of all this? Joshua, if they catch you—"

"They're not going to catch me. I'm going to cross the river into Missouri and give Warsaw and Quincy a wide berth. I'll travel under a different name." He took her hand. "I'll be all right. Really I will."

"Don't go, Joshua," she pleaded. "Please! I don't care about those businesses. We'll be all right. We can get by."

He took a deep breath, looking around the circle now, looking as tired and defeated as Nathan had ever seen him. "There's something else you need to know, Caroline."

She half closed her eyes, not wanting to hear any more.

"When I was buying up those businesses down there—the construction company, the cabinet mill, and so on—so we'd have employment for the family when we left here?"

"Yes?"

"Well, I borrowed a lot of money in order to do that. Not even Walter knew that."

Nathan leaned forward, his face intent. "What are you saying, Joshua?"

He rubbed his eyes with the heels of his hands, pressing them in tightly as though he were trying to staunch a wound. "I used the freight business as my collateral."

Benjamin, who was standing behind Mary Ann, looked as if he had been struck. He groped for the chair back and then sat down slowly. "How much?" he asked.

"Fifty-six thousand dollars."

There was an audible gasp from each of them.

Joshua went on now, thoroughly weary. "I've paid back about ten thousand of that. Actually, I wasn't going to trade in that cash I got from Walter for specie. I was going to use it to pay down the debt."

"And now it's gone," Lydia said in a small, horrified voice.

"And the freight business with it," Nathan said, equally horrified at the implications of what Joshua had just told them.

"I've got more than enough to cover the balance with my equity in those other businesses," Joshua explained, still looking at Caroline. "More than enough." There was a long pause. "If . . ." It hung there, like a bomb about to explode. "*If* I can get fair market value for them. But if Ben Barber gets a whiff of what's happened . . . ?" He didn't finish it. "I have to go, Caroline, and I have to go now."

She lowered her head, the sickness showing on her face. "I understand, Joshua."

Chapter Notes

Edmund Durfee, a faithful Latter-day Saint from the early days of Kirtland, was killed in the Morley Settlement on 15 November 1845 in the manner described here (see HC 7:523, 528; *Edmund Durfee*, p. 22). He was one of the first, if not the first, to be martyred for the cause of truth following the deaths of Joseph and Hyrum and Samuel Smith.

The carriage driver pulled the single seater hack up in front of a large brownstone building. He leaned down from his upper seat and peered at Will and Alice. "This is it."

Will climbed stiffly out, feeling the cold all the way down into his bones. Half snow, half sleet was coming down out of a leaden sky. He helped Alice down, then reached for their two bags and set them on the cobblestone street.

"That'll be four bits, please."

Will fumbled in his vest pocket and found a half-dollar and handed it up. "Thank you."

The man touched his hat, then clucked to the horse. The carriage rattled away.

The man who opened the door to their knock was a slight man, not quite as tall as Will's nearly six feet, but twenty or thirty pounds lighter. He had a high, receding hairline, and wore a Greek-style beard, with one tuft of whiskers just below his lower lip. He was young, in his mid-twenties, Will guessed. Will thought he looked familiar, but wasn't sure.

"Yes?"

"We're looking for Mr. Samuel Brannan."

"I'm Mr. Brannan."

That helped explain the familiarity. Will had probably seen him while he was in Nauvoo. "I'm Will Steed, Brother Brannan," Will said, "and this is my wife, Alice."

"Yes?" There was no sign that the name meant anything to him.

"We've just come from Nauvoo."

His eyes momentarily widened; then his face broke into a warm smile. "Nauvoo? Why, bless my soul." He stepped back, opening the door wider. "Come in."

They stepped inside and Will set down their cases. "You haven't received a letter from President Young concerning us?"

There was a moment's reflection. "No, I don't believe so."

Alice spoke for the first time. "We made very good time. The Ohio was still open almost to Pittsburgh. President Young's letter is probably coming overland."

"What does it say?" Brannan asked.

Will smiled slowly. "Well, we're here to help. I think we'd better sit down and talk."

———————

Savannah sat on the edge of the bed, her legs crossed, elbows on her knees, her chin resting in her hands. Her mother had piled her red hair on top of her head and tied it with a ribbon. She wore a green dress with a white pinafore and looked quite bewitching, which was exactly what she hoped to be. She had come to wheedle something out of her grandfather because everyone else had told her no.

She watched Mary Ann, who was fussing around him, making sure he looked just fine. As she finished, Savannah began her quest.

"Grandpa, why can't I go to the temple dedication?"

Benjamin turned around and smiled. "Honey, this is just a partial dedication of the temple. And it's only for a small group of priesthood leaders. There just isn't room for a large crowd in the attic story."

She wrinkled up her nose. "The attic story?"

"Yes, the top floor of the temple. It's called the attic story."

"Why? Do they keep old things up there?"

"No," Mary Ann laughed. "It's just the top floor of the temple. So they call it the attic floor."

"Please, Grandpa. You could ask President Young if it's all right. I could sit on your lap."

He stepped to the bed and bent over to give her a quick peck on the cheek. "I'm afraid not, Savannah. No children this time."

"When the full temple is dedicated in April, then we will all go, Savannah," Mary Ann explained.

"Why don't we wait until April and do it all at once?"

"Because Brigham is very anxious to start giving the endowment, and he can't do that until that part of the building is dedicated." He held up his hand, cutting off the inevitable next question. "The endowment is a sacred ordinance of the priesthood, Savannah. That's all I can tell you about it." And then to try and deflect her thinking he changed the subject. "No word from your father yet, I suppose?"

"Not yet. It's been almost two weeks now and Mama is very worried."

"We all are, Savannah," Benjamin said, following them out. "We are praying hard for your father."

"So am I," she said gravely. "I'm also praying that Papa will let us go west with you, Grandpa."

"I know, Savannah. We're all praying for that too."

———— ◆ ————

"This special meeting of the Steed family women's council will now come to order," Mary Ann intoned. The low buzz of conversation died and they all turned to look at her.

"My," she said a little sheepishly, "that sounded awfully official, didn't it?"

They laughed. In actuality, all of their women's meetings were pretty informal. And this would be no different.

There were nine of them besides Benjamin and Mary Ann. On his return from the temple that afternoon, Benjamin had spent almost an hour telling Mary Ann all that had transpired.

It had so excited her that she proposed that they convene an immediate meeting with the women of the family. So Benjamin had gone from house to house, trailing an air of mystery and pointedly suggesting this was for ladies only and that the men should stay home with the children. That ensured that the women came—with the exception of Melissa, who declined the invitation—and that they came with an air of more than a little anticipation.

"Father Steed, as you know, has just returned from the temple dedication," Mary Ann went on. "He has something I think we all need to hear. Rebecca, would you open our meeting and ask the Lord's blessings to be with us? Then we'll turn the time over to you," she finished, looking at Benjamin.

As Rebecca finished her prayer and sat down again, Benjamin stood up and moved behind his chair. He leaned forward, using the back of the chair as a podium. "Well, before I say what it is your mother feels needs discussing, let me just say a word or two about the service. It was a wonderful meeting. I wish all of you could have been there."

"Who was there, Father Steed?" Lydia asked.

"Well, all of the Twelve who are in town, of course. Uncle John Smith was there as a patriarch. Bishops Whitney and Miller were both there. Joseph Young, President of the Seventy, members of the stake presidency, some of the temple committee. Actually that was why I was invited. W. W. Phelps was there too. And William Clayton, of course, as clerk to the Twelve."

He paused, letting his mind run back over the morning's meeting. "Brigham gave the dedicatory prayer. It was brief, just as it was at conference. It would come as no surprise to you to know that he pled with the Lord to sustain and deliver us from the hand of our enemies until we can finish the temple and complete the work God expects of us there." He grew more thoughtful. "In Brother Brigham's mind, the giving of the endowment has to receive the same attention, maybe even more so, as the preparations for going west. It is a matter of the utmost urgency to him."

"Now that the upper floor is dedicated," Jessica asked, "did he say how soon they will start to give the endowment?"

"Yes, and that is why we are here. He wants the rooms ready in order to begin administering the ordinance by the tenth."

"Of December?" Caroline asked in surprise. "Tomorrow is December first. He's talking that soon?"

"Yes."

"I can't believe it," Jessica whispered. "We've waited so long, and now it's really going to happen."

"And not only that," Benjamin smiled, "you are going to play a role in getting the rooms ready. Brigham has called upon the sisters to help so that the work can begin on the day he has set." He looked down at Mary Ann. "I think you should tell them the rest."

He sat down and Mary Ann stood up. Her face was infused with excitement and happiness. "We are very blessed that, as a family, we are being given an opportunity to help in the final preparations of the temple. As you know, many of the sisters, including some of us, have been busy making curtains and other furnishings for the temple. We have also been helping sew the temple clothing. Now President Young has made another request of us."

They were all watching her closely, the feeling of anticipation rising higher.

"I don't fully understand this. Perhaps Benjamin can explain more, but there are different rooms that will be used for the ceremonies."

"Yes," Benjamin spoke up, "this will make much more sense to you once you have been endowed, and I can't say too much about it here, but the endowment symbolically represents man's eternal journey, his moving from premortal existence through mortality and back into the presence of God. So as part of the endowment there are different rooms, and you actually move from one room to another to symbolize the progression from one state to another. There will be a garden room, representing the Garden of Eden. There will be one room which represents the world, and one—which is the largest room in the attic—which will be the celestial room. When you enter the celestial room it represents returning to the presence of God."

"When you received your endowment from Brother Joseph," Jenny asked of Benjamin, "did you do all that?"

"After a fashion. Joseph administered the ordinance to a few of us in the upper floor of his store. We had to improvise somewhat."

"It all sounds so wonderful," Lydia said. Without thinking, she rubbed her hand across her stomach, now starting to show the first signs of the life within her.

Mary Ann continued again. "Well, here's the problem. Brigham has asked the wives of the Twelve to supervise getting the rooms ready. As you know, a call already went out to families all around Nauvoo to contribute rugs and carpets that can be used in the various rooms. Vilate Kimball has asked our family group if we could meet immediately with some other sisters to make the cotton veil that will be hung for the main ordinance room."

"A veil?" Kathryn asked curiously. "What will it be for?"

"You'll have to wait and see," Benjamin said with a knowing smile.

"Anyway," Mary Ann said, "President Young has also asked families to contribute potted plants or small evergreen trees which can be placed in the garden room so that it will have the feeling of an actual garden. He also has asked for a few of our finest pieces of furniture and lamps that could be used in the celestial room. He is especially concerned about that room because he feels like it needs to symbolize the glory of the celestial kingdom. It must be very beautiful."

She stopped and they all began to talk at once. Benjamin let it go on for a minute or two, then raised his hands. "It is exciting, isn't it?" he exulted. "Think of it. The endowment has not been on the earth for nearly two thousand years, and not only will we be among the first to receive it, we shall be privileged to help prepare the place where it is to be given."

He stood. "I shall leave you." He grinned sheepishly. "I won't be of much help to you now. You have some planning to do, and it sounds to me like this particular assignment has already been put in good hands."

When Lydia opened the door and saw Joshua standing there, she took one look at his face and the cry of joy that had started within her died in her throat.

"Hello, Lydia," he said heavily.

Recovering somewhat, she opened the door wider. "Joshua, when did you get back?"

"Just a while ago." He looked past her. "Are Caroline and the children here?"

"The children are, but Caroline is over at Derek and Rebecca's helping put together some things for the temple."

"How about Nathan?"

She stepped back, motioning him in. "He's in the kitchen. Go sit down. I'll get him."

Joshua nodded, looking numb, and went into the sitting room. A moment later, as Nathan appeared, Joshua heard Lydia rounding up all the children and suggesting they go upstairs to read a story.

Joshua took the hardback chair by the lamp table. Nathan sat down on the sofa so he would be facing him directly. For a moment he studied his brother's face, then spoke. "Not good?"

There was a slow, heavy shake of the head.

"Tell me about it. What happened? We've been worried sick about you. How are the ribs, by the way?"

Joshua waved that away. "A little tender, but I'm all right." Then he continued, his voice dropping to a dull monotone. "First of all, you have to understand how things are in St. Louis. The news about Alice and Will is all over town. Judith had sent out the letters of invitation for the weddings already. Walter had bragged to everyone about hiring a riverboat and bringing the whole family down. So when Alice and Will showed up with their news, it became a major scandal. Everyone is outraged." His dark brows knitted together even more. "Unquestionably, it was having to face all those people that was part of Judith's illness. But aside from that, I can tell you that the Steeds are not high on anyone's list of favorite people down there right now. And having the whole situation be caused by a call to follow some Mormon missionary assignment doesn't help any either. Not in Missouri."

Nathan felt sick for Joshua. He and Walter were, if not at the very pinnacle of St. Louis society, then very close to it. To fall from there would be long and precipitous. That it had been exactly that showed in the dullness in Joshua's eyes. He looked as if he had endured an extended whipping, then been dragged behind a team of horses. "So what happened on your loan?" Nathan asked softly.

"Well, to no one's surprise," Joshua went on, his voice void of life, "Ben Barber had already been around town, talking to people we do business with about the awful thing Joshua Steed had done. How could you ever trust a man like that? Even his own lifelong business partner, the venerable Walter Samuelson, had broken things off with him because his word means nothing now."

Feeling was coming back into his voice now, but it was dark, bitter, every word coming out as though it tasted of bile. "You'd have to know Ben Barber. He's water moccasin, cobra, and prairie rattlesnake all rolled into one. He's a harlot in a business suit, smooth as silk and deadly as arsenic. And he's been after our businesses for two years now."

"I can't believe Walter sold out to him, knowing that he's that kind of a person."

"Walter was betrayed, at least in his mind. He feels that selling out to Barber was no more than what I deserved."

"Was he still there?"

"He and Judith left the day after I arrived. He wouldn't see me."

Joshua leaned forward now, elbows on his knees, and put his face in his hands. He began to rub his eyes. "I've had a lot of dealings with my banker over the years, so at first I thought it would be all right."

He looked up, and his eyes were dark and withdrawn. The look in them shocked Nathan. He had never seen him look so vulnerable, so totally beaten.

"But," Joshua continued, "when I explained about my stables being burned out, the bank panicked. Note how I said that. The banker assured me that he still trusted me completely, that he knew I was good for the debt. But the bank? Now, that was a different story. It was not in the best interests of the bank, he was most sorry to say, to have that big a loan outstanding with only a burned-out business for collateral. I tried to tell him that I'll have another raft of lumber coming downriver first thing next spring, which will bring in more than enough to pay back what I owe. I was even willing to consign the whole thing to him."

"But he wouldn't accept that?"

"Well, at first I thought he was going to go for it. But two days later he called me back to the bank." There was a long silence. Joshua was staring at the wallpaper now, letting his eyes trace the spiraling pattern. "Barber and his little weasel brother were there. They had heard about the fire and 'come to help.'" His voice dripped with needle-sharp sarcasm. "They told the banker they wanted to buy out my share of all the businesses we were now 'partners' in, thanks to Walter. That would pay off the debt to the bank and leave me free and clear."

He finally looked at Nathan. "The fact that their offer was worth about thirty cents on the dollar was purely incidental, of course."

"No," Nathan said slowly. "And the banker did it? Couldn't you refuse to sell to them?"

"Yes, if I hadn't owed the bank forty-six thousand dollars."

Nathan sat back, deeply shaken. "So it's done?"

There was a bitter laugh. "Signed and delivered. Joshua Steed no longer owns business or property in St. Louis, Missouri. None. Zero! Not a single bale of cotton."

"I can't believe it," Nathan said, his voice thin and strained. "Just like that and it's all gone?"

"Gives one thought, doesn't it?" Joshua said with a mocking

smile. "Here, just a few days ago, I was offering to bankroll the family's trip west. Now . . ." He shook his head. "Caroline and I will be lucky if we can make it through the winter until I can get that lumber down here and sold."

For several moments there was silence as each considered all that this meant. Finally Nathan leaned forward. "The store is yours, Joshua."

His head came up with a start.

"Caroline put twenty thousand dollars of her money into it."

"We're not going to take the store," he said shortly.

"Why not? It's half yours anyway. We're leaving. We've got to sell it."

"Carl wants it."

Now the sick feeling in Nathan deepened even more as he began to realize just how profound this disaster was proving to be. "Carl can't buy it. To no one's surprise, the construction business has collapsed here in Nauvoo. Carl hasn't had an order of bricks for two weeks. He still wants Derek's farm, but he won't be able to pay him anything for it until spring, when hopefully things will pick up again."

Joshua just stared at him.

"We're still pretty well off," Nathan went on quickly. "We have the store. We've had people coming to look at the house. We used those three wagons that were partially burned to make two good ones."

And then suddenly his chin lifted and his eyes widened. "Come with us, Joshua!" Nathan said.

"What?" Joshua said, startled out of his thoughts.

"Come west with us. There's nothing to hold you here now."

There was one soft hoot of derision. "No thank you."

"Why not? You've got to make a new start anyway. Why not out west? Why not with the family?"

Abruptly, Joshua stood up, his face hard. "Well, in the first case, I've got some scores to settle. There's that little matter of burning me out. I've learned the names of at least some of the men who did it. And then there's the Barber brothers."

"Don't, Joshua."

"No," he said, his voice cracking like a whip. "Don't you give me that turn-the-other-cheek business, Nathan. They've ruined me. I can understand Walter's part in this. It was a terrible thing he did, but I can understand why he did it. But the others? No, there's a very large score to be put to rest on that account."

"You're not only going to put yourself in danger again, but you're going to break Mother's heart if you go after them."

He shrugged. "Once you leave Nauvoo, Mother won't know."

Nathan blew out his breath, wanting to grab him and shake him as if he were one of the children. "Think about what Brigham said, Joshua. A whole new civilization. A brand-new start. It's what you do best. Come with us."

Joshua turned away. "It's been a long two weeks, Nathan. I'd better round up Caroline and the children and go home."

Nathan stood now. "I'm sorry, Joshua. I know this isn't the time to talk about that. But will you at least think about it? If you've got to start again anyway, at least—"

Joshua's look stopped him short. His eyes were like the smouldering coals left after the rest of the stables were gone up in smoke. "Let me tell you something, Nathan," he said in a very low voice. "I've been pretty cooperative with your God lately. I let Will and Caroline be baptized. I gave in on Savannah. I was willing to help the family with anything I had. I even went toe to toe with Samuelson so that things would work out between him and Alice. And what has all of that got me?"

He rubbed his hand along his jaw, looking very old now. "I lost a daughter in a terrible accident. My son is on his way to California and I may never see him again. And now I'm back where I was in life fifteen years ago."

"Joshua, I—"

"You go ahead and be faithful to what you believe, Nathan. But from now on, I think I'll try it on my own."

"Watch it, Kathryn, your foot's catching on the rug." Peter started to rise. "Here, let me move it."

"No," she cried. "Please, Peter, don't."

He sank back down, still poised to leap out of the chair and catch her if she tripped.

"If I can't even lift my foot above a throw rug, how will I ever get around a campground?" Gripping the crutches, she adjusted her feet slightly to balance her body, then swung the crutches forward, setting them down solidly before pulling the rest of her body forward again. Barely waiting to get set again, she repeated the action, coming smoothly forward another foot, then another.

He clapped his hands. "Good, Kathryn. That's very good."

She was beaming now, more pleased than a child who has just mastered her first step. She did it again. And a fifth time.

He stood, applauding loudly. "Bravo! I think you've got it."

Breathing in short, quick gulps, straining with the concentration of making her body obey her mind, she crossed the remaining distance and fell into Peter's arms. She let the crutches slip from her grasp and clatter to the floor. "I'm getting it, Peter," she breathed excitedly. "I really am getting it."

He kissed her on the nose. "You are, Kathryn. I can see that you are."

He meant it, and she saw that he meant it. Letting him take her weight in his arms, she threw her head back and laughed triumphantly. "I can walk!" she cried. "I can walk."

"I think with some more practice you will have it mastered."

"I have to," she said, her expression sobering. "I can't use a wheelchair on the trail. Even the best of campgrounds will be too rough. I have to be able to get around at least somewhat."

"I'll be there to help you, Miss McIntire."

"Mrs. Ingalls to you, sir," she murmured airily, still euphoric.

He helped her over to the bed and saw her seated comfortably, then pulled a chair around to face her. They were living in the small house that had once been Benjamin and Mary Ann's first home in Nauvoo. Benjamin and Mary Ann now lived in the two-story "second house" to the side of this one, and this house had become the traditional home for newlyweds in the family.

Her face was still flushed with excitement and with the effort it had taken to cross the room. He watched her, marveling at her beauty, still a little dazed that she had finally consented to marry him. Others might complain about a bad hailstorm, he thought with a smile, remembering that terrible, wonderful evening in early September, but he never would again.

"What are you thinking?" she said.

"Well, I wanted to talk with you about an idea that's been percolating in my mind."

She laughed merrily. "Percolating? You should write poetry, Mr. Ingalls."

He smiled, then went on, earnest now and a little concerned as well. "Do you remember Levinah Murphy?"

Kathryn's lips pursed slightly. "I don't believe I do."

"She's a widow. She and her children lived here in Nauvoo for a time, but they've all since moved back to Tennessee—all, that is, except for her married daughter Sarah, who I think now lives in St. Louis."

"Oh?" Kathryn couldn't figure out why Peter was telling her about this family.

"Anyway, a few years ago, back when we were doing baptisms for the dead in the river, Sister Murphy was one of the first to participate. So was I. That's how I met her and her children, and learned about their situation. Seeing all those children, seven of them, and knowing they had lost their father not long before that—well, it reminded me of how I lost my parents, and it made me feel bad. So now and then I tried to find opportunities to help the Murphys out around their place. It wasn't much, but I tried." He suddenly got an embarrassed look on his face. "I guess Sister Murphy's always felt grateful to me for that, and so I've gotten an occasional letter from her since she moved away."

Kathryn nodded. She wasn't surprised that she had not heard about this from Peter before. It was just like him to do something nice for another person and not talk about it. So why would he be telling her about it now? Before she could ask, Peter went on.

"I recently received a letter from her. She'd heard that the Saints plan to head west, and she would like to join us. But given her circumstances—she's a widow with five unmarried children now, living in Tennessee, far from the main body of Saints—it seemed like a difficult proposition. One of her concerns is that she not be a burden. She is determined not to be a burden to the Church."

Kathryn was listening carefully to him, wondering again why he had brought these matters up. It seemed to be more than just idle conversation. "So what is she going to do?"

"Well, that's what is interesting. She says in her letter that she's now found a possible way for getting herself west so she can meet us there."

"What? You mean go alone?"

"Not alone, just a different way. She says there are many emigrant trains that will be headed to California and Oregon in the spring, and she plans to take her children and go with one of those trains. If she has to, she says she can even hire on as a laundress or cook. But she may not have to do that if her two married daughters and their husbands go. So she sees this as an opportunity to make the journey west and at the same time not be a burden on the Saints."

"Yes," Kathryn said slowly. That was the third time he had used the word *burden*, and now she thought she knew where this might be leading. Her chin lowered and she stared at her legs. "I don't want to be a burden either."

He jumped a little, then was instantly contrite. "Kathryn, it's not you I'm worried about."

She gaped at him. "Then who?"

"Me!"

"You! How would you be a burden?"

"Well, first of all, I have nothing. No money, virtually no job now, no wagons, no food. Unfortunately, Kathryn McIntire Ingalls, you married the absolute poorest member of this family. I was hoping that I could do things for Joshua and Carl, help pay for their assistance." He shook his head. "But now that neither of them has money, I don't know quite what to do."

Her eyes were soft and misty, touched by his honesty about himself, and more touched that he hadn't thought of her when he was thinking of burdens.

"And that's only part of it," he went on. "Oh, I know the family will help us. We won't be left, but think about this. We will have six families going, seven if Joshua and Caroline decide to accompany us by some miracle."

"Yes?"

"The ideal number for a wagon is a family of four or five. More is a real challenge."

"So?"

"Think about it. Mother and Father Steed will likely go with someone, most probably Matthew and Jenny, since they have only two children."

She started to interrupt, but he held up a finger and went on quickly. "Derek and Rebecca make a family of five. Nathan and Lydia have seven, so they'll be more than full. And Jessica and Solomon have eight."

Now she saw clearly why he was troubled. "That doesn't leave much room for us, does it?"

"No," he responded. "Derek says we'll go with them, or just get another wagon. But you know we'll be lucky to have five wagons. And that's not to say anything about food and a hundred other items."

The euphoria she had felt a few minutes before had totally evaporated.

Peter went on in deep dejection. "And if that's not bad enough, there's one other thing. I'm going to be the least helpful person on the trail. I can't make anything. I've never driven a team." He held out his hands, staring at them. They were soft and stained with ink. "I'm a printer. Don't suppose there'll be much use for that on the road west."

"That's not true," she exclaimed. "You're not useless. Look at all you're doing now. Keeping a record of everything. Making sure everything is accounted for. Everyone knows you are valuable to the family."

"I don't deny that. But once we cross the river, how much bookkeeping will there be? We'll be eating our inventory, not recording it. Who's going to need to keep track of how much money we do or don't have then?"

She waited, hurting for him, wanting to reach out and smooth away the lines around his mouth. "So what are you suggesting?" And then, remembering that he had started this conversation with mention of Sister Levinah Murphy, her eyes grew wide. "You're not thinking of us going separately!"

"Just hear me out, Kathryn. It's just an idea."

"I'm listening," she said, looking suddenly very dubious.

"A few weeks ago, I saw an article in one of the Springfield papers. It reported that there are some wealthy farming families around the capital who are talking of going to California and Oregon in the spring. They're having weekly study meetings, reading all the books and looking at the maps, so they'll be better prepared. One of the men they interviewed said that once the weather breaks, they'll be looking for others to go with them, especially young men they could hire to help along the trail. He said they'll be looking for tutors for the children, drovers, teamsters."

"Not go with the family?" she said in a small voice. It completely overwhelmed her. "Besides, as I understand it, we're not going to either Oregon or California, Peter. I thought Brother Brigham said we're going to the Rocky Mountains."

"I know, I know. But most of the way it's the same trail. I'm not saying this is what we're going to do, Kathryn, but think about it for a minute. Suppose we could hire on as tutors. We both helped Jessica when she had the school here. That's one thing I can do. Then we'd have a way, we'd not have to worry about having our own outfit. We . . ." He stopped, overwhelming himself with the breadth of his thinking. "We could go with them as far as Fort Laramie, or something like that, then wait for our group to come."

"They'll not want a cripple with them any more than our family will."

He gave her a sharply critical look. "My worry is convincing them to hire *me*," he said. "But we could teach the children, Kathryn. Then neither one of us would be a burden to them. I know it's slim, but maybe there's a chance it would work."

She didn't have the heart to discourage him, so she finally nodded. "I think you're right, Peter. I think it is something to think about."

His face lit up. "I think so too. Maybe it will never happen, but it is something to think about."

Chapter Notes

On 30 November 1845 the Twelve met with other priesthood leaders and dedicated the attic story of the temple in preparation for its being used for the administration of the endowment (see HC 7:534–35). At this time the Saints worked busily to provide the temple's attic story with plants, mirrors, paintings, and other furniture (see *Women of Nauvoo*, pp. 150–51). On 7 December 1845, the cotton veil that the sisters sewed for use in the endowment was hung in the attic story.

The tenth of December, 1845, dawned dazzling bright. As the day wore on it became pleasantly warm, at least ten degrees warmer than the blustery cold of the day before. The snow from a previous storm was gone, and had it not been for the bareness of the trees and the brown grass, it might have passed for an early spring day. It was a fitting day to begin the administration of the endowment to the general membership of The Church of Jesus Christ of Latter-day Saints.

With hundreds upon hundreds of Saints anxiously awaiting their turn to participate in the ordinance, the Twelve were faced with the decision of where to begin. In May of 1842, Joseph Smith had introduced a small group of men to the endowment. So now, until they could share the ordinance with more men and women in the temple, there were only a limited number to help in giving it to others. That limited the numbers of who could receive it at first and raised the question of who should be first.

Finally, it was determined that they would start with those of the Twelve who had not received it under Joseph's hand, their wives, and a few of the other General Authorities and their wives.

The work began at 3:00 p.m. on the afternoon of December tenth. It would take twelve and a half hours before the thirty people—fifteen men and fifteen women—were finished. Two widowed sisters were also present at that first session—a singular and yet well-deserved honor. Agnes Smith, wife of Don Carlos Smith, Joseph's beloved younger brother, was there. She was accompanied by her sister-in-law Mary Fielding Smith, wife of the martyred Hyrum Smith.

As a member of the temple committee, Benjamin and his wife, Mary Ann, had been invited by President Young to be there as well on that first night. Benjamin had been there on that day in 1842 when Joseph first introduced the endowment, but Mary Ann had not. Sorely tempted to be part of this historic occasion, they finally opted to wait for a few days so that the rest of the adult members of the Steed family could all receive their endowments at the same time.

At about three-thirty a.m. on the morning of the eleventh of December, a very tired but jubilant Brigham Young and Heber C. Kimball left the temple with their wives. They went to the Joseph Kingsbury home, just a short distance from the temple, rested for a few hours, had breakfast together, then returned to the temple and started the second group.

This day more leaders and their wives came—the seven Presidents of the First Council of Seventy, presidents of the priesthood quorums, members of the high council. Fifteen more people—seven males and eight females—were endowed on that day. Among them were two additional widows from Joseph Smith's family. Lucy Mack Smith, beloved mother of the Prophet and revered Saint in her own right, was there. She was accompanied by Mercy Fielding Thompson Smith, plural wife to Hyrum after her husband, Robert Thompson, had died, and sister to Mary Fielding Smith.

In later life, Brigham Young would observe how some Saints said, "We never began to build a temple without the bells of hell beginning to ring." That lesson was reaffirmed in December 1845, for on the very day the long-awaited giving of the endowment began, Brigham received a letter from Samuel Brannan in New York City. It was filled with much news of his progress in chartering a ship to go to California. It also contained news that showed that Satan's opposition had flared up once again.

———•———

Brigham was standing outside the main door to the temple talking with several people. The moment he spied the Steeds coming up the walkway, he excused himself and strode over to greet them. "There you are!" he boomed pleasantly. "How good to see you all here!"

He moved from couple to couple, shaking hands and speaking briefly with each one—Matthew and Jenny, Peter and Kathryn, Derek and Rebecca, Solomon and Jessica, Nathan and Lydia, and finally, Benjamin and Mary Ann. Caroline had been invited to come, but decided under the circumstances—Joshua was still under a dark cloud following his return to Nauvoo—that it was best that she wait.

Brigham turned to Mary Ann. "I received a letter from New York a few days ago."

She brightened instantly. "From Will and Alice?"

"No, from Samuel Brannan. But he scribbled a quick note at the bottom of his letter saying that our young couple had just arrived that afternoon. It was dated the twenty-eighth of last month."

"Oh, good. Caroline will be so relieved."

"So how are the preparations for their voyage coming?" Nathan inquired.

"Good. They have chartered a ship, the *Brooklyn* by name, and plan to leave in mid-January. They are enrolling the Saints in the East now. However," he said, his face darkening, "there is news that is not so good."

"What is that?" Benjamin asked.

"Well, two things. The first didn't come from Sam Brannan, but it's news from Springfield. Have you heard about the indictment handed down by the United States circuit court there?"

Benjamin harrumphed in total disgust. "Yes, Brother Pratt told me about that yesterday. Eight members of the Twelve were indicted for bogus-making."

"What?" Nathan cried. "I haven't heard about this. Counterfeiting? Surely that's some kind of a joke."

"I wish it were," Brigham said grimly. "Unfortunately, we have had trouble with counterfeiters in this area, transient river traffickers who have preyed on our people. Now someone has sworn we are in league with them and supporting their evil efforts."

"And there's more bad news besides that?" Solomon inquired.

Brigham's countenance fell even further. "Yes, and far more serious. Brother Brannan was down in Washington recently, visiting the Saints there. He learned that the secretary of war and other members of the cabinet are laying plans against us."

"No!" several of them cried at once, alarm sharpening their voices.

"They claim it is against the law for an armed body of men to leave the United States and go to some other government. Since Upper California belongs to Mexico, and ownership of Oregon is still being disputed between the United States and Great Britain, they plan to prevent us from leaving."

"How can they do that?" Lydia cried. "It's the people here who are driving us out. We don't want to go."

"You assume we are dealing with just and rational men," Brigham answered somberly. "According to Brannan, they say it will not do to have us go, but neither can they let us stay within the United States."

"So what do we do, hang from the sky somewhere?" Jenny asked tartly.

"Actually, according to what Brannan was told, they are saying we must be obliterated from the face of the earth."

A pall fell over the group and they looked at each other in grave concern. Brigham laid a hand on Benjamin's arm. "Brother Ben, I'd like you and Nathan to come to a meeting in a day or two. We are praying that the Lord will stay their hand and allow us to finish our work here. We shall go out, in spite of what they say. It is God's will that we do. But now . . ." He sighed heavily. "With these two new developments, we may not have the luxury of waiting until April or May."

"You mean you want to leave before then?" Nathan exclaimed. "But there won't be any grass on the prairie yet. We—"

"I know, I know," Brigham soothed. "That's why we need to meet. I'll send word to you."

They nodded. After a moment, Brigham smiled and it was warm and full again. "But enough gloom for now. This is a glorious day. We've been working day and night. It's only been five days and we've already given the ordinances of the endowment to almost two hundred people."

Matthew, who of all the family knew Brigham best, nodded thoughtfully. "You look tired, Brother Brigham."

"Tired!" he retorted with impatience. "Who's got time to be tired?" He turned to the women. "In fact, dear sisters, we have a request to make of you."

"What is that?" Mary Ann asked for all of them.

"We had planned to take Saturday off so we could wash the temple clothing. However, it means we will lose that day for ordinance work. We are going to ask the sisters to take the clothing home and wash them during the night."

"We would be delighted to do that," Jessica spoke up.

"Yes, of course," exclaimed Rebecca and Lydia together.

"It would mean staying up most of the night," Brigham warned.

"Like you and the others have been doing?" Mary Ann scoffed, brushing his warning aside. "You count on the five of us for sure."

He reached out and gave her a quick hug. "Oh, bless you. Bless you all! Now, let's go inside. A glorious experience awaits you."

Peter started to lift a hand, but Brigham was ahead of him. "Kathryn, we'll have Peter wheel you inside to the stairs. Then we'll ask Matthew and Nathan to carry your chair up while Peter carries you. Once you're up in the attic story, you will be able to move around as required."

"Thank you, President Young," she said softly. "I've been so worried that I might have to stay down."

"Nonsense. If these men can't get you up those stairs, I'll carry you myself."

He looked around once more, then was suddenly misty-eyed. "Let the wolves of Washington and Springfield howl until their throats are raw. Who can stop the work of the Lord when we have people like you as part of it?"

———•———

Lydia walked briskly up the walk to the east door of the Homestead and rapped on the door. Her breath made little puffs of vapor in the air. It had snowed the night before, then cleared and turned quite cold. She was dressed in a long woolen coat, woolen mittens, and a winter bonnet. Her cheeks and the tip of her nose were touched with red, but as she looked around, she breathed deeply, tipping her head back slightly. She loved mornings like this—the air crisp and perfectly clean, the snow crunching softly underfoot. It reminded her of her girlhood days in Palmyra. Whenever it snowed, she would, much to the dismay of her mother, immediately get dressed and go for a long walk.

There was the sound of footsteps, then the door opened. Julia, Emma's oldest child, and now fourteen years old and a lovely young woman, opened the door. "Good morning, Sister Lydia."

"Good morning, Julia. Is your mother—"

But Emma appeared behind her. She too had on her winter coat and bonnet and was pulling on leather gloves. "Good morning, Lydia. It looks like a beautiful morning. Do you mind if we walk?"

"Oh, no. I love to be out on a day like this."

"Good." Emma gave Julia a kiss on the cheek. "We shouldn't be more than an hour. If little David Hyrum gets hungry, you may give him some bread and jam."

"Yes, Mother."

Emma stepped out onto the small porch and Julia shut the door behind her. Lydia turned and they walked together past the small well (known for having some of the sweetest water in all of Nauvoo) through the gate and out onto Main Street. As Emma shut the gate, she breathed deeply, half closing her eyes. "You are right, Lydia. It is a glorious morning."

"I love it when everything is so white and clean."

Emma nodded, then looked around. "Would you mind if we walked toward the south today? I . . . I would like to have it be just the two of us together this morning. I don't feel like having to stop and talk with others."

Lydia masked her surprise. "Of course. South would be fine."

They moved to the corner of Main and Water Street, directly across from the Mansion House, and turned east. They walked in silence until they came to Durphy Street, which became the road south to Warsaw and Quincy once it left town. They turned onto it, walking slowly, savoring the morning together. One wagon had passed, its tracks making two endless trails in the road, the hoofprints of the single horse making a dotted line between them.

"How is Joshua?" Emma asked after a moment.

Lydia shook her head. "He's gone, you know."

"Gone?"

"Yes. He and Carl left yesterday for Wisconsin."

"Oh, my. No, I hadn't heard that."

"The lumber mills are all that he has left now," she explained sadly. "He felt he had to go north and make sure everything is all right there."

"You don't think . . . ," Emma started.

Lydia shook her head. "No, he's not worried about anyone going that far to try and harm him. He's going to make sure they cut a large supply of logs this winter. It will be his only source of income next spring."

Emma's dark eyes were even darker now as she spoke. "The children and I were up past his stables a day or so ago, out for a carriage ride. I just felt sick when I saw that pile of rubble and ashes."

"Yes. I've never seen Joshua quite like this. Caroline is really worried. She was almost glad to have him go north. It will get his mind off all that has happened."

"And Carl went with him?"

"Yes, much to Melissa's disappointment. But the brickyards are shut down now. There is just no business at all anymore. He almost jumped at the chance to go with Joshua."

Emma merely nodded. After a moment, she glanced sideways at Lydia. "And how is Melissa?"

Understanding exactly what she meant, Lydia sighed. "Still troubled. She hasn't been to a worship service now for several months. She . . ." Lydia's hesitation was more for Emma than for Melissa. "She has never recovered from the idea of plural marriage."

There was a low, bitter laugh, but Emma said nothing, and Lydia decided to change the subject. "We saw Mother Smith at the temple the other day."

"She told me. She was very pleased that Brigham had asked her to be one of the first." She gave Lydia a quick sidewards glance. "It's no secret that Brother Brigham and I don't see eye to eye on a lot of things, but he and the Twelve have been wonderful to Mother Smith."

"Yes," Lydia responded warmly, pleased that Emma would acknowledge it. Normally when they met, the topic of Brigham Young was carefully avoided.

"So you had your endowment? How was it?" Emma's voice was lifeless and without real interest.

"It was wonderful," Lydia said, not wanting to be less than

totally honest. "It was a little overwhelming at first," she went on, "but the imagery is so beautiful, Emma. I came out so inspired."

"I'm glad for you."

Lydia took a quick breath, debating whether to pursue this further, but one of the things that made their friendship so dear to the both of them was that they had always been completely honest with each other. "You seem unhappy about that. Do you not approve of what's happening in the temple now?"

Emma reached out and briefly touched Lydia's arm. "I'm sorry, Lydia. I know how you feel, and I don't mean to make it seem as if I don't have similar feelings anymore. It's just that . . ." She was staring out across the river, which now ran with patches of slush and an occasional chunk of ice. "Things are so different now. I'm not sure Joseph would approve."

Lydia couldn't help it. She couldn't not say what was in her heart. "I think he would be very pleased to see what is happening in the temple now, Emma. I do. That was *his* dream. I just wish he could have lived to see it fulfilled."

There was no answer, and they walked on for several minutes before Lydia spoke again. "What are you going to do, Emma?" There was no need to explain that. It was the question on the lips of every person, every family in Nauvoo—When spring comes, what are you going to do?

"I'm not leaving, Lydia," came the quick and stubborn reply. "I have five children to worry about."

If the incongruity of that statement struck Emma, she gave no sign. Lydia had five children too and was carrying her sixth. It was due in April. If Brigham was right about leaving earlier than that, it would be born out on the plains. And it wasn't just her. Jessica would be taking six children, including a year-old baby. Rebecca and Jenny both had babies not yet a year old.

"We have a home here." Emma's voice caught momentarily. "Joseph is buried here."

"I know," Lydia said sadly. "I know, Emma."

"I'm not sure that Mother Smith will go either."

Lydia's head came around sharply at that. At the October conference, Brigham Young invited Lucy Mack Smith, upon her request, to speak to the Saints. Mother Smith being universally beloved by all, it had been a sweet and tender moment for those assembled in the temple. She had rehearsed briefly the story of her family, for many there in that congregation of five thousand did not know the Smiths personally. She asked the congregation if they considered her a mother in Israel. Brigham had immediately sprung up and called out, "All who consider Mother Smith a mother in Israel, signify it by saying yes." There was an instant cry of acclamation. She had ended by saying that she would be going west with them, but requested that when she died her bones be brought back to Nauvoo to be interred beside those of her husband and sons. Deeply moved, Brigham had pledged himself to honor that request, and called upon the people to signify how many were willing to enter a covenant to do the same. The vote had again been instantaneous and unanimous in the affirmative.

"I know," Emma sighed. "I know that she told the people she would be going, but her health is such that I don't think she can. Even she is beginning to accept that now." Her head came up, chin thrust out and eyes filled with a touch of anger. "It's a mistake, you know."

"Going west?" Lydia asked softly, not surprised at all by Emma's words. "It's not like it's our choice."

"Yes, it is. We can live in peace with others. We don't have to go."

Lydia had heard from more than one person that Emma was adamantly opposed to the coming exodus and spoke against it frequently. She had also heard that Joseph's three sisters—Lucy, Sophronia, and Catherine—had determined not to go. Their husbands owned farms out away from Nauvoo and they were not willing to leave them. She decided to focus on another part of the family. "But Mary will be going?" she asked.

Emma turned and looked squarely at Lydia. There was just a touch of wistfulness in her eyes. "Dear Mary. So strong. So faithful. Yes, she won't hear of doing anything else. Even Brigham is saying that the widows of the Smith family need to wait until later in the spring, when the weather is warmer. He has offered to come back for us. But Mary won't hear of it. I wouldn't be surprised if she beats Brigham across the river."

"She is a strong woman," Lydia agreed.

Emma looked away. "And I'm not strong, Lydia. Not anymore."

Lydia's hand shot out. "I didn't mean that," she exclaimed. "I only meant that—"

Emma smiled sadly. "I know you didn't mean to imply that I'm not strong, but I'm not. I'm worn out, Lydia. It's like I have no strength left in me."

"You have always been strong, Emma," Lydia said earnestly. "You have been an inspiration to all of us." When there was a quick, almost imperceptible shake of Emma's head, Lydia rushed on. "You have! Remember when I went to Palmyra? Nathan had gone with Zion's Camp. I had lost the baby." She looked away, fighting the sudden urge to cry.

When she turned back, her face was filled with a fierce intensity. "I was at the bottom, Emma. I wasn't sure I could come back and face life and the family anymore. It was your letter, the one where you talked about the Lord's revelation to you, about being an elect lady, that changed everything. You had endured so much more than I had faced. You had so many more challenges than I did. I wept with shame and determined that I would try to be more like Emma Smith."

They had stopped. They stood alongside the snowy road, looking out across the river, a wide ribbon of brown dividing the snowy landscape. Emma looked at Lydia for several moments, her own eyes glistening now. "Thank you, Lydia."

On impulse, Lydia threw her arms around the woman who had been such an example to her for so many years. She was weeping openly now. "I'm going to miss you so, Emma. I'm going to miss you more than I can ever say."

Emma clung to her, and Lydia felt her body beginning to shake convulsively. "I will miss you too, Lydia. I will miss you all."

It was just after noon of the twenty-third of December, 1845. Nathan and Benjamin Steed stood on the front step of the temple, along with a few other men. They seemed to be gathered there as an afterthought, lingering to talk after a meeting had been dismissed. In reality, they were on assignment as door-keepers and guards. Brigham Young and others of the Twelve were inside, upstairs in the attic room. With the recent indictments handed down in Springfield, the Twelve now had a guard with them round the clock. And since there was only one entrance to the temple, the brethren were not about to leave it unattended so the Twelve could be trapped inside.

Of equal concern, and perhaps an even greater source of tension, was the rising crisis with the federal government. The news from Samuel Brannan had been independently confirmed. Governor Ford had written a letter to Brigham saying he had learned that federal troops in St. Louis were planning to intercept the Mormons and stop them from leaving the United States. The orders were not only to stop the Saints but to destroy them. Then word came from friends in the East. The reports were that the federal government planned to seize the Mormons, and those were taken very seriously.

Benjamin stamped his feet against the cold, hugging himself tightly. "Do you think the fire this morning was an accident?" he asked Nathan in a low voice.

Nathan shook his head. "I don't know." As if things weren't bad enough, this morning Charles C. Rich, captain of emigrating company number thirteen, had raced up to the temple to report that one of the sheds used by his company for drying their wagon lumber had caught fire and burned to the ground. Three hundred dollars' worth of badly needed lumber had been lost along with the shed. Normally it would have been accepted as nothing other than an accident. Fires in lumber kilns and drying sheds were common enough. But after the destruction of Joshua's freight business, the whole city was jittery, and this morning's news had sent a chill through everyone.

All of this combined to raise the question of whether or not they could wait until April or May to leave. It was a question under heavy debate right now. Yet it left Nathan feeling greatly depressed. Leaving sooner than expected had three serious consequences—first, there would not be sufficient grass on the prairies for their stock; second, they would have to leave Nauvoo before they were fully prepared, always a risky enterprise; and third, the weather would be a critical factor, even if they left only a month earlier than planned. But what did any of that matter if there was no choice? And that was what so depressed him. It was a grim set of alternatives.

"Uh-oh!" someone behind him muttered.

Nathan turned around and stiffened. Riding up Mulholland Street toward them was a party of ten to twelve men. All but two were in the uniform of the state militia. Instinctively, the small band of men moved in together to block the door, watching the approaching group with a sense of deep foreboding.

They rode into the yard of the temple, and at a grunted command from the lead rider, they all dismounted. Without a moment's hesitation, the leader strode up to the group of brethren. Benjamin, as the oldest present, and as a member of the temple committee, stepped forward.

The leader pulled back his coat to reveal a silver star pinned on his jacket. "My name is Thomas Horne. I am the United States deputy marshal for the state of Illinois." He withdrew a folded paper from inside his jacket. "I have a writ here for the arrest of one Brigham Young, and others of his associates, on charges of counterfeiting United States coin."

When Benjamin said nothing, the marshal turned and gestured toward the others. "I have brought a posse of militia with me so there will be no trouble. We have the writ and we mean to have our man."

Benjamin looked around the circle of men surrounding him. "Brigham Young is not here," he said.

Horne let his eyes gaze up at the tower of the temple. "I know he is not here. I was told he is in the temple. Is that true?"

"I have not been inside," Benjamin said truthfully.

The marshal started forward, trying to push around Benjamin. "Then I shall go in and look for myself." The Mormon men instantly closed ranks around Benjamin, cutting off any path to the temple doorway.

"The temple is the house of God," Benjamin explained, still amiable enough. "Only worthy members of the Church are allowed to enter."

Horne's eyes narrowed, but there was something in the determined look of the men in front of him that told him that he would not go through them easily. "All right," he said, stepping back, "but you send word up immediately to Mr. Young that we are here. I know he's up there."

Benjamin turned, catching the eye of the man nearest the door. "Brother Babbitt, would you go upstairs and if President Young is present tell him that he has someone who wants to see him down here."

Brigham was in the small room on the southeast corner of the temple which served as his office. There was a knock on the door and it immediately opened. Almon Babbitt was standing there, hat in hand. Through the open doorway, Brigham saw Heber and John Taylor and others of the men who were in the larger outer room. They stared at Babbitt, concern clearly written on their faces.

"President, there is a federal marshal outside the front doors of the temple."

Brigham's face fell. There were audible gasps from the men outside his door. "A marshal?" Brigham said slowly.

"Yes, sir. He is the deputy federal marshal for Springfield. He has a company of state militia with him. He has a warrant for your arrest and the arrest of others of the Twelve and says he must take you to Carthage for arraignment."

Brigham sat back slowly. "Thank you, Brother Babbitt," was all he said.

Brother Babbitt stood there for a moment in confusion, then nodded and backed out of the room, pulling the door shut behind him. For almost a full minute, Brigham Young sat there in silence, staring at nothing. Outside, he could hear the anxious whisperings, but gave them no heed. Finally, he pushed his chair back and fell to his knees. His head bowed, his eyes closed.

After several minutes, Brigham got back to his feet and sat down heavily in his chair. In a moment, the door pushed open again. This time it was George D. Grant, his carriage driver. "President, what shall we do?"

As the door opened wider, out in the hallway, beyond Brother Grant, Brigham saw William Miller—a seventy, and a faithful member since his baptism eleven years before—leaning against a pillar, looking greatly dejected. There was something about his pose, something about the way that he was standing.

Brigham stood abruptly. "Brother Grant, is my carriage at the front door?"

Grant's mouth opened in dismay. "Yes, President, but—"

"Just do as I say," he said gently. He turned his head slightly. "Brother Miller, will you come in here for a moment?"

William Miller was at the doorway in an instant. "Yes, President?"

"William, as you heard, the marshal is downstairs waiting for me. But I have an idea. Will you do exactly as I tell you? If you do, we shall play a little trick on our marshal friend."

"Of course, President."

———•———

When the door opened, every head swung around. George D. Grant blinked at the brighter light, seeming not at all surprised at the assembly of men. "Excuse me, brethren," he called. "Please make way."

Marshal Horne stiffened, watching carefully. He was about
to grab Grant's arm, when a second figure stepped out of the
doorway. The militia were alert now, hands on pistols or swords.
It was Brigham who came out of the temple. Nathan felt his
heart drop. Once before he had watched as their prophet sur-
rendered to the officers of the state. The results had proven to
be unbearably tragic.

Then suddenly, Nathan leaned forward, staring. Brigham
wore his long cloak tied around his neck and wrapped around
his body. The hat that was Brigham's peculiar trademark was
pulled down low over his eyes. But . . . there was something
strange . . .

As the two men started for the carriage, Horne leaped forward, peering at Brigham, who had his head half-turned away.
Grant climbed up into the carriage. Then Brigham lifted his head
to look up at Grant, and Nathan gasped in shock. It wasn't
Brigham Young at all. The clothes were those of the President of
the Quorum of the Twelve, but the face was that of William
Miller.

The marshal laid a hand on Miller's shoulder, turning him
around. "Mr. Young?" he demanded in a harsh voice.

Miller looked calmly into the man's eyes, but said nothing.
George Grant looked down with some impatience at the substi-
tute Brigham. "Are you ready, sir?"

That was enough for Horne. He clamped a hand on Miller's
shoulder firmly. "Brigham Young, you are my prisoner." He
turned and motioned. The other man not in uniform who had
come with the marshal came forward. "Benson," said Horne, "is
this the man we're after?"

Benson, who had been introduced to the crowd at the doorway as being from Augusta, had evidently been brought along
for this very purpose. He stepped forward, peering at William
Miller, who stood without flinching. There was momentary
uncertainty, but then a quick nod. "Yes, that's Brigham Young."

Miller climbed into the carriage, which was surrounded now
by the militia. "Marshal, I shall come with you, but I must stop

at the Mansion House first for a moment. You may accompany me in the carriage if you'd like."

Pleased that this had gone so easily, the marshal nodded. "I shall indeed."

Suddenly Benjamin stepped forward. "I should think there would be some value in President Young's having someone to accompany him. I would be happy to do so, if invited."

Miller looked surprised, then pleased. Nathan leaped forward. "Father, no!"

Benjamin smiled. "It will be all right," he said.

The marshal, noting that Benjamin was older and not very threatening, nodded. "That will be acceptable," he said.

"Then, Brother Grant," Miller said comfortably to the carriage driver, "let's be off to the Mansion House."

It was after dark when the marshal's party rode up to the Hamilton House in Carthage, Illinois. They came into town with a large crowd of jeering, yelling citizens lining both sides of the road. That was thanks to Horne's decision to pause at the outskirts of town, then send his jubilant riders ahead yelling, "We've got him! We've got him! We've got him!"

Benjamin felt a little shudder. This was exactly the kind of greeting Joseph and Hyrum had received when they came to Carthage. And the Hamilton House had been the place the bodies of Joseph and Hyrum were taken after the martyrdom.

William Miller seemed to sense his feelings and laid a hand on his knee. "It will be all right, Brother Steed. Let us have faith."

On horseback beside them, Marshal Horne gave them a look of disgust. In his mind, faith had nothing to do with this. He swung down. "We shall stay here for the night and have you arraigned in the morning."

"Whatever you say," Miller said with equanimity.

Once they were settled comfortably in a corner of the main room of the hotel, across the room from their captors, Benjamin leaned over to William Miller. "How did you do it?" he asked.

"It was President Young's idea."

"But at the Mansion House?"

He shrugged. "The Youngs and the Kimballs have some very bright children."

Benjamin nodded. When they had arrived at the Mansion House, Brigham's two sons, Joseph A. and Brigham, Jr., were playing outside with some of Heber's sons and other friends. There had been a momentary look of surprise as the carriage and its military escort drove up, but then instantly the young men had sensed what was happening and played along. They followed the carriage up to the Mansion House, crying and pleading. "Oh, Father," Brigham, Jr., wailed, "where are they taking you?" "President Young," some of the others cried, "what is happening?" It had been so convincing, that Benjamin had fought the temptation to look at his companion to make sure it was still William Miller.

"So what shall become of us now?" Benjamin asked.

"We shall be fine. Sooner or later, someone is going to come in who knows Brother Brigham, and then I think we shall have one very embarrassed deputy marshal on our hands."

It took nearly half an hour before Miller's prophecy was fulfilled. A steady stream of people came into the hotel, wanting to see the infamous prisoner. They would cluck their tongues, shake their fists, mutter imprecations, then file out again. For a time, Marshal Horne beamed with pleasure; then, tiring of the game, he went to another room to rest. As Benjamin and Miller were eating a meager dinner served by the Hamiltons, another man entered. "Where is Brigham Young?" he said in a loud voice.

Benjamin looked up. "Uh-oh," he said softly. It was a man by the name of Thatcher. Benjamin recognized him as a member of the Church who had once lived in Nauvoo but had apostatized and moved to Carthage.

"He is over there," one of the militia said, pointing.

"Where? I don't see anyone that looks like Brigham."

The landlord, Artois Hamilton, looked irritated. "There, at the table eating. The fleshy man. That's Brigham Young."

Thatcher leaned forward slightly, staring. Miller, by now, had laid down his fork, and looked back at the man with a calm expression. Suddenly, Thatcher gave an incredulous hoot. "That's not Brigham Young. That's William Miller. And Benjamin Steed."

That brought everyone up short. Hamilton, swearing, ran out of the room, and a moment later came back in with the marshal. Horne's face was bright red. He ran up to William Miller and thrust his face into Miller's. "Come with me," he sputtered. Smiling now, Benjamin and William Miller stood and followed him down the hallway to a small room. He slammed the door and spun on them.

He swore bitterly. "Why didn't you tell me your name wasn't Brigham Young?"

"You never asked me my name," Miller answered calmly.

"But . . . well, what is your name?"

"William Miller."

"I thought you were Brigham Young. You swear this is a fact, that you are not him?"

"I do."

"Why didn't you tell me before?" he roared. His face was a flaming red now. "Why didn't you tell me you weren't Brigham Young?"

"You didn't ask me who I was, and I was under no obligation to tell you on my own. I am William Miller. I am not Brigham Young."

For several moments, the marshal stood there, his mouth working, no words coming out. Then, cursing bitterly, he spun on his heel and left the room, slamming the door behind him. Even through the closed door, they heard the great roar of laughter that went up in the dining room. Miller looked at Benjamin and smiled, like a fox that had just eluded the cleverest of the hounds. "I think it could be said that we have done a good night's work here," he said. "Don't you?"

Chapter Notes

Mother Smith's address to the Saints in the October 1845 conference is found in the official history (see *HC* 7:470–73; also Ronald W. Walker, "Lucy Mack Smith Speaks to the Nauvoo Saints," *BYU Studies* 32 [Winter and Spring 1992]: 276–84). By spring, due to her growing age and failing health, she determined that she needed to stay in Nauvoo with her children and grandchildren. She still maintained that she believed Brigham led the people west under direction of the Lord. She lived with her daughter Lucy for some time, and then spent her final years with Emma. She died shortly before her eighty-first birthday on 14 May 1856. (See *Encyclopedia of Mormonism*, s.v. "Smith, Lucy Mack"; also Gracia N. Jones, *Emma's Glory and Sacrifice: A Testimony* [Hurricane, Utah: Homestead Publishers and Distributors, 1987], pp. 167–71.)

Once the endowment work began, a great urgency seemed to grip the Saints. The records show how quickly the work progressed. Between 10 December and 20 December a total of 561 men and women received the endowment. Plans to cancel ordinance work on Saturday the twentieth so that the clothes could be washed were changed, and instead many sisters spent the night laundering temple clothing. On Friday the nineteenth, Brigham Young called twenty-six elders to help officiate in the temple. (See *HC* 7:542–48; *Women of Nauvoo*, p. 152.) The names of those, both men and women, who received their endowments on the first and second days of the ordinance work are listed in the official history of the Church (see *HC* 7:542–44).

In his journal entry for 11 December, Brigham mentions the letter from Samuel Brannan which contained the report of the federal government's opposition to the move of the Saints. However, he states that he read it to the brethren that morning at their eight o'clock meeting. This means he would have had to receive it the previous day—which would have been the very day the endowment work began. (See *HC* 7:544.) Brigham's statement about the bells of hell starting to ring whenever the Saints began to build a temple was made after the Saints arrived in the Salt Lake Valley (see *Journal of Discourses*, 26 vols. [London: Latter-day Saints' Book Depot, 1854–86], 8:355–56).

Later events indicate that there was no truth to the rumors of imminent action by federal troops. The stories seem to have been started by enemies of the Church in hopes of hastening the departure of the Saints. (See *American Moses*, pp. 126–27.)

The "bogus Brigham" incident, as it came to be known, was told with great relish in the Church for many years, and always with wry amusement by Brigham himself. No name is given in the sources for the marshal, so the name of Thomas Horne was created by the author for purposes of the narrative. Even in Warsaw, where hatred of the Church ran deep, they saw the incident as a minor triumph for Brigham and the Church. Thomas Sharp, one of the Church's bitterest enemies, wrote of the incident in his paper in some detail, calling it "the best joke of the season." (See "Journal of Thomas Bullock," pp. 38–39. See also Andrew Jenson, comp., *Latter-day Saint Biographical Encyclopedia*, 4 vols. [1901–36; reprint, Salt Lake City: Western Epics, 1971], 1:482–83.)

The beginning days of 1846 could easily have been viewed by the Steed family as pretty grim. It was almost certain now that the Church would be leaving much earlier than previously planned. That gave new urgency to their preparations. The disastrous fire at Joshua's stable had destroyed horses and oxen and mules and wagons that would have been almost priceless on the trail. Joshua had been wiped out financially and Carl's business had collapsed. Nathan and Lydia's store was still operating, but virtually all cash money in Nauvoo was being expended for wagons and teams. The barter system had always been a mainstream of the economy, but now everyone needed the same essential commodities and were trying to trade off those things that were not essential for the coming journey. That didn't help the Steeds. Filling the shelves with nonessentials was not a profitable way to run a store.

Several prospective buyers had looked at Derek's land (now no longer within Carl's financial reach) and the various houses, but the prices offered were so ridiculously low that they decided to hold out a little longer to see if they could make a better sale. Carl and Joshua were gone to Wisconsin and weren't expected back for another week or so. The lumber mill in the Pineries provided some hope for the future, but it would come far too late to help the family leave with the rest of the Saints, which they were determined to do. The family had never planned to be dependent on the largesse of Carl and Joshua, but it had been a cushion of safety for them if worse came to worst. Now the worst had come and there was nothing to fall back on.

But there was no sense of despair, no deep discouragement. In fact, just the opposite was true. They were determined to be ready when the call came, and the days and nights were spent working to make that happen. In the meantime, they looked forward with great anticipation to another milestone of the Restoration.

During the first week of the new year, Brigham announced that since the giving of the endowment was proceeding in good order, they would now begin sealing husbands and wives together for both time and eternity. This had been promised for some time, and the news swept across the city like a breath of spring.

On the seventh of January, an upholstered altar was completed and installed in a small room on the upper floor of the temple. The coverings for the altar were sewn by the wives of several of the General Authorities, assisted by Mary Fielding Smith, her sister Mercy Thompson Smith, and Agnes Smith, the widow of Don Carlos Smith. On that same day, following the installation, four couples were sealed together in keeping with the principles and practice revealed earlier through the Prophet Joseph Smith. Also on that day, invitations went out to others, and the work of sealing was extended to the Saints along with the endowment.

On the tenth day of January, Benjamin Steed received a brief note from Willard Richards, secretary to the Quorum of the Twelve, inviting him and all other worthy married couples in the Steed family to come to the temple on the fourteenth of the month at four p.m. There they would receive the sealing ordinance.

———•———

They walked slowly up Mulholland Street. They had gotten ready in plenty of time so that there was no need to rush. It was later in the afternoon and the air was cold. There were six couples in all. Benjamin and Mary Ann led the way. Derek and Rebecca, Solomon and Jessica, Matthew and Jenny, Peter and Kathryn all followed. Nathan and Lydia, at the specific invitation of Brigham Young, accompanied them, even though they had been sealed together by Joseph Smith in May of 1842. Peter pushed Kathryn in her wheelchair, but Matthew carried her crutches. Since their marriage, Kathryn had worked for one or two hours every day practicing with her crutches. She had improved immensely and now did quite well, even out in the open, unless there was snow on the ground. Today, she had decided she would let Peter wheel her to the temple and get her up the stairs, but then she was determined to get around on her own once they were in the attic rooms.

They talked softly as they walked, their quiet happiness tinged with sorrow as well. Caroline had come to see them off and wept openly at the thoughts that this being sealed as husband and wife for eternity was a privilege she might never have. Melissa knew about their going as well, but there was no sign of her as they walked past her house. On the other hand, the couples were ecstatic to think that it was finally going to happen. They had all been envious of Nathan and Lydia. Joseph had sealed a few selected couples, then shut it off again until it could be done in the temple. Now at last the time had come.

"Did you know that Jessica and I were there that night when Joseph taught the principle of eternal marriage over in Ramus?" Solomon asked as they started climbing the low hill that led up to the top of the bluff.

"Oh, yes," Lydia said. "I remember you telling us that a while back. But I can't remember the details."

"Yes," Jessica answered. "It was while Joseph and some others had come out to visit the Saints. That would have been . . ." She looked to Solomon. "When?"

"May of '43, almost three years ago now. He was staying at the home of Benjamin F. Johnson. I think you know the Johnsons."

Benjamin nodded. "The Johnsons were close friends to the Prophet for a long time. In fact, Benjamin Johnson was Joseph's private secretary for a time."

"That's right. We had a larger meeting at the Perkins' home earlier; then Jessica and I walked Joseph and those with him back to the Johnsons'. He invited us in and we were just sitting around visiting. Anyway, what happened next very much surprised us all. William Clayton was sitting beside Joseph. We had been talking about the importance of eternal marriage and other such things. Then Joseph did an unusual thing. He reached out and laid his hand on Brother Clayton's knee. 'Your life is hid with Christ in God, and so are many others,' he said. 'Nothing but committing blasphemy against the Holy Ghost, the unpardonable sin, can prevent you from inheriting eternal life, for you are sealed up by the power of the priesthood unto eternal life, having taken the step necessary for that purpose.'"

Solomon stopped, shaking his head. "By 'the step necessary' we assumed he meant being sealed together as husband and wife. But you could tell his words really stunned Brother Clayton."

"Those were the words he used?" Nathan asked, quite taken aback.

"Yes, as near as I can recollect."

"He said 'sealed up to eternal life'?"

"Yes," Jessica said. "I remember that clearly."

Nathan shook his head, looking at his father. "Isn't that like having your calling and election made sure?"

"That's my understanding."

"Well," Solomon went on, "it was a very solemn moment. And then Joseph looked at the rest of us. We knew a little about the idea that a man and woman could be joined together forever, but that was all. I can still remember the thrill that shot through my whole body as I heard him explain just what the possibilities were."

"What did he say?" Jenny asked eagerly.

"Yes, what?" Rebecca and Derek said together.

Solomon looked at Jessica, motioning for her to answer.

She nodded and looked at the family. "He told us that except a man and a woman enter into an everlasting covenant and be married for eternity by the power and authority of the holy priesthood, not only will their marriage end when they die, but they will not have increase either."

"Increase?" Rebecca echoed. "You mean children?"

"That's right. He said that those who have not been sealed will not have any children after the resurrection. But—" Suddenly her voice was husky and filled with a quiet joy. "But he said that those who *are* married by the power and authority of the priesthood and who continue faithful, especially not committing the sin against the Holy Ghost, will continue to increase and have children in the celestial glory. For those, the family will continue on into the eternities forever and ever."

Solomon reached inside his jacket and withdrew a flat purse. He opened it and took out a folded piece of paper. "That's when Joseph made this statement. Someone wrote it down—Brother Clayton, I think. I later asked if I could make a copy. I've carried it with me, waiting for the day when we would see it come to pass." His voice went suddenly soft. "And now it's here."

"Read it to us," Peter urged.

He unfolded the paper. They all stopped now, circling around Solomon. He lifted it so he could watch them as he read. "'In the celestial glory there are three heavens or degrees; and in order to obtain the highest, a man must enter into this order of the priesthood—' Joseph let us know that meant the new and everlasting covenant of eternal marriage. 'And if he does not, he cannot obtain it. He may enter into the other, but that is the end of his kingdom; he cannot have an increase.'"

"I've read that," Peter exclaimed. "Elder Taylor thinks it is so significant that it ought to be included in the next edition of the Doctrine and Covenants. So he had me typeset a copy."

Solomon nodded, folded the paper, took out the wallet again, and put it away. No one spoke for a moment. Then finally Benjamin reached out and took Mary Ann's hand. "When I married this woman," he said to his family, "I knew I loved her and wanted to spend my life with her. Now, after all these years of being together, I can tell you this. If I could not spend eternity by her side, I would know the true meaning of hell."

Mary Ann just looked at him, her eyes brimming with tears. "And I as well," she whispered.

He shook his head and cleared his throat, turning again to face the temple. "Come on, Mrs. Steed," he said gruffly. "We've got an appointment with eternity."

They filled every chair in the small room except for three chairs that sat behind the altar and that had ribbons draped across them so they couldn't use them. There were not enough chairs, and so Nathan and Solomon and Derek had to stand behind their wives. Willard Richards had shown them to the room but left again immediately. A few moments later, William Clayton, who was the temple recorder, came in and sat in one of the three empty chairs. No one spoke. The room was plainly furnished except for the altar that stood near the center of the room. Every eye was drawn to it.

The altar was about two and a half feet high and that same width across the front. It was no more than a foot wide and had a platform of eight or nine inches in height attached all around it to provide for a convenient and comfortable place to kneel. The top of the altar and the place for kneeling were covered with cushions of scarlet damask cloth. The upright sides, or body, of the altar were covered with white linen. It was beautifully simple, and yet carried such a feeling of sacredness that they could not take their eyes from it.

After about five minutes, the door opened and Brigham Young and John Taylor came into the room. Smiling, speaking in low murmurs, they went around the room, shaking hands and greeting each couple. When finished, Brigham went to stand behind the altar and faced them.

"I can see from your eyes that I do not need to tell you what a wonderful and special occasion this is. Nathan and Lydia were among the privileged few to be sealed under the hand of the Prophet Joseph. Now, the time has come for the rest of you to have this sacred and remarkable privilege and promise. Now you can begin to sense why we have felt that we must finish the temple at all costs, even though we shall soon abandon it. Yes, sooner than we thought. Sooner than we hoped. But even under threat of destruction by federal troops, we cannot stop this work, for without the temple, we could not endow and seal our people. That is worth whatever it costs us."

He looked around the group, his eyes resting briefly on each one. "As a family you have been with the Church from the beginning. Nathan and Mary Ann and Lydia and perhaps others of you were baptized two years before I was wise enough to join the Church. You have been faithful members in all that time, through all that the Lord has seen fit to lay upon us. How fitting that you should come here this day to kneel before the Lord and receive this highest of earthly blessings."

He paused and looked around once more, letting his gaze stop on Benjamin and Mary Ann. "I assume the family will have no objections if we begin with your mother and father?"

They all shook their heads. Several had tears in their eyes.

"Then Benjamin Steed, will you bring your wife here to the altar. You kneel on this side. Mary Ann, you kneel opposite him so that you face one another."

They stood and did as instructed.

"Nathan? I would like you and Solomon to act as witnesses. As you know, in the Lord's kingdom all things are done in order. Brother Clayton will record the proceedings this day. It will be noted that witnesses made certain that all was done in order. If you'll come and sit here." He motioned at the two vacant chairs behind him."

They did so.

"Now, just before we begin, may I remind you that the keys of the sealing power were brought back from heaven on the third day of April, 1836. They were brought by the hand of the ancient prophet Elijah and given to the modern prophet Joseph Smith, Junior. Shortly before his death, Joseph bestowed those keys upon the members of the Twelve. He gave us full power and authority to carry on this work after he was gone.

"Those are the keys that I hold and the power by which I shall act this day. If it were not so, it wouldn't matter what words I said or what I did. It would not be recorded in heaven. Peter, James, and John received those keys on the Mount of Transfiguration by the hand of Elijah as well. The Savior taught Peter that with those keys, whatsoever he bound on earth would be bound in heaven. And whatsoever he loosed on earth would be loosed in heaven. This is the only way wherein we can bind the heavens and pronounce that what is done here today will be recognized there forever."

He stopped, smiling down now on Benjamin and Mary Ann. He stepped forward, moving closer to the altar where they knelt. "And now, Benjamin, if you will take Mary Ann by the right hand, we shall proceed."

As they walked slowly back home, their feet crunching in the snow, their breath trailing in clouds around them, the stars hung above them in the immense blackness, so close as to be touchable, and yet so vastly far away as to fill the soul with thoughts of eternity.

As they reached Steed Row, they all stopped in front of Benjamin and Mary Ann's gate. The air was still now and the night filled with silence. It was as though the whole city were hushed by the sacredness of what had transpired that night.

Finally Benjamin looked around at his family. He reached out and took Mary Ann's hand. "This has been a wonderful evening," he said softly, not wanting to disturb the silence. "Now each of us as couples have been joined together through eternal and sacred covenants. Remember the Lord's own words. 'I am bound when ye do what I say, but if ye do not what I say, ye have no promise.'

"We received marvelous promises today, promises that very few in the history of the world have been privileged to receive. Now it is up to us to keep the covenants we have made. If we do, by his own word, the Lord is bound to honor his word."

There were grave nods and soft murmurs of assent. Each couple stood close together, either holding hands or having an arm around the other's waist or shoulder.

"Today we were sealed together as husbands and wives. Soon we shall have our families sealed to us as well. Think about that. If there is one thing I have learned in my years of fumbling through life, it is this. When it comes down to it, all that really matters both here and in the world to come is our family. Let us go into the wilderness." He waved his hand, taking in the houses along Steed Row. "Let us leave all this. Even if we don't get a dime for it. What does that matter? I think of your children. Will and Alice, filled with enough faith to follow a prophet's voice. Emily and Rachel, now women in their own right." He smiled. "Savannah, who as you all know is the apple of her grandfather's eye." He turned to Derek and Rebecca. "I think of Christopher and little Benjamin and your sweet, sweet little Leah." He looked at the others. "There's not time to name them all. But you know how you feel about them, and you know how we feel about them. They are all that really matter."

Now they were all nodding.

"Do you know what I was thinking as we finished tonight?"

They watched him quietly, waiting for him to answer his own question.

"I remembered that day several weeks ago when your mother and I got off the boat. How terribly disappointed we were as we looked at the faces in the crowd and saw no one we knew! Think of that. Think of entering the spirit world and having no one there.

"And then I picture going around the side of the Nauvoo House and seeing all of those grandchildren standing there waiting for us." His voice caught and he had to look away. When he spoke again, it was with difficulty. "I think of all of you stepping out to greet us." His body started to shake a little as he fought to hold back his emotions.

Several were wiping at their eyes now, and there were more than just a few sniffles to be heard.

"The Lord has promised us a fulness of joy if we are faithful," he finally went on. He stepped nearer to Mary Ann and pulled her close to him. "Well, if that's the case, he's going to have to give me a lot bigger bottle to hold it in than I have now, because I can't imagine being happier or more joyful than I was at that moment. And if there's more joy than that to be found, I will just simply burst."

They laughed with him through their tears, all of them deeply touched.

Benjamin straightened, his face calm and serene. "We must continue to pray for Carl and Melissa and Joshua and Caroline so that they someday will be with us. And other than that, it doesn't matter what happens now. We have obtained the blessings that the Lord has designed for us. We shall seal our children to us and become one great, eternal family. And then no one can take it from us and we can go from here in peace."

"Amen!" Nathan said in a near whisper.

"Amen!" murmured the others.

Chapter Notes

While on a trip to the outlying settlements, Joseph Smith pronounced the doctrine of the new and everlasting covenant of marriage in Ramus. This eventually became section 131 of the Doctrine and Covenants (see HC 5:391–93). Though Joseph Smith had sealed a few couples for time and eternity before his death—Brigham and Mary Ann Young, Heber and Vilate Kimball, Parley and Mary Ann Pratt, and a few others—the ordinance of sealing couples together for time and eternity, revealed in what is now sections 131 and 132 of the Doctrine and Covenants, was not administered to the general membership until 7 January 1846 (see HC 7:565–66).

The description of the altar comes from the official history of the Church (see HC 7:566).

Chapter Twenty-Nine

Brethren!"

Those assembled in the largest room of the upper floor of the temple stopped their quiet whisperings and turned to face Brigham Young.

"Thank you for coming. If our count is right we have all but one or two of the captains of companies here. We also have several captains of tens and other leaders with us. We appreciate your coming. We know that you are busy and that every minute away from your workshops is time away from your preparations, so we shall keep this meeting short."

He looked tired. Two days before, Heber Kimball had told Nathan that with the time growing shorter and with the huge numbers of Saints who wished to have their temple ordinances, Brigham had been working day and night in the temple. Heber said that he had been home only once in the past week and was averaging no more than four hours of sleep each night.

"We regretfully inform you that the news from our friends in high places is not good. They say that the federal troops in St. Louis are ready to march on us at any time. We know not how much longer we can stay safely in our city."

He stopped, letting the soft cries of alarm play out, his fingers drumming softly on the small table he was using as a podium. "A few days ago, we called for a report from the captains as to who in their respective companies were ready to leave immediately. We learned that we now have about a hundred and forty horses or other draft animals and seventy wagons. That is terribly disheartening in a way. We estimate that we are going to have to eventually move close to fifteen thousand Saints, so this is a pittance. And time is running out."

He squared his shoulders, looking at the men through narrowed eyes. "We are now certain that we can no longer delay our departure, certainly not until there is grass on the plains. If evil descends upon us, our only safety will be in our departure from this place. So I am asking, How many of you captains are ready and willing to start immediately?"

Heads turned as men looked at each other in dismay. "How soon is immediately, President?" someone called out.

"Two weeks, maybe less."

That brought a rumble of surprise. Men gaped at each other. Some just shook their heads. Nathan Steed turned and looked at his father. Two weeks! Today was the eighteenth of January. Two weeks meant about the first of February, two and a half months sooner than they had been planning.

"I'm not talking about having every single nail and piece of rope you're going to need. I'm talking about who is close enough in their preparations to leave immediately if the call comes. Let me see by raise of hands."

Benjamin gave Nathan a long appraising look, and then, not waiting for an answer, raised his hand.

"There's no way we can be ready that soon," Derek said, reflecting the discouragement they all felt at hearing the news

Nathan and Benjamin had brought back from the temple. "We only have three wagons thus far and still need more oxen to pull them."

"We have two more yoke now," Matthew said, raising his hand.

Nathan nodded at him. "What do you mean, Matthew?"

"We sold the cabinet shop today."

"You what?" Nathan cried. The others were equally shocked and began to pepper him with questions.

He waited patiently until the voices in the room died away into silence again. Nathan noted that Jenny's head was down and her hands were twisting at the edge of her apron. "A gentleman from Peoria offered us two yoke of oxen and a pepperbox pistol with fifty rounds of ammunition."

"And that's all?" Lydia exclaimed. "For the whole shop?"

Jenny's head came up. "Tools, lumber, unfinished furniture. Everything."

Matthew's face was impassive, but one could sense the deep struggle to hide his pain. "I knew we needed the animals. What good is a wagon without something to pull it? I made him agree to wait until we're gone before he takes possession."

Now they were all staring at their hands. Derek spoke without looking up. "Does Carl know?" And then he answered his own question. "Of course Carl doesn't know. Carl is in Wisconsin with Joshua."

"I talked with Carl before he left," Matthew explained. "He wishes desperately that he could buy it, but there's no way he can. Not now."

Benjamin had to fight the urge to sit down, such was the weariness that hit him at that moment. Nathan and Lydia were giving the store to Joshua and Caroline, since they owned part interest in it anyway, so that was settled. But nothing else in Nauvoo was taken care of. Solomon's land in Ramus was sold, but for a mere two hundred dollars—about a tenth of what it was worth. The man had sent seventy-five dollars as a down payment, and so far had sent nothing more. Solomon had talked about going to Ramus to see about it, but there likely would not be time now.

"Brigham asked something else of us," Nathan said quietly.

"What?"

"He's appointed a committee of five. He wants us to turn any unsold properties over to them as we leave, and give them power of attorney to sell it for whatever they can get. They will then use that money to help others who have little or nothing."

"Better than just giving it away," Derek murmured.

"That's what Nathan and I thought too," Benjamin said. "We signed the papers."

Peter and Kathryn had been sitting quietly in the corner. Now Peter stood up slowly. A little surprised, everyone turned. Kathryn's eyes were glistening as she looked up at him.

"Peter?" Benjamin said. "Do you have something you'd like to say?"

"Yes, I do." There was no mistaking the air of gloom that hung upon him. "Kathryn and I have a suggestion on how to solve one of your problems."

"What?" Derek said, taken aback by this sudden boldness of his younger brother.

Peter fumbled in his trouser pockets for a moment, then withdrew a small piece of paper. It was a half sheet of foolscap, folded in half again. "This advertisement will appear in the *Sangamo Journal* in a few weeks. That's a Springfield newspaper. I was sent a copy after sending off inquiries to one of the members of the Church there."

He lifted it, turning it toward the lamplight, and began to read in a clear, flat voice devoid of all emotions. "'Westward, Ho! For Oregon and California!'" He looked up. "That will be the headline." Down his eyes went again. "'Who wants to go to California without costing them anything? As many as eight young men, of good character, who can drive an ox team, will be accommodated by gentlemen who will leave this vicinity about the first of April. Come, boys! You can have as much land as you want without costing you anything. The government of

California gives large tracts of land to persons who have to move there. The first suitable persons who apply, will be engaged.'"

He folded the paper calmly and returned it to his pocket. Only then did he look up into their astonished faces.

"Are you saying . . . ?" Nathan started, but he was so completely dumbfounded that he didn't finish.

"I'm saying that this is a partial solution to a family problem. We are short of wagons and have no more money to buy them. We need additional teams to pull them. You will be lucky to find transportation for each of you and your families. Kathryn and I could—"

"California?" Mary Ann interrupted him. "You would go to California?"

"No, Mother Steed. We'd go only as far as we have to, then we'd drop off and join up with you."

"You're serious about this?" Derek asked, still not believing what he was hearing.

"Yes!" Peter said forcefully. "Of all the family, Kathryn and I will be the most difficult to care for. And not just because of Kathryn either. We have no skills, very little money, no way to really contribute."

"It says you have to be able to drive an ox team," Matthew broke in. "Have you ever driven an ox team, Peter?"

He flushed, but didn't back down. "I would like one of you to teach me."

Jenny was staring at her sister in horror. "Do you agree with this?" she asked.

Kathryn nodded, biting at her lower lip. "Not happily, but it's a way we will not be a burden." She took a quick breath. "And if we have to leave earlier than planned, as Brigham says we will, it will be one less thing for all of you to worry about."

"You can't!" Rebecca cried. "You can't go alone without us. We'll just make do."

"Tell them the rest, Peter," Kathryn said.

"These people that I know in Springfield have been making some discreet inquiries. These are wealthy farmers and businessmen. One of the families, by the name of Reed, has several children. They are very well-to-do. The mother is talking about hiring a tutor for her children."

Now several conversations erupted at once. Peter watched sadly as the family reacted to his startling proposal. Nathan finally held up his hands and the noise died away again. He appeared grim as he looked around the room. "I know that what we have just heard sounds awful, but . . ."

"No!" Lydia cried. "There are no buts, Nathan. Peter and Kathryn have to go with us."

He wanted to reach out and hold her, stroke her hair, tell her it was all going to be okay. But he couldn't. The realities were too gloomy.

Mary Ann was whispering urgently to Benjamin, but he too was shaking his head. He then turned to the others. "Peter is right. If we are forced to leave in the next two weeks, we will be facing a crisis. You've all seen our lists. You've heard the numbers. We have barely enough food to see us into July, or August at the latest. What if it takes us longer than that to find a home?"

"And what if we have to load it all into just three wagons?" Nathan came back again. "We have over thirty people we have to move. Aside from the food, we have no hardwood for making any more wagons. And even if we did, we can't find, nor afford, the animals to pull them."

"If we go with this other group, it will be two less mouths to feed," Peter said, glad that Nathan could see the wisdom of their thinking. "Two less beds to carry. Basically, one less wagon you will need."

"One less person who cannot walk," Kathryn said calmly.

"We can't just leave you to make it on your own," Mary Ann said firmly.

Now Caroline, who had said nothing through all of it, raised her head. "At least they will be going."

That stopped all further comment. The realities of even more difficult decisions hit them hard.

Nathan turned to Peter. "You know if there is any way that we can take you with us, we will. But thank you. Thank you for looking for other solutions."

Peter gave one curt nod. "If they know we are Mormons, it may hurt our chances of being accepted. So . . ." He took in a breath. "There's a stage to Springfield on Wednesday. We have about forty dollars saved. I think we'll go there now and find somewhere to stay for a time. We won't deny we're Mormons, of course, but if we're living in Springfield when the advertisement is finally put in the paper, maybe they won't think to ask."

"Wednesday?" Jenny cried in alarm. "That's just three days from now."

"If it doesn't work out," Peter went on doggedly, "we'll come back. Otherwise, we'll write and let you know what our plans are."

Now the room was silent. Hopes and reality were being split asunder on this night, and no one knew quite what to do about it. Caroline did not look up. The pain for her was too great, and she couldn't bear to even think about it.

———•———

Savannah sat on the piano bench, her fingers running lightly and soundlessly over the piano keys.

"Savannah?" Her mother's voice floated to her from the kitchen. "Why aren't you practicing?"

"I am, Mama." She plunked out a quick scale. But in a moment she was staring out the window again. There were footsteps behind her, but she didn't move.

"Savannah, you have got to practice. I need you to go to the store for me in a few minutes."

"Mama?"

"What?"

"Is it true that we have to leave in two weeks?"

"Who told you that?"

"Sarah."

"Oh." Which meant Melissa had heard the news from someone and talked about it with her children.

"Sarah says she's not going."

"That's right, Savannah. Uncle Carl and Aunt Melissa are going to stay in Nauvoo."

"But why, Mama? If Heavenly Father wants us to leave, why do they want to stay?"

"Because they're not sure that Heavenly Father wants that for everybody." She was tempted to say more, but knowing Savannah's penchant for talking openly to anyone about anything, she let it go.

"Are *you* sure that's what Heavenly Father wants?"

"Yes, I am," Caroline murmured, feeling a sudden ache inside.

"Then we're going, aren't we, Mama?"

With a sigh, she sat down on the piano bench beside her daughter. "We don't know yet, Savannah. Your papa and I haven't decided."

"We have to go, Mama! We have to. If it's what Heavenly Father wants, we have to."

"Your father isn't sure it is what God wants for us either," she said sadly.

"Well, I'm going!" Savannah said, folding her arms in defiance.

"Savannah."

"Well, I am. I'm going to tell Papa when he gets home that we have to go. We have to."

"Savannah, I want you to listen to me. When you were baptized, you promised your Heavenly Father that you would try to live a good life and do what he asks of you. That's what baptism means. It means we try to live as Jesus and Heavenly Father want us to."

"Yes, I know. I've been trying to do that."

"I know you have. You've been wonderful. I've been very proud of you. Even your father has commented on it. But one of the things that Heavenly Father wants us to do is to honor our fathers and mothers. You've learned about that in the Bible, haven't you?"

Now Savannah saw what was coming. "Yes, Mother," she said meekly.

"I know you want to go, Savannah, and so do I, but there'll be no more running away, no more hiding. If we decide it is not best to go right now, then you need to honor your father and me in that decision. Is that clear?"

"Yes, Mama."

Caroline reached over and kissed her on the top of the head. "I know Heavenly Father wants the Church to go west, but in our case, he may want us to stay behind. For your papa's sake. Do you understand what I mean?"

"Yes, Mama."

Caroline reached out and rubbed her hand along the polished wood. "If we do go, Savannah, we can't take your piano with us."

She flinched. "We can't?"

"No. It's much too big and heavy. It would take one wagon just to carry it."

That hit her hard. Her mouth twisted into a deep frown, and her eyes looked hurt. "But I love my piano," she cried.

"I know you do," Caroline said, lifting her hand now to touch Savannah's hair. "But if we go, the piano will have to stay. Would that make a difference about whether or not you want to go?"

"Can I have a piano when we get to the Rocky Mountains?"

Caroline smiled, but it was sad and filled with wistful longing. "Probably not. At least not for a long time."

Savannah twisted her fingers round one strand of her red hair where it fell over her shoulders. The deep blue eyes weighed that information carefully.

"Well?"

"I think pleasing Heavenly Father is more important than playing the piano."

Caroline hugged her, trying not to cry. "I think pleasing Heavenly Father is more important than most things, Savannah."

Savannah started plunking a single note with her right little finger. "I'm praying that Papa will change his mind," she said after a moment.

Caught off guard, Caroline nodded. "I am too, Savannah. Every morning and every night."

Savannah stopped playing and looked up at her mother. "Then we'll get to go," she said simply.

———•————

They stood together in Matthew's cabinet-shop-turned-wagon-factory—Nathan, Solomon, Derek, and Matthew. No one said much now. The pile of lumber they were looking at was sufficient to make one more wagon box—barely—but they had not a single piece of hardwood. Not one. Pine and spruce were all right for the wagon box, but the axles, the tongue, the hubs—unless they were of ash or hickory or oak, they would wear down like butter too close to the fire. Matthew and Derek had just returned from a two-day trip to Peoria. They had come back with nothing. Not a single board. That was the fierceness of the competition for the wood required to make a good wagon.

"Well," Nathan finally said, "there's not much point in making the box until we're sure we can get the rest of what we need. I say we go help the women with the final work on the tents."

Solomon Garrett didn't move. He thought of his own small farm wagon. Could they strip it for parts? But he knew the answer even as he thought of the question. Brigham had asked that every wagon have a span of five feet from wheel to wheel so that the roads would not have to be made to handle a variety of wheelbases. Solomon's wagon had hardwood pieces, all right, but they were all on too small a scale for what they needed. If they had no choice, he might have to take that one anyway, but it was only slightly better than having nothing at all.

Matthew looked up as the sound of a wagon and team was heard outside. When it stopped, he moved a few steps so he could look out the window. There was a soft exclamation, and then he whirled. "It's Joshua and Carl. They're back."

"I was hoping to find more than one, Nathan," Joshua said ruefully. "Last year we had several wagons and teams that I could have spared. But this year we're having to range out farther and farther from the river to get good timber. That means more wagons and mules to get it down to the water."

"This is more than we expected, Joshua," Nathan said. "A wagon and two good mules. It's like an answer to prayers."

"I only wish I could do more."

Carl looked at Matthew. "Melissa said you've sold the shop here."

"Yes, I'm sorry, Carl. I—"

Carl held up one hand quickly. "You don't have to explain. I'm just sorry it didn't work out so I could help you."

Joshua gave a soft, mirthless hoot. "Old Carl and me are a couple of paupers, aren't we now? There were even a couple of times on this trip that we had to go without meals and had to sleep in someone's barn before we got up to Frenchie's camp and got enough money and food to get us back home again."

"How does it look for this spring?" Solomon asked.

"Good," Joshua said, forcing a brightness into his voice. "We'll have a big raft. Maybe two. If the price of lumber will just hold, I'll be back in business again." He turned to Nathan and frowned deeply. "Thanks to you and Will, I'm going to have to find me another lumber foreman for next year."

"Thanks to me?" Nathan said in surprise. "Why? Where's Jean Claude going?"

"West."

"West? You mean with us?"

Joshua jerked his head up and down in one swift motion. "Says he'll bring these rafts down and make sure he's got me a good replacement; then he plans to buy him a wagon with the wages he's saved and go find you."

"Well, well," Nathan said slowly. Actually, he got little credit for the conversion of Jean Claude Dubuque. It had been Will that had taught him the gospel.

Joshua grunted, half in disgust, half in respect. "Says he wants to go out there and find him some land, marry a good, stalwart Mormon woman, have half a dozen children or so, and become a solid citizen."

"Good for him," Solomon said.

"Yes," Matthew agreed. "Good for Jean Claude."

Joshua turned to Nathan again. "Caroline told me about Peter and Kathryn. What's going on?"

Nathan told him briefly, giving Peter's reasoning. "They left yesterday on the stage."

"He's got grit," Joshua said with admiration. "They both do. You've got to hand it to them for even having the courage to look into it. By the way, who is it that's talking about going to California? I know a few people in Springfield."

"'G. Donner and others' is the way the coming advertisement was signed. I guess they plan to run it in the paper down there."

"George Donner?" Joshua asked in surprise.

"I suppose," came the answer. "It just said G. Donner."

"I'll bet it's George. He's got a brother named Jacob. They've been talking about going off somewhere and getting free land. In fact, now that I think about it, I heard they went to Texas once but didn't like the country there."

"They're the ones," Matthew said. "Peter mentioned that about Texas. They said the land wasn't that good and came back to Springfield."

"My, my," Joshua said, half to himself. "The Donner brothers. Well, they're well enough off, all right. They could easily hire someone to help drive their wagons."

"We don't know whether to pray that they succeed or fail," Derek said glumly.

Carl pulled at his lip. "It's hard to consider them going on alone a blessing, but it's a partial answer to some of your problems, isn't it?"

"Yes, it is." Nathan leaned forward, catching Joshua's eye. "I suppose you haven't changed your mind?"

There was a quick and emphatic shake of his head. "No, although I have to admit, I'm not angry anymore. I guess I was looking for someone to blame for all that's happened. I'm sorry for sounding off like that about your God, Nathan."

He waved that aside. "Leave religion out of it. Just think about the opportunities, Joshua. A whole new world to build. You too, Carl. I'll bet that once the Saints are gone, Nauvoo will never recover. You may not be able to support a family making bricks any longer."

Carl's frown deepened. "Actually, I've been worrying about the same thing." Then he shook his head. "But even if we have to find something else to do, Melissa and I are not interested in going into the wilderness and starting all over again."

"I understand." Nathan decided not to push either one of them further. "Well, we thank you for the wagon and mules. That will make it possible for us to be ready now."

"I'm glad we could find that much," Joshua answered. "I wish to heaven it was more."

"Well," Carl said, "I've been gone a long time. I'm going to go spend some time with the family." He waved and headed for the door.

"Thank you, Carl."

Joshua followed him to the door, but stopped after Carl had stepped outside. "You ready for a shock, little brother?" he said to Nathan.

"What kind of a shock?"

"I think I've hit on a compromise for me and Caroline."

That was enough to make Nathan's mouth drop open. "You have?"

"Yes. I've been thinking a lot about what Brigham said that night, and about what you keep harping on. It could be an interesting opportunity out there."

"A hundred interesting opportunities," Nathan said eagerly.

Matthew piped in now, just as eagerly. "You could do anything you wanted to, Joshua. Hauling freight. Commerce. Mining. Construction."

Joshua laughed easily, no longer taking offense with their attempts to sway him over. "There's only one problem. I've got nothing, absolutely nothing, now. I couldn't outfit even half a wagon, let alone get enough to take my family out of here in two weeks, or even two months."

"Keep the one you brought us. If you go, we'll share. We'll make do," Nathan cried, hardly believing what he was hearing.

"No. Not yet. But let me get that lumber down here next spring, let me get some cash in my pocket again. By then Brigham will have found his promised land, and then, just maybe . . ." He shrugged. "At least it's enough to give Caroline some hope that the separation from the family won't be permanent."

Nathan drew in his breath, wanting to say so much more. "I think she will be very pleased, Joshua. Very pleased."

Chapter Notes

While it would not appear in the Springfield papers until March of 1846, the advertisement read here by Peter attempting to recruit drivers for the George and Jacob Donner party is quoted word for word from the original (see *Sangamo Journal*, 19 March 1846; also Walter M. Stookey, *Fatal Decision: The Tragic Story of the Donner Party* [Salt Lake City: Deseret Book Co., 1950], pp. 59–60).

I love you for trying, Nathan," Lydia said, "even if I'm not very hopeful."

Nathan paused at the door. "I'm not very hopeful either, but . . ." He shrugged. "We do have to try."

"What did Jane say when you asked her?"

"She was very pleased to try and help. She still has very fond feelings for Carl and Melissa and the children."

"She's a good woman, and they think a lot of her."

"I know. That's why I thought of it." He put on his hat. "Well, let's hope they don't throw me out."

Lydia's smile was filled with love. "If they do, you're always welcome here."

As he stepped out on the porch, Jane Manning James was waiting by the gate. He waved and ran lightly down the walk. "Good evening, Jane."

"Good evening, Nathan."

As they started up the street toward Carl and Melissa's house, Nathan said, "I really appreciate your coming. Was it all right with your husband?" Jane had married since leaving Carl and Melissa to work for President Young.

She nodded quickly. "Yes. And Brother Brigham said to tell you he'll be praying for us."

"Good. I think we're going to need all the prayers we can get."

———•———

"Have you heard the latest news?"

Carl and Melissa both shook their heads.

"Well, you've seen for yourselves how the state militia, thanks to Governor Ford, keep prowling around the city, looking for Brigham or any of the other Church leaders so they can arrest them and drag them off to Carthage."

"Yes," Carl said. "Some came poking through my drying sheds yesterday looking for who knows what."

"Well, Brother Brigham and the Twelve can hardly move about, but that's not the worst of it. There's been another letter from Samuel Brannan in New York. He says that the order has been given for the federal troops to march against us."

"Has any of that been confirmed?" Carl asked quietly. "We keep hearing the rumors, but so far we've not seen evidence of one federal militiaman."

"Who knows?" Nathan replied in discouragement. "There are so many stories flying around. But can we take the chance that it's not true?"

There was silence. Then, "So what is Brigham planning to do?" Carl asked Jane.

"They've called a meeting of all the Twelve tomorrow to decide. I'm not sure, but I think they'll call on the Saints to leave in the next day or two."

Melissa looked stricken. "A day or two?"

"Yes," Nathan answered slowly.

Carl shook his head. "Can you be ready to leave that soon?"

"Well, we don't have everything we need, but we're better off than many."

Melissa had started to weep. "That soon?" she whispered.

Carl looked at Jane. "And you'll be going with President Young?"

"Perhaps. Thankfully, President Young has invited me and my husband to go with his company. But we may not be quite ready."

"Including all his wives?" Melissa said, a touch of anger mingling with her tears.

Jane wasn't fazed at all by that. "I'm not sure we'll be ready so soon, but Brother Brigham will be taking all of his household," she said. "Would you want him to leave them behind?"

"No," Carl spoke up, surprising both of them. "I don't agree with the practice, but I'll hand it to Brigham. He's doing what's right by them."

Now Nathan redirected the conversation. "Carl?"

Carl looked away, running his fingers through his hair. "I know what you're going to say, Nathan. And I know why you feel you need to say it, but we've made our decision."

"I know you have. I just want to say a thing or two, and then I'll honor whatever you decide. Tell me about Israel Barlow, Carl."

He blinked, caught completely by surprise by that question. "Israel Barlow?"

"Yes. Remember the buggy whip?"

He still seemed a little nonplussed, but he finally nodded. "I remember it well."

"The buggy whip?" Jane asked.

Carl told her the story quickly. He had been helping carry rock from the quarry up to the temple. He had joked with Israel Barlow about never using a buggy whip with his teams, and Barlow retorted that he controlled his high-spirited team by word alone. Only a fool needed a whip. Then one day, as they were preparing to leave the quarry, Joseph Smith casually recommended that Israel stop in town and buy a buggy whip. To Carl's utter amazement, Israel had done so, then bristled defensively when Carl tried to tease him about it. He would do what the Prophet asked, he said shortly, and refused to discuss it further.

Carl's voice dwindled off. He was clearly lost in the memory of that day.

"So what happened?" Jane asked.

Melissa answered for him. "On their very next trip, Israel's team got spooked. They were above the quarry and they started backing up right toward the edge of the cliff." Now she stopped too, watching Nathan carefully.

"If he hadn't had the new buggy whip," Nathan concluded, "Israel Barlow and his team would have been killed."

The silence in the room was total for several seconds. Then Carl straightened. "So what's your point?"

"I'll make it in a minute." Nathan glanced at Jane. "I asked Jane to come tonight for two reasons. First, of course, she wanted to say good-bye to the family."

Jane broke in. "It was so good to see the children again. They're so grown up. Young Carl? I can't believe it. He's already a man, and not yet fourteen."

"They were so glad when I told them you were coming," Melissa said warmly. "We really loved having you with our family, Jane."

"I know. And you were very good to me."

"The second reason," Nathan went on, "is that Jane has a story of her own to tell. When I asked her, she said that she had never shared it with you. At least not in detail. I wanted you to hear it."

Now Melissa was curious. "What is it, Jane?"

Jane looked a little embarrassed, so Nathan smiled his encouragement. "Go on, Jane. I know you're reluctant to talk about yourself, but I think they need to hear this."

"All right." She turned so she was facing Carl and Melissa more squarely, took a breath, and began. "As you know, my family and I came here from New England in the fall of eighteen forty-three." She stopped, letting her mind go back.

Melissa watched her closely. Jane Elizabeth Manning James had eyes so dark they looked as if they were large pools of liquid lampblack. Though her skin was quite brown, her eyes made the rest of her face seem pale in comparison. Melissa was fascinated as tiny points of light danced across the blackness of the pupils. No wonder Joseph and Emma had taken this woman into their house to help Emma. No wonder Melissa's own children had come to love her so. Her very presence cheered the soul.

"I was born at Wilton, Fairfield County, Connecticut," Jane began. "My family were free blacks. Not *freed* blacks," she emphasized proudly, "freeborn. My grandfather and grandmother had been given their freedom and came north before my mother was born. None of my family are slaves, freed or otherwise. We are freeborn."

"I knew that," Carl answered.

"We lived in the home of a prosperous white family. We worked there as household servants—not slaves, but servants. It was a good life for us and we were very happy. Then one day, two men from the West came to our town. They were the Mormon missionaries. We had joined the Presbyterian faith about a year and a half before, but I was not really satisfied with it. When I heard them speak at a meeting in town, I was convinced that they were presenting the true gospel, and not long after, I joined the Church. The rest of my family also joined."

Carl seemed a little impatient. "Yes, I knew that too."

Jane just smiled. "In the fall of '43, a group of members came west to Nauvoo to live with the Saints. We decided we would come with them."

Melissa's brow furrowed. "I remember when the group arrived, but I don't remember a colored family being with the group."

"That's because we weren't, not when they arrived in Nauvoo." She was no longer looking at Melissa, but was staring straight ahead. Her head was high and the muscles in her neck were like cords, revealing the tension in her. "We traveled together up the Hudson River to Albany and then across New York on the Erie Canal. It was a glorious trip. Never having been out of Fairfield County, we were all very excited." There was a soft, bitter sigh. "But when we reached Buffalo and the rest of the group took tickets on a steamer to Chicago, we were denied passage."

"Because you were Negroes?" Carl said in surprise.

There was a quick, curt nod and the pain was back on her face.

"So what did you do?" Melissa asked.

"Well, the rest of the group went on, of course. We talked about going back to Connecticut, but decided that we wanted to be with the Saints."

Carl's mouth opened in astonishment. "You didn't walk!"

"We did," came the answer. "We didn't have sufficient money to bring that many of us that far by stagecoach or other means of conveyance."

"But that is . . ." He stopped, aghast.

"About eight hundred miles," Jane finished for him softly.

"They walked every step of it," Nathan affirmed.

"How many of you were there?" Melissa said, as shocked as Carl now.

"There were nine of us, counting me. That included two children, one a babe in arms." Now Jane's voice took on a ring of caustic irony. "You have to remember, Melissa. We weren't slaves. We hadn't spent our lives barefoot out in the fields weeding cotton or cutting tobacco. We lived in the home of a wealthy family who treated us kindly and with respect. Our feet were not the feet of slaves or farmworkers."

Jane was far away now, back on those roads again. "We had blisters and sore feet, but at least we had shoes. Then after a time our shoes wore out. We needed every dime we had for food, so we couldn't buy new ones, and we started going barefoot. Our feet soon cracked open and bled until you could see the whole print of our feet in the blood on the ground."

"How did you ever do it?" Melissa whispered. She was surprised to see that Jane's eyes were glistening now, and Melissa felt a wave of shame. Here she was asking questions, making her dredge up the painful memories all over again. But she had misread the tears.

Jane turned to her fully now, and to Melissa's surprise her face was infused with joy. "We stopped one day, right there by the roadside, out in the middle of nowhere. And we united ourselves in prayer to the Lord." She stopped, her voice low and husky.

"Go on, Jane," Nathan urged. "Tell them what happened."

Her head came back around and she smiled radiantly at both Carl and Melissa. "We asked God, our Eternal Father, to heal our feet, and our prayers were answered." There was a long pause. "Our feet were healed forthwith."

The word caught Carl totally by surprise. He jerked forward. "You mean right there? Right then?"

There was a slow nod. "Not in one instant. But forthwith." As Carl sat back, incredulous, Jane spoke to him. "Have you ever known me to lie, Mr. Rogers?"

"No. I—" He shook his head. "No, you've always had the highest integrity, Jane."

"Well, I'm telling you. That day, somewhere in the middle of Ohio, or Indiana—we didn't know exactly where we were—we had a miracle. We got an answer to our prayers that told us in a wonderful way that we were not making this journey in vain."

"And you had no more trouble with your feet?" Melissa asked in wonder.

"None." Jane threw back her shoulders, lifting her face to look directly at Carl and Melissa. "We went on our way rejoicing, singing hymns, and thanking God for his infinite goodness and mercy."

"What a wonderful story," Melissa exclaimed, reaching out to take Jane's free hand. "Why didn't you ever tell us that before?"

"That's not the end of it," Nathan said softly. He looked at Jane. "Tell them the rest."

Jane nodded immediately, eager now to comply. "When we finally reached Nauvoo, we inquired as to where we might go to meet the Prophet Joseph Smith. We were directed to the Mansion House. Emma answered the door and invited us inside, then sent someone upstairs for the Prophet." There was a slow shake of her head, and the look of wonder in her eyes was arresting. Melissa could not take her gaze from her.

"We were standing there, in the parlor, when two men came downstairs and into the room. One was Doctor Bernhisel, the other was the Prophet Joseph. But I did not need an introduction. I knew it was Joseph Smith immediately."

"You did?" Carl asked in surprise.

"I did," Jane said quietly. "You see, back in Connecticut, about three weeks after I was baptized . . ." There was a long moment before she spoke again. "I was shown the Prophet Joseph Smith in a dream. When he walked into the room that night, I didn't need any introduction." There came that soft, radiant smile again. "I already knew him."

She sat back, calm and serene, pleased that both Carl's and Melissa's faces showed that her account had impacted them deeply.

After several moments of silence, Nathan spoke. "Carl, I know that if you were convinced that what we are doing now was God's will, you would come. Well, think about it. There's the simple thing of a buggy whip. There's the miracle of feet healed in a moment. Don't you think that says something about God's power being in this work? Joseph was a prophet, Carl. How else do you explain the Israel Barlow story? A lucky guess? I don't think so. And do you think God would show Jane the Prophet Joseph in a dream if there were nothing to the work?"

Carl stirred, but said nothing. He was watching Nathan, his face without expression. Melissa's head was down, however, and she was scrutinizing her hands with meticulous care.

Nathan suddenly stood. "I'm not asking you to answer, Carl. You have no obligation to answer to me. I'm just asking you to think about it. Jesus told the disciples that signs of power would follow the faithful. If this *is* God's work, then don't let it pass you by." He looked at Melissa, wanting to cry. "You knew once,

Melissa. Just think about that. We don't want to see our family split apart. But much more important than that is the question of doing what God wants you to do."

Jane stood up too and gave Melissa a quick hug. "Good-bye, Melissa. It was wonderful working for your family. Thank you for listening tonight."

Melissa nodded, but neither Carl nor Melissa followed them to the door as they let themselves out.

For a long time after Nathan and Jane had left, Carl and Melissa stood at the window, looking out into the night. Finally, Melissa took Carl's hand. "Tell me what you're thinking."

He shrugged. "About the buggy whip."

"How *do* you explain it?" she asked softly.

He thought about it for a moment before answering. "I guess I have to admit that there is evidence that at times Joseph Smith had the Spirit of the Lord. And I think the healing of the feet was the result of Jane's faith, and her family's. They had made a great sacrifice for their beliefs."

"And the dream?"

He shook his head. "I don't know. The mind can play funny tricks on you."

She didn't turn. "Nathan's right, Carl. I did know once. I knew it was all true."

"Well," he said, wearily now, and with just a trace of anger. "If Nathan wants to talk about evidence, then let's talk about the fact that when Brigham Young rolls out of here, he'll have several wives with him. So will Heber Kimball and who knows how many others. What of that?"

Her thoughts were already there. "I don't know, Carl. You know how that makes me feel. It just makes me sick inside."

"Isn't it possible to be a prophet and then fall? It's happened before."

"I suppose."

He swung on her. "Do you want to leave? Do you want to take our children out of here and go to some wild place a thousand miles from nowhere, facing the threat of Indians, not knowing if you're going to survive the next winter?"

"No, you know I don't. But . . ."

"I know how you feel about your family, Melissa, but we have our family to think about too. Do you want to go? Is that what you're saying?"

There was no sound, but as he turned to look at her, he saw the tears making streaks on her face. "No," she said finally, in a small, barely audible voice. "I don't want to go, Carl. And that's what frightens me the most."

Nathan was in the back room of the store, checking on the bags of beans they were trading to John Browning for one of his new rifles. He heard the door open at the front of the store and the soft jingle of the bell. Only half listening, he went on working. Then he heard his father's voice.

"Good afternoon, Lydia. Is Nathan here?"

"In here," he called. He set down the small record book and pen and wiped his hands on his leather apron. When his father appeared at the doorway, he started across the room, then stopped at the sight of Benjamin's face. "What?"

"Brigham has called for a meeting of all captains at four o'clock."

Lydia had come up behind her father-in-law. "A meeting?" she asked in alarm. "Do you know what it's about?"

He shook his head, his mouth tight. "No, but I can guess."

"Brethren, if we can have your attention. I know there is a lot of excitement, but if you'll quiet down, we'll only have to say this once."

It took another minute, but finally the noise died away.

Brigham barely waited for the last whisper to fade. "Brethren, we met in council this morning. We have come to a decision. As you know, the news from Washington is not good. Our enemies prowl around the city like wolves on the trail of blood. Therefore—" He stopped, suddenly looking overwhelmed by the enormity of what he was about to say. He took a quick breath and bored on. "Therefore, as the Twelve, we have agreed that it is imperative that we start as soon as possible."

There were no gasps, no indrawn breaths, no shocked looks of incredulity. The only real question for the last week had been merely, When shall it be?

"Our enemies have resolved to intercept us whenever we start and to disarm us. If we stay here many days, our way will be hedged up. Therefore, I should like as many as possible to push on as far as possible as quickly as possible. Before we are closed in."

"How soon is that?" someone cried out.

Brigham looked grim. "I have counseled the brethren to procure boats and hold them in readiness to convey our wagons and teams across the river. You captains, get with your families immediately. Tell them to have all things in readiness. I want a family to be in such a state that when the call comes, they can have everything loaded in no more than four hours and start for the river crossing. We suspect that the call to move will come tomorrow or the next day."

He stopped, waiting for a response, but there was not a sound.

"No one is to leave until they are called to do so. I shall start loading my wagons as well. The plan is that the Twelve and I shall cross first so that the Saints will know that they are following their appointed leaders." There was a brief, fleeting smile. "That will also confound the governor's troops, who keep sniffing around for Brigham like a puppy dog looking for an old slipper."

That brought a laugh, but it quickly died out. "Brethren, you have your charge. You are dismissed."

As they walked slowly out the front door of the temple, Nathan turned to his father. "Today is the second day of February."

Benjamin looked at him curiously. "Yes?"

"This is madness, you know," Nathan said quietly. "Utter madness. There won't be grass on the prairies for another two months."

"Are you saying that we shouldn't go?"

"Oh, no. We have no choice. But it's still madness."

"Seems to be a constant bedfellow in our lives, doesn't it?"

Nathan nodded. "Have you ever noticed something, Father?"

"What?"

"When we were driven out of Jackson County it was in November and December. When Kirtland fell and we had to flee for our lives, it was December and January. Far West fell in November and we had to leave there in January and February. Now it's February again. Does it seem to you like something's missing here?"

Benjamin gave a mirthless little chuckle. "I don't remember you mentioning April or May. Early September would also have been nice."

"Do you think the Lord is trying to tell us something?" Nathan mused, half to himself now.

"No."

His head came around. "You don't?"

"No, I think he's trying to *make* us into something."

———◆———

When Jenny opened the front door of the house the next morning, she blinked for a moment. President Brigham Young was standing on their porch, hat in hand, his eyes bright and alert and filled with some hidden amusement.

"Good morning, Jenny."

"Oh! Good morning, President Young."

The smile spread from his eyes to his mouth. "Is Matthew about or has he gone to the wagon shop already?"

"No, he's upstairs with Betsy Jo. Won't you come in?" She

was holding Emmeline in one arm and pushed the door open with her free hand. "I'll go get him."

"Here. Let me take this little beauty while you do so." And then, seeing the look in Jenny's eyes, he laughed lightly. "It's nothing critical," he said. "It's just been so busy of late, that I never get to see this young friend of mine anymore. I was hoping he might just walk up with me to the temple this morning so we would have a chance to visit."

"You're in the fourth company?" Brigham asked.

"Yes."

"And your preparations?"

"As good as could be expected. We have four wagons, now that Joshua brought that one down from Wisconsin. We have the required amount of flour and foodstuffs, with one or two small exceptions."

"Good for you. Would that every family was as ready!"

Matthew looked sideways at his mentor, business partner, and friend. "So how soon do you think we'll be leaving?"

Brigham seemed surprised. "I thought you'd heard. The first company will start tomorrow morning."

It was no less than Matthew expected. He blew out his breath slowly. "It is an enormous task, isn't it?"

There was a quiet grunt of frustration. "More than I ever dreamed possible. I'll tell you, Matthew. I have a whole new appreciation for Moses lately."

"I'll bet you do."

"We are modern Israel, you know," he mused. "And we are about to leave Egypt and strike out into the wilderness."

"For forty years?" Matthew asked, straight-faced.

Brigham hooted. "Might take us that long just to get the people ready to leave." Then he sobered again. "In fact, I have been reading a great deal in the Old Testament about the Exodus. There are some interesting parallels."

"Like what?"

"Well, just this morning, I was reading something that cheered me up greatly. It's in the book of Numbers. Do you remember the time that Moses got so discouraged?"

Matthew's brows knitted into a puzzled expression. "No, I guess I don't."

"Well, there they were, getting manna from heaven every day, one miraculous sign after another being shown to them, and what were the people doing? They were moaning and groaning and complaining. The scriptural word is *murmuring.*" His voice went into a high, mimicking whine. "'We're tired of eating manna all the time. We want fish and the onions. Where are the vegetables of Egypt? Give us flesh to eat.'"

His voice dropped again and he blew out his breath with some disgust. "They were like children, wanting Moses to meet their every need, satisfy every whim. Moses got really discouraged. And that's what cheered me up. He went to the Lord and said something like this: 'What have I done wrong that you have afflicted me with this people? Why should I be asked to carry such a burden? Where am I going to find flesh for them to eat? If you really love me, Lord, why not take my life now and spare me all of this?'"

Matthew was chuckling. "Did he really?"

Brigham smiled back. "Well, I've taken a few liberties with the text, but not many." He looked at Matthew directly, his eyes grave now. "And then Moses said, 'I am not able to bear this burden alone, because it is too heavy for me.'" He sighed heavily. "I know what he means, Matthew. I know exactly how he felt."

Matthew waited, knowing that Brigham had more he wanted to say.

After a moment, he straightened and looked at Matthew again. "But the Lord reminded Moses, and he reminded me at the same time, that we do not carry the burden alone. The Lord is with us, and if we are faithful, we shall be borne up as on eagle's wings, as Isaiah tells us."

He clapped a hand on Matthew's shoulder. "Thank you for letting me unload my cares on you, Matthew. I know it won't shake your testimony to know that old Brother Brigham is human."

Matthew laughed softly. "Never."

They were just starting to climb the hill that led to the top of the bluff and the temple site. They walked on in silence for a moment, each lost in his own thoughts. Then Brigham cleared his throat. "Has Joshua definitely decided to stay?"

"Yes. He's saying that maybe after he gets his lumber down here next spring and after we have found where we're going to be, maybe then he'll come join us. Caroline is, of course, disappointed with that, but at least there is some hope for her."

"And Carl?"

Matthew just shook his head.

"That's a tragedy. He's a good man. And Melissa is a jewel."

"Mother is having a very difficult time with this," Matthew said. Then his voice lifted. "But we heard from Peter yesterday."

"You did? From Springfield?"

"Yes. They have been inquiring around. One family is definitely interested in getting a tutor for their children. The husband is traveling right now, but the wife wants them to come back when he returns and to interview with him."

"Really! That's wonderful."

"In the letter Peter seemed very pleased. He's also found work at one of the newspapers there to earn a little money in the meantime." He started to chuckle. "Peter did say that he provided a group of local boys considerable amusement when he tried to drive three yoke of oxen for the first time."

Brigham was chuckling too. "Peter's got a lot of pluck. Kathryn too. They'll be fine."

They were now just half a block away from the temple, and the front door was clearly in sight. A large crowd of people were gathered there. Brigham slowed his step. "I was afraid of that," he muttered. He took Matthew's elbow. "This is what pains me the most, Matthew. The administration of the temple ordinances is going to have to come to an end."

As they approached, someone spied them coming and an excited cry went up.

Matthew stood back as Brigham pushed into the crowd, shaking hands and answering questions. In a moment, he climbed the front steps of the temple, which put him above the rest of the crowd. He turned to face them and raised his hands. In a moment they quieted, every face looking up in anticipation.

"Brethren and sisters, I was afraid I might find such a gathering here this morning. Did you not hear the announcement that we would not be attending to the ordinances of the temple today?"

A cry of disappointment went up and many were shaking their heads.

"We are preparing to depart. Our enemies are going to try and hedge up the way and prevent us from leaving. If we continue giving the endowment, we shall not be able to get away."

"But how, then, can we get this blessing?" a woman cried out.

Brigham raised a hand. "It is not wise that we stay longer. We shall build other temples, and you shall have further opportunities to receive the blessings of the Lord, as soon as you are able to receive them."

The murmurs of disappointment formed a mournful chorus.

"Brethren and sisters, I am going back home to get my wagons ready and start west tomorrow morning. I urge you to do the same. It is time for us to leave."

Without another word, he stepped into the crowd again and made his way back to Matthew. "Let us return home, Matthew," he said, his voice heavy with discouragement. "I have wagons to load."

As they walked away, Matthew looked over his shoulder. No one in the crowd moved. They stood in clusters, watching their leader leave again. It was as if they were watching their captain boarding the lifeboat and leaving them to sink with the ship.

"It is a wonderful testimony of their faith," Brigham said in a low voice, "but we must prepare to leave."

They walked on silently all the way to the edge of the bluff before Brigham turned around. Matthew turned with him. The crowd had not moved. They still stood there at the front door to the temple, their eyes fixed on Brigham, now nearly a block away.

For a long time, Brigham didn't move. Matthew could see his mouth working, but he didn't speak. Then there came a deep sigh, filled with pain, filled with surrender. "Look at them," he said, not speaking to Matthew, but to the people. "How they hunger and thirst for the blessings of the Lord!"

"Would you like me to go speak to them again?" Matthew asked.

There was a slow shake of the head. Then, "Matthew, could I ask a favor of you?"

"Of course."

"Would you go by the house and tell Sister Young and my family that I will be up here for a time? I'll try to get down this afternoon to continue with the loading of the wagons."

"Yes, Brother Brigham."

Chapter Notes

The story of the conversion of Jane Manning and her family and of their arduous trip from Connecticut to Nauvoo, Illinois, is true (see *Women of Nauvoo*, pp. 19–20; also Linda King Newell and Valeen Tippetts Avery, "Jane Manning James: Black Saint, 1847 Pioneer," *Ensign* 9 [August 1979]: 26–29). Though the modern preference is to call African-Americans "blacks" and not "Negroes" or "colored folk," in the nineteenth century the other terms prevailed, and the author felt to follow that convention here in order to be authentic to the times.

Brigham's conversation with Matthew about Moses is not based on any particular known speech or any of his writings. However, we do know that there were times when he became greatly discouraged with the burden placed upon him. One entry in his history reads: "Unless this people are more united in spirit and cease to pray against counsel, it will bring me down to my grave. I am reduced in flesh so that my coat that would scarcely meet around me last winter now laps over twelve inches. It is with much ado that I can keep from lying down and sleeping to wait the resurrection." (Cited in Susan W. Easton, "Suffering and Death on the Plains of Iowa," BYU Studies 21 [Fall 1981]: 435; capitalization standardized.)

On 29 January, Brigham Young received a letter from Samuel Brannan stating that while in Washington he had confirmed the intent of the federal government to intercept the Mormons and prevent them from leaving. With that discouraging news, on 2 February, Brigham called a meeting of the captains of hundreds and captains of fifties and announced that they would leave in a short time and asked them to be ready to leave on four hours' notice. (See HC 7:577–79.) The following day, Brigham went to the temple and found a large congregation waiting there for the ordinance work, even though he had previously announced there would be none. When they would not disperse, Brigham reopened the temple for endowment work. He records in his journal that 295 people received ordinances on that day. (See HC 7:579.) He did not leave the next day, but stayed another two weeks. By then, nearly six thousand people had been endowed in the house of the Lord since the work had started on 10 December 1845.

They're going! They're going!"

Young Joshua Steed came whooping up the middle of Steed Row, hollering at the top of his lungs, his breath puffing out like smoke from a railroad engine. A door opened and Melissa Rogers stepped out, dressed in a winter coat. Across the street, Benjamin appeared for a second or two at a window; then a few moments later he stepped out, putting on his coat. Mary Ann appeared right behind him, wrapping herself as well.

In five minutes every member of the family was there, Carl and Joshua included. The older children ran on ahead, but the rest walked together the five blocks south to Parley Street, then turned right toward the river crossing. It was a cold morning and there had been a hard frost. Puddles from the thaw of the previous day were now irregular circles of shining ice along the way. By the time they reached the west end of Parley Street, noses were touched with red, and ears tingling.

There was already a crowd, as though they had come for a parade. But there were no bands, no marching soldiers, no clowns to run up and down and amuse the children. Except for the creak of the wagons and the soft plopping of oxen hooves on the frozen ground, and now and then a muted cry of farewell, there were hardly any sounds at all. Those in the wagons waved a limp hand from time to time when they saw someone they knew. Those lining the road watched mutely, knowing that this day signaled the finality of what was coming for each of them.

"Who is it?" Joshua finally asked Nathan quietly. "Who leads out?"

"Charles Shumway and his company."

Joshua didn't know him and said no more.

"How far will they go today, Papa?" Emily asked in a subdued voice.

"The first camp is at a place called Sugar Creek. It's about nine miles west of here."

"Is your departure date set for sure?" Melissa asked her father.

Benjamin nodded once. "Yes. We leave on the ninth. Five more days."

The family fell silent again. When the last of the nearly two dozen wagons passed and the sound died away, the people silently turned and started back towards their homes. A heavy gloom seemed to settle over the city. It was February fourth, 1846. The exodus of the Camp of Israel had officially begun.

Wednesday, February 4th, 1846

As I write these lines with pen and ink by candlelight, I, Alice Samuelson Steed, sit alone in a tiny cabin down in what is called the "passenger deck" of the sailing ship "Brooklyn." I am alone because all the rest of our company, two hundred thirty-eight Saints—seventy men, sixty-eight women, and one hundred children—are up top lining the rails and saying farewell to the United States of America. For a time I was with them, standing beside my beloved Will, but as I saw the white mounds of Staten Island and the bristling guns of Fort Lafayette pass slowly by, and knew that I was leaving my country behind, I could not bear the sight any longer. Who knows what this beginning day portends? Shall we land in six months' time in Upper California or shall we perish in the sea? I feel that the Lord will watch over us, but it is a long and perilous voyage, and one cannot say with any certainty what the future holds.

I have decided to keep a daily journal of our experience. Perhaps someday I shall send it to my parents. I have written them every single week since our departure from St. Louis. There has been no response. So whether they read it or not, I shall write it as though I write to them.

We leave New York City about a fortnight behind schedule. The outfitting of the ship and the task of changing her from a merchant ship to a passenger packet took more time than at first was proposed. Sadly, the refitting has left conditions quite uncomfortable. Our quarters are terribly cramped, the floor of the deck above being no more than four feet above the floor of the deck below. We cannot so much as stand up straight, and have to scuttle about like crabs whenever we are down here.

I must say a word or two about Elder Samuel Brannan, who is the "first elder"—his choice of titles—for our company. I shall keep this journal secreted away, as I wish no one except for Will to read it. Elder B. is not yet twenty-seven years old, which makes him young to lead such an enterprise as this. He is only five years older than Will. He is dashingly handsome and dresses like a dandy. Always his clothes are meticulously cut and cared for. His hair is black; his eyes are dark and flash with enormous energy. When he speaks he tends to roar like an orator and can be very compelling, though I find him somewhat pompous and arrogant. He definitely holds an exalted opinion of himself.

However, I must also admit that he does have some remarkable leadership qualities. He is strongly faithful in believing we carry out the will of the Lord. Will says he is shrewd and quite beyond other men in managing detail and arranging things. He has the vision of a man possessed and the courage to carry it out. While others might have worried only about foodstuffs and other essentials needed on our journey, he has planned for the time when we arrive in California. In addition to the five-ton printing press we carry in the hold below us, he has collected enough agricultural and mechanical implements for a company about three times the size of ours. There are scythes, plows, hoes, forks, shovels, nails, glass, blacksmith's tools, carpenter's tools, millwright's and cooper's tools. We have seeds of numerous kinds, enough to plant our first crops when we arrive. He has brought books and slates enough to start a large school and food sufficient to keep us healthy for a year. We have two milk cows on board along with forty pigs. There are also crates of chickens and ducks to provide us eggs on the journey and a start of fowls in our new home.

Will is at times greatly concerned about Elder B.'s judgment, however. Elder B. can be brash and quite unreasonable, especially if he feels he is right. The refitting of the ship and the stocking of it took about $16,000. Somehow he managed to raise this staggering sum. Will learned just a few days ago that while he was in Washington, Elder B. made a deal with Amos Kendall there. Kendall is the former postmaster general of the United States. Elder B. agreed to sign a contract—in the name of the Church, mind you—with Kendall and his agent. The contract states that once we get wherever we are going, every even-numbered unit of land or town building lot acquired by the Mormons will be deeded over to them.

We've only been married a short time, but this was the first I had seen Will truly angry. It was frightening in a way, but also I loved him all the more when I saw how indignant he was. He told Elder B. that he had no right to bind the Church to such an outrageous contract. Elder B. just pushed it aside, claiming that it was the only way to get Kendall to use his influence in our behalf. Kendall claims to have the president of the United States as a silent partner in this contract, and, according to Elder

Brannan, if we had not signed, the president would stop the Mormons from leaving Illinois. Will does not believe that, but Elder B. airily dismisses any objections.

Enough about Elder B. Things shall be fine. He is good to the people and has inspired us all to undertake this "grand adventure," as he calls it, in the name of the Lord. And the people are wonderful. Most are from New England, but some are from the southern Atlantic coast states as well. There has been some murmuring—especially when people saw the conditions under which we must live for the next six months—but all in all our spirits are high.

Will has astonished me and many others in another way. He has come alive with the thoughts of being at sea again. In some ways he is like a young boy. He amazed the sailors as he scrambled up the rigging like a squirrel and helped them secure the sails. He is—

I must close now. Will is calling down and saying that we are passing Sandy Hook, the last spit of land before we head into the Atlantic Ocean. He wants me to come and be with him and bid farewell to our beloved country.

———◆———

James Frazier Reed was an aristocrat, not only by bearing, which was plain for anyone to see, but also by blood, if there was any truth to the tales told about him. When Peter casually asked about him at the office of the *Sangamo Journal*, where Peter now served as copy editor and typesetter, he quickly got an earful. The Reeds were wealthy, Mr. Reed having prospered greatly as a merchant, railroad contractor, and furniture manufacturer. Though he had been born in the north of Ireland, they said he descended from Polish nobility and that the family name had originally been Reedowsky. He had come to America as a boy, and when he was in his twenties he had moved to Illinois. He served in the Black Hawk War with another of Sangamon County's more well-known citizens, the lanky and affable lawyer and state legislator Abraham Lincoln.

There were two primary reasons James Reed was talking about joining the Donner brothers and going to California, according to the town gossip. First, the whole of the Mississippi Valley was undergoing economic hard times and his business ventures had faltered somewhat. Second, his wife was in ill health (a semi-invalid, some said) and he hoped that California's wondrous climate—"even in December and January vegetation is in full bloom," the accounts claimed, "and December there is as pleasant as May here"—might improve her health.

The semi-invalid part worried Peter a great deal. If that was true, having another person along who was limited in physical capacity might be seen as too much of a burden to deal with. On the other hand, perhaps someone who had physical challenges of her own might be more inclined to show understanding and favor toward Kathryn.

Peter had been tempted to try and get an interview with Mr. Reed alone, to see how he would respond to the idea of a tutor before introducing him to Kathryn. But that seemed underhanded to Peter, and, more important, it made him feel like he was being disloyal to Kathryn. So they came together.

As they approached the gate of the Reeds' home, a finely built two-story brick Georgian, Peter let the wheelchair roll to a stop. The yard was fenced with wrought iron and had what in the spring must have been spectacular flower gardens.

"I will walk from here, Peter."

"Kathryn, I—"

"I won't try and hide the wheelchair from them, Peter. But I will not have you wheel me up to the door."

He nodded, knowing that her showing that she could get around quite well on her crutches would likely work in their favor. He untied the crutches from the back of the chair, braced his foot against the wheel, and helped her up. She got herself firmly planted, gave him a brave smile, then bowed her head and closed her eyes for just a moment. He saw her lips move slightly and heard a soft murmur. Then she looked up. "All right. I'm ready."

"Oh dear!" Margret Reed said softly as Kathryn and Peter entered the sumptuously furnished parlor. James Reed was frowning deeply and trying not to stare at Kathryn.

"Mr. and Mrs. Reed," said the woman servant who had answered the door, "may I present Mr. Peter Ingalls and his wife."

Reed stood swiftly, his face smooth again, and came across the room to shake Peter's hand. "How do you do?"

"I am pleased to meet you, Mr. Reed," Peter said in his best voice. "Thank you for agreeing to see us. May I present my wife, Mrs. Kathryn Ingalls."

Kathryn shifted her weight easily and held out her hand. "Good evening, Mr. Reed. It's a pleasure to make your acquaintance."

Peter turned and looked at her in surprise. Her Irish accent had become suddenly distinct and pronounced.

Mr. Reed's eyebrows went up sharply. "Are you Irish?" he said, letting his own brogue roll out.

Kathryn looked totally surprised. "Why, yes. And you also?"

"I am." He was smiling now. "From what part?"

"South of Dublin, a small place called Kilkenny."

"Aye," he said, enjoying himself now, "I've not been there. We were from the north, up near Londonderry, but I came to America as a boy."

"I too came when I was a child. My father had died, and my mother brought my older sister and me across and we settled on a homestead in western Missouri."

Turning to Peter, Reed inclined his head. "And did I hear a touch of English accent with you, Mr. Ingalls?"

"Yes, sir. I was born and raised in Preston, just north of Liverpool."

Reed stepped back, considerably more cordial now than he had been when he first came across the room. "Please come in and sit down."

Kathryn sat down smoothly, without hesitation, and laid the crutches down beside her chair. She seemed perfectly calm and composed. Peter fought not to stare at her in amazement as he sat beside her.

As Mr. Reed sat down again, he turned his head toward his wife. "Since this involves finding a tutor for our children, I've asked Margret to be present. She will be asking many of the questions."

"We very much appreciate your willingness to consider us," Kathryn said with her prettiest smile.

James Reed was in his mid-forties and was a handsome man with neatly trimmed beard and mustache. Margret Reed looked like she might be about ten years younger than him. She was a pleasant-looking woman with long dark hair, parted in the center and plaited into long circular braids on both sides of her head. She half reclined on the sofa, and her feet and legs were covered with a blanket. Though she appeared somewhat frail, her color was good and her eyes clear. Peter decided that the "semi-invalid" description was an exaggeration.

"Well," Reed began after a moment, "how did you come to hear about our little expedition? We haven't posted the advertisement at the paper yet."

"A friend of ours had heard about the study meetings you and the Donners were holding, and mentioned to me that you might be looking for help as you go west. Then I was given a copy of the advertisement you plan to post with the paper next month."

"Ah. Well, we do plan to find eight or ten young men who can go with us. But you come not as a 'bull-whacker,' which is our primary need, but as a schoolteacher?"

"Not only me, but my wife as well. We have both taught school. I currently work at the *Sangamo Journal* as copy editor and typesetter."

"Can you drive a team?"

Peter had fully expected that one and didn't hesitate. "It would be an exaggeration to say that I have a lot of experience in this area, Mr. Reed, for I have not. However, in anticipation of this possible employment, I have been availing myself of the opportunity to learn down at the Mueller livery stables."

There was a surprised look, then a touch of amusement. "And what have you learned so far?"

"That horses are the most expensive way to pull a wagon, selling at one hundred fifty to two hundred dollars per head for a good workhorse. They are the fastest but also the weakest of draft animals. They need costly grain, they are prone to get distemper from bad water, and they are most likely to be stolen by Indians. A mule runs about fifty to ninety dollars per head. They too are fast, but are given to mayhem, especially at river crossings. They tolerate alkaline water the best of the three choices, but are likely to bolt for home if not watched carefully. They have one other advantage. If a wagon breaks down they can be used as a pack animal."

He smiled fleetingly at Kathryn, who was now staring at him with wide eyes. "Oxen, which are favored by about sixty to seventy percent of all emigrants, cost only fifty to sixty-five dollars per yoke. They are stronger and have great endurance but are considerably slower than either horses or mules. They do very well on prairie grass but have low tolerance for alkaline water. If things get desperate, they can be eaten, but I am told that they are the most difficult to shoe. I don't know if Mr. Mueller was trying to pull my leg, but he claims that you even have to turn them upside down to do it."

Mr. Reed was nodding as Peter finished. "That's exactly right. Shoeing oxen is not a job for the fainthearted."

"I also have learned from my own personal experience that a soft voice is the best ox goad."

"Well," Reed said, obviously impressed. "Are you that thorough with your teaching as well?"

"He is," Kathryn answered for him. "He also keeps books and accounts, if you have a need for that on the trek. He is very good at numbers, sir."

Reed stood up suddenly. "Come with me, young man. I'd like to show you something." He smiled at Kathryn. "That will give you and Margret a chance to visit as well."

He took Peter through the back of the house, stopped at the

pantry near the back door to get a lantern and light it, then led him across the yard to a large barn. He opened the big doors and they stepped inside.

There in the center of the large, open area was a larger than normal wagon. Peter stared curiously. It was slightly higher than usual and had odd extensions on each side. There was also a set of steps extending out of one side.

"What is that?" Peter exclaimed in surprise.

That seemed to be exactly the response Reed was hoping for, for he smiled broadly. "This is what I have heard my daughter call the 'pioneer palace car.' I've had it specially constructed for our trip. Come, let me show you."

As they moved around the front of it, Peter examined the wagon carefully.

"As you may have surmised, my wife is in ailing health. That's one of the reasons we are anxious to make a new home in California. Her mother, Mrs. Keyes, who is an aged widow, shall also be traveling with us. Her health is most certainly not good, and so I have had this wagon built to my specifications. It is designed to make the trip west as comfortable and trouble free as possible."

Peter was no expert on wagons, but he knew that this creation would have impressed even someone with as much experience as Joshua. The wheels were oversized on both front and back, and the tires—banded with steel—were wider than the width of a normal wagon wheel.

With evident pride, Reed reached down and pulled the steps up. They folded flush with the side of the wagon box. Then he lowered them again. "Go on up. I want you to see inside."

The first thing that was evident to Peter's eye was why he had called it the "palace." The whole center of the wagon was a sumptuously fitted room, much like a miniature parlor or sitting room. In the center was a small table, its feet bolted to the floor. Along both walls were padded benches for sitting. Only they were not attached to the sides of the wagon box but to the floor.

"Look," Reed said, sitting on one of them and bouncing up

and down. There was a soft squeaking noise. "These are spring seats, just like you find in the finest of stagecoaches." He patted the seat beside him. "Try it."

Peter did so, amazed at how comfortable they were. Most wagons had no springs at all, and often those traveling with them found it more pleasant to walk than to endure the jolting ride.

Turning, Reed gestured toward the far corner. There was a sheet-iron stove there, with a stovepipe going straight up and through the canvas cover. It was not a full-size stove, but about half-size. "It will likely get cold on some nights," he said. "I didn't want my wife and mother-in-law to get chilled."

"I can't believe it," Peter said. "I've never seen anything like it."

Reed seemed pleased. He looked around at his creation for a moment, then stood and went down the steps. Peter followed, still visibly impressed.

Reed laid a hand on Peter's shoulder. "Well, shall we go back in and see how the ladies are faring?"

"Good night. Thanks again for letting us come speak with you."

"Good night," Reed called, waving cordially. "We shall be in touch and let you know of our decision, but we are most impressed."

"Thank you." Peter and Kathryn turned out the gate and started up the walk. Only when they heard the door shut did Kathryn look at Peter. She was trying to appear very demure, but the grin broke out and spread across her face in an instant. "'We are most impressed,'" she said, in a deep voice that sounded surprisingly like Mr. James Frazier Reed's.

Peter stepped to the spot where they had left the wheelchair. He got Kathryn settled, then started pushing her back toward their own street. "So tell me," he whispered loudly, "what all did she say?"

"Well," Kathryn said, tipping her head back and half closing her eyes in pleasure, "we talked about teaching school, of course. And I told her about both of us teaching for Jessica."

"Did she ask where?"

"Yes. I told her it was in Nauvoo."

He groaned. "Did she ask if we were Mormons?"

"No. I got the distinct impression she already knew. She did tell me not to mention Nauvoo to Mr. Reed, though. That it would be better that way."

He pursed his lips. "She did? Does that mean she's considering you and doesn't want to have our being Mormons influence him against us?"

"Not just me, Peter. She's considering us. And yes, I think that's exactly it. She liked me. I could tell. And I like her. We got along quite famously, actually."

"Wonderful!"

"She was much too polite to ask me about my legs, but I told her anyway. I told her about the lightning and how at first I couldn't do anything. That seemed to impress her. I even told her about my wheelchair."

"I can't believe it," he said. "So you don't think it's going to discourage her?"

"She seemed a little concerned about convincing her husband that I won't be another problem for him. But as for her, she said she was sure it would work out. She has four children—one older daughter by a previous marriage, and three younger ones. She is determined that their education not be neglected while they travel west. She is a very determined woman."

"I can't believe it, Kathryn," he said again, his voice light with wonder. "I think we've got it."

"So do I, Peter. So do I." She opened her eyes and turned back to look at him. "Did Mr. Reed give you any idea of when they will be leaving?"

"Yes. In a little over two months. Evidently, there's a large party of emigrants forming up to go to Oregon and California at Independence, Missouri, in May. They want to leave here in time to join up with them. He says he thinks it will be about the middle of April."

"Good. That will mean we are not that far behind your family."

"I'm telling you, Kathryn, these people are excellent planners. They have money. I don't know how many extra yoke of oxen they are taking just for emergencies. They have riding horses, beef and milk cattle. And that wagon, Kathryn. Oh, that wagon! You won't believe it."

"Mrs. Reed told me that he's very proud of what he had done there."

"Very proud. And from what he says, the Donner brothers are just as well-to-do as the Reeds are." He laughed aloud. "We are going to travel in style."

She threw back her head and laughed with him in pure delight. "Oh, Peter. You're right. I think we've done it."

Benjamin waited at the window of the sitting room, watching through the curtains to the house across the street. He already had his coat and scarf on. After about five minutes, he grunted softly. "Caroline is leaving."

Mary Ann looked up from carding wool. "Are the children with her?"

"Yes. Do you think he suspects anything?"

Mary Ann smiled. "No. She's told him she's going over to Lydia's to help with the packing. Joshua is working on the books from the lumber camp. He'll be grateful for the time to be alone."

Benjamin was carrying a copy of the Book of Mormon in one hand. He tucked it under his arm, walked to Mary Ann, and bent down and kissed her forehead. "Any last minute words of advice?"

She shook her head. "Just follow your heart, Benjamin. That's all that matters."

He pulled a face, far less confident than she was. "It didn't work with Melissa and Carl."

She shook her head. "You don't know whether it did or not. We may not know that for a long time."

He kissed her again. "How did I ever manage to get you?" he said softly.

She smiled sweetly up at him. "I guess it was just your lucky day."

———◆———

Joshua looked up as he heard the front door open. "Caroline? Are you back already?"

"Want to guess again?" said a deep voice.

He pushed a large ledger book aside and stood up. Benjamin stepped around the corner into view, already shedding his coat. "Hello, Joshua."

"Hi, Pa. What's up?"

"I know you're busy, but if you've got a minute, I'd like to talk."

A little surprised, Joshua shrugged, nodding toward the table full of books. "I'm glad for any excuse to get away from this." He pointed toward where two chairs flanked a small lamp table. "Let's sit down."

As they did so, Joshua saw the copy of the Book of Mormon in his father's hand. One eyebrow lifted slightly, but he said nothing. When they were settled into their chairs, Joshua sat back to wait, suspecting what might be coming.

"I saw Caroline go. I thought about waiting until tomorrow, but . . ." Benjamin shook his head. "Tomorrow will probably be pretty hectic."

"What time are you scheduled to be at the ferry?"

"Two o'clock. They're hoping we'll be across by three."

"And it's for sure?"

"Yes. Our captain sent confirmation this morning. We leave tomorrow."

Joshua leaned forward, elbows on his knees, and began to drum his fingers together softly. "It's going to be hard, Pa."

Benjamin's head went up and down slowly.

"The family has been so close this past year and a half since Carl and Melissa came back. All of us together except for that time you were in Nashville."

"It's been wonderful. It's not easy leaving tomorrow, knowing that we won't be together any longer."

"I know." There was a fleeting smile touched with sadness. "Did you come to try and talk me into reconsidering?"

"No."

"No?"

"No. I didn't come to try to persuade you to come with us."

"Perhaps in a year or two."

"We hope so. Your mother is finding this very difficult."

"So are we. Caroline can hardly bear to talk about it. And Melissa? She's already falling to pieces."

He nodded again, watching Joshua closely. "Do you remember the last time we said good-bye?" he suddenly asked.

Joshua was momentarily startled. "You mean when you and Ma left for Nashville?"

"No. Before that."

"When?" But it was obvious he already knew.

"It's been almost seven years ago now, Joshua. It was July of eighteen thirty-nine. I think people would say I was on my deathbed."

"I remember." It came out barely loud enough for him to catch.

"You didn't like what I had to say, but you listened to me then because you thought I was dying."

"You were!" Joshua shot back. "We all thought you were gone."

"Well, I'm not dying now, but by tomorrow afternoon, I will be gone. Your mother will be gone. The rest of the family will be gone. And who knows when we will see each other again." There was a challenge now in his voice. "And since this is our last day together, I thought you might listen to me again."

Joshua's smile was rueful, but genuinely filled with love and affection. "Of course I'll listen, Pa."

"Oh, no," Benjamin chided. "I'm not just talking about being polite to me. I'm talking about listening."

He sobered. "All right, I'll listen. But there are no promises."

"I don't remember asking for any," came the dry response.

"All right, then, I'm listening."

"Tell me about the Savior, Joshua."

He reared back slightly. "The Savior? Me?"

"Yes." Benjamin waited, his face impassive.

"I don't know," Joshua said, almost stammering. "What do you mean?"

"Tell me about the Savior."

"I . . . I'm not religious, Pa. I don't know if I believe all that stuff."

"Stuff? What stuff?"

"About him dying for our sins and giving his life for us."

Benjamin nodded thoughtfully. "Do you think it's possible a man could love others enough that he would do something like that?"

Joshua thought about that. "Well, yes, I suppose. I would gladly die for Caroline if it came to that."

"And the children?"

"Yes." There was no hesitation.

Benjamin nodded and fell silent. Joshua watched him, fighting the temptation to start to fidget a little.

"Do you remember Cincinnati, Joshua?"

That one came out of nowhere and he looked puzzled. "Cincinnati?"

"Yes, you told me about it once. You said you still carry a six-inch scar on your shoulder from it."

His face fell. "Oh. Yes, the fight." It had been in those first years after running away from Palmyra. There had been a barroom brawl. A professional gambler had been jumped by several men and Joshua didn't like the odds. He had come away with a new friend, a vicious cut, and a warrant for his arrest for nearly killing one of the men.

"And Independence?"

Joshua's eyes narrowed.

"The whiskey. The gambling. Striking Jessica."

"What are you doing, Pa?" he asked in a low voice.

Benjamin seemed not to hear. He was almost musing. "You were so filled with hate that you drove your wife and baby daughter out of their house into a winter's storm."

"Pa," he said sharply, "that's over now. I'm not proud of that."

"Do you think I'm condemning you, Joshua? Well, I'm not, because I'm the one who drove you out of my house and into that life. You were young and foolish and way off the beaten path. And me? Well, I was old and foolish and way off the beaten path."

"That's all in the past now."

Benjamin smiled softly. "Yes, it is, isn't it?" He began to finger the copy of the Book of Mormon in his lap, but his thoughts were still far away. Finally he came back, looking directly at Joshua. "Let's suppose that someone came to you today and proposed to help you."

"Help me? In what way?"

"Let's suppose they had heard about all that had happened to you—Samuelson's ruination of your partnership, the burning of the stables, the loss of the twenty-five thousand dollars—everything! And suppose that this person said he wanted to be your benefactor, that he wanted to help restore everything you had lost."

Joshua was openly skeptical. "I'm sorry, that's a little hard for me to imagine."

Benjamin looked surprised. "Why? Isn't that what you did for us after we lost everything in Missouri?"

Joshua blinked, looking almost stunned. "But you were family."

"All right. Let's say this benefactor was family. Let's say that Nathan was extremely wealthy. Do you think he would do something like what I just described?"

There was no need to even question that. "Yes, he would," Joshua admitted quietly.

"Why?"

"Because he is family."

"It's called love, Joshua."

"Yes, I suppose that's what it comes down to, isn't it?"

Benjamin leaned forward now, his face almost radiant with a quiet joy. "That's what the Savior did for you, Joshua. You've been restored. You were rebellious, angry, a drunkard, violent. You had lost everything. Everything! And now, look at you."

"I've lost everything now."

Benjamin's look shamed him instantly. "Why is it you want to blame God for the bad things, and not give him credit for the other—Caroline, a beautiful family, a comfortable home."

"You're right, Pa," he murmured. "The only thing I've lost that really matters is Olivia."

"And the Savior is going to restore her to you as well, Joshua. You know that, don't you?"

"No, I—"

"Yes, you do, Joshua. Just listen to what your heart is telling you. You don't believe that Olivia is no more. You don't believe that she has become nothingness. That her smile is gone. That her laugh that lifted everyone around her is forever silenced. You don't believe that, do you? Not really."

"I don't want to believe it."

"No! You *don't* believe it. And that's part of what the Savior has done for you, Joshua. That's why he died on the cross. That's why he suffered so terribly in the garden. He wanted to be able to restore people. Restore them to life. Restore them to goodness and happiness. Just as he has restored you, Joshua. Just as he restored me."

Joshua's head had lowered and he was staring at the floor.

"Suppose Nathan had used his wealth to give you everything back. How would you feel toward him? What would you do?"

He still did not look up. "That's obvious."

"Tell me."

"I would be forever grateful. I would do . . ." He stopped, seeing where his words were leading him.

"You would do anything for him."

There was a mute nod.

Now at last Benjamin opened the book on his lap. His fingers moved slowly, opening to the center of the book. He already had a slip of paper there. There was an inaudible sigh. "In the Book of Mormon, two men named Alma and Amulek were teaching a group of people called the Zoramites. Alma taught them about faith and how to get it. Amulek talked about the Atonement and how the Lord's infinite mercy could save them."

He looked down. "I was reading this last week and one part just hit me hard, Joshua. It hit me hard for you. Here is what Amulek says. 'And now my beloved brethren—'" He looked up. "Or I would say, 'Now my beloved son.'"

Joshua's head came up. He looked as if he wanted to escape.

Benjamin continued. "'Now my beloved son, I desire that ye should remember these things, and that ye should work out your salvation with fear before God, and that ye should no more deny the coming of Christ.'"

There was a long pause; then very slowly Benjamin went on. "'That ye contend no more against the Holy Ghost, but that ye receive it, and take upon you the name of Christ; that ye humble yourselves even to the dust, and worship God in whatsoever place ye may be in—'" His voice now rose in both power and solemnity. "'And that ye live in thanksgiving daily, for the many mercies and blessings which he doth bestow upon you.'"

He closed the book and sat back, saying no more. The silence stretched out for a full minute, then two. Joshua was no longer looking at him, but staring beyond him at nothing.

Finally Joshua drew in a breath. It was filled with pain. "So you came over to call me to repentance?" he asked softly. There was no bitterness, only a quiet sadness.

"No!" Benjamin said fiercely. "You've already repented, Joshua. Don't you see that? Your heart has been changed. No, Joshua, all I've come to do is call you to remembrance."

His words struck Joshua hard and he looked suddenly bewildered.

Benjamin stood slowly. Joshua watched him, but didn't move. "Joshua," Benjamin said, his voice heavy with emotion. "Tomorrow we start west. We're like Israel of old. We leave Egypt now to find the promised land. If you and Caroline and Carl and Melissa are not with us, we will be sad, but it is not a tragedy. But someday, this life will be over, and we'll be going to another place of rest."

Suddenly his voice broke and he had to take in a deep breath to regain control. "If we do not have you with us then, then it *will* be a great tragedy, one that I cannot bear to contemplate."

He moved across the room to stand beside Joshua, whose head had dropped again. "Oh, my beloved son," he said in a whisper, laying his hand on his shoulder. "That's what I want you to remember as we leave tomorrow. Your mother and I can stand this farewell. We could never bear the other."

He squeezed his son's shoulder briefly, then went quietly out into the hall, got his coat, and let himself out.

Chapter Notes

By some strange irony, because of various delays, the *Brooklyn* did not set sail from New York harbor until 4 February 1846, the very day the first wagons crossed the Mississippi River on ferryboat and started the long trek across Iowa Territory (see *CHFT*, pp. 326–27).

The description of Samuel Brannan's character, the company of Saints, the ship, and the supplies it carried comes from Paul Bailey's work on Samuel Brannan (see *Sam Brannan and the California Mormons* [Los Angeles: Westernlore Press, 1943], pp. 25–31). He gives the numbers of passengers at 238. Another source says it was 234 (see Lorin K. Hansen, "Voyage of the *Brooklyn*," *Dialogue* 21 [Fall 1988]: 52). In the *History of the Church* it is put at only 175, with 55 additional crew (see HC 7:587–88). This is probably an error, perhaps given out by the ship's captain to disguise the fact that the ship carried more than the allowed load of passengers (see Hansen, "Voyage of the *Brooklyn*," p. 52).

Details of the land deal made by Brannan with Amos Kendall and the

United States government are described in letters and the actual contract sent to Brigham Young by Samuel Brannan (see *HC* 7:587–91). The Twelve rejected the contract outright, seeing it for the extortion that it was.

While some of the minor details given in this chapter about the Reeds and their wagon and supplies (such as the placement of furniture in the wagon) had to be created by the author, the majority of the material comes from historical sources on the Donner-Reed Party. Reed was Irish but was thought to be of Polish aristocracy. His wife, Margret, was in failing health but would prove to be a courageous woman. The "pioneer palace car," with its stove and spring seats and commodious beds, was all part of Reed's design to make the trip as comfortable as possible for her and his invalid mother-in-law. (See Walter M. Stookey, *Fatal Decision: The Tragic Story of the Donner Party* [Salt Lake City: Deseret Book Co., 1950], pp. 60–61; and George R. Stewart, *Ordeal by Hunger: The Story of the Donner Party* [Boston: Houghton Mifflin Co., 1988], pp. 11–12, 16–17.) Other sources question whether the wagon was as large and spacious as some would suggest (see Kristin Johnson, "The Pioneer Palace Car: Adventures in Western Mythmaking," *Crossroads* 5 [Summer 1994]: 5–8).

The scripture Benjamin quotes to Joshua is now Alma 34:37–38.

Bᵧ early afternoon of the ninth day of February, the air had warmed enough that the hard freeze of the night before was gone and one's breath showed only for a moment in the air. The sky was still overcast, but it was high and thin and held no promise of immediate snow. On Granger Street, between Mulholland and Ripley Streets—that block commonly known as Steed Row—four wagons were lined up along the west side of the street. Three of the wagons looked exactly the same. The odd one, and the last in line, was the wagon Joshua and Carl had brought down from Wisconsin. Built for hauling timber out of the woods, it was three feet longer and the wagon box had slightly higher sides than the others. Also, the canvas cover was darker and more weathered than the new canvas that sheltered the other three.

When it came to the teams, however, there was no match at all. The two mules that came down from Wisconsin were not hitched to the lumber wagon. They were pulling the lead wagon, which carried Benjamin and Mary Ann, Matthew, Jenny, and the young couple's two children. The largest wagon had three yoke of oxen—six in all—hitched to it. Because they had the greatest number of people, Jessica and Solomon Garrett were given the lumber wagon. They also carried three hundred more pounds of flour than the others because of the extra room. That much weight was too much for the two mules.

Nathan's wagon, the second in line, had only two yoke of oxen, the minimum for pulling a fully loaded wagon. Three would have been better, but they simply had not been able to purchase another yoke. Of greater concern was the fact that Derek and Rebecca had only a team of horses to pull their wagon. They were a heavy-shouldered pair of draft horses that had proven their worth on some of Joshua's freight hauls, but for a trek of such long duration, oxen would have been better. But here again it was a case of necessity making the decisions for them.

The family's array of stock was rounded out by one milk cow tied to the back of Nathan's wagon, and a riding horse tied at the rear of Derek's. The horse wore its saddle so as to save space and weight in the wagon. Once across the river, the men and older children would take turns riding the horse to lighten the loads in the wagons.

All morning long, Steed Row had looked like a colony of prairie dogs. People ducked out of the houses carrying boxes, bags, or piles of clothing. They would poke their heads into the wagons, disappear momentarily, then scurry back to the houses again. The flour, seeds, and heavy tools had been loaded the day before. Now came the household and personal goods—bedding, clothing, kitchen utensils, water buckets, pistols, rifles, ammunition, matches carefully wrapped in waxed paper, sugar, salt, pepper, other spices, baskets and tins of dried fruit, medications. Inside the houses, there were debates—sometimes heated, sometimes tearful—about whether this or that could be taken or had to be left behind. Usually, the latter decision held sway.

By one o'clock, the last item had been stowed, the last grease bucket tied to the side of the wagon, the last mess in the house tidied up and put away. As Benjamin looked around and saw that at last it was done, he motioned for Savannah. She scampered over to him.

"Savannah. Will you go tell everyone that we're going to have family prayer before we leave? We'll meet in Grandma's living room."

"Yes, Grandpa." And away she went.

They all came, even those who would not be leaving this day. They crowded in, faces sorrowful, voices subdued. Benjamin watched until the last were seated either in chairs or on the floor, then stood up.

"The hour of our departure has finally come," he said gruffly. "This is the time we have been dreading for months now, the time when our family will be separated again." He paused and looked around the room. Every eye was fastened on him. "Most of us undertake a difficult journey to a place we know not. I felt it was appropriate that we have this one last opportunity to have prayer together so we can ask the Lord to watch over all of us. I would suggest that we kneel."

It took several moments for the moving and shuffling to stop and for everyone to find a place. He saw that for the most part, they knelt together as families, and that seemed appropriate. When they were finally settled, Benjamin bowed his head. All the rest followed suit.

"Our Father in Heaven, hallowed be thy name. As we kneel here this day, prepared to follow thy call into the wilderness—a call that now separates us from each other—we remind ourselves that we are here to see that thy will is done on earth as it is in heaven.

"Our hearts are filled with sorrow, Father, when we consider that we will be separated as a family. How we thank thee for this family! How we thank thee that it has been our special privilege to be a part of it! We thank thee for the children that were sent to our home. We thank thee that they have found husbands and wives who have likewise become part of our family. We thank thee for the numerous grandchildren who are gathered around us. In this rising generation, we have great hopes for the future. We find each one a joy and a delight and pray for them. We are thankful for those who have been joined to our family through circumstance and who have become part of us as though they were our own."

He stopped, hearing the first of the sniffles sounding around him. "Father, we are mindful that already members of our family have been taken on different paths. We pray for them, Father. We pray for Will and Alice on their voyage to California. Smooth the seas and chart their path clearly. May it be our privilege to meet them again in that place thou hast designed to be our new home. We are grateful for the news received just yesterday that Kathryn and Peter have found a way west. We are grateful for thy tender mercies unto them and plead for thy protective care to overshadow them until they can join us again."

Now the room was filled with the sound of sniffling and stifled sobs and Benjamin had to stop for a moment. Finally, he took a breath and went on. "O Holy Father, we pray for those who will be left behind here in Nauvoo. We pray a special blessing on Melissa and Carl and their children. Keep them safe from any danger and help them prosper. Let them know of our deep love for them and that they shall always be in our prayers. Be with Joshua and Caroline and their children. Protect and care for them. Let them know of our great love and concern for them and keep them safe until we can meet again."

He stopped once more and took a deep breath. "Now, Father, we express our gratitude to thee for thy house which is not far from us and which we leave now this day. How grateful we are that we could see it completed to this point so that we could be endowed with power in preparation for our departure into the wilderness."

His voice caught and he knew there was no way he could stop his own tears from coming. "How grateful we are that under the sealing power of thy priesthood our family has been sealed together for time and for all eternity! Be with those who have not yet had this wonderful privilege, that someday they too may join that eternal circle."

Beside him, he could feel the shudders running through Mary Ann's body. Without opening his eyes, he reached out and took her hand. "Now, Father, we prepare to depart. We commend ourselves to thy over-watching care. As Israel of old was guided by thee, we ask that thou wilt oversee our journey and protect us from our enemies and from any danger. Be with us as we seek a place of refuge where we can raise our children in peace. Keep us safe. Make us strong. Buoy up our feeble and fainting hearts so that we may have the courage to do thy will. And this we pray for in the name of our beloved Lord and Savior, Jesus Christ, amen."

One by one the doors were shut and locked, and the family members walked slowly out to the wagons. There they turned their keys over to Carl and Joshua, who would work with the committee of trustees charged with selling what property was not already disposed of.

Finally the moment arrived. Nothing more could postpone that moment they had all been dreading. Even the children, excited and giggling all morning, were subdued now as they filed back out into the street.

Benjamin looked up at the sky. It was still overcast, and the sun was no more than a brighter spot of gray in the sky. It was clearly past its zenith. He turned to the family. "We'd better get started. We're to be at the ferry by two o'clock. Children, you'd better say good-bye to your cousins."

He looked at Mary Ann. Her eyes were shining, and her lip started to tremble. "It's time, Mother," he added softly.

Amid wails and cries, the children swarmed around each

other. For Melissa's and Caroline's children, there was no mistaking the envy that mingled with their sorrow. In their minds, this was an adventure that came along only once in a lifetime and they were the ones who were missing out. The parents saw it as something far more tragic than that. It was the breakup of the family.

As they watched their offspring hugging each other and making outrageous promises to write every day, Joshua finally turned to his parents. "I'm going to accompany you across the river," he said. "I'll say my good-byes there."

Savannah spun around. "Can I go with you, Papa? Can I? Please?"

He shook his head. "No, I'm just going to cross over on the ferry and see them off. Then I'm coming right back."

Caroline looked at her daughter. "We'll go down to the ferry landing with them, but not across the river."

"Oh, please, Papa," she begged, wringing her hands. "I want to see Grandma and Grandpa off too. Please. I've been so good. I've not said anything about not going. Please, Papa. Please!"

Joshua looked at his father, who was smiling in spite of himself. "Don't look at me," Benjamin said. "She's purely yours."

"I want to go! I want to go!" Sarah cried out.

But Carl squashed that immediately. "We're not going down to the river, Sarah." He glanced at Melissa, who was weeping copiously now. "It's better if we say good-bye here."

Benjamin turned to Joshua and Caroline as Savannah jumped to his side and threw her arms around him. "If Joshua's coming across with us, I guess it wouldn't hurt."

Joshua shook his head in surrender. He looked at Caroline, who nodded. The bond between these two—a redheaded imp and a gray-haired patriarch—had always been unusually strong. Caroline remembered that first time in Missouri when Savannah had slipped out of her mother's arms and trotted into Benjamin's—a thing unheard of for her. "All right," she said, "but you stay right with your father."

"Oh, thank you, Mama. Thank you, Papa."

Now Carl stepped forward to face Nathan. He stuck out his hand and Nathan gripped it firmly. "Thank you for the other night, Nathan. I know you think it didn't do any good, but it meant a lot to me and Melissa that you cared enough to try."

Nathan started to answer, then suddenly couldn't speak. He pulled Carl forward and threw his arms around him, holding him tightly to himself. "Take care, Carl," he finally managed. "Take care of our Melissa."

"I will."

All around now the tears were flowing. Melissa was the most affected. Tears were streaming down her face. Her body shuddered as she fought to keep at least some control. She went to Matthew, who took her by the hands and then gently kissed her on the cheek. "Good-bye, dear, dear Melissa," he said in a low, strained voice. "Oh, how we'll miss you!"

That did it. She began to sob and could say nothing as Jenny took her in her arms. Then Jessica and Solomon moved in, as did Derek and Rebecca. Carl stepped to Melissa's side and put his arm around her, steadying her as her body was swept by great shudders. After she had clung to each of them, Carl gently turned her around to face her parents. With a great cry, she threw herself into her father's arms. "Oh, Papa, I'm sorry. I'm so sorry."

He took her face in his hands, tears welling up in his own eyes. "Sweet Melissa. You will always be in our thoughts and in our prayers." He pulled her to him with a sudden fierceness. "Don't stop believing, Melissa. Whatever else happens, don't stop believing."

She couldn't answer. She buried her face against him and wet his shoulder with her tears. Finally, he stepped back and turned her toward her mother. Now any semblance of control that was left to her totally collapsed. Mary Ann opened her arms, and Melissa fell into them, her body shaking, the sobs coming out in great cries of pain. "Oh, Mama!"

"It's all right, Melissa. It's all right."

"We're not coming down to the river," Melissa gasped, between sobs. "I can't bear it. I can't!"

"I know." Mary Ann reached up and stroked her daughter's hair, tasting the salt of her own tears as they streamed down her face. "We'll never stop praying that you'll come, Melissa. Never!"

Melissa said nothing, just clung to her all the more fiercely.

Caroline was saying her farewells too. She was weeping, but still was in control of herself. For the longest time, she and Lydia held each other, not saying anything. Then finally, Lydia pulled back to look at her. "You'll come, Caroline. You will. I feel it."

"Yes. I think so too. Give us a couple of years and I think we'll be there." Now a fresh burst of tears overflowed. "Otherwise, I would be like Melissa. I could not bear to see you go."

She turned to Nathan. As he hugged her, she looked over his shoulder. Joshua was standing aside, waiting for the good-byes to be said. She went up on tiptoes. "I don't know if the fire and what happened with Walter Samuelson was the Lord's doing or not, Nathan," she whispered, "but I do know that before the family started fasting, I had no hope. Now I have hope, Nathan. Thank you."

He shook his head, deeply moved. "No, Caroline. It is your faith and your goodness that the Lord is responding to." He laughed softly. "And somehow, I think the Lord was afraid that if he didn't do something, he might have Savannah to contend with."

Caroline smiled at him through her weeping. "Yes. She won't give up."

Suddenly, Nathan's eyes began to burn. "Shall I tell you the greatest miracle, Caroline?"

"What?"

"What you have done for Joshua. Don't give up on him."

She stepped back, wiping at her eyes with the back of her hand. "I won't," she whispered. "I won't."

The scene at the ferry dock at first seemed as chaotic as the one on Steed Row, but after watching for a few minutes, Nathan could see that there was underlying order here as well. There was a large crowd milling around the landing area. Many of these, like the Steeds, were leaving the city. Others were clearly family and friends come to see them off. There were several men, obviously not Mormons, who stood in a cluster on one end of the dock, smoking cigars or working their jaws steadily as they chewed on wads of tobacco stuffed inside their cheeks. These were the river transients, the riffraff that plied the river towns all up and down the Mississippi. They watched the crowd around them with obvious disgust, muttering or making mocking remarks. The Mormons tried to ignore them.

When the Steeds arrived with their four wagons, they became the thirteenth through the sixteenth wagons in line. That was a little before two o'clock. Now, as it approached half past three, they were next up for loading. There were two large flatboats ferrying back and forth to the Iowa side. These carried up to four wagons and as many as thirty people at a time. There were also two smaller boats that could take one wagon and family each trip. Numerous lighter craft—skiffs, rowboats, canoes— seemed to be taking individuals and small groups across with nothing more than what they carried with them. The river was running with slush, and there were large chunks of ice coming down from the upstream breakup. A few blocks were almost as big as some of the smaller boats and presented a real threat to crossing. A jagged corner could puncture the side of a canoe like a knife piercing soft leather.

The largest of the flatboats—empty on its return trip—was pulling in to the ferry dock. Right behind it came a second, smaller boat, empty now as well. The lead captain jumped off the boat and onto the shore. He came up to Benjamin, Joshua, and Nathan. "How many?" he barked.

"Four," Benjamin answered.

The man stepped back and eyed the line. "The fourth one is yours too?"

Joshua nodded.

"I can't get all four of you on my boat," he said, "not with that many oxen." He glanced quickly at the other flatboat, which was just tieing up, then spoke to Benjamin. "Who's the fourth driver?"

"Solomon Garrett."

"Hey, Garrett!" the man called. "Bring your rig up here and put it on this other boat."

Solomon looked momentarily surprised, then nodded. He took the lead span of oxen, calling out softly, pulled out of line, and came up to where they were. As he did so, the captain eyed the other three men. "You're still a little long, I think. Let's unhook one span of oxen off that second wagon and send them with this big one. Also, you'll have to untie the cow and horse. Lead them on first and take them up to the prow. We'll be nose to wagon end as it is."

"All right." Nathan turned, looking for the young men of the family. "Luke. Mark. Untie the cow and horse and take them on first. Young Joshua, help me unhitch the lead span off our wagon. They'll go with Solomon."

As the boys sprang to obey, the captain turned to Benjamin and Joshua. "That'll be four dollars, fifty cents." He spat. "The fifty cents is for the extra animals."

Joshua nodded, reached in his pocket, and took out some coins; then he and Benjamin turned to help.

Solomon led the oxen while Jessica sat on the seat above him with little Solomon on her lap. Once they were on board, Nathan led the extra span of oxen on behind them and snubbed the rope to the back of Solomon's wagon. He stepped off again as the captain shouted at the three men crewing that boat, and they shoved off into the current.

On the other side of the dock, Matthew was leading his team of mules forward. They snorted and pawed as they reached the gangplank, but Matthew rubbed their noses and coaxed them on. Mary Ann and Jenny were on the wagon seat, with Savannah between them. Jenny held Emmeline in her arms, and three-year-old Betsy Jo poked her head out between her mother and Savannah. Lydia sat on the seat of the second wagon, holding the reins. Emily, Elizabeth Mary, and Josiah sat beside her, all of them grinning widely with the excitement as Nathan took the remaining yoke of oxen and led them forward. As he got them into position, Lydia smiled down at him. "Little Joseph fell asleep. Can you believe he's missing all of this?"

Nathan laughed. His two-year-old had been so excited for days that he had finally given out. Then, turning back to the task, Nathan moved his wagon up until the noses of the oxen almost touched the tailgate of his parents' wagon.

Two minutes later, Derek had his team and wagon aboard as well.

"Be sure and lock the brakes," the captain bawled, as he jumped on board the rear of the flatboat.

At this point, the river was too wide to use a rope ferry, so the large flatboats became the means of crossing the river. This larger boat carried a crew of five. More like a great raft with a gangplank on each end and sideboards down its length, it was propelled by the current. Steering and docking were done by means of a great "rudder" oar at one side of the back end and two long "walking" side oars—oars that were worked not by sitting but by walking them back and forth in great arcs. There were also two "pole men." Using fifteen-foot stout poles while close in to shore, they would help move the boat out into the river, or slow her down when they landed on the opposite side. Out where the water was too deep to hit bottom with the poles, they stood on the upriver side and used the poles to shove away the larger chunks of ice before they hit the boat.

At a shout from their captain, these last two men pulled the gangplank up and secured it. They picked up their poles and, grunting mightily, leaned into them and began to shove off. Just as the boat began to move away from the dock, two of the river transients suddenly grabbed their bags and jumped aboard. They made the leap nimbly, reaching in their pockets for the ten-cent individual fare even as they saw the captain glower at them.

The rest of the family climbed down from the wagons now and moved to the rear of the boat where there was room to stand together. Matthew stayed with the two mules, but Benjamin came back to join Nathan and Joshua at the head of Nathan's yoke of oxen. Derek's team of horses were getting skittish, not liking the movement of the boat beneath their feet, and he stayed beside them, talking quietly to them and stroking their foreheads.

"Well," Benjamin said, glancing back, "this makes it pretty official."

"Yes," Joshua said.

Nathan was peering toward the far side. "I think we're going to have to camp in Montrose for the night. It's too late to start for Sugar Creek."

"I agree," Benjamin said. "They say there's a temporary camping site just half a mile from the river."

Just then Savannah came back to stand beside her grandfather. She put an arm around his waist and leaned against him. "How long does it take to cross, Grandpa?"

"Oh, with this big boat about twenty minutes, I'd guess."

"Uncle Solomon's boat is faster, isn't it?" she said, pointing.

The smaller ferry was well out into the river now and making good time.

Benjamin nodded. "They'll be unloaded and on their way back again before we even reach shore."

Joshua started to say something, but then saw that the two transients were moving forward on the opposite side of the boat from them. Joshua jerked his head, motioning for Benjamin and Nathan to pay attention. It was hard not to grimace, Nathan thought. They were heavily bearded. Their hair, beneath filthy hats, was matted and greasy. Their buckskin shirts were likewise stained and soiled. As they passed across from them, the one looked at the Mormons in disgust, turned his head, and spat out a long stream of dark brown liquid.

Joshua turned his head to follow them, watching them with guarded eyes. Young Joshua and Jessica's two boys were up front with the milk cow and the riding horse, but when the men saw them there, they moved over to the side and stayed clear.

"I don't like the look of those two," Joshua muttered, relaxing a little.

"I'll be glad to see them off on the other side," Nathan agreed.

After a moment, they turned to watch the boat's progress toward the landing site across the river. There was a stiff wind blowing out of the west, and it was slowing them considerably. The crew worked hard, two walking back and forth with the side oars, the captain steering at the rudder oar, and the two pole men warding off the blocks of ice. Ahead of them by three or four hundred yards now, the smaller boat with Jessica and Solomon's wagon aboard was out of the main current and approaching the shore.

They had cleared the secondary channel, passed the southern tip of the island that lay in the river directly west of Nauvoo, and were into the main current and the swiftest part of the river, when they heard a cry. They all turned to see where it had come from. Behind them and about fifty yards downstream, they saw a small skiff. An older man and two boys—probably twelve and fifteen—were rowing frantically, trying to move against the current. The boat rode low, far lower than it should have with the weight of only three people, and Nathan knew they were taking on water. They were holding their own but making no headway.

"Help! We're sinking!"

"Pull around! Pull around!" the captain shouted to his crew, pushing the long rudder hard to the right. Almost immediately they felt the nose of the big boat start to turn to the left.

Joshua, Nathan, and Benjamin went racing back past the wagons. As they joined the captain and one of the pole men, there was a solid *thunk*. A large block of ice hit the side of the skiff squarely and nearly overturned it. The boys screamed and clutched the side of the boat as it rocked violently. When it finally righted itself, it sat several inches lower in the water, and now the water—choppy from the wind—was spilling into their boat.

The captain swore, then yelled at his side oarsmen. "Harder! Come around!" He glanced at Joshua, shaking his head. "Idiots! What are they doing out on the river on a day like today?"

"Trying to kill themselves," Joshua said with equal disgust. "Look at that boat. That's not fit for sailing across a puddle."

Now the man and his sons were pulling frantically on the oars, the nose of the skiff pointed toward the flatboat bearing down on them. The ferry was now running straight downriver with the current, and the distance between them was closing rapidly.

"Watch it!" the captain cried. "Don't run them down."

But he had steered the flatboat right. In a moment the skiff came alongside. Nathan and Joshua went down on their knees, leaning out over the low sides of the flatboat. They grabbed the outstretched arms and pulled them up, first the two boys and then their father. Behind them, the two river transients had come back to watch. They stood by the women and children, who watched with wide, frightened eyes. The two men made no move to come over and help.

Gasping, drenched from head to foot, the man and the two boys staggered to their feet. As they stared in horror, their tiny skiff, freed now of the extra weight, started to turn in the current. When it was broadside of the swirling, muddy water, the current lifted it up and overturned it. It disappeared without a sound.

"Thank you," the man stammered. Hugging themselves tightly, teeth chattering violently, the three of them moved close together, numbed into a trance-like state.

Mary Ann turned to Rebecca. "Let's get some blankets. We have to get them warm or they'll be in serious trouble."

Lydia and Rebecca moved quickly to the back of Rebecca's wagon, and in a moment returned with two blankets. They handed one to the man, the other to the two boys. "Here. Wrap up."

As they did so, Joshua straightened and gave the two bearded men a withering look. "Thanks for your help," he said sarcastically. "Couldn't have done it without you."

They glowered at him for a moment, and then the one spat again. The brown stream of tobacco hit the deck and splattered. The captain jerked up. "You two want to find your own way across from here?" he asked in a cold voice.

They tried to stare him down for the moment, but the captain had risen to his full height.

"Stupid Mormons," the one man finally muttered. Then they turned away and moved back up towards the front of the boat.

The captain turned and called to his two oarsmen. "All right, pull her around again. Let's head for shore."

It was five minutes later that another shout brought everyone up short. This time it was Savannah. She was staring back across the river, her eyes wide, her mouth registering shock. "Look, Papa!"

They swung around to look where she was pointing. There was a collective gasp, then cries of shock and astonishment. Back across the river, Nauvoo was clearly visible. What drew every eye was the temple, which stood like a majestic monument on the far bluffs. From its roof a great column of black smoke was billowing upwards.

"The temple is on fire!" Lydia cried.

"No!" Benjamin exclaimed hoarsely. "It can't be."

But there was no question about it. Now, even from this distance, they could see the flickering flames through the smoke.

For a moment, even the captain and crew forgot about getting the boat in to shore. Everyone stood there, mouths agape, watching what their eyes could scarcely comprehend. For those who were members of the Church, it was sickening. Not the temple. Not after everything they had done to build it.

Finally the crew went back to work, glancing back from time to time to watch. The family stood together in silent horror watching the great column of smoke rising into the sky. Then about five minutes later, Benjamin jerked his hand up. "Look! They're fighting it."

As they peered eastward, they saw that he was right. Now in front of the smoke and the flames, they could see tiny figures scuttling across the temple roof. From their movements it was obvious they were bringing buckets of water forward to dump on the fire, then racing back for more.

They watched, breathless, wishing they could be part of the massive effort being put forth on the far side of the river. Gradually their horror began to subside as the column of smoke thinned and turned from dark black to a pale gray.

"Thank heavens," Mary Ann murmured.

"It looks like it's just one spot on the roof," Nathan noted. "I don't think it's any more than that."

Jenny breathed a sigh of relief. "Wouldn't that be terrible if it all burned?"

Suddenly Rebecca reached out and thumped her father's arm. "Look, Papa!" she cried in a low voice.

Nathan and Benjamin both turned. In the excitement of the fire, the two transients had been forgotten. Now Nathan saw that one of them was at the back of Benjamin's wagon, peering inside the flap.

"Hey!" Nathan shouted. "Get away from there."

The man jumped guiltily and stepped back a little. Joshua came around, anger darkening his eyes. "You heard him!" he snarled. "Get away from that wagon."

The second man moved over to stand next to his companion, and they glared defiantly at the assembly at the back of the boat. Neither of them moved.

"Come on," Joshua growled, starting forward.

Lydia reached out and clutched at Nathan's sleeve. "Nathan, little Joseph is asleep in our wagon. He's there alone."

Nathan and Joshua were already moving, following after Benjamin, headed for the two men. The others were staring, the temple now forgotten.

As Joshua strode up one side of the boat and Nathan the other, the two men finally backed away. "We ain't doing nothin'," the one growled. He held up his hands to show that they were empty.

"Then get away from that wagon!" Joshua warned.

At the back of Nathan's wagon, the flap opened and Nathan's son poked his head out. He was rubbing sleepily at his eyes and looked bewildered. "Mama," he called out.

Derek, who had stayed with his team through the excitement to keep them calm, left them now and pulled Joseph out of the wagon. "Take him to Lydia," Nathan commanded. Derek nodded and started back. Savannah was coming forward to see what was happening. She stepped back so Derek could pass, reaching out to touch the boy's hand. "It's all right, Joseph. Your mama's right back here."

Nathan and Joshua now closed in on the two men, Nathan from one side of his team of oxen, Joshua from the other side. Matthew, who had also stayed at the head of his mules, came around from the front of the wagon. Benjamin stepped in behind Nathan as backup. Derek moved back to the head of his team, watching the developments but still needing to make sure his team did not spook.

"Why don't you boys just move to the back of the boat and stay there until we've got these wagons unloaded?" Joshua said in a low voice.

The two men didn't move, but their heads swung back and forth between Nathan and Joshua and there was fear in their eyes now. Finally, the one man spoke. "A bit touchy, aren't we?" he muttered.

"You might say that," Joshua said shortly. "Now, move!"

The man who had spoken dropped his eyes and pushed past Nathan, who stepped aside to let him pass. The second one stood his ground for a moment, his jaw working furiously as he chewed his tobacco. Then he swore under his breath and started to follow his companion. As he approached Nathan, who was now standing at the side of his yoke of oxen, the man turned and squirted a stream of tobacco juice between his teeth at the nearest ox. The foul-smelling liquid hit the animal squarely in the left eye. Stunned, it let out a bellow of pain and jerked its head around, nearly pulling its companion off its feet.

Nathan grabbed the man by the shoulders and slammed him

around against the wagon wheel. But there wasn't time for retaliation. The ox went wild in its traces, kicking violently, swinging its head back and forth, trying to escape the searing pain in its eye. The man jerked free of Nathan's grasp and darted away.

Joshua leaped forward, grabbing at the yoke, trying to get the oxen under control. But both animals were bellowing and blowing, pawing wildly, throwing their powerful necks against the yoke in an attempt to free themselves. The one lifted its back leg, trying to kick free, and got tangled in the traces. Down it went with a crash, dragging the other one with it.

That jerked Nathan's wagon around, its locked wheels skidding across the decking. Since Derek's team of horses had their noses almost right up against the back of Nathan's wagon, the sudden movement startled them. The one snorted loudly and reared up.

"Whoa, boy!" Derek shouted, leaping for its head and grabbing at the reins. Already frightened by the unsteady platform beneath them, the horses fought back, eyes rolling, snorting wildly, trying to buck. Now the flatboat was rocking sharply as the oxen and horses both fought to get free.

"Get their heads! Get their heads!" the captain was shouting. He didn't dare abandon the rudder oar, since they were now only thirty or forty yards from shore and closing fast.

Derek fought the horse down again, hanging on to the harnessing. Nathan was having less success in controlling his animals. He grabbed at the horns of the blinded and crazed ox as it lunged to its feet again, dragging its yokefellow up as well. He was dimly aware of children screaming, the captain shouting wildly at him, the oarsmen running forward to help, Savannah standing just behind the wagon, ashen-faced and staring. But before he could bring the ox under control, the animal gave one massive yank of its head, bawling with pain. He heard something in the yoke snap and felt himself go flying.

"Watch out!" Joshua yelled.

As Nathan scrambled frantically to stop from pitching over the side of the boat, his feet tangled and he went down on the deck hard, slamming up against the sideboard. Out of the corner of his eye he saw the wagon slewing around as the oxen plunged forward. He rolled away, trying frantically to get clear. Slashing hooves came within inches of taking off his scalp. Then the front leg of one of the oxen hooked up and over the sideboard. That part of the boat was meant only to keep people from stepping off into the river, not to take the weight of a thousand pounds of wildly thrashing animal. The sideboard snapped like a twig and broke free. Down went the ox, its front legs plunging into the river. It would have been able to pull back except that the second ox, feeling the terrible yank of its teammate throwing its weight to the right, lunged now in the same direction. For one awful moment, the two oxen teetered on the edge of the boat, bawling and pawing for a grip with their back feet; then they toppled over the side, dragging the wagon with them as the steel-rimmed tires gouged great gashes in the planking of the flatboat.

As Derek had passed with little Joseph, Savannah had stepped back to let him by. Now, rooted to the spot in horror, she stood against the opposite sideboard. When Nathan's wagon jerked around, the back end nearly sideswiped Savannah, and with a cry, she jumped back to get clear. The top of the sideboard caught her right at the back of her knees. She screamed, flailing her arms to try and catch her balance, then flipped over the side and hit the dark, icy water with a splash.

"Savannah!" Mary Ann screamed.

Joshua was on his knees, staring at Nathan across a now empty deck, making sure he was all right. His mother's scream spun him around. All he saw was a flash of blue and the splash from a body hitting the water. In one mighty leap he was up and sprinting toward the spot. "Savannah!" There was a swirl of hair, a momentary glimpse of a terrified face, one hand clutching at the air. Like a madman, Joshua tore his coat off and flung it aside. He dove into the river, shouting her name again even as he hit the water.

It was like throwing himself against a stone wall. The shock of the icy water was so violent, so stunning, that for a moment he couldn't get his breath. He groped wildly in the water around him. There was nothing. He opened his eyes, but the water was so dark and murky, he could see nothing. He kicked hard, shooting upward to break the surface. "Savannah!" It was a primal scream.

Benjamin leaped to the side of the boat. The women were screaming. Children were shrieking in terror. Derek was still fighting to get his team under control so they didn't lose a second wagon. Nathan staggered to his feet, shaking his head in a daze. A moment later, Joshua broke the surface, gasping, looking around wildly. "Where is she? Where is she?"

Not waiting for an answer, he took in a huge gulp of air and went under again.

Benjamin leaned over the side, searching the swirling, muddy black water. There was nothing.

"Row! Row!" the captain was screaming. With the one sideboard off, water was gushing into the flatboat and the decking was already two inches under water. They were nearly to shore now, and the men there waiting were shouting at them. Several, including Solomon Garrett, leaped into the river and started wading out to help the boat come in.

Benjamin raced across to the other side of the boat. They were out of the main part of the current now, but the water still moved beneath them at a steady rate. The thought flashed into his mind that Savannah might have been swept beneath the boat. He stared down, frantically searching the water. There was a momentary flash of blue cloth, then it was gone again. It was enough. He never even thought to remove his heavy coat. Over the side he went, keeping his eye on the spot where the blue had appeared. Behind him he heard Mary Ann cry out, but it barely registered. He had one thought and one thought only. Get his hands out. Catch that blue dress. Hold on no matter what.

The shock of the cold made him gasp. Unfortunately, his body plunged deep into the water and when he gasped, he took in not air, but water. He tasted mud and felt the choking cold shoot down into his lungs. But he also felt his hands close on something soft. He clamped his fingers tight, sinking them into the cloth like an eagle clutching with its talons. In a moment he broke the surface and felt a thrill of elation to see Savannah's face in front of him.

"He's got her! He's got her!" he heard someone above him shouting.

Choking, spitting, fighting desperately not to lose his grip, Benjamin started kicking his feet, moving toward the shore. Then he saw a head coming toward him. It was Solomon. He felt big hands brush past him and take the weight of Savannah from him.

"I've got her," Solomon shouted. "Hold on to my coat, Father Steed. Swim!"

"I can't," Benjamin gasped. The weight of his coat made it seem like he carried a hundred pounds of flour on each shoulder. He couldn't feel his hands now. His feet were a vague impression of pain and leaden weight somewhere far removed from him.

"Hold on!" Solomon shouted over his shoulder.

But Benjamin had already lost his grip on Solomon's coat. He felt the current take him and turn him over. Down he went again, into the blackness. He fought it, kicking out, clawing with his hands. In a moment he saw light above him and thrust his head back, breaking out into air again.

"Benjamin!" It was Mary Ann, screaming out his name. He saw Matthew's body arcing through the air, then heard a splash. He tried to turn his head to see, tried to raise an arm so it could be seen. But once again the current took him, pulling him down and down into its cold embrace.

Chapter Notes

Though the incidents in this chapter are shown as having happened to the Steed family, they are based on real events. On the ninth of February, the temple roof did catch fire about three-thirty in the afternoon. It was caused by someone drying temple clothes too close to a stovepipe in the upper room of the temple. Fortunately, it was seen immediately and the alarm sounded. Men came from all over the city and the fire was extinguished in about half an hour. It burnt a hole some sixteen feet long by ten feet wide in the roof. (See HC 7:581.)

At the same time as the fire, a flatboat filled with wagons and Saints leaving Nauvoo was hailed by a passing skiff in danger of swamping in midriver. It was a man and two boys. Barely had the man and boys been rescued, when a person whom Brigham later described as a "filthy wicked man" squirted tobacco juice into the eyes of one of the oxen on board the flatboat. The animal, crazed with pain, kicked off one of the sideboards and dragged a second ox and the wagon into the river. Both oxen drowned. In the case of this actual incident, the flatboat sank a short distance offshore. The wagon was later recovered, though most of the contents were ruined. (See HC 7:582; also "Journal of Thomas Bullock," p. 49.)

Brigham Young, in company with John Taylor and Parley P. Pratt, arrived shortly after dark. Caroline, Carl, and Melissa had already come across an hour before. Word of the accident had swept through Nauvoo like a storm, and they left immediately, leaving the older children in charge of the younger.

When the Apostles reached the little encampment—three wagons in a half circle around a blazing fire—it was a grim and stricken camp that greeted them. Joshua, Matthew, and Solomon were stripped to the waist and wrapped in blankets, seated nearest the fire, their hair not yet dry. Caroline sat across from them, holding Savannah—also wrapped in a blanket—rocking her slowly back and forth and singing softly to her. One tent had been pitched and it glowed a warm yellow from a lamp. A shadowy figure could be seen moving inside. Though it was still early, all but the older children had been bedded down in the wagons. The adults stood around the fire in numbed silence, staring into the crackling flames.

Brigham paused for a moment, taking in the scene, then strode up immediately to Caroline. Elder Taylor and Elder Pratt stayed back for the moment. When Caroline saw who it was, she straightened, and Savannah slid off her lap to stand beside her. Brigham dropped to his knees and took Caroline's hands. "I just received word," he said softly. "We came as quickly as we could."

"Thank you, President Young."

He turned to Savannah. Her red hair was still damp and there were smudges of mud on one cheek. "Are you all right?" he asked.

She nodded mutely, then great tears welled up and spilled over. "Grandpa saved my life," she whispered.

"I know," Brigham said, taking her in his arms and holding her tight, weeping with her now as well. "I know. Your grandfather was a brave man."

Caroline started to sob, and Joshua stood and came over. He reached out and touched Brigham's shoulder. "Thank you for coming," he said; then he put his arms around Caroline and held her to him.

"I am so sorry," Brigham said, still holding Savannah. "What a tragedy."

Matthew and Solomon came over to join them. Brigham stood, sending Savannah back to her mother's embrace, and looked at Matthew. "Are you all right?"

Matthew nodded. "I . . . I got to him." He stopped, and then his face crumpled and he turned away, great shudders racking his body. "It was too late."

Brigham stepped forward and threw his arms around Matthew. They stood that way for almost a minute, neither speaking. Elders Taylor and Pratt stepped closer to the fire. "The ferry captain told us what happened," Elder Taylor said to Joshua and Solomon. "What about the two men who started all this?"

Solomon's face turned hard as flint. "They didn't even wait for the boat to dock. They jumped off and swam ashore. They've not been seen since."

"They'd better keep running," Joshua muttered. "A long, long ways."

Brigham pulled away from Matthew and they turned to face the group. "Everyone else is all right?"

"Yes," Joshua said.

"The wagon?"

"We've got it located and a rope tied to it. We'll pull it out in the morning."

Parley spoke up. "The ferry captain said both oxen drowned."

Solomon nodded. "Thank heavens there wasn't room for the other yoke, or we would have lost them too."

"Where's your mother?" Brigham asked Matthew.

He turned and gestured toward the tent. "She's in there with Papa and Nathan."

Brigham nodded and moved away. He walked to the tent, stopped at the door, and called out softly. "Nathan, it's Brigham Young. May I come in?"

Immediately the flap opened and Nathan was there. Brigham stepped inside. Along the far side of the tent, there was a straw mattress laid out on the ground. It was filled with the form of a man covered with a blanket. Mary Ann sat on a stool beside it, her head down, her hands folded neatly in her lap. When she looked up and saw who it was, she rose to her feet. Brigham went to her quickly. "No, no, Mary Ann, just sit there. Please."

She sank back down again. "Thank you for coming," she said, her voice hollow and empty.

He put an arm around her and pulled her against him. "How could I not come? One of the truly great ones of the kingdom has fallen."

She buried her face in her hands and her shoulders began to shake silently. "I know," she finally whispered. "I know."

Again for a long time, Brigham just held her, rocking slowly back and forth, letting her weep against him. Finally, her trembling subsided and she straightened. Brigham stepped back. "Have you decided where you want the burial?"

She nodded immediately. "Here."

Brigham's eyebrows came up.

She nodded more vigorously. "Here on the bluffs, so he can look back at Nauvoo. He would like that. To know that he left . . ." She had to stop again. "That he died while doing what God asked us to do."

Now it was Brigham who was nodding. "Yes," he said simply. "I think you're right." He turned to Nathan. "In the morning?"

"Yes. If you could be here, we'd like you to say a few words."

"Of course. I would be honored."

There was silence for a time. Finally Brigham, still speaking to Nathan, asked, "And then what?"

Nathan sighed. "We'll go back across in the morning, take everything with us. We can salvage the wagon, but all the food is ruined, of course. We hope we can save the bedding and the clothes." He rubbed a hand across his eyes. "We'll have to find another yoke of oxen."

"Yes."

"It will take a week or more to get ready again. It's just as well we still have homes to go back to."

"But as soon as possible," Mary Ann said, her voice firm and steady now, "we'll be crossing again."

Brigham nodded, obviously touched and pleased. "I understand."

"Ben wouldn't have it any other way."

Brigham had to turn away, his eyes misting up.

"Thank you, President," Mary Ann said after a moment. "Thank you for calling us to Nashville."

He turned back, a little surprised. "You're welcome, but I think the call came from the Lord."

"I know. That's why it meant so much to him. He was always afraid that he wasn't of that much value to the kingdom."

Brigham just stared at her in astonishment.

"He did," Nathan explained. "He always felt like he was good for the building committee, or for the city council, or the temple committee. But when it came to serving as a priesthood leader, he felt that he couldn't contribute much. Nashville changed all that. He talked about it all the time."

Brigham was slowly shaking his head. "What an epitaph," he observed. "Would to God that we all might have such a tribute written about us when we die." He paused only for a moment. "'He found joy in the service of the Lord. He was beloved of his family. He died saving the life of another.'"

———◆———

As Nathan came down the stairs of their home and into the sitting room, Lydia looked up. "Is she asleep?"

He nodded. "I think so. I stood outside her door for several minutes, and she didn't even stir."

"Good." Lydia turned to young Joshua and Emily. "You be really quiet so you don't wake Grandma up. If anything happens, you come right over to Aunt Caroline's and get us."

"Yes, Mama."

"Papa?" Emily's large dark eyes held great concern.

"What?"

"How are we going to go west now?"

"That's what we'll be talking about with the family, Emmy."

"We're not going to stay, are we." It was not a question.

Nathan shook his head and stood up. He took a deep breath. "We may be late. You don't have to wait up for us."

Joshua would be fifteen in a few months now. He was as tall as Nathan and still growing. Sober, thoughtful, and sensitive by nature, he was a wonderful combination of the best of Nathan and Lydia. He was a son that brought much joy to his parents. He looked at his father now. "We'll wait up," he said.

———◆———

Nathan looked around the room with some sadness. He had thought they had held their last Steed family council. He had been wrong. They were in Joshua's house, and all the adults, including Carl and Melissa, had come.

As Nathan and Lydia got seated, Solomon Garrett bent over

and started to cough. He threw his arms about his chest, his face twisting into a grimace of pain as the deep, barking sound racked his body. Jessica held him by the hand, trying to steady him, as the rest watched gravely until the spasm passed him. Jessica looked around the circle. "I think he has pneumonia."

Melissa leaned forward. "Have you tried the mustard poultice?"

"Yes, all afternoon."

"You need to be in bed," Joshua said.

Solomon waved one hand weakly at them. "I will, as soon as we're done."

Nathan looked at Matthew, who still looked a little pale and drawn. "And how are you?"

"I'm okay."

Jenny reached up and laid a hand on his forehead. "He's got a slight fever, but I think he'll be all right."

Turning to Joshua, Nathan raised one eyebrow. "You were in the water the longest."

"I'm fine." Then, at the dubious looks, he said more firmly, "I am. Aren't I, Caroline?"

"So far," she said.

"And Savannah?" Lydia asked.

"She'll be all right," Caroline said softly. "There seems to be no effect from the cold." Then her voice went suddenly hoarse. "I had to sit with her for a long time tonight. She didn't want to close her eyes." She looked away as suddenly her eyes were shining. "She said it reminded her of being under the water."

There was a long silence; then Nathan turned to Joshua. "Shall we start?"

Joshua nodded. "Yes. Go ahead."

Nathan swallowed, took a deep breath, and stood up. "All right. We know the issues before us. Let's see if we can find a way to solve them."

Melissa tentatively raised her hand and Nathan nodded in her direction.

"Before you talk about getting more food and another team and all of that, can I ask another question?"

"Yes." Nathan thought he knew what it would be.

"Why can't you all just stay now? Papa's gone." Her voice went suddenly shrill. "He's gone from us. Why can't you just stay?" She dropped her head, her body visibly trembling.

"If only for another season," Carl came in. "Let Brigham find you a place, then you can go next year."

Joshua was nodding. "It's not a bad idea, Nathan. Especially now."

Nathan was silent for a time, looking at the faces around him. "Do you know what Mother's last words to me were tonight before she fell asleep?"

Matthew answered for them all. "Go."

"Yes. She took both of my hands and held them tightly. And then she said, 'Nathan, don't let them talk you out of it. You know what we have to do.'"

Melissa just shook her head and began to cry quietly. Nathan waited for a moment. "We don't know what the federal troops are going to do. If they come in and try to take action against us, there may not be another season, Carl. But," he went on quickly as Joshua stirred, "let's hear the voice of the council. Solomon? Jessica? Stay or go?"

Solomon opened his mouth but another spasm of coughing hit him before he could speak. He let it pass, looked at Jessica, who nodded at him, then looked back at Nathan. "We're going."

"Matthew? Jenny?"

"We're going with Mother," Matthew said softly.

"Derek? Rebecca?"

It was Rebecca who spoke, and she spoke to her sister. "I'm sorry, Melissa," she said, her eyes also filled with tears, "but if Papa were here right now, he'd be chiding us for even having this discussion. You know that, don't you?"

Melissa stared at her for several seconds, and then whispered, "Yes."

"We'll be going," Derek answered, taking Rebecca's hand in his.

"And so will we," Lydia said. "The only question we have is, how soon can we restock our supplies and find a team?"

Carl was shaking his head, but it was not without admiration. "I've located a yoke of oxen for you."

They swung on him, dumbfounded. "You what?"

Carl just looked at Nathan steadily. "I traded my team of grays for it."

Nathan stared. "But—"

"I'm not delivering much brick right now. Come spring, I'll find me another team."

For a moment, Nathan considered protesting, but then he knew their situation was too desperate for such posturing. "Thank you, Carl," he said quietly, deeply moved.

Carl merely nodded.

Joshua came in now, accepting what he already knew would be the answer. "The bigger question is finding the supplies you need. I think your wagon is all right. We'll have to watch for warped boards and such, but it'll be okay. But the other? Flour especially." He paused. "I have a proposal."

"What?" Nathan asked.

"Why don't you and I and maybe Derek go down to Quincy tomorrow with the two wagons I have left. We'll try and buy enough food to resupply what you lost."

"But we don't have any money," Matthew replied, "and nothing to trade."

"I'll talk to my banker there," Joshua answered evenly, "have him give me credit enough for what we need."

Now several started talking at once. "Will he do that?" Derek asked in surprise.

"No, Joshua," Lydia said. "You can't do that."

"But I thought no one would give you credit," Jessica blurted out.

"He'll give me credit," Joshua growled menacingly.

Nathan considered that. "I don't think they'll sell to Mormons."

"I'll tell you what, Nathan," Joshua answered, grim now. "I've had about all the anti-Mormon sentiment I can handle. If they refuse to sell us what we need, maybe I'll burn *their* houses down."

That brought a smile all around. Finally Nathan nodded. "I suppose we don't have a lot of choice. All right, we'll try it."

Caroline lifted her hand. Nathan turned to her. "Yes?"

"Joshua and I have another proposal."

"What?"

"Joshua is going with you." And then at Nathan's blank look, she hurried on. "I'm not talking about Quincy. He'll go west with you."

"What?" several of them cried at once.

"Yes," Joshua said. "Caroline and I have talked about it all afternoon. I'll go and help take care of Mama. I know Matthew plans to do that, but he has his own family to worry about."

"And you'd stay here, Caroline?" Lydia asked, eyes wide. "Is that safe?"

"We'll have Carl and Melissa," Caroline answered, her voice level. "And with Joshua gone, they're not going to bother us."

Carl saw the inevitability of it immediately. "Yes," he said. "That's best. We'll take care of Caroline and the children." He turned to Joshua. "What about the lumber you've got coming this spring?"

Joshua grinned. "You said things at the brickyards were slow. How would you like to become a lumber merchant?"

Carl rocked back, stunned. "You'd trust me to do that?"

Joshua just nodded. Then he swung back. "You don't have to think about this, Nathan. You know it's right. You need another man. Mama needs someone to look after her."

Nathan's thoughts were a wild tumble, the possibilities racing in his mind. But finally, he just inclined his head in Joshua's direction. "Yes, we do." And then his voice suddenly caught and his eyes were glistening. "If Papa were here, you know what he'd say right now, don't you?"

Joshua's head dropped and he didn't look up.

"He wouldn't say anything," Lydia whispered, looking at Joshua. "He'd just throw his arms around you and hold you tight."

Chapter Thirty-Four

Saturday, February 14, 1846

Today is the day called by many St. Valentine's Day. It is a day when love between men and women is honored and remembered. It is a day when I sit in my tiny cabin and shed tears as I write, for never has Will had less reason to love me than on this day.

We have been at sea now for ten days. We had hoped and prayed that the weather would be kind until those of us who have spent our entire lives on land grew accustomed to the constant rolling and pitching and pitching and rolling of the floor beneath our feet. Alas, it was not to be. Hardly had five days passed when a great storm descended upon us. This was not just any storm. Even Will said it was a bad one. The sky at midday was as black as midnight. The winds howled with a fury I have never before known. For four days and nights we were tossed about helplessly on the monstrous waves. For a time it looked as though our brave little company was to come to a premature end and that I would die without my parents ever knowing what had happened to me.

Life on the "passenger deck," as they call our quarters, became not only unbearable, but unbelievably horrible. Remember that the remodeling of our ship from a merchantman to a packet ship left the ceilings—the sailors call them the bulkheads—no more than four feet high. In the best of circumstances we crawl around like monkeys in order not to crack our heads. But with the storm, it became a nightmare. Everywhere people were sick—violently, violently sick. Children screamed or lay in their beds moaning piteously. Pots and pans, dishes, luggage of every description, even whole eating tables were thrown out of their places and hurled about frightfully. One could scarce move about without risking life and limb.

This is when I learned that I had married a total stranger. I have heard people say that being seasick makes you wish you were dead. Such mild, unremarkable language does not begin to describe my feelings. I not only wished I were dead, I longed for it like a baby longs for its mother's breast. I cried out for it like a young kid bleating for its nanny goat. And in the midst of this indescribable suffering of body and spirit, a stranger named Will Steed stood by me, smiling down at me with ruddy cheeks and sparkling eyes. He would go up top, stand on the deck, feet braced, gripping the rigging while the rain lashed his face, and he would laugh into the teeth of the storm. At night, while I lay groaning like a dying woman, he would come tripping down the stairs, his face as rosy as a baby's after its bath. He would be chomping on an apple, or carrying some gigantic slab of bread smeared with butter. Smacking his lips, he would then have the effrontery to suggest that if I would but partake with him, I would be instantly and forever cured.

What terrible accident of fate created such a disparity as this between a woman and her husband? The irony of St. Valentine's Day now rests upon me and my soul cries out, "Why oh why couldn't I have married a man who knew not the sea?" Fortunately, Will has not cast me off for being the whimpering lass that I am. He even claims that he loves me all the more—a likely story!!

Though I clearly let my pen run away with itself, in a more serious note, it was indeed a most terrible storm. Our vessel, completely helpless before the lashing gale, was driven closer and ever closer to the Cape Verde Islands, where many a ship has met its watery doom. Elder Brannan became a man possessed. He exhorted us to prayer. He would come down and call upon us to sing a hymn of praise to God, convinced that we could turn the elements through the song of faith.

I digress for a moment. I said Elder B. comes "down." Let me explain. Elder B. assigned himself one of the stateroom cabins in the officer's quarters. In fact, he cabins beside Captain Richardson, captain of our vessel. At first he vowed that he would take mess with us, but that lasted no more than a few days. The smell of bilgewater and the howling babies who were by then already sick were too much for him. Now he eats at the captain's table and comes down among us only occasionally. I make no further comments. Some are murmuring, but Will reminds me that it is not Christian to harshly judge another.

Now back to the singing. Elder B. would come down in the passenger's deck, amid the crying and the moaning, amid the terrible clatter of things flying about. "Let us sing!" he would bellow. "Let us all sing!" And we would sing. Amid the retching stomachs, amid the shrieking children, amid the howling of the wind, we would sing. We would sing at the top of our lungs such songs as "The Spirit of God," or "We Are Going to California." (I confess I found greater solace in the first than in the latter.)

On the last night, Captain Richardson, with his hair flying and salt water dripping from his beard, came down to speak to us. Even he was in despair. And though I make light of it now (only in order to stop from weeping), it was a most awful circumstance. By then we had some dead, mostly the old, their bodies no longer able to bear up under the never-ending misery in which we found ourselves. "Prepare for the worst," the captain cried. "We shall be dashed upon the rocks before the night is over."

But to his surprise, in spite of the terrible, terrible situation in which we found ourselves, Elder Brannan's call to sing had kept our faith up. Not only was the captain astonished that we were not in despair, but he was chagrined to find us more composed and hopeful than he. It was after he left that I came to know why I had chosen to marry this stranger with whom I share my bunk. Will stood before us and told us of that day when another shipload of Saints came across the great Atlantic to America. He told how in the midst of another great storm, President Young and the Twelve gathered in a circle and petitioned the Lord to calm the elements.

I need not tell the reader of this journal what happened next. As one, we bowed our heads—as we had done many times before—and prayed for a cessation of the storm. Only this time we prayed with even greater faith. Nor is the end of my story a surprise either. Within a very short time, the wind shifted, blowing us away from the islands and the reefs that awaited. Then they died down to no more than a stiff sailing breeze. The seas that were like mountains around us calmed. The sun appeared again. Our first thoughts were to those who had died. We saw them buried in their watery grave, then gathered together on deck and knelt in a prayer of thanksgiving.

So as I close this Valentine's Day entry, I do express my love for the man that I have married. I also thank my God for watching over us and answering our prayers.

Brigham Young's original plan was to take his family across the river with the first wagons on February fourth, leading the exodus out of Nauvoo as an example for all to follow. However, on the third, when he could not disperse the crowds at the temple, he postponed his departure and stayed for nearly two more weeks. He spent that time almost day and night in the temple, overseeing the work there so that as many Saints as possible could have their temple ordinances.

It is often the case that those in leadership positions seem unable to escape criticism from one hand or the other. So it was that when Brigham was supposedly leaving on the fourth, some—those who were not ready to leave with him—murmured because he was abandoning the city in the face of danger. Then when he decided to stay, those who had already crossed the river stopped their forward movement and complained that they had no leader to guide them. Of greater concern, Brigham learned that many in the city were postponing their departures as well, using him as the justification for doing so. Obviously, they reasoned, there was no immediate danger, because Brigham was still here. When Brigham went, they would go.

So finally, during the evening of Sunday, February fifteenth, 1846, Brigham Young crossed the river and took his family to join the company to which he had been assigned. This company was camped at Sugar Creek, nine miles into Iowa Territory. There were fifty people in the Young party, including his wives, children, foster children, and a few others who were actually taken along because they had no other way to go. He had five separate and well-provisioned wagons to carry them west.

Heber C. Kimball stayed behind to secure some of the Church property and supplies that were needed on the trail. Then on Tuesday morning, February seventeenth, Elder Kimball walked out of the beautiful two-story brick home that he and Vilate had completed just four months previously. He locked the door, left the key with the committee assigned to try and sell the remaining property, and walked away.

When Heber arrived at the Sugar Creek camp shortly before noon of that same day, he became the seventh Apostle in the camp. With a majority of the Quorum now present, Brigham called for a council meeting. There were serious problems to discuss. The first stemmed from the numbers of people who had completely ignored the counsel of the brethren not to leave until they were sufficiently prepared. Panicked at the thought that they might be trapped—which was only heightened by the departure of Brigham and the Twelve—they left Nauvoo with whatever they had. Charged to be ready for as much as a year in the wilderness, they came barely able to last a fortnight. Some tents had not been completed and were open on both ends. A few families hadn't even brought that much and tried to shelter themselves from the wintry weather by rigging up bedclothes between trees.

The second concern, which was even more serious than the first, was the fact that now, two weeks after the exodus had started, there were still only a few hundred Saints out of Nauvoo. And these were camped a scant nine miles from their former homes—hardly a protective buffer against the marauding armies of federal soldiers that were expected. Part of the reason for that was that there simply were not enough boats to get the people across the river, even though the ferries and flatboats were working around the clock. Part of it seemed to be that once the Twelve started west, the carefully constructed organization of companies and captains started to break down. The leaderless minions in Nauvoo were milling around like sheep in a rainstorm. It was decided that Brigham, Heber, and John Taylor would return to Nauvoo the following day to expedite the exodus and get things in hand once again.

The first two weeks of February had seen relatively mild weather, with days in the low fifties or high forties and the nights not falling far below freezing. Occasional rain or snow left the ground muddy and difficult for travel, but the temperate weather was a great blessing to people traveling out in the open or sleeping in tents and wagons.

The day after Brigham returned to Nauvoo, the respite ended with a vengeance. A massive winter storm swept out of Canada, lashing the Great Plains with bitter cold, howling winds, and blinding blizzards. In Nauvoo, the citizens retreated to their houses. They stood around their stoves and fireplaces, listening in awe as the winds shrieked around them and the snow began to pile up in drifts. But in the Sugar Creek camp, the fledgling pioneers were about to learn that Mother Nature is not forgiving of the unprepared. Blowing straight out of the northwest, untrammeled by hundreds of miles of open prairie, the gale-force winds toppled trees, snatched the makeshift tents away like twigs of straw, and toppled even those tents which were sturdily made and properly pitched. Many a family spent the night huddled together with nothing but coats or blankets to shield them from the storm.

When the storm finally blew itself out, there were seven or eight inches of snow on the ground and temperatures plummeted like a stone. Where before the highs had been in the forties and fifties, now they were in the teens or low twenties. Where the nights had seen frost, but little more, now the thermometer dropped close to zero. In less than thirty-six hours, the smaller channels on the river were frozen over with a thin skiff of ice. In the main channel, the river was running heavily with slush and the large chunks of ice from upstream, making the crossing to Iowa in anything but the largest flatboats a dangerous matter.

Then on the evening of February twenty-third, the skies cleared and the temperature plunged even further. What had been unseasonably cold before became frigid beyond anything ever seen for this late in February. When the sun came up on the morning of the twenty-fourth, the temperature was still below zero. By seven p.m. that night, Brigham Young recorded in his journal that the temperature stood at twelve degrees below zero on the Fahrenheit scale.

———◆———

Derek Ingalls walked swiftly, swinging his arms vigorously back and forth to keep warm. His breath came in big explosions of mist, turned golden by the rays of the rising sun. Beneath his boots, the snow not only crunched, it squeaked. That was something he had never experienced in England, and only two or three times since coming to America. That alone told him how cold it was. He raised his gloved hands and covered his nose and mouth. He blew into them softly, letting the warmth of his breath temporarily ease the tingling in his cheeks.

He turned off Parley Street, north onto Granger, letting the jubilation move him forward with great strides. As he reached

Steed Row, he went through the gate of Nathan and Lydia's home, not even pausing at the front porch. He strode around the back of the house and headed for the barn. He reached the small side door, threw it open, and stepped inside.

There were three wagons down the center portion of the barn, and several people, all dressed heavily in winter coats, hats, gloves, and scarves, swarmed around them. At the sound of the door, they all stopped and turned toward Derek.

"Well?" Nathan said, when Derek just stood there grinning.

"Solid as stone."

Joshua was loading a bag of flour into the nearest wagon. He dropped it into place, gave it one last shove, then straightened. "Did you go out on it?"

"Didn't have to," Derek answered exultantly. "The wagons are already going across."

Matthew and young Joshua came forward, followed by Carl Rogers and his three sons. Matthew smiled broadly. "Wagons? Not just people?"

"Yes! Wagons! There must have been thirty or forty spread out across the river. I'm telling you, that ice is as solid as if the river had turned to stone."

Nathan stood there for a moment, letting the significance of that sink in; then he turned to his son. "Joshua, go tell Mama and the others. We'll finish loading here, then hitch up the teams. We'll leave in about an hour."

"Yes, Papa."

Carl turned to his sons. "You go with Joshua and help him spread the word. Tell Mama."

"Tell them to meet at our house by ten o'clock," Nathan called as they started away. "Oh, and fetch Solomon. He's at the blacksmith shop."

As the boys left, Joshua jumped down from the wagon and came to stand with Matthew, Derek, Nathan, and Carl. "What a blessing!" Derek said. "We'll be able to get hundreds of wagons across the river now. No more waiting days or weeks for a turn on the ferry."

"I'm not sure that leaving your homes when the temperature is no more than zero at high noon is a blessing," Carl said quietly. "Especially for Mother Steed."

Joshua looked at his brother. "I'm going to try and talk her out of leaving, Nathan. At least leaving right now."

"I won't fight you on that," Nathan answered, "but I think we both know what she's going to say."

"Maybe so, but I'm going to try."

"Fine." Nathan gave him a piercing look. "And if she won't change her mind?"

Joshua shrugged. "That's decided. I'll be going with you until you get to wherever it is Brigham Young has got it in his head to stop. Then I'll come back to my family."

"You don't have to go, you know," Matthew said. "Jenny and I will take care of her."

"She can also come with us," Nathan and Derek said at the same moment.

Joshua turned away, looking at the wagons. After several moments, he spoke, his voice far away and distant. "When I see Pa again, how could I ever face him and tell him that I let Mother go alone? Especially after what he did for Savannah." And then before anyone could answer, he turned to Carl. "We'd better go to your barn and make sure that fourth wagon's ready."

Carl nodded and they moved away. When the door to the barn shut again, Nathan looked at Derek and Matthew. "Did you hear that?" he asked with a satisfied smile.

"What?" Matthew asked.

"He didn't say *if* he sees Pa again."

Derek and Matthew reared back a little, then smiled too. "Yes," Derek said, "he did say *when*, didn't he?"

With that quiet gentleness that was as soft as fine goose down and as unbendable as the best of tempered steel, Mary Ann Steed let it be known that she would not be staying behind with Joshua and Caroline, nor would she consider delaying her departure even so much as one day in hopes that the weather would temper somewhat. She too tried to convince Joshua that she would be fine with either Matthew or Nathan and that he should stay in Nauvoo with Caroline. But in that, Joshua was as immovable as his mother.

They finished packing the wagons, hitched the mules and the oxen and the horses, and moved them out to the street in front of Joshua's house. Then they gathered inside Joshua's house, more than thirty of them crowded into the sitting room for one last time. By silent acclamation, they turned to Nathan to say what had to be said.

He cleared this throat, knowing that this was going to be difficult. "We went through the pain of saying good-bye once," he started. "And now that pain is mingled with the pain of the loss of our father and grandfather. I don't think any of us have it in us to go through another prolonged farewell. I would therefore suggest that we have one final family prayer, and then quietly say our farewells here. It is very cold outside, and coming down to the river will be a difficulty."

He paused to see if anyone disagreed with that. When no one did he nodded gravely. "Then let us kneel and petition the Lord to be with us."

When they reached the top of the bluff above Montrose, Iowa, Joshua, who drove the lead wagon, pulled out of line and turned to the left, driving the mules across the snow-covered landscape. The other three wagons turned off as well and followed in a line.

Joshua was peering ahead but still almost missed it. It was Mary Ann who pointed to the rounded hump of snow. "There," she said quietly. "There by the small oak tree."

He pulled the team to the left a little. "It looks like the marker has fallen down."

She nodded. "Probably in that terrible wind we had."

Swinging the mules clear around so they were headed back the way they had come, Joshua pulled them up. He hopped down lightly, then reached up to help his mother. As the others came up behind them, the two of them moved over to stand beside the grave. Joshua dropped to one knee, brushing at the snow with his hand. In a moment he found the short length of wooden planking on which crude letters had been scraped. He made no effort to stand it upright, but rather laid it on the snow-covered rocks they had used to cover the burial place.

He turned and looked for Nathan, and waved a hand. Nathan was at the back of his wagon and Solomon and Matthew were with him. They waved back and disappeared behind the wagon. In a moment they reappeared. Nathan carried something large and flat and heavy. Matthew had a pick. Solomon had a shovel. The rest of the family had climbed down now as well and moved in behind the three of them as they came over to the grave site. They spread out to form a silent semicircle around Mary Ann and Joshua.

Nathan stepped forward to stand beside Joshua. Now all could see that what he carried was a large, flat black piece of slate. "Here," he said, starting to hand it over to Joshua.

Joshua tried to wave him off. "You do it, Nathan."

Nathan shook his head firmly. "This was your idea."

He sighed and took the heavy piece of stone from Nathan. Their mother was watching with some surprise. Joshua turned the stone slate around and faced the group. It was smoothed and polished on the front, and neatly chiseled into the face of the stone were several lines of lettering. Joshua tipped it back so the light made the words clearly readable, but he kept his arm across the bottom half, obscuring what was there. What they could see was this:

Benjamin Steed
Born: May 18, 1785
Died: February 9, 1846

"We decided," Joshua said in a husky voice, "that we wanted something more permanent than a board to mark this spot."

Mary Ann's eyes were wide and filled to overflowing. "Thank you," she whispered.

Joshua withdrew his arm, revealing what was written on the lower half. It was the words of Brigham Young paid in spontaneous tribute to the life of Benjamin Steed:

> *He found joy in the service of the Lord.*
> *He was beloved of his family.*
> *He died saving the life of another.*

And there was one final line, which was Joshua's alone.

> *Good-bye until we meet again.*

The families were in the wagons, with the flaps closed, trying to keep out some of the cold. Only the four drivers—Nathan, Joshua, Matthew, and Solomon—waited outside, watching the solitary figure kneeling at the grave. Nathan turned. From below them came the sounds of an army on the move. There was the bellowing of oxen, the whinnying of horses, the braying of mules. Drivers shouted, children yelled, women cried out to one another. Wagons creaked and rattled across the ice. Traces cracked, singletrees and doubletrees jingled.

On the far shore, Nauvoo sat in the sunshine, mantled in white, crowned with the magnificent building on the opposite bluffs. The river was like a silver mirror frosted by someone's breath. In a long black line which started just a short distance from where they were and stretched all the way back across the great sheet of ice to Parley Street and beyond, the wagons of Nauvoo were on the move. A hundred wagons had already crossed, and there were twice that many more still coming.

"It's not exactly the Red Sea," Nathan murmured, as much to himself as to the others, "but we'll take it."

"What was that?" Joshua asked.

Nathan flung out a hand at the panorama before them. "Doesn't this strike you as a pretty strange coincidence? I mean, here we are in the last week of February. Some years we're starting to see the first riverboats by now, but the ice is thick enough to carry a hundred wagons and teams."

Joshua grunted, squinting down at the scene before them. It was a sound that was impossible to read and Nathan decided not to press him. But Solomon was not willing to simply let it go. "Brigham says we are the Camp of Israel. Why shouldn't we expect the Lord to bless us as he did ancient Israel?"

"Is that what you think this is?" Joshua asked. "Another miracle?"

"Without question," Solomon answered calmly. "Without the slightest question."

"Do you not see anything strange in it at all, Joshua?" Matthew asked.

Joshua gave him a sharp look, then, to their surprise, turned and gazed on the scene before them thoughtfully. "Strange, yes. I'll grant you that. It is highly unusual. But I'm not ready to write it in my book of miracles yet."

"Why not?" Matthew said with great solemnity. "It's the second one in two weeks for you."

"The second one?" Joshua asked with a quizzical look. "What was the first?"

Matthew turned and looked to where his mother still knelt at the graveside. He did not turn back as he answered Joshua's question. "The first was when Papa saw Savannah beneath the water and was able to dive in and reach her."

———— ••• ————

Mary Ann rubbed her hands softly across the polished stone, letting her fingers touch the lines of rough-cut lettering. She knelt in the snow, oblivious to the cold, unheeding of the wetness that she felt through her dress at the knees.

"It's time to go, Ben," she murmured. "We have to make Sugar Creek camp by nightfall. The family's waiting for me."

Half turning, she looked out to the east, to the long, snaking line of wagons and teams and families walking along beside them. Then she looked back at the headstone, now firmly buried in the frozen ground. "I'm glad you can see all this, Ben. It's happening. It's finally happening."

She stood slowly, wearily. "I don't know how I can bear it without you, but . . ." She laughed softly in spite of the tears. "I know, I know. You don't like me talking like that. How grateful I am that we were sealed before this happened. I know that I shall see you again, and let you hold me. But, oh, how I shall miss you until that day, Ben Steed."

She had a sudden insight. "Have you ever thought how many of your grandchildren carry your name? There's Charles *Benjamin* Steed, and John *Benjamin* Griffith, and Joshua *Benjamin* Steed, and David *Benjamin* Rogers, and *Benjamin* Derek Ingalls. Every family has a Benjamin now except Matthew," she smiled, "and he says they will too, as soon as they get a little boy."

She blinked quickly, fighting the sudden blurriness. "Does that tell you how much you were loved, Ben?"

She stood silently for several more moments, feeling now the cold wind tugging at her scarf and piercing through her dress. She was unaware that the tears had started again and were leaving cold streaks down her cheeks. She pulled the shawl more tightly around her, not wanting to leave, not wanting to have to face the family again quite yet. She looked down one last time, then turned to go.

She started away, back toward the wagons, her steps heavy and slow. She felt as though she were too tired to make it.

When it came she had gone only three or four steps. It came as softly and as gently as the softest and gentlest touch of a summer breeze on one's face. It was two words. Two words only. "Mary Ann."

She whirled, staring at the mound of snow and the black stone that stood at the head of it. There was nothing there. No one there. But then she nodded. She didn't need to see. There

"Good-bye Until We Meet Again"

was only one voice in all the world that had ever spoken to her with such love and sweet gentleness.

She stared for several moments, feeling a great, soaring sense of joy and peace fill her soul. Finally, she smiled, tears of sorrow now turned to tears of joy. "Good-bye, Benjamin Steed," she called softly. "Good-bye until we meet again."

Chapter Notes

In what was considered a miracle for that late in the season, a terrible cold descended on the Great Plains in the last week of February 1846. At one point the temperature was measured at twelve degrees below zero. The river froze solid, making it possible for literally hundreds of families to cross in a short time. (See *HC* 7:585–98; Orson F. Whitney, *Life of Heber C. Kimball*, Collector's Edition [Salt Lake City: Bookcraft, 1992], pp. 351–54; "Journal of Thomas Bullock," pp. 50–54; *American Moses*, pp. 121, 127–28; and Susan W. Easton, "Suffering and Death on the Plains of Iowa," *BYU Studies* 21 [Fall 1981]: 431–35.)

ABOUT THE AUTHOR

Gerald N. Lund received his B.A. and M.S. degrees in sociology from Brigham Young University. He also did extensive graduate work in New Testament studies at Pepperdine University in Los Angeles, California, and studied Hebrew at the University of Judaism in Hollywood, California.

During his thirty-five years in the Church Educational System, the author served as a seminary teacher, an institute teacher and director, a curriculum writer, director of college curriculum, and zone administrator. His Church callings have included those of bishop, stake missionary, and teacher.

Gerald Lund has written nineteen books, including such novels as *Fire of the Covenant*, *The Alliance*, *The Freedom Factor*, *Leverage Point*, *One in Thine Hand*, and *The Kingdom and the Crown*, *volume 1: Fishers of Men*. He has also written several books on gospel studies, including *The Coming of the Lord* and *Jesus Christ, Key to the Plan of Salvation*. He has twice won the Independent Booksellers "Book of the Year" Award and has received many other honors for his works.

He and his wife, Lynn, are the parents of seven children and live in Alpine, Utah.